University of Liverpool

Withdrawn from stock

Accounting

Fourth Edition

Accounting

Understanding and Practice

Fourth Edition

Danny Leiwy and Robert Perks

McGraw-Hill Higher Education

London   Boston   Burr Ridge, IL   Dubuque, IA   Madison, WI   New York   San Francisco   St. Louis
Bangkok   Bogotá   Caracas   Kuala Lumpur   Lisbon   Madrid   Mexico City
Milan   Montreal   New Delhi   Santiago   Seoul   Singapore   Sydney   Taipei   Toronto

Accounting. Understanding and Practice, Fourth Edition
Danny Leiwy and Robert Perks
ISBN-13 9780077139131
ISBN-10 0077139135

 **McGraw-Hill
Higher Education**

Published by McGraw-Hill Education (UK) Limited
Shoppenhangers Road
Maidenhead
Berkshire
SL6 2QL
Telephone: 44 (0) 1628 502 500
Fax: 44 (0) 1628 770 224
Website: www.mcgraw-hill.co.uk

British Library Cataloguing in Publication Data
A catalogue record for this book is available from the British Library

Library of Congress Cataloging in Publication Data
The Library of Congress data for this book has been applied for from the Library of Congress

Acquisitions Editor: Tom Hill
Development Editor: Stephanie Frosch
Production Editor: Alison Davis
Marketing Manager: Alexis Thomas

Text Design by HL Studios
Cover design by Adam Renvoize
Printed and bound in Spain by Grafo Industrias Gráficas.

ISBN-13 9780077139131
ISBN-10 0077139135

Dedication

To Malki
Kate and Menachem
Jonny and Natalie
and
David and Jo

Brief Table of Contents

The following additional material is available online at
www.mcgraw-hill.co.uk/textbooks/leiwy:

Chapter 19: Incomplete Records
Appendix: Developments in Management Accounting

Detailed Table of Contents

The following additional material is available online *at www.mcgraw-hill.co.uk/textbooks/leiwy:*

About the Authors

Danny Leiwy ['lu:i] teaches at the London School of Economics and Political Science and on the University of London's International Programme at City University, London. He is a Senior Teaching Fellow at the School of Oriental and African Studies (SOAS), University of London. Danny is currently in practice as a Chartered Accountant. He was a Principal Lecturer in Accounting and Tax at the University of Westminster for 30 years, teaching at both undergraduate and postgraduate level.

Robert Perks formerly taught Accounting and Finance at the International Business School on the Isle of Man. Robert also held chairs at the following universities: Queen's University, Belfast, Middlesex University, Aberdeen University, Birkbeck College University of London and University of Westminster.

Preface

This book is intended to help readers understand accounting and to see how it can be used in practice, particularly in the interpretation and management of company finances. It should appeal to future managers, rather than to those who simply want to become accountants. It is intended to be 'user-friendly' for those who are put off by conventional presentations of the subject based on arcane rules and procedures. Non-specialist accounting students, for whom figures are sometimes a painful necessity, will probably find that this is as good as it gets with accounting textbooks.

It is an introductory text, which is particularly suitable for degree courses in management and business studies, including MBAs and other masters degree programmes. It is suitable for year-long introductory accounting modules or semester-long modules on financial accounting and management accounting. The approach is analytical, critical and evaluative, amply illustrated with real-world examples and for those modules that include the preparation of accounts, there is an extended section on bookkeeping and the preparation of financial accounts at the end of Part 1 (Chapters 9 and 10).

The book is divided into three parts and begins with financial accounting (Chapters 1–10) and then moves on to financial management (Chapters 11 and 12) and then to management accounting (Chapters 13–18). Readers may be interested in the application of published financial reports in relation to the stock market (Chapter 5), financing a company (Chapter 11), investment appraisal (Chapter 14), or current issues in the rapidly developing area on financial accounting (Chapters 3 and 8). In response to requests from users, this 4th edition provides a new introduction with an explanation of characteristics of a limited liability company that result in the need for public disclosure to various stakeholders of every company's financial accounts. The production of accounts from incomplete records has been moved online and some more advanced management accounting developments such as backflush accounting and balanced scorecards are briefly explained in an online Appendix.

Interpretation of accounts is a problem for many students and a simplified 'ready reference' guide to accounting 'ratios' is now provided in Chapter 4, with more advanced issues dealt with in a separate chapter (Chapter 7). After covering the basics of statements of financial position and income statements (Chapters 1 and 2), the book is designed so that any chapter can be studied in almost any order according to the readers' particular interests, or the requirements of a course.

Ample resources are provided to enable readers to understand and apply financial accounting. Self-testing questions (numerical, theoretical and analytical) are included in each chapter, with answers at the end of the book. Assessment questions are provided without answers. Discussion questions and group activities are included to encourage readers to become involved in exploring important questions; and these can be related to current issues in the press by analysing the 'Accounting in context' illustrations. There is also an extensive glossary at the back of the book.

All companies produce annual reports and accounts that include a great deal of valuable information if only managers, analysts, financial journalists, economists, bankers and everyone with an interest in business and management would take the time and trouble to understand them. This book is intended to help. Similarly, students who produce projects and dissertations, and politicians and journalists who analyse particular companies and industries, can benefit from the thorough understanding of published financial statements that this book provides. In the main it explains financial accounting as an important resource that has valuable applications and gives an understanding of management accounting techniques used widely in businesses everywhere; but its approach is also critical, and it encourages readers to think about important issues and to reach their own conclusions.

Danny Leiwy

Acknowledgements

Author's acknowledgements

First, I would like to thank Bob Perks who wrote the first two editions of this book. Bob is a deeply admired former colleague of mine and a friend for many years.

Additionally, I'd like to thank my colleagues John Silverstone and Mark Pilkington for their advice on some management accounting issues, and my friend Jeremy Shaw.

And my thanks to Tom Hill, Stephanie Frosch and Leonie Sloman at McGraw-Hill for nagging me in the nicest possible way! Needless to say, any mistakes can't be blamed on anyone but myself.

Publisher's acknowledgements

Our thanks go to the following reviewers for their comments at various stages in the text's development:

Jock Anderson, Queen Margaret University
Stuart Cooper, Aston University
Siobhan Goggin, University of Lincoln
Louise Gracia, University of Warwick
Lindsey Hamilton, University of Keele
Qile He, University of Bedfordshire
Andreas Hoepner, University of St Andrews
Elisavet Mantzari, University of Westminster
Paul Marambos, University of Hertfordshire
Jim O'Hare, University of Leicester
Mohammad Rajjaque, University of Sheffield
Ane Ripoll-Zarraga, University of Keele
Deirdre Ruddy, National University of Ireland, Galway
Sheeja Sivaprasad, University of Westminster
Anne Stafford, University of Manchester
Grigorios Theodosopoulos, University of Hertfordshire

Every effort has been made to trace and acknowledge ownership of copyright and to clear permission for material reproduced in this book. The publishers will be pleased to make suitable arrangements to clear permission with any copyright holders who it has not been possible to contact.

Guided Tour

Chapter contents

A brief list of key chapter contents is highlighted at the start of each chapter.

✓ Learning objectives

After studying this chapter you will be able to:
- ✓ Understand the different ways in which profit is see
- ✓ Appreciate and critically assess the role of accountin
- ✓ Evaluate the various attempts to base accounting o
- ✓ Understand the two main ways of approaching prof
- ✓ Define assets and liabilities and understand some m
- ✓ Define revenues and expenses and understand som
- ✓ Understand the effects of price changes on financia
- ✓ Appreciate different ways of adjusting for price chan

Learning objectives

Each chapter opens with a list of learning objectives, summarizing what you will learn from that chapter.

4.1 Introduction

This chapter shows how financial a financial strength of a company, an ability in a straightforward way. Con with in Chapter 11.

 This chapter also introduces the mance of a company's shares on the

 Interpretation of accounts is not It is about examining a set of accoun ing the evidence to answer those qu

Introduction

Each chapter opens with an introduction, which sets the scene and introduces you to the issues that will be addressed in the chapter.

ILLUSTRATION 1.1

	£
What I own	
House	300,000
Furniture	4,000
Car	10,000
Premium bonds and shares	6,000
Food and drink	200
Cash and bank	4,800
Total	325,000
What I owe	
Mortgage	222,000
Bills (gas and electricity, etc.)	1,000
Credit card	2,000

Illustrations

Figures, tables and statements of financial position illustrate and summarize important concepts, helping you apply theory to accounting practice.

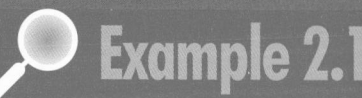

Example 2.1

At the beginning of March, Raj's shop had inventories o
for resale costing £10,000.[9] His sales figure for March
Raj, therefore, had £11,000 worth of goods availa
goods he had available for sale were not sold, and w
know the closing inventory figure.

His stock of unsold goods at the end of March was
The cost of the goods which he sold can now be c

Opening inventory
Purchases

Examples

The chapters contain varied examples, including
real-life accounting situations and worked problems which bring accounting to life.

Summary

This briefly reviews and reinforces the main
topics you will have covered in each chapter to
ensure you have acquired a solid understanding
of the key topics.

 Summary

One of the main objectives of financial managem
which are dependent on profits, contribute to t
the value of their shares. Directors and chief ex
increase their company's share price: they ow
shares at predetermined prices; and their remun
share price performance. If they fail, and the sha
ers, and leave themselves open to a hostile takeo

Accounting measures of solvency and profit
If a company is seen as having excessive debt,
maintaining and increasing share prices, althou
return on capital employed (ROCE). Growth, ar
dividends make a major contribution to increa
tions of share price increases are the main cause
expectations, rumours and many other factors t

Review of key points

- Profit is not the same as cash flow. The
  justification and explanation of the diffe
- A cash flow statement provides a reconcil
  increase or decrease in cash during the ye
- A company's operating profit may be use
  to pay interest, taxation and dividends, a
- A detailed cash flow statement shows oth
  ardized format.
- A cash flow statement should be interpr
  tion and income statements, and can rev
- Some differences between cash flow and
  receipts and payments compared with th

Review of key points

These bullet points at the end of each
chapter are ideal for revising accounting
concepts.

Self-testing questions

1 What are the main differences between a stat
2 What is an expense? How does an expense d
  In what sense could it be argued that an asse
3 How are inventories valued? Why does it ma
  selling price?
4 Why is depreciation charged?
5 What is the difference between capital expen
6 Which of the profit figures shown in a simplif
  ers likely to be most interested in, and why?
7 The Kingsdun Company buys a delivery van
  decide that the delivery van should be depr
  balance basis, and that the boring machine s
  straight-line basis. Calculate the depreciatio

Self-testing questions

These questions encourage you to review and apply the
knowledge you have acquired from each chapter. Answers
are provided at the back of the book.

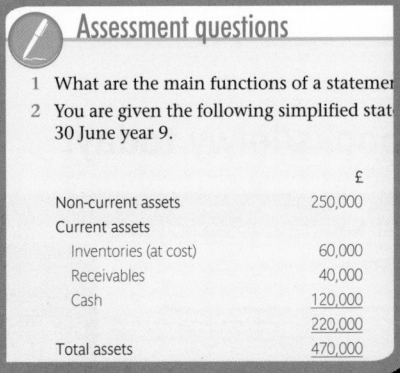

Assessment questions

This section provides a multitude of questions you may be asked in an exam. They can be used as helpful revision questions or to check progress as you cover the topics throughout the text.

Group activities and discussion questions

These questions are ideal for sparking debate in class and also help readers think around the topic.

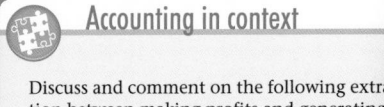

Accouting in context

Each chapter ends with an article from the press that aims to illustrate the main themes of the chapter, allowing you to appreciate how the theory applies to real life.

References and further reading

A list of references from the chapter, plus useful websites, which can be used for further research.

Online Learning Centre

Visit www.mcgraw-hill.co.uk/textbooks/leiwy today!

Students – Helping you to Connect, Learn and Succeed

We understand that studying for your module is not just about reading this textbook. It's also about researching online, revising key terms, preparing for assignments, and passing the exam. The website above provides you with a number of **FREE** resources to help you succeed on your module, including:

- *Web links* to online sources of information to help you prepare for class
- *Additional press articles and questions* for self-study
- *Glossary* of key terms to revise core concepts

Lecturer support – Helping you to help your students

The Online Learning Centre also offers lecturers adopting this book a range of resources designed to offer:

- **Faster course preparation** – time-saving support for your module
- **High-calibre content to support your students** – resources written by your academic peers, who understand your need for rigorous and reliable content
- **Flexibility** – edit, adapt or repurpose; test in EZ Test or your department's Course Management System – the choice is yours

The materials created specifically for lecturers adopting this textbook include:

- *Solutions manual providing answers to the assessment questions and the group activities and discussion questions in the textbook*
- *PowerPoint presentations to use in lecture presentations*
- *Image library of artwork from the textbook*
- *Additional exam questions and solutions*

To request your password to access these resources, contact your McGraw-Hill representative or visit www.mcgraw-hill.co.uk/textbooks/leiwy.

Test Bank available in McGraw-Hill EZ Test Online

The testbank for this new edition has been expanded and hundreds of questions are available to lecturers adopting this book for their module through the EZ Test online website. For each chapter you will find:

- A range of multiple choice, true or false, short-answer or essay questions
- Questions identified by type, difficulty and topic to help you to select questions that best suit your needs

McGraw-Hill EZ Test Online is:

- Accessible anywhere with an internet connection – your unique login provides you access to all your tests and material in any location
- Simple to set up and easy to use
- Flexible, offering a choice from question banks associated with your adopted textbook or allowing you to create your own questions
- Comprehensive, with access to hundreds of banks and thousands of questions created for other McGraw-Hill titles
- Compatible with Blackboard and other course management systems
- Time-saving – students' tests can be immediately marked and results and feedback delivered directly to your students to help them to monitor their progress

To register for this FREE resource, visit www.eztestonline.com

Make our content your solution

At McGraw-Hill Education our aim is to help lecturers to find the most suitable content for their needs delivered to their students in the most appropriate way. Our **custom publishing solutions** offer the ideal combination of content delivered in the way which best suits lecturer and students.

Our custom publishing programme offers lecturers the opportunity to select just the chapters or sections of material they wish to deliver to their students from a database called CREATE™ at

www.mcgrawhillcreate.co.uk

CREATE™ contains over two million pages of content from:
- textbooks
- professional books
- case books – Harvard Articles, Insead, Ivey, Darden, Thunderbird and BusinessWeek
- Taking Sides – debate materials

Across the following imprints:
- McGraw-Hill Education
- Open University Press
- Harvard Business Publishing
- US and European material

There is also the option to include additional material authored by lecturers in the custom product – this does not necessarily have to be in English.

We will take care of everything from start to finish in the process of developing and delivering a custom product to ensure that lecturers and students receive exactly the material needed in the most suitable way.

With a Custom Publishing Solution, students enjoy the best selection of material deemed to be the most suitable for learning everything they need for their courses – something of real value to support their learning. Teachers are able to use exactly the material they want, in the way they want, to support their teaching on the course.

Please contact your local McGraw-Hill representative with any questions or alternatively contact Warren Eels **e: warren_eels@mcgraw-hill.com.**

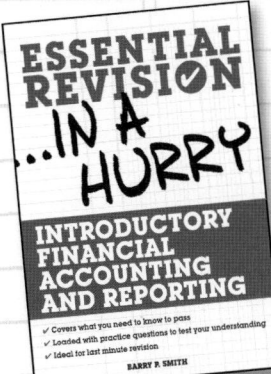

Part 1

Introduction to Financial Accounting

Introduction

Contents

What is Accounting?

Accounting is the process of producing financial information about a business that will enable those with rights to that information to make informed economic decisions. An 'economic decision' relates to how scarce resources should be best used. For example, an investor, who is an example of someone with rights to information about a business, will need to assess whether or not to invest his money in Company A or Company B. A bank will need information to help decide whether or not to lend money to that business.

The process of accounting, like any process, has many stages. First, the transactions of the business are **recorded.** Then, these transactions are **classified.** Payments from the bank account of the business might be for buying inventory, the goods it buys in order to sell them, or perhaps to pay the wages of the employees of the business. Then, sales, expenses, profits, assets, liabilities and expenses will be **measured**. Since businesses, such as Marks and Spencer or BP are owned and financed by shareholders, who are investors who have purchased a share of the business but are not involved in running the business, the directors of such companies have been appointed by the shareholders to run their business. But directors cannot just run away with the shareholders' money; they are made accountable to the shareholders by the requirement to produce annual reports and accounts. In a sense these documents are the 'election address' of directors, who hope to present themselves in a good light so that they will be re-elected. These directors are the stewards of these investments. The notion of **stewardship** is that the directors are accountable to the shareholders for how their investment has been managed. The resources of the business must be *monitored and controlled* to ensure the resources of the business are effectively and efficiently used. The resources and performance and the risks attached to the business need to be *evaluated*. And periodically, the accounting information showing, for example, the assets and liabilities and sales revenue, expenses and profits are **communicated** to those with rights to that information.

Private Business – Accountability

In this book, we are mainly focused upon accounting of privately owned, for profit businesses. Such organisations come in different legal structures. A *sole trader* is a business organization with a single owner with no legal structure separate from the owner. In fact, there are no legal formalities involved in forming such a business. I might start buying and selling goods on eBay. I am obliged to inform the tax authorities that I am self-employed and am in business. If, for example, I am in business as a builder anyone owed money by the business can, if the business is unable to pay them, recover the sum owed from the sole trader of the business. That is because there is no legal distinction between the business and the owner. Hence if the nature of the business is risky, like that of a builder, running a business as a sole trader is very worrying because any activity such as building a wall which could fall on a passer-by could lead to the builder being sued for not only the assets of the business but all his personal assets, too. A *partnership* is much like a sole trader with more than one owner. Again, partnerships can be formed with no legal formalities. Here the resources and skills of more than one owner are available to the business but in much the same way as the entire personal 'fortune' of a sole trader is at risk and can be at the mercy of any creditors of the business, that is, anyone owed money by the business for whatever reason, exactly the same situation applies in a partnership. The partners are liable 'jointly and severally' for the debts of the business, that is, the personal fortunes of *all* the partners are available to the creditors of a partnership in the event that there are insufficient funds to pay and creditors. A *limited liability company*, however, has, as a lawyer would put it, 'a separate legal personality' from those that own it. A company is formed by a legal process, filling in forms submitted to Companies House, an Executive Agency of the Department for Business, Innovation and Skills (BIS). Because a company is separate from its owners, called 'shareholders', the creditors of such a business do not have the right to chase the owners or shareholders of the company for any sums owing by that business. There is no limit to the number of shareholders in a company and so a company has the possibility of inviting thousands of potential shareholders to invest in the business and the shareholders, as a group, to elect directors to run their business. And it is for these two reasons that creditors of a company are in a weaker position and are less well-protected than creditors of a sole trader or partnership and that while a sole trader or partners are likely to be involved in managing the business on a daily basis while shareholders in a company like Marks & Spencer are not involved in running the business that in the UK, the Companies Act 2006 requires all companies to produce a set of accounts each year disclosing specified information in a required form and by a specified date and which is made available to all shareholders. And since these accounts have to be 'filed' at Companies House, and are available for 'public inspection' so all creditors and anyone else interested in the company's 'annual report' can download the accounts via the Companies House website www.companieshouse.gov.uk. Unincorporated businesses (sole traders and partnerships) are not required by law to produce financial statements, but most find it useful to do so.

A *limited liability partnership* (llp) is in most respects a cross between a partnership and a limited liability company and is most commonly used by accountants and lawyers. Each partner is only liable for debts arising from their own activities but the llp is also required to submit its accounts to Companies House.

Users of Accounting Information

Businesses, particularly companies, produce statements of financial position, income statements and detailed financial reports, because in addition to the legal requirement to do so, they are assumed to be useful to a range of 'users'. Published financial statements are supposed to meet the information needs of a variety of different 'users'. The main groups of users, and their information needs, are summarized below.

1 Shareholders, including potential shareholders, who are considering buying or selling shares in the company. They are interested in such things as the value of the company, the profits, dividends and cash flows that it has generated in recent periods, what its performance is likely to be in future periods and its financial position and survival prospects.

   Directors are also accountable to shareholders, and annual financial reports fulfil a 'stewardship' role, showing how well the directors have acted as 'stewards' of their money.

2 Creditors and suppliers including potential creditors. They are interested in the company's cash flows and ability to meet their liabilities in general and to pay their creditors on time.

3   Lenders both short (e.g. banks in relation to overdrafts) and long term (e.g. debenture holders and those considering lending) have similar information needs to other creditors. They want to know about the company's ability to repay the loans, and their future prospects. They are interested in financial position (statements of financial position), performance (income statements) and cash generation (cash flow statements).

4   Employees, and potential employees, want to know about the future prospects of the company, whether they will survive and prosper and be able to pay wages and salaries and provide expanding career prospects in the future. They are also interested in companies' pension schemes, and whether they are viable or in deficit. When going for an interview with a company, applicants are well advised to find out all they can about their potential employer's business and their proposed developments.

5   Customers may be interested in the financial position and prospects of a company, although this is a bit unlikely in relation to most consumer goods. If a government or large company is considering entering into a substantial or long-term contract they will want to know if proposed contractors are reputable, and in a strong enough financial position to meet the commitments that are being considered.

6   Government and public sector bodies are interested in companies in various ways. They gather information about businesses in relation to a whole range of public policy concerns, including employment levels and policies, research and development, investment and growth, their impact on the balance of payments, pricing and inflation, mergers, takeovers and competition policy, and environmental and public health. Wherever politicians see a public policy impact, or evidence of voters' concerns, they are likely to want to know what companies are doing, and to consider gathering more information, and implementing additional regulations.

7   HM Revenue and Customs are responsible for collecting corporation tax, income tax, value added tax, and customs and excise duties, which they do on the basis of specific forms and information requirements. But as part of their general checking and control procedures they are likely to be interested in the published accounts of companies, and to investigate any apparent discrepancies.

8   Managers and directors of companies are likely to be interested in the annual financial statements and even more interested in monthly statements. But financial accounting information is primarily designed for people outside the business. Managers should have access to specially produced internal management accounting information on a regular basis. But there are many small companies that produce little management accounting information other than monthly income statements, statements of financial position and cash flow statements that are relied on by managers and directors.

9   Financial analysts and advisers come in all shapes and sizes, and have many different information needs. Some may be advising the companies about raising additional finance, or on a potential takeover bid. More generally, there are investment analysts who carry out fundamental analysis of the financial information about a company and produce recommendations for those considering buying or selling shares in the company. They are interested in the financial position and performance, and still more interested in its future prospects. They may attempt to value a company based on the future cash flows that it is expected to generate, and in assessing whether or not the current share price represents good value in relation to future prospects.

10 Competitors usually like to compare their own results with those of their rivals, perhaps to gloat where they are doing better, and to learn what they can in order to improve their own performance. They are interested in how much their competitors are expanding, their profit margins and in how the different segments of the business are performing.

11 The public, special interest groups and students may want a very wide range of information about a company, much of which can be found in annual reports and accounts. There are environmental lobby groups, animal welfare groups, local people interested in possible building expansion,

trade unions acting on behalf of employees, people concerned with health, safety and accidents and many others. The internet is usually the first port of call for students undertaking projects; but they should not overlook the company's annual report and accounts, which is the company's official information, intended mainly for investors, and includes much more than students usually expect.

The information needs of some of these groups should not be taken too seriously because they are in a position to get most of what they want to meet their specific needs directly from the company. These groups include governments, HM Revenue and Customs, managers and directors. Lenders such as bankers demand and are usually given much more information than is included in published financial statements, including forecast information, monthly breakdowns and cash budgets. Similarly, financial advisers are likely to be given most available information if they are acting for the company concerned (but not if they are acting for competitors!).

In some cases the information that particular groups want is so detailed and specific that it would be impractical to include it in a general purpose annual report. Expansion plans at a supermarket site, safety records at a particular factory and employment prospects at a particular location may all be matters of interest locally, but it would be impractical to expand annual reports to include all the detail that some groups might want in respect of a particular location. Annual reports are necessarily 'general purpose'. Many of the supposed information needs of the various groups are a matter for legitimate public concern, but perhaps it should be governments who act on behalf of the public and obtain appropriate information; it is unrealistic to expect everything to be included in a company's annual report and accounts.

A major problem with the information needs of the various groups is that most want to know what is going to happen in the future. Shareholders, creditors, lenders and employees all want to know what the company's future prospects are. Will they be able to meet their liabilities? Will shares be a good investment? Will the company thrive, and provide good career prospects? These are all legitimate questions, but financial statements deal almost entirely with what has already happened. Many users are concerned to assess the value of published, historic financial information by assessing the extent to which it provides an effective basis for future forecasts, and there are increasing pressures for companies to publish additional forecast information. Some see the role of financial statements as being to provide a basis for predicting future cash flows.[1]

As it is not possible for a company to publish exactly the information that everyone wants, the emphasis is on statements of financial position, income statements and cash flow statements that are primarily designed for the benefit of shareholders and creditors.

It may be assumed that, by focusing on the interests that investors have in the financial performance and position of a company, the needs of a wide range of users will be met. The income statement, statement of financial position and cash flow statement are assumed to meet most information requirements of general users of financial statements. This is a bit like a truism: the statements that are available are the ones that are used and so must be the statements that users want. These three statements, the income statement, the statement of financial position and the cash flow statement, are introduced in Chapters 2, 1 and 6, respectively.

---

[1] Cash flows are, of course, different from profits. These differences are explained in Chapter 6.

Chapter 1

The Statement of Financial Position (Balance Sheet) and What it Tells Us

Chapter contents

✓ Learning objectives

After studying this chapter you will be able to:

✓ Explain the structure and terminology of straightforward statements of financial position

✓ Understand how statements of financial position can indicate financial weaknesses and strengths

✓ Demonstrate how transactions and profits affect statements of financial position

✓ Discuss the uses and limitations of statements of financial position

1.1 Introduction

The term 'balance sheet' is widely used, although most people have never seen one and have little idea of what it shows. First, it should be noted that in the last year or two, the balance sheet is more commonly called 'a statement of financial position'. This chapter provides a gentle introduction to statements of financial position by showing how individuals can prepare their own personal statement of financial position, and how similar these are to company statements of financial position. Second, it also gives some indication of the usefulness of statements of financial position: they can give an indication of what an individual or company is worth (but with severe limitations). They also show what liabilities there are, which can help to predict future bankruptcy.

1.2 An Individual's Statement of Financial Position (Balance Sheet)

If you want to know how much you are worth as an individual you would probably start by drawing up a list of everything that you own, and then try to put a value on each item. After working for a few years you might own a house, some furniture, a car, some premium bonds and shares that you intend to keep on a long-term basis, and perhaps some short-term investments. You might also have a good stock of food and wine in the kitchen as well as some money in the bank. But you may have debts: a mortgage owed to your bank or building society, an overdraft, money you owe on your credit card, and bills not yet paid for such things as electricity, gas, telephone and council tax.

It is easy to produce a list of what you own, and a list of what you owe. You can then deduct what you owe from what you own to show your 'net worth'. An example is given in Illustration 1.1.

We can summarize this as:

What I own *minus* what I owe = what I am worth

If you are a full-time student this might be more difficult, or more embarrassing. It may be that the most valuable things that you own are items such as CDs, clothes, books, an iPhone and a laptop. You may have paid a lot for them, but their value now is questionable – especially if you suddenly need to sell them. They would cost a lot to replace, and if they were all stolen you would probably claim quite a high value for them if they were insured. But if you try to sell them, their second-hand value would probably be very disappointing: it is likely to be only a small fraction of what you paid for them. Worse still, you may well have a student loan and an overdraft and owe other amounts of money, which means that your net worth is zero, or even negative: you owe more than you own. But it is all worth it, you tell yourself, because all the time you are spending money on your education, that is an investment, and what you are really worth is your future earning power. If you go to your bank wanting to borrow money, they will be much more interested in your future earning power than they are in a pile of second-hand clothes and some CDs. Three main problems arise in trying to establish what any individual or business is worth:

1　What items are we going to list? Are we going to include our five-year-old computer, our CDs, all the food in the kitchen, our educational qualifications and our children? We might think of these as being some of the best things we have, but we would probably exclude them. We need some basis, or principle, for deciding what to include and what to exclude.

2　How do we establish what particular items are worth? We attempt this in several different ways; for example, by looking at what they originally cost, or what the second-hand value is, or what it would cost to replace them.

ILLUSTRATION 1.1	
	£
What I own	
House	300,000
Furniture	4,000
Car	10,000
Premium bonds and shares	6,000
Food and drink	200
Cash and bank	4,800
Total	325,000
What I owe	
Mortgage	222,000
Bills (gas and electricity, etc.)	1,000
Credit card	2,000
Total	225,000
What I am worth	100,000

3 What is our future earning power worth? Whether we look at an individual or a company, in many cases the money that they can earn in the future is worth a lot more than a collection of bits and pieces that they own. If you want to borrow money, you could tell your bank that you expect to earn at least £1 million during your working life, and ask to borrow the £1 million now. The bank's response is likely to be short and not very sweet.

You can, of course, make up your own rules, and decide that you are worth £100,000. But if you want to compare your own wealth with someone else's, then you need to agree how the calculation is to be made. Are you going to show your house at the amount you paid for it, or at the market value now? Are you going to show your car at the amount you paid for it, or allow for the fact that it has depreciated since you bought it? If you attempt any comparisons like this you will soon find that you need some agreed rules on what to include, and the basis of valuation to be used. You will need accounting principles.

It is difficult to know what something is really worth until you sell it. I might boast that my house is worth £500,000, but we might agree that it is more objective to show it at cost; and it cost £300,000 a few years ago. The accounting principle would be to list everything that we own, and show everything at the original cost price.

Deciding what principle to adopt for furniture and for a car is more difficult. They have only a limited life, and are likely to depreciate over time as we 'use them up'. We could decide that a car has a five-year life and write it down by one-fifth each year.

1.3 A Company's Statement of Financial Position (Balance Sheet)

A company's statement of financial position is very much like an individual's statement of financial position, except that a standard layout is used, and more impressive terminology is applied.

The layout and terminology probably look quite confusing at first and it may be hard to believe that Illustration 1.2 really is the same statement of financial position as Illustration 1.1. By using standardized terminology and presentation, accountants say that they are making it easier to compare

ILLUSTRATION 1.2

Statement of financial position of A Company as at 31 December year 1

Assets	£
Non-current assets	
Freehold land and buildings (at cost)	300,000
Furniture (at cost)	4,000
Vehicles (at cost)	10,000
Investments	6,000
	320,000
Current assets	
Inventories	200
Cash and bank	4,800
	5,000
Total assets	325,000
Equity and Liabilities	
Liabilities	
Current liabilities	
Trade payables	1,000
Short-term borrowings	2,000
	3,000
Non-current liabilities	
Mortgage	222,000
Total liabilities	225,000
Equity	
Share capital and reserves	100,000
Total equity and liabilities	325,000

one company with another. You might think that they are just making it more complicated so that it is 'impenetrable' to non-accountants. But professionals can no longer hide behind their terminology, conventions and so-called 'expertise'. These days many patients question their doctor's recommendations (perhaps by looking things up on the internet and becoming instantly more 'expert' than the doctor). Similarly, you are learning to question accountants (and other management 'experts'), and now is the time to make sure that you understand the basic terminology of financial statements.

The terminology used on statement of financial positions has become more standardized since the widespread application of International Accounting Standards (IASs) in 2006. Illustrations 1.2 and 1.3 are both consistent with international standards; the first is in the format illustrated in International Accounting Standard 1 (IAS 1). The second one also complies with the standard, and is also fairly conventional. Unfortunately, we have to be able to cope with statements of financial position presented in different ways.[1]

In accountant's jargon, what a company controls and what they owe are called *assets* and *liabilities*, and the statement showing assets and liabilities (and *net assets,* or *net worth*, or *equity*, or *capital*)

---

[1] That is the price of international 'standardization', prior to which there was a standardized UK form of statement of financial position which, unfortunately, differed from that of other countries.

ILLUSTRATION 1.3

A Company statement of financial position as at 31 December year 1

	£	£
Assets		
Non-current assets		
Freehold land and buildings (at cost)	300,000	
Furniture (at cost)	4,000	
Vehicles (at cost)	10,000	
Total of tangible assets	314,000	
Financial assets (investments)	6,000	320,000
Current assets		
Inventories	200	
Cash and bank	4,800	5,000
Total assets		325,000
Current liabilities		
Trade payables	1,000	
Credit card	2,000	3,000
Non-current liabilities		
Mortgage		222,000
Equity		
Share capital and reserves		100,000
Total liabilities and equity		325,000

is called a *statement of financial position* – formerly a 'balance sheet'. The idea is that it 'balances'; the total of assets used to be shown on the one side, and the total of liabilities and equity on the other side: the two sides balance. But nowadays it is usual to show the one 'side' at the top, and the other 'side' underneath.

In everyday English we have seen that what I am worth is the total of what I own, minus the total of what I owe. In accountancy terms we would say that the statement of financial position value of a company is the total of assets minus liabilities. We could call this 'equity', or net assets, or capital, or net worth. Accountants sometimes talk about the 'statement of financial position (or balance sheet) equation' that has three items (assets, liabilities and equity), which can be arranged in different ways, as follows:

(a) assets = liabilities *plus* equity

This shows a total of assets, and then how they were financed: partly with other people's money, and partly with the owners' equity;

    or

(b) assets *minus* liabilities = equity

This emphasizes the amount of equity

It is easy enough to establish the 'statement of financial position value' of a company, or its 'net asset value', or 'equity', or 'net worth'. In Illustration 1.2 it would be £100,000. It is much more

difficult to establish what a company is really worth, because of the same three problems already identified:

1 What items are we going to include on the list?
2 How do we establish what particular items are worth?
3 What is the future earning power of the company as a whole worth?

These problems are addressed more fully later in the book.

1.4 Short- and Long-term Classification

The usual formats for statements of financial position make it relatively straightforward to compare one company with another. Both assets and liabilities are classified as being long or short term. Anything that is intended to be around for more than a year is long term. Anything that changes within a year is short term.

Assets

An **asset** is a resource controlled by a business as a result of past events and from which future economic benefits are expected.

Long-term assets are called 'non-current assets'. They are still often referred to as 'fixed assets', although there is nothing fixed about them: they include cars and aeroplanes just as much as they include land and buildings. The main categories within the non-current assets section of a statement of financial position are:

1 *Intangible assets* – for example: goodwill; patents; trademarks; licences.
2 *Property, plant and equipment (tangible fixed assets)* – for example: land and buildings; plant, machinery and equipment; vehicles; furniture, fixtures and fittings.
3 *Financial assets or investments* – items such as shares in other companies or loans that have been made.

We can say that things like vehicles or furniture are *usually* classed as non-current assets, but that is not always the case. If a business intends to use them for a period of years, then they are non-current. But if someone is in business to buy and sell vehicles, or furniture, then any items held short term, awaiting sale, are not fixed assets. Stocks of goods held for sale are labelled as 'inventories' and shown as current assets.

The same arguments apply with investments. Any surplus funds invested in shares, or loaned to someone or another business, might be intended to be long term, and so are 'non-current'. Or they might be intended to be short term, and so are shown as current assets.

Current assets are short term. They include cash and any assets intended to become cash within a year. They include:

1 *Inventories (or stocks)* – merchandise, production supplies, materials, work in progress and finished goods.
2 *Trade receivables (or debtors)* – money owed to the business by customers and others.[2]
3 *Investments* – (those that are not fixed assets).
4 *Prepayments* – expenses such as rent or insurance, paid before the statement of financial position date from which the benefits will arise in the following accounting year.
5 *Cash.*[3]

---

[2] And even prepayments, and accrued income if you want to be technical!

[3] Cash includes money in the bank, and petty cash in hand. Obviously the two are quite distinct and a bookkeeper needs to account for them separately. But for the sake of simplicity, in interpreting statements of financial position, the two can be lumped together.

Current assets are short term, and constantly circulating. They are all cash, or cash equivalents, or things that are expected to become cash within a year. We intend that all our inventories will be sold; even raw materials and components will be incorporated into finished goods that are sold. Investments that are shown as current assets are assumed to be temporary, and so will be sold and converted into cash. The amounts shown for receivables should be received from debtors within a few months.

Liabilities

Liabilities are also categorized as current and non-current (short and long term).

A **liability** is a present obligation arising from past transactions that are expected to be paid in the future.

1 Current liabilities are creditors where the amount is due to be paid within a year. They include:

- most ordinary trade payables (creditors for goods and services who have not yet been paid);
- corporation taxation payable;
- accrued charges – expenses, such as electricity, which are paid in arrears and for which no invoice has been received at the statement of financial position date;
- bank overdrafts.

The statements of financial position shown in Illustrations 1.2 and 1.3 clearly show current and non-current assets and liabilities separately from each other.

2 Non-current liabilities include long-term borrowings such as mortgages and debentures.

The distinction between what is short term and what is long term is important in assessing the financial strength or solvency of a business in assessing whether or not it is likely to go bust!

Equity

Equity is the assets less the liabilities and is the owners' interest in the business. In a company it will include:

1 Share capital – the book (or par) value of the shares subscribed for.

2 Share premium – any excess paid into the company on the issue of shares in excess of the book (or par) value of the shares.

3 Retained profits – profits after tax made by the business not yet distributed to the owners as a 'dividend'.

4 Other reserves, such as a revaluation reserve.

1.5 Statement of Financial Position: Financial Strengths and Weaknesses

A statement of financial position may suggest that a business is financially strong, although it does not prove it. It can also show signs of weakness – and we ignore these at our peril. Accountants are often criticized when a company gets into financial difficulty because they did not warn in big red letters, 'This company is dodgy. Avoid it like the plague.' But, in most cases, the signs of financial difficulty are there for all to see, long before a much publicized collapse, if only the trouble is taken to try to understand the statement of financial position.

Companies collapse in one way or another when they cannot pay what they are required to pay: when they are unable to meet their financial liabilities. Many factors may contribute to this situation: poor management, poor marketing, poor planning, trying to do too much with too little money, bad luck, dodgy customers, changes in the world economy and so on. There is usually someone, or something, to blame. But, in the end, either a company can pay its bills or it cannot. The statement of financial position gives a pretty good guide to what bills are due to be paid – and the resources available for paying them.

Although there may be question marks about the reliability of some figures in published accounts, the liabilities[4] figures are among the most reliable. A company needs to have sufficient funds readily available to meet its liabilities when they fall due. A company's 'current liabilities' are shown clearly on the statement of financial position. The important question is: does the company have enough short-term assets to be able to pay its short-term liabilities as they fall due?

A company's current assets include money in the bank, receivables[5] that are due to become money in the bank within a few months, and inventories, or stocks of goods that the company plans to sell and convert into money in the bank within a matter of months. If a company has a lot more current assets than current liabilities, it should be able to pay its current liabilities when they fall due. If their current assets are two or three times as much as their current liabilities, then they appear to be fairly strong; or in the terminology of accounting, they have a high current ratio.

In Illustrations 1.1–1.3, current assets are £5,000, and short-term liabilities are £3,000. The current ratio is 1.67 : 1.[6] This is not particularly high, but it looks as if there is enough cash and near cash available in the short term to be able to pay the short-term liabilities as they fall due.

Although all current assets should become cash within a matter of months, this is more difficult with some items than others. Not all inventories (or stocks of goods) are easily and quickly turned into cash. A half-baked loaf will probably be finished and sold for cash within a matter of hours. A half-built house, in an area where no one wants to live, could remain unsold for a long time. If most of a company's 'current assets' are actually inventories, its ability to pay trade payables and other creditors quickly may be less than its current ratio suggests. A useful approach to assessing a company's ability to pay its short-term liabilities is to exclude inventories from current assets, and to assess the company's 'liquidity', by comparing its 'liquid assets' with its current liabilities. This is known as the liquidity ratio, or acid test, or quick assets ratio.

Long-term liabilities are also important – a company or individual can go bankrupt because of the weight of long-term creditors. It is difficult to say how much debt is too much – some people, and some companies, seem to manage with huge amounts of debt,[7] whereas others (like a number of airlines recently or even governments) collapse. An individual who has lots of money can afford to borrow lots of money. Similarly, a company with a large amount of equity, or shareholders' funds (the company's 'own' money) can afford to borrow more money than a company with very little equity. In Illustrations 1.1–1.3 the amount of equity is £100,000, so it would seem reasonable to borrow another £100,000. If a business is financed half by borrowing and half from its own shareholders' equity (or funds), then the borrowing is high, but probably not excessive. But in these illustrations, the borrowing is much more than the equity. If we add together all the long-term funds (shareholders' funds plus long-term creditors = £322,000), then we can see that the assets of the business are mainly[8] financed by borrowing. In accounting terminology such a company is 'high geared', which usually means high risk.

But high gearing, or high amounts of long-term debt, does not particularly matter if the individual or company has a substantial amount of income with which to pay the interest, and to repay the creditors (or borrow more!) when repayment is due. Individuals who have to pay mortgage interest of £20,000 a year should have no problems if their annual income is £100,000 a year or more. Someone who has to pay £20,000 a year mortgage interest from an annual income of £25,000 is likely to have real problems! It is worth comparing the amount of interest that has to be paid each year, with the

---

[4] There are occasions when crooked accountants and directors omit liabilities completely, or hide them as some form of 'off statement of financial position finance'. These 'creative accounting' issues are addressed in Chapter 8.

[5] Receivables are debtors; these are customers who have not yet paid for the goods and services with which they have been supplied.

[6] £5,000 ÷ £3,000 = 1.67.

[7] At the end of 2010 GlaxoSmithKline had long-term borrowings of £14,809m; shareholders' equity amounted to only £8,887m. This is most unusual!

[8] £222,000 of £322,000 is almost 69 per cent.

income available to pay that interest. If the interest is covered, say, five times by the income, then it is probably alright. But if the interest is covered only 1.25 times by the available income, then there are likely to be problems.

In assessing the financial strength of a company, or how likely it is to go bankrupt, it is worth calculating the current ratio, the liquidity ratio, the capital gearing ratio and the interest times cover.

1.6 Depreciation and Statement of Financial Position 'Values'

Before looking at the published statement of financial position of a real company, it is useful to know that all assets are not simply shown at cost. Some non-current assets, particularly land and buildings, are revalued from time to time. Most property,[9] plant and equipment ('tangible non-current assets') are depreciated each year.

If you buy a car for £10,000, you might decide that you will keep it for four years, and expect that at the end of the four years you will be able to sell it for £2,000. This is a plan, or an accounting policy. After one year you can show the car as being £8,000; after two years it would be £6,000 and so on. This does not mean that the car is 'worth' £8,000 after one year. What we need to do is to show three things:

1 The car cost £10,000.
2 After one year the cumulative depreciation is £2,000 (after two years it would be £4,000; after three years it would be £6,000).
3 After one year the net book[10] value of the car would be £8,000 (after two years it would be £6,000; after three years it would be £4,000).

It is important that *all three* of these can be found on the statement of financial position, or in notes to the statement of financial position: the cost of an asset, the cumulative depreciation and the net book value. As the above example shows, the net book value is not an attempt to show what the asset is really worth now. We decided to write off the initial cost of the car, down to an estimated trade in value when we have finished with it, and to charge the same amount of depreciation each year[11] for four years. A published statement of financial position does not, of course, show individual assets; totals for groups of similar assets are shown.

In Illustrations 1.1–1.3 depreciation has been ignored to simplify it. The car is shown at £10,000. If we decided that a depreciation charge, or expense, of £2,000 is appropriate, there would be *two effects* on the statement of financial position: (i) the car (assets) would be reduced by £2,000; and (ii) the equity would be reduced by £2,000. The basic balance sheet equation, shown below, would still balance.

$$\text{Assets} - \text{liabilities} = \text{equity}$$

Illustration 1.4 shows how the statement of financial position changes as a result of charging expenses, earning income and making a profit.

1.7 Statements of Financial Position and Profit

A successful individual or business is likely to show an increase in capital or equity or net worth each year.

---

[9] Yes, even property.

[10] The amount shown in the 'books' of the company, or its statement of financial position value.

[11] Depreciation does not have to be on a 'straight line' or 'equal annual instalments' basis. Businesses can choose to charge more depreciation in the early years by using a 'diminishing balance' basis.

ILLUSTRATION 1.4

Statement of financial position of A. Reader Company Ltd as at 31 December

	Year 1		Year 2	
	£	£	£	£
Non-current assets				
Tangible assets:				
Freehold land and buildings (at cost)	300,000		300,000	
Furniture (at cost less depreciation)	4,000		3,200	
Vehicles (at cost less depreciation)	10,000		8,000	
	314,000		311,200	
Investments	6,000	320,000	6,000	317,200
Current assets				
Inventories	200		9,000	
Trade receivables	–		20,000	
Cash and bank	4,800		5,000	
		5,000		34,000
Total assets		325,000		351,200
Current liabilities				
Trade payables		3,000		4,200
Non-current liabilities				
Mortgage		222,000		222,000
Total liabilities		225,000		226,200
Equity				
Capital and reserves		100,000		100,000
Retained earnings for year 2				25000
		325,000		351,200

Expenses, such as depreciation, decrease assets and decrease equity. Most expenses reduce the asset of cash when they are paid.[12] If they have not yet been paid, then there is an increase in liabilities – shown as payables (which has the same effect as a reduction in assets). Whether they are paid out in cash or not, the effect of all expenses is to reduce equity.

Revenues, mainly from sales, increase assets and increase equity. If they come in the form of cash, then the asset of cash is increased. If the customers have not yet paid, then the increase in assets shows up as an increase in receivables.[13] Whether they are received in the form of cash or not, the effect of all revenues is to increase equity.

In a successful business revenues should be greater than expenses. This means that profit is earned; the net effect is to increase equity. Profit is added to equity.

If we take the statement of financial position at the end of one year, and compare it with the statement of financial position at the end of the next year, we can get a fairly good idea of the amount of profit that was made in the period between the two dates. All we do is compare the figure for equity (or net assets, or shareholders' funds) on the most recent statement of financial position with the equivalent figure a year ago. This is shown in Illustration 1.4. The profit has shown up in additional

---

[12] Depreciation is an expense that reduces the non-current asset; it does not reduce the cash – it is not paid.

[13] Or debtors.

inventory, receivables and cash: they have increased by £29,000. But non-current (or fixed) assets have gone down by £2,800 (depreciation), and there are additional liabilities of £1,200; the total effect of these is an increase in net assets of £25,000. That £25,000 should be added to equity: until the question mark has been replaced by £25,000 of 'retained earnings', the statement of financial position will not balance.

Without more evidence we cannot always be sure that the increase in net assets is the profit for the year, for three main reasons:

1 It could be that the amount of equity has increased because shareholders have put more money into the business; there has been a new issue of shares. Any extra coming in from the issue of shares does not count as profit, and so should be deducted from the increase in equity shown on the statement of financial position to arrive at the profit figure for the year.

2 All the profits that have been made do not necessarily stay within the business. Most companies pay out dividends. They can make a substantial profit, and pay most of it out as dividends. Dividends do not reduce profits, but they do mean that the whole of the profit for the year does not increase equity. If we are to calculate the amount of profit for the year using the statement of financial position, dividends must be added to the amount of retained profit for the year to arrive at the total profit for the year.

3 Sometimes the amount shown for equity has increased because the company has revalued its assets. An increase in the value of assets does not count as profit. In Illustration 1.4 if the company had wanted to revalue its land and buildings from £300,000 to £350,000 there would be two effects: the amount for the asset would increase by £50,000; and the amount of equity would have increased by £50,000. This has not happened in Illustration 1.4.

If there has been an increase in the amount shown for equity from one year to the next, this is an indication of profit; but adjustments may need to be made for the three items listed above to arrive at the correct profit figure for the year.

A statement of financial position is not the most convenient way of calculating profit, but it can be done! Profit for the year is the increase in equity during the year, minus any additional shares that have been issued, plus any dividends that have been distributed to shareholders, minus any amounts resulting from the revaluation of assets.

Some may argue that even an increase in asset values should count as profit. But the traditional accountant would not be impressed with such an 'all-inclusive' view of profit.

1.8 A Company's Published Statement of Financial Position

A recent published statement of financial position of the Marks and Spencer Group plc for the year ended 2 April 2011 (slightly simplified) is shown in Illustration 1.5. It provides useful indications in relation to several aspects of a company, especially when comparing one year with another.

1 *Size and growth*[14]: The book value of the Marks and Spencer Group net assets decreased from £26.0m in June 2010 to £19.3m in January 2009, a decrease of 25.8 per cent. There has been an increase in current assets but a decrease in non-current assets.

2 *How the business is financed*: The balance sheet equation, assets *equals* liabilities *plus* equity, shows that a business finances its assets partly with other people's money (liabilities), and partly with the owners' money (equity). The Marks and Spencer Group's decrease in assets has been financed by an 11.8 per cent increase in liabilities but a 25.8 per cent decrease in equity. The

---

[14] In assessing size and growth it is useful also to look at sales revenue, profits and market capitalization. On Monday 10 October 2011 the market capitalization of Marks and Spencer Group was shown in the *Financial Times* as £5,172m.

ILLUSTRATION 1.5 Marks and Spencer Group plc	2 April 2011	3 April 2010
	£m	£m
Non-current assets		
Intangible assets	527.7	452.8
Property, plant and equipment	4,662.2	4,722.0
Other	512.5	458.2
	5,702.4	5,633.0
Current assets		
Inventories	685.3	613.2
Trade and other receivables	250.3	281.4
Other	235.9	219.8
Cash and cash equivalents	470.2	405.8
	1,641.7	1,520.2
Total assets	7,344.1	7,153.2
Equity and liabilities		
Current liabilities		
Trade and other payables	1,347.6	1,153.8
Borrowings	602.3	482.9
Current tax liabilities	115.0	129.2
Provisions	22.7	25.6
Other	122.7	99.0
	2,210.2	1,890.5
Non-current liabilities		
Retirement benefit deficit	14.1	366.5
Trade and other payables	262.3	280.3
Borrowings	1,924.1	2,278.0
Other non-current liabilities	37.5	–
Provisions for liabilities	22.0	25.5
Deferred tax liabilities	196.5	126.5
	2,456.5	3,076.8
Total liabilities	4,666.7	4,967.3
Equity		
Share capital	396.2	395.5
Share premium	255.2	247.5
Capital redemption reserve	2,202.6	2,202.6
Other reserves	6,053.7	5,958.9
Retained earnings	5,873.2	5,281.9
Total shareholders' equity	2,673.5	2,168.8
Non-controlling interests in equity	3.9	17.3
Total equity	2,677.4	2,185.9
Total liabilities and equity	7,344.1	7,153.2

decrease in equity was as a result of a substantial loss in the year; no additional shares were issued.

The increase in current assets (£6.8m) was financed partly by an increase in current liabilities (£5.9m).

3 *Profits*: Comparing statement of financial positions of two different dates does not show the amount of profit (or loss) made in the intervening period, unless a few adjustments are made, as explained above. It does not show what dividends were paid; but even after deducting the dividends we can see a substantial decrease in Marks and Spencer Group's retained profits (£6.6m).

4 *Solvency*: Statements of financial position show the amount of liabilities, and give some indication of whether or not these are excessive. This can be done in two stages, as follows.

Current liabilities

Are these excessive in relation to current assets? The amounts are as follows:

	2011 £m	2010 £m
Current assets	1,642	1,520
Current liabilities	2,210	1,891

Current liabilities are amounts that have to be paid out in the short term. Current assets include cash and items that should become cash within a year. As the Marks and Spencer Group has more current liabilities than current assets, there could be a problem in paying those liabilities as they fall due. This is often expressed as the *current ratio*, which is the ratio of current assets to current liabilities, which is:

$$0.74 : 1 \quad 0.80 : 1$$

The ratio has fallen slightly during the year but is still in line with other similar retailers.

With some current assets, such as inventories, it could take many months before they are turned into cash, although not in clothing retailers, perhaps. Liquidity can be assessed by taking only 'quick assets' and comparing them with current liabilities. This is the 'acid test'. If inventories are excluded from current assets, the *liquidity ratio* is calculated as follows:

	2011 £m	2010 £m
Current assets excluding inventories	956	907
Current liabilities	2,210	1,891
Liquidity ratio	0.43 : 1	0.48 : 1

The liquidity ratio has fallen in the year but even though there are not enough current assets to pay the current liabilities, this is still in line with similar businesses so it would not be considered to be a problem in this case.

Non-current liabilities

The Marks and Spencer Group's statement of financial position shows that borrowings within non-current liabilities (or '*debt*', D) are significant, amounting to £1,924m. The total shareholders' equity ('E' or shareholders' funds) amounted to over £2,674m in 2011. This can be expressed as a *gearing ratio*

for each year by asking the question: what proportion of long-term finance was borrowed (as opposed to being part of shareholders' funds)? This can be expressed as: what is D as a proportion of D + E?

	2011 £m	2010 £m
D Long-term borrowings	1,924	2,278
E Equity	2,674	2,169
D + E Total long-term finance	4,598	4,447
D as a percentage of D + E	42%	51%

The gearing is quite high, meaning that the company is significantly dependent on long-term borrowings, but this is not out of line with other retailers. Many companies have gearing ratios of 40 per cent or more without any problems. A company might be regarded as being highly geared, and so more risky, if the ratio is around 50 per cent but, again, this depends on the business sector in which the company operates.

In assessing whether there is too much borrowing it is important to see how much interest the company has to pay, and if its operating profits are high enough to ensure that the interest is amply covered by the earnings available to pay it.

The published annual reports of companies show a lot more detail than the simplified statement of financial positions included in this chapter, and it can look frighteningly complex. A great deal of additional information is shown in notes to the accounts. In studying statements of financial position it is important to have a few clear questions in mind; to concentrate on the larger figures; and not to become lost in detail that is hard to understand.

1.9 Role and Limitations of Statements of Financial Position

Statements of financial position can be useful in a number of ways:

1 We saw that the statement of financial position, or a statement of assets and liabilities, can be useful in showing what a person or business is worth. But there are problems in establishing agreed rules as to exactly which assets (and perhaps even which liabilities) should be included, and in determining the basis upon which they should be valued. There is also the problem that the value of a business as a whole is likely to be different from the value of all of its assets (less liabilities) added together. The real value of a business (or an individual) might depend more on the income that it can generate (as a whole entity) in the future than on whatever amounts might be shown for individual assets and liabilities.

2 We also saw that, in listing the various liabilities that have to be paid, short and long term, we can get an idea of the financial strength of a business. If its liabilities are too high, and it cannot pay them, it is likely to get into serious financial difficulties, and perhaps go out of business. Statements of financial position can give a good indication of whether liabilities are too high, or whether the business is reasonably strong. The statement of financial position is the basis for assessing the financial position of a company.

3 We can also measure profit using the statement of financial position. There are easier ways of measuring profit, but it is useful to calculate it in two different ways so that one checks the other. The statement of financial position approach to measuring profit is one of the two main approaches, and one that may increase in importance.

4 Statements of financial position play an important role in 'stewardship'. Shareholders put their money into a company; directors and managers are the 'stewards' of that money; and shareholders

want to know what has happened to their money. The statement of financial position shows what money has been put in by the shareholders, and what retained profits have been added to it; this amount is shown as equity (or shareholders' funds). Examination of the statement of financial position, the assets and liabilities, shows what that money is now financing or, if you like, what has happened to it.

5 In order to produce a statement of financial position it is necessary to produce a listing of all the company's assets and liabilities. This can be useful in keeping track of various assets, and ensuring that all are being put to good use and are earning their keep. When a company gets into financial difficulties it sometimes seems that they manage to find assets that they had previously forgotten about, or done nothing with. There may be investments that are not much use; sports and social facilities that are hardly used; receivables (debtors) who have been neglected and have got away with not paying for too long (perhaps because of a half-forgotten dispute); a workshop developing a new product that made little progress; machinery, or components and raw materials that were specially bought for a new product that was quietly abandoned; too many premises or branches; an expensive head office in the centre of London; a training centre, kitchens, computer work-shops and maintenance facilities that should have been sold or redeployed when these activities were outsourced.

Many companies do not even know what assets they own, or how many laptop computers have 'walked' out of the door, and they do not even have an up-to-date non-current assets register. The process of producing listings of assets in order to compile a statement of financial position can be a useful housekeeping exercise.

6 In addition to providing a basis for assessing the financial *position* of a company, the statement of financial position also provides a basis for assessing the financial *performance* of a company. The shareholders of a company are likely to be concerned about performance in terms of profitability. They are not concerned merely with the amount of profit the company makes; they are concerned with how much profit the company makes in relation to the amount of capital employed. A profit of £1m may look good for a company with capital employed of £5m; it would look pathetic in relation to capital employed of £100m. It is the statement of financial position that shows the amount of capital employed. The ratio of profit to capital employed is a key ratio in assessing and improving a company's financial performance.

7 Financial accounting is a whole system, and the statement of financial position is an essential part of it in checking, balancing and controlling other parts of the system. If a company's statement of financial position does not balance, there is definitely something wrong! Accountants are only (or nearly!) human, and inevitably some mistakes are made with figures. The financial accounting system is designed to show up errors, and to find where they occurred. An accounting system can also show up fraud and theft. When a statement of financial position does balance, we cannot be sure that there is no fraud or error. If it does not balance, we can be sure that something is wrong; and if we do make a mistake, it will probably show up during the accounting processes before producing a statement of financial position.[15]

But we should not expect too much from statements of financial position. They were never properly designed to achieve anything very useful. When double-entry bookkeeping first became widely used, the statement of financial position was just a matter of bookkeeping convenience. It was not even necessary to produce one every year. Until the eighteenth century a statement of financial position was often not produced until the ledger was full; then a statement of financial position was a summary of the assets and liabilities that were transferred to the new ledger. Any remaining old balances, mostly revenues and expenses, were written off. The balances shown on the statement of financial position are items that are continuing, but they tend to be shown at the cost price when they are first entered in the business's books.

---

[15] Mistakes usually show up in the trial balance – if it does not balance!

By the end of the nineteenth century the production of statements of financial position on an annual basis became normal. During the nineteenth century it became a requirement for companies to publish annual statements of financial position; and during the twentieth century legislation became increasingly specific about what should be shown on a statement of financial position. Towards the end of the twentieth century accounting standards laid down more detailed requirements, and since 2006 large companies have been following IASs in the same way as in many other countries.

The main limitations of statements of financial position have already been referred to:

1 What items are we going to include?
2 How do we establish the value of particular items?
3 The value of a company as a whole is likely to be very different from the total net value of the individual assets and liabilities.

Sometimes it is very difficult to decide whether or not an item should appear on the statement of financial position. If a company running a number of hotels buys an additional hotel, that is clearly an extra non-current asset that would be shown on the statement of financial position, and the amount shown would be the amount paid for it. If such a company pays for routine cleaning of a hotel, there is no additional asset, and the amount paid should not appear on the statement of financial position as an additional asset. A payment for cleaning will reduce assets (cash) and also reduce equity. Routine redecoration, like cleaning, is an expense that does not appear on the statement of financial position. Improvements, such as installing double-glazing, an extension or additional bathrooms, are 'capital expenditure': the amounts are added to non-current assets on the statement of financial position. Sometimes the boundary between 'capital expenditure' (which appears on the statement of financial position, and does not reduce equity) and 'revenue expenditure' (which does not appear on the statement of financial position, and does reduce equity) is not clear and there may be scope for creative accounting.

Where there is a lack of clear principles to determine what should be included on a statement of financial position, and the basis or valuation that is to be used for the various items, the value of statements of financial position is restricted. A series of official Financial Reporting Standards (FRSs) in the UK and International Financial Reporting Standards (IFRSs) have been produced to deal with this problem, and the development of financial accounting has steadily encouraged users to expect more from statements of financial position. It would be difficult for them to satisfy all the different expectations that interested parties might have. But we cannot even begin to assess a company's financial position and performance without a good understanding of the statements of financial position.

1.10 Financial Accounting and Management Accounting

Financial accounting is mainly concerned with producing financial statements for shareholders, creditors and others who are outside the organization concerned. The main financial statements are the statement of financial position, the income statement and the cash flow statement. In published accounts these are supported by substantial additional information, notes and explanations. The Companies Act, and official accounting standards, regulate the information that is published. Within the company a sophisticated bookkeeping system is required to record all the transactions that form the basis of these financial statements. Bookkeeping systems are explained in Chapter 9. In large-scale businesses managers do not rely very much on published financial accounting information; they have access to much more detailed and relevant management accounting information.

Management accounting is concerned with producing information for managers who are concerned with planning, decision-making and control. Management accounting information is not usually published, and it is designed to meet the needs of the managers of the organization concerned; it does not have to comply with official regulations. The subject of management accounting is introduced in Chapter 13, where it is clearly distinguished from financial accounting.

📖 Summary

A statement of financial position shows the assets and liabilities of a company, and can provide useful information about a company's financial position. Solvency ratios can give an indication of whether a company is likely to become insolvent. Assets are not usually shown at their current value, and care is needed in using the statements of financial position as an indication of the value of a company. A business as a whole, as a going concern, is usually worth much more than the total of its net assets.

➡ Review of key points

- ▪ A statement of financial position shows what a company controls (assets) and what it owes (liabilities).
- ▪ By deducting liabilities from assets we arrive at the figure for 'equity', or 'capital', or 'net assets'.
- ▪ Assets and liabilities are classified as being long (non-current) or short term (current). UK statements of financial position usually begin with non-current assets, followed by current assets. The second part of the statement of financial position shows how the assets were financed: by liabilities (current and non-current) and by equity.
- ▪ A successful business is usually worth more than the statement of financial position figure for its net assets.
- ▪ A statement of financial position shows how a company is financed and may indicate if a company has excessive liabilities.
- ▪ Comparing this year's statement of financial position with last year's can provide a basis for calculating profit.
- ▪ The main financial accounting statements are published; management accounting information is different, and is internal to the organization.

❗ Self-testing questions

1 Which of the following are shown on a statement of financial position: assets; expenses; liabilities; sales; share capital; profit for the year?

2 What is the difference between a non-current asset and a current asset? *Within a year*

3 Give examples of non-current (or 'fixed') assets. In what circumstances would some of the items you have listed be current assets? *for equipments   some equipment you won't use*

4 Arrange the three main statement of financial position items (assets, liabilities, equity) as an equation. *assets − liabilities = equity / net asset / capital*

5 A statement of financial position appears to show what a business is worth. What are the main problems with this statement? *the value of company as a whole is likely to very different*

6 You are given the following simplified statement of financial position of the Sandin Castle Company:

from the total value of the individual
assets and liabilities −

	£	£
Non-current assets		50,000
Current assets		
Inventories (at cost)	24,000 *20,000*	
Receivables	12,000	
Cash	9,000 *17000*	
		45,000 *49,000*
Total assets		95,000 *99,000*
Current liabilities		
Payables		22,000
Equity		
Share capital	50,000	
Retained earnings	23,000 *27000*	
		73,000 *77,000*
		95,000 *99,000*

a   Calculate the current ratio. *45000/22,000*

b   Calculate the liquidity ratio. *21000/22,000*

c   After preparing the statement of financial position, the company sells inventories, which had cost £4,000, for £8,000, which it immediately receives in cash. Show how the statement of financial position would appear after this transaction.

d   How does the above transaction affect the current ratio and the liquidity ratio?

7   You are given the following simplified statements of financial position of the Windysand Company as at 31 December:

Simplified[16] statement of financial position of the Windysand Company as at 31 December

	Year 1	Year 2
	£	£
Non-current assets	320,000	350,000 *↑30000*
Current assets	5,000	45,000 *↑40000* *↑70000*
Total assets	325,000	395,000
Non-current liabilities	222,000	202,000 *↘20,000* *↘13,000*
Current liabilities	3,000	10,000 *↗7000*
	225,000	212,000
Equity	100,000	183,000 *↑.83,000.*
	325,000	395,000

a   How much profit does it at first seem that the company made during year 2? *83000*

b   How would your answer to (a) be affected if you found out that the company had paid £10,000 in dividends; that additional shares with a value of £20,000 had been issued; and that non-current assets had been revalued upwards by £30,000? *113,000*   *↗ ? 93,000*

[16] The order of items on this statement of financial position follows the illustration given in IAS 1; it differs from the order given in the Marks and Spencer Group's published statement of financial position. We have to be prepared for statements of financial position that show items in a different order.

8 You are given the following simplified statements of financial position of two very similar companies, Domer Castle Company and Warmer Castle Company as at 31 December year 1.

	Domer Castle Ltd £	Warmer Castle Ltd £
Non-current assets		
Tangible assets		
Freehold premises (at cost)	300,000	100,000
Furniture (at cost less depreciation)	4,000	80,000
Vehicles (at cost less depreciation)	10,000	90,000
	–	44,000
Investments	314,000	314,000
Current assets		
Inventories	8,000	9,000
Receivables	12,000	10,000
Cash	14,000	5,000
	34,000	34,000
Total assets	348,000	348,000
Current liabilities		
Trade payables	17,000	17,000
Non-current liabilities		
10% debentures	100,000	200,000
Total liabilities	117,000	217,000
Equity		
Share capital	100,000	100,000
Retained earnings	131,000	31,000
	231,000	131,000
Total liabilities and equity	348,000	348,000

During year 1 the operating profit (earnings before interest and taxation) of the Domer Castle Company amounted to £31,000. The operating profit of the Warmer Castle Company amounted to £32,000.

Which of the two companies appears to be financially weakest, and why? You should calculate the current ratio, the liquidity ratio, the capital gearing ratio and the number of times interest is covered by operating profit.

9 You are given the following simplified statement of financial position of the Stonefolk Company as at 31 March year 4.

	£
Non-current assets	158,000
Current assets	
Inventories (at cost)	110,000
Receivables	120,000
Cash	20,000
	250,000
Total assets	408,000

Current liabilities				
Trade payables	120,000		120,000	100,000
Equity				
Share capital	250,000		250,000	
Retained earnings	38,000	38,000	88,000	
	288,000	308,000	338,000	
Total equity and liabilities	408,000	428,000	458,000	

a The following transactions took place in April year 4. Show how each would affect the statement of financial position. (Each transaction must affect two or more figures, and the statement of financial position must continue to balance.)

  i A building, which had cost £80,000, was sold for £100,000, which was immediately received in cash.

  ii Inventories, which had cost £30,000, were sold to Mr Spliff for £80,000. Mr Spliff agreed to pay for the goods by the end of May year 4.

  iii The company paid £40,000 of the amount that it owed to creditors, which is shown on the statement of financial position as 'payables'.

b Show how the statement of financial position would appear after these transactions have been recorded.

Assessment questions

1 What are the main functions of a statement of financial position?

2 You are given the following simplified statement of financial position of the Hackin Company as at 30 June year 9.

	£
Non-current assets	250,000
Current assets	
Inventories (at cost)	60,000
Receivables	40,000
Cash	120,000
	220,000
Total assets	470,000
Current liabilities	
Payables	100,000
Equity	
Share capital	250,000
Retained earnings	120,000
	370,000
Total equity and liabilities	470,000

a Calculate the company's current ratio and liquidity ratio.

b The following transactions take place during July year 9:

i New plant and equipment are bought for £80,000, and payment is made in cash.

ii Additional inventories of goods are bought for £15,000; it is agreed that they will be paid for in August.

Prepare a revised statement of financial position after these transactions have been recorded.

c How do these transactions affect the current ratio and the liquidity ratio?

3 You are given the following simplified statements of financial position of the Fourpine Company as at 31 December.

	Year 1	Year 2
	£	£
Non-current assets	520,000	450,000
Current assets	45,000	55,000
Total assets	565,000	505,000
Equity		
Share capital	300,000	310,000
Retained earnings	35,000	60,000
	335,000	370,000
Non-current liabilities	200,000	100,000
Current liabilities	30,000	35,000
Total equity and liabilities	565,000	505,000

a How much profit does it at first seem that the company made during year 2?

b How would your answer to (a) be affected if you found out that the company had paid £25,000 in dividends?

4 You are given the following simplified statements of financial position of the Port Andrew Company and the Port Edward Company as at 31 December year 1.

	Port Andrew Ltd	Port Edward Ltd
	£	£
Non-current assets		
Tangible assets		
Freehold premises (at cost)	100,000	200,000
Plant (at cost less depreciation)	200,000	100,000
Vehicles (at cost less depreciation)	100,000	100,000
	400,000	400,000
Investments	200,000	30,000
	600,000	430,000
Current assets		
Inventories	70,000	40,000
Receivables	50,000	90,000
Cash	10,000	60,000
	130,000	190,000
Total assets	730,000	620,000

Current liabilities		
Trade payables	70,000	80,000
Non-current liabilities		
10% debentures	300,000	100,000
Total liabilities	370,000	180,000
Equity		
Share capital	300,000	300,000
Retained earnings	60,000	140,000
	360,000	440,000
Total equity and liabilities	730,000	620,000

During year 1 the operating profit of the Port Andrew Company amounted to £61,000. The operating profit of the Port Edward Company amounted to £40,000.

Which of the two companies appears to be the financially weaker, and why? You should calculate the current ratio, the liquidity ratio, the capital gearing ratio and the interest times cover.

5 You are given the following simplified statement of financial position of the Whiting Company as at 31 August year 6:

	£	£
Non-current assets		350,000
Current assets		
Inventories (at cost)	90,000	
Trade receivables	80,000	
Cash	30,000	200,000
Total assets		550,000
Current liabilities		
Trade payables		130,000
Equity		
Share capital	380,000	
Retained earnings	40,000	420,000
Total equity and liabilities		550,000

a The following transactions took place in September year 6. Show how each would affect the statement of financial position. (Each transaction must affect two figures, and the statement of financial position must continue to balance.)

i A new machine costing £10,000 was purchased and paid for in cash.

ii Inventories, which had cost £50,000, were sold to Mrs Fish for £90,000 and paid for immediately in cash.

iii £30,000 was received from debtors, which were shown as 'receivables' on the statement of financial position.

b Show how the statement of financial position would appear after these transactions have been recorded.

Group activities and discussion questions

1   Each individual in the group should attempt to answer the question 'How much am I worth?' There is no need to disclose actual figures or personal information. The objective is to determine – and for members of the group to agree – the way in which the question would be answered. What principles or rules would you use?

2   Each member of the group should choose two listed companies, and obtain their published statement of financial position (from the companies' websites or by using the *Financial Times* Annual Reports Service). Try to assess how financially strong each company is (or is it likely to collapse?). The group should rank each of the companies that members have examined from the strongest financially, to the weakest. The group should discuss, and try to agree, criteria to form the basis for this assessment.

3   Is it possible to calculate the value of a company? If not, why not? If so, how?

4   Which of the following should be included as assets on a company's statement of financial position: money that is owed to the company; the cost of an advertising campaign; machinery that is over 20 years old but which is still used occasionally; key employees who have a high market value; money paid as 'commission' to a government minister in Wayawayaland that has helped to secure a lucrative contract; brand names; money receivable under a contract that was signed yesterday and that will be earned next year; machinery that the company does not own, but for which they have signed a five-year lease.

Accounting in context

Discuss and comment on the following article with particular reference to the nature and accounting value of a company's assets.

BHP Billiton may write down shale

By Emma Rowley

BHP Billiton, the world's biggest miner, hinted that it faces writing down the value of its shale-gas assets, after spending billions investing in the energy sector.

The FTSE 100 miner entered the shale-gas arena last year by spending around $17bn (£11bn) buying producer Petrohawk Energy and assets from Chesapeake Energy. It has described the gas as a "game changer".

But its foray into the gas – extracted from shale rock through the controversial practice of "fracking" – has been affected by a fall in natural gas prices to a decade low.

The plunge is largely due to the abundance of shale gas entering the market.

BHP will review its assets on June 30, the end of its financial year, said J Michael Yeager, chief executive of its petroleum division, when asked about potential writedowns.

"If we have to take an accounting snapshot here, we hope everybody knows that we'll take another accounting snapshot in the future and whenever those circumstances are changed, that whatever action we take now, may get reversed later on," he said.

Steven Robinson, at Australian fund manager Alleron Investment Management, told Bloomberg: "It looks like they have paid a lot of money for those shale assets."

BHP shares dropped 66 or 3.6pc to close at £17.98 in London, as economic fears provoked a wider sell-off.

Source: The Daily Telegraph, 15 May 2012

References and further reading

International Accounting Standard 1 (2003, amended 2012). *Presentation of Financial Statements*. IASB.

Melville, A. (2011) *International Financial Reporting* (3rd edn.). Harlow: FT Prentice Hall.

Wood, F. and A. Sangster (2012) *Business Accounting* (vol. 1) (12th edn.). Harlow: FT Prentice Hall.

www.frc.org.uk (gives details of the Financial Reporting Council and arrangements for accounting standards in the British Isles)

www.ifrs.org (gives details of international financial reporting standards)

http://annualreport.marksandspencer.com/ (gives the Marks and Spencer Group accounts in full)

When you have read this chapter, log on to the Online Learning Centre website at *www.mcgraw-hill.co.uk/textbooks/leiwy* to explore chapter-by-chapter test questions, further reading and more online study tools.

The Income Statement (Profit and Loss Account)

Chapter contents

✓ Learning objectives

After studying this chapter you will be able to:

- ✓ Explain the structure and terminology of straightforward income statements
- ✓ Understand that there are different reasons for measuring profit, and different views of what profit is
- ✓ Describe the main categories of expenses
- ✓ Assess some possibilities for 'creative accounting' in measuring profit
- ✓ Discuss the role and limitations of income statements

2.1 Introduction

In Chapter 1 we saw that the amount of profit a company makes during a year can be calculated by comparing the statement of financial position at the beginning of the year with the statement of financial position at the end of the year. Some additional information may be needed, and it is not the easiest way of calculating profit. Income statements (or profit and loss accounts) provide more straightforward presentations of profit figures. But even a brief examination of the published income statement of a company shows a complex assortment of different profit figures, and it can be difficult to know where to start.

At first sight the notion of profit seems very straightforward. If you buy something for £6 and sell it for £10, you have made £4 profit. But accountants would say that this is 'gross profit', which is the first of the profit figures shown on an income statement. We need to deduct expenses before we arrive at operating profit. There are more deductions, and profit is shown both before and after tax.

To begin with, we need to be clear about (a) terminology, and (b) the usual formats for presenting the information. Most people are clear that they want to know the profit figures, but they are much less clear about exactly what profit means, and what the profit figures are to be used for. If we are clear about the function(s) of profit figures, we can then see what principles for measuring profit are appropriate.

2.2 Terminology and Format

Income statements show profit for the year[1] and the term 'income statement' has now generally replaced the term 'profit and loss account', following international accounting standards (IAS).

An income statement shows the calculation on the basis that expenses are deducted from revenues.

Revenues *minus* expenses = profit

'Revenues', 'turnover' and 'sales' are much the same thing, and are shown on an income statement along with any 'other income'.[2] The words 'expenses' and 'costs' mean much the same thing, but payments (of cash) are quite different. It sometimes seems as if accounting terminology is designed to be confusing!

One thing we need to be very clear about is that the word 'receipts' is nothing to do with income or profit; it means receipts of cash. Similarly, the word 'payments' is nothing to do with expenses or profit measurement; it means payments of cash. The differences between receipts and payments of cash, and profit are essential to an understanding of financial accounts. They are dealt with in Chapter 6.

The standard format appearing in IAS 1 is shown in Illustration 2.1.

Another commonly seen format of the income statement, a variation of the IAS 1 format in Illustration 2.1, can be seen in Illustration 2.2 in which profit is presented in four main stages.

First, there is 'gross profit', which is the difference between the sales figure and *the cost of the goods that have been sold*.[3] This phrase, more simply expressed as *cost of sales*, is very important in profit measurement.

---

[1] An income statement can be for a year, a month or any period you like. A statement of financial position is never for a period – it is always 'as at' a given date.

[2] It is easier to think of 'income' as being revenues for the period, before expenses are deducted; but, unfortunately, some accountants use the word 'income' to mean profit. Accounting terminology can be very confusing!

[3] It excludes the cost of goods that have not been sold (inventory or closing stock), which is carried forward to be treated as an expense in the following period.

ILLUSTRATION 2.1

Income statement of IAS1 Company Ltd for the year ended 31 December Year 3

	£000
Revenue	100
Cost of sales	60
Gross profit	40
Other income	2
Distribution costs	(12)
Administration expenses	(9)
Other expenses	(2)
Financing costs	(3)
Profit before taxation	16
Tax on profit for year	(4)
Profit for the year	12

Statement of changes in equity of IAS1 Company Ltd for the year ended 31 December Year 3

Balance at 31 December year 2	500
Add Profit for the year	12
Deduct Dividends for the year	(5)
Balance as at 31 December year 3	507

Second, there is 'operating profit', which is arrived at after deducting the main categories of expenses, which are distribution costs and administrative expenses. Operating profit is an important figure: it shows how much profit has been made from the normal operations of the business before deducting any interest payable. Operating profit is not shown explicitly in the IAS 1 format in Illustration 2.1 but can be computed by the reader.

Third, there is 'profit before taxation', which is arrived at after bringing in interest receivable and interest payable – usually shown as 'finance costs'.

Fourth, there is 'profit after taxation', which obviously comes after deducting the company's tax charge for the year, and is the net amount that has been earned for the shareholders.

Each of the above four versions of profit may be useful in assessing different aspects of a company's performance. The fourth figure shows profit available after taxation that is the basis for determining the amount of dividend to be paid to shareholders.

The dividend[4] for the year is shown on a separate 'Statement of changes in equity for the year'. As we saw in Chapter 1, we can compare the statement of financial position at the beginning of the year with the statement of financial position at the end of the year to show the amount by which 'equity' has changed: it is increased by the amount of profit earned during the year; it is reduced by the amount of dividends to be paid for the year; and it may be changed by other items such as a revaluation of assets. The 'Statement of changes in equity for the year' shows these items and anything else that has changed the amount of equity during the year.

Although company income statements can be almost infinitely complex, it is also possible to have versions that look relatively simple, as shown in Illustrations 2.1 and 2.2. Each of the different profit figures has its uses, but the two marked with asterisks are perhaps the most important in assessing the

---

[4] The dividend for the year is the amount paid to shareholders; it is usually part of the profit (after tax) for the year. The remaining profits are 'retained' within the business.

ILLUSTRATION 2.2

Income statement of Simple Company Ltd for the year ended 31 December year 3

	£000
Revenue	100
Cost of sales	60
Gross profit	40
Distribution costs	(12)
Administration expenses	(9)
Operating profit	19
Financing costs	(3)
Profit before taxation	16
Tax on profit for year	(4)
Profit for the year (i.e. after taxation)	12

Statement of changes in equity of Simple Company Ltd for the year ended 31 December year 3

Balance at 31 December year 2	500
Add Profit for the year	12
Deduct Dividends for the year	(5)
Balance as at 31 December year 3	507

---

overall performance of a company. It is useful to compare the profit figures for the current year with those of previous years to see what improvement (if any) there has been. It is also useful to compare the profit figures with the amount of resources invested in the company to see if a reasonable return has been achieved.

The income statement emphasizes what profit has been earned for the shareholders. The final figures on a published income statement show the 'earnings per share' (EPS). This is the total amount of profit after tax that the company has earned during the year, divided by the number of shares that the company has. This figure is widely used as a measure of a company's success. Not all of the EPS is paid out to shareholders as dividends: the total earnings for the year can be compared with the dividends for the year on the statement of changes in equity. In Illustration 2.2 the Simple Company Ltd made profits of £12,000 during the year; £5,000 of this was paid to shareholders as dividends; the remaining £7,000 was retained in the business for the maintenance and expansion of the business.

An income statement might show a substantial increase in profits, but this does not necessarily mean that the shareholders are going to be better off. If profits have increased by 50 per cent, but the number of shares has doubled, then the EPS will be reduced. EPS is sometimes seen as being the most important figure in assessing company performance. Shareholders expect to see it increase year after year, and some companies even aim for 'double-digit' growth in EPS – they want it to increase by at least 10 per cent each year. Not many companies manage to achieve this for more than a very few years.

2.3 Reasons for Measuring Profit

There are many good reasons for measuring profit. It is a symbol of success for companies and their managers. A company that shows steadily increasing profits is likely to go from strength to strength. A company that shows losses, or falling profits, is likely to find itself in difficulties.

More specifically, the main reasons for measuring profit, or functions that profit measurement may serve, are as follows:

1 It is a measure of *performance*. Shareholders want to know how well the directors and managers of a company are doing, running the company for its owners (the shareholders).

2 It is a guide to dividend policy. A company chooses how much profit is paid out as dividends. Occasionally, a company pays out more dividends than it earns in profits, but it cannot do that for very long. A company must earn profits if it is to continue paying dividends. There is a Companies Act requirement that dividends should be paid only when there are sufficient accumulated realized, retained earnings to justify them.

3 Directors and managers may have a direct interest in such a performance for their own reasons: they are often shareholders themselves, and they may have some sort of performance-related pay, which means that they get extra salaries or bonuses[5] if profits achieve specified levels.

4 It is a measure of the *efficiency* of a company. Efficiency is about the relationship between inputs and outputs. To maximize efficiency is to minimize the cost per unit of output; or to maximize the outputs per £ of cost. For a company the inputs are shown as costs; outputs are shown as sales; the difference between sales and costs is shown as profit. Maximizing profits, therefore, maximizes efficiency.

5 It is a measure of the *effectiveness* of a company. Effectiveness is about the relationship between outputs and objectives. An effective organization (or individual) is one that achieves what it is intending to do. If we assume that companies intend to maximize profits, then maximizing profits maximizes effectiveness.

6 It is a guide to the financial strength of a company. A company that is profitable is more likely to survive, and be able to pay its liabilities when they fall due, than one which is loss-making.

7 It is a basis for taxation. The government lays down various rules for taxation purposes (e.g. what rate of depreciation or 'writing-down allowance' should be used), which means that the profit figure shown in a company's published accounts may be quite different from the figure used in calculating the amount of corporation tax payable.

8 It is relevant in pricing decisions. In most circumstances prices are determined more by what the market will bear, and the company has to find ways of keeping costs below the market price (and/ or ways of pushing up what the market will bear). In some circumstances (e.g. in public utilities that were previously publicly owned) there might be official restrictions on price increases that are related to profits.

9 Employees have an interest in profits. They may believe that a profitable company is the best guarantee of long-term employment. They may also believe that good profits present an opportunity for pressing for increases in wages and salaries.

10 Profits are sometimes seen as being the key to a successful economy and a successful country. Companies that are most profitable find it easier to raise capital, at lowest cost; and so resources in the country flow into the most profitable companies, which are also the most efficient and effective. Companies that are least profitable find it hardest to raise additional capital, have to pay more for it, and so the least efficient and effective companies tend to decline.

Some of the above may be questionable, or political, and you are, of course, free to take very different views. You may believe that profit is a measure of the success of the strong in exploiting the

---

[5] Or they may have share options. Or they may be 'fat cats' who get good bonuses even when the company does badly. Or their bonuses may depend on the share price achieving a particular level. Or they may have share options that are valuable only when the share price achieves particular levels. As directors are supposed to be accountable to shareholders, it is worth considering the effectiveness of accountability arrangements; these are discussed later.

weak; that big business makes too much profit; that more should go to the workers; that profit fails to measure social costs; and all of the above ignores issues such as health and safety, child labour, damage to the environment and non-sustainable development. You can, if you wish, take the view that profits are a 'bad thing'. It is probably a 'good thing' if this book encourages you to think about these issues!

It is, however, worth being explicit about the general assumptions that seem to lie behind the measuring and reporting of profit. Many different people and groups in society are likely to be in favour of companies making good and increasing profits for many different reasons. In some circumstances governments may try to restrict the amount of profit that monopolies (or near monopolies) are allowed to make. But increasing profits are generally favoured by shareholders, managers (and the Treasury who are usually happy to rake in more in taxation), and the company's bankers and professional advisers (whose fees seem to keep going up), the financial press, many employees and anyone else who can jump on the gravy train. There is enormous pressure on managers to perform, and to produce profits. And if they cannot, they are liable to be replaced by others, sometimes by managers who can produce profits out of thin air,[6] like magicians. There are always some who can make use of creative accounting techniques for their own advantage. But, like magicians, such managers do not want to be watched too closely, and the more successful ones move on rapidly to other companies to display their tricks and illusions.

Given that profit figures are likely to be used for many different purposes, it is not surprising that there are different approaches to profit measurement. The principles of profit measurement could be based mainly on comparing statement of financial position values from one period to the next. They can also be based on the income statement, and how revenues and income are defined and measured.

2.4 What is Included as Revenues (or Income)

The income statement begins with the figure for revenue, which could also be called sales or turnover. It includes all the sales that have been made during the period, not just of goods, but, depending on what kind of business it is, also of services, and it can include other items such as rents receivable. The turnover figure is shown net of such things as value added tax.

It includes all sales that have been made during a period, even if the money for those sales is not received until a later period. This principle is important. It means that a rapidly expanding business might be making very good sales each month, and good profits, but the amount owed by receivables (debtors) will increase each month, and the cash that comes into the business lags behind the profits that are being earned. This could mean that a rapidly expanding and profitable business has much less money than the sales figures suggest.

It is also important because it is sometimes not clear exactly when a sale has been made. It could be that a sale is initially agreed by telephone; a few days later an order is received; then a few weeks later the goods are completed ready for despatch; then, a few days later, the goods are received by the purchaser; then the seller sends out the invoice. Payment for the goods is probably not made for another month or two. There is a need for a clear accounting principle that determines the exact point, or the critical event, at which a sale is recognized. In practice, an accounting system usually recognizes a sale when the invoice is sent out, signifying ownership of goods has been transferred from seller to buyer or that services have been delivered. But it is easy to see that temptations can arise to recognize sales at an earlier date. When sales are below target, perhaps in the last month of the year, and managers see their bonuses disappearing, or even their jobs, it is not difficult to create a few extra sales by bringing some forward, or sending invoices out early; they can be reversed

---

[6] Such 'creative accounting' is examined in Chapter 8.

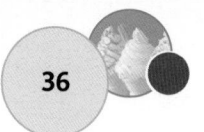
the following month. It is a bit like a shop assistant borrowing from the till, with the intention of paying back before the final reckoning comes: you can get away with it for a while, but eventually it will catch up with you. You can bring forward your revenues one year, but you cannot bring them forward more and more each year.

Other items of income are included in published income statements such as profits on sales of non-current assets, investment income, interest receivable, various 'exceptional items' and any share of profits from associated companies.

2.5 What is Included as Expenses

There are more problems with defining and measuring expenses, and no shortage of accounting standards or principles attempting to deal with them. Expenses are recognized in accordance with the *accruals concept*, which means that it is not the amount of cash paid out during a period that is counted; it is the amount incurred in earning the revenue that is recognized during the period. This is also about *matching*: after recognizing the turnover for a period, we match against it those expenses that have been incurred in earning that turnover. This is particularly important with cost of sales and with depreciation.

Cost of sales

The first expense on the income statement is cost of sales, or cost of goods sold. This means that if you buy 100 items, but sell only 70 of them, only the 70 count in the cost of sales. The other 30 are 'closing inventory' (stocks remaining at the end of the period), and are carried forward as a current asset in the statement of financial position to be treated as an expense in the following period (see Example 2.1).

As the calculation of gross profit (or any other profit) is dependent on the closing inventory figure, the way in which this is determined is important. If, in Example 2.1, Raj had made a mistake, and his closing inventory figure was really £3,000, then his cost of sales would be only £8,000, and the gross profit would be £7,000.

If his real closing inventory figure was only £1,500, then his gross profit would be only £5,500. If a higher closing inventory figure is shown, then the profit figure will be higher, and the assets[7] and equity figures on the statement of financial position will be higher. If a lower closing inventory figure is shown, then the profit figure will be lower, and the assets and equity figures on the statement of financial position will be lower. This has important consequences: if Raj overstated his closing inventory figure by £1m, his income statement and statement of financial position would look better by £1m. Clearly, we need some clear rules and principles for determining closing inventory figures. The general rule is that the inventory of goods is shown at cost price.[8]

In a retailing business it is relatively easy to establish the cost price of goods. In a manufacturing business it is more difficult because we need to establish the cost of manufacturing the goods, which involves some difficult decisions in allocating overheads.

The cost of sales figure includes only the costs of buying, or producing goods and services. It includes an appropriate share of production overheads, including the costs of running the factory or other production facilities (including rent, lighting, heating, depreciation and maintenance of machinery, and factory supervision costs). Cost of sales does not include the general administration costs of the business, or the selling and distribution costs.

---

[7] Closing inventory is shown as an asset on the statement of financial position.

[8] Or, more precisely, closing inventories are shown at the lower of cost and net realizable value.

Example 2.1

At the beginning of March, Raj's shop had inventories of goods amounting to £1,000. During March he bought goods for resale costing £10,000.[9] His sales figure for March was £15,000.

Raj, therefore, had £11,000 worth of goods available for sale. But that is not the cost of sales figure. Some of the goods he had available for sale were not sold, and we cannot calculate the cost of sales or the gross profit until we know the closing inventory figure.

His stock of unsold goods at the end of March was £2,000.

The cost of the goods which he sold can now be calculated as follows:

Opening inventory	£1,000
Purchases	£10,000
Cost of goods available for sale	£11,000
Deduct Closing inventory	£2,000
Cost of goods sold (or cost of sales)	£9,000

The cost of sales figure is then compared with the sales figure, and the difference, £6,000, is the gross profit.

Sales	£15,000
Cost of sales	£9,000
Gross profit	£6,000

Gross profit ratio

In examining the income statement of a business, analysts usually calculate the gross profit ratio. This expresses gross profit as a percentage of sales as follows:

$$\frac{£6,000}{£15,000} = 40\%$$

Mark-up

The cost of the goods that Raj sold was £9,000. He marked them up by £6,000 and sold them for £15,000. The mark-up can be expressed as a percentage as follows:

$$\frac{£6,000}{£9,000} = 66\tfrac{2}{3}\%$$

It is important not to confuse percentage mark-ups with gross profit percentages, and it is worth playing with a few calculations to become familiar with them. A 25 per cent mark-up becomes a 20 per cent gross profit ratio (e.g. buy for £80, sell for £100). A 33⅓ per cent gross profit ratio comes from a 50 per cent mark-up (e.g. buy for £100, sell for £150).

---

[9] That is what he bought during March. He probably did not pay for them until April. But actual payments of cash, and receipts of cash, are quite distinct from revenues and expenses, that are used in profit measurement.

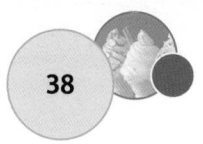

Depreciation

Figures for depreciation are less obvious on a published income statement; they are usually included under several headings with the detail hidden away in the notes to the accounts. When a business buys a non-current asset (a fixed asset) such as a piece of machinery, it is not immediately treated as an expense. The asset is shown on the statement of financial position; the business decides how long the useful life of the asset is expected to be; and the figure is written down, or depreciated, each year. If machinery is purchased for £12,000 and is expected to have a useful economic life of four years; that is, to produce revenue for four years, the cost of £12,000 will be written off, as an expense, over the four-year period in accordance with the accruals, or matching principle. On the day it is purchased it is an asset expected to produce future benefits for four years. After one year, one-quarter of its benefits have arisen and the depreciation expense will be £3,000, leaving a net book value in the statement of financial position of £9,000, reflecting, at that point, that there are three years of expected benefits remaining. Depreciation is an expense in calculating profit that sounds straightforward enough. But it causes problems to students of accounting because:

1 They often think that expenses are paid out in cash; but depreciation is not paid out in cash. The non-current asset has already been bought, and the cash has already flowed out. Depreciation is a bookkeeping entry, not a flow of cash. Profit is always calculated *after* charging the depreciation expense. If we want to know what cash flow a business is generating, then we have to add depreciation back on to profit. Some people say that a business's cash flow is its profit plus depreciation, which is roughly right. Some even see depreciation as being an inflow of cash, but that is completely wrong: depreciation is something that, in calculating profit, we treat as if it had been paid out as cash (but it hasn't) so we add it back to profit to indicate the cash that has been generated during the period.

2 They see depreciation as part of a process of valuing assets, which it is not. The objective is to write down the cost of a non-current asset, year by year, as the useful life of the fixed asset is being used up. Usually[10] this results in asset figures being shown on the statement of financial position that are closer to current values, but that is incidental. The main point is to charge, as an expense in calculating profit, the amount of the non-current asset that has been 'used up'.

3 They think that a provision for depreciation is a pool of money that can be used to replace non-current assets when they come to the end of their lives. But there is no money in a provision (or in 'reserves'). If you want to know what money (or cash and bank) there is in a business, you have to look in current assets. The provision for depreciation is a book keeping entry, not an allocation of cash. It reduces profits, and as companies usually relate dividend decisions to the level of profits, the fact that depreciation is charged may limit the amount of dividends paid out – a way of achieving 'capital maintenance'.

Even for sophisticated users of accounts, there are problems with depreciation. Different companies have different depreciation policies, and we never really know how long a non-current asset will last, or how long we will keep it, or how much it will be sold for when we have finished with it. We might buy a car for £10,000, and *plan* to keep it for four years, and then to sell it for £2,000. But that might change; we might keep it much longer, or sell it much earlier; and the amount we sell it for might be much more, or less, than we planned.

The easiest approach to depreciation is to use the 'straight line' method. If we buy a car for £10,000, and plan to sell it for £2,000 after four years, then the total amount to be depreciated is £8,000, which works out at £2,000 a year for four years.

---

[10] But not always. Companies are expected to depreciate buildings as their effective lives are 'used up', even if they are increasing in value.

Slightly more complicated, but still reasonably popular, is the 'diminishing balance' method.[11] If we charged 33 per cent[12] per annum on this basis, the figures would be as follows:

	£
Initial cost of car	10,000
Year 1 depreciation 33% of £10,000	3,300
Balance at end of year 1	6,700
Year 2 depreciation 33% of £6,700	2,211
Balance at end of year 2	4,489
Year 3 depreciation 33% of £4,489	1,481
Balance at end of year 3	3,008
Year 4 depreciation 33% of £3,008	993
Balance at end of year 4	2,015

This method of depreciation results in higher depreciation in the early years, and lower depreciation in the later years than depreciation calculated using the straight-line basis. Occasionally, depreciation is calculated in more obscure ways. A vehicle could be depreciated in relation to the number of miles it does each year.

If a company suddenly changed its policy and planned to keep its vehicles (or ships, or aeroplanes, or machinery) for twice as long as it had previously planned, that could halve its depreciation charges, and produce a very significant increase in profits. Such a change in policy, and its financial effects, would have to be disclosed in a note to the financial statements. But there is inevitably some scope for individual judgement or manipulation as there is no certainty in the future lives, or residual values, of non-current assets.

Depreciation figures and policies should be disclosed fully in the notes to the financial statements, but they do not usually appear on the face of a published income statement. The three main categories of expenses (cost of sales, distribution costs and administration expenses) may all include some depreciation as there may be non-current assets involved in producing the goods and services, in selling and distributing them, and in the administration of the business.

Impairment of goodwill

When one company buys another business, the amount of money it pays is partly for the net assets of the business, and partly for its 'goodwill', a term that covers a multitude of attributes of a business that enable it to earn profits. If a company buys a business with excellent prospects, it may pay a lot for 'goodwill', and the amount must be shown on the statement of financial position as a non-current asset; and, as with other non-current assets, it is likely to be 'used up' over a number of years. Traditionally, accountants would 'amortize' goodwill in much the same way as they depreciated other non-current assets. But it is difficult to know how long the goodwill will last, and so it is difficult to decide whether it should be written off over 5 or 20 years, or some other period. What happens now is that any goodwill appearing on the statement of financial position will be assessed each year. This valuation is known as the 'impairment test'; the company assesses the extent to which the goodwill has been impaired, or used up, during the year. An impairment charge is then made, which is, in effect, depreciation or amortization of goodwill.

Goodwill and its amortization are controversial areas in accounting. The traditional view was that if goodwill is an asset, its value is dubious and it should be written off as soon as possible. A more

---

[11] Also known as the reducing balance method.

[12] Thirty-three per cent. Not $33\frac{1}{3}$ per cent – that would give a different answer.

current view is that, provided the business is well run, goodwill should last indefinitely, and there is no need to amortize it each year – especially as this can lead to massive reductions in reported profits. The present requirement is that goodwill should be subject to an annual impairment test, and then written down accordingly. A business may decide that it has been impaired very little during the year or not at all. Some subjectivity is inevitable, and the door is wide open for creative accounting. Companies are not allowed to *increase* the amount they show for goodwill. Regardless of the requirements of financial reporting standards, many companies and investment analysts choose to emphasize profit figures that have not been charged with impairment of goodwill.

Classification and disclosure of expenses

A business can produce an income statement showing as much detail as it wishes – with separate figures for wages and salaries, repairs and maintenance, cleaning, rent and rates, lighting and heating, insurance, telephones, stationery, postage, newspapers, directors' fees, auditors' fees, lawyers' fees and many other things. But the published accounts of companies are in standardized formats, such as the one shown in Illustration 2.1, which group most expenses under the general headings 'cost of sales', 'distribution costs' and 'administrative expenses'. The income statements included in the published annual reports and accounts of companies probably look more complicated, but the basics are the same as shown in Illustration 2.1.

If you plough through the notes to the accounts, and the directors' report, you will find lots more detail and further analysis of expenses, including wages and salaries, directors' remuneration, costs of hiring plant and machinery, auditors' remuneration, depreciation and amortization, and charitable and political donations. Other items disclosed include exceptional items such as profits or losses on disposals, the results of discontinued operations, and new acquisitions, and an analysis of results classified as different segments for the various activities of the company and the geographical areas in which it operates.

As long as an expense is clearly recognized as such, which heading it is included under is less important. The chief executive may spend part of his time dealing with production issues (arguably part of the cost of sales), part dealing with distribution issues and part dealing with administration. But there is no need to bother with allocating the costs of employing him to these different headings, and it is acceptable to treat the whole cost as being administrative expenses. Gross profit ratios[13] may be important, but it is sometimes difficult to be clear about just which expenses have been included in cost of sales.

2.6 A Company's Published Income Statement

The income statement for Marks and Spencer Group plc is shown in Illustration 2.3. It is called a 'group income statement' because it includes the results of subsidiary companies that the Marks and Spencer Group Company controls.

The main feature to note, from the shareholders' point of view, is that the 'profit for the period' has increased from £523m to £586.6m, an increase of 12 per cent. Although sales revenue has increased by 2.1 per cent (from £9,536.2m to £9,740.3m), the cost of goods sold has only increased by 1.6 per cent, the selling and distribution costs (which Marks & Spencer have chosen to combine) have risen by 4.5 per cent, while the finance income has risen by 228 per cent, the finance expenses have fallen by 39 per cent, while taxation has only increased by 1.3 per cent. The statement of financial position (shown as Illustration 1.5, p. 17) shows that equity has increased from £2,168.6m to £2,673.5m (an increase of 23 per cent). Shareholders would be quite happy to see an increase in sales but they might be even happier to see the increase in profit for the period resulting from the other relative

---

[13] Gross profit expressed as a percentage of sales revenue.

ILLUSTRATION 2.3

Group income statement of Marks and Spencer Group plc for the 52 weeks ended 2 April 2011

	Note	52 weeks ended 2 April 2011 £m	53 weeks ended 3 April 2010 £m
Revenue	2, 3	9,740.3	9,536.6
Cost of sales	3	(6,015.6)	(5,918.1)
Gross profit		3,724.7	3,618.5
Selling and administration expenses		(2,959.7)	(2,831.5)
Other operating income		59.9	56.9
Other adjustments	5	12.0	8.1
Operating profit		836.9	852.0
Finance income	6	42.3	12.9
Finance expenses	6	(98.6)	(162.2)
Profit before tax	4	780.6	702.7
Income tax expense		(182.0)	(179.7)
Profit for the period		586.6	523.0
Attributable to			
Equity shareholders of the company		612.0	526.3
Non-controlling interests		(13.4)	(3.3)
Profit for the period		586.6	523.0
Earnings per share			
Basic	8	38.8p	33.5p
Diluted	8	38.4p	33.2p

Group statement of changes in equity of Marks and Spencer Group plc (simplified extract) for the 52 weeks ended 2 April 2011

	£m
Balance at 4 April 2010	5,281.9
Add Profit for the period	612.0
Add Actuarial gains on retirement benefit scheme	286.0
Deduct Other items	(59.2)
Deduct Dividends	(247.5)
Balance at 2 April 2011	5,873.2

improvement in expenses. Together with the increase in profit for the period, the company benefited from substantial gains in the pension scheme amounting to £286m and these factors have caused a substantial increase of £591.3m in group retained profits, which amounts to 11.2 per cent with an increase in shareholders' equity of 23.3 per cent.

The main categories of expenses shown are:

- Cost of sales
- Selling and administration costs
- Finance expenses

Finance expenses relate to interest payable by the company. The Marks and Spencer Group's borrowings are very low, and so there is little interest to pay; in the most recent year they paid more interest than they received (finance expense is greater than finance income). In Chapter 1 we saw that some companies are very dependent on borrowings; interest costs can be high in relation to profits; and such companies may be at risk if they are unable to pay their liabilities as they fall due. The Marks and Spencer Group is very lowly geared and with no real risk in relation to borrowings.

We can see that total profits have increased, and that most of the various categories of expenses have increased. This is not surprising as the business has expanded: total revenues have thus increased. It is worth examining whether or not expenses have increased faster than revenues; whether expenses seem to be carefully controlled, or whether they are rocketing upwards even faster than turnover. The main expenses are expressed as a percentage of sales, including cost of sales. It is more usual to express gross profit as a percentage of sales; both are shown as follows:

Ratio	2011	2010
Cost of sales/revenue	6,015.6/9,740.3	5,918.1/9,536.6
	61.8%	62.1%
Gross profit/revenue	3,724.7/9,740.3	3,618.5/9,536.6
	38.2%	37.9%
Selling and administration expenses/revenue	2,959.7/9,740.3	2,831.5/9,536.6
	30.4%	29.7%

The gross profit ratio seems fairly high. It would be interesting to compare it with other clothing retailers. The selling and administration expenses have increased as a percentage of sales. There was a substantial gain from the valuation of the pension scheme amounting to £286m, while in the previous year there were losses from the pension scheme valuation of £251m. From the notes to the accounts other information about expenses, and some explanation of the increases, can be found.

2.7 Income Statement Detailed Items

Examining the published income statement of a company usually reveals more complexities than have been outlined so far. These can be seen in the accounts of most listed companies; that is, those whose shares are traded on a stock exchange. You could download the accounts of such a company from its website. The annual report of Marks & Spencer can be found on www.annualreport.marksandspencer.com/.

Company or group

Most large companies that are listed on the stock market own a number of subsidiary companies. It is most useful to look at the group results that include all the results of the subsidiary companies.

Non-controlling interests

A company often owns only, say, 90 per cent of a subsidiary company, but the income statement includes 100 per cent of the results of all the subsidiaries. At the end of the income statement, after profit for the period has been calculated, an item for 'non-controlling interests', formerly known as 'minority interests', is shown. This is the part of the group's profit that belongs to shareholders outside the group (e.g. 10 per cent of the shareholders of a subsidiary company). The amount of profit

remaining (after deducting the non-controlling or minority interest) belongs to the shareholders of the parent company.

Associates and joint ventures

A company (e.g. H) may invest in other companies (e.g. A or J), but own only between, say, 20 per cent and 50 per cent of A or J's shares. H is likely to have significant influence over A or J. But H does not include 100 per cent of A or J's profits in its income statement. Instead, H includes, say, 20 per cent to 50 per cent, according to the proportion owned.

Dividends receivable

A company (e.g. H) may have only a small shareholding in another company (e.g. I) as an investment. If H has no significant influence over I, then I is not part of the group, and the group's income statement does not include a share of I's profits. Instead, the group income statement includes dividends (not profits) from such companies.

Acquisitions, discontinued operations and continuing operations

Large companies often sell off parts of the business, and buy new businesses. If you want to assess the future performance of a business, it is not much use doing so on the basis of information that includes parts of the business that have been closed down or disposed of. If you want to assess the past performance of a business, it is not much use comparing last year's figures with this year's figures if there has been a major acquisition; in that case we would expect to see a significant increase in this year's figures. To make meaningful comparisons we need to separate the figures for new acquisitions from continuing operations, and we need to separate the figure for operations that have been discontinued or disposed of.

Income statements provide the information under the three headings (acquisitions, discontinued operations and continuing operations) for sales and for operating profit.

Segmental reporting

Many large companies combine together a number of different businesses, perhaps with very different products, or with very different geographical areas. International Accounting Standard (IAS) 14 requires companies to disclose their revenues, profits and capital employed for each major geographical and business segment. This can be very useful if you are trying to forecast a company's future performance and you believe that one area of business is going to perform better than another in the future. It can also be useful in assessing whether the management of one company has been as successful as others in dealing with areas of growth, and areas of decline and in assessing different prospects for growth or levels of risk in different activities or different geographical areas. The Marks and Spencer Group accounts show segmental analysis in terms of 'general merchandise' and 'food', split between 'retail' and 'wholesale' and in geographical segments, between 'UK' and 'international'.

Exceptional items

A company's results are sometimes affected by 'one-off' exceptional items such as a profit on selling part of the business or some assets; inventories being written down; some write-offs to reflect the impairment of non-current assets; or the costs of redundancies and reorganization. These are usually shown as a separate item on the income statement, with more detail shown in the notes. The profit for the year and the basic EPS are shown after deducting (or crediting) all exceptional items. However,

companies sometimes show a second EPS figure that may exclude any bad news that they have managed to label as 'exceptional items'.

2.8 Subjective Measurement and Creativity Problems

Creative accounting is an important subject in its own right, but even an introductory look at income statements reveals several areas where subjective judgements are required, and where there may be scope for creative accounting.

Capital expenditure and revenue expenditure

Capital expenditure adds to the amount for non-current assets (sometimes called fixed assets) that are shown on the statement of financial position as 'property, plant and equipment', under the heading 'non-current assets'. The statement of financial position shows the amount of assets that the company owns at the year end. In an expanding company this usually increases each year because the company buys additional non-current assets during the year. 'Capital expenditure' is the term used for buying additional non-current assets; its effect on profit figures is delayed, and spread over a number of years as depreciation. The net effect of capital expenditure and depreciation is shown on the statement of financial position, and more detail is shown in the notes to the accounts. Revenue expenditure appears on the income statement, not the statement of financial position, and is an immediate charge against profit. Buying a new car, premises or machinery is capital expenditure. Maintaining them, and the costs of using them, are revenue expenditure.

The important distinction between capital expenditure and revenue expenditure is usually clear, but there are some grey areas and sometimes there may be a temptation to 'capitalize'[14] expenditure that is more like revenue expenditure and should be treated as an expense immediately. If a company can make most of its 'repairs and maintenance' expenditure look more like improvements and additions to non-current assets, they can avoid charging them as expenses on the income statement, boost profits and show higher asset figures on the statement of financial position.

There are areas, such as research and development, where companies can capitalize large amounts of development expenditure in this way. It is also possible, when constructing a non-current asset (perhaps building a new hotel), to treat the cost of interest during the period of construction as part of the capital expenditure rather than revenue expenditure.

Depreciation

There is inevitably scope for differences of view on the lives of non-current assets, likely values at the end of their lives and in choosing what method of depreciation to use.

Valuation of inventories

The value of inventories at the end of the year affects profits: if closing inventories are overstated, then profits and assets are overstated. Although the general rule is that inventories are shown at cost price (or net realizable value if it is lower), there may be some room for manoeuvre, especially when the company has itself manufactured the unsold items. There are important rules to determine which costs should be included in the cost of production, and which costs should be treated as expenses immediately. There is also a grey area in assessing 'net realizable value'. If an item has cost £100 to make or buy, it should continue to be included in the accounts at that price, until it seems that it can only be sold for a lower figure. It is possible for a company to be too optimistic in assessing net realizable values or to be too pessimistic; either approach can lead to unrealistic profit figures.

---

[14] Treat it as adding to non-current assets.

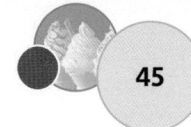

Timing

The rules on when sales should be recognized are not very clear and there is sometimes scope for bringing forward the recognition of sales, and so boosting the sales figure for the year.

2.9 Role and Limitations of Income Statements

The main role of the income statement is to set out the profit that a business has made during the period, and its component parts. The old term 'profit and loss account' may still be preferred because it shows the profits and losses from the various activities undertaken by the company. There are many good reasons for measuring profit, as set out in Section 2.3.

The income statement also has a role in indicating how and where profits might be increased. Comparing this year's results with last year's is a useful monitoring exercise. Most businesses expect their sales figure to increase each year, with an increase in cost of sales and an increase in gross profit. But they also hope to at least maintain their operating margins: that gross profit as a proportion of sales will be maintained or increased. The same kind of analysis should be applied to the main categories of expenses. As sales increase, expenses might also be expected to increase. But management should be monitoring the various expenses as a proportion of sales, and trying to ensure that expenses, as a percentage of sales, do not increase. Sometimes, as a matter of policy, a business might decide to increase particular items of expense (e.g. spending more on marketing). But, more generally, a business should expect some economies of scale as it expands, and monitor the results to see if each category of expense really is declining as a proportion of sales.

The information shown in the income statement can be useful in comparing this year's results with last year's as part of the financial control.[15] It can also be useful in comparing one company's results with another. Of course, a large supermarket chain makes more profits than a small one; but detailed analysis of the income statement, looking at the various expenses as a proportion of sales, can show where one company is doing better than another, and where there is room for improvement.

In comparing companies with each other, we need to look carefully for explanations of difference in performance. One company might lease all its premises and equipment while another owns them. One might have very old non-current assets, and so have very low depreciation charges, while another has much newer non-current assets. One company might be financed wholly by shareholders' funds, and so have no interest charges, while another is largely financed by borrowing (i.e. it has high gearing) and so have high 'finance expenses' (interest charges). There might also be different accounting policies, and where there is scope for 'creative accounting', it may be difficult to make meaningful comparisons between one company and another. Among the functions of the International Financial Reporting Standards (IFRSs) and International Accounting Standards (IASs), referred to in Chapter 1, are to aid comparisons between different companies, and different countries, and to minimize the scope for manipulation and creative accounting.

It is also important to realize that profits are not the same as cash flow. A company might do very well in selling equipment and civil engineering products to what the Americans call 'rogue states'; but there could be massive delays in receiving the money from these sales, which rather takes the shine off the performance. Income statements should be interpreted together with cash flow statements. Indeed, the main published financial accounting statements should be taken as a whole. Making profits is not enough. Profits need to be sufficient when compared with the amount of money invested in the business, to justify that investment. Companies need to make a good return on capital employed (ROCE), and assessing the performance of a company requires the use of figures both from the income statement and from the statement of financial position.

---

[15] The exercise is often carried out comparing budgeted (or planned) income statements with the actual results achieved.

📖 Summary

An income statement (previously known as a profit and loss account) shows the profit for a period, typically a year. Profit is based on the difference between revenue (or sales or turnover), and the costs incurred in earning those sales. Profit figures are useful in many different ways, and care is needed in interpreting the information. Profit is calculated after charging cost of sales (which requires a value to be put on closing inventories) and depreciation; these are examples of expenses where there is an element of subjectivity.

    IASs permit a variety of different ways of presenting statements of financial position and income statements, provided the same information is disclosed (sometimes on the face of statements; sometimes in the notes to the accounts). Illustration 2.1 will probably prove to be the most popular way of presenting income statements in the UK, but, with additional items, many look much more complex.

⮕ Review of key points

- The income statement (or profit and loss account) shows the profit for a period by deducting from sales (and any other revenues) the costs incurred in earning those revenues.
- It is useful to measure profit as an indication of a company's performance and as a basis for dividend decisions.
- Profit figures are also useful to a range of different groups in society.
- There is some subjectivity in profit measurement; for example in depreciation and in valuing closing inventories.
- Profit figures are most useful when they are used in making comparisons.
- Profit is different from cash flow.

❗ Self-testing questions

1 What are the main differences between a statement of financial position and an income statement?

2 What is an expense? How does an expense differ from an asset? Can an asset become an expense? In what sense could it be argued that an asset is an expense waiting to happen?

3 How are inventories valued? Why does it matter? Would it be a good idea to show inventories at selling price?

4 Why is depreciation charged?

5 What is the difference between capital expenditure and revenue expenditure?

6 Which of the profit figures shown in a simplified income statement (Illustration 2.2) are shareholders likely to be most interested in, and why?

7 The Kingsdun Company buys a delivery van for £25,000 and a boring machine for £25,000. They decide that the delivery van should be depreciated at 25 per cent per annum on a diminishing balance basis, and that the boring machine should be depreciated at 10 per cent per annum on a straight-line basis. Calculate the depreciation charge for each of the first four years of the assets' lives, and the net book value of each at the end of year 4.

8 The Dargate Retailing Company sells a range of different products, some with modest gross profit margins, and some with much higher gross profit margins. For example, they buy Fargs for £100 each, apply a 25 per cent mark-up, and sell them for £125 each; the gross profit on Fargs is, therefore, 20 per cent (£25 gross profit is 20 per cent of the selling price). Employees often confuse percentage mark-ups with percentage gross profit. To avoid confusion you are asked to produce a definitive list showing the cost, mark-up percentage, selling price and gross profit percentage of each product by completing the gaps in the table that follows:

Product	Cost price	Mark-up	Selling price	Gross profit
	£	%	£	%
Fargs	100	25	125	20
Gargs	100	10	110	9.09
Hargs	50	100	100	50%
Jargs	40	100	80	50%
Kargs	80	50	120	33⅓
Largs	50	20	60	16⅔
Margs	30.77	30	40	23
Nargs	45	11.1	50	10
Pargs	75	33⅓	100	25

(handwritten annotation: x–80)

9 Banterbury Company Ltd

Income statement of the Banterbury Company Ltd for the year ended 31 December

	Year 3	Year 4
	£000	£000
Revenue	100	120
Cost of sales	(60)	(73)
Gross profit	40	47
Distribution costs	(12)	(14)
Administration expenses	(9)	(12)
Operating profit	9	21
Finance expenses	(3)	(3)
Profit before taxation	16	18
Taxation	(4)	(3)
Profit for the year	12	15

Statement of changes in equity of Banterbury Company Ltd for the year ended 31 December

	£000	£000
Balance at beginning of year	93	100
Profit for the year	12	15
Dividends paid	(5)	(6)
Balance at end of year	100	109

The chairman of the company boasts that sales, profits and dividends are at record levels and that the amount of shareholders' funds in the business has increased to £109,000 at the end of year 4.
Critically assess the performance of the company.

 ## Assessment questions

1 The Broadstores Company:

Income statement of Broadstores Company for the year ended 31 December

	Year 7	Year 8
	£000	£000
Revenue	200	220
Cost of sales	(120)	(131)
Gross profit	80	89
Distribution costs	(22)	(24)
Administration expenses	(40)	(41)
Operating profit	18	24
Finance expenses	(10)	(18)
Profit before taxation	8	6
Tax on profit for year	(3)	(2)
Profit after tax for the year	5	4

Statement of changes in equity of Broadstores Company for the year ended 31 December

	£000	£000
Balance at beginning of year	50	51
Profit for the year	5	4
Dividends paid	(4)	0
Balance at end of year	51	55

The chairman of the company states that the management of the company has performed well in a very difficult economic climate, and that increased profits have been retained within the business to finance profitable expansion.

A shareholder at the annual general meeting of the company claims that the reduction in profits and the absence of dividends prove that the management of the company is a disaster.

Assess the evidence for each point of view.

2   The Billygate Company operates with a 40 per cent mark-up on the goods that it buys. What is its gross profit ratio?

The Sillygate Company operates with a 40 per cent gross profit margin. What percentage mark-up does it use?

3   Roger, a graduate of the University of South East England, has been running a business called 'SuperSoftService' since he completed his information technology (IT) degree six years ago. He sells software and prides himself on providing fast delivery using his sports car, and he has an extensive stock of software, catering for the latest developments as well as meeting demand for software for old operating systems – he still can supply most things for Windows 95 and makes the occasional sale of old software.

About half of his sales are on a cash basis, and about half are on credit. He sells on credit only to friends, graduates and people he knows, and has no experience of bad debts.

The business is very profitable, and is almost entirely financed by borrowing from his father. But his father is concerned that Roger keeps borrowing more and more money to keep the business afloat.

His summarized financial statements are shown as follows:

Income statement of SuperSoftService for the year ended 31 December year 6

Revenue		£100,000
Cost of goods sold		
Opening inventories	60,000	
Purchases	40,000	
	100,000	
Less Closing inventories	(80,000)	20,000
Gross profit		80,000
Administration and distribution expenses		(50,000)
Net profit		30,000
Drawings for personal expenditure		(29,000)
Retained profit for year		1,000

Statement of financial position of SuperSoftService as at 31 December year 6

Non-current assets		
Car at cost 1 January year 1		£18,000
Less Provision for depreciation		(9,000)
		9,000
Current assets		
Inventories at cost	80,000	
Receivables	80,000	
		160,000
Total assets		169,000
Current liabilities		
Payables	3,000	
Overdraft	3,000	6,000
Loan from father		150,000
Equity		
Roger's capital	6,000	
Roger's retained earnings	7,000	13,000
		169,000

a Comment on the financial position and performance of the business.

b How 'real' are the profits?

4 The Depreciation Company

The directors of the Depreciation Company are deciding on their accounting policy on the depreciation of their non-current assets.

They have just purchased some new assets that cost £200,000 and which they expect to sell after five years for £20,000.

a Calculate the depreciation expense in the income statement and the figures that will appear in the statement of financial position of the company assuming:

(i) They adopt the straight-line basis of depreciation

(ii) They adopt the diminishing basis at 30 per cent

b Advise the directors which method is the more appropriate and why.

5 The Chinese Motor Company

The Chinese Motor Company runs a UK branch and a China branch. Both branches run three departments for sales, car servicing and the sale of parts.

Advise the management of the company

a why the users of the company's financial statements would find a segmental report useful

b what information it should contain

c how this information would improve the users decision-making process

Group activities and discussion questions

1 Profit figures are wanted by so many different groups of people for so many different purposes that it is not possible to define and measure profits in such a way as to meet all of those different needs. Discuss.

2 Attempt a definition of 'profit'. You can use other books. Can all members of the group agree on the definition? Is the definition clear and robust enough to provide a basis for measuring profits in all businesses? You could have a formal debate with two people arguing in favour of a particular definition of profit, and two could argue against that definition. Or two could argue that it is possible to produce a workable definition, and two could argue that it is not.

3 Last year a company's statement of financial position showed freehold land and buildings at cost, the amount being £4m. This year the properties have been revalued at £7m. Is the company £3m better off? Have they made £3m profit?

4 Why do companies aim to earn profits? Should all organizations attempt to earn profits? If you think that some organizations should not attempt to earn profits, on what basis would you decide which should earn profits, and which should not?

5 Do companies have too much freedom to determine the methods and rates of depreciation that they use for their published accounts? Where governments specify methods and rates of depreciation to be used to calculate profits for taxation purposes, should companies be required to use those same rates in their published accounts?

6 You are a shareholder in a listed company and are told that last year the company's net profit after tax increased from £100m to £130m, and that the management of the company is therefore performing extremely well.

a What additional information would you want in order to assess the effectiveness of management? (Produce a list, and do not look at (b) until you have done that!)

b Obtain the published annual report and accounts of a listed company. How much of what you wanted to know does it tell you?

7 Examine Marks and Spencer Group's results since 2010. Has the expansion of the company been successful in leading to a big enough increase in profits?

8 Compare the gross profit ratios of a number of different retailers. Are the differences very substantial? How do you explain or justify such differences?

 ## Accounting in context

Discuss and comment on the following article from the press with particular reference to the importance of turnover, operating profit and expenses in assessing the effectiveness of an organization and its future prospects.

Spurs go private to fund their new stadium

Club to 'delist' from stock market to help borrowing
Move could raise £350m for Northumberland Park

By Paul Kelso, Chief Sports Reporter

Tottenham's owners are to take the club off the stock market to help their prospects of borrowing to fund their new stadium development.

Majority owners ENIC, owned by billionaire speculator Joe Lewis, will put the club into private hands as they begin the task of meeting the £300–£350 million cost of building a new ground adjacent to White Hart Lane.

The announcement of plans to 'delist' the club from the Alternative Investment Market came as Spurs revealed record revenues for the 2010–2011 season.

Following the club's first season in the Champions League, revenue rose almost £44 million to £163.5 million in 2010–11, with operating profits up 42 per cent to £32.3 million.

The encouraging rise in revenue is balanced by a sharp increase in wages that emphasise [sic] the importance of regular Champions League football if the club are to maintain their playing strengths.

The cost of maintaining a large squad for European football saw overall costs, largely made up of wages, rise 35 per cent to £131.2 million, up from £97.1 million in 2009–10.

Failure to qualify for the Champions League last season means that to maintain a wage bill that now includes an increase for Luka Modric, persuaded to stay in the summer, and the addition of Emmanuel Adebayor and Scott Parker, will be a challenge.

The Europa League provides some income but even an extended run could struggle to raise £10 million, leaving a shortfall that prudent chairman Daniel Levy will want to alleviate with improved commercial performance.

Tottenham have not specified their precise salary outgoings but the rise in costs appears to have pushed the wages-to-earnings ratio to between 70 and 80 per cent, an uncomfortable level.

The club will point to their earnings before tax, interest and player amortisation of £35 million as evidence that the club is in a sound position.

The challenge of balancing the cost of ambition with the uncertainty of short term results is one of ▶

the factors that makes [sic] a move to a new stadium a priority.

Tottenham were the first football club to be floated on the stock market in 1983, but Levy has concluded that the costs and restrictions of remaining on the AIM hampers that ambition.

The move follows discussions with potential investors and financial institutions who suggested that it will be easier for Spurs to piece together the funding package required for a new ground in private hands.

Tottenham need to raise revenue to build the new stadium at Northumberland Park, much of which will come from borrowing.

Having lost the Olympic Stadium bid to West Ham, Spurs are now focused on Northumberland Park but the huge investment required is complex given the troubled economic climate and the challenges facing Tottenham in the wake of the summer riots.

The stadium is likely to be funded by a mix of sponsorship, equity and some form of borrowing, with naming rights a crucial part of the package.

The club have begun testing the market for naming rights in the hope of attracting a package worth around £150 million over 10 years.

Source: The Daily Telegraph, 17 November 2011

References and further reading

International Accounting Standard 1 (2003, amended 2012). *Presentation of Financial Statements*. IFRC.

Melville, A. (2011) *International Financial Reporting* (3rd edn.). Harlow: FT Prentice Hall.

Wood, F. and A. Sangster (2012) *Business Accounting* (vol. 1) (12th edn.). Harlow: FT Prentice Hall.

www.frc.org.uk (gives details of the Financial Reporting Council and arrangements for accounting standards in the British Isles)

www.ifrc.org (gives details of international financial reporting standards)

http://annualreport.marksandspencer.com/ (gives the Marks and Spencer Group accounts in full)

Online
Learning Centre

When you have read this chapter, log on to the Online Learning Centre website at *www.mcgraw-hill.co.uk/textbooks/leiwy* to explore chapter-by-chapter test questions, further reading and more online study tools.

Chapter 3

The Development of Financial Reporting

Chapter contents

✓ Learning objectives

After studying this chapter you will be able to:

- ✓ Understand the different ways in which profit is seen to be important
- ✓ Appreciate and critically assess the role of accounting standards
- ✓ Evaluate the various attempts to base accounting on a number of concepts
- ✓ Understand the two main ways of approaching profit measurement
- ✓ Define assets and liabilities and understand some measurement difficulties
- ✓ Define revenues and expenses and understand some measurement difficulties
- ✓ Understand the effects of price changes on financial statements
- ✓ Appreciate different ways of adjusting for price changes

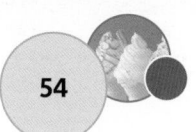

3.1 Introduction

Most people are familiar with the idea of profit, and may have assumptions about the usefulness of profit figures. Some, even journalists, seem to assume that there is a single agreed definition of 'profit', and that the rules for measuring it are clear and unambiguous uncontroversial/generally accepted.

This chapter explores the importance of profit figures by outlining the various functions that it is expected to serve. The role of accounting standards in improving financial reporting is explored, and the idea of generally accepted principles and concepts as a basis for financial accounting is examined.

Two main approaches to measuring profit are then explored: one based on the statement of financial position and the amounts shown for assets and liabilities (as indicated in Chapter 1); the second based on the income statement and the amounts shown for income and expenses (as indicated in Chapter 2).

Finally, the effects of inflation on financial statements, and possible methods of dealing with them are examined.

3.2 Functions of Profit Measurement

Annual financial statements contain a great deal of financial and other information that is of interest to different users, but profit figures are central. The widespread belief that profit is important is based on the idea that it tells us something useful. Profit figures may be useful in many different ways:

1 *As a guide to dividend decisions* – The more profit a company makes, the more it can pay out as dividends. The idea of capital maintenance is important: dividends are paid out of profits, not out of shareholders' capital. Profits must be calculated after making provision for depreciation so that, as the useful life of assets declines, the amount of shareholders' funds invested in assets does not. Charging depreciation ensures that an equivalent amount stays within the business, whether in the form of cash or other net assets, and is not paid out as dividends.

When companies decide how much of their profits to pay out as dividends they consider other factors, not just the current year's profit. In some years, even if profits are very low, they may maintain, or even increase, dividends. But they cannot do this indefinitely. In the long run, profits are the main guide to dividend decisions. The Companies Act limits the amount a company can distribute as dividends to the total of accumulated, realized profits, less accumulated losses.

Measuring the amount of profit available for distribution as dividends may also be seen as measuring how much can be consumed during a period without reducing the amount of capital at the beginning of the year; that is, without 'living off capital'.

2 *To indicate cash generated* – Many people talk about making money as if it is the same as making profits. The differences between cash flow and profit are central to financial accounting, and are explained and illustrated in Chapter 6. To some extent we could argue that it is mainly a matter of timing: in the end, all profits should eventually show up as cash. Profits may be tied up in inventories and receivables, but, in due course, the inventories are sold, and customers (should) pay up. But profits may also be tied up in additional non-current assets and used up in other ways (such as paying off long-term debt; or reducing the company's own share capital). Although we can say that profits do generate cash, there is no reason to expect profits will still be around as cash at any given time.

The Companies Act requirement that dividends should be paid only out of *realized* profits goes along with the idea that profits turn up as cash, and are 'available'. Profits are realized when a sale is made. Unrealized profits, such as those that result from revaluing buildings and other non-current assets, are not available for distribution as dividends until the assets are sold, and the profits are realized.

The idea that profits are 'available' for dividends does not mean that there is a pool of cash. It is one of the hardest things for non-accountants to understand: reserves or retained earnings are not cash. The fact that reserves are not usually available as cash is shown in Example 3.1.

The company has made £90,000 profit,[1] but none of it is 'available' to pay out dividends because, as the profit and cash flow was generated, it was all paid out, and more cars were bought. Legally, £90,000 is 'available' to pay out as dividends; but in cash terms there is nothing available – only cars.

Although the idea of using profit figures to indicate the amount of cash that a company has generated may have some popular appeal, it must be rejected as misleading, impracticable and simply wrong. It is more useful to examine cash flow statements to see what has happened to the profits that have been generated.

3 *To indicate how (un)successful the management of the company is* – Companies are expected to make profits. Shareholders elect directors to run the company for them. If the directors manage the company successfully they will make a lot of profit for the shareholders. If they do not make decent profits, then they are failing and should be got rid of. This might be a bit simplistic, but it is essentially what companies are about.

A more sophisticated version would be that the aim of the financial management of companies is to maximize shareholder wealth; shareholder wealth is made up of dividends and the value of the shares; maximizing profits is likely to maximize dividends and share price. It is easy to make a lot of profit if the company has a lot of capital employed; profits as a proportion of capital employed are therefore most important.

It is difficult to maximize shareholders' wealth for very long without good and increasing profits. We should not be surprised if we find that directors sometimes try to manipulate profit figures to make their performance look better. Some naïve economists seem to believe that there are such things as 'correct' profit figures, and if we have proper accounting and auditing standards, directors would not be able to indulge in such creative accounting. But, as will become increasingly clear, there are no 'correct' profit figures; there are many difficult areas in profit measurement; and profit figures in practice are, at least in part, the result of negotiation rather than 'economic reality' (whatever that is!).

Example 3.1

The Quirkar company was established on 1 January year 1 with £10,000 capital. The business bought and sold second-hand cars. All profits generated were either paid out as dividends, or used to increase the stocks of cars. At the end of year 3 the company's statement of financial position was as follows:

	£
Inventories of cars	100,000
Share capital	10,000
Retained earnings	90,000
	100,000

---

[1] It probably made much more, some of which was paid out as dividends; the £90,000 is retained earnings, after paying out dividends.

4 *As a basis for taxation* – Governments expect companies to pay corporation tax on their profits and so have an interest in the way in which profits are measured. In the UK, HM Revenue and Customs lays down rules for profit measurement for taxation purposes, and these rules are to some extent different from those used for financial reporting.

In some countries companies are required to use published profit figures as the basis for taxation; but this view is not generally favoured.

5 *To guide investors in deciding to buy or sell a company's shares* – The main users of financial accounts are supposed to be investors, particularly (a) those who are thinking of buying shares in the company and (b) those who already have shares in the company and are deciding whether to sell or retain them. These investors want to know about future performance and hope that the profits of the last few years will provide the appropriate guidance. The priority is therefore to find profit figures that have a predictive value. One way of forecasting future profits is to analyse previous years' profits in terms of various elements, some of which are likely to continue along with known trends, some of which are one-off, some of which are coming to an end. In recent years official segmental disclosure requirements have specified increasingly detailed analysis of the various different elements of profit, as shown in Chapter 7.

6 *To guide creditors* – Creditors may be more interested in the statement of financial position, to calculate current ratios, liquidity ratios and gearing ratios. But, in assessing a company's ability to pay amounts due to creditors, it is not just the assets available at the statement of financial position date that matter; it is also the company's ability to generate assets, particularly in the form of profits. If a company is making losses, the security that creditors see in assets can soon disappear.

We could say that investors and creditors are mainly interested in the future cash flows that the company will generate, and that principles for profit measurement should be selected to provide the best basis for prediction. Perhaps the companies themselves should provide more predictions.

Profit figures are used as a survival indicator. A company that makes profits is more likely to survive than one that makes losses. Various sophisticated versions of 'Z-Scores' have been developed to predict corporate failure that incorporate measures of working capital, debt and equity; but the biggest single element is usually some measure of profitability.

7 *To indicate economic efficiency* – Efficiency is concerned with the relationship between inputs and outputs. An organization that maximizes the ratio of outputs to inputs is maximizing efficiency. There are of course difficulties in defining the inputs and outputs that should be counted, and how to measure them. In a company, the simplest approach is to say that the main output is sales or revenues; and the main input is costs. The difference between sales and costs is profit. Maximizing profit therefore maximizes efficiency. Efficiency can be increased by (a) increasing sales; (b) reducing costs; (c) increasing sales and costs, but increasing sales by more than the increase in costs; or (d) reducing sales and costs, but reducing costs more than the reduction in sales. This is all very simplistic, and the overall approach could ignore many inefficiencies. It also ignores costs to society, and costs to employees and other interested parties. This idea does, however, underlie much of our thinking: a profitable company is efficient; an unprofitable company is inefficient. In organizations that are not primarily intended to make profits it is more difficult to assess efficiency.

A profitable company is also assumed to be an effective company. Effectiveness is concerned with the relationship between outputs and objectives. An effective organization is one that achieves its objectives. If we assume that profitability is a primary objective of companies, then it is also a measure of effectiveness.

Profits are also assumed to be concerned with efficiency in the economy as a whole, particularly the allocation of resources in the economy. The most profitable companies will attract investment and resources most easily; companies that are not profitable will have difficulty in finding funds for investment. Investment in the economy therefore goes to the most profitable, and so the most efficient organizations.

This idea is also rather simplistic, but in attempting to understand what goes on in the economy, and how it is justified, these arguments about efficiency and effectiveness should not be ignored.

8 *To indicate anything you like* – Profit figures seem to be quoted in many different contexts to indicate a wide variety of different matters of concern to individuals, groups or society. Employees and their representatives are likely to look at profits as an indicator of how much companies can afford to pay out in wage increases, or as an argument against closures and redundancies. Socialists may see profits as an indicator of how much companies exploit others. Profits are also relevant in any government-imposed price controls; for example, with privatized utility companies. Such companies are usually allowed to make a reasonable return on capital, but are not expected to use their near monopoly positions to make excessive profits.

Different profit figures seem to be required for different purposes. It is reasonable to expect financial statements to identify different versions of profit to meet the needs of the various different users of financial statements.

3.3 Setting Accounting Standards

Profit figures themselves are important, and they are the product of all the other figures in statements of financial position and income statements. Financial statements themselves are important to a range of users who need to have confidence that the figures shown represent 'economic reality' and are not just the opinions of some optimistic directors or accountants. Governments have long recognized that directors should not be allowed to produce financial statements in their own individual ways, and a series of Companies Acts has prescribed the information that they are required to publish. Companies Acts tend not to be very specific with accounting rules, and company directors have sometimes been tempted to produce annual reports that seem more intended to present their companies' performance in a flattering light than to hold the directors to account. The problems of such 'creative accounting' are addressed in Chapter 8.

It is sometimes argued that governments do not have the expertise to set detailed accounting rules, and that the financial world changes too rapidly for governments to be able to respond in time to deal with problems. The development of accounting 'standards' has been left largely to the accountancy profession.

Accounting standards first came into being following the establishment of the Accounting Standards Steering Committee in 1969. They were intended to provide guidance additional to the requirements of the Companies Acts by specifying additional definitions and rules for measurement and disclosure, and to narrow the areas of difference and variety in accounting practice. A series of accounting scandals in the 1960s had shown that different accountants could come up with very different profit figures, based on the same data, because there was so much flexibility in accounting.

The professional accountancy bodies set up the Accounting Standards Steering Committee that promulgated a series of 'accounting standards', or Statements of Standard Accounting Practice (SSAPs). Twenty-five SSAPs were produced. They started off as Exposure Drafts (EDs) for consultation, and, when agreed by the main professional accountancy bodies, they became authoritative statements. They did much to clarify definitions and alternatives, and to improve disclosure practice. But too often they allowed more than one treatment, and there was no effective enforcement mechanism. By the 1980s they were losing credibility as 'creative accounting' became well known.

A new accounting standards regime was established in 1990. The Accounting Standards Board (ASB) produced Financial Reporting Exposure Drafts (FREDs), which, after consultation, became Financial Reporting Standards (FRSs). It worked under the supervision of the Financial Reporting Council, alongside the Financial Reporting Review Panel (FRRP). Overall, the new arrangements worked better than the old Accounting Standards Committee. The FRSs (together with the SSAPs that they adopted) had more legal backing, and auditors are required to state if they have been followed; the number of permitted alternatives is being reduced; and the FRRP developed an enforcement role.

The ASB was essentially British. Other countries developed their own standards, and by the beginning of the twenty-first century two main approaches had been established: the US Financial Accounting Standards Board (FASB), and the International Accounting Standards Board (IASB). There is often a need for a reconciliation statement where companies are following the requirements of both regimes. The two bodies signed a Memorandum of Understanding (MOU) in 2006 to develop a convergence programme with the intention of developing good quality accounting standards for all companies in the world's capital markets.

The International Accounting Standards Committee was formed in 1973 and issued 41 International Accounting Standards (IASs). It was reconstituted as the IASB from 2001, which now issues International Financial Reporting Standards (IFRSs). These are increasingly like the US FASB's accounting standards as we move towards international harmonization. By 2011 the IASB had issued 13 IFRSs, which are:

- IFRS 1 First time adoption of IFRSs
- IFRS 2 Share Based Payment
- IFRS 3 Business Combinations
- IFRS 4 Insurance Contracts
- IFRS 5 Non-current Assets Held for Sale and Discontinued Operations
- IFRS 6 Exploration for and Evaluation of Mineral Resources
- IFRS 7 Financial Instruments: Disclosures
- IFRS 8 Operating Segments
- IFRS 9 Financial Instruments
- IFRS 10 Consolidated Financial Statements
- IFRS 11 Joint Arrangements
- IFRS 12 Disclosure of Interests in Other Entities
- IFRS 13 Fair Value Measurement

The IASB has also adopted the IASs that remain extant.

It is easy to criticize accounting standards, especially in their early years. Many were imprecise, or permitted different treatments. Some were revised, or withdrawn, or reissued in a different form. There was a lack of enforcement mechanisms. Difficult issues and decisions were avoided. And there was no consistent theoretical framework to support them. Often it seemed that standard-setters were like firefighters rushing from one problem to the next without a clear overall strategy.

Over the years they have steadily become more professional and effective, tackling difficult issues, reducing the number of permissible different treatments, and with widespread general acceptance and more effective enforcement. Their standards have also become increasingly complex and voluminous, and there is still a tendency for issues not to be 'finally' resolved. The requirement for truly international standards requires extensive discussion and agreement, and it sometimes seems that drafts are passed from one group to another, and then revised, and reissued almost indefinitely.

3.4 Concepts and Principles

The idea of a 'conceptual framework' that underlies all accounting standards is appealing and various attempts have been made to produce such documents, culminating in the *Framework for the Preparation and Presentation of Financial Statements* (1989).[2] Such statements usually begin by defining the objectives of financial reporting (to help users to make economic decisions), sometimes listing

---

[2] *The IASB's Framework* (1989) is comparable with the British ASB's *Statement of Principles for Financial Reporting* (1999).

who the users are. The Corporate Report (1975)[3] included almost everyone as user – at least once (investors, potential investors, employees, potential employees), all of whom were seen as having 'a reasonable right to information' about an organization. This emphasized that financial statements are 'general purpose', and may not serve the needs of particular individuals. It is useful to try to define general purpose information needs, and the usual conclusion is that a statement of financial position and income statement are required. The difficult part is to establish how the items on those statements (assets, liabilities, revenues, expenses) should be defined and measured.

The idea that financial reporting is based on four fundamental accounting concepts was established for many years[4] (about 1971 to 1999). These were as follows:

1. *Going concern* – Assumes that the business will continue in operational existence for the foreseeable future; that there is no intention to liquidate the business or to curtail it significantly. This was used to justify showing assets at cost (adjusted for such things as depreciation), rather than attempting to show them at the amount for which they could be sold at the statement of financial position date.

2. *Accruals* – Revenues and costs are recognized as they are earned or incurred, not as money is received or paid; they are matched with one another and dealt with in the income statement of the period to which they relate. Profit measurement is based on accruals and matching, not on receipts and payments of cash. This is used to justify a whole range of accounting adjustments, including accruals and prepayments; capitalization of fixed assets and annual depreciation charges; and carrying forward the cost of unsold inventories to be treated as an expense when they are sold.

3. *Consistency* – There is consistency of accounting treatment of like items within each accounting period, and from one period to the next. This means, for example, that it is not acceptable to depreciate some vehicles but not others; or to change depreciation policies from one year to the next (unless full details are disclosed).

4. *Prudence* – Revenues and profits are not anticipated, but are recognized only when realized as cash (or other assets, the ultimate cash realization of which can be assessed with reasonable certainty[5]); provision is made for all known liabilities (expenses and losses) whether the amount of these is known with certainty or is a best estimate. This conservatism is intended to ensure that profits, assets and income are not overstated; and that expenses and liabilities are not understated. The assumption is that the financial position of a business should be *at least* as good as the financial statements show.

A fifth concept, 'separate valuation', is usually added because it was specifically referred to in the 1985 Companies Act along with the other four. It requires that the amount for each item included in the financial statements should be determined separately. One item should not be offset against another; and (for example) a fleet of vehicles should not be valued as a whole: the amount for each vehicle should be determined separately, and then added together.

Over the years a whole range of other concepts, doctrines, principles, postulates, statements of the obvious and pieces of nonsense have been added. *The Corporate Report* stated that financial statements should be relevant, understandable, reliable, complete, objective, timely and comparable. The entity concept is widely accepted; it means only that financial statements are produced for a business entity that is separate from the owners or managers. The materiality concept suggests that minor items will not affect 'a true and fair view', so that, for example, there is no need to capitalize and depreciate a pencil sharpener although it might last for several years. The historic cost concept suggests that items are shown in accounts at their original cost (adjusted for such things as depreciation), not at a current

[3] *The Corporate Report*, Accounting Standards Steering Committee (1975).

[4] Beginning with SSAP 2 'Accounting concepts' (ASC, 1971).

[5] It is acceptable to recognize sales before the money has been received from customers, provided it is reasonably certain how much cash will be received.

market value (although market values are given for some assets). Duality indicates that every transaction must have two aspects so that it can be recorded twice in a double-entry system, as a debit and as a credit. Disclosure suggests that all information should be disclosed that is likely to be relevant to the needs of users. Verifiability suggests that items should be included only where there is verifiable evidence (such as documents) of their existence. Objectivity and neutrality suggest that those responsible for producing financial statements should not be biased in favour of a particular point of view. Money measurement indicates that items in financial statements are given monetary values. Substance over form suggests that financial statements should show the economic reality of an item rather than its legal form. Odd writers have suggested that financial accounting is based on other conventions such as the arithmetic convention, which seems to be a statement of the obvious, and the assumption that the value of the pound is constant, which is nonsense.

Even the old Accounting Standards Committee recognized contradictions within their own four fundamental concepts, and argued that the prudence concept should prevail over the accruals concept. Other 'concepts' indicated above do not form any coherent framework or basis for accounting.

The (British) ASB's *Statement of Principles for Financial Reporting* (December 1999) refers to Objectives and Constraints rather than Concepts. In producing financial accounting statements, the most appropriate accounting policies are those that meet four objectives:

1 *Relevance* – to the needs of users in predicting the future or confirming the present or past.

2 *Reliability* – which means that accounting information should represent faithfully the substance of the underlying transactions; is neutral (there is no deliberate or systematic bias); is free from material error; is complete within the bounds of materiality; and, where conditions are uncertain, judgements and estimates have been made with a degree of caution.

   There is something of a conflict between these two: the more relevant information is for decision-making, the less reliable it is likely to be (perhaps because it is based on forecasts); and the more reliable it is (e.g. historic cost), the less relevant it is for decision-makers.

3 *Comparability* – which means that the financial statements of one entity can usefully be compared with those of another; this requires a combination of disclosure and consistency and is likely to need adjustment to the published figures since companies adopt different accounting policies, such as the method or date of depreciation.

4 *Understandability* – suggests that users should be able to understand financial statements (provided they have a reasonable knowledge of business, economics and accounting; and a willingness to study the information diligently).

The idea of prudence has been downgraded from being a fundamental accounting concept to being only part of reliability, and applying only in conditions of uncertainty; it means only that a degree of caution should be used in making judgements and estimates. The idea of general prudence has gone; it has been dismissed as being likely to result in systematic bias in financial statements. Similarly, consistency has been downgraded to being part of comparability. The accruals concept continues to be central to financial accounting. With regard to the going concern concept, companies are now required to disclose information where there may be uncertainties about its continuance as a going concern.

The idea of understandability may be rather optimistic: the published financial statements of companies are now generally more complex and more difficult to understand than ever before.

With the FASB and the IASB increasingly working together a new conceptual framework is in the process of emerging. It is likely to include four principal qualitative characteristics of information that is useful for making decisions. These are:

1 relevance;

2 faithful representation, which replaces reliability. It means that the accounting measures and descriptions used in financial reports should correspond with the economic phenomena that they are supposed to represent;

3 comparability;

4 understandability.

These are subject to two 'pervasive constraints': (i) materiality; and (ii) benefits that justify costs.[6]

3.5 The Statement of Financial Position Approach: Definition and Measurement of Assets and Liabilities

There are two basic approaches to profit measurement. One is based on the statement of financial position (Chapter 1); the second is the income statement approach (Chapter 2). Conventional accounting practice uses both at the same time, and both (should!) produce the same profit figure.

In the first approach, the *statement of financial position* would take priority. The emphasis would be on correct definition and valuation of assets and liabilities. Any increase in a company's net asset value would be the profit figure.[7] This is an 'all-inclusive' version of profit. The emphasis of financial accounting would change from being mainly the recording and summarizing of transactions (at cost price) to being mainly concerned with the valuation of assets and liabilities. The income statement would be downgraded, but would provide some detailed breakdown of the elements that have made up the overall gain.

Profit would be calculated as the increase in net assets during a period (after deducting any additional share capital subscribed, and adding back any dividends paid), as shown in Illustration 3.1.

Assets: definition

It is easiest to think of a company's assets as being anything that they own. They may be short term (current assets such as inventories, receivables, money in cash or in the bank); or they may be long term, intended for use for more than a year (non-current assets such as land and buildings, plant and machinery, furniture and fittings, and vehicles). Most are tangible, but there are also intangible assets (such as goodwill, patents and trademarks). A company may also own financial assets (such as shares in another company, or debentures).

However, a company's statement of financial position should include all assets that it controls, even if it does not own them. 'An asset is a resource controlled by the enterprise as a result of past events and from which future economic benefits are expected to flow to the enterprise.'[8] This definition includes items such as machinery that are leased, not owned. The definition should be borne in mind when considering problem assets (below).

ILLUSTRATION 3.1

Net assets at 31 December year 4	£45m
Net assets at 1 January year 4	£35m
Increase during year	£10m
Minus proceeds of share issue	(£5m)
Plus dividends paid	£7m
Profit for year	£12m

---

[6] It is usually possible to produce 'better' information but the benefit of so doing should be greater than the costs of producing it.

[7] Except that any additional share capital has to be deducted, and any dividends have to be added back.

[8] *Framework for the Preparation and Presentation of Financial Statements* (IASB, 1989).

Assets: measurement

An accounting system records transactions; that is, what things cost. Traditionally, items are shown on a statement of financial position at the amount recorded in the books, which, at least to begin with, is the cost price. But many users of financial statements want to know that 'prudent' asset values have been used, and that the assets are worth *at least* as much as the statement of financial position shows. As machinery and vehicles get older their value is 'used up', and depreciation is charged. The statement of financial position shows non-current assets at net book value (which is usually cost, minus the depreciation accumulated over a number of years).

Similarly, inventories are originally recorded at cost price. But if a business buys an item of inventory for £100 (perhaps intending to sell it for £150), and if it remains unsold for a long period, it may deteriorate, or become out of date, and its resale value may fall to (say) £70. It would be misleading to continue to show such an item at cost, £100; it has to be written down to £70. The rule for inventories is that they should be shown at the *lower* of cost and net realizable value.

Sometimes companies are required to revalue assets; sometimes they choose to do so. If a company bought a building many years ago for £100,000, it is probably misleading to continue to show it at cost (or at cost minus depreciation) if its market value has increased to £1m pounds or more. If companies understate the value of their assets on their statements of financial position there is also the possibility that they will attract unwelcome takeover bids. A company's statement of financial position may show total net assets as being £10m, but if really they are worth £25m another company may try to buy the company for (say) £15m, just to do an 'asset stripping' operation, and sell off the assets for a substantial profit. With listed companies, the market value on the stock market (or 'market capitalization') is likely to be much higher[9] than the statement of financial position shows. But with unlisted companies, statement of financial position figures may be an important determinant of what a company is seen to be worth.

When it is decided to 'revalue' assets, it is necessary to determine the basis for such a valuation, and there are many possibilities. Often some sort of 'market price' is preferred to historic cost figures, but there are different versions of market price: buying prices ('input' values) may be very different from selling prices ('output' or 'exit' values); and the selling price of an asset in the normal course of business is likely to be much higher than in a forced sale (liquidation values).

If there is a 'true' value of an asset, it is the amount that a willing buyer is willing to pay to a willing seller. This was the historic cost at the time the original transaction took place. Later we may say that the value to the business of an asset is what the business can make from that asset, which is based on the future cash flows that the asset is expected to generate. The net present value of the future cash flows that an asset (or a business) is expected to generate is its 'economic value'. If the asset is an item of inventory that the business expects to sell, then the value to the business of that item is its net realizable value – the amount for which it can be sold. The final part of this chapter deals with 'value to the business' (or 'deprival value'), and with the idea of 'fair value'.

One approach is to say that the value of an asset depends on whether you are going to buy it, sell it or use it. If you are going to buy it, it is the *replacement cost* that matters. If you are going to sell it, it is the *net realizable value* that matters. If you are going to use it, it is the *value in use* that matters; this is sometimes referred to as the *economic value*, or the *net present value of the future cash flows* that the item will produce.

The idea of *deprival value* was popular during the current cost accounting debates. This is the lower of replacement cost and recoverable amount. The recoverable amount is the higher of value in use and net realizable value. The idea is that, if you were deprived of an asset, what value would you have lost? If you would replace it, the deprival value is the replacement cost. But if it is not worth replacing (because the replacement cost is too high), the deprival value is what the business could have recovered from the asset, either by using it, or by selling it.

More recently the idea of 'fair value', which is really market price, has found favour. It is examined in the final part of this chapter.

---

[9] Unless the company is doing very badly.

Problem assets

Goodwill

Goodwill arises in financial statements when one company buys another business. If a business has a statement of financial position value of £10m it is unlikely that the owners will sell it for only £10m, especially if the business has a good profit record. The agreed price might be £15m, which leaves an accounting problem. The company has paid £15m, but has acquired only £10m of net assets; an extra £5m has been paid for something, which they hope is worth £5m, and which is labelled on the statement of financial position as goodwill.

There are many different reasons why a company might pay to acquire a business's goodwill: the company might have a good profit record, reputation, trained workforce, specialist manufacturing capacity, established customer base, particular products and brand names, and assets that are underused or undervalued. Perhaps it has unused borrowing capacity. Perhaps the acquiring company simply paid too much. Goodwill is an intangible asset, and sometimes one of doubtful value. In the past, prudent accountants have written it off, sometimes as quickly as possible.[10] More recently it has been amortized systematically in the same way that a non-current asset is depreciated.

In the past a lot of 'goodwill' arose where the assets of an acquired business were undervalued. Now, when a business is acquired, the assets of the business should be restated at 'fair value'. Where fair value is above book value, the amount of apparent goodwill is reduced. IFRS 3 also requires that different intangible assets should, where possible, be separately identified and accounted for, and not be included in 'goodwill'. The standard provides a long list of such assets, including patented technology, software, trade secrets, franchise agreements, trademarks, literary and musical works, videos and television programmes, construction permits, broadcasting rights, customer contracts and relationships.

IFRS 3 defines goodwill as 'future economic benefits arising from assets that are not capable of being individually identified and separately recognized'. It should be shown as an asset on the statement of financial position, initially at cost, which is the excess of the price paid for the business acquired over the net fair value of the identifiable assets[11] acquired. It must then be tested for impairment, with an annual impairment charge if appropriate. This supersedes systematic annual amortization charges.

It is sometimes argued that a business is creating goodwill all the time by developing and advertising products, recruiting and training employees, making profits and in many other ways. This 'internally generated' goodwill is not recognized in financial accounting. Goodwill is recognized only where it is the result of a transaction, buying another business.

Development costs and other intangibles

The days have gone when a company (like Rolls-Royce) could spend a lot of money on research and development, and treat it as capital expenditure (creating a non-current asset), and continue to show profits while getting into serious financial difficulties. Accounting standards require that all research expenditure is charged as an expense, and not capitalized. The position with development expenditure is more complex because sometimes it really is creating an asset.

For any 'intangible' to be recognized as an asset there must be the probability of it generating future economic benefits, and these must be capable of being measured reliably. With development expenditure it should be recognized as an asset, and shown on the statement of financial position (rather than being written off immediately in the income statement) if the following apply: it is technically feasible and will produce something that will be used or sold, and that the business has sufficient resources to be able to complete the development and obtain the economic benefits.

If development costs are capitalized they must subsequently be amortized or subject to impairment reviews.

IAS 38 is clear that other internally generated intangible assets such as brands, customer lists, mastheads and publishing titles should not be capitalized.

---

[10] By deducting it from retained earnings.

[11] Minus liabilities.

Human assets

It is sometimes argued that a company's employees are its most important asset and should be recognized in some way, or valued, on the statement of financial position. There may be circumstances in which some contracts of employment may be recognized as an asset, but these are unusual. IAS 38 recognizes some employment contracts as intangible assets, where these are beneficial to the employer because their pricing is below market level. It is also possible to recognize the cost of buying professional footballers. But these are very much the exception, and the idea of widespread recognition of employees as assets for accounting purposes is unlikely.

Capitalized interest

There is no doubt that creating a new non-current asset (such as a building) is capital expenditure, even if the company itself does the work and creates it. When it takes a long time to construct an asset, substantial borrowing costs are often incurred during the construction process. If a company bought such an asset from a builder, the price would have to cover the interest costs incurred by the builder. Where the company constructs assets for itself, the interest costs during construction may be regarded as part of the cost of the building and capitalized (rather than treated as an expense). IAS 23 defines conditions for such treatment, and specifies information to be disclosed. It attempts, however, to remove the discretionary element by defining when capitalization should take place.

Liabilities: definition

It is easiest to think of a company's liabilities as being anything that they owe to people outside the company. They may be short term (current liabilities such as trade payables and overdrafts), or they may be long term, that the company does not have to pay for more than a year (non-current liabilities such as loans and debentures). There are also liabilities for taxation, which may be current or non-current. It is usually not difficult to list the amounts that a company owes.

The IASB[12] defines a liability as 'a present obligation of the enterprise arising from past events, the settlement of which is expected to result in an outflow from the enterprise of resources embodying economic benefits'. An outflow of economic benefits usually means a payment. The important part is that the liability is a *present* obligation, meaning that the obligation must exist at the statement of financial position date; this may restrict the use of vague 'provisions' if they may or may not require the payment of an unknown amount at an unknown future date.

Liabilities: measurement

With most liabilities there are no problems in determining the amount owed.

If a liability is not due to be paid for some years it may be appropriate to 'discount'.[13] If, for example, a company owes £10m that is due to be paid four years in the future, and the appropriate discount rate is ⑩ per cent, the amount could be shown on the statement of financial position at its 'present value', which would be (£10 × 0.683 =) £6.83m.

Problem liabilities £10 > 90%

There can, however, be problems in dealing with some items such as provisions and deferred tax.

Provisions

The term 'provision' is sometimes used for amounts deducted from assets, such as provision for bad debts, or provision for depreciation on non-current assets. There is likely to be some subjectivity in determining the amounts of such 'provisions', but otherwise it should be straightforward. The

---

[12] *Framework for the Preparation and Presentation of Financial Statements* (IASB, 1989).

[13] Using the principles of DCF, as explained in Chapter 13.

amounts relate to assets, not liabilities; the amount of the asset could be reduced to zero, but we should not have 'negative assets'. Provisions as liabilities are more problematic. The Companies Act 1985 defined provisions as 'amounts retained as reasonably necessary to cover any liability or loss which is either likely or certain to be incurred'. This gives companies a fair amount of freedom to reduce profits in one year[14] and create a provision against which expenses can be charged in a subsequent year (without reducing profits in that year). This could be seen as an application of 'prudence'. It could also be used for 'income smoothing', and is discussed in Chapter 8.

Provisions were often created for future reorganizations, redundancies, legal liabilities, decommissioning costs, and future costs and losses of various sorts.

The more recent, stricter definition of liabilities refers to a 'present obligation', which would exclude current *proposals* to incur liabilities or losses in future periods. IAS 37 defined a provision as 'a liability of uncertain timing or amount'. The definition assumes that an outflow of resources is probable, and that a reliable estimate of the amount can be made. The obligation may be legal or 'constructive', which allows provisions to be made where there are no legal commitments, but where the company has by its actions and announcements committed itself to a course of action.

The accounting standard-setters are in a difficult position. If they allow too much freedom in creating, increasing and reducing provisions, they leave the door open to creative accounting. But if they are too strict in not allowing provisions, there would often be cases where companies knew of some likely bad news, and kept quiet about it. A prudent set of financial statements would disclose all potential liabilities, including 'contingent liabilities'.

Warranties

Companies may make specific provisions for the cost of guarantees or warranties and other after-sales service that they are expected to provide. This may appear on a statement of financial position as a provision; or it may not be separately disclosed. Sometimes companies deduct appropriate provisions from the figure for sales; sometimes it is included in a more general provision.

Contingent liabilities

Contingent liabilities can arise as a result of legal action. Maybe the company will have to pay out a lot of money as a result of losing a case; the result may not yet have been determined. A contingent liability is a possible obligation whose existence will be confirmed only by the occurrence of an uncertain future event; or it can be where a transfer of economic benefits is not probable, or the amount cannot yet be measured reliably. Contingent liabilities should not be shown on a statement of financial position. They should be disclosed as a note to the accounts (unless it is only a remote possibility).

In assessing the solvency or creditworthiness of a company, it is worth looking not only at the actual liabilities shown on the statement of financial position, but also at the contingent liabilities; there may be a risk of substantial payments having to be made.

Deferred taxation

Deferred taxation arises because the rules for calculating profit for inclusion in annual reports and accounts are different from the rules for taxation purposes. Depreciation allowances for taxation purposes ('writing-down allowances') are typically quite high in the early years of a fixed asset's life; these high allowances reduce taxable profits, which means that the amount of corporation tax payable is much reduced in the first years after substantial acquisitions of fixed assets. Profits for tax purposes are much lower than the profits reported in the annual accounts, which would make the tax charge look peculiarly low, and might mislead shareholders by exaggerating the after-tax profits available for dividends.

---

[14] By debiting the income statement with the 'expense' of the provision, and creating a credit balance, which is shown as a provision on the statement of financial position.

As the non-current assets get towards the end of their lives (and if there have been few additional purchases of non-current assets) the position reverses: allowances for tax purposes are smaller; the amount of tax payable is larger; and this might mislead shareholders by showing low after-tax profit being available for dividends.

Deferred taxation is a bit like a taxation equalization account. In the early years after acquisitions of fixed assets, the tax actually payable is low; but a higher charge against profits is made; this extra 'deferred taxation' is not yet payable but is shown as if it is a liability. After a few years it may reverse: the tax actually payable is higher, but only a modest 'equalized' charge is made against profits; the extra is charged against the balance for deferred taxation that was built up for that purpose in the early years of the non-current asset's life.

In many cases the amount shown as a long-term liability for deferred taxation will never actually be paid. If a company continues to invest in additional non-current assets it is likely that the writing-down allowances on the new non-current assets will have the effect of building up the credit balance on the deferred taxation account faster than it is used up by the smaller writing-down allowances on the older non-current assets. The old Accounting Standards Committee experimented with a 'partial provision' for deferred taxation, based on the idea that provisions should be made only for amounts that it was reasonably probable would become payable. But this was rather subjective and not consistent with international practice.

IAS 12 requires full provision for deferred taxation for all[15] timing differences. The effect can be to build up a substantial provision on the statement of financial position that might never actually become a liability. This makes interpretation of financial statements, and the calculation of accounting ratios, rather difficult. Some people simply ignore it: they exclude it from capital employed, and from liabilities, but this can lead to inconsistent ratios that never properly add up or reconcile.

Deferred taxation is normally shown as a non-current liability, identified separately from other liabilities. As in so many areas of interpretation of financial statements, there may be no definitive, 'right' answer. The important thing is to treat it in a consistent way in comparing one company with another, and comparing one year with another.

3.6 The Income Statement Approach: Definition and Measurement of Revenues and Expenses

In the second approach, the *income statement* takes priority. The emphasis is on reporting revenues, and carefully determining the costs that should be matched against those revenues in order to determine the amount of profit. The statement of financial position is a statement of left-over balances with no attempt to show them as the current *value* of assets and liabilities. Depreciation is necessary for profit measurement: the cost of an asset is spread over its estimated useful life; there is no pretence that the remaining balance represents the current value of the asset.

Profit may be defined as sales and any other revenues earned during a period, minus the costs incurred in earning those sales and revenues. This seems straightforward enough. Sales are not very hard to identify, and most costs are obvious. Both are shown on an income statement as seen in Chapter 2.

Determining exactly which costs should be 'matched' against the revenues of a period is, in most cases, done with little difficulty, although it does mean dealing with asset values, or 'unexpired costs'.

If a company buys goods for £100 and sells half of them for £120 it has made £70 profit. The cost of goods was £100, but half of the costs are 'unexpired', or unsold: those inventories are still there to be shown as assets on the statement of financial position. The gross profit requires the 'cost of goods sold' to be deducted from sales.

---

[15] There are some limited exceptions.

Accountants have traditionally been prudent in valuing closing inventories. They may be difficult to sell, and they may eventually have to be sold for less than the cost price of £50. The net realizable value of seasonal, perishable and fashionable items can rapidly fall below cost price. When the net realizable value of the inventories is less than the cost price, the closing inventory must be written down. In the above example, if the net realizable value of the closing inventory, which had cost £50, was only £35, then the cost of goods sold[16] would be £65, and the gross profit would be £55. If the closing inventory value falls by £15, then profit falls by £15.

There are also problems in the treatment of non-current assets, and calculating depreciation based on estimates of how long the asset's useful life will be, and what its scrap value will be at the end of its life. With receivables it is necessary to assess what provisions for bad debts is appropriate, and estimates in relation to other assets and unexpired costs[17] may be needed.

The income statement approach to profit measurement is the most popular. Businesses and accounting systems record revenues that have been earned and the costs incurred, and profit seems naturally to be the difference between the two. Unfortunately, it is not possible to measure profit in this way without considering the amounts to be shown for various assets (e.g. closing inventories, and as a result of depreciation).

Revenues, income and gains

It is easiest to think of a company's revenues as being anything that is credited to the income statement. They may be normal sales revenues, including professional fees earned, and various other income such as rent, interest and dividends receivable, or from sources such as royalties. IAS 1 is fairly permissive, but most income statements have separate headings for (1) revenue (from sales), (2) other income and (3) finance income.

Normally income statements include only income that has been *realized*. This means that a transaction has taken place and an item has been sold. It may be that inventories that had cost £100 are worth £150 at the year end, but that 'gain' of £50 is not included in the income statement until the items have been sold. Similarly, if a building cost £1m, but at the statement of financial position date is revalued at £1.5m, that gain of £0.5 is not realized until the building is sold.

Revenues are normal sales; income comes from other sources; both are recognized when 'realized'. Other 'gains' of various kinds may or may not be realized, and may or may not be recognized.

Statement of changes in equity

The IASB adopts an 'all-inclusive' (or statement of financial position) approach to the definition of income: 'Income is increases in economic benefits during the accounting period in question in the form of inflows or enhancements of assets or decreases of liabilities that result in increases in equity, other than those relating to contributions from equity participants.' They include increases in the value of assets as 'income', but these would not normally be included as 'revenue' on the income statement. Here the US FASB approach is useful: it defines revenues as being from 'delivering or producing goods, rendering services, or other activities that constitute the entity's ongoing major central operations'. Other gains (which are part of an all-inclusive concept of income, but which are not included as revenues on the income statement) are shown on the 'Statement of Changes in Equity', which is required by IAS 1.

During the year the total amount for equity can change because:

1 additional shares are issued or redeemed;

2 profits or losses are made (as shown on the income statement);

---

[16] Cost of goods sold, or cost of sales, is opening inventory (zero), plus purchases (£100), minus closing inventory (£35) = £65.

[17] Sometimes the benefit from paying for something (such as advertising, or development expenditure) may extend over several periods and it is necessary to determine how much of it is to be treated as an expense in the current period, and how much should be carried forward as an unexpired cost, or asset, to future periods.

3 dividends are paid;

4 a variety of other gains and losses are made, including those resulting from the revaluation of property, and available-for-sale investments.

An example of a Statement of Changes in Equity is shown in Chapter 2 (Illustration 2.1).

Revenue recognition

There is sometimes a problem in determining the date on which a sale takes place and thus when revenue is recognized. If a company's year end is 31 December and a substantial order is received on 28 December year 1, but the goods are not despatched until 3 January year 2, it can make an important difference to year 1 results if the sale is included in that year. Accounting systems usually record a sale as taking place when the invoice is issued, but that may not be the 'critical event' in determining when a sale should be recognized. Where management is under pressure to improve financial results in the short term they might be tempted to amend their accounting systems to record sales at as early a date as possible. As in so many other areas, the accounting standard-setters are in the process of producing clear rules on revenue recognition, but the results have yet to be finalized.[18]

Expenses

Expenses are the costs incurred in earning the revenue that is recognized during a period and which are shown on the income statement. Thus 'cost of sales' is the correct expense figure, not purchases. The cost of acquiring a machine (or other non-current asset) is not recognized when the machine is bought or paid for; it is spread over the asset's life as it is used up and recognized as depreciation.

There may be other losses or 'impairments', which look a bit like expenses, but which are not recognized on the income statement. Where these are recognized they are shown on the Statement of Changes in Equity.

The IASB adopts a wider, or all-inclusive, definition of expenses. They are 'decreases in economic benefits during the accounting period in the form of outflows or depletions of assets or incurrences of liabilities that result in decreases in equity, other than those relating to distributions to equity participants'. This would include all decreases in the value of assets, some of which are not normally recognized in financial accounting.

Problem areas

There are a number of problem areas with expenses, including the following:

1 *Depreciation* – The expense charged for depreciation of a particular asset depends on assumptions about its future life, pattern of usage and final salvage value. As these cannot be predicted with certainty, there is inevitably some subjectivity in determining depreciation charges. There are also different methods of calculating depreciation (see Example 3.2).

2 *Impairment of goodwill* – Most large, listed companies are really groups of companies with a number of subsidiaries. When a subsidiary company is first acquired it is usually the case that the price paid to acquire the business is higher than the statement of financial position value of the net assets acquired. If the statement of financial position of a successful company shows a net asset value of £10m, the owners of the company are unlikely to be willing to sell it for as little as £10m. They will expect an extra payment for the goodwill of the company. Perhaps the agreed price will be £22m, of which £12m is paid for goodwill. Goodwill is an intangible non-current asset, and, like other non-current assets, it should be written off as it is used up.

The treatment of goodwill has varied over time, and the amounts involved have tended to increase. It used to be regarded as being very questionable, and was typically written off immedi-

---

[18] A new standard is expected in 2012.

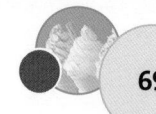

Example 3.2

The Adle Company buys a new machine for £256,000 and intends to use it for five years, after which it is expected to have a trade-in value of £36,000. Calculate the amount of depreciation using:

a the straight-line method; and
b the reducing (or diminishing balance) method at 25% per annum.

a	£256,000 – £36,000 = £220,000 ÷ 5 = £44,000 per annum _annum_				
b	Year 1	25% of £256,000	= £64,000	leaving net book value	£192,000
	Year 2	25% of £192,000	= £48,000	leaving net book value	£144,000
	Year 3	25% of £144,000	= £36,000	leaving net book value	£108,000
	Year 4	25% of £108,000	= £27,000	leaving net book value	£ 81,000
	Year 5	25% of £ 81,000	= £20,250	leaving net book value	£ 60,750

ately by deducting it from retained earnings; it did not pass through the income statement. That was a problem when the amount of goodwill was greater than the amount of retained earnings! In the last few decades of the twentieth century the usual policy was to recognize goodwill as a non-current asset, but to amortize it systematically, as an expense, via the income statement, over its expected useful life (which could be 10 years, or 20 or more years).

Now, IAS 36 requires that there should be an annual impairment review of goodwill, although it is recognized that goodwill does not generate cash flows separately from the assets with which it is associated. The impairment review is of a cash-generating unit, and any impairment is recognized as an expense in the income statement. This, of course, leaves open the possibility that a company will decide that there has been no impairment and so no charge is required.

3 *Capitalization of interest* – There is no doubt that creating a new non-current asset is capital expenditure, even if the company creates their own new non-current assets. When it takes a long time to construct an asset, substantial borrowing costs are often incurred during the construction process. If a company bought such an asset from a builder, the price paid would have to cover the interest costs incurred by the builder. But if the company constructs the asset itself, it may regard the interest cost as being part of the cost of the building (a non-current asset) rather than an expense. The idea of capitalizing interest may be controversial, but it is permitted in circumstances specified by IAS 23, provided appropriate disclosures are made.

4 *Share options* – Some companies have chosen to give part or all of their employees' remuneration in the form of options to buy shares rather than in cash. This was popular during the dotcom boom, when companies were expanding rapidly, and their share prices were increasing, but they found it difficult to pay the high levels of remuneration that some key employees expected. If a company's shares are trading at £2 each, an option to buy 100,000 of them at £2.50 would at first not be attractive. But if the company's share price increased to, say, £12.50, the employee could make £1m by buying the 100,000 shares at £2.50, and then selling them at £12.50. That is more attractive than most salaries!

At first that seems to be a cost-free way of paying employees generously. But there is a cost to the original shareholders: suddenly they own a smaller proportion of the company. The standard-setters require that this cost must be recognized and specified how to do this in IFRS 2 Share-based Payments.

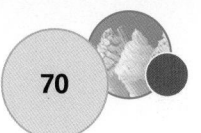

3.7 Adjusting Financial Statements for Price Changes

The problem

Both statements of financial position and income statements are affected by changing prices, and the resultant profit figures need to be interpreted with care. During a period of rising prices, profits are usually overstated and there are a number of problems with using conventional financial statements based on historic cost (see Illustration 3.2).

- Cost of sales is understated. If a business buys oil for £120 a barrel, and a month later sells it for £130 a barrel, it seems to have made a profit of £10. But if, during that month, the cost of replacing that oil increases from £120 to £129, the business is not much better off. It has made a 'holding gain' of £9, but its 'operating gain' or profit is only £1.

- Depreciation is understated. If a business buys a machine for £100,000, which is expected to last for 10 years, it seems reasonable to charge £10,000 a year depreciation. But if, at the end of 10 years, it comes to replace the machine, it might cost a lot more – perhaps £200,000. Depreciation based on historic cost was much lower than it would be using current costs, and in that sense profits have been overstated.

- Excessive dividends might be paid if profits are overstated. This would reduce the company's capital in real terms.

- Excessive taxation might be paid if it is based on overstated profits, which would reduce the company's capital in real terms.[19]

- Liquidity problems are likely to arise if a company pays excessive dividends and taxation and needs to finance the extra cost of replacing various[20] assets.

- Statement of financial position values of assets are understated during a period of rising prices, especially freehold property.

- Return on capital employed is overstated; this is true if profits are overstated and asset values are understated.

- It is wrong to add together items on a statement of financial position that are expressed in different units of currency. Obviously dollars are not added to euros. But, on a statement of financial position, items expressed in £s of 20 years ago are added to items expressed in £s of this year, although the value of the currency has changed significantly in the meantime.

- Gains from borrowing. When a business borrows money, the interest payable is correctly recorded as an expense. But if the borrowed money is used to purchase a tangible asset (such as freehold property), the gain on that asset (as prices increase) is not recorded.

ILLUSTRATION 3.2		
	Historic cost	Current values
Profit for year	£12,000	£8,000
Net assets	£100,000	£133,333
Return on capital employed	12%	6%

---

[19] HMRC's rules for measuring profits for corporation tax purposes are different, and in some ways more realistic than conventional accounting.

[20] Including receivables, which are likely to increase in line with inflation; the resulting extra amount of debt has to be financed.

Some of these problems are to do with the measurement of profit, some with assets, and others to do with the consequences; and some are inherent in the nature of accounting. It would be difficult to devise a satisfactory system of accounting that would solve all the problems.

Possible solutions

Various piecemeal and *ad hoc* solutions have been suggested, such as being careful about dividends (i.e. do not pay out all profits as dividends; some need to be retained to finance the increased cost of assets); revaluing fixed assets and increasing depreciation accordingly; and using last in first out (LIFO) (so that cost of sales is based on recent prices).[21]

An important principle in finding a solution is 'capital maintenance'. Profit is the amount that a business can afford to pay out as dividends without making itself less 'well off'. If a business starts a year with equity of £1m (using the statement of financial position approach to measuring profit), and ends the year with equity of £1.2m, we may say that it has made £0.2m profit, it can pay out £0.2m as dividends, and it will have maintained its capital at £1m. This is true in historic cost terms; but in real terms (allowing for inflation) the value of the capital will be less.

If a business starts the year with equity of £1m, and there is 5 per cent inflation, at the end of the year it needs £1.05m to maintain capital in 'real terms', and it can pay only £0.15m as dividends, not £0.2m. Current purchasing power (CPP) accounting is designed to maintain capital in real terms. It adjusts all items in the financial statements to reflect inflation; that is, changes in the general price level.

A different approach is to deal with the effects of *specific* price changes on the entity, rather than general inflation. There are various ways[22] of doing this, but the best known is intended to maintain the *operating capability* (capital) of the business, based on changes in the prices of the actual assets that the business used. The best known method of doing this is current cost accounting, applying four adjustments to the income statement, and showing items on the statement of financial position at current cost. Profit is calculated in the usual way, then the following adjustments are applied:

1 Cost of sales adjustment that reduces profit by calculating the cost of financing the increase in inventories required by price increases.

2 Depreciation adjustment that reduces profit by calculating the additional depreciation required to finance the increase in the cost of non-current assets.

3 Monetary working capital adjustment that reduces profit by calculating the cost of financing the increase in receivables[23] required by price increases.

During a period of rising prices, the total of the first three adjustments will reduce historic cost profits, as if the whole of the additional finance required is provided by equity shareholders. To the extent that a business is financed by borrowing:

4 A gearing adjustment is applied that reduces the effect of the other three adjustments.

In current cost accounting statement of financial position items are shown at their 'value to the business', or 'deprival value', which is often their replacement cost.[24] These figures are more realistic than historic cost (adjusted in various ways), but there may be more subjectivity. They are more relevant to the needs of users, but perhaps less reliable than good old historic cost.

---

[21] In a period of rising prices, LIFO gives more realistic profit figures than FIFO; but LIFO statement of financial position figures for inventories are more unrealistic.

[22] ASC SSAP16 Current Cost Accounting (1979).

[23] Net receivables (receivables minus payables), or, more strictly, net monetary working capital. Where payables are greater than receivables, the adjustment would *increase* profits (offsetting the cost of sales adjustment because additional inventories are financed by payables).

[24] If replacement cost is higher than 'deprival value', then economic value (net present value of future cash flows), or net realizable value, is used, whichever of the two is higher.

Example 3.3

Two companies, A Ltd and B Ltd, each buy an identical asset for £100,000 during Year 1. Immediately before the year end, A Ltd sells the asset at its market value of £125,000. B Ltd retains the asset, and a few months later the asset falls in value to £90,000.

Each company reports a profit of £25,000 for Year 1. For A Ltd it is a realized profit. B Ltd has missed an opportunity and subsequently has an unrealized loss.

Another problem is to define and measure 'fair value'. It has long been recognized that 'pure' historic cost (although 'fair' at the time of the transaction) may be very different from 'fair value' at the statement of financial position date. Accounting standards already require that a number of items are shown on the statement of financial position at fair value, including pension assets and liabilities, some other financial assets and liabilities such as derivatives, assets acquired as a result of a business combination, assets that have been revalued, perhaps because of impaired value, investment properties and provisions.

In establishing 'fair value' based on market values there is often a difference between buying prices (entry values, or replacement cost) and selling prices (exit values, or net realizable value), and it is the latter that seems to be favoured by standard-setters. It is likely that we will continue with statements of financial position showing a mixture of cost-based and 'fair value' figures.

However fair or accurate the measurement of assets and liabilities may be, the total of the amounts shown for individual assets and liabilities will not be the same as the value of the firm (or its market capitalization).

There has been extensive discussion about which theoretical system for financial accounting would be better than traditional accounting, based on historic cost. Several different systems may be theoretically superior, but there is a lack of agreement on which, and with inflation falling to low levels the problem no longer seems urgent, and making major changes does not seem to be a priority.

Fair value

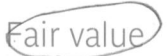

The idea of 'fair value' is currently fashionable among standard-setters, and some academics, together with an 'all-inclusive' concept of profit. This means that if all items on the statement of financial position are stated at 'fair value', an increase in equity is regarded as profit.[25] One problem with this approach is that it would include in profit any increase in the value of assets – even if they are not sold (see Example 3.3).

📖 Summary

Published financial statements are designed to give useful economic information to users of accounts to enable them to make informed decisions in relation to the business. On the whole, the level and detail of disclosure arises from regulation, including the Companies Act and accounting standards. It is easy to criticize accounting standard-setters for not yet coming up with a 'final solution' to all the problems of profit definition measurement, and definitions that have universal acceptance. Progress has been made with developing theoretical frameworks, the setting of underlying assumptions and definitions. This has resulted in standards that narrow the differences in accounting practice, define terms and methods and have increased the level of information disclosed. The statement of financial position and the income statement approaches to the calculation of profit are contrasted. In times of inflation, accounts under the historical cost convention have serious difficulties but every inflation-adjusted method of accounting has serious inadequacies.

---

[25] After allowing for any dividends paid and any additional equity capital.

⊜ Review of key points

- Published financial statements may be used by many different groups in society, but the principal users are investors and creditors.
- Profit figures are assumed to be useful in various ways including making investment decisions, assessing creditworthiness and evaluating the effectiveness of management.
- It is difficult to establish a theoretical basis for profit measurement and financial reporting.
- There are different approaches to profit measurement based mainly on the statement of financial position, or on the income statement.
- Definitions have been established for assets, liabilities, revenues and expenses, but some items still present difficulties.
- Financial statements can be seriously affected by inflation and various methods have been developed to tackle this.

Self-testing questions

1 Who are the main users of financial accounting information, and what are their information needs?
2 Define assets and liabilities.
3 Why are 'provisions' a problem?
4 What is 'goodwill', and how does it arise?
5 Why do we not have 'pure' historic cost accounting?
6 Distinguish between 'revenues', 'income' and 'gains'.
7 Why is 'profit' seen as being important?

✎ Assessment questions

1 What is 'profit'?
2 Explain the meaning of 'relevance' and 'reliability' in financial reporting.
3 Examine the main methods of measuring (or valuing) assets.
4 Define revenues and expenses. What other sorts of gain are there?
5 What are the tests for recognizing an intangible asset?
6 Is profit usually overstated when historic cost accounting is used? Explain.

Group activities and discussion questions

1 To what extent is it possible for published financial statements to meet the needs of different user groups?
2 Does financial accounting have any fundamental accounting concepts? Is it more helpful to establish objectives and constraints?
3 Financial statements are part of the process of making the directors of companies accountable to their shareholders. How accountable do you think they really are?

4 Examine the idea of accountability in relation to an organization with which you are familiar (e.g. a university, a church, a football club, a national government).

5 Why is it not easy to define and measure profit?

 ## Accounting in context

Discuss and comment on the following article. What are contingent liabilities and why are they such an important factor to consider when assessing published accounts? Can you identify other examples of contingent liabilities from other companies you are interested in?

Stringfellow has a bare grasp of currency trading

By Jonathan Russell

Peter Stringfellow sells all sorts of things at his chain of lap dancing clubs, not all to everyone's taste, even though he does claim his steaks are the "finest in London".

However the most profitable line could be neither the meat nor the flesh on offer.

Buried in the latest set of accounts for his company Stringfellow Restaurants is the small matter of a £970,000 contingent liability.

All that heavenly money that Stringfellow has put through his profit and loss account comes directly from Heavenly Pounds, the cash that his clubs insist punters use to pay for the, er, entertainment.

The liability relates to the amount of Heavenly Pounds customers have failed to redeem over the last 12 years.

They must have taken it home, where, presumably, it's been found by the wife. Whatever happens to it, until it's redeemed Stringfellow gets to keep the real stuff.

A licence to print money.

Source: The Telegraph, 4 July 2009

References and further reading

Elliott, B. and J. Elliott (2011) *Financial Accounting and Reporting* (14th edn.). Harlow: FT Prentice Hall.
Melville, A. (2011) *International Financial Reporting* (3rd edn.). Harlow: FT Prentice Hall.
Wood, F. and A. Sangster (2012) *Business Accounting* (vol. 1) (12th edn.). Harlow: FT Prentice Hall.
www.frc.org.uk (gives details of the Financial Reporting Council and arrangements for accounting standards in the British Isles)
www.ifrs.org (gives details of international financial reporting standards)
www.annualreport.marksandspencer.com/ (gives the Marks and Spencer Group accounts in full)

 **Online LearningCentre**

When you have read this chapter, log on to the Online Learning Centre website at *www.mcgraw-hill.co.uk/textbooks/leiwy* to explore chapter-by-chapter test questions, further reading and more online study tools.

4

Ratios and Interpretation: A Straightforward Introduction

Chapter contents

4.2 Financial Strength/Solvency （償債能力）   77

4.3 Profitability   81

4.4 Stock Market Ratios   86

4.5 Working Capital Management   88

4.6 Financial Structure/Gearing   88

4.7 Limitations and Comparisons   89

4.8 Ratios Ready Reference   91

✓ Learning objectives

After studying this chapter you will be able to:

- ✓ Calculate and interpret four solvency ratios from a company's published financial statements
- ✓ Calculate and interpret four overall profitability ratios; three dealing with the profitability of sales; and five dealing with the utilization of assets
- ✓ Calculate and interpret four stock market ratios
- ✓ Understand the role of working capital management and apply relevant ratios
- ✓ Appreciate the importance of financial structure and apply relevant ratios
- ✓ Understand the limitations of ratio analysis and the importance of suitable bases for comparison

4.1 Introduction

This chapter shows how financial accounts provide information that can be useful in assessing the financial strength of a company, and in analysing and improving its performance in terms of profitability in a straightforward way. Complexities, and more advanced aspects of interpretation, are dealt with in Chapter 11.

This chapter also introduces the use of financial accounting information in interpreting the performance of a company's shares on the stock market. These issues are dealt with more fully in Chapter 5.

Interpretation of accounts is not about memorizing a number of ratios and then calculating them. It is about examining a set of accounts, with some clear questions in mind, and then carefully arranging the evidence to answer those questions.

Presentation of 'ratios'

Accounting 'ratios' are presented in a number of conventional ways, most of which are percentages or some other measures, rather than 'ratios' in the strict sense of the word:

- *Ratios* – Current ratio and quick (or acid test) ratio are presented as ratios in the form 1.8 : 1.
- *Percentages* – Many so-called ratios are really expressed as percentages. A dividend yield might be 3.5 per cent. Return on capital employed (ROCE) might be 12 per cent. The gross profit ratio is also expressed as a percentage (e.g. 25 per cent).
- *Number of times* – Dividend cover is expressed as a number of times, for example 2.2 times. Interest cover and asset turnover ratios are also expressed as, for example, 6 times, 1.9 times. The 'price/earnings ratio' (P/E) (e.g. 16) is the share price divided by earnings per share, indicating that the share price is a number of times earnings (per share).
- *Number of days* – The trade receivables (trade debtors) 'ratio' is often shown as being, for example, 36 days,[1] being the average time customers take to pay for the goods sold to them. Similarly, the inventory (stock) turnover ratio is often expressed as the number of days, on average, goods are in stock before being sold. The trade payables (trade creditors) ratio is often shown as being the average period taken to pay trade payables.
- *Sum of money* – Earnings per share are expressed as a sum of money (e.g. 10p).

There are three main groups of question in interpreting financial statements and a number of related ones:

i *Financial strength/solvency* – Is the business likely to survive? Can it pay its liabilities as they fall due? Is it financially strong? Is there too much debt?

ii *Profitability* – Is the business sufficiently profitable? Is it making the best use of the resources available to it? How can profitability be increased?

iii *Stock market* – How are the company's shares performing on the stock market? Are they likely to be a good investment?

The chapter demonstrates how ratios can be used to tackle each of these questions in relation to Druisdale plc for year 5. Readers are invited to calculate and interpret the equivalent ratios for year 6. (The answers are provided at the end of the book, pp. 482–485.)

Other related questions include different aspects of profitability, working capital management, financial structure and cash flows. This chapter introduces most of these issues. Cash flows are dealt with in Chapter 6. Stock market ratios are dealt with more fully in Chapter 5. More advanced interpretation of financial statements and some complexities are dealt with in Chapter 11.

---

[1] Alternatively, it could also be expressed as sales divided by trade receivables, giving perhaps 10 times per annum.

The final part of the chapter provides an overview of ratio analysis, followed by a 'ratios ready reference' section.

4.2 Financial Strength/Solvency

A statement of financial position shows what a company owns or controls (assets) and what it owes (liabilities). Unless the company is a complete disaster, it should have more assets than liabilities, and the excess of assets over liabilities is called 'equity'. If someone owns a house worth £200,000, and has a mortgage of £120,000, their 'equity' in that house is £80,000.

A business can collapse in many different ways: bankruptcy of the owner, liquidation, receivership, winding up, reorganization and takeover. Many different reasons are put forward to explain what went wrong, including bad management and bad luck. But, in the end, a company collapses if it is unable to pay its liabilities as they fall due. Statements of financial position show liabilities clearly, and it is worth trying to assess if those liabilities are excessive – if the company owes so much that it is likely to get into financial difficulties and become insolvent.

The statement of financial position clearly separates short-term assets and liabilities from long-term assets and liabilities, and the assessment can be done in two stages: short term and long term.

Short term

The key question is: can a company meet its short-term liabilities as they fall due? Current liabilities are clearly shown on statements of financial position. If a company has current liabilities of £1m, and they have £2m in the bank, then there should not be a problem. There are companies with so much money in the bank that they do not know what to do with it, but that is not the norm. Even if a company does not have lots of money in the bank, it is worth looking at its current assets as a whole. Current assets include cash, and things like inventories and receivables that are expected to become cash within a matter of months. If a company has a lot more current assets than current liabilities, then it looks reasonably strong.

If we look at the Druisdale plc statement of financial position at the end of year 5 (Example 4.1), we can see that current liabilities amount to £60m. If all their current assets are turned into cash there should not be a problem: current assets amount to £120m. Current assets are twice as much as current liabilities – a ratio of 2 : 1. This relationship between current assets and current liabilities is called the current ratio.

In some businesses inventories are not easily, or quickly, converted into cash. In looking at what money is immediately available with which to pay current liabilities we should, perhaps, exclude inventories. Some inventories, such as stocks of food in a supermarket, should be sold and converted into cash within a few weeks. Other inventories may take a long time to be converted into cash; for example, raw materials and components that have not yet been incorporated into saleable products, or partly built houses – perhaps where demand is currently slack. In Druisdale plc there is £20m of cash, and £40m of trade receivables that should become cash within a month or so. In other words 'liquid assets' of £60m (excluding inventories) are just enough to meet current liabilities of £60m as they become due. This is a quick (or acid test) ratio of 1 : 1.

On year 6 statement of financial position there are not enough liquid assets (£60m) to meet current liabilities (£80m). The quick ratio has gone down to 0.75 : 1. Their liquidity position has deteriorated, and problems could arise.

Long term

A company is likely to find itself in financial difficulties if it has too much debt, whether it is short or long term. One way of assessing if debt is too high is to compare it with equity. If someone has a mortgage (debt) of £120,000 it is probably not serious if the house is worth £200,000 – there is £80,000 of the owner's equity. It is still less of a problem if the house is worth £500,000: the owner's equity would amount to £380,000. The more equity there is in relation to the total value of the house, the less risky the borrowing is. The more borrowing there is in relation to the total value of the house, the more risky the borrowing is.

Example 4.1

Statement of financial position of Druisdale plc as at 31 December		
	Year 5	Year 6
	£m	£m
Assets		
Non-current assets		
Property, plant and equipment	180	200
Current assets		
Inventories	60	60
Trade receivables	40	50
Cash	20	10
	120	120
Total assets	300	320
Liabilities and equity		
Current liabilities		
Trade payables	60	80
Non-current liabilities		
Long-term borrowing	60	40
Total liabilities	120	120
Equity		
Share capital	100	100
Retained earnings	80	100
Total equity	180	200
Total liabilities and equity	300	320

Income statement of Druisdale plc for the year ended 31 December		
	Year 5	Year 6
	£m	£m
Revenue	300	350
Cost of sales	(200)	(230)
Gross profit	100	120
Distribution costs	(15)	(20)
Administrative expenses	(25)	(31)
Operating profit	60	69
Finance costs	(5)	(4)
Profit before tax	55	65
Income tax expense	(15)	(15)
Profit for the period	40	50

Continued >>>

Example 4.1

Continued >>>

Statement of changes in equity of Druisdale plc for the year ended 31 December		
Balance at beginning of year	165	180
Profit for the period	40	50
Dividends	(25)	(30)
Balance at end of year	180	200

Additional information

Druisdale plc's share capital consists of 100 million ordinary shares with a nominal value of £1 each. Assume that the share price on 31 December year 5 was £5.60, and on 31 December year 6 it was £7.50.

It is also necessary to look at an individual's, or a company's, ability to service the loan. If interest of 8 per cent per annum is payable on a loan of £120,000, the cost of the loan is £9,600[2] per annum. If an individual or company earns only £10,000 a year, they are going to have problems paying the interest. If they earn £30,000 a year we can say that the interest is 'covered' just over three times, which might be satisfactory. It would be much more comfortable if the income available to pay the interest was £96,000 a year: we could say that the interest is covered 10 times since a future reduction of income will not seriously jeopardize the likelihood of being able to pay the interest.

Statements of financial position show the relationship between equity and long-term borrowings. At the end of year 5 Druisdale plc's equity amounted to £180m; their long-term borrowings were £60m. We could say that as long as equity is a lot more than borrowings, the position is satisfactory. Or we could present a 'gearing ratio' that relates debt (long-term borrowings) to equity. The total amount of long-term funding available to Druisdale is (180 + 60 =) £240m. Of this total, £60m is borrowed: the gearing ratio is therefore 25 per cent.[3]

Druisdale should have little difficulty in servicing their loan. The income statement for year 5 shows 'finance costs' of £5m. The profit available to provide that interest amounted to £60m. We could arrive at this figure simply by taking profit before tax, and adding back the interest. Or we could use the 'operating profit' figure (which is the same), which is gross profit minus operating costs for distribution and administration (100 − 15 − 25 =) £60m. Interest is covered 12 times,[4] which should be very safe.

An overall view

The approach so far has been to calculate four widely used 'ratios' for year 5, which are as follows.

1 *Current ratio* (or working capital ratio)   2 : 1
2 *Quick* (or acid test ratio)   1 : 1
3 *Capital gearing ratio*   25%
4 *Interest cover*   12 times

---

[2] 8% × £120,000 = £9,600.

[3] 60 ÷ 240 × 100 = 25%.

[4] 60 ÷ 5 = 12.

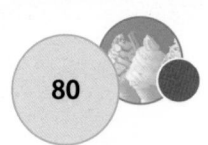
Example 4.2

Ratio	Tesco plc	GlaxoSmithKline
Current ratio	0.7 : 1	1.3 : 1
Quick ratio	0.5 : 1	1 : 1
Capital gearing ratio	37%	64%
Interest cover	8 times	6 times

It is not sensible to state what are acceptable or benchmark levels for these ratios since what would be considered acceptable in one industry might be thought to be far too high or too low in another. In Example 4.2, we can see two highly regarded companies in different sectors with different results and in order to assess these ratios, the only sensible approach is to compare Tesco with another supermarket group and GlaxoSmithKline with another pharmaceutical company.

If the current ratio and quick ratio are lower than other similar companies, that tends to indicate that the company is not liquid enough while if these ratios are higher than similar companies, that indicates that the company is not using its liquid resources in an effective way.

If the gearing ratio is higher than similar companies, that indicates that the company's borrowing begins to look a little risky, while if it is much lower than similar companies, that indicates the company is risk averse. Companies with very reliable income, such as property companies, often have very high gearing (with loans secured on property and the rental income receivable from it). Companies in the motor trade cannot afford a high level of gearing since their profits tend to fluctuate with the economic cycle.

Interest cover of 12 times looks fairly safe. Cover of much less than 5 begins to look risky since a downturn in the company's profit would put its ability to service its loans in doubt.

The above comments need to be interpreted with care, and what is satisfactory depends on the type of business. It is also useful to look at trends rather than at just a single year.

Activity 4.1

Complete the following table for Druisdale plc by inserting the figures for year 6, and commenting on the changes that have taken place.[5]

Ratio	Year 5		Year 6	Comment
1 Current ratio	120 : 60	2 : 1		
2 Quick ratio	60 : 60	1 : 1		
3 Gearing ratio	60/240	25%		
4 Interest cover	60/5	12 times		

This conventional approach separates short-term liabilities from long-term liabilities. It may also be important to look at the total of all liabilities in forming an assessment of a company's financial strength and survival prospects.

---

[5] A completed table is provided at the end of the book (see p. 482).

In assessing the financial strength of a company there are many other factors to take into consideration; indications of many of these can be found in the financial accounting statements. The statement of financial position alone will not tell us all we want to know. We also have to look at the income statement in order to calculate interest cover. Profit is by no means a guarantee of survival, but creditors of a profitable company are likely to be much more secure than creditors of a loss-making company. A company that is making profits is much more likely to survive than one that is making losses.

Suppliers are interested in whether or not they are likely to be paid on time. A calculation of the average time it takes to pay trade payables (creditors) is provided in ratio 16 (see p. 82).

In terms of survival, it may be that cash flow matters more than profit, or any of the above ratios. As long as a company is generating lots of cash it can pay its liabilities and survive. The calculation and interpretation of these ratios and the evaluation of solvency are considered more fully in Chapters 7 and 11.

4.3 Profitability

Profitability is examined here in three sections:

■ Overall profitability
■ Profitability of sales
■ Utilization of assets

Overall profitability

An income statement shows how much profit a company has made for the shareholders in a given period. Druisdale plc's profit for year 5 was £40m, after finance costs and taxation (but before deducting dividends, which are shown on a separate statement). Shareholders may reasonably ask: was that enough? Should the company be more profitable?

Druisdale's statement of financial position shows the total equity as being £180m at the end of year 5. If the shareholders' funds had been put into a deposit account at a bank, they might have been paid about 4 per cent per annum interest, with virtually no risk. Shareholders would expect a company to earn a much better return than that[6] in view of the risk inherent in investing in companies. A return of 4 per cent per annum on £180m would produce £7.2m profit a year. As Druisdale earned £40m in year 5, the shareholders may be satisfied. The return earned for them is as follows:

5 *Return on shareholders' funds*

$$\frac{\text{Profit for the year}}{\text{Equity at year end}} \times 100 \qquad \frac{£40}{£180} \times 100 = 22.2\%$$

We might consider that any ROCE of more than about 10 per cent is satisfactory; anything over 20 per cent is good.

It is important to consider the *total* of shareholders' funds (£180m), not just the share capital (£100m). This ratio considers the shareholders' point of view. The ratio measures the return on *shareholders'* capital employed, or the return on equity.[7]

In assessing management, however, we should consider all the funds for which they are responsible more generally, and look at the return on *total long-term capital*. The return of total long-term capital employed, ROCE, is often regarded as being the most important, or key, or primary ratio, particularly in measuring profitability. Where there is a good, and increasing ROCE, we can conclude that

---

[6] Even if much of the profit or income earned is retained in the business and not paid out to shareholders as dividends.

[7] When there are preference shares the return on equity (ordinary shareholders' funds) will be different from the return on total shareholders' funds (ordinary shareholders' funds plus preference shares).

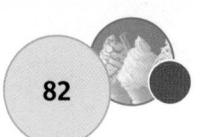
the management of the company is using its resources effectively. The statement of financial position at the end of year 5 shows that, in addition to shareholders' funds of £180m, the company had long-term borrowings of £60m. Profit is earned for the shareholders; interest is the return to lenders. If we are going to calculate a return on total long-term capital, we must include interest, in addition to profit, as being part of the return; that is, the return before remunerating either of the suppliers of capital, lenders or shareholders. In year 5 the profit was £40m, and the finance cost (presumably interest) was £5m. Rather than just adding the two together, it is easier to consider the return before taxation; sometimes the figure is described as earnings before interest and taxation (EBIT), or as operating profit.

6 *Return on total long-term capital employed*

Profit £40m, plus tax expense £15m, plus finance cost £5m = £60m

Or gross profit of £100m, minus £15m distribution costs, minus £25m administrative expenses = £60m

Total capital employed is equity (£180m), plus long-term borrowings (£60m) = £240m operating profit

$$\frac{\text{Operating profit or EBIT}}{\text{Equity + long-term borrowings}} \times 100 \qquad \frac{£60m}{£240m} \times 100 = 25\%$$

As is the case with most ratios, this figure is most useful when making comparisons with previous periods (or other companies). It is important to ensure that all ratios are calculated in the same way when making comparisons, but it is particularly relevant with ROCE as there are several different ways of doing it.

Directors and shareholders often want to see an increase in the ROCE and there are two[8] ways of achieving this: by increasing the numerator, return; or decreasing the denominator, capital employed.

- Increasing the return, or profit, in relation to the amount of capital employed. This can be done by reducing costs, and/or increasing sales. The important thing is to increase the difference between costs and sales; in other words, to increase profit as a percentage of sales. This is assessed in ratio 7, and considered in more detail using ratios 9–11 on p. 83.

- Reducing the amount of capital employed (in relation to the amount of sales); or increasing the amount of sales (in relation to the amount of capital employed. This means making more intensive use of assets, or capital employed; or increasing 'asset turnover'. This is assessed in ratio 8, and considered in more detail using ratios 12–16 on pp. 84–85.

7 *Operating profit[9] as a percentage of sales*

In year 5 Druisdale's operating profit as a percentage of sales was

$$\frac{\text{Operating profit}}{\text{Sales}} \times 100 \qquad \frac{£60m}{£300m} \times 100 = 20\%$$

8 *Asset turnover*

In year 5 Druisdale's asset turnover may be measured by relating the sales figure to net operating assets.[10]

Non-current assets plus current assets minus current liabilities (£180m + £120m – £60m) = £240m

Or, equity plus long-term borrowings (£180m + £60m) = £240m

---

8 Perhaps *only* two.

9 Profit before deducting finance charges.

10 Net operating assets may be defined as total assets (current plus non-current) minus current liabilities. This should be equal to equity plus non-current liabilities.

The £240m may be shown as Non-CA + CA − CL
Sales revenue £300m

$$\text{Asset turnover} = \frac{\text{Sales}}{\text{Non-CA} + \text{CA} - \text{CL}} \qquad \frac{£300m}{£240m} = 1.25 \text{ times}$$

The last three ratios considered can be related together as follows:

6 Return on total long-term capital employed 25%

7 Operating profit as a percentage of sales   20%
   25 ÷ 20 = 1.25

8 Asset turnover   1.25 times

Activity 4.2

Complete the following table for Druisdale plc by inserting the figures for year 6, and commenting on the changes that have taken place.[11] Check the relationship between ratios 6, 7 and 8.

Ratio	Year 5		Year 6		Comment
5 Return on shareholders' capital employed	40/180	22.2%			
6 Return on total long-term capital employed	60/240	25%			
7 Operating profit as a percentage of sales	60/300	20%			
8 Asset turnover	300/240	1.25 times			

When these four ratios have been calculated for each of the two years, it will be clear whether profitability has increased, and why.

In order to increase its profitability it is necessary to consider (a) the profitability of sales (and analyse costs), and (b) the utilization of capital employed, or asset turnover (and analyse 'activity ratios').

Profitability of sales

Any costs can be expressed as a percentage of sales. The first cost on an income statement is cost of sales, but it is more usual to express gross profit as a percentage of sales. If cost of sales is two-thirds of sales, then gross profit is one-third of sales. The figures for Druisdale plc for year 5 are as follows:

9 *Gross profit ratio*

$$\frac{\text{Gross profit}}{\text{Sales}} \times 100 \qquad \frac{£100m}{£300m} \times 100 = 33\tfrac{1}{3}\%$$

It may be more useful to express the cost of raw materials or labour as a percentage of sales. But the most readily available costs from published accounts are distribution costs and administrative expenses. The ratios for Druisdale plc for year 5 are shown below. A decline on gross margin might indicate that the company is operating in a more competitive market and, perhaps, cannot pass on its purchase price increases in a similar proportion to its customers. This could occur, for example, if £ sterling has fallen on imported goods but the company finds it is unable to increase its selling prices in a similar way. Or perhaps the company's sales mix has altered and it is selling a higher proportion of its sales in products with a lower margin.

10 *Distribution costs as a percentage of sales*

$$\frac{\text{Distribution costs}}{\text{Sales}} \times 100 \qquad \frac{£15m}{£300m} \times 100 = 5\%$$

---

[11] A completed table is provided at the end of the book (see p. 482).

11 *Administrative expenses as a percentage of sales*

$$\frac{\text{Administrative expenses}}{\text{Sales}} \times 100 \qquad \frac{£25\text{m}}{£300\text{m}} \times 100 = 8\tfrac{1}{3}\%$$

Whether or not these ratios are satisfactory depends on the business; the figures mean little, except by comparison.

Activity 4.3

Complete the following table for Druisdale plc by inserting the figures for year 6, and commenting on the changes that have taken place.[12]

Ratio	Year 5		Year 6		Comment
9 Gross profit ratio	100/300	33⅓%			
10 Distribution costs as a % of sales	15/300	5%			
11 Administrative expenses as a % of sales	25/300	8⅓%			

Utilization of assets

Where there is a problem with the asset turnover ratio (number 8 above), there is a need to improve the utilization of assets. The first step is to see whether the problem lies with non-current assets or with current assets.[13] This can be done by comparing one year with the next, as demonstrated in Activity 4.4 below.

12 *Sales/non-current assets*

$$\frac{\text{Sales}}{\text{Non-current assets}} \qquad \frac{300\text{m}}{180\text{m}} = 1.67 \text{ times}$$

If it is established that there is a problem with fixed assets (there are too many fixed assets in relation to the amount of sales), further analysis can be done by comparing different categories of fixed assets with sales.

13 *Sales/current assets*

$$\frac{\text{Sales}}{\text{Current assets}} \qquad \frac{300\text{m}}{120\text{m}} = 2.5 \text{ times}$$

If it is established that there is a problem with current assets (there are too many current assets in relation to the amount of sales), further analysis can be done by comparing different items of current assets, and current liabilities, with sales. The most widely used ratios are in relation to inventories, receivables and payables. These may be measured in terms of the number of times the item is 'turned over' in a year (e.g. inventory turnover ratio). However, it is preferable to express each of inventory, trade receivables and trade payables as a number of days.

14 *Inventory (stock) turnover ratio*

The stock or inventory figure taken from the statement of financial position is shown at cost price (not selling price), and so must be compared with the cost of sales figure (not the sales revenue figure). The inventories are divided by cost of sales to give a proportion of a year (365 days):

---

[12] A completed table is provided at the end of the book (see p. 482).

[13] The problem might also lie with current liabilities. Increasing current liabilities can increase profitability (it reduces the amount of capital employed), but it might make solvency ratios look weaker.

$$\frac{\text{Inventories}}{\text{Cost of sales}} \times 365 \qquad \frac{60m}{200m} \times 365 = 110 \text{ days}$$

This figure seems rather high, but it does depend on the type of business. A supermarket would probably have only a few weeks' inventory on hand at any one time: Tesco had 21 days' inventory in 2011, while GlaxoSmithKline had 193 days' inventory. Generally, the quicker the inventory is sold, the better.

15 Trade receivables (debtors) ratio

The trade debtors or trade receivables figure taken from the statement of financial position is shown at selling price (that is, the amount that the customer owes, not the cost price), and so must be compared with the sales revenue figure (not the cost of sales figure). Again, it is expressed as a proportion of a year:

$$\frac{\text{Trade receivables}}{\text{Sales revenue}} \times 365 \qquad \frac{40m}{300m} \times 365 = 49 \text{ days}$$

If all sales are on credit, and customers are expected to settle their accounts by the end of the month following the month in which the sale takes place, perhaps 49 days is reasonable.

If some or all sales are on a cash basis (as is the case with most retailers), a much lower average figure would be expected. If possible, credit sales should be separated from cash sales, and the debtors figure should be compared only with the credit sales figure. Generally, our intention is to collect our trade receivables quickly and this can be encouraged, for example, by offering discounts for prompt payment.

16 Trade payables (creditors) ratio

The trade creditors, or trade payables, figure taken from the statement of financial position is shown at cost price (that is, the amount owed to suppliers), and so must be compared with the cost of sales figure in the same way as with the inventory turnover ratio above:

$$\frac{\text{Trade payables}}{\text{Cost of sales}} \times 365 \qquad \frac{60m}{200m} \times 365 = 100 \text{ days}$$

On the statement of financial position of Druisdale plc, it happens that the amount for inventories is the same as the amount for payables, and so the two payment periods are the same.

We do not necessarily know what is included in payables. Ideally, we should compare like with like, and payables for raw material purchases would be compared with amount of raw material purchases. As always, we have to use the best information available, and even relatively crude measures can provide valuable information, such as: is the company taking longer to pay its trade payables than it did a year ago? On the face of it, one might think that paying one's suppliers more slowly than in the previous year would be better and although it is in terms of the effect on the bank balance, paying slowly implies we are not taking advantage of any prompt payment discounts, it is likely to put our relationships with our suppliers under strain and might be because we do not have the bank facility to pay and could be an indication that we are in serious financial difficulties.

Activity 4.4

Complete the following table for Druisdale by inserting the figures for year 6, and comment on the changes that have taken place.[14]

---

[14] A completed table is provided at the end of the book (see p. 483).

Ratio	Year 5		Year 6	Comment
12 Sales/non-current assets	300/180	1.67 times		
13 Sales/current assets	300/120	2.5 times		
14 Inventory turnover ratio	60 ÷ 200 × 365	110 days		
15 Trade receivables ratio	40 ÷ 300 × 365	49 days		
16 Trade payables ratio	60 ÷ 200 × 365	110 days		

4.4 Stock Market Ratios

Investors can compare the share price of a company with information from that company's financial statements to assess how expensive the share is in relation to the last known level of earnings (income), dividends and underlying asset values.

17 Price/earnings (P/E) ratio

'Earnings per share' is a widely used measure and is calculated by dividing the profit for the period by the number of shares that the company has. This shows how much profit was earned for each share. The amount of profit that Druisdale plc earned for its shareholders in year 5, after deducting all expenses and taxation, was £40m. The company had share capital of £100m, all in £1 shares.

$$\text{Earnings per share} = \frac{\text{Profit for the year}}{\text{Number of shares}} \qquad \frac{£40m}{£100m} = 40p \text{ per share}$$

Investors in that company might think that earnings per share will continue at 40p for the foreseeable future, and be willing to pay five or ten times as much as that for each share; that would result in the share price being £2 or £4. If shareholders are optimistic that future earnings will increase substantially, they might be willing to pay more than 10 times as much as the earnings per share figure. At the end of year 5 investors were paying £5.60 for each share, so they must have been reasonably optimistic.

$$\text{P/E ratio} = \frac{\text{Share price}}{\text{Earnings per share}} \qquad \frac{£5.60}{40p} = 14$$

A P/E ratio of 14 means that the amount investors are willing to pay for shares is 14 times the last known earnings per share figure. That is not particularly high. If shareholders are very optimistic about the future of a company, they would be prepared to pay much more for the shares, and P/E ratios of 20 or 30 are not unusual. A high P/E ratio suggests that investors are optimistic about the future prospects of the company.

18 Dividend yield

Investors are interested not only in the amount of profit that has been earned for them, but also in how much dividend is being paid. Companies usually pay out only a part of their profits as dividends. Druisdale plc paid out dividends of £25m in year 5 (as shown on the statement of changes in equity). This amounts to 25p per share (there are 100 million shares).

$$\text{Dividend per share} = \frac{\text{Total dividends}}{\text{Number of shares}} \qquad \frac{£25m}{100m} = 25p \text{ per share}$$

This may seem like only a modest return for shareholders. They have to pay £5.60, and at that time the last known dividend per share was 25p. The dividend yield is calculated by expressing the dividend per share as a percentage of the share price.

$$\text{Dividend yield} = \frac{\text{Dividend per share}}{\text{Share price}} \times 100 \qquad \frac{£0.25}{£5.60} = 4.5\%$$

Investors hope for higher dividends in the future and pay a lot more for shares where substantial growth is expected. If Druisdale's share price doubled (to £11.20), the dividend yield would halve (to about 2.25%).

19 Dividend cover

Some companies pay out a higher proportion of their profits than others. If a company pays out only a quarter of its profits as dividends it is more likely to be able to maintain dividend levels in the future than a company that pays out most or all of its profits as dividends. Investors may want to know to what extent their dividends are 'covered' by earnings.[15]

Dividend cover[16] can be measured on a 'per share' basis, or in total for the company.

$$\frac{\text{Earning per share}}{\text{Dividend per share}} \quad \text{or} \quad \frac{\text{Total profit for the period}}{\text{Total dividends}}$$

$$\frac{40p}{25p} \quad \text{or} \quad \frac{£40m}{£25m}$$

$$\text{Dividend cover} = 1.6 \text{ times}$$

Companies typically pay out about half of their profits as dividends; on average dividend cover is around 2 (i.e. dividends are covered twice by profits). Shareholders who buy shares for income will be inclined to invest in companies with a low dividend cover, while shareholders motivated by higher future share price growth will prefer to invest in companies with a high dividend cover.

20 Net assets per share (or statement of financial position value per share)

Investors may be interested in the asset value underlying the share price. The statement of financial position of Druisdale at the end of year 5 shows net assets as being £180m. This may be calculated in two different ways, each giving the same answer:

i Non-current assets, plus current assets, minus non-current liabilities, minus current liabilities. £180m + £120m – £60m – £60m = £180m.

ii Total equity = £180m. Obviously it is easier to do it this way, but it is worth making the point that (1) above, which is usually called 'net assets', is equal to total equity.

The amount of net assets per share is calculated as:

$$\frac{\text{Net assets}}{\text{Number of shares}} \qquad \frac{180m}{100m} = £1.80$$

The value of the shares on the stock market at the time, at £5.60, was much higher. This is usually the case with a successful company: it is worth significantly more than the statement of financial position indicates.

---

[15] Just as debenture holders may want to know to what extent their interest is 'covered' by operating profits, which are available to pay that interest (ratio 4).

[16] Here it is assumed that there are no preference shares.

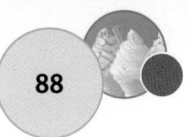

Activity 4.5

Complete the following table for Druisdale plc by inserting the figures for year 6, and commenting on the changes that have taken place.[17]

Ratio	Year 5		Year 6		Comment
17 Price/earnings ratio	£5.60 ÷ 40p	14			
18 Dividend yield	25p ÷ £5.60 × 100	4.5%			
19 Dividend cover	40/25	1.6 times			
20 Net assets per share	£180/100	£1.80			

4.5 Working Capital Management

Working capital management is concerned with balancing two contradictory pressures:

i The need to ensure that there are sufficient funds to pay liabilities as they fall due. Having large sums of money in the bank, and plenty of money due from trade receivables (plus additional money tied up in inventories) should reassure creditors. If creditors are paid rapidly, the figure for creditors is minimized, and that contributes to maximizing the amount of working capital. The larger the amount of working capital, the more creditors are reassured about the company's solvency.

ii The need to ensure the profitable use of capital employed. Having large sums of money tied up in current assets undermines profitability (by increasing capital employed). Similarly, minimizing the amount of creditors undermines profitability (also by increasing capital employed). The smaller the amount of working capital, the greater the profitability is likely to be.

The first of these is about maximizing solvency, and the usual ratios for assessing this are dealt with above.

1 Current ratio: are there enough current assets to cover current liabilities?

2 Quick ratio: are there enough liquid assets to cover current liabilities?

16 Trade payables ratio: how long does it take to pay creditors? Are we paying them too slowly?

The second is about maximizing profitability, particularly in the utilization of assets (ratio 8, asset turnover). More specifically the main ratios are:

13 Sales/current assets ratio: are current assets excessive in relation to turnover?

14 Inventory turnover ratio: is inventory excessive in relation to turnover?[18]

15 Trade receivables ratio: are customers taking too long to pay?

16 Trade payables ratio: are we paying suppliers too quickly to maximize profitability?

Working capital management is considered more fully in Chapter 12.

4.6 Financial Structure/Gearing

The way in which a business is financed is often called *financial structure*. It is particularly concerned with the balance between equity (shareholders' funds) and debt (long-term borrowing). This is also called capital gearing, and is introduced previously as ratio number:

3 Capital gearing ratio: is there too much borrowing in relation to the amount of equity?

---

[17] A completed table is provided at the end of the book (see p. 467).

[18] More specifically, inventory in relation to cost of sales.

From the point of view of creditors, the lower the gearing (the lower the amount of borrowing), the greater is their security. Low gearing may be seen as an aspect of solvency or financial strength. High gearing suggests high risk.

But high gearing can be advantageous in maximizing profitability. A company may be able to borrow money at modest interest rates, perhaps 6 per cent per annum; it may then be able to invest that money in the business to earn a return[19] of more than, say, 10 per cent. In that situation, increasing borrowings will increase profits. But this can be a risky strategy and companies usually seek to avoid excessive borrowings.[20]

Capital gearing is considered more fully in Chapter 11.

4.7 Limitations and Comparisons

A systematic use of ratios can provide valuable insights into a company's financial position and performance. It is better to have some clear questions in mind than to simply read through the financial statements as presented by the company. Annual reports often emphasize the favourable aspects of a company's performance, and some systematic investigation is required to arrive at a more balanced view. Financial statements provide substantial and increasing amounts of detail, but they can still leave important questions unanswered. A detailed ratio analysis is likely to indicate areas for further investigation at least as much as it produces full and final answers.

Bases for comparison

The figures and ratios from an analysis of financial statements are meaningful only by comparison with something. The easiest thing, in all companies' accounts, is to compare this year's results with last year's; they are presented side by side for that very purpose. We can immediately see whether a company's financial position and performance are improving or deteriorating, as a whole, and in detail, using many different figures and approaches. The following comparisons may be used:

- with previous years for the same company. Published financial statements always show one previous year, but a comparison over a number of years is more valuable. Listed companies show five years of figures;
- with other (similar) companies;
- with other divisions or branches within the same company;
- with stock market or sector averages;
- with market levels; a return on shareholders' funds may be compared with the general level of interest rates;
- with policy: a company may have a policy of requiring credit customers to pay within 45 days;
- with budgeted or planned results. This can indicate the success of management in implementing their plans and achieving the intended results.

Limitations of ratio analysis

The main limitations of ratio analysis are as follows:

- What basis for comparison should be used? To know that a company's inventory turnover ratio is 64 days does not mean much, except by comparison. Is it better or worse than last year? Or than

---

[19] Ratio 6: Return on total long-term capital employed. The return is measured before deducting the cost of interest.

[20] Profit before deducting tax and interest, or EBIT, or gross profit minus operating expenses.

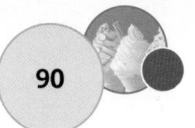

planned? Or than a similar company? Inventory turnover of more than a few weeks would be unacceptable for a fresh food business, but might be quite good in a gift shop.

- Comparisons may be limited where companies have different accounting policies. Some companies may capitalize software or development expenditure, where others write them off, as expenses, immediately. There may be differences on approaches to depreciation of non-current assets. Some companies' accounting policies are more prudent than others, and some may indulge in 'creative accounting'.

- Comparisons may be limited where companies have different financing policies. Some companies rely more on overdrafts and short-term borrowing; others rely more on long-term borrowing; others have little or no borrowing. Some companies own most of their non-current assets; others lease them on finance leases (which show up in the financial statements); others lease them on operating leases (which do not show up in the financial statements). Some companies spend substantially on non-current assets every year; others have major expenditure only every three, or five, or ten years. Some companies sell on a cash only basis; others sell partly or mainly on credit. Ratio analysis shows up many of these differences, but care is needed in interpretation, for example, where a company changes its policy in a particular year (e.g. reducing short-term debt by issuing shares or debentures).

- Comparisons may be limited where companies have different policies to achieve growth. Where internal growth is pursued, there may be substantial investments in non-current assets in a particular year that do not earn their keep at first. Where external growth is pursued, substantial amounts may be paid for goodwill in acquiring other companies, with a subsequent charge for impairment; and there may be substantial one-off benefits from rationalization (e.g. closing down operations in some locations where there is duplication).

- Comparisons may be limited where companies have different operating policies. Some companies do most of their manufacturing in the UK (and so have substantial amounts of non-current assets); others subcontract their manufacturing, perhaps to overseas companies, and so have less money tied up in non-current assets. Some companies produce only for specific orders, or in batches, while others have mass production of standard items: this is likely to affect profit margins and stock levels.

- Comparisons may be limited where companies have different accounting dates, especially in seasonal businesses. Retailers with a year end a few weeks before Christmas are likely to have substantial inventories and trade payables shown on their statements of financial position, and perhaps some short-term liquidity problems. The statement of financial position of a retailer a few weeks after Christmas is likely to show lower inventory levels, and more liquid resources.

- Results may be influenced substantially in particular years by 'exceptional items', such as losses incurred in closing down a production facility, or profits made in selling particular non-current assets (especially land and buildings).

- Statements of financial position show the position only on a given date. They are not necessarily typical for the whole year. Some companies indulge in 'window dressing' to try to make the position look better at the year end when the financial statements are published.

- Statements of financial position are usually based on historic cost, and the amounts shown for assets are not necessarily their current values. Some non-current assets are revalued from time to time, and in comparing results with different companies, we cannot always be sure that we are comparing like with like. The amount shown for 'equity' on a statement of financial position does not usually reflect the current value of the assets; nor does it indicate the market value of the equity (the 'market capitalization') on the stock market.

- Most of the information included in financial statements is for the business as a whole and so most ratios are an average for the business. Some parts of it are likely to be performing much better than others. Companies produce some 'disaggregated' or 'segmental' information about different parts of the business, but this is rather limited.

- Financial statements do not normally show the effects of inflation. A company's sales and profits may increase every year, but a 3 per cent increase is not an indication of success if the inflation rate was 4 per cent.

- Financial statements and their analysis are based on information relating to the past; much of it is inevitably out of date. And the past is not necessarily a guide to the future.

- Ratio analysis is usually limited to the information that companies are required to show in their published annual reports. There is likely to be a great deal of other information, financial and non-financial, that would be important in evaluating the financial position and performance of a company.

4.8 Ratios Ready Reference

The ratios in Examples 4.3 and 4.4 are illustrated taking the figures from the financial statements of Garwick Ltd for year 7. Activity 4.6 lists these ratios and invites readers to calculate the equivalent ratios for year 8, and to comment on them. A solution is provided at the end of the book (see p. 484).

Example 4.3

Statement of financial position of Garwick Ltd as at 31 December		
	Year 7 £000	Year 8 £000
Assets		
Non-current assets		
Property, plant and equipment	50	60
Current assets		
Inventories	10	13
Trade receivables	14	16
Cash	18	1
	42	30
Total assets	92	90
Liabilities and equity		
Current liabilities		
Trade payables	17	20
Non-current liabilities		
Long-term borrowing	40	30
Total liabilities	57	50
Equity		
Share capital	20	20
Retained earnings	15	20
Total equity	35	40
Total liabilities and equity	92	90

Example 4.4

Income statement of Garwick Ltd for the year ended 31 December	Year 7 £000	Year 8 £000
Revenue	101	110
Cost of sales	(70)	(74)
Gross profit	31	36
Distribution costs	(7)	(7)
Administrative expenses	(5)	(6)
Operating profit	19	23
Finance costs	(4)	(3)
Profit before tax	15	20
Income tax expense	(4)	(5)
Profit for the period	11	15

Statement of changes in equity of Garwick Ltd for the year ended 31 December		
Balance at beginning of year	32	35
Profit for the period	11	15
Dividends	(8)	(10)
Balance at end of year	35	40

Additional information

Garwick Ltd's share capital consists of 100,000 ordinary shares with a nominal value of 20p each. Although the company is too small to be listed on a stock market, for the purpose of this question assume that the share price on 31 December year 7 was £1.87, and on 31 December year 8 it was £2.85.

Four financial strength/solvency ratios

1   Current ratio (or working capital ratio)

Current assets : Current liabilities

£42,000 : £17,000

2.47 : 1

2   Quick ratio (or acid test)

Current assets excluding inventories : Current liabilities

£32,000 : £17,000

1.88 : 1

3   Capital gearing ratio (financial gearing, or leverage)

$$\frac{\text{Long-term borrowings}}{\text{Equity plus long-term borrowings}} \times 100$$

$$\frac{£40,000}{£75,000} \times 100 = 53.3\%$$

4   Interest times cover

$$\frac{\text{Profit before deducting interest}}{\text{Interest}} \qquad \frac{£19,000}{£4,000} = 4.75 \text{ times}$$

Four overall profitability ratios

5   Return on shareholders' funds

$$\frac{\text{Profit for the period}}{\text{Total equity}} \times 100 \qquad \frac{£11,000}{£35,000} \times 100 = 31.4\%$$

6   Return on total long-term capital employed

$$\frac{\text{Operating profit}^{20}}{\text{Total equity plus long-term borrowings}} \times 100 \qquad \frac{£19,000}{£75,000} \times 100 = 25.3\%$$

7   Operating profit as a percentage of sales (or profit/sales ratio)

$$\frac{\text{Operating profit}}{\text{Sales}} \times 100 \qquad \frac{£19,000}{£101,000} \times 100 = 18.8\%$$

8   Asset turnover

$$\frac{\text{Sales}}{\text{Operating assets}^{21}} \qquad \frac{£101,000}{£75,000} = 1.35 \text{ times}$$

Three profitability of sales ratios

9   Gross profit ratio

$$\frac{\text{Gross profit}}{\text{Sales}} \times 100 \qquad \frac{£31,000}{£101,000} \times 100 = 30.7\%$$

10   Distribution costs as a percentage of sales

$$\frac{\text{Distribution costs}}{\text{Sales}} \times 100 \qquad \frac{£7,000}{£101,000} \times 100 = 6.9\%$$

11   Administrative expenses as a percentage of sales

$$\frac{\text{Administrative expenses}}{\text{Sales}} \times 100 \qquad \frac{£5,000}{£101,000} \times 100 = 5\%$$

---

[21] Non-current assets plus current assets minus current liabilities. This is the same as equity plus non-current liabilities.

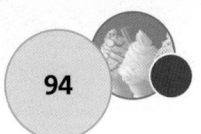

Five utilization of assets ratios

12 Sales/non-current assets

$$\frac{\text{Sales}}{\text{Non-current assets}} \qquad \frac{£101,000}{£50,000} = 2.02 \text{ times}$$

13 Sales/current assets

$$\frac{\text{Sales}}{\text{Current assets}} \qquad \frac{£101,000}{£42,000} = 2.4 \text{ times}$$

14 Inventory turnover ratio

$$\frac{\text{Inventories}}{\text{Cost of sales}} \times 365 \qquad \frac{£10,000}{£70,000} \times 365 = 52.1 \text{ days}$$

15 Trade receivables ratio

$$\frac{\text{Trade receivables}}{\text{Sales}} \times 365 \qquad \frac{£14,000}{£101,000} \times 365 = 50.6 \text{ days}$$

16 Trade payables ratio

$$\frac{\text{Trade payables}}{\text{Cost of sales}} \times 365 \qquad \frac{£17,000}{£70,000} \times 365 = 88.6 \text{ days}$$

Four stock market ratios

17 Price/earnings ratio (P/E ratio)

$$\frac{\text{Share price}}{\text{Earnings per share}} \qquad \frac{£1.87}{11 \text{ p}} \qquad \text{P/E} = 17$$

18 Dividend yield

$$\frac{\text{Dividend}}{\text{Share price}} \times 100 \qquad \frac{8\text{p}}{£1.87} \times 100 = 4.3\%$$

19 Dividend cover

$$\frac{\text{Earnings per share}}{\text{Dividend per share}} \qquad \text{or} \qquad \frac{\text{Profit for the period}}{\text{Dividends for the period}}$$

$$\frac{11}{8} \qquad \text{or} \qquad \frac{£11,000}{£8,000} = 1.4\% \text{ times}$$

20 Net assets per share (statement of financial position value per share)

$$\frac{\text{Total equity}}{\text{Number of shares}} \qquad \frac{35,000}{100,000} = £0.35 \text{ per share}$$

Activity 4.6

Calculate the ratios for Garwick Ltd for year 8 and comment on them.

Ratio	Year 7	Year 8	Comments
1 Current ratio	2.47 : 1		
2 Quick ratio	1.88 : 1		
3 Capital gearing ratio	53.3%		
4 Interest cover ✓	4.75 times		
5 Return on shareholders' funds	31.4%		
6 Return on total long-term capital employed	25.3%		
7 Operating profit as a % of sales	18.8%		
8 Asset turnover	1.35 times		
9 Gross profit ratio	30.7%		
10 Distribution costs as a % of sales	6.9%		
11 Administrative expenses as a % of sales	5%		
12 Sales/non-current assets	2.02 times		
13 Sales/current assets	2.4 times		
14 Inventory turnover ratio	52 days		
15 Trade receivables ratio	51 days		
16 Trade payables ratio	89 days		
17 Price/earnings ratio	17		
18 Dividend yield	4.3%		
19 Dividend cover	1.4 times		
20 Net assets per share	£0.35		

📖 Summary

There are a number of conventional ratios that can be calculated from statements of financial position and income statements that give a good indication of a company's solvency and profitability. Care is needed in selecting and interpreting the most appropriate figures, and the exercise is more useful if comparisons are made over a number of years. Companies need to be solvent to survive. But profitability is also important, and is best indicated using figures for ROCE. Careful analysis of gross profit, operating profit and various costs as a percentage of sales can indicate where improvements may be made. But utilization of assets is also an essential part of profitability: there should not be excessive assets in relation to the amount of sales generated. Ratio analysis also provides useful insights into the management of working capital and financial structure. Accounting ratios often raise as many questions as they answer, but are a valuable tool of analysis, particularly in making comparisons, provided their limitations are recognized.

There is no limit to the number of ratios that can be calculated. This chapter has concentrated on a few key questions, and a total of 20 widely used ratios that help to answer those questions.

➡ Review of key points

- The current ratio, quick ratio, capital gearing ratio and interest cover can be used to assess a company's solvency, but care is needed in calculating and interpreting them.
- There are two main ways of calculating ROCE; each can be used to assess a company's profitability and how it might be improved.
- One side of ROCE can be used to assess all costs as a proportion of sales.
- The second side of ROCE can be used to assess the utilization of each group of assets by relating them to sales.
- Stock market ratios can be used to assess how expensive shares are in relation to the most recent levels of earnings, dividends and net asset values.
- The chapter is based around 20 widely used ratios and provides opportunities to practise calculating and interpreting them.
- Accounting ratios are most useful when used in making comparisons, but care is needed in comparing different types of business and in realizing the limitations of the figures.
- Published financial statements often contain a lot of detail that is hard to understand; it is important to be clear about key questions, to select the most appropriate figures and to focus on those.

❗ Self-testing questions

1. Describe how to calculate:
   a current ratio;
   b quick ratio;
   c capital gearing ratio;
   d interest cover.
2. Why are inventories excluded from current assets when calculating the quick ratio?
3. How is the return on ordinary shareholders' capital employed calculated?
4. If debentures are included as part of capital employed, what figure is used for 'return'? How and why does it differ from the 'return' figure used for calculating return on ordinary shareholders' capital employed?
5. If a company's gross profit ratio has increased, what does that tell us about the volume of sales and selling prices?
6. You are given the following statement of financial position information about the Nikkigra Company.

   You are required to comment on the financial position and performance of the company, making use of appropriate ratios.

Statement of financial position of Nikkigra as at 31 December

	Year 1 £000	Year 2 £000
Assets		
Non-current assets		
Property, plant and equipment	1,000	900
Current assets		
Inventories	1,200	1,000
Trade receivables	600	500
Cash	68	600
	1,868	2,100
Total assets	2,868	3,000
Liabilities and equity		
Current liabilities		
Trade payables	294	451
Taxation	60	65
Interest payable	80	84
	434	600
Non-current liabilities		
10% debentures	1,000	900
Total liabilities	1,434	1,500
Equity		
Ordinary 50p shares	1,000	1,000
Retained earnings	434	500
Total equity	1,434	1,500
Total liabilities and equity	2,868	3,000

Income statement of Nikkigra for the year ended 31 December

	Year 1	Year 2
Revenue	3,600	3,780
Cost of sales	3,225	3,396
Gross profit	375	384
Distribution costs	(50)	(48)
Administrative expenses	(30)	(31)
Operating profit	295	305
Finance costs: interest	(100)	(90)
Profit before tax	195	215
Income tax expense	(60)	(65)
Profit for the period	135	150

Statement of changes in equity of Nikkigra for the year ended 31 December

	Year 1	Year 2
Balance at beginning of year	1,379	1,434
Profit for the period	135	150
Dividends	(80)	(84)
Balance at end of year	1,434	1,500

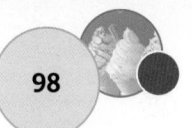

 ## Assessment questions

1   Why would you expect retailers to have lower current ratios than manufacturers?

2   What information (in addition to the current ratio, quick ratio, capital gearing ratio and interest times cover) would you want to assess a company's solvency?

3   Accounting ratios are said to be most useful when making comparisons. If you had a set of ratios for a company, what comparisons would you make?

4   What are the main limitations of accounting ratios?

5   How could a company increase its profitability when sales are falling (assuming that it is unable to increase sales)?

6   You are given the following statement of financial position information about Jackdan Ltd. You are required to comment on the financial position and performance of the company, making use of appropriate ratios.

Statement of financial position of Jackdan Ltd as at 31 December

	Year 1	Year 2
	£000	£000
Assets		
Non-current assets		
Property, plant and equipment	300	330
Current assets		
Inventories	70	90
Trade receivables	50	70
Cash	30	40
	150	200
Total assets	450	530
Liabilities and equity		
Current liabilities		
Trade payables	38	45
Taxation	32	40
Interest payable	30	35
	100	120
Non-current liabilities		
8% debentures	100	150
Total liabilities	200	270
Equity		
Ordinary 50p shares	200	200
Retained earnings	50	60
Total equity	250	260
Total liabilities and equity	450	530

Income statement of Jackdan Ltd for the year ended 31 December

	Year 1	Year 2
	£000	£000
Revenue	492	550
Cost of sales	(369)	(410)
Gross profit	123	140
Distribution costs	(12)	(12)
Administrative expenses	(10)	(9)
Operating profit	101	119
Finance costs: interest	(8)	(12)
Profit before tax	93	107
Income tax expense	(32)	(40)
Profit for the period	61	67

Statement of changes in equity of Jackdan Ltd for the year ended 31 December

	Year 1	Year 2
Balance at beginning of year	239	250
Profit for the period	61	67
Dividends	(50)	(57)
Balance at end of year	250	260

Group activities and discussion questions

1 Which is more important: increasing ROCE, or increasing earnings per share, and why? Can a company increase its earnings per share year after year, although its ROCE is steadily falling?

2 In what circumstances can a substantial improvement in a company's position result in a reduction in their ROCE?

3 In what circumstances can a steady increase in a company's ROCE be a symptom of a company being in decline?

4 Many companies' profitability is lower than it should be because they have too much money tied up in assets. They should aim to have a zero level of assets. This would lead to a ROCE of infinity. Discuss the practicability of these suggestions.

5 Most efforts to reduce the amount of funds tied up in assets are wasted because one type of asset is turned into another: inventories and surplus buildings become receivables and cash. The total capital employed, and the total profitability is unaffected. Discuss the validity of these statements.

6 The Executive Service Company has high levels of inventory, and impressive premises; their sales/net assets ratio is 1 : 1. The QuickValue Service Company has low levels of inventory, and back-street premises; their sales/net assets ratio is 2 : 1. Does that mean that the QuickValue Service Company is more profitable?

Making use of this example, discuss the idea that the use of ratios shows the effects of companies choosing to do business in different ways; ratios do not indicate how businesses should be run.

 ## Accounting in context

Discuss and comment on the following article. Why must ratio analysis be considered in the context of the company's sector, wider issues affecting that sector and the company's main competitors?

Bovis provides opportunity to plot for the long term

Yesterday, Bovis Homes became the latest house builder to issue an upbeat trading statement.

By Garry White

Bovis said that it had delivered 'significant' profit growth in 2011 and was well positioned to improve returns further in 2012 and beyond. A consensus view sees pre-tax profits up almost 70pc in the current year – admittedly from a low base. Consensus sees profits rising around 45pc in 2012.

The statement followed on from positive updates from sector peers Barratt Developments and Persimmon.

All of the key performance measures look reassuring. Bovis legally completed 2,045 homes in 2011, an 8pc year-on-year rise, of which 1,624 were private homes and 421 social housing.

The average private sales price increased by 4.5pc to £180,100 – but this was 'almost entirely' down to the mix. In common with most sector players, Bovis has moved away from building flats to focus on family homes in the South.

Margins are expected to see a boost because of savings on the cost of building and the fact that cheaper plots bought in the recession of 2009 are now being completed.

For 2011, the operating margin will be around 10pc, compared with 7.3pc in 2012. Management are focusing on return on capital employed (ROCE), a measure that compares the company's earnings with the amount of capital invested in the business.

If volumes and prices remain relatively stable, the company should be able to get a ROCE this year of above 7pc. In 2011, the ROCE was 'approaching' 5pc. This is not spectacular, but given the backdrop it is a good achievement and progress this year should show the company is on its way back to double-digit returns.

Bovis actually has quite a large land bank. One way that ROCE could be boosted is for targeted disposals should the need arise.

Of course, what all the house builders really need is an improvement in lending and a more active market.

These two things should improve over time. However, research from the Council of Mortgage Lenders out yesterday said that falling prices had made property more affordable for first-time buyers.

Indeed, the proportion of loans advanced to first-time buyers has remained remarkably steady, fluctuating between 34pc and 40pc of the total since 2005. However, overall sales have fallen.

The shares have been very volatile since they were tipped at 460p in November, rising as high as 500p and falling as low as 408p. They are now back at the same level as they were when tipped.

This proves that an investment in the sector is not for the faint hearted – but Questor believes there is long term value in the sector.

The UK is structurally short of housing – there are not swathes of empty homes as can be seen in areas of the US and Ireland where housing stock was overbuilt during the boom. Also, the government is trying to bolster the construction of new homes with investment and mortgage guarantees.

Tipped at 460p on November 9 last year, the shares are down 2pc compared with a FTSE 100 up 4pc.

The shares are still a buy.

Source: The Telegraph, 17 January 2012.

References and further reading

Lewis, R., D. Pendrill and D. Simon (2004) *Advanced Financial Accounting* (7th edn.). Harlow: FT Prentice Hall.

McKenzie, W. (2010) *Financial Times Guide to Using and Interpreting Company Accounts* (4th edn.). Harlow: FT Prentice Hall.

Melville, A. (2011) *International Financial Reporting* (3rd edn.). Harlow: FT Prentice Hall.

Sugden A., P. Gee and G. Holmes (2008) *Interpreting Company Reports and Accounts* (10th edn.). Harlow: FT Prentice Hall.

www.cifc.co.uk (select: benchmarking and interfirm comparison; a standardized basis for using ratios to compare different firms)

Online LearningCentre

When you have read this chapter, log on to the Online Learning Centre website at *www.mcgraw-hill.co.uk/textbooks/leiwy* to explore chapter-by-chapter test questions, further reading and more online study tools.

Chapter 5

How the Stock Market Assesses Company Performance

Chapter contents

✓ Learning objectives

After studying this chapter you will be able to:

- ✓ Discuss various factors that influence share prices
- ✓ Understand the main information shown by the *Financial Times* London Share Service
- ✓ Calculate and interpret P/E ratios, dividend yield and dividend cover
- ✓ Explain why cash flows may influence share prices
- ✓ Understand the relationship between share prices and statement of financial position values
- ✓ Critically assess the possible influence of a variety of other factors on share prices

5.1 Introduction

The performance of companies' shares on the stock market is part of our everyday news agenda, but it is difficult to be sure about what really influences share prices, and why it is important. Share prices are determined by supply and demand for a company's shares, much like any other commodity on an open market. These are influenced by a number of factors, and the information revealed in financial accounts is perhaps the most important. It is easy to see which companies are doing well, but by the time this is obvious, their shares are usually already quite expensive. Similarly, by the time a company's performance is obviously poor, the share price has already fallen. Unfortunately, this chapter cannot teach you how to 'beat the market', but it does a lot to explain what happens.

5.2 Investing in Shares

When we talk about investing in shares, we usually mean buying shares that are listed on the London Stock Exchange (LSE), or other leading international stock markets. There are more than two million private companies in the UK, most of them very small, typically with only about two shareholders; their shares are not available on any stock market. There are also many public companies, some quite large, which are also not listed on stock markets. You may be invited by friends or family to buy shares in an unlisted company; you may set up your own company; and you may inherit some shares. But unless the company is a listed one, buying and selling the shares is usually difficult because there is no ready market.

The shares in listed companies are bought and sold frequently, sometimes every few minutes or seconds, on the stock market, and it is easy to buy and sell them. If you want to buy or sell shares in listed companies, you need to have a stockbroker; or you could ask your bank to act for you; or you could register with a stockbroker who arranges for you to deal directly on the internet. In the bull[1] market of the 1990s many private individuals became 'day traders', buying and selling shares on the same day, and making more profit than they could earn by working for a living. It is not difficult to make profits when share prices are rising.

Companies do not buy and sell shares themselves except when issuing additional shares such as a rights issue, as explained in Chapter 15. If you go to Marks & Spencer or Mothercare and ask to buy some shares, you will be referred elsewhere. Shares are already in existence, and, in effect, are bought and sold by investors (companies, institutions and individuals) via an established stock market. The price or current value of the shares is not calculated, or determined, by the company or individual. It constantly changes as a result of supply and demand for a particular company's shares. If demand for a share is very high, the price will be marked up; this will encourage some investors to sell their shares so that others can buy. When the price goes up too high, demand for the company's shares will slacken, and an equilibrium is reached. If a company's shares are not in demand, the price will fall until some investors decide that the shares have become good value.

Sometimes there are exaggerated short-term effects on share prices. If there is a rumour that there will soon be a takeover bid for a particular company, demand for those shares might increase rapidly until the situation is resolved. When a company has some bad news, or there is bad news from comparable companies, there might be a sudden, exaggerated decrease in the share price, which may prove to be only temporary.

---

[1] A bull market is when share prices are rising; a bear market is when share prices are falling.

5.3 What Influences Share Prices?

Many different factors influence share prices. Some factors might relate to the company alone, such as those listed above, while others have nothing directly to do with the company itself but are more to do with general sentiments about investing and the economy. Such factors include expectations about interest rates, growth or recession in the economy, and exchange rates. To some extent stock markets in different countries move in line with each other, and it often seems that the UK stock market follows that of the USA.

The most widely used measure of share price performance is the FTSE 100 ('Footsie'). This is the *Financial Times* index[2] of the share prices of the 100 largest companies, based on their market capitalization. The FTSE 250 covers the next 250 largest companies and the FTSE All Share is the index for all listed companies. The constituent companies of the index change slightly on a regular basis as the value of their shares changes or when two of the companies in the list of 100 merge, leaving a vacancy. During the 1990s and up until 2008, there were substantial increases in share prices and the index reached an all-time high at the end of 1999 when the FTSE 100 index reached 6950. The index fell to 3392 in January 2003, rose to 6377 in May 2008, had fallen to 3461 by March 2009 and had recovered to 4462 in May 2009. By February 2011, the FTSE 100 index stood at 6091 and had fallen to 4944 in October 2011, and risen again to 5896 in October 2012. So you can see that share prices, in recent years, have moved like a roller-coaster.

The FTSE 100 is widely used, and some 'tracker' investment funds simply buy shares in the companies that make up the index; the performance of these funds is often better than funds where the managers use their own expertise to select the best investments. Inclusion, or non-inclusion, in the index can affect a company's share price. It may be partly a matter of prestige and status. It is also a result of increased demand for shares that are going into the index; the managers of tracker funds have to buy them. And when companies are about to be removed from the index (because of a relative fall in their market capitalization), the share price is hit by the need for tracker funds to sell those shares.

A company's share price is also influenced by what is happening to other companies in the same sector. When one retailer reports relatively poor results, the share prices of many retailers may suffer too because it is anticipated that their results will also be poor. In 2011 bank shares were 'hit' because of the recession and the collapse of the Greek economy and its effect on the euro and general economic confidence but bank shares recovered later in the year. It also seems that sectors go in and out of favour.

Other factors influencing a company's share price are more directly to do with the company itself. Fundamentals of solvency and profitability are important, and so is growth. The (perceived) quality of management can also affect share prices. When a company has been through a bad time, chief executives often lose credibility and their jobs. When new chief executives are appointed they, and the company's share price, often enjoy a honeymoon period while the market awaits the delivery of improved results. Share prices are also influenced by the reputation of the company, by actual or rumoured takeover bids and by all sorts of rumours, speculation, scandal and gossip.

As we do not know what will happen to share prices in the future, there is inevitably some risk in investing in shares. Some risk is because of what happens to the market generally: this is known as systematic risk. Other risk is because of what happens with particular companies: this is known as unsystematic risk, and it is possible to have a balanced portfolio of shares in different companies that eliminates this unsystematic risk.

There may be individuals who really understand how the various factors operate and affect share prices. If such individuals exist, they are likely to keep their advice to themselves, and to act on it, and to become extremely rich. When you read advice from investment analysts, bankers and other

---

[2] The index is calculated by taking the average share prices of the 100 largest companies on the LSE. The index is 'weighted' so that the largest companies have most influence on the index.

'professionals' you may be tempted to believe them. But you might also wonder why they are giving you this advice or selling it to you so cheaply. Why do they not simply take their own advice and make more money that way?

There are a number of possible explanations for this:

■ Investment analysts are fair-minded individuals, solely interested in pursuing the truth, with no interest in making money for themselves, and with more interest in helping others to make money.

■ They do not really know. Like journalists, they are just writing for a living and putting out any credible stories for which they get paid.

■ For some reason they want you to follow their advice and buy and sell shares when they suggest that you should.

There are infamous tales of financial journalists who offered share tips to readers. They would choose a company with a credible story about its future prospects; then they would buy themselves a few thousand shares at the current price, say £1 each. Then they would recommend readers of the *Daily Whatsit* to buy the shares at £1 each. Once such a recommendation is published (unless it is total rubbish) the share price is likely to go up immediately – even prior to publication. By the time the poor readers of the *Daily Whatsit* get their shares, the price has gone up to, say, £1.10, and they are likely to stay at this increased level for at least a few days. The journalists then sell their shares at, say, £1.10, having made a nice little profit. They can then boast to readers that the share price increased as they predicted it would. Financial journalists may be influential enough to cause temporary price increases, but readers receive the advice too late to act on it. Some might argue that the market is too 'efficient' for individuals to influence share prices. But if we are talking about a major investment bank, or the chief executive of the company concerned, what they say, and what is reported in the financial press, may have a significant effect on share prices.

At any one time there are likely to be hundreds or thousands of theories around about which shares are going to do particularly well in the future. Some of those theories will prove to be correct, while most will be quietly forgotten.

Most investors want to buy shares when they are cheap, and sell them when they are expensive. If you think that the true value of a particular share is £2, and you can buy it for £1.80, then it seems 'cheap', and you might buy some. If, soon after buying them, you still think that they are worth £2 each, but the market price has risen to £2.20, it seems 'dear' and you would make a decent profit by selling. The problem is determining what a share is really worth.

Unfortunately, there is no 'true value' with which the market price of shares can be compared. It does not mean much to say that a share with a market value of £2.50 is cheaper than a share with a market value of £3. We can, however, say that a share price is expensive or cheap in relation to key information such as the amount of earnings, or dividends, or net assets per share.

5.4 Accounting Information and Share Prices

Investors and investment analysts make their investment decisions and recommendations using financial accounting information, and whatever other relevant and/or credible information they are able to find. Share prices reflect the information that is available to investors, and financial accounting information is central to this. Share prices may be influenced by any information that a company discloses, but the most important figures are probably:

■ The profits earned by a company;
■ The dividends paid out by the company;

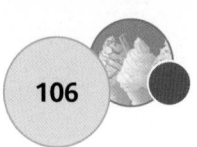
- The net asset (or statement of financial position) value of the company;
- The cash flows generated by the company.

Each of these can be related to the most recent share price that gives an indication of whether a share is 'expensive' or 'cheap' in relation to that information. Investors are guided by the most recent figures for each of these; predictions are also sometimes available, which is what investors really need; but predictions have varying degrees of credibility, and should be compared with the actual results when they become available.

Profits

From the shareholder's point of view, the most relevant profit is the amount that was earned for them in the most recent financial year. It is the figure after all expenses, including interest and any exceptional items, have been deducted, and after charging taxation for the year. It usually has a straightforward label such as 'profit for the year', and that is the amount that has been earned for the shareholders during the year. Some of it is paid out, or distributed, as dividends; the rest remains in the business and becomes part of the retained earnings shown on the statement of financial position.

If there are preference shareholders, then part of the profit earned for the year belongs to them; preference dividends have to be deducted from profits for the year to arrive at the amount earned for ordinary shareholders.

There is a relationship between the value of a company, and the amount of profits that the company earns. If a company earns £1m a year, the company might be worth, say, £10m or £15m. The relationship is called the 'price[3]/earnings ratio', which, in this example, would be 10 or 15. It can be calculated by relating the company's *total* earnings for the year to the *total* market value for all of its shares.[4] Alternatively, it can be calculated by relating the earnings *per share* to the market price *per share*.

Dividends

Some shareholders, particularly those like the elderly who buy shares for income, are more interested in the dividends that a company actually pays out than in how much profit the company makes. If a shareholder needs the income, profits are all very well, but it is the cash dividend that the shareholder actually receives that helps to pay the bills.

Companies usually declare dividends in pence per share, perhaps 4p per share. This means that the shareholders receive a 4p dividend for each share that they own. The amount varies from year to year, and companies usually try to increase it a little each year.

A company usually pays a dividend twice a year: an 'interim' dividend in the year and a 'final' dividend early in the following year. The shareholders are most interested in the total amount for the year.

Dividend yield

There is a relationship between the value of a company's shares and the amount of dividend paid. If a company pays a dividend of 4p per share and each share is worth, say, £1, then the 'dividend yield' is 4 per cent. If the share price increased to £2, the dividend yield would fall to 2 per cent. The dividend yield is usually calculated by showing the most recent annual dividend per share (interim plus final) as a percentage of the current share price. The same dividend yield figure would be produced if the company's total dividends for the year are expressed as a percentage of the company's market capitalization. As share prices fell in early 2011, and dividends, on the whole have remained steady, so dividend yields rose.

---

[3] The 'price' is the price of one share: in this example it is worth 10 or 15 times the amount of profits earned per share.

[4] The total market value of all the shares is called the market capitalization.

Dividend times cover

There is also an important relationship between the amount of profits a company earns and the amount that they choose to pay out as a dividend. If a company pays out a lot less than half of its profits as dividends, then the dividend looks reasonably secure: the dividend is well covered by profits. If a company pays out nearly all its profits as dividends, then the dividend looks less secure. Analysts divide the profit by the dividend and say, for example, that the dividend is covered 1.6 times by profits. If a company earned £100m profits, and paid out £62.5m as dividends, then the dividend is covered 1.6[5] times by profits.

Dividend cover[6] can be calculated using earnings and dividend figures for the company as a whole or on a per share basis. Shareholders who invest in shares because they are particularly interested in dividends will be attracted to those with a relatively low dividend cover, while those shareholders who are more interested in long-term growth in share price would be more attracted to companies distributing a smaller proportion of their profits as a dividend, which therefore have a relatively high dividend cover.

Net asset (or statement of financial position) value

A company's statement of financial position clearly shows the amount for equity or shareholders' funds, which is the same as the amount for 'net assets'. But the total value of the company's shares on the stock market is likely to be very different from what the statement of financial position shows. Share prices result from the interplay of supply and demand for shares, rather than from recording financial transactions within the business. If a company's prospects are seen to be very good, there is a strong demand for the shares, and the share price tends to increase. Generally, with a successful company, the market price of the shares is much higher than the net asset value per share (based on statement of financial position values).

Cash flows

Many analysts do not rely on profit information alone, but also analyse the company's cash flow statement, and are likely to have more confidence in a company that has healthy cash flows.

5.5 The *Financial Times*

The *Financial Times* shows key figures and ratios in respect of each listed company on the LSE[7] on a daily basis. On Tuesdays to Saturdays the P/E ratio and the dividend yield are shown for each company, together with various other information (see Illustration 5.1).

All these four companies' share details are printed in bold type indicating that each of these companies is among the 100 shares in the FTSE 100 index. We can access the latest annual report of companies in the *Financial Times* Share Service via www.ft.com/ir.

On the day that the figures in Illustration 5.1 were published[8] the average yield for the FTSE 100 companies was 3.44 per cent and the average P/E ratio was 9.93.

In Illustration 5.1 we can see that Tesco and Morrison have very similar P/E ratios that are rather higher than the stock market average. Marks & Spencer's PE ratio is lower than the other three companies indicating a lower expectation in the market on the future than of the other three companies. The content of the columns is as follows:

---

[5] £62.5 × 1.6 = £100m.

[6] Dividend cover should not be confused with interest cover.

[7] Comparable information is shown on preceding pages for many other shares and markets in the world.

[8] The two FT extracts are from Saturday 7 November and Monday 9 November 2011.

ILLUSTRATION 5.1

Company	Notes	Closing price on previous day (pence)	Change in price (pence) since previous day	2011 high	2011 low	Yield %	P/E	Volume '000s
Marks & Spencer		323.5	−1.7	411.2	296.2	5.3	8.2	17,082
Morrison		312.2ˣᵈ	+5.1	348.8	178.6	3.7	12.1	14,251
Sainsbury	✠	302	−0.1	395.7	258.0	5.0	10.6	5,640
Tesco	✠+	405.55ˣᵈ	−1.15	490.5	280.4	3.6	13	19,063

1 name of company, usually abbreviated;

2 various notes. The '✠' symbol indicates that the company is among the FT Global 500 companies. The '†' symbol indicates that the interim dividend has been increased or resumed since the previous year;

3 share price at close of business on the previous day (closing mid price[9]);

4 amount by which the share price changed during the previous day;

5 the highest the share price has been during the previous 52 weeks;

6 the lowest the share price has been during the previous 52 weeks;

7 yield: the latest known dividend per share expressed as a percentage of the share price;

8 P/E: expresses the relationship between the share price and the latest known profit, or earnings, per share;

9 volume: the number of shares traded on the previous day in thousands.

On Mondays, as there was no previous day's trading, the *Financial Times* provides different information as follows, and as shown in Illustration 5.2:

1 name of company as above;

2 various notes as above;

3 price at the close of business on the previous Friday;

4 the percentage change in the share price during the previous week;

5 the amount of the last known annual dividend expressed in pence per share;

6 the dividend cover: earnings per share (EPS) divided by dividend per share;

7 market capitalization: the share price multiplied by the number of shares that the company has in issue;

ILLUSTRATION 5.2

Company	Notes	Closing price on Friday	% change during last week	Dividend in pence per share	Dividend cover	Market capitalization £m	Date when share last became ex-dividend
Marks & Spencer		323.5	−1.7	17	2.3	5,129	1.6
Morrison		312.2ˣᵈ	+3.6	11.54	2.2	7,978	28.9
Sainsbury	✠	302	−0.6	15.10	1.9	5,670	18.5
Tesco	✠+	405.55ˣᵈ	−	14.72	2.1	2,513	2.10

---

[9] There is always a 'spread' between the buying price and selling price: the mid-point is shown.

8 the date when the share became 'ex-dividend'. The most recent dividend was payable to whoever owned the shares on the day before the 'xd' date. If the dividend is 4p per share, we might expect the share price to fall by about 4p on the 'xd' date, because whoever owns the share on that date will not receive the 4p dividend, and will probably have to wait six months before another dividend is due;

9 City line. This is a four-digit telephone number that gives live, up-to-the-minute share prices, if you dial 09058 171 690, followed by the four-digit number. Normal trading hours are 8.00 a.m. – 4.30 p.m.

On the date that these figures were published[10] the average dividend times cover among FTSE 100 companies was 2.93.

In Illustration 5.2 we can see that Morrison shares had the biggest increase during the week. Sainsbury's paid the largest dividend of the four companies, but this piece of information by itself does not mean much since the dividend should be related to the market price of the shares. What matters is the dividend yield: the dividend as a percentage of the share price. On this measure Marks and Spencer looks the best since its dividend yield at 5.2 per cent is much higher than the other three companies.

The dividend cover indicates how safe the dividend is. Marks and Spencer, Morrisons and Tesco dividend cover look reasonably safe: they were paying out less than half of their profits as dividends (i.e. dividends were covered three times and twice by their profits). Sainsbury's paid out the highest proportion of last year's profits as a dividend, perhaps anticipating an increase in profits in the following year.

The market capitalization is a measure of the size of a company. It is the current share price multiplied by the number of shares in issue. Using this measure we can see that Marks and Spencer, Morrisons and Sainsbury's are companies of a similar size while Tesco is a much larger company in terms of total value. Other measures of the size of a company include turnover, net asset (statement of financial position) value, profits and number of employees.

When a company declares a dividend it is payable to all who own the shares on a particular date. Anyone buying the shares after that date will not receive the company's most recent proposed dividend. If the dividend is, say, 20p per share, we can expect the share price to drop by 20p on the day that it becomes ex-dividend. It is important to know the date that a share becomes ex-dividend (and the amount of the dividend), if we are to make sense of share price movements.

For information about net asset values and cash flows, it is necessary to look at the annual report and accounts; alternatively, information produced by investment analysts and in the financial press can be examined.

5.6 Price/Earnings (P/E) Ratios

Calculating the P/E ratio

The 'P/E' ratio is perhaps the most widely used stock market indicator. It shows clearly the relationship between the last known EPS figure and the most recent share price. Example 5.1 shows how the P/E ratio can be calculated on a per share basis (g) or for the company as a whole (e).

What the P/E ratio can tell us

In Example 5.1, Cronky plc has a P/E ratio of 10. If we pay £2 for a share, and the company earns 20p per share each year, the share will have paid for itself[11] in 10 years. That seems rather a long time for

---

[10] 7 November 2011 in the *Financial Times*.

[11] In terms of profit that the company earns, not in terms of dividends that the company pays out.

Example 5.1

		Cronky plc	Voddy plc
a	Number of ordinary shares	1,000,000	1,000,000
b	Current share price	£2.00	£3.20
c	Market capitalization (a × b)	£2,000,000	£3,200,000
d	Total profits after taxation attributable to ordinary shareholders	£200,000	£160,000
e	P/E ratio (c ÷ d)	10	20
f	EPS (d ÷ a)	£0.20	£0.16
g	P/E ratio (b ÷ f)	10	20

an investment to pay for itself. But the position with Voddy plc is even worse: it would take 20 years. These figures are not unusual. Currently, the average P/E ratio on the London Stock Market was about 13. This could mean that most shares are hopelessly overpriced. It is more likely to mean that investors expect EPS to increase significantly in the coming years. The share price looks high in relation to the previous year's earnings, but (hopefully) not in relation to future earnings.

If share prices seem high it is because demand for them is high; and if demand is high it is usually because investors are optimistic about the future prospects of the company. Investors in Voddy plc do not assume that the EPS will remain at 16p for the next 20 years: they expect or demand *growth* in EPS.

If earnings grow at a constant rate of 10 per cent per annum, they will double in less than eight years. If they grow at 15 per cent per annum, they will double in just less than five years. Not many companies manage to maintain such rates of growth in earnings, but they may be needed to justify high share prices, that is, to justify high P/E ratios. We can assume that, generally, a high P/E ratio means that investors are expecting high rates of growth, although they may, of course, be disappointed. In recent years, many share prices were very high, with high P/E ratios, particularly biotechnology, media and telecommunications, together with computing, and anything vaguely connected with the dotcom bubble. But many such companies failed to deliver the rapid growth in earnings that was needed to justify the high P/E ratios, and many high share prices crashed. Many investors jumped on the bandwagon of high P/E ratios, only to be disappointed. In recent years, more modest P/E ratios and more realistic expectations of growth were the order of the day and several years of steadily increasing share prices followed until the collapse in early 2009.

We can get a feel for P/E ratios by looking at the FTSE Actuaries Share Indices table in the *Financial Times*. It gives the average for the London Stock Market as a whole, the average for the top 100 companies (the FTSE 100) and the average for about 35 different sectors. Currently, the average P/E ratio for the FTSE 100 was 9.93. Sectors with high P/Es included oil equipment, personal goods, technology, hardware and equipment and equity investment. Sectors with low P/Es included mining, automobiles and parts, mobile communications and electricity utilities.

We can generalize that high P/E ratios are associated with expectations of high rates of growth. If the average P/E is 9.93, then any company with a P/E of much more than about 15 is expected to deliver high rates of growth if investors are not to be disappointed. A company with a P/E of less than about 6 is not expected to produce so much growth in EPS.

Most companies have a P/E of between about 5 and 20. But care is needed in interpreting these, especially if the P/E is unusually high or low. Sometimes P/E ratios are abnormally high – so high as to be meaningless. In Example 5.2 Sudndip plc had four very successful years. Profit increased each year

Example 5.2

Sudndip plc has 10 million ordinary shares in issue. Their total profits after tax and EPS, are shown below. The share price and P/E ratio shortly after the results were published are also shown.

	Year 1	Year 2	Year 3	Year 4	Year 5
Net profit after tax	£1m	£1.1m	£1.25m	£1.45m	£50,000
EPS	£0.10	£0.11	£0.125	£0.145	£ 0.005
Share price	£1.20	£1.43	£1.87½	£2.61	
P/E ratio	12	13	15	18	

by more than 10 per cent, and at an increasing rate. This raised expectations, and the P/E ratio went up from 12 to 18 during the period. Then, in year 5, earnings collapsed; EPS are minute. We could be fairly sure that the share price would collapse too. Maybe it would go down to £1 or even to 80p. But with a tiny EPS figure, even at 80p the P/E ratio would still be 160, which is so far out of the normal range as to be misleading. It still means that the share price is very high in relation to the latest EPS, but the explanation is more to do with exceptionally low earnings than it is to do with a high share price.

The drop in earnings shown in Example 5.2 is rather extreme, but it is often the case that a high P/E ratio signifies that the previous year's earnings were unusually low, and better results are expected soon.

Although International Financial Reporting Standards (IFRSs) lay down clear rules on how EPS should be calculated, it is not always clear which EPS figures have been used in calculating the P/E ratio, particularly in the financial press. Unusual P/E ratios are often the result of unusual earnings figures, such as exceptional profits, or losses on the sale of a subsidiary, or charges for the impairment of goodwill. Companies often produce two different EPS figures, choosing to exclude particular items for one of them. In the financial press use is sometimes made of P/E ratios based on future forecast earnings that may be referred to as prospective or forward P/E ratios.

5.7 Dividend Yield

Calculating the dividend yield

The dividend yield is another widely used stock market indicator. It shows clearly the relationship between the last known amount of annual dividend and the most recent share price. It can be calculated on a 'per share' basis, by dividing the most recent annual dividend by the most recent share price.[12] Alternatively, it can be calculated for the company as a whole, by dividing the company's total dividends payable for the most recent year[13] by its 'market capitalization' (the most recent share price multiplied by the number of shares that the company has in issue).[14]

The calculation, for two companies, is shown in Example 5.3.

---

[12] And multiplying by 100 to express it as a percentage.

[13] After deducting any preference dividends.

[14] And multiplying by 100 to express it as a percentage.

Example 5.3

		Cronky plc	Voddy plc
a	Number of ordinary shares	1,000,000	1,000,000
b	Current share price	£2.00	£3.20
c	Market capitalization (a × b)	£2,000,000	£3,200,000
d	Total ordinary dividends	£100,000	£100,000
e	Dividend yield (d ÷ c × 100)	5%	3.1%
f	Dividend per share (d ÷ a)	£0.10	£0.10
g	Dividend yield (f ÷ b × 100)	5%	3.1%

In this example, Cronky has a significantly higher dividend yield than Voddy, but care is needed in interpreting this. It does not mean that Cronky's dividends are higher than Voddy's; both companies are paying the same dividend per share; that is, 10p. Cronky's higher dividend yield means that it has a lower share price than Voddy. A high dividend yield means that the share price is low (in relation to dividends); a low dividend yield means that the share price is high in relation to dividends.

What the dividend yield can tell us

In the 1990s, little attention was given to low dividend yields. The average dividend yield on shares was only around 2 per cent at a time when it was possible to get 5 per cent or more from a bank or building society deposit account. Dividend yields looked very low, partly because share prices were very high. Although interest rates can vary, there is no 'growth' in the amount of interest paid on deposit accounts. But the hope and expectation is that dividends will increase, year after year, and in the majority of companies they still do. If someone invests £100 in shares, and the only dividend they get is £2, that is a yield of 2 per cent but it looks miserable. But the following year it might be £2.15, then £2.35 the next year, then £2.55; and, after a number of years (hopefully before the investor retires!), the dividend might look very respectable in relation to the original £100 invested, with every prospect that it will continue to increase, at least in line with inflation. With a successful investment, the share price also increases, which means that the dividend yield still looks low: it is the *amount* of dividend that the investor hopes to see increasing each year, not the dividend yield. And with interest rates on bank deposits in 2011 at a historical low, dividend yields running at an average of 3.44 per cent seem quite high.

It is 'normal' for the average yield on shares to be lower than interest rates on deposit accounts, because investors expect there to be growth in dividends on ordinary shares. So, in 2011 it was possible to invest in shares that yielded more than bank deposit account rates.

Low dividend yields are mainly the result of high share prices, and low dividend yields go hand in hand with high P/E ratios. Shares that are expected to deliver rapid and sustained growth have high prices, and, therefore, high P/E ratios, and, therefore, low dividend yields. It might be a rational strategy for investors to choose companies with high dividend yields, provided they can be sure that the dividends will continue to be high. We do not know what future dividends will be and it might be with the economic growth expected to be minimal there was no guarantee that present levels of dividend will continue.

At present, interest rates are still very low. Although the average yield on shares is only 4.79 per cent, one might expect future earnings and therefore dividends to fall. Many individual and institutional investors are attracted to 'good value' shares with a reasonable dividend yield. It is possible to get some guidance on how sound such an investment might be by looking at the company's record over a number of years (profits and dividends), and by looking at their cash flow statements.

5.8 Dividend Cover

The easiest and most widely used indicator of how likely it is that a company's dividend will be maintained and increased is 'dividend cover'. This is the relationship between profits and dividends. If a company pays out only a small proportion of its profits as dividends, then the dividend looks reasonably secure: even if profits fall in the following year, there should still be more than enough to pay the same level of dividend.

Dividend cover is calculated by dividing EPS by dividend per share. It can also be calculated by dividing the total profits attributable to ordinary shareholders by the total amount of ordinary dividends payable for the year.

The calculations for Cronky plc and Voddy plc are shown in Example 5.4.

On this basis, Cronky's dividend looks more secure than Voddy's. We must expect profits to fluctuate from time to time. Cronky can afford a bigger percentage reduction in profits before the dividend looks threatened than can Voddy. If each company suffered a 40 per cent reduction in profits, the EPS would be:

	Cronky plc	**Voddy plc**
Earnings per share	£0.12	£0.096

If each company continued with a 10p per share dividend, the dividend cover would be:

Dividend cover	1.2 times	0.96 times

Although it is acceptable for a company to pay out more in dividends than it earns in profits from time to time, perhaps when there is an unusually bad year, clearly this cannot continue for very long. A dividend that is not well covered by profits looks insecure. The average company on the stock market had a dividend cover that increased from about 2.3 times in 2006 to 2.9 times in 2011. Many companies try to maintain the amount of dividend that they pay, even in years when profits are not good; their dividend cover then looks weaker.

Example 5.4

		Cronky plc	Voddy plc
a	Total profits after taxation attributable to ordinary shareholders	£200,000	£160,000
b	Total ordinary dividends	£100,000	£100,000
c	Dividend cover (a ÷ b)	2 times	1.6 times
d	EPS	£0.20	£0.16
e	Dividend per share	£0.10	£0.10
f	Dividend cover (d ÷ e)	2 times	1.6 times

5.9 Net Asset (or Statement of Financial Position) Value

It is easy to calculate the net asset value of a company, or the value of its equity, from the statement of financial position. It is simply the total figure for equity, including share capital and all retained earnings and reserves. The amount for preference shares (if there are any) should be deducted because we are usually assessing only the value of the ordinary shareholders' funds.

This amount can be compared with the company's 'market capitalization' – the total value of all the company's shares, using the most recent share price. The comparison can be made using these total figures for the company as a whole. Alternatively, it can be made on a per share basis, comparing the net asset value per share with the share price.

In most cases the market value of a company is much higher than the net asset value shown on the statement of financial position. This is for two main reasons:

1 Statement of financial position values may be understated, often being based on historic cost (HC) rather than current values; and some assets are not shown on the statement of financial position – human assets, skills, brands and any 'internally generated'[15] goodwill.

2 Share prices are determined by supply and demand for the shares, and the statement of financial position usually has a minor influence on demand for shares. The major influence is expectations of future profits and dividends, and expectations that the share price will rise in the future.

Some traditional manufacturing companies may have huge amounts of assets, and their market capitalization may not be very much more than their net asset value. Many modern companies have relatively small amounts of tangible assets, and their value lies in their skills, expertise, reputation, brands and other intangibles not shown on the statement of financial position. Such companies might easily be worth 5 or 10 times their net asset values, especially at the height of a bubble!

The *Financial Times* does not regularly publish net asset values – which might be taken as an indication that they are not seen as being particularly important. They can easily be calculated from a company's statement of financial position, and usually feature in reports by investment analysts, and are published by journals such as the *Investors Chronicle*. Some examples are shown in Illustration 5.3.

In a successful company it is normal for the market price of the share to be higher than the net asset value per share. In many companies a large part of the net assets consists of 'intangible assets' (mainly the amounts paid for goodwill when another company is taken over). If such intangible assets are excluded, then the tangible assets of a company may be very low indeed compared with the share price.

ILLUSTRATION 5.3

Company	Share price (pence)	Net asset value per share	Intangibles included in net asset value
Halfords (Retailers)	340	152	348
Ted Baker (Retailers)	767	175	1
GlaxoSmithKlein (Pharmaceuticals)	1379	157	12,138
Land Securities (Real estate)	691	887	–
ITV (Media)	65	170	969
WPP (Advertising)	664	510	11,011

---

[15] When a company buys another business, any amount paid for 'goodwill' has to be shown. But when a company generates its own goodwill, this is not shown on a statement of financial position.

In a minority of cases the net asset value of a company falls below its market capitalization. If the difference is substantial, this might invite an asset-stripping takeover bid: it may be possible to buy up the company at a bargain price, and then sell off all the separate parts of it at a profit. Investment analysts often assess the market value – not just the statement of financial position value – of the separate parts of a business, and when this falls below the market capitalization, there are danger signs for management: another management team may be able to take over and do a better job for the shareholders.

In some cases, such as property companies, the market capitalization is usually significantly less than the market value of the underlying assets. In part this may be because the statement of financial position shows properties at fairly full current valuations, and it may be difficult to sell the properties at those prices. It may also be because it is difficult to generate much growth in profits: rental income is relatively stable, and safe, but does not produce 'double-digit' growth in profits.

5.10 Cash Flow

Cash flow may be a better indicator of a company's performance than profit. A company that generates substantial profits on paper, but cannot back them up with cash flows, raises serious questions. A company that makes profits year after year, but has to keep raising more money (by borrowing or making rights issues) may be unpopular with investors. Cash flow statements explain how and why a company's cash flow differs from its profit, as explained in Chapter 6.

The first question is: does the company generate cash from its normal operations? If it does not, there is a need to establish why not.

The second question is to do with expansion. Is the company investing in more non-current assets and buying other businesses? This is clearly shown on the cash flow statement. Such expansion may require additional borrowing or the issue of more shares. Amounts invested in expansion can be compared with the amounts raised as additional share capital and borrowings. It is a danger sign if the company is raising lots more capital, without any evident increase in profitable investment. It is more healthy if a company is investing in additional capacity and this is partly financed from operating cash flows, and not totally dependent on raising additional funds.

Cash flow statements show three categories of cash flow:

1 *Cash generated from operating activities* – Investors expect to see a positive figure here, even after financing any increases in working capital.
2 *Cash flow from investing activities* – Investors expect to see a negative figure here, with the company investing in additional non-current assets and perhaps buying up other businesses.
3 *Cash flow from financing activities* – Investors want to know about the company's financing, how any expansion has been financed, and whether the company has been increasing or reducing borrowings.

Some analysts emphasize profit plus depreciation and amortization as being the key figure. The cash flow from the operations figure is perhaps the most useful and readily available. Others look for 'free cash flow' that can be deduced from somewhere in the middle of the cash flow statement by estimating how much of the amount paid for additional non-current assets is essential, and how much is for expansion.

5.11 Other Indicators/Predictors of Performance

There is no shortage of investment analysts, experts and charlatans giving advice on how to pick winners when investing on the stock market. Most accountants are more cautious, but not all! It is

difficult to be clear about who is an expert, who is a charlatan and who is advising investing in particular shares for reasons of self-interest. Even the 'experts' do not seem to be able to get it right, and are often carried along with the fashionable conventional wisdoms of the day. At the end of 2010, there were not many experts predicting the significant collapse in share prices and, much like other crashes in the past, those still jumping on the bandwagon lost the most.

All financial accounting information can be analysed with a view to guiding investment decisions. Many different ratios can be calculated, and an examination of trends over a number of years can be revealing.

The relationship between a company's turnover figure and its market capitalization is one of many ratios that might be worth following. The idea is that, if a company's market capitalization is higher than its turnover, the shares are overpriced. If a company's turnover is very much higher than its market capitalization, the shares are good value. The theory is that if a company has a high level of sales (in relation to share price), profits will follow. The hardest thing is to achieve a high level of turnover. If the present management cannot make good profits from a high level of sales, a future management will. This may be no more than a hypothesis. It would probably turn out to be a good basis for investment in some companies, in some years, but not for other companies in other years. This is probably true for most decision rules that are supposed to form the basis for investment decisions.

During the period of enthusiasm for shares in telecommunications companies, emphasis was given to measures such as earnings before interest, taxation, depreciation and amortization.[16] A decision rule emerged that a company should be worth about three times this figure; but ideas like this soon faded.

The more fully past data are analysed, the more models can be developed that appear to predict future share prices. It is not difficult to find past data which, if analysed in a particular way, would have predicted share prices. But we cannot assume that such relationships will hold good in the future. In choosing between different accounting policies, accountants often favour those policies that seem to have most predictive value; but we can know only those that would have had most predictive value in the past. Markets are constantly changing. Companies and activities that did well in recent years, such as banks and the insurance sector, have proved to be the worst in the 'credit crunch'. Past performance is no guide to the future.

The same arguments apply with technical analysis: it is difficult to believe that graphs of share prices over time show patterns that enable us to predict future share prices.

Although financial accounting cannot give us all the answers that we might like, the information that it provides is central in making investment decisions, and in monitoring how successful those decisions turn out to be.

5.12 A Further Illustration

The main stock market ratios are shown in Illustration 5.4. The figures suggest a typical, average company, and may be used to make comparisons with other companies and to see how the ratios have been calculated. The P/E ratio, the dividend cover and the dividend yield may all be calculated using figures for the company as a whole, or on a per share basis.

The figures for Stoutmouth plc are in many ways typical of a listed company. Currently, the average P/E ratio of the 100 largest companies quoted on the LSE was 9.8; the average dividend yield was 4.8 per cent; and the average times cover for dividends was 2.13. The market capitalization of each of the companies in the largest 100 is between £0.5 and £100b. But the market capitalization of most listed companies is nearer to that of Stoutmouth plc.

---

[16] Known as EBITDA.

ILLUSTRATION 5.4

	Stoutmouth plc
Share capital (25p shares)	£ 5,000,000
Retained earnings	£31,000,000
	£36,000,000
Net profit after tax for year	£6,400,000
Dividends for year	£4,000,000
Number of shares	20,000,000
Market price of shares	£5.44
Market capitalization	£108,800,000
EPS	£0.32
Dividend per share	£0.20
P/E ratio	17
Dividend times cover	1.6 times
Dividend yield	3.7%
Net assets per share	£1.80

📖 Summary

One of the main objectives of financial management is to maximize shareholders' wealth. Dividends, which are dependent on profits, contribute to this. But the main element of shareholders' wealth is the value of their shares. Directors and chief executives are usually well motivated to maintain and increase their company's share price: they own shares themselves; they may have options to buy shares at predetermined prices; and their remuneration may include substantial incentives related to share price performance. If they fail, and the share price languishes, they risk the wrath of shareholders, and leave themselves open to a hostile takeover bid with a new management team replacing them.

Accounting measures of solvency and profitability are central to the performance of share prices. If a company is seen as having excessive debt, the share price will suffer. Profitability is essential to maintaining and increasing share prices, although more attention seems to be paid to EPS than to return on capital employed (ROCE). Growth, and expectations of future growth in sales, profits and dividends make a major contribution to increases in share prices. Sometimes it seems that expectations of share price increases are the main cause of share price increases. Share prices are influenced by expectations, rumours and many other factors that are difficult to define and measure, particularly in the short term. In the long run, sound finances and growth in EPS are likely to be the main contributors to increasing share prices.

➡ Review of key points

- Many different factors influence share prices.
- A company's P/E ratio, dividend yield and dividend cover are widely used measures of share price performance.
- Growth and expectations of growth of sales and profits help to boost share prices.

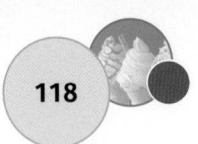
- Many influences on share prices are difficult to quantify.
- Company directors and shareholders have an interest in maintaining and increasing share prices.
- Claims to be able to predict share prices should be treated with caution.
- Financial accounting information helps to explain changes in share prices.

Self-testing questions

1 Explain the meaning, calculation and significance of each of the following:
   a P/E ratio;
   b dividend yield;
   c dividend times cover.

2 Is a company's statement of financial position value (net asset value) likely to be higher or lower than its market value? Explain.

3 If a company currently has a dividend yield of 10 per cent, does that mean that someone investing £100 today will receive £10 dividend in the coming year? Explain.

4 You are given the following information about two companies. You are required to fill in the missing items for Beermouth plc.

	Alemouth plc	Beermouth plc
Share capital (20p shares)	£1,600,000	£ 2,000,000
Retained earnings	£3,200,000	£18,000,000
	£4,800,000	£20,000,000
Net profit after tax for year	£3,520,000	£1,200,000
Dividends for year	£3,200,000	£800,000
Number of shares	8,000,000	10,000,000
Market price of shares	£4.40	£1.80
Market capitalization	£35,200,000	£18,000,000
EPS	£0.44	£0.12
Dividend per share	£0.40	£0.08
P/E ratio	10	–
Dividend times cover	1.1 times	–
Dividend yield	9.09%	–
Net assets per share	£0.60	–

5 Comment on the dividend yield of Alemouth plc.

6 Comment on the relationship between the net assets per share of Beermouth plc and its share price (or on the relationship of the total of shareholders' funds to the market capitalization).

Assessment questions

1 What is the level of the FTSE 100 today? What is the average P/E ratio of the top 100 companies? What is their dividend yield and dividend cover? You are given the following information about the FTSE 100:

	Index	P/E	Dividend yield (%)	Dividend cover
16 September 2003	4299	17.6	3.3	1.72
19 June 2006	5597	12.8	3.4	2.3
8 May 2009	4462	9.8	4.8	2.13
7 Nov 2011	5527	9.9	3.4	2.93

What do you think are the main causes of the changes

a between September 2003 and June 2006?

b between June 2006 and May 2009?

c since May 2009?

2 You are given the following information about two companies, partly extracted from their most recent statement of financial position and income statement, and partly taken from the financial press. You are required to fill in the missing items for Drinkmouth plc.

	Cidermouth plc	Drinkmouth plc
Share capital (20p shares)	£ 4,000,000	£1,200,000
Retained earnings	£14,000,000	£2,400,000
	£18,000,000	£3,600.000
Net profit after tax for year	£3,400,000	£1,800,000
Dividends for year	£2,000,000	£ 900,000
Number of shares	20,000,000	6,000,000
Market price of shares	£3.40	–
Market capitalization	£68,000,000	£45,000,000
EPS	£0.17	£0.30
Dividend per share	£0.10	–
P/E ratio	20	25
Dividend times cover	1.7 times	–
Dividend yield	2.9%	2.0%
Net assets per share	£0.90	–

3 You are given the following information about Swin Gin plc:

	Year 1	Year 2	Year 3	Year 4	Year 5*	Year 6	Year 7
EPS	£0.50	£0.55	£0.62	£0.01	£1.20	£ 0.83	£ 0.90
Share price	£6.00	£7.70	£9.92	£6.00	£7.20	£12.45	£15.30

(after publication of results for year)

* In year 5 the company sold its head office building in London making a profit that amounted to 45p per share.

You are required to calculate the P/E ratio for each year, and comment on how the market appears to have reacted to changes in EPS.

4 Assess the usefulness of P/E ratios and suggest how they might be misleading.

5 Select a recent takeover bid (e.g. Kraft and Cadbury). Assess the various factors that determined the price that was eventually agreed for the company which was taken over.

 ## Group activities and discussion questions

1 Look at the shares listing in the *Financial Times*. What is an average P/E ratio? Select some companies with high P/E ratios. Do they seem to have anything in common? How useful are the P/E ratios given for different sectors in the 'FTSE Actuaries Share Indices'? Select some companies with low P/E ratios. Do they seem to have anything in common?

2 Look at the shares listing in the *Financial Times*. What is an average dividend yield? Select some companies with high dividend yields. Do they seem to have anything in common? How useful are the dividend yields given for different sectors in the 'FTSE Actuaries Share Indices'? Select some companies with low dividend yields. Do they seem to have anything in common?

3 Each member of the group selects one or two companies in which they believe the shares are likely to increase in price during a selected period. A long period may be preferable, but in a 10-week module the selection could be made in week 3; the shares monitored for 6 weeks; and the 'final' results assessed in week 8.

   Each member of the group is required to give a justification for selecting a particular share in week 3. Then, in week 8, each member should present an explanation of what has happened to their company's share price.

   There would be a competitive element (who would have made most money?). There should also be an assessment of the quality of the presentations; this assessment could be done partly or wholly by the students themselves.

4 Each group forms one or more hypotheses about how to select companies where the increase in share prices is expected to be higher than the average for the FTSE 100 companies. Examples might include (with variations) such things as:

   a companies with a dividend yield of between 4 per cent and 5 per cent where the cover is not less than 2

   b companies where sales have increased by more than 20 per cent per annum (over a given number of years), but profits have not (yet) increased

   c companies where profits have increased by more than 10 per cent since last year, but the share price is lower

   This exercise might be more fun if it is done live. But it is difficult to complete it during the 10-week period of a typical module. It is easier to do it historically. The decision rules are selected first, then they are applied to a sample of companies.

   Some competition between different groups can produce interesting results. The results produced by the winners might need careful scrutiny.

5 Each group chooses three different sectors (e.g. pharmaceuticals and biotech; construction and materials; travel and leisure and retailers). The key stock market indicators are found for each sector and compared with the average for the FTSE. These are shown in the *Financial Times* as 'FTSE Actuaries Share Indices'. Suggest factors that make each sector different from the FTSE average.

Accounting in context

Discuss and comment on the following extract from the press with reference to why movements in share price should be judged in the light of movements in the market as a whole and what factors affect the move in share price.

Unearth some treasure at mine operator Hargreaves

Yesterday's full-year numbers from coal mine operator Hargreaves Services were, as usual, excellent.

By Garry White

Annual pre-tax profits jumped 20pc – and analysts expect profits to rise almost 30pc in the current year. Indeed, Hargreaves has an exemplary track record of profit delivery – with earnings per share increasing by about 40pc a year since the group floated in 2005. The company has always hit or beaten consensus forecasts.

Hargreaves is a growth share and should be rated as such – but it is not. It is currently trading on a May 2012 multiple of just 8 times, falling to 6.9 times. This does not reflect the growth potential.

Of course the recent risk aversion prompted by the crisis in the eurozone has hit the shares hard. They are now almost £1 lower than their July peak of £10.76. However, Questor reckons this valuation appears derisory.

Revenues in the year to May rose 20.1pc to £552.3m and net debt fell by a quarter to £66m. Hargreaves has finished the major investment in its Maltby Colliery, and the fall in debt underscores the cash generative nature of the business.

The final dividend is 10.4p, bringing the total for the year to 15.5p, an increase of 14.8pc on the preceding year. The final payment will be on November 16 and new investors need to buy the shares before October 12 to qualify.

However, this is not an income share, it is a growth stock – as the company is investing in its business. The yield is therefore 1.8pc.

The group has moved its trading operations into Europe and the business is growing fast. Operating projects in the region grew by 106pc to £9.9m.

When the company first entered Europe, it aimed to grow the business to the same size as its UK operations within five years. Hargreaves now expects that to happen in four years. Also, the group is looking at a move into Asia – and it expects to be able to announce a strategic beachhead in the region in the current financial year.

The management has time to focus on Asia now the group has secured the permits for its Tower Colliery surface coal joint venture in Wales. Hargreaves will operate the site on behalf of the venture on a proposed "cost-plus" 10pc basis. [...]

The shares are up 81pc since their initial recommendation on February 22 2009, at 542½p, compared with a FTSE 100 up 34pc, although they have been tipped as a buy as high as £10.40. Hargreaves is a well managed business that delivers.

Questor sees plenty of growth in the business and believes the shares are undervalued. Buy.

Source: The Telegraph, 15 September 2011.

References and further reading

Arnold, G. (2010) *The Financial Times Guide to Investing* (2nd edn.) Harlow: FT Prentice Hall.

Boakes, K. (2010) *Reading and Understanding the Financial Times.* Harlow: FT Prentice Hall.

Financial Times (daily newspaper). Available online at www.ft.com.

Hillier, D. and S. Ross et al. (2010) *Corporate Finance* (1st European edn.). Maidenhead: McGraw-Hill Education.

Investors Chronicle (weekly magazine).

Lumby, S. and C. Jones (2003) *Corporate Finance: Theory and Practice*. London: Thomson Learning.

McKenzie, W. (2010) *Financial Times Guide to Using and Interpreting Company Accounts* (4th edn.). Harlow: FT Prentice Hall.

Vernimmen, P. et al. (2011) *Corporate Finance: Theory and Practice* (3rd edn.). Chichester: Wiley.

Watson, D. and A. Head 2009. *Corporate Finance: Principles and Practice* (5th edn.) Harlow: FT Prentice Hall.

www.londonstockexchange.com

When you have read this chapter, log on to the Online Learning Centre website at *www.mcgraw-hill.co.uk/textbooks/leiwy* to explore chapter-by-chapter test questions, further reading and more online study tools.

Chapter 6

Cash Flow Statements: Understanding and Preparation

Chapter contents

 Learning objectives

After studying this chapter you will be able to:

- ✓ Understand the differences between cash flow and profit
- ✓ Explain the accruals concept
- ✓ Understand and interpret cash flow statements
- ✓ Compare the statement of financial position at the beginning of the year with that at the end and explain how the amount of cash has changed during the year
- ✓ Produce cash flow statements in a format suitable for publication

6.1 Introduction

This chapter begins by explaining the difference between *cash flow* and *profit*. Non-accountants often think they are the same thing: making money means making profits and generating cash. Often the two go hand in hand. A successful company generates lots of cash. An unsuccessful company runs out of cash. If a company's success was judged by the amount of cash generated, the accountant's job would be very easy: there would be no need to do more than record all receipts and payments, and to report on a regular basis which is higher. The analyst's job would also be easy: the company that generates most cash is most successful. There would be no problems of credibility or subjectivity, or manipulation of asset values and exaggeration of profits. Everything could be easily checked by looking at the company's bank statement.

But generating lots of cash is not necessarily a sign of success. Few of us would be impressed by a company that massively increased its cash balances simply by selling off assets and borrowing lots of money. A company that succeeds in generating large amounts of cash is not necessarily a successful company.

Similarly, a successful company might pay out far more cash than it receives. A profitable company might be paying out substantial sums of cash to buy assets that are going to increase future profit; the company performs well, even though it is using up lots of cash.

The distinctions between cash flow and profit are not easily understood, but are vital to an understanding of financial accounting – and to the survival of a business. This chapter begins by explaining the theoretical difference, as in the accruals concept. Cash flow statements are then explained and interpreted. The final section explains how to produce cash flow statements in a form suitable for publication in accordance with IAS 7 Cash Flow Statements.

6.2 The Accruals Concept

Statements of financial position and income statements are based on the *accruals concept,* which means that profit is the difference between the revenues earned during a period (regardless of when the money is received), and the costs incurred in earning those revenues (regardless of when cash is paid out).

The accruals concept has long been regarded as a *fundamental accounting concept.*[1] It requires that revenues and costs are accrued, and matched with one another so far as their relationship can be established or justifiably assumed. They are dealt with in the income statement of the period to which they relate, which is often not in the period when cash is received or paid.

The profit figure for a particular period is therefore likely to be very different from the amount of cash generated in that period. A naïve, non-accountant might think that:

$$\text{Profit} \ = \ \text{Receipts of cash} \quad \text{less} \quad \text{Payments of cash}$$

But they would be seriously mistaken.

Financial accounting is based on the accruals concept, which means that for a particular period:

$$\text{Profit} \ = \ \text{Revenues earned} \quad \text{less} \quad \text{Costs incurred in earning those revenues}$$

The words are important. Receipts and payments apply to cash. Revenues or income and costs or expenses apply to profit calculation.

The accruals concept is applied throughout financial accounting. Gross profit is the difference between sales and the cost of goods sold. In calculating profit, it is the amount of sales revenue

---

[1] SSAP 2 specified four fundamental accounting concepts: going concern; accruals; consistency; and prudence (or conservatism).

earned during a period that matters, not when the money is received. The cost of goods sold uses the purchases figure, which is the total amount purchased during the period, regardless of when they are paid for. The cost of goods sold figure also adjusts for inventories. The expense *cost of sales* is based on the cost of the goods which were actually sold during the period. Unsold inventories from one year become a cost for the following year as they are included in cost of sales as opening inventory. Closing stocks of unsold inventory of goods at the end of one period are the opening inventory of unsold goods at the beginning of the next year.

Any payment made to buy non-current assets that is made this year (or which it is agreed will be paid in another year) is not an expense for this year. The cost is spread out over the life of the non-current asset and is charged as depreciation each year. The timing of cash paid out for buying non-current assets is very different from the timing of the depreciation expense that is charged in calculating profit.

It is important to be clear that:

1 Not all payments of cash are expenses; some payments are not a charge against profits

2 Not all receipts of cash are revenues; some receipts do not add to profits

3 Not all expenses are payments of cash; some expenses are charged against profits although no payment of cash is required in the year that the expense is charged

4 Not all revenues are receipts of cash; some revenues are added to profits although there is no receipt of cash in the year that credit is taken for the revenue.

There are examples of each of the above four differences. But, in interpreting financial statements, it is important to look for the big differences. Substantial inflows of cash are likely to come from borrowings, issuing share capital and selling off assets;[2] none of these count as revenues for the purpose of calculating profit. Substantial outflows of cash are usually for buying non-current assets; but such payments are not charges against profit for the year. The biggest expense, which is not paid in cash, is depreciation and that can easily cause confusion!

Some of the examples of differences are relatively minor timing differences. But they are all important in explaining the difference between cash flow and profit. And, in some circumstances, 'minor' items can become very significant.

1 *Payments of cash that are not expenses* – purchase of non-current assets; investing in other companies; repaying loans; payments to buy stocks of goods that are not sold until the next period; payments to creditors for expenses incurred in the previous period.

2 *Receipts of cash that are not revenues* – sale of non-current assets; borrowing money; proceeds from issuing shares; receipts from receivables this period in respect of sales for the previous period.

3 *Expenses that are not payments* – depreciation and amortization;[3] expenses incurred this period but which are not paid for until the next period; creating a provision; increase in a provision for bad debts; discount allowed to customers for settling their accounts promptly.

4 *Revenues that are not receipts* – sales that are made during this period, but the money is not received until the next period; discount allowed by suppliers for settling accounts promptly; reduction in a provision.

There are also examples where the cash receipt is very different from the revenue figure. When a non-current asset is sold, all the cash received is credited to the cash account. But in calculating profit, only the difference between book value and the sale proceeds is credited to profit, as shown in Example 6.1.

---

[2] Any profit on selling a non-current asset counts towards income for the year; the full amount of the sale proceeds does not.

[3] Amortization is really the same as depreciation, but the word is usually applied to leasehold property, and to intangible non-current assets such as goodwill. 'Impairment' of goodwill or other assets is comparable.

Example 6.1

The Floughin Company has a small assembly plant at Jurbeigh that originally cost £30,000; cumulative depreciation is £6,000. The government decided to develop an international airport nearby, and the company was able to sell its plant for £40,000.

The receipt of cash is £40,000. The net book value of the plant is (£30,000 – £6,000 =) £24,000. Only the profit of £16,000 is credited towards profit for the year.

It is sometimes argued that cash flow would be a better basis for accounting than the accruals concept because it is more objective. But total cash flows (including receipts from borrowing, and payments to acquire non-current assets) mean little unless there is some classification of the receipts and payments. The need for classification would remove the supposed objectivity. Almost all accountants agree that profit measurement[4] and the use of the accruals concept are essential.

6.3 Cash Flow Statements

A *cash flow statement* provides a reconciliation between the amount of profit generated during a period, and the amount by which cash balances have increased or decreased during that period. The idea is that profits generate cash; but cash tends to flow away. The statement shows where it has gone.

It starts off by showing how much profit before tax was generated during the period; then it shows what happened to the profits. Some of it may be tied up in additional inventory and receivables; some may have gone in paying interest and taxation; some may have gone in buying more non-current assets, or repaying loans. The final figure shows how much cash is left; that final figure at the end of a cash flow statement is the same as the cash balance shown on the statement of financial position at the year end.

It is useful to bear in mind that cash *in*flows are decreases in assets and increases in liabilities, while cash *de*creases are increases in assets and decreases in liabilities. Think that when buying a car, cash reduces while when selling a car, cash increases. Most of the information required to prepare a cash flow statement can be found by comparing two statements of financial position. In Illustration 6.1 we can see that Ebbing plc made a profit in year 2.[5] But, as the illustration shows, a company may be making, and retaining, decent profits, but because of the need to finance more non-current assets, and higher levels of inventory and receivables, it ends the year with less cash than it started with. In Illustration 6.2 (Ebbing plc) the company started year 2 with £160,000 in the bank; it retained profits of £15,000 during the year; but it ended the year with only £35,000 in the bank. By comparing the two statements of financial position it is easy to see where the money went: £100,000 extra was tied up in non-current assets; there was additional inventory of £40,000; and there was an additional £30,000 tied up in receivables. How were these additional assets financed? The money came partly from retained profits, partly by reducing cash balances, and partly by owing more to trade payables.

The above reconciliation is rather simplified, and the cash flow statements published by companies are in a standardized format so that businesses can readily be compared with each other. They start by identifying cash flows from operations, which are as follows.

---

[4] The reasons why profit is measured are explored in Chapter 5.

[5] Retained earnings increased from £120,000 to £135,000. Profits retained in year 2 amounted to £15,000; that figure is after deducting dividends and taxation. Pre-tax profits would be much greater.

ILLUSTRATION 6.1

Statement of financial position of Ebbing plc as at 31 December

	Year 1	Year 2
	£000	£000
Assets		
Non-current assets	200	300
Current assets		
Inventories	80	120
Trade receivables	60	90
Cash	160	35
	300	245
Total assets	500	545
Liabilities and equity		
Liabilities		
Current liabilities		
Trade payables	90	110
Non-current liabilities		
Long-term borrowings	50	60
Total liabilities	140	170
Equity		
Share capital	240	240
Retained earnings	120	135
	360	375
Total liabilities and equity	500	545

Income statement of Ebbing plc for the year ending 31 December Year 2

	£000
Operating profit	48.5
Interest expense	4.0
Profit before taxation	44.5
Taxation	13.5
Profit for the year	35.0
Notes: Depreciation expense	£16,000
Dividends paid	£16,000

Operating activities

1 Profit before deducting taxation
2 Depreciation
3 (Increase) or decrease in working capital
4 Interest expense
   = *Cash flow from operating activities*

5 Interest paid

6 Taxation paid

7 Dividends paid

  = *Net cash flow from operating activities.*

1 *Profit* is normally positive and is an inflow of cash. Where the business makes a loss, this outflow of cash is shown in brackets.

   Any increase in retained profits can be established by comparing the statement of financial position at the end of the period with the statement of financial position at the beginning of the period. The figure required for a cash flow statement is profit before deducting taxation, which is found from the income statement

2 *Depreciation* is shown as an inflow of cash. Profit is shown as if all expenses are outflows of cash. But depreciation is an expense that is not paid; there is no outflow of cash for depreciation. It is therefore necessary for depreciation to be added back to profit. It is an oversimplification to say that cash flow consists of profit plus depreciation; but it is useful to remember this as being the first part of a cash flow statement.

3 Any *increase in working capital* is an outflow of cash, or a negative cash flow, and so it is shown in brackets. This usually means that profits have been used to finance higher levels of inventories and payables. Any reduction in working capital is shown as a cash inflow.

   The main components of working capital are inventories, receivables and payables and these can be shown individually instead of using a single figure for working capital.

   Any increase in inventories and receivables is shown as an outflow of cash; any decrease in inventories and receivables is shown as an inflow of cash.

   Any increase in payables is shown as an inflow of cash; any decrease in payables is shown as an outflow of cash. This is explained as follows:

   a *Receivables* – Not all the revenue from sales (which is included in the profit figure) is immediately a cash inflow. Where the receivables have increased, this is treated as an outflow of cash (to reduce the inflow included in profit arising from sales). Where the receivables have gone down during a period, more money has been received from them, and the reduction is treated as an inflow of cash.

   b *Payables* – Not all the expenses that have been recorded in arriving at the profit figure have in fact been paid. Where the amount of payables has increased, this is treated as an inflow of cash (to reduce the outflow included in profit in respect of purchases and expenses). Where the amount of payables has decreased during the period, this is treated as an outflow of cash (because more has been paid out than has been charged as an expense in calculating profit).

   c *Inventories* – In calculating profit, only the cost of goods that have been sold is treated as an expense. The cost of goods that have not yet been sold (closing inventory) is not yet an expense; but those goods still have to be paid for. Any increase in inventory is therefore treated as an outflow of cash. Any reduction in inventory is treated as an inflow of cash.

4 *Interest expense* is added back since it might not have actually been paid but might be payable at a later date and have been, at least to a degree, accrued.

   = Cash generated from operating activities. Items 1 to 4 are subtotalled to show the cash flow from trading activities

5 *Interest paid* is an outflow of cash, and is shown in brackets. Any interest receivable is an inflow of cash. In some cases the interest receivable is greater than the interest payable, and so the net figure is an inflow of cash.

6 *Taxation paid* is an outflow of cash, and is shown in brackets. Sometimes there is a cash inflow where there has been a tax rebate, perhaps after the company has been making losses.

7 *Dividend paid* in the year

   = *Net cash flow from operating activities*

The first part of a cash flow statement, dealing with cash flows from *operating activities*, is often the most complex. The second and third parts of the cash flow statement deal with *investing activities* (buying and selling non-current assets and investments) and *financing activities* (raising additional finance by issuing additional shares or debentures; or perhaps reducing share capital and borrowings). The reconciliation of cash flow and profit for Ebbing plc is shown in the form of a cash flow statement in Illustration 6.2. Some additional information[6] has been included to make it more realistic.

International Accounting Standard 7 specifies that cash flow statements should report inflows and outflows of cash under three headings, as follows:

1 *Operating activities* – This should include all the receipts and payments resulting from sales and costs based on the profit figure. Not all the profit figure shows up as cash because of changes in current assets and current liabilities, as was illustrated with Ebbing plc in Illustrations 6.1 and 6.2.

ILLUSTRATION 6.2

Cash flow statement of Ebbing plc for the year ended 31 December year 2

Operating activities	£	£	
Profit before taxation		44,500	
Depreciation		16,000	
		60,500	
Increase in working capital			
Inventories	(40,000)		
Receivables	(30,000)		
Payables	20,000	(50,000)	
Interest expense		4,000	
Cash flow from operating activities		14,500	
Interest paid	(4,000)		
Taxation paid	(13,500)		
Dividends paid	(16,000)		
		(33,500)	
Net cash flow from operating activities		(19,000)	(A) Total inflow from operating activities
Investing activities			
Purchase of non-current assets[7]		(116,000)	(B) Investing outflow
Financing activities			
New loan issued		10,000	(C) Financing outflow
Decrease in cash		(125,000)	Net outflow A – B – C
Cash at beginning of year 2		160,000	
Cash at end of year 2		35,000	

---

6 Additional information: depreciation £16,000; interest paid £4,000; taxation paid £13,500; dividends paid £16,000. The increase in retained profits for year 2 is still £15,000, but profit before taxation is (£15,000 + £13,500 taxation + £4,000 interest + £16,000 dividends =) £48,500.

7 Non-current assets at the end of year 1 were £100,000. In year 2 the amount deducted for depreciation was £16,000. This would have reduced the amount to £84,000. But at the end of year 2 the amount shown for fixed assets was £200,000; expenditure on additional non-current assets must therefore have been £116,000.

Depreciation has to be shown separately. It is treated as an expense in calculating profit as if cash has been paid out. But, unlike other expenses, no cash is paid out for depreciation. To arrive at a cash flow figure it is therefore necessary to add depreciation (and amortization) to the net profit figure.

Interest and taxation paid and dividends are also usually included as operating activities since they are likely to occur every year, although dividends can be shown as a financing activity.

Ebbing plc made a decent enough profit which, when added to depreciation, produced a cash flow of £60,500. But after financing the increase in working capital, and paying interest, taxation and dividends, there was a deficit of only £19,000, which was clearly not enough to pay for additional non-current assets.

2   *Investing activities* – This includes all payments for additional non-current assets, and expenditure on buying investments in other businesses. Cash inflows include receipts from disposals of non-current assets. Ebbing plc spent £116,000 on additional non-current assets.

3   *Financing activities* – The main cash flows here are from issuing or redeeming shares and long-term loans. Cash outflows include redemption of loans and a company may buy back some of its own shares.

Ebbing plc raised a loan of £10,000 but did not raise any share capital during the period as it had enough cash to meet its needs in this year since, fortunately, it had sufficient money to pay for them because it started the year with £160,000 in the bank.

The cash flows arising from operating activities is perhaps the most important figure, and it should be positive, even after paying interest, taxes and dividends. There is a cash deficit from operating activities in Ebbing plc (Illustration 6.2) but there is a cash surplus from operations in Reet Aylor plc (Illustration 6.3).

In year 3 Reet Aylor plc generated £2.8m from operating activities. But this was not enough to finance the £9.3m it spent on property and equipment. It raised some money from selling off equipment (£0.4m); but the net payment for investing activities was £8.9m. In most businesses this would lead to the need to raise additional funds through long-term loans or issuing shares. But Reet Aylor plc started the year with £7m of cash in the bank, which was more than enough to finance the shortfall, and to pay the dividend for the year. The company decided to pay back some of its borrowings, and ended the year with a £1m overdraft.

The financing activities in year 4 were rather different. The cash generated from operating activities was higher at £4.1m, but this was still not enough to finance the £6.3m of additional non-current assets in year 4. The shortfall was financed by a substantial share issue which raised £3.3m. The additional funds raised were also used to pay off the £1m overdraft.

In a reasonably successful company the cash generated by operating activities should be enough to pay the regular annual payments of interest, tax and dividends, and some increase in non-current assets. Where there is a substantial increase in non-current assets it is usually necessary for some financing activities to raise additional long-term funds.

In Reet Aylor plc the increase in dividend was very small considering the substantial increase in share capital. If the additional shares were issued towards the end of year 4, a substantial increase in the amount of dividends paid might be expected in year 5.

6.4 Interpreting Cash Flow Statements

Free cash flow

The term 'free cash flow' is widely used by financial journalists. The idea is that profit plus depreciation generate additional cash flows; some of this has to be used to finance increases in working capital, and to pay interest and taxation. What then remains is free cash flow: companies are free to use it how they wish: to pay dividends; to invest in non-current assets or other businesses; and to repay borrowings or share capital.

ILLUSTRATION 6.3

Cash flow statement of Reet Aylor plc for the Year Ended 31 December

	Year 3	Year 4
	£000	£000
Cash flows from operating activities		
Profit before tax	6,800	7,300
Depreciation	5,700	6,100
	12,500	13,400
Increase in trade receivables	(2,000)	(1,700)
Increase in inventories	(4,100)	(3,800)
Increase in trade payables	200	300
Interest expense	1,100	900
Cash flow from operations	7,700	9,100
Interest paid	(1,100)	(900)
Income taxes paid	(2,500)	(2,700)
Dividends paid	(1,300)	(1,400)
Net cash flow from operating activities	2,800	4,100
Cash flows from investing activities		
Proceeds from disposal of equipment	400	300
Purchase of property and equipment	(9,300)	(6,600)
Net cash outflow from investing activities	(8,900)	(6,300)
Cash flows from financing activities		
Proceeds of issue of shares	200	3,300
Repayment of borrowings	(2,100)	–
Net cash used in financing activities	(1,900)	3,300
Net (decrease)/increase in cash	(8,000)	1,100
Opening cash	7,000	(1,000)
Closing cash	(1,000)	100

It is perhaps easiest to regard free cash flow as being the net amount of cash arising from operating activities. For example, in Reet Aylor plc (Illustration 6.3) the amount was £4.1m in year 3.

Unfortunately, there is no clear definition of what is meant by free cash flow. Most companies do not identify such a figure. Some companies who show it use a variety of different definitions. Although companies are generally 'free' to decide whether or not to pay dividends, care is needed in interpreting cash flow statements: some companies show a free cash flow figure *before* deducting dividends while others show free cash flow *after* dividends, as in Reet Aylor plc.

The treatment of non-current assets is also a problem. Businesses regularly need to replace some of their non-current assets as they come to the end of their lives; cash flow is not free if it has to be used for essential replacements. But some non-current assets are purchased as part of an expansion plan, and companies are free to decide whether or not to go ahead with such expansions. It would be sensible to say that free cash flow is arrived at after payment for essential replacements of non-current assets, but before funding any expansion. Unfortunately, the distinction between essential replacements, and non-current assets for expansion is hard to determine. Sometimes an arbitrary compromise is used, such as deciding that one-third of expenditure on non-current assets is for essential replacements; free cash flow is arrived at after deducting such a proportion of expenditure on non-current assets.

Cash flow ratios

Conventional ratio analysis can be adapted to use cash flow figures rather than profit figures. It is important that, in such analyses, a clear definition of cash flow is used consistently. The most straight-forward figure to use is the net cash flow generated from operations in the first part of a published cash flow statement. It is seen as being a key indicator of a business's ability to generate cash flows from its operations to pay dividends, repay debt and finance investments in fixed assets to maintain and increase its operating capability (without having to raise additional long-term share or loan capital).

Unfortunately, IAS 7 does not have a firm definition of what is to be included in net cash flow generated from operations with regard to interest and dividends. Interest paid is probably best included under operating activities, but the standard also allows it to be included under financing activities.

Interest and dividends received are probably best included under operating activities, but the standard also allows them to be included under investing activities (as they are the product of investments that have been made). Dividends paid are probably best included under financing activities, but the standard also allows them to be included under operating activities.

The following cash flow ratios are useful provided the definition used for cash flow is clear and consistently applied. The term is sometimes used to mean simply profit plus depreciation. It would be better to use the total figure for operating activities taken from the cash flow statement.

Interest and dividend cover

These figures can be calculated to indicate the extent to which interest and dividend payments are covered by cash flows generated. The figures for Reet Aylor plc are as follows:

	Year 3	Year 4
Net cash from operating activities plus dividends[8]	£4.1m	£5.5m
Dividends paid	£1.3m	£1.4m
Dividend times cover	3.15 times	3.93 times

The dividend cover has increased because, although the dividend payment has increased a little, the operating cash flow has increased by a bigger proportion.

	Year 3	Year 4
Net cash from operating activities plus dividends[9]	£4.1m	£5.5m
Interest	£1.1m	£0.9m
Cash flow available to cover interest	£5.2m	£6.4m
Interest times cover	4.73 times	7.11 times

The cover has increased because the amount of interest payable has reduced (because some borrowings have been repaid) and operating cash flow has increased.

Cash return on capital employed

This figure can be calculated to indicate the extent to which the business generates cash (as opposed to profit) for the shareholders.

$$\frac{\text{Net cash from operating activities}}{\text{Equity}} \times 100$$

---

[8] This figure is taken before deducting dividends; it is all available to cover dividends.

[9] This figure is provided *after* interest has been deducted; the interest is therefore added back to establish the amount available to cover interest.

Cash flow per share

This figure can be calculated in the same way as earnings per share (EPS), but using cash flow from operating activities instead of profit. The cash flow figure is divided by the number of shares in issue. Comparing cash flow per share with EPS is much the same as comparing total cash flow with total earnings.

Published cash flow statements

Published cash flow statements can be quite daunting and include many details and complexities that are hard to understand, even after wading through pages of complicated notes. Generally, figures shown in brackets are outflows of cash, and figures not shown in brackets are inflows of cash. But the proliferation of subtotals and negative figures (outflows) can be confusing, and sometimes the use of brackets is not consistent. It can be helpful to begin by summarizing the main figures, and then asking a number of key questions. The following are likely to be helpful in respect of Reet Aylor plc.

	Year 3	Year 4
	£000	£000
Cash from operating activities	2,800	4,100
Cash (used in) investing activities	(8,900)	(6,300)
Cash (used in)/from financing activities	(1,900)	3,300
(Decrease)/increase in cash	(8,000)	1,100

Suggested questions in interpreting cash flow statements:

1 Was there a positive cash flow from operating activities? If so, how was it used? If not, why not?
2 Has working capital increased, and how was it financed? Has there been a reduction in working capital, and what is the significance of this reduction?
3 Have there been significant investing activities? Is there a substantial increase in non-current assets? Have there been substantial investments in other businesses? How were these financed?
4 Has there been a reduction in investments in non-current assets and other businesses? How much money was raised, and how was this used?
5 Has the business been raising substantial long-term financing? Why do these funds seem to be needed? Have they been invested in long-term assets? Were they needed to finance shortfalls in cash flows from operating activities? Were they needed to pay off overdrafts?
6 Are the cash flows from financing activities negative (i.e. has there been a reduction in long-term funding)? What does this suggest? Is the business contracting? Or are cash flows from operating activities sufficient to finance expansion?
7 Has one form of long-term capital been used to redeem another (perhaps issuing shares to repay debentures)? Why might this have been done?
8 Was the amount of dividend covered by cash flows from operating activities? Does the dividend appear to be justified by available cash flows?
9 Did the cash balance increase or decrease during the year? Why – what were the main contributors to this?

A cash flow statement provides useful information in relation to questions such as these, but it may not provide full answers. It is important (as always with interpretation of financial statements) to compare this year's figures with the previous year's and to identify trends. It is also usually necessary to examine the statement of financial position and income statement for further explanation. All three statements should be considered together.

ILLUSTRATION 6.4

A published cash flow statement

Statement of group cash flows of Thorntons plc, the chocolate retailer, for years ended June

	2011	2010
	£000	£000
Net cash outflow from operating activities[10]		
Profit before tax	852	7,582
Depreciation and amortization	12,197	11,244
Loss/(profit) on disposal of non-current assets	148	(76)
Other items	(110)	379
Increase in inventories	(6,625)	(5,023)
Decrease/(increase) in receivables	264	(1,723)
Increase in payables	7,265	3,265
Increase in provisions	2,162	609
Increase in post-employment benefit obligations	(1,330)	(1,134)
Cash generated from operations	14,823	15,123
Interest received	12	177
Interest paid	(1,802)	(1,890)
Taxes paid	(1,392)	(2,255)
Dividends paid	(4,054)	(4,553)
Net cash outflow from operating activities	7,587	6,602
Cash flows from investing activities		
Purchase of property, plant, equipment	(4,208)	(4,605)
Proceeds of sale of property, plant, equipment	46	136
Net cash outflow from investing activities	(4,162)	(4,469)
Cash flows from financing activities		
Net proceeds from issue of shares	–	18
Capital element of finance leases rental payments	(2,499)	(3,613)
Borrowings (repaid)/advanced	(800)	2,500
Net cash outflow from financing activities	(3,299)	(1,095)
Net increase in cash and cash equivalents	126	1,038
Cash and equivalents at beginning of year	1,626	588
Cash and equivalents at end of year	1,752	1,626

Interpretation

A quick overview of Thorntons' 2011 cash flow statement (see Illustration 6.4) shows that it generated a small profit from operations but its cash flow from operations, after paying interest, taxation and dividends, was substantial and not much lower than in 2010. Although there was a substantial increase in inventories, there was also a substantial increase in payables. This might have an effect on Thorntons' relationship with its creditors. There were substantial purchases of non-current assets and repayments of loans and payments against assets acquired on long-term lease arrangements.

In 2010, the pattern of cash flows is quite similar, although there was a significant improvement in credit control since the receivables were reduced in the year. In both years there were substantial repayments of loans and no share issues. Perhaps, given the state of the economy and difficulties experienced in the retail sector, the company was happy to increase its cash balances and survive the period.

---

[10] Taken from Note 32, regrouped and simplied.

6.5 Format for Cash Flow Statements

A company's statement of financial position shows how much cash (bank) it has. Comparing this year's statement of financial position with last year's shows whether it has more or less cash now than a year ago, or whether its overdraft has increased. It is worth comparing the profit that the company has made with what has happened to its cash balances.

The Stuaper Company (Illustration 6.5) made a profit during year 2, but it ended up with less cash at the end of the year than it had at the beginning. This is not unusual. If we compare the statements of financial position at the end of years 1 and 2, we can see what has happened to a lot of its cash. Where assets have increased (items 1, 2 and 3 below), we can assume that cash has flowed out of the business to pay for them. Where liabilities have been reduced (items 4 and 5), we can assume that cash has flowed out of the business to (re)pay them. In total £140,000 has flowed out of the business to buy more assets or to pay liabilities.

ILLUSTRATION 6.5

Simplified statement of financial position of Stuaper Company as at 31 December

	Year 1		Year 2	
	£000	£000	£000	£000
Non-current assets		200		250
Current assets				
Inventories and	60		80	
Receivables	40		60	
Cash	160	260	40	180
		460		430
Current liabilities				
Trade payables		40		30
Non-current liabilities				
Borrowings		70		30
Equity				
Share capital	200		200	
Retained earnings	150	350	170	370
		460		430

Simplified income statement of Stuaper Company for the year ended 31 December

	Year 2
	£000
Sales revenue	660
Cost of sales	440
Gross profit	220
Operating expenses	120
Operating profit	100
Finance expenses	(7)
Profit before tax	93
Corporation tax	(30)
Profit after tax	63

Cash balances have decreased from £160,000 to £40,000: an outflow of £120,000. But these outflows of cash have been partly offset by the fact that the company has made a profit. The statement of financial position shows that retained earnings have increased from £150,000 to £170,000: the company must have made (at least) £20,000[11] profit.

	£000
1 Non-current assets have increased, so it seems that it has bought more non-current assets during the year	50
2 Inventories have increased, so it seems that more money is tied up in inventories	20
3 Receivables have increased, so it seems that more money is tied up in receivables	20
4 Current liabilities have gone down, so it seems that more money has been paid out	10
5 Borrowings have gone down, so it seems that cash has been paid out to repay them	40
6 Total outflows of cash	140
7 Reduction in cash balance	120
8 Increase in retained earnings	20

One way of preparing a cash flow statement is simply to compare each item on this year's statement of financial position with last year's. Every increase in assets, or reduction in liabilities,[12] is an outflow of cash. Every decrease in assets, or increase in liabilities,[13] is an inflow of cash. Arithmetically this will reconcile this year's cash balance with last year's. But this is not satisfactory for a number of reasons:

1   A reconciliation is not an explanation and it is better to present a cash flow statement in accordance with international accounting standards to make comparisons easier.

2   One simple figure for an increase (or decrease) in non-current assets is not satisfactory because (at least) two things have usually happened:

   a   additional non-current assets have been bought (and some may have been revalued or disposed of);

   b   non-current assets have been depreciated.

   Careful examination of the notes to the accounts might show that the depreciation charge for the year was £25,000, and £75,000 was spent on buying additional non-current assets. The net figure of £50,000 does not tell us what we want to know.

3   The £20,000 increase in retained earnings is not a very useful figure. It is more useful to need to know how much the **profit before tax** was (before deducting taxation and dividends) as a first step to finding out how much cash was generated from operations. If we find that the company paid dividends of £43,000 during the year, the total profit after tax would be £63,000, leaving additional retained earnings of £20,000.

IAS 7 requires that cash flows should be classified under three headings:

1   Operating activities

2   Investing activities

3   Financing activities

Although international standards are not totally prescriptive about what should be included under each of the three headings, Illustration 6.6 complies with generally accepted practice.

---

[11] Some profits have been paid out as dividends. The statement of financial position shows only the *retained* earnings.

[12] Or equity.

[13] Or equity.

ILLUSTRATION 6.6

Summarized statement of financial position of Kione Halby as at 31 December

	Year 1		Year 2	
	£000	£000	£000	£000
Non-current assets				
Machinery at net book value	20		15	
Vehicles at cost	–	20	45	60
Current assets				
Inventories	30		50	
Receivables	30		35	
Cash	10	70	–	85
Total assets		90		145
Current liabilities				
Trade payables		20	18	
Overdraft			4	22
Non-current liabilities				
Debentures				50
Equity				
Share capital	40		40	
Retained earnings	30	70	33	73
		90		145

Summarized income statement for the year ended 31 December year 2

	£000
Sales revenue	200
Cost of sales	(170)
Gross profit	30
Profit on sale of non-current asset	1
Depreciation of machinery	(5)
Other operating expenses	(11)
Profit for the year	15

Additional information

1 During the year machinery, which had a net book value of £3,000, was sold for £4,000.

2 The motor vehicles were bought on the last day of year 2, and no depreciation will be charged on them until year 3.
3 Dividends paid were £12,000.

Ignore interest and taxation.

Kione Halby Cash flow statement for the year ended 31 December year 2

	£000	£000
Cash generated from operating activities		
Profit before tax		15
Depreciation		5
Other items		
Profit on sale of machinery		(1)
		19

Continued

ILLUSTRATION 6.6 (Continued)		
Increase in working capital		
Increase in inventories	(20)	
Increase in receivables	(5)	
Decrease in payables	(2)	(27)
Interest paid	–	
Dividends paid	(12)	(12)
Net cash outflow from operations		(20)
Cash used in investing activities		
Purchase of machinery	(3)	
Purchase of vehicles	(45)	
Proceeds of disposal of non-current assets	4	(44)
Cash used in financing activities		
Debentures issued	50	50
Decrease in cash during year		(14)
Opening cash balance		10
Closing cash balance		(4)

The net book value of machinery at the beginning of the year was £20,000; machinery with a net book value of £3,000 was sold, and depreciation of £5,000 was charged; these would reduce the balance to £12,000. The balance at the end of the year was £15,000, indicating that additional machinery of £3,000 had been purchased.

In the above statement the convention has been adopted that outflows of cash are shown in brackets.

Cash generated from/used in operating activities

The above presentation shows cash generated from operating activities in three stages:

1 *Profit before tax plus depreciation and similar items and interest expense* – This is almost always an inflow of cash. Even when a business makes a loss this is often more than offset by the depreciation charge for the year. The figure for Kione Halby is an inflow of £19,000.

2 *Changes in working capital* – This is typically an outflow of cash when a business is expanding. But careful management, reducing inventories and receivables, and delaying paying payables, can produce an inflow of cash. Kione Halby had an outflow of £27,000.

3 *Interest, taxation and dividends paid* – These are usually outflows of cash. However, sometimes a company receives more interest than it pays out; and negative tax charges do exist (for example, after losses, and/or substantial writing-down allowances for new non-current assets).

Illustration 6.6 is simplified, and Kione Halby made no payments for interest or taxation. Overall, in a successful business, there should be a cash inflow from operating activities. But with Kione Halby there was an overall outflow of cash of £8,000 from operating activities because of the substantial increase in working capital.

Cash generated from/used in investing activities

The main items here are purchase of non-current assets, or other businesses, which are outflows of cash. There are usually some inflows as well resulting from sales of non-current assets or parts of the

business. Kione Halby paid £48,000 for additional non-current assets, which was slightly offset by receipts of £4,000 for selling old non-current assets. The net cash outflow was £44,000.

Cash generated from/used in financing activities

Inflows and outflows are about equally likely under this heading. Dividends paid are classified as payments of operating activities, although it can also be classified as an outflow of cash under financing activities. The repayment or redemption of debentures and shares. Inflows result from additional borrowings, or from raising more share capital. Kione Halby obviously needed a lot more cash (to finance the increases in working capital and the additional non-current assets), and it raised £50,000 by issuing debentures.

The total of the three categories of cash flow added together show a net outflow of £14,000, as follows:

	£
Cash used in operating activities	(20,000)
Cash used in investing activities	(44,000)
Cash generated from financing activities	50,000
Net cash outflow	(14,000)

The total of the cash flows in each of these categories must be equal to the difference between the cash that the business had at the beginning of the year, and the amount at the end of the year. Kione Halby started the year with £10,000 in the bank; it ended the year with an overdraft of £4,000; this means that £14,000 had flowed out of the business. The cash flow statement shows the main items that made up that outflow.

6.6 How to Prepare a Cash Flow Statement

In order to prepare a cash flow statement it is important to have a clear format in mind, such as the one shown in Illustration 6.6. Then it is helpful to list each of the items that have to be found from the statement of financial position, income statement or notes to the accounts, as shown in Illustration 6.7. It is a good idea to leave a line or two between each item as there are likely to be additional figures or 'adjustments'[14] to be slotted in.

There is almost no limit to how complicated financial statements can be, and a competent and experienced accountant would be needed to produce a decent cash flow statement for any large, listed company. The following provides a guide to how the main figures can be found in reasonably straightforward situation. The items are numbered in Illustration 6.7 for convenience; this numbering has no official status. The format illustrated complies with international standards, but some variations are also acceptable.

1 Profit before tax should be easy to find on an income statement, even if it is not separately labelled as such.

It may be useful to see what cash flows have been generated before deducting interest, taxation and dividends, but these obviously have to be paid. They are usually shown as separate items (8, 9 and 10 above).

2 Depreciation is regarded as being a cash inflow because profit before tax is calculated after charging depreciation for the year, as if depreciation was an outflow of cash. But it is not an outflow; it is charged as an expense, and so has to be added back to profit as if it is a cash inflow.

---

[14] It sounds better if you are 'making an adjustment' rather than just correcting a mistake!

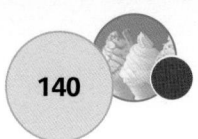

ILLUSTRATION 6.7

Cash generated from operating activities

1 Profit before tax

2 Depreciation

3 Other items such as profit or loss on the sale of non-current assets

4 Interest expense

(Increase)/decrease in working capital

5 (Increase)/decrease in inventories

6 (Increase)/decrease in receivables

7 Increase /(decrease) in payables

   = *Cash inflow/(outflow) from operating activities*

8 Interest paid

9 Taxation paid

10 Dividends paid*

   = *Net cash inflow (outflow) from operating activities*

Cash used in investing activities

11 Purchase of non-current assets

12 Disposal of non-current assets

Cash used in financing activities

13 Issue/(repayment) of loan

14 Issue/(redemption of shares

Increase/(decrease) in cash during year

+ Opening cash balance

= Closing cash balance

* Can be shown as a financing activity

Depreciation is not usually shown as a separate item on the face of an income statement. It is tucked away in the note; usually the note that applies to non-current assets on the statement of financial position. There is a schedule that shows the balance at the beginning of the year[15] for non-current assets: the balance at the end of the year, and the explanation of the differences; additional non-current assets acquired during the year; and disposals of non-current assets during the year. There is a similar schedule for depreciation showing the total cumulative depreciation at the beginning of the year, the depreciation charge for the year, the amount of depreciation for non-current assets disposed of, and the total cumulative depreciation remaining at the end of the year.

3 There are often other items, such as depreciation, which have been charged as expenses, but there has been no outflow of cash. These have to be added back to profit. They include: amortization; write-offs for impairment of goodwill and other assets; and increases in provisions.

Some of these items can be the other way around: profits have been boosted by items that produce no cash flows, and which therefore have to be deducted from operating profit. A reduction in a provision is an example of this.

There is also a problem with any profit or loss arising from the sale of non-current assets. If a non-current asset is sold during the year for more than its net book value, the profit arising is

---

[15] The non-current assets are shown at cost (or revalued amount).

correctly treated as part of profit in preparing the income statement. The total amount of cash received on disposal of a non-current asset is shown under item 10, and this includes the amount of profit as part of the cash inflow. As the profit on disposal cannot be included twice on a cash flow statement (as part of profit, and as part of the proceeds of disposal), it has to be taken out of the profit figure; this is done by deducting it from profit – as if it is a cash outflow.

If a non-current asset is sold for less than its net book value, the loss is correctly charged against profit when the income statement is prepared (even if it is not separately identified). But as there is no cash outflow for that loss, the amount has to be added back to profit in preparing the cash flow statement. The proceeds of disposal are shown under item 10 in the cash flow statement.

4 The interest expense must be added back, too, because it might be an accrued expense and not paid at all or to an extent in the year.

5 The increase or decrease in inventories is easily calculated by comparing this year's statement of financial position with last year's. If the difference between the two inventories figures is an increase, the amount is shown on the cash flow statement as an outflow of cash. If inventories have decreased, the cash flow statement shows this as an inflow.

6 The increase or decrease in receivables is easily calculated by comparing this year's statement of financial position with last year's. If the difference between the two receivables figures is an increase, the amount is shown on the cash flow statement as an outflow of cash. If receivables have decreased, the cash flow statement shows this as an inflow.

7 The increase in payables is easily calculated by comparing this year's statement of financial position with last year's. If the difference between the two payables figures is an increase, the amount is shown on the cash flow statement as an inflow of cash. If payables have decreased, the cash flow statement shows this as an outflow.

8 It is easy to find the interest charge for the year on the income statement: it is labelled 'finance costs'. In some cases there is also 'finance income' (interest receivable), and it is acceptable to show a single net figure for interest on a cash flow statement.

The amount shown on the cash flow statement should be the amount actually paid (or received) during the year, which is sometimes different from the amount shown on the income statement. The income statement should show the amount *due and chargeable as an expense* during the year; the cash flow statement should show the amount actually paid. Sometimes an amount due for the year ended on 31 December is not actually paid until January of the following year. The interest paid, to be shown in the cash flow statement, is the interest payable in the opening statement of financial position, plus the interest expense in the income statement less the interest payable in the closing statement of financial position.

9 It is easy to find the taxation charge for the year on the income statement. Sometimes this might not be the same as the amount actually paid during the year, which is required for the cash flow statement. The amount actually paid can be calculated if sufficient information is available, as shown in Illustration 6.8. It is much like the calculation of interest paid. The tax paid in the year, to be shown in the cash flow statement, is the tax liability at the beginning of the year, plus the tax charge in the income statement minus the tax liability at the year end.

10 The dividend paid in the year is usually disclosed in a note to the accounts, very often in the 'movements in equity' note.

11 The amount paid for additional non-current assets can be found in the (statement of financial position) notes to the accounts, as explained in 2 above (additional non-current assets acquired during the year). There may be several different items included under the general heading of non-current assets.

Any increase in the amount of non-current assets that is due to a revaluation involves no cash flows and is not included on a cash flow statement.

12 The amount included on a cash flow statement for disposals of non-current assets must be the actual amount of cash received, not the book value. The book value of assets disposed of is easily

ILLUSTRATION 6.8

Statement of financial position extract from current liabilities

	At 31 December Year 5	At 31 December Year 6
Corporation tax	£50,000	£60,000

The income statement showed a tax charge of £58,000 for the year ended 31 December year 6.

To calculate the amount actually paid during year 6 we can assume that the whole of the £50,000 shown as a current liability at the end of year 5 was paid during that year.

During year 6 an additional £58,000 became payable, making a total of £108,000 due to be paid. By the end of year 6 only £60,000 was still due to be paid. We can therefore assume that the difference, £48,000, was actually paid, and this is the figure to be shown on the cash flow statement. A similar calculation is made to determine the interest actually paid in the year.

---

established. As explained in 2 above, the statement of financial position notes to the accounts in respect of non-current assets show both the cost[16] of the assets disposed of, and the depreciation relating to them; the difference between the two is the net book value. The sale proceeds are the book value, plus any profit arising, or minus any loss arising. Profits or losses on disposals of non-current assets are included in the income statement, but it may be necessary to hunt around in the notes to find the amounts.

13 If any loans have been repaid the amounts can be established by comparing this year's statement of financial position with last year's. There may be increases or reductions in non-current borrowings, or both. Details are provided in the notes to the financial statements.

14 Other items include the cash inflows arising from issue of any shares during the year, including the amount of any premium. The company may also have bought its own shares and cancelled them, which involves an outflow of cash. The overall picture is easily seen by comparing two years' statements of financial position, and more detail (such as the number of shares issued or redeemed) is provided in the notes to the accounts.

📖 Summary

In many businesses, generating profits and generating cash flows go hand in hand. Good profits are likely to result in healthy cash flows. But the two are unlikely to be identical. In many circumstances the profit (or loss) for the year can be very different from the increase (or decrease) in cash. The differences between the two show up well on a cash flow statement. Having cash available to meet liabilities as they fall due is essential for business survival, and healthy businesses should generate healthy cash flows. Businesses also need to generate profits if they are to survive and be healthy. If a business makes a profit, its wealth increases. That increase in wealth is used in many different ways (such as paying dividends, and investing in more assets); it is unlikely to be matched by an exactly equal increase in cash.

It is vital that users of accounts can see where cash has been generated and how it has been spent in terms of operating activities, investment in non-current assets and elsewhere and in financing, in order to see the 'quality' of profits.

We could debate whether cash flow or profit is more important to the survival and success of businesses. That would be a bit like debating whether eating or drinking is more important to the survival and success of people. Both are essential.

---

[16] Or revalued amount.

➡ Review of key points

- Profit is not the same as cash flow. The accruals concept may be seen as being the theoretical justification and explanation of the difference.
- A cash flow statement provides a reconciliation between profit before tax for the year and the net increase or decrease in cash during the year.
- A company's operating profit may be used to finance higher levels of inventory and receivables; to pay interest, taxation and dividends, and to buy additional non-current assets.
- A detailed cash flow statement shows other differences between cash flow and profit in a standardized format.
- A cash flow statement should be interpreted alongside the related statements of financial position and income statements, and can reveal important aspects of a company's performance.
- Some differences between cash flow and profit are relatively minor, relating to the timing of receipts and payments compared with the timing of recognition of revenues and expenses.
- Depreciation is an important expense in calculating profit; there is no equivalent payment in cash terms.
- Cash *in*flows are decreases in assets and increases in liabilities, while cash *de*creases are increases in assets and decreases in liabilities.
- Some of the biggest receipts and payments (such as issue of shares; purchase of non-current assets; paying back loans) have no direct effect on profit.
- The availability of cash to meet liabilities as they fall due is essential to business survival. Making profits is essential if the business is to become 'better off'.

! Self-testing questions

1 What is meant by the 'accruals concept'? Why is it important in financial accounting?

2 In what circumstances is a very profitable business likely to find that it has serious cash shortages?

3 Is it possible for a company to make losses year after year, but still to increase its cash balances? Explain.

4 What is meant by 'free cash flow'? Estimate the amounts of free cash flow for

   a Ebbing plc for year 2 (Illustration 6.2)

   b Reet Aylors for years 3 and 4 (Illustration 6.3)

5 You are given the cash flow statements for the last two years for Deek Lining plc, which are as follows:

Cash flow statement of Deek Lining plc for the year ended 31 December

	Year 3 £000	Year 4 £000
Cash flows from operating activities		
Profit before tax	3,200	(1,350)
Depreciation	2,600	2,800
	5,800	1,450
Interest expense	200	150
(Increase) Decrease in trade receivables	(600)	300
(Increase) Decrease in inventories	(400)	200
(Decrease) Increase in trade payables	(100)	100
Cash inflow from operations	4,900	2,200
Interest paid	(200)	(150)
Income taxes paid	(1,300)	(100)
Dividend paid	(600)	(700)
Net cash flow from operating activities	2,800	1,250
Cash flows from investing activities		
Proceeds from disposal of equipment	100	1,100
Purchase of property and equipment	(3,700)	(150)
Net cash from investing activities	(3,600)	950
Cash flows from financing activities		
Proceeds of issue of shares	–	–
Increase (Decrease) in borrowings	200	(1,000)
Net raised cash from (used in)		
financing activities	200	(1,000)
Net (decrease)/increase in cash	(600)	1,200
Opening cash	700	(100)
Closing cash	100	1,100

An extract from the chairman's statement reads as follows:

> Year 4 was another successful year, producing a positive cash flow which enabled us to pay off a substantial amount of borrowings, to invest in new fixed assets, and to increase the dividend for ordinary shareholders.

Critically appraise this statement.

6 You are required to produce a cash flow statement for Daubyhaven Ltd for the year ended 31 December year 2.

Summarized statement of financial position of Daubyhaven Ltd as at 31 December

	Year 1 £000	£000	Year 2 £000	£000
Non-current assets				
Machinery at cost	120		130	
Provision for depreciation	(60)	60	(68)	62
Current assets				
Inventories	30		50	
Receivables	30		35	
Cash	10	70	–	85
Total assets		130		147
Current liabilities				
Trade payables		20	18	
Overdraft			12	30
Non-current liabilities				
Debentures		30		20
Equity				
Share capital	50		60	
Retained earnings	30	80	37	97
		130		147

During the year ending 31 December year 2

a   A machine that had originally cost £15,000, and on which £12,000 depreciation had been charged, was sold for £4,500.

b   Operating profit, including the profit on the sale of the machine, was £35,000.

c   Interest of £2,000, taxation of £8,000 and dividends of £18,000 were paid.

7   You are required to prepare a cash flow statement for Fistard Neash plc for the year ended 31 December Year 6

Summarized statement of financial position of Fistard Neash plc as at 31 December

	Year 5		Year 6	
Non-current assets	£m	£m	£m	£m
Intangible assets		100		90
Property, plant and equipment	120		140	
Provision for depreciation	(50)	70	(66)	74
Current assets				
Inventories	40		65	
Receivables	60		55	
Cash	10	110	8	128
Total assets		280		292
Current liabilities				
Trade payables		45		40
Non-current liabilities				
Debentures		55		6
Equity				
Share capital	150		170	
Share premium	–		40	
Retained earnings	30	180	36	246
		280		292

Income statement for year ended 31 December year 6

	£m
Sales revenue	440
Cost of sales	(330)
Gross profit	110
Profit on sale of Scottish factory	7
Distribution costs	(47)
Administrative expenses	(40)
Impairment of goodwill	(10)
Operating profit	20
Finance costs	(2)
Profit before taxation	18
Corporation tax	(4)
Profit for the year	14

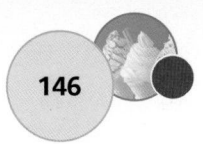
During the year ending 31 December year 6

a The Scottish factory had originally cost £24m, and depreciation of £8m had been charged on it. It was sold for £23m.

b Dividends paid were £8m.

c Interest of £2m and taxation of £4m were paid.

Assessment questions

1 Explain the effect of the accruals concept on the treatment of inventories, capital expenditure, receivables and payables.

2 Shareholders are mainly interested in a company's ability to pay dividends. If a company increases the amount of cash it has available during the year, it is able to pay more dividends. A company should therefore aim to maximize the amount of cash it has available. Explain the flaws in these statements.

3 You are given the following cash flow statements for Ink Reasing plc.

Cash flow statement of Ink Reising plc for the year ended 31 December

	Year 1	Year 2
	£000	£000
Cash flows from operating activities		
Profit before financing costs	1,800	2,500
Depreciation	1,500	1,900
	3,300	4,400
Increase in trade receivables	(800)	(1,200)
Increase in inventories	(600)	(1,300)
Increase in trade payables	100	200
Cash from operations	2,000	2,100
Interest paid	(600)	(600)
Income taxes paid	(400)	(600)
Net cash from operating activities	1,000	900
Cash flows from investing activities		
Proceeds from disposal of equipment	–	100
Purchase of property and equipment	(2,100)	(4,000)
Net cash from investing activities	(2,100)	(3,900)
Cash flows from financing activities		
Proceeds of issue of shares	2,000	–
(Repayment of) increase in borrowings	(600)	2,200
Dividends paid	(400)	(500)
Net cash (used in) raised from financing activities	1,000	1,700
Net (decrease)/increase in cash	(100)	(1,300)
Opening cash	400	300
Closing cash	300	(1,000)

a   Write a report explaining what the above cash flow statements reveal.

b   The company's bankers stated that, in view of the £1m increase in the company's overdraft, and the additional borrowings of £2.2m, the increase in the amount of dividends paid is not justified. Do you agree? Explain.

4   Ballamauda Ltd

Summarized statement of financial position as at 31 December

	Year 1		Year 2	
	£000	£000	£000	£000
Non-current assets				
Machinery at cost	80		70	
Provision for depreciation	(40)	40	(44)	26
Current assets				
Inventories	50		35	
Receivables	38		28	
Cash	–	88	90	153
Total assets		128		179
Current liabilities				
Trade payables	30		39	
Overdraft	16	46	–	39
Non-current liabilities				
Debentures		–		40
Equity				
Share capital	40		40	
Retained earnings	42	82	60	100
		128		179

During the year ending 31 December year 2

a   A machine, which had originally cost £10,000, and on which £6,000 depreciation had been charged, was sold for £3,400.

b   The profit before tax, after deducting the loss on the sale of the machine, was £35,200.

c   Interest of £2,400, taxation of £6,400 and dividends of £6,000 were paid.

You are required to produce a cash flow statement for Ballamauda Ltd for the year ended 31 December year 2.

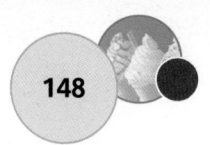

5 Soldriction plc

The summarized statement of financial position as at 31 December

	Year 3		Year 4	
Non-current assets	£m	£m	£m	£m
Intangible assets		50		55
Machinery at cost	90		104	
Provision for depreciation	(30)	60	(44)	60
		110		115
Current assets				
Inventories	30		36	
Receivables	44		48	
Cash	–	74	8	92
Total assets		184		207
Current liabilities				
Trade payables	28		20	
Overdraft	13	41	–	20
Non-current liabilities				
Debentures		–		38
Equity				
Share capital	90		90	
Retained earnings	53	143	59	149
		184		207

Income statement for year ended 31 December year 4

	£m
Sales revenue	216
Cost of sales	(144)
Gross profit	72
Loss on sale of machinery	(4)
Distribution costs	(24)
Administrative expenses	(20)
Impairment of goodwill	(6)
Operating profit	18
Finance costs	(3)
Profit before taxation	15
Corporation tax	(4)
Profit for the year	11

So

During the year ending 31 December year 4

a The company sold machinery, which had cost £12m, and on which £5m depreciation had been charged, for £3m.

b The company bought a number of manufacturing businesses in South Asia for £37m, of which £26m was for property, plant and equipment, and £11m for goodwill.

c Dividends paid were £5m.

d Interest of £3m and taxation of £4m were paid.

You are required to produce a cash flow statement for Soldriction plc for the year ended 31 December year 4.

6 You are given the following summarized statements of financial position and income statements for the Solverham Company for the past two years.

Statement of financial position as at 31 December

	Year 1		Year 2	
	£000	£000	£000	£000
Non-current assets at cost		200		220
Provision for depreciation		(60)		(82)
Net book value		140		138
Current assets				
Inventories	95		70	
Receivables	80		50	
Cash	–	175	25	145
Total assets		315		283
Liabilities and equity				
Current liabilities				
Payables	40		60	
Overdraft	80	120	–	60
Non-current liabilities				
12% debentures		110		135
Equity				
Share capital	50		50	
Retained earnings	35	85	38	88
		315		283

Income statement for the year ended 31 December

	Year 1	Year 2
Sales	520	500
Cost of sales	376	375
Gross profit	144	125
Administration expenses	(35)	(36)
Depreciation	(20)	(22)
Distribution costs	(22)	(24)
Operating profit	(67)	(43)
Interest paid	(14)	(17)
Net profit before tax	53	26
Taxation paid	16	8
Net profit after tax	37	18

Dividends paid in year 1 were £10,000, and in year 2 were £15,000

a Prepare a cash flow statement for the year ended 31 December year 2.

b Explain how cash flow differs from profit.

c The company's managing director is pleased that the company has money in the bank having paid off a significant overdraft. He is particularly pleased that he ignored his chief accountant, who said that the company could not afford to buy more fixed assets or to increase the dividend. Critically assess the chief accountant's advice.

7 Malcolm, the son of the founder of Solverham plc, is aware that the managing director of the company believes that the company is strong, and is doing well, but the chief accountant says that the company's position is rapidly deteriorating. You are required to produce a report on the company's financial position and performance, based on the information given for question 2. Your answer should include calculations of the ratios shown below for each year, and comments on them.

a Current ratio

b Liquidity ratio

c Capital gearing ratio

d Interest times cover

e Return on shareholders' funds

f Return on total long-term capital employed

g Operating profit as a percentage of sales

h Asset turnover

i Gross profit ratio

j Distribution costs as a percentage of sales

k Administrative expenses as a percentage of sales

l Sales/non-current assets

m Sales/current assets

n Inventory turnover ratio

o Trade receivables ratio

p Trade payables ratio

 Group activities and discussion questions

1 A small business is more likely to prosper and to control its operations effectively by monitoring cash flows than by listening to its accountant. Discuss.

2 In what ways is a cash flow statement likely to be useful?

3 Why should small businesses produce accruals-based accounts (as opposed to relying on controlling cash and banking)?

4 The published accounts of companies have steadily become more complicated, with additional statements, notes and disclosures, as required by accounting standards. Conventional financial accounting is a waste of time and effort for small businesses. Discuss.

5 Analyse a number of companies' cash flow statements. Which figures seem to give the best indication of a company's performance? Can 'free cash flow' be assessed, and does it provide a useful indicator?

6 Analyse a number of companies' statements of financial position and calculate their current ratios, liquidity ratios and capital gearing ratios for the last two years. What do these ratios tell you about the companies' liquidity problems or strengths? What useful information does the companies' cash flow statements add to this?

7 The financial statements of a small business are likely to reveal any liquidity problems; the financial statements of a major listed company are more likely to disguise them. Discuss.

8 It is useful for companies to have detailed analysis and control of all cash flows. Why would they want additional, accruals-based information?

Accounting in context

Discuss and comment on the following extract from the press with particular reference to the distinction between making profits and generating cash and an analysis of the sources and uses of cash.

Mafia is biggest business in Italy

By Nick Squires, Rome

The Mafia is now Italy's biggest business enterprise, with an annual turnover of €140 billion ($A174 billion), according to an authoritative report.

The country's four Mafia groups have broken out of their traditional strongholds and spread across the whole country, taking advantage of the economic crisis to snap up ailing businesses and ramp up their loan-shark operations.

They have estimated cash reserves of €65 billion and estimated annual profits of €100 billion, about 7 per cent of Italy's GDP, says a study released by Confesercenti, an employers' association.

It seems the average mobster is no longer a machine-gun-toting hoodlum but a savvy businessman with a smart phone and a sophisticated knowledge of finance. "Mafia Inc is Italy's No.1 bank with €65 billion in liquidity," the association said in its report, *Criminality's Grip on Business*.

With the economic crisis meaning banks are loath to lend, Mafia dons have profited as desperate businesses turn to loan sharks demanding crippling rates of interest.

"Among the illegal activities of Mafia organisations is loan-sharking, which with the economic crisis has become a national emergency," said Marco Venturi, the president of Confesercenti. "According to our estimates, loan-sharking caused the closure in 2010 of 1800 businesses and destroyed thousands of jobs. Right now, Mafia Inc is the only business enterprise willing to make substantial investments."

Small business owners with tight margins and limited cash flow were the most vulnerable – some 200,000 had fallen victim to usury, Mr Venturi said.

They were also being hit by extortion and straightforward robbery by the mob – at a rate of one crime a minute.

The Mafia's influence was felt not only in its traditional strongholds such as Palermo and Naples but also increasingly in the wealthy north of Italy.

Confesercenti, which represents 270,000 small-to-medium businesses, said the new technocrat government of Mario Monti had to help firms "retake territory occupied by the Mafia".

But it will be an uphill battle. Organised crime controls everything from gambling to construction and the disposal of industrial and household waste.

Source: Sydney Morning Herald, 12 January 2012.

References and further reading

Black, G. (2009) *Introduction to Accounting and Finance* (2nd edn.). Harlow: FT Prentice Hall.
Elliott, B. and J. Elliott (2011) *Financial Accounting and Reporting* (14th edn.). Harlow: FT Prentice Hall.
IAS 7 *Cash Flow Statements* (revised 2009). IASB.
Wood, F. and A. Sangster (2012) *Business Accounting* (vol. 1) (12th edn.). Harlow: FT Prentice Hall.
www.ifrs.org (international accounting standards)
www.frc.org.uk (UK accounting standards)

When you have read this chapter, log on to the Online Learning Centre website at *www.mcgraw-hill.co.uk/textbooks/leiwy* to explore chapter-by-chapter test questions, further reading and more online study tools.

Chapter 7

Advanced Interpretation of Company and Group Accounts

Chapter contents

✓ Learning objectives

After studying this chapter you will be able to:

✓ Identify key information in published financial statements required to assess companies' solvency and profitability

✓ Understand the terminology used in consolidated accounts and produce straightforward group statements of financial position

✓ Explain how financial accounting information can be used to calculate Z-scores and predict financial distress and understand the main elements included in Z-scores

✓ Analyse the performance of companies using most of the detailed information included in published financial statements

✓ Describe segmental reporting and make use of the information disclosed to assess the performance of different segments

✓ Make use of financial information disclosed by companies in addition to that included in statements of financial position, income statements and cash flow statements

7.1 Introduction

Chapter 4 showed how 20 widely used 'ratios' can be used to assess three key aspects of a company:

- Its solvency and ability to meet its liabilities as they fall due.
- Its profitability and how this can be increased.
- How its shares are rated on the stock market.

It is not too difficult to calculate these ratios when the information is provided by a textbook in a convenient format. It is more difficult to find and use appropriate information from a complex-looking annual report and accounts.

This chapter begins by providing extracts from the 2011 published annual report of Marks and Spencer plc. The 20 ratios are calculated for 2010, together with guidance on selecting the appropriate figures, and some interpretation. Students are invited to calculate the equivalent 20 ratios for 2011 and to provide a more detailed interpretation.

The second part explains how group (or consolidated) statements of financial position are produced. The third and fourth parts of the chapter provide more detailed guidance on assessing solvency and profitability. More detailed consideration of a company's performance on the stock market is provided in Chapter 6. The final part of this chapter examines other information available from annual reports and accounts.

7.2 Calculating Ratios from Published Accounts

The information provided in respect of Marks and Spencer plc is from pages 74 and 75 of their 2011 annual report and accounts and part of notes 2, 3, 5, 19 and 21. The information in respect of ratios 17–19 assumes the share price to be 370p in 2010, and 337p in 2011. These figures show a 9 per cent fall in that one-year period. Share prices, as a whole, as indicated by the FTSE 100 index rose by 4 per cent in that period. Hence, Marks & Spencer shares performed very badly in comparison with the market, as a whole (see Illustrations 7.1 and 7.2).

Comments on 2010 figures

1 The **current ratio** is the ratio of current assets to current liabilities. It is lower than many companies but its inventory is readily saleable and goods are sold for immediate payment. The current ratio of this company is higher than that of a supermarket group, such as Tesco.

2 The **liquidity ratio** is the ratio of current assets excluding inventories to current liabilities. This is also low because the company has few trade receivables (customers pay for their purchases on sale yet the company buys its goods on credit). These two liquidity ratios are neither too high nor two low when judged against similar companies.

3 The **gearing ratio** relates debt (or borrowings) to equity. In this instance, for convenience, the total amount for non-current liabilities has been used. Non-current liabilities are shown as a percentage of total long-term capital (non-current liabilities plus equity). It is also acceptable to use borrowings as a percentage of equity. Although gearing is on the high side, Marks and Spencer has the strength and reputation to maintain such a level of gearing.

If current liabilities are added to non-current liabilities (£1,890.5m + £3,076.8m = £4,967.3m), the total amount of 'debt' is seen to be higher than the amount of equity, which may be a cause for concern.

ILLUSTRATION 7.1

Marks and Spencer plc

Consolidated statement of financial position 2 April 2011

	Note	2011 £m	2010 £m
Assets			
Non-current assets			
Intangible assets	14	527.7	452.8
Property, plant & equipment	15	4,662.2	4,722.0
Investment property	16	16.0	22.4
Retirement benefit asset	11	182.6	–
Other		16.0	15.2
Trade and other receivables	18	276.1	287.7
Derivative financial instruments	23	21.8	132.9
		5,702.4	5,633.0
Current assets			
Inventories		685.3	613.2
Other financial assets	18	215.9	171.7
Trade and other receivables	19	250.3	281.4
Derivative financial instruments	23	18.4	48.1
Cash and cash equivalents	21	470.2	405.8
Other		1.6	-
		1,641.7	1,520.2
Total assets		7,344.1	7,153.2
Liabilities			
Current liabilities			
Trade and other payables	21	1,347.6	1,153.8
Borrowings	22	602.3	482.9
Partnership liability to the pension scheme	12	71.9	71.9
Derivative financial instruments	23	50.7	27.1
Provisions	24	22.7	25.6
Current tax liabilities		115.0	129.2
		2,210.2	1,890.5
Non-current liabilities			
Retirement benefit deficit	11	14.1	366.5
Trade and other payables	21	262.3	280.3
Borrowings	22	1,924.1	2,278.0
Derivative financial instruments	23	37.5	–
Provisions	24	22.0	25.5
Deferred tax liabilities	25	196.5	126.5
		2,456.5	3,076.8
Total liabilities		4,666.7	4,967.3

Continued

ILLUSTRATION 7.1 (Continued)

Equity

Share capital	26	396.2	395.5
Share premium		255.2	247.5
Capital redemption reserve		2,202.6	2,202.6
Hedging reserve		(11.3)	11.6
Other reserve		(6,042.4)	(5,970.5)
Retained earnings	31	5,873.2	5,281.9
Total shareholders' equity		2,673.5	2,168.6
Non-controlling interests in equity		3.9	17.3
Total equity		2,677.4	2,185.9
Total liabilities and equity		7,344.1	7,153.2

The financial statements were approved
by the Board on 23 May 2011.

Mark Bolland   Alan Stewart
Chief Executive Officer   Group Finance Officer

Marks and Spencer plc, Consolidated income statement for the year ended 2 April 2011

	Note	2011	2010
		£m	£m
Revenue	2,3	9,740.3	9,536.6
Cost of sales	2,3	(6,015.6)	(5,918.1)
Gross profit		3,724.7	3,618.5
Selling and administrative expenses	3	(2,959.7)	(2,831.5)
Other operating income		71.9	65.0
Operating profit		836.9	852.9
Financed income	6	42.3	12.9
Finance costs	6	(98.6)	(162.2)
Profit before tax		780.6	702.7
Tax	7	(182.0)	(179.7)
Profit for the year		598.6	523.0
Basic earnings per share	8	38.8p	33.5p
Dividends per share	9	15.7p	15.0p
Total dividend paid	9	247.5	236.0

Marks and Spencer plc, Notes to the financial statements

19 Trade and other receivables

	2011	2010
	£m	£m
Current assets		
Trade receivables (net)	98.3	88.5
Other receivables	25.5	27.3

	126.5	165.6
Prepayments and accrued income	**126.5**	165.6
	250.3	281.4

21 Trade and other payables
Current liabilities

Trade payables	**919.2**	792.2
Social security and other taxes	**57.2**	79.4
Accruals and deferred income	**371.2**	282.2
	1,347.6	1,153.8

26 Share capital
Allotted and issued ordinary shares of
25p each fully paid:1,584,863,882
(2010: 1,582, 316, 581)

ordinary shares of 25p each	**396.2**	395.5

ILLUSTRATION 7.2

Ratio	2010	2010	2011	2011
1 Current ratio	$\dfrac{1,520.2}{1,890.5}$	0.8 : 1		
2 Liquidity (quick) ratio	$\dfrac{907.0}{1,890.5}$	0.5 : 1		
3 Capital gearing ratio	$\dfrac{3,076.8}{2,168.6}$	142%		
or	$\dfrac{3,076.8}{3,076.8 + 2,168.6}$	59%		
4 Interest times cover	$\dfrac{852.9 + 12.9}{162.2}$	5.4 times		
5 Return on shareholders' funds	$\dfrac{523.0}{2,168.6}$	24%		
6 Return on total long-term capital employed	$\dfrac{852.9 + 12.9}{3,076.8 + 2,168.6}$	16%		
7 Operating profit as a % of sales	$\dfrac{852.9}{9,536.6}$	9%		
8 Asset turnover	$\dfrac{9,536.6}{7,153.2 - 1,890.5}$	1.8 times		
9 Gross profit ratio	$\dfrac{3,618.5}{9,536.6}$	38%		
10 Selling and administrative expenses as % of sales	$\dfrac{2,831.5}{9,536.6}$	30%		
11 Other operating expenses as % of sales	not shown			
12 Sales/non-current assets	$\dfrac{9,536.6}{5,633.0}$	1.7 times		
13 Sales/current assets	$\dfrac{9,536.6}{1,520.2}$	6.3 times		

Continued

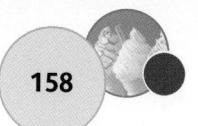

ILLUSTRATION 7.2 (Continued)		
14 Inventory turnover ratio	$\dfrac{613.2 \times 365}{5,918.1}$	38 days
15 Receivables ratio	$\dfrac{88.5 \times 365}{9,536,6}$	3 days
16 Payables ratio	$\dfrac{792.2 \times 365}{5,918.1}$	49 days
17 Price/earnings ratio	$\dfrac{370}{33.5}$	11.0
18 Dividend yield	$\dfrac{15.0}{370}$	4.1%
19 Dividend cover	$\dfrac{523.0}{236.0}$	2.2 times
20 Net assets per share	$\dfrac{2,168.6}{1,582.3}$	£1.37

4 Interest cover is calculated by taking the profit available for paying interest and dividing it by the amount of interest paid (shown as finance costs). Although it depends on the type of business, interest cover of more than about 5 looks reasonably comfortable.

5 The profit for the period (after tax) is expressed as a percentage of the total amount for shareholders' equity. It is the return earned for ordinary shareholders. A return of more than 20 per cent is quite impressive, given the state of the retail sector.

6 Operating profit and finance income (before deducting interest paid and taxation) is expressed as a percentage of total capital employed, using the figure from number 3 above. It is the return earned by the company on the total of its long-term capital employed. It is important to use equivalent figures when comparing one year with another, and also when relating income statement figures to statement of financial position figures. As the assets generating finance income have been included on the statement of financial position[1] the 'return' must include all returns on those assets.

It is difficult to be completely consistent and correct. The figure used for capital employed includes all non-current liabilities. It excludes those 'loans and borrowings' that are part of current liabilities. The figure provided for finance costs includes interest on both non-current and current liabilities. It would be possible to estimate how much of the finance costs relate to short-term borrowings, and treat these as an operating expense. In ratio analysis there is inevitably some approximation, and it is necessary to be consistent. In this analysis all interest has been treated as if it is in respect of non-current liabilities.

The return, using both ratios 5 and 6, looks reasonable. It is more useful to compare two or more years and to note trends.

7 Operating profit is expressed as a percentage of sales revenue (turnover). This calculation, as with most profitability ratios, means little except when compared with other years, or with other companies in a similar line of business.

8 Sales revenue (turnover) is divided by operating assets; this includes all operating assets regardless of what long-term financing was used. It is usually taken as the total of all assets (current and non-current), *minus* current liabilities. It is equal to equity plus non-current liabilities.

---

[1] It would be included in 'investments accounted for using the equity method'.

9 Gross profit is expressed as a percentage of sales revenue (turnover).

10 and 11 Most companies disclose two categories of operating expenses: distribution costs, and administrative expenses that can be expressed as a percentage of sales revenue (turnover). In this instance only selling and administrative expenses have been separately identified and disclosed.

12 Sales revenue (turnover) is divided by the total for non-current assets to show the number of times that non-current assets were 'turned over' during the year.

13 Sales revenue (turnover) is divided by the total for current assets to show the number of times that current assets were 'turned over' during the year. This is then analysed in more detail in ratios 14 and 15 (and 16).

14 Cost of sales is used here, not sales, because the inventories figure is shown at cost price (not selling price). Inventories are divided by cost of sales (which is sales *minus* gross profit); this is then multiplied by 365 to show how many days inventories are held.

15 The sales figure is used here (not cost of sales) because receivables are shown at selling price. Trade receivables are divided by sales (turnover) and then multiplied by 365 to express the amount of receivables in days, which indicates how long receivables take to pay. Here, the figure for receivables is very low because people pay for their purchases as they buy them. When a company sells goods and is paid by credit card, the seller receives the money almost immediately.

16 Cost of sales is used here, not sales, because the amounts owing as trade payables are at cost price. Trade payables are divided by cost of sales, and then multiplied by 365 to indicate the number of days taken to pay trade payables.

17 This is calculated as the share price (current, perhaps taken from the *Financial Times*) divided by the amount of earnings per share, as shown in Chapter 5. The higher the price/earnings (PE) ratio, the more confident the stock market is in the company's growth prospects.

18 The dividend paid in the year usually comprises last year's final dividend, which is paid in the first half of this financial year, and this year's interim dividend, which is paid in the second half of this financial year. The dividend is expressed as a percentage of the current share price.

19 This can be computed as the profit after tax dividend by the dividend paid, or the earnings per share is divided by the dividend per share. Marks and Spencer's policy is to pay out almost half its profit after tax as a dividend.

20 The amount shown for total shareholders' equity is divided by the number of shares, which is taken from note 26. The share price on the stock market was higher than the statement of financial position value per share, reflecting that the expected benefits of owning these shares exceeds the carrying value of the net assets as reflected in the statement of financial position.

7.3 Consolidated (Group) Financial Statements

Most large, listed, public companies are really groups: a parent company with a number of subsidiary companies. When interpreting their financial statement it is usually better to use the figures for the group, rather than just for the (parent) company. In order to interpret these it is necessary to know some of the principles and terminology of consolidated accounts.

Illustration 7.3 shows the simplified statements of financial position of Quinnie plc and Krown Ltd on 31 December year 1 immediately after Quinnie bought all the shares of Krown. The group statement of financial position, which combines the two companies, looks like that of Quinnie, except that Quinnie's investment in Krown (£240,000) has been replaced by the net assets[2] of Krown (which also happen to be £240,000).

---

[2] Non-current assets, plus current assets, minus current liabilities.

ILLUSTRATION 7.3

Summarized statements of financial position of Quinnie plc and Krown Ltd at 31 December year 1

	Quinnie plc	Krown Ltd
	£000	£000
Non-current assets	260	200
Investment in Krown Ltd at cost	240	–
Current assets	80	100
Total assets	580	300
Current liabilities	100	60
Ordinary share capital	300	200
Retained earnings	180	40
	580	300

Quinnie bought 100 per cent of the shares of Krown Ltd on 31 December Year 1. Prepare the group statement of financial position as at that date.

Group statement of financial position of Quinnie plc and its subsidiary at 31 December year 4

	£000
Non-current assets	460
Current assets	180
	640
Current liabilities	160
Ordinary share capital	300
Retained earnings	180
	640

It is unlikely that when one company buys another company the price that they pay would be exactly the fair value of the net assets acquired. If the company that is acquired is doing reasonably well,[3] the acquiring company will have to pay something extra for *goodwill*. In Illustration 7.4 the net assets of Fourthing are shown as £70,000,[4] but Pinnie paid £90,000 to acquire all the shares; on the group statement of financial position goodwill is therefore shown as £20,000.

Some of the main principles are shown in Illustration 7.4. There are two separate companies, Pinnie plc and Fourthing Ltd, and each produces its own statement of financial position. Pinnie is the parent company: it owns all of Fourthing's shares, and controls it. A group statement of financial position combines the statements of financial position of the two companies in a particular way: the first part of the group statements of financial position includes all the assets and liabilities of both companies; the second part shows who owns them all, and how it was financed. Goodwill appears on the group statement of financial position where the parent company has paid more for the subsidiary company than the fair value of the net assets that it acquires.

The rules for consolidated accounts may be summarized as follows:

i Goodwill is the difference between the price paid for the subsidiary company (£90,000) and Pinnie's share of the net assets acquired. In this instance Pinnie acquired 100 per cent of the

---

[3] In 2009 many companies were doing badly, and it was possible to buy companies for less than the statement of financial position value of their assets; the assets should be valued at 'fair value', but that may be difficult to determine in a depressed market.

[4] $50 + 60 - 40 = 70$.

ILLUSTRATION 7.4

Summarized statements of financial position of Pinnie plc and Fourthing Ltd at 31 December year 4

	Pinnie plc	Fourthing Ltd
	£000	£000
Non-current assets	100	50
Investment in Fourthing Ltd at cost	90	–
Current assets	80	60
Total assets	270	110
Current liabilities	30	40
Ordinary share capital	100	50
Retained earnings	140	20
	270	110

Pinnie bought 100 per cent of the shares of Fourthing Ltd on 31 December year 4. Prepare the group statement of financial position as at that date.

Group statement of financial position of Pinnie plc and its subsidiary at 31 December year 4

	£000
Non-current assets	150
Goodwill	20
Current assets	140
	310
Current liabilities	70
Ordinary share capital	100
Retained earnings	140
	310

---

net assets. The net assets of Fourthing are £50,000 + £60,000 − £40,000 = £70,000. It is probably easier to think of this as being the amount of equity (which is £50,000 + £20,000).

Goodwill must be calculated at the date of acquisition (in this case it is easy: 31 December year 4); it will subsequently be reassessed for impairment.

ii Share capital: the group statement of financial position shows only the parent company's share capital, not the subsidiary's.

iii Retained earnings: the group statement of financial position shows only the parent company's share of retained earnings at the statement of financial position date. The group statement of financial position will show the parent company's share of any retained profits made by the subsidiary *after* the date of acquisition. In the case of Pinnie and Fourthing, the statements of financial position are prepared as at the date of acquisition; Fourthing has not yet made any 'post-acquisition' profits.

iv The figures shown on the group statement of financial position for non-current assets, current assets and current liabilities are simply the amounts shown for each company, added together. This applies even if the subsidiary company is only partly owned.

A subsidiary company is one that is controlled by a parent company, usually by owning a majority of its shares. In Illustration 7.5 Florrie plc owns 80 per cent of the shares of Tanner Ltd. There is an

additional complication in this illustration: the subsidiary was acquired on 31 December year 4; a group statement of financial position is now required for 31 December year 6.

The principles are much the same when a subsidiary is only partly owned. In Illustration 7.5 the holding company owns 80 per cent of the subsidiary, and so there is a 'non-controlling interest' of 20 per cent. The first part of the group statement of financial position still includes 100 per cent of the non-current assets, current assets and current liabilities. The second half includes an item 'non-controlling interest' that shows (as at the statement of financial position date) the amount of net assets owned by shareholders outside the group.

The main difficulty is with retained earnings. All of Florrie's retained earnings (£125,000) belong to the group, and so are included on the group statement of financial position. But only part of Tanner's belong to the group: only 80 per cent of the retained earnings that Tanner has accumulated since it was acquired are included on the group statement of financial position. Retained earnings have increased from £65,000 to £90,000 since acquisition, meaning that post-acquisition retained earnings are £25,000. The group's share of this (80 per cent) is £20,000.

The principles for calculating goodwill are the same. The price paid for Tanner was £118,000. Florrie's share of Tanner is 80 per cent; but it is necessary to calculate the net asset value of Tanner *at the date of acquisition*. This was share capital of £60,000, plus retained earnings that were £65,000. Equity at the date of acquisition was therefore £125,000; Florrie's share of that (80 per cent) was

---

ILLUSTRATION 7.5

Summarized statements of financial position of Florrie plc and Tanner Ltd at 31 December year 6

	Florrie plc	Tanner Ltd
	£000	£000
Non-current assets	162	120
Investment in Tanner Ltd at cost	118	–
Current assets	20	80
Total assets	300	200
Current liabilities	15	50
Ordinary share capital	160	60
Retained earnings	125	90
	300	200

Florrie bought 80 per cent of the shares of Tanner Ltd on 31 December year 4. At that date Tanner's retained earnings were £65,000. Prepare the group statement of financial position at 31 December year 6.

Group statement of financial position of Florrie plc and its subsidiary as at 31 December year 6

	£000	Workings
Non-current assets	282	162 + 120
Goodwill	18	118 – 80% (60 + 65)
Current assets	100	20 + 80
	400	
Current liabilities	65	15 + 50
Non-controlling interest	30	20% (90 + 60)
Ordinary share capital	160	Florrie only
Retained earnings	145	125 + 80% (90 – 65)
	400	

£100,000. Goodwill was therefore the difference between the £118,000 paid, and the £100,000 that was the group's share of the net assets as at the date of acquisition.

Negative goodwill

Sometimes a company buys another for less than the net book value of its assets. Perhaps it pays £2m for £3m worth of assets. Traditionally, this was regarded as 'negative goodwill'. But in the world of international accounting standards (IASs), this should not arise. Assets and liabilities should be revalued to 'fair value' at the date of acquisition. The assets shown at £3m were probably worth a lot less; and there may have been substantial unrecognized liabilities. Most of what was regarded as negative goodwill should disappear when assets and liabilities are restated at 'fair value'. If, on revaluation, there is still a 'profit' left,[5] then it should be taken to the income statement.

Group accounts in practice

The basic principles of group accounts as outlined here apply in what are frequently much more complex situations. Many companies have a number of subsidiaries, which, in turn, have their own subsidiaries, or 'sub-subsidiaries' of the parent company, all of which may be owned in different proportions, with part or all acquired or disposed of on different dates. The first part of a group statement of financial position shows 100 per cent of the assets and liabilities of parent and subsidiary companies; the second part shows who owns them: part belongs to the non-controlling interest – shareholders who own the minority part of the subsidiary.

The first part of a group income statement shows 100 per cent of the revenues, expenses and profit of the group. The second part shows that part of them are attributable to the non-controlling interest; the rest belong to the group.

In addition to subsidiaries, there may be *associates* and *joint ventures*. Here, the parent normally owns between 20 per cent and 50 per cent of the shares, and full consolidation does not take place. The group statement of financial position would show an amount for investment in such companies, which would reflect their share of net assets. The group income statement shows the group's share of the profits[6] of the associate or joint venture. When interpreting published financial statements it is normally best to use the figures for the group as a whole, including the results for associates and joint ventures. These may be shown as 'investments accounted for using the equity method'.[7] More detailed analysis may exclude them. The important thing, as always with interpretation, is to ensure that comparisons are made on a consistent basis.

7.4 Solvency and Predicting Financial Distress

The words 'financial distress' are widely used to cover a variety of different situations in which a company may find itself when it is unable to meet its liabilities as they fall due. Liquidation, receivership, bankruptcy and voluntary or compulsory winding up are all variations on a theme. Companies can negotiate arrangements with their bankers and other creditors. A few years ago the debts of companies like Marconi and Eurotunnel were too great and the companies gave their creditors substantial amounts of share capital in return for cancelling debt, so that previous shareholders soon held only a tiny proportion of the companies, the value of which was much reduced. By 2012 many well-known companies were in serious financial difficulties. Barratt Shoes simply ceased trading while Blacks Leisure

---

[5] If you have paid £2m for net assets that really are worth £2.1m, then you show the difference as £100,000 profit.

[6] Or losses.

[7] Joint ventures may be shown using either the equity method, or proportional consolidation.

is in administration and hoping for a buyer. Many professional football clubs have got into serious financial difficulties. In recent years major banks collapsed and were taken over by the government or by foreign banks.[8] Sometimes companies may be the unwilling victim of a takeover bid; an agreed bid or merger may be sought; or parts of the business may be sold off to a variety of different companies, venture capitalists and other investors and institutions. When a company is in financial difficulties the ordinary shareholders can lose most or all of their investment; creditors can suffer direct financial loss; and employees and suppliers suffer in different ways.

In the end, a company gets into financial difficulties for one reason only: they are unable to pay their debts. All sorts of factors can lead to this situation: bad management, poor products, a weak economy, problems with exchange rates, government policies, poor industrial relations, and changes in demand for products and services. There is usually no shortage of explanations for poor performance, and it can be difficult to identify these various factors – until it is too late. But the warning signs of impending financial difficulty are usually there for those who take the trouble to interpret financial information, and are brave enough to heed it.

Some of the warning signs are:

1 *Excessive debt* – This can be inferred from current ratios, liquidity ratios, gearing ratios and interest cover, especially if there is a deteriorating trend. It is important also to look at total debt, including both short and long term.

   Some aspects of published accounts can be hard to interpret – such as deferred taxation.[9] Obligations under finance leases can also be a problem. The important thing is to treat items consistently so that ratios are comparable. There are also companies, such as privatized utilities, which are not endangered by high levels of debt.[10]

   It may be useful to compare the amount of interest paid by a company with the amount of debt shown on its statement of financial position. An unusually high figure may suggest that, for most of the year, the level of debt was much higher than the amount shown at the year end. An unusually low figure may suggest that debt built up substantially before the year end, and may still be increasing.

2 *Falling profits, or losses* – A one-off loss, perhaps due to exceptional items, may not be a problem. But a profitable company is generally more safe, and able to pay its liabilities, than one that is making losses.

3 *Cash flows* – Sometimes companies generate profits that never seem to show up as cash – perhaps the company keeps pouring money into expansion. If there is 'creative accounting' the profits may be questioned. In the end it is cash that pays the bills. Creditors such as bankers are usually interested in cash budgets to monitor the company's ability to repay what is due.

4 *Assets* – Assessments of solvency depend on the quality and valuation of the assets shown on the statements of financial position. Some assets are very specialized, and may be of doubtful value in a forced liquidation.

5 *Share price* – When a company's share price goes down significantly more than the market generally, that is a warning sign. Companies do not suddenly get into financial difficulties, and the market price usually reflects problems well in advance.

6 *Other factors* – The financial press may draw attention to other warning signs, such as key executives leaving, difficulties in renegotiating loan agreements or significant loss of market share.

---

[8] Notably the bank of Santander. The government took a majority shareholding in the Royal Bank of Scotland that owned NatWest and the Isle of Man Bank. Halifax Bank of Scotland became part of the Lloyds Group.

[9] Deferred taxation is a 'liability' that may never have to be paid.

[10] Because of their near monopoly positions, and near certain revenues.

None of these warning signs alone necessarily indicates that a company will fail. A number of models exist that combine the various factors to give more or less reliable predictions of financial distress, including the 'Z-score'.

Z-scores

It is possible to find out which factors have been most closely associated with companies finding themselves in a situation of financial distress. A list of companies that have 'failed' in one way or another is produced. The financial data for those companies is compiled for a number of years, including amounts of profit, equity, working capital (WC), cash flows, and so on. The data is then manipulated until a way of selecting it and arranging it is found that would best have predicted impending failure.

Altman (2006) found that the key data were:

- working capital;
- total gross assets;
- retained profits;
- earnings before interest and tax;
- market value of equity;
- book value of debt;
- sales.

By arranging these as five ratios, and giving a weighting to each, he calculated a Z-score, which gave the best prediction of corporate failure.

Ratio	Weighting
1 Working capital ÷ total gross assets	× 1.2
2 Retained profits ÷ total gross assets	× 1.4
3 Earnings before interest and tax ÷ total gross assets	× 3.3
4 Market value of equity ÷ book value of debt	× 0.6
5 Sales ÷ total gross assets	× 1.0

Altman did not claim to be stating the causes of failure; it was a statistical calculation which, in his sample, gave the best results. Companies with a Z-score of more than 2.99, using the above calculation, did not fail; companies with a Z-score of less than 1.81 did fail. The outcome of companies with a score of between 1.81 and 2.99 was less predictable, but overall the prediction was accurate in 96 per cent of cases.

Altman's model suggests that the following are important in predicting failure:

- the amount of working capital (in relation to total assets);
- the amount of retained profits (in relation to total assets);
- some measure of return on capital employed (ROCE);
- some measure of gearing, and the market value of equity;
- some measure of utilization of assets (or turnover of assets).

ILLUSTRATION 7.6

Z-score for Marks and Spencer plc 2011

	£m			Weighting	
Current assets	1,642				
Current liabilities	(2,210)				
Working capital (WC)	(568)				
Non-current assets	5,702				
Current assets	1,642				
Total assets (TGA)	7,344				
Retained profits (RP)	5,873				
Profit before interest and tax (PBIT)	837				
Market capitalization (MV):					
1,585 million @ £3.37	5,341				
Current liabilities	2,210				
Non-current liabilities	2,457				
Total liabilities (BV)	4,667				
Sales	9,740				
1 WC/TGA	$\dfrac{(568)}{7,344}$	=	(0.077)	1.2	(0.093)
2 RP/TGA	$\dfrac{5,873}{7,344}$	=	0.800	1.4	1.120
3 PBIT/TGA	$\dfrac{837}{7,344}$	=	0.114	3.3	0.376
4 MV of equity/BV of debt	$\dfrac{5,341}{4,667}$	=	1.145	0.6	0.687
5 Sales/TGA	$\dfrac{9,740}{7,344}$	=	1.326	1.0	1.326
Z-score					3.416

This calculation suggests that Marks and Spencer are well above the 'safe' level of 2.99 (see Illustration 7.6). It is likely that the book value figures for non-current assets understate their market value and, as a result, the Z-score calculated is understated.

Altman's sample was based on manufacturing companies in the USA more than 40 years ago. But similar work has been done by Taffler (1983) and Taffler and Tisshaw (1977) more recently in the UK. Taffler found that the key ratios included:

	Weighting %
1 Profit before taxation ÷ current liabilities	53
2 Current assets ÷ total liabilities	13
3 Current liabilities ÷ total assets	18
4 (Immediate assets ÷ current liabilities) ÷ operating costs excluding depreciation	16

Taffler did not publish full details on the calculations but it is clear that the key information, manipulated in different ways, could give very good indications of corporate failure in a different environment.

The message is clear: published financial statements, if interpreted with skill and care, can give very good indications of a company's solvency, or how safe it is from financial collapse. Important information is available from financial statements, the most important being profits, assets, liabilities, cash flows and Z-scores. But other information is also important, including trends, quality of management, competition and what is happening the markets in which the company is operating.

7.5 Selective Performance

At an introductory level, most interpretation of accounts concentrates on the performance of a company as a whole. Profitability is measured using return on capital employed, and this is analysed into its various components showing (a) costs and profits in relation to turnover;[11] and (b) utilization of assets,[12] relating sales or cost of sales to different categories of assets in varying degrees of detail. Cash flows are also analysed for the company as a whole.

There are good reasons for wanting to analyse selectively the performance of different parts of the business. If investors and analysts are interested in forecasting the future sales, profits and cash flows of a company, they are likely to assume different growth rates, different rates of profitability and varying amounts of risk for different types of business – even if they are unable to do it exactly. At the end of the twentieth century it was assumed that there were great growth prospects in areas like telecommunications, pharmaceuticals and leisure. But investors were disappointed in the short run.

Investors are also concerned with assessing the competence of management. Many companies are becoming increasingly diversified, making money in one area where they have expertise and success, then investing it in other areas that need careful monitoring.

In many cases diversification is very successful: as one area declines another expands. But some attempts at diversification are not successful, and it is useful to monitor the performance of different parts of the business. To facilitate this there are official disclosure requirements that enable us to find out about different *segments* of a business, about *continuing and discontinued* operations, and about the results of investments in *associates* and *joint ventures*.

The idea that the financial performance of a company can be distilled into a single figure is appealing, and the *earnings per share* (EPS) figure is the most suitable for this purpose. If the EPS increase each year, that must be a good thing. If they fall, that must be a bad thing.

But a single measure of performance is likely to cover a multitude of sins. Investors who are trying to forecast future EPS figures need to consider whether or not this year's EPS figure has taken into account the following:

- the results of parts of the business that have since been discontinued;
- the results of new acquisitions that have yet to come fully on stream;
- any exceptional items such as large, one-off profits on the sale of non-curent assets or investments;
- exceptional write-offs of goodwill or other assets;
- exceptional provisions for future reorganizations and redundancies;
- impairment of goodwill;
- depreciation;
- interest;
- unrealized profits on revaluation of assets;
- exchange rate gains or losses on translating the financial statements of overseas subsidiaries.

---

[11] Chapter 4, ratios 7, 9, 10 and 11.

[12] Chapter 4, ratios 8, 14 and 15.

Although IAS 33 clearly specifies how EPS should be calculated, companies are free to show additional versions of the figure, and it is important to be clear which version is being used, and how the above items have been treated.

Segments

Most large companies have a number of different 'segments', which may be geographical (e.g. UK, Europe, Asia, USA), or 'business' segments (e.g. women's clothes, men's clothes, children's clothes). It is difficult to have a standard approach for defining segments for very different businesses, and the standard-setters have continuously revised their rules and guidelines on how segments should be defined, and what information should be disclosed for each. IFRS 8 Operating Segments is intended to be a step towards a world-wide accounting standard.

A careful examination of the annual report and accounts of most large companies reveals information about the different segments of the business that enables us to assess the performance of the different parts of the business using both business segments and geographical segments. Marks and Spencer discloses information for only two business segments: general merchandise and food. It provides a great deal of segmental information, but care is needed in comparing one year with another. The information that it provided in 2011 is summarized in Illustrations 7.7 and 7.8.

These figures must be treated with care but we can see the degree to which the sales and the profits arise from the different activities in which the company is engaged and where the assets are located. This information gives us an analysis of the degree to which the company depends on its various activities and the locations in which it operates. This can help in assessing risks and growth prospects.

The use of conventional accounting ratios provides more useful information to the extent the company provides information. For example, we can compute ratio 7 (from Chapter 4) for UK and for international activities and we can compute sales/total assets. These are shown as Illustration 7.9 for the year 2010. Readers are invited to calculate equivalent figures for 2011, and to comment on them. Answers are provided at the end of the book in Self-testing Question 5 in Chapter 7.

The international activities appear to be more profitable than the UK activities but we must bear in mind that the international activities are a much smaller percentage of the total activity.

It is worth analysing the performance of the different segments of a company in this way, and comparing this with the comments made by the chairman or directors about the progress and prospects of different parts of the company. Producing detailed analyses for a number of years can

ILLUSTRATION 7.7

	2011 £m	2011 %	2010 £m	2010 %
General merchandise	4,233.6	43	4,152.0	44
Food	4,499.4	46	4,415.9	46
UK revenue	8,733.0	89	8,567.9	90
Wholesale	353.7	4	297.7	3
Retail	663.6	7	671.0	7
International revenue	1,007.3	11	968.7	10
Group revenue	9.740.3	100	9,536.6	100
UK operating profit	679.0	87	701.1	100
International operating profit	157.9	20	150.9	21
Group operating profit	836.9	107	852.0	121
Finance income	42.3	5	12.9	2
Finance costs	(98.6)	(12)	(162.2)	(23)
Profit before tax	780.6	100	702.7	100

ILLUSTRATION 7.8

Other segmental information

	2011 UK £m	2011 International £m	2011 Total £m	2010 UK £m	2010 International £m	2010 Total £m
Additions to property, plant and equipment and intangible assets other than goodwill	463.6	27.9	491.5	360.0	29.3	389.3
Depreciation and amortization	434.5	33.0	467.5	398.7	29.2	427.9
Assets	6,287.6	1,056.5	7,344.1	6,242.7	910.5	7,153.2
Non-current assets	4,751.1	951.3	5,702.4	4,843.9	789.1	5,633.0

give a better indication of trends, but the way in which the information is produced can change from year to year, making such comparisons difficult.

Readers are invited to calculate percentage figures for Illustration 7.8 similar to the percentage figures in Illustration 7.7 and, for Illustration 7.9, the 2011 figures and to monitor the progress and changes of dependence of the different divisions.

IASs require companies to publish more information, and on a more comparable basis so that the published financial statements of major international companies are a mine of information, providing an ever-increasing resource for more detailed analysis.

Investments

It is possible to assess how successful management has been in making investments in other companies, although the information required for this may not be as full and clear as necessary. It is usually possible to establish a value for each category of investment, and the return earned on that investment. There are three categories of investment:

i Subsidiaries where control is usually achieved by owning 50 per cent or more of shares. Group accounts are prepared as shown in Section 7.2.

ii Associates where significant influence is exercised, usually by owning between 20 per cent and 50 per cent of the shares; and joint ventures where two or more jointly control a company in which they have invested. These are mostly[13] accounted for using the equity method, with the proportion owned (the investment) shown as an asset on the group statement of financial position, and the share of profit earned shown on the income statement.

ILLUSTRATION 7.9

Marks & Spencer	2011 UK	2011 UK	2011 International	2011 International	2011 Total	2011 Total	2010 UK	2010 UK	2010 International	2010 International	2010 Total	2010 Total
Operating profit as a % of sales							$\frac{701}{8,568}$	8%	$\frac{151}{969}$	16%	$\frac{852}{9,537}$	9%
Sales/Assets							$\frac{8,568}{6,243}$	1.37 times	$\frac{969}{910}$	1.06 times	$\frac{9,537}{7,153}$	1.33 times
Operating profit/Assets							$\frac{701}{6,243}$	11%	$\frac{151}{910}$	17%	$\frac{852}{7,153}$	12%

[13] Proportional consolidation is also permitted for joint ventures.

iii Investments in companies where there is no significant influence, where only a small proportion of the shares is normally held. An amount for the investment is shown on the statement of financial position, and dividends receivable (not a share of profits) are shown on the income statement.

7.6 Other Information from Annual Reports

Users of financial statements may be concerned with other aspects of a company's activities, not just their solvency and profitability. They may be seeking a more detailed explanation of what is revealed by the statement of financial position, the income statement and the cash flow statement, and they may be looking for information about future prospects and performance. Companies may choose to disclose all sorts of things in their annual reports and there is often a chairman's statement full of fine-sounding information in the style of advertising and public relations. But there is also quite a lot of useful additional information that is required by law, and which is presented by companies in a fairly standard way.

Directors' report

Companies are also required to produce a directors' report that contains a great deal of fairly standardized formal information, including the following:

- *principal activities* of the company, and any changes;
- *business review* of the activities during the year and of the position at the year end;
- *future developments*;
- *research and development activities*;
- *statement of events after the reporting periods*: any important changes and events since the statement of financial position date;
- *value of land and buildings*: significant differences between statement of financial position values and market value of land and buildings;
- *statement about employee involvement*: policies on providing information to employees, consulting them, any schemes for employees' shares, and increasing understanding of shared ideas about factors affecting the company's success (in companies with over 250 employees);
- *number of disabled employees* and employment policies regarding disabled employees (in companies with over 250 employees);
- *donations* to charities and to political parties are each disclosed separately;
- *purchase of own shares*: number of shares purchased, amount paid and reasons for doing it;
- *information about directors*: their names and the number of shares held by each at the beginning and end of the year;
- *supplier payment*: the company's policy should be disclosed and a calculation of the average number of days taken to pay trade payables.

Substantial information is also provided about directors' remuneration and how it is determined, and about corporate governance and how the directors run the company. There is an auditor's report that usually looks fairly complicated, but uses standard wording and says very little. The principal point of interest is if the auditors state whether or not it is their opinion that the financial statements show a 'true and fair view' (an unqualified or 'clean' audit report) or, alternatively, express some specific or general reservations (a 'qualified' opinion), and a statement of directors' responsibilities, which makes it clear that the financial statements are the responsibility of the directors, not the auditors.

The financial statements include an income statement, a statement of financial position, a statement of *changes in equity* and a cash flow statement. With large listed companies there are usually Parent Company versions of these statements together with a consolidated version (which includes all the subsidiary companies). These are followed by substantial *notes to the financial statements* that include complex but vital information, which may sometimes lead to more obfuscation than clarification. There is usually also a *five-year summary* of results, although these vary considerably: it may not be for five years, and the companies may disclose very little, or a great deal of information for previous years in a standardized format. Serious analysts may want to analyse previous years' financial statements for themselves, or to follow up particular items; most large listed companies now have good websites from which it is possible to download previous years' annual reports and financial statements.

Summary

It is not very difficult to learn to calculate a dozen or so standard accounting ratios based on the simplified versions of company accounts that are usually presented in textbooks and examinations. But when examining the complexities of real companies' financial statements it is easy to be overwhelmed. Relatively straightforward real company financial statements were introduced early in the book. More complicated financial statements, many of which are for groups of companies, should be seen as a challenge and as an opportunity: a challenge to answer the same basic questions about solvency and profitability that have already been introduced; and an opportunity to make use of more detailed information that is available to produce a fuller analysis.

Substantial and detailed information is available to assess the solvency of a company; its performance and how its profitability might be improved; and the performance of its shares on the stock market. The amount of information disclosed is generally increasing, partly in response to official requirements, and partly because companies want to enhance their social, environmental and political reputations and, not least in the market place, to support their share price.

Review of key points

- Interpreting published financial statements is more complex than most textbook examples, and the exact information required is not always available.
- Group or consolidated statements of financial position show goodwill and non-controlling interests. Retained earnings for the group include all those of the parent company, but only the appropriate proportion of retained profits made by subsidiaries since acquisition.
- More sophisticated assessments can be made of a company's solvency than the main ratios shown in Chapters 1 and 4, particularly by using Z-scores.
- Companies disclose key information that enables us to analyse the performance of the different business and geographical segments in which the business operates.
- The published annual reports of most large companies include a wealth of useful information that companies are required to publish, including the notes to the accounts and the directors' report.
- Many annual reports include additional information that is not required by law, about such matters as the company's products and progress, directors, and environmental and social performance. Much of this is of a public relations nature and needs to be interpreted with care.

Self-testing questions

1   Calculate the 20 ratios for Marks and Spencer plc for 2011 to complete the table in Illustration 7.2, and write a report on the company's financial position and performance based on those ratios.

2   What accounting information is most useful in assessing a company's solvency?

3   The summarized statements of financial position of Grand plc and Pony plc at 31 December year 6 were as follows:

	Grand plc	Pony plc
	£m	£m
Non-current assets	180	75
Investment in Pony plc at cost	90	–
Current assets	80	20
Total assets	350	95
Current liabilities	30	15
Ordinary share capital	150	45
Retained earnings	170	35
	350	95

Grand bought 60 per cent of the shares of Pony on 31 December year 3. At that date Pony's retained earnings were £55m. Since that date, the fair value of goodwill has been impaired by £20m. Prepare a group statement of financial position as at 31 December year 6.

4   What key information is disclosed to assess the profitability of the various segments of a company?

5   Calculate the appropriate ratios for Marks & Spencer for 2011 to complete the Table in Illustration 7.9, and comment on the figures produced.

6   You are given the following information about Gobbiediggan International plc:

Segment	UK		Africa		South America	
	Year 1	Year 2	Year 1	Year 2	Year 1	Year 2
	£000	£000	£000	£000	£000	£000
Sales	800	860	300	270	100	180
Operating profit	80	78	40	44	20	21
Operating assets	900	760	200	175	40	60

Making use of appropriate ratios, comment on the performance of each of the geographic segments.

One of the directors of the company considers that the UK market should be abandoned because profits are declining. A second director considers that the Africa market should be abandoned because sales are declining. A third director considers that the South America market should be abandoned because it keeps needing additional investment. Critically assess each of these views.

7   Calculate the Z-score for Marks and Spencer for 2010 and 2011. What are the main reasons for the change between 2010 and 2011?

Assessment questions

1 Select one or two companies' annual reports and accounts and assess the financial position and performance of its various segments and investments in as much detail as the information permits.

2 If a company analyses the ROCE of every division, branch, investment or segment that it operates, and closes down all those with a below average ROCE, then the average ROCE for the company as a whole is bound to increase. Assess this approach to managing a large business.

3 The summarized statements of financial position of Yourow plc and Sentus Ltd at 31 December year 6 were as follows:

	Yourow plc	Sentus Ltd
	£000	£000
Non-current assets	700	400
Investment in Sentus Ltd at cost	450	–
Current assets	250	300
Total assets	1,400	700
Current liabilities	220	170
Ordinary share capital	1,000	430
Retained earnings	180	100
	1,400	700

Yourow bought 75 per cent of the shares of Sentus on 31 December year 2. At that date the retained earnings of Sentus were £70,000. At 31 December year 6 the original value of goodwill had been impaired by £32,000. Prepare the group statement of financial position as at 31 December year 6.

4 You are given the following segmental information about the Willaston Company:

Segment	Men's things		Women's things		Children's things	
	Year 1	Year 2	Year 1	Year 2	Year 1	Year 2
	£000	£000	£000	£000	£000	£000
Sales	400	405	800	820	60	130
Operating profit	80	95	90	92	(20)	(4)
Operating assets	200	180	250	260	10	11

Making use of appropriate ratios, comment on the performance of each of the segments.

5 You are given the following information about the Goodwynne Company:

	Year 2	Year 3
	£000	£000
Sales	1,000	1,100
Operating profit	100	115
Operating assets	700	800

Making use of appropriate ratios, assess the view that the company should concentrate on reducing its operating assets.

6 Interpretation of accounts tends to concentrate on statements of financial position, income statements and cash flow statements. Critically assess the value of other information included in annual reports *either* (a) for companies in general, *or* (b) for one or two particular companies.

Group activities and discussion questions

1 What information would you like to see disclosed in company annual reports and accounts in addition to that which is at present required? Examine the annual report of a few companies that provide a lot more information than the minimum required. To what extent does that information provide you with what you want?

2 It is possible to calculate an almost infinite number of ratios from a company's annual report. What ratios other than the 20 emphasized in this chapter do you think would be useful? Why?

3 Think of a number of companies, or types of company, that have gone bankrupt or have found themselves in serious financial difficulties recently (perhaps airlines, banks or retailers). What do you think led to their financial difficulties? Try to identify some comparable companies, and examine their annual report and accounts. Is there evidence of impending financial difficulties?

4 It is unrealistic to assess the performance of a company on the basis of one figure, such as EPS. To what extent do the complexities in producing this figure undermine its usefulness?

5 Companies that generate cash surpluses can afford to diversify, but they should return the money to the shareholders, and it is for the shareholders to decide the extent to which they wish to diversify their investments. Companies that cannot afford to diversify often borrow money that they cannot afford and make their shareholders' investments more risky; it is for the shareholders to decide whether or not they want more risk. Critically assess these statements.

6 Z-scores are only the beginning. Sophisticated statistical models that produce accurate predictions of share prices are becoming available. Discuss the practicability, limitations and implications of these statements.

Accounting in context

Discuss and comment on the following article in the press. How does the 'beta' factor affect the comparison of an investment in one company or sector with another?

Better bet on beta to get the best out of your portfolio

By Garry White

Volatility over the past few months has been exceptional, as politicians wrangle to find a solution to the debt turmoil. Should a resolution fail to materialise, some sectors will be hit harder than others. The reverse is also true – should agreement be made, then some sectors will benefit more.

One good way of looking at such volatility is through "beta", a measure of the volatility of a particular share or sector against the market as a whole.

The index is assigned a beta of 1. The higher the beta, the more a share moves when the market moves. Shares with low betas are the place to be in a downturn because they fall less than the market falls, but in order to outperform when the market rises, you need more beta in your portfolio at that time. Managing beta is an important part of managing your portfolio.

Here Questor looks at the betas in the FTSE 350 supersectors, to see where the most volatility lies.

Miners have been trapped in a perfect storm of late, as rising costs and falling commodity prices look set to crimp profit margins. It should come as no surprise that the sector is the most volatile in the market. Miners have the highest beta, at 1.705.

Of course, the mining story is more about China than Europe, but the EU imported Chinese goods worth €281.9bn (£176.8bn) in 2010. The total of EU direct investment into China last year also stood at €4.9bn.

In a globalised world, the European and Chinese economies are therefore intrinsically linked. Yesterday, it was also revealed that Chinese manufacturing activity remained weak in October. An implosion in Europe could hence hit the Chinese economy hard – and this would be bad for miners. However, with the medium-term outlook for the sector being particularly strong, a solution to the eurozone crisis should send miners significantly higher.

Automobiles and parts

When times are good, things are fine for car-makers. But when times are bad, then things are very bad indeed. The FTSE 350 auto index is unusual as it contains just one share, GKN. This is a depressing reflection of what has happened to the UK car industry over the past decades.

However, despite a lift from scrappage schemes early on, car-makers have been suffering. This means a cloudy outlook for GKN, a major part of the supply chain.

Last week, we saw a profit warning from French carmaker Peugeot. The group is shedding 6,000 jobs and stopping production for a week to limit oversupply. Volkswagen's recent numbers were good, but it said customers were "worried" about buying cars. However, high-beta GKN will benefit from a successful solution to the eurozone crisis.

Banks

The crisis in Europe is about sovereign debts and the fact that countries such as Spain, Italy and Greece cannot afford to repay creditors.

European banks have been feeling the strain and fears of contagion are very real. It is not surprising that banks have a much higher beta than other sectors, at 1.296.

Last week, when the euro crisis summit came up with a deal to recapitalise banks, Barclays' shares soared by a massive 18pc. This highlights the opportunity in the sector should a political solution be forthcoming. But the high beta also underscores the downside should things turn to dust.

Retail

Perhaps the most surprising sector to be in the low-beta category is retail. That's because the sector is not particularly defensive. Indeed, the FTSE 350 retail sector is down 12pc this year, compared with the FTSE 100 down 9pc.

The reason for the relatively low beta – at 0.641 – is that the sector is more a reflection of what is going on in the UK and European factors are peripheral, and a lot of negativity was factored in to sector valuations last year.

Healthcare

THE FTSE 350 healthcare index is obviously dominated by the two large players – GlaxoSmithKline and AstraZeneca. These two companies have a weighting of more than 85pc – and the sector's beta is 0.554.

Despite the turmoil, they have been a relatively safe home for your cash, but the shares are not likely to be propelled significantly higher should any debt resolution occur.

Utilities

The safest shares to hold in a downturn are utilities. Investors do not need a Nobel Prize in economics to work that out, but the beta figure underlines this fact. Utilities have the lowest beta of all 19 FTSE 350 supersectors, at 0.456.

A slowdown in economic activity will obviously hit manufacturing, so utilities exposed to industrial activity will suffer.

However, cash flows look relatively safe and the sector is all about dividends and an income stream. Some utilities, such as Pennon and SSE, have said they will raise payments by more than the retail price index, which is welcome at a time of high inflation and low interest rates.

Beta demonstrates that utilities are where widows and orphans really should be.

Source: The Telegraph, 2 November 2011.

References and further reading

Altman, E. and E. Hotchkiss (2006) *Corporate Financial Distress and Bankruptcy* (3rd edn.) Hoboken, NJ: Wiley.

Boakes, K. (2010) *Reading and Understanding the Financial Times*. Harlow: FT Prentice Hall.

Financial Times (daily newspaper). Available online at www.ft.com.

Gray, R., J. Bebbington and S. Gray (2010) *Social and Environmental Accounting* (SAGE Library in Accounting and Finance).

McKenzie, W. (2010) *Financial Times Guide to Using and Interpreting Company Accounts* (4th edn.). Harlow: FT Prentice Hall.

O'Regan, P. (2006) *Financial Information Analysis* (2nd edn.). Chichester: Wiley.

Rees, B. (2011) *Financial Analysis* (4th edn.). Harlow: Pearson Education.

Sugden, A., P. Gee and G. Holmes (2008) *Interpreting Company Reports and Accounts* (10th edn). Harlow: FT Prentice Hall.

Taffler, R.J. (1983) The assessment of company solvency and performance using a statistical model – a comparative UK-based study, *Accounting and Business Research*, 15(52): 295–308.

Taffler, R.J. and H. Tisshaw (1977) Going, going, gone – four factors which predict, *Accountancy*, March, p. 6.

www.cifc.co.uk (select: benchmarking and interfirm comparison; a standardized basis for using ratios to compare different firms)

www.experian.com (a credit rating agency)

www.investorschronicle.co.uk/public/home.html (a variety of information about companies, interpretation and performance)

www://annualreport.marksandspencer.com/ (gives Marks and Spencer Group accounts in full)

When you have read this chapter, log on to the Online Learning Centre website at *www.mcgraw-hill.co.uk/textbooks/leiwy* to explore chapter-by-chapter test questions, further reading and more online study tools.

Chapter

8

Current Issues in Financial Reporting

Chapter contents

✓ Learning objectives

After studying this chapter you will be able to:

✓ Explain what is meant by *creative accounting* and understand that the term is sometimes applied to very different practices

✓ Explain why creative accounting has developed

✓ Give examples of a number of creative accounting practices

✓ Describe and evaluate the various approaches to dealing with creative accounting

✓ Explain what is meant by *corporate social reporting,* and understand its relationship with corporate social responsibility

✓ Appreciate the application of corporate social reporting in particular areas, such as employees and the environment

✓ Discuss the role of accountants in corporate social reporting

✓ Describe and assess corporate social reporting in practice

8.1 Introduction

Financial accounting and reporting has gradually developed over the last two centuries to help to make the directors of companies accountable to their shareholders. In the mid-nineteenth century, when companies first became popular entities, it was relatively easy for directors to set up companies that did little more than defraud shareholders and creditors of their money. In return for the privilege of 'limited liability', governments steadily introduced stricter requirements for accounting, financial reporting and auditing. As new and more complex abuses developed, so stricter accounting regulations were introduced through a series of Companies Acts.

In the last few decades of the twentieth century 'creative accounting' became a fine art, and developed more quickly than governments were able to regulate through Companies Acts. The accounting profession took on the role of producing 'accounting standards' that specified definitions, measurement and disclosure in financial accounting. By the first decade of the twenty-first century these bodies had become more powerful, with the backing of governments, and more international.

It has long been recognized that companies are accountable to both shareholders and creditors who have an interest in the survival and prospects of companies. But other groups in society, and indeed society generally, also have an interest in the activities of companies, and it may be argued that companies are accountable to society generally for both their social and environmental activities and impacts.

The first part of this chapter deals with creative accounting, its continuing problems and attempts to control it. The second part deals with endeavours to develop social and environmental reporting. In conventional financial accounting 'the bottom line' refers to the profit for the year figure, or perhaps earnings per share (EPS). Many now advocate a 'triple bottom line' showing performance in three areas: (1) financial or economic; (2) ecological or environmental; and (3) social. This may be characterized as concerns with profit, the planet and people.

The section on creative accounting shows how difficult it is to establish and enforce rules that measure financial or economic performance. The second part of the chapter deals with the issue of social and environmental accounting.

8.2 What is Creative Accounting?

When the financial and banking crisis, and 'credit crunch', hit the world in 2008/9, it was bankers, not accountants, who were seen as the main culprits. But, as with so many financial scandals, questions were asked about the reliability of published accounting statements. In the $50bn Bernard Madoff fraud in the USA, the financial records were said to be 'utterly unreliable'. In the UK some of the biggest banks made substantial rights issues, before the crisis hit, using financial statements that some, later, said were dubious. It was even alleged that one bank was insolvent at the time it issued an optimistic-sounding prospectus. It is not surprising that sometimes companies are tempted to bend the truth, to put a favourable gloss on things, or worse, when they present financial information.

The term 'creative accounting' is used in relation to a variety of different accounting practices. At one extreme it is used to describe fraudulent and criminal activities. At the other extreme it might be viewed more benignly: as being no more than producing an honest presentation that emphasizes the favourable aspects of a company's performance. There is a natural desire for companies to put a positive spin on their financial position and performance.

It is unlikely that a company's annual report will say:

> *The company has three divisions. Division A is the largest and is a complete disaster; losses continue to mount. Division B is going downhill and is now running at a loss. Division C is small, but it did make a tiny profit.*

A more optimistic version, such as the following, is more likely to appear:

> *Division C has expanded rapidly and sales and profits are at record levels. Division B is*
> *coping well with difficult world economic conditions. Division A has made good progress in*
> *meeting its targets and is expected to show further progress in the coming year.*

Investors and other users of annual reports and accounts can look at the published, audited figures to establish the relationship between management claims and the 'real' financial performance and position.

The development of creative accounting

In the late 1960s there were some serious and high-profile accounting scandals from which it seemed that companies could choose almost any accounting principles they liked. What was a profit to one accountant would be a loss to another, and confidence in the accountancy profession was at a low ebb.

The accountancy profession set up the Accounting Standards Committee (ASC) which, in the 1970s and 1980s, produced a series of Statements of Standard Accounting Practice (SSAPs) which were intended to raise standards of financial reporting, and to reduce the areas of difference and variety in accounting practice. They had some success in improving financial reporting, but it was in the 1980s that the term 'creative accounting' came to be widely used, even in the popular press.

Popular books on creative accounting by Griffiths (1986), followed by Jameson (1988), argued that companies had a wide choice of accounting principles, policies and practices, and could justify almost any profit figures that they wished. The reputation of the ASC suffered, and, following the recommendations of the Dearing Committee (1988), the accounting standards-setting arrangements were revamped, and the Accounting Standards Board (ASB) was established.

The situation improved in the 1990s, but the scandals did not go away. In a new version of his book, Griffiths (1995) argued that some order had been brought to the chaos of the regulatory framework of accounting, and that the ASB had made tremendous progress in restoring the integrity and credibility of accounting standards. The more flagrant abuses had been banned, but an extensive range of techniques was still available that could be used to massage the figures. The Financial Reporting and Review Panel (FRRP) was demonstrating that it could be effective in enforcing the application of accounting standards. But, he argued, 'creative accounting still flourishes ... there is still tremendous scope for manipulation'. He concluded that his basic 1986 premise still held: companies were still fiddling their profits.

Other books popularized the idea that creative accounting was (and probably still is) widespread. Smith and Hannah (1991) highlighted a number of creative accounting practices. They produced a list of major companies, and put a number of 'blobs' against them; one blob for each of the questionable practices that the company adopted. Some companies came out with a clean bill of health, but serious questions were raised about the credibility of the financial statements of others. More recent versions by Smith show that the problems have not gone away. Other books in the 1990s (e.g. McBarnet and Whelan, 1999; Pijper, 1993) continued to highlight the problems of creative accounting in the UK.

But, in 2001/2, the limelight was taken by US companies with a number of major accounting scandals that overshadowed what came to be seen as relatively minor problems in the UK.

In November 2001 Enron, one of the world's largest energy groups, admitted that between 1997 and 2000 various 'special purpose entities' should have been included in the group's accounts, which would have substantially reduced profits. In December 2001 they filed for bankruptcy. Arthur Andersen, Enron's auditors, admitted shredding or deleting thousands of relevant documents and were found guilty of obstructing the course of justice. Arthur Andersen, one of the world's largest accountancy firms, collapsed, and its business was split up and taken over by rival firms. Enron had paid Andersen $25m in audit fees for 2001 and another $27m for other non-audit services. Many of the accounting policies that were criticized at the peak of the controversy had previously hardly been a matter for comment. Suddenly the climate changed and they were presented as scandals or abuses. The main problems seemed to be in the USA, and action was taken by establishing stricter requirements under the Sarbanes–Oxley Act. Former Enron chief executives, Kenneth Lay and Jeffrey Skilling, were found guilty of the biggest fraud in corporate history after their energy giant collapsed into bankruptcy. Others became more cautious as the effects of the Sarbanes–Oxley Act were felt, and the enhanced role of the International Accounting Standards Board (IASB) became effective, with more clear-cut accounting standards and moves towards international harmonization. Other scandals have occurred since 2001 including Bernie Madoff, Anglo Irish Bank and Olympus Corporation. The most notorious scandal at the centre of the global economic crisis involved the financial services giant, Lehman Brothers. Lehman had borrowed huge sums to finance loans in sub-prime housing mortgages. At first, the company disclosed huge profits from this activity but did not recognize in their accounts the risks attaching to these loans, ignoring the accounting concept of 'prudence'. And when the housing market collapsed, massive losses arose on these loans. During 2008, as the horrible truth of the overvaluation of these assets became apparent, Lehman's share price collapsed and in September 2008, the company filed for Chapter 13 bankruptcy protection. However, in spite of the collapse of Enron, Lehman Brothers, and other names that now trip off the tongue of newspaper readers, and the humiliation of their senior executives, creative accounting has not disappeared and a number of problem areas remain.

The effects

Creative accounting is sometimes used to:

1 *Boost reported profits (or reduce reported losses)* – As long as the profits are credible, this is likely to lead to higher share prices; but share prices can collapse rapidly when credibility goes. Senior managers and directors often have remuneration packages, bonuses, shares and options, the value of which is increased by higher profits. The temptations of 'aggressive accounting' are obvious.

2 *Smooth profits* – In a year of very high profits the creative accountant might understate them, and keep something back to supplement reported profits in leaner years. Investors are probably more impressed by a company that manages to increase its profits every year than by one that seems to swing from profits to losses. 'Income smoothing' may help to maximize shareholders' wealth. It is, of course, contrary to accounting rules, but it is likely that, at the margin, judgements in some companies are exercised in a more prudent way when the profits are very good, and in a less prudent way when profits have fallen.

3 *Manipulating ratios* – Creative accounting can also be used to manipulate key ratios that are used by analysts, and to produce more healthy-looking statements of financial position. If a company wants to demonstrate that it has a high return on capital employed it will want to maximize profits; but it will not want to see high figures for capital employed. Such companies may avoid increasing asset values, and find ways of reducing asset values that do not hit profits too hard, particularly in relatively lean years.

4 *Facilitate borrowing* – Creative accounting can show higher asset values to support borrowing, and reduce gearing levels. Borrowings often come with covenants, to protect lenders, requiring specified gearing or current ratios. If land and buildings are revalued (upwards), that automatically increases the figure for equity and shows lower gearing.

5 *Flattering management* – Directors and managers want to look good, and to keep their jobs. After a takeover bid, the new management team are likely to be under pressure to prove that they are more successful than their predecessors. Poor performance can be blamed on the previous management while strikingly better results appear to have been produced by the new management.

Judgement becoming creative

There is inevitably a need for judgement in many areas of accounting. With depreciation we can rarely be sure how long a non-current asset will be used, or what its residual value will be. If an airline changes its depreciation policy so that aircraft are depreciated over 25 years rather than 15 years, it will make a massive difference to profits. In a year when profits are a little low it would not be surprising if a company suddenly decides that non-current assets will have longer lives so that depreciation is reduced and profits are increased.

We cannot be sure what the net realizable value of inventories of unsold goods are.[1] When a company is doing well it may have time to check that all inventories really are written down to net realizable value. When profits are looking a little low, there may be other priorities than estimating the latest net realizable value figures and ensuring that everything has been written down accordingly.

Perhaps provisions for bad debts are more prudent in some years than others. Similarly, in a year of low profits, there may be no harm if a few repairs and renewals get classified as capital expenditure. And it is only natural to delay doing repairs when times are hard. It can all start off fairly harmlessly and almost unconsciously: where there is a margin for error or judgement, profits can be understated a little in the good years, so that when the bad years come, accounting policies can be reviewed to release something held back by previous caution.

Gradually, there can be more pressure to increase profits and accounting policies seem to be twisted in one direction only. At first this might all be legitimate, and within the rules. But it can become, dubious, illegal and even criminal.

A company might operate a number of hotels and be reasonably successful for many years. Then occupancy levels drop. Keeping the hotels in a good state of repair, and maintaining their appearance is a major expense that hits profits. At first the company might decide to try to maintain profits by deferring all but essential repairs. Carpets are not replaced until they are threadbare and dangerous; rooms are not redecorated until the paper is peeling off the walls and the smart white paintwork has either turned to a gentle shade of puce, or gone mouldy; and the furniture is starting to fall apart. After a few years it is not repairs that are needed, but a total refurbishment. Fortunately, refurbishment can be classified as capital expenditure, and does not hit profits. A new policy emerges: the expense for repairs virtually disappears; all hotels are refurbished every four or five years.

If there are still no profits from running the hotels, more extreme accounting policies are needed. Suppose that the company owns a hotel that originally cost £8m, but now needs £2m spending on it for refurbishment. It has a market value of £10m. The company sells the hotel to a friendly building company for £10m. The building company does the refurbishment, and sells the hotel back to the hotel company for £13m. The building company is happy with the contract: it has made £1m profit. The hotel company is happy with the arrangement: what might have been an expense for repairs, over the years, of £2m has become a profit (on sale of the hotel) of £2m. And its statement of financial position looks better. Instead of having a tatty old hotel shown at £8m, it has a newly refurbished one shown at £13m. And it had to borrow only £3m to achieve this.

It could get worse and more dubious, and illegal. Maybe the hotel is not really worth £10m. But there may be ways of finding a building company willing to enter into a contract to buy it for £10m, if there is a guaranteed profit of £1m. Perhaps there is more profit to be made from specialized arrangements to buy and sell hotels than there is from actually running hotels.

Other strange contracts can be created. A hotel might find that it expects spare room capacity worth £1m at quiet times of the year. It might be glad to sell that spare capacity to a package holiday company for £500,000 – giving the hotel company £500,000 of revenues that it would not otherwise have had. The package holiday company might then find that it has more capacity than it needs, and sell on half of what it has bought to a conference company for £600,000 (making £100,000 profit for doing almost nothing). Then the conference company sells part of what it has bought – and the conference company buys some surplus capacity on an airline's routes from London to one of the places where it has hotel capacity; the airline has bought that spare capacity from another airline, and it had bought it from a hotel that had bought it from another airline – or perhaps it was the original airline, or hotel, or conference company. This had happened, similarly, in earlier years with telecommunication companies making profits by selling spare capacity to each other.

---

[1] Inventories should be shown at the lower of cost and net realizable value. It is, of course, necessary to know what the net realizable value is if it is to be compared with cost.

Creative accounting can start with cautious use of judgement that varies a little from year to year, depending on the circumstances. It can end with serious fraud and criminal activity; and with the company going into liquidation – with lots of people losing their livelihood, their pensions and their savings. But some people probably manage to get out in time, after making a lot of money. Creative accounting can be a mechanism for redistributing wealth from the poor, weak and vulnerable to those who are strong, clever and ruthless. Financial accounting has an important role to play in trying to prevent and disclose such activities.

How bad are the various techniques?

Where there are suggestions or accusations that creative accounting has been used, we could ask, on a scale of 1–10, how bad is it? Number 1 would be almost nothing wrong at all; number 10 would be the worst possible. The following is not intended to be authoritative or definitive. But it does give an idea of the range of different activities that some might classify as being 'creative accounting':

1 There is nothing questionable about the financial statements, but information has been presented to emphasize the more favourable aspects of financial position and performance, and to de-emphasize the least favourable.

2 The emphasis on the favourable aspects is so strong as to suggest more of a propaganda exercise than a balanced report.

3 All financial statements are properly drawn up, but somehow the rules seem to flatter the company's performance whereas a different selection of accounting policies and measurements would be less flattering.

4 All financial statements have been properly drawn up in accordance with the requirements of company law and accounting standards. Where the official accounting requirements allow choice or flexibility, the company selects those options that tend to flatter the financial statements.

5 There are departures from accounting standards, but these have been properly disclosed and explained, and the financial effects have been quantified.

6 There is a suspicion that there are departures from accounting standards that have not been disclosed. Some of the figures are questionable.

7 Rules and definitions have been pushed to the limit, and perhaps a little beyond. Judgements have been exercised to come up with treatments that the auditors have been persuaded to accept, but which, on the face of it, other accountants would find unacceptable.

8 Transactions and arrangements seem to have been deliberately designed to take advantage of, or to avoid, particular rules or accounting treatments.

9 *Clear* breaches of accounting standards without proper disclosure of departures or reasons for them.

10 Criminal activity, fraud and deception.

8.3 Some Problem Areas

One of the difficulties of describing the problem areas and neatest tricks of creative accounting is that by the time they come to be described in books such as this, they have become so well known that the accounting standard-setters have brought in measures to limit them.

Non-recurring items

In the 1970s we had a plethora of 'extraordinary items', which were 'below the line' and so did not affect profit or EPS. These non-recurring items might include: losses on the sale of a manufacturing plant; exceptional write-offs of goodwill and other non-current assets; inventory write-offs; foreign currency losses; and costs of reorganizations and closures. Such 'extraordinary treatment' has now been effectively banned. Even exceptional items must be shown as part of profits (or losses); these are often separately disclosed, and there may be different profits after tax, and EPS[2] figures, before and after non-recurring items. Companies are also required to show separately profits from continuing operations, and from discontinued operations. If an investor is seeking a profit figure that is not unduly influenced by unusual items, as a basis for forecasting future profits, it can be difficult to know which figure to choose. When profits are poor, it must be tempting to highlight 'unusual' items that have affected them, and to try to give the impression that next year things will be back to normal, and much better.

At the height of the banking crisis, when some banks were losing billions of pounds, Barclays did relatively well: it made £6bn profit in 2008.[3] *Investors Chronicle*[4] greeted these results with the headline '*Barclays' earnings flattered by one-off gains*', and stated the following:

> *Barclays' shares rose over 7 per cent on the back or these figures after the bank reported a bigger-than-expected rise in second-half profits. However, earnings were flattered by a number of one-off gains. These included a £2.26bn gain from acquiring Lehman Brothers' North American businesses (reflecting the excess of the fair value of the net assets over the consideration) and a £326m profit on the disposal of Barclays' closed UK life assurance business.*
>
> *There was also £219m of gains from the VISA IPO and from selling shares in MasterCard.*

This all makes it very difficult for the investor to decide what is a normal level of profits, the basis for forecasting future years. The creative accountant might be tempted to say that all good news is normal, and whenever there is bad news, it is exceptional, nonrecurring, and outside the control of the company.

Provisions

Strange things can happen when one company is taken over by another company. The 'victim' company may have been pottering along quite nicely with modest profits. Then along comes a new management, and what looked like last year's profits suddenly become substantial losses. The new management say that inventories and fixed assets are mostly obsolete and write them down to much lower values. There will have to be reorganizations and redundancies, and a provision must be made against the most recent profit figure to allow for this. Some of their customers look in poor shape, and might not pay up, so a large provision for bad debts is created. Any intangible assets that the 'victim' has paid for are likely to be virtually worthless, and so are written down to very low values, or written off completely. Last year's expected profits are suddenly converted into a substantial loss, and it is all blamed on the previous management.

The new management, perhaps they are company doctors,[5] are able to transform the company's performance. The following year, inventories can be sold for much more than their new, written-down value; the costs of reorganizations and redundancies can be charged against the provision that was created; the provisions for bad debts were not needed as customers 'unexpectedly' pay up; and depreciation, amortization and impairment charges are substantially reduced because of write-offs the previous year. The dreadful losses that they inherited are suddenly turned into substantial profits the next year.

---

[2] There should always be two earnings per share figures: one 'basic', and one 'diluted' showing the effects of an increase in the number of shares due to such things as conversions.

[3] Down from £7bn the previous year.

[4] 13–19 February 2009.

[5] Perhaps even witch doctors who can create a massive improvement in a company's performance, as if by magic.

For some managements there may be a temptation to throw all sorts of dubious expenses and write-offs into a 'big bath', or massive provision. All the bad news can be got rid of in one year; future years can then only appear to be better. IAS 37 Provisions, Contingent Liabilities and Contingent Assets is intended to curtail such (ab)use of provisions. For a provision to be recognized, there must be a present obligation (legal or constructive) involving a probable outflow of economic resources of which a reliable estimate can be made. This may be based on past practices, or published policies, which lead to a valid expectation that a payment will be made. This is all rather more subjective than is desirable and still allows some scope for creative accounting.

Goodwill

Goodwill arises in financial statements when one company buys another company, and pays more for it than the net asset value as shown on its statement of financial position. This is normal practice. If a company has a net asset value of, say, £10m, it is very unlikely that the owners of that company would be willing to sell it for £10m, especially if the company has had a good profit record for a number of years. Assets are often undervalued on statements of financial position, and when there is a takeover, the assets should be revalued to 'fair value'. A company might have net assets with a statement of financial position value of £10m, and a 'fair value' of, say, £12m. But if the company is successful and profitable, anyone wanting to take it over should expect to pay more than £12m. Perhaps they pay £15m.

If a business has net assets of £12m, and £15m is paid for that business, there is no problem recording the payment of £15m, or the net assets of £12m. But £3m has been paid for goodwill. Is this to be recorded as an expense, or as an asset? Treating it as an expense would hit profits too hard. Showing it as an asset might be open to question: does the business really own something worth £3m? Standard practice for accounting for goodwill has varied over the years. Now IFRS 3 has no requirement for systematic amortization. Instead, there is an annual impairment review. The company decides by how much goodwill has been impaired (if at all!) over the previous year, and the amount of the impairment is an expense in calculating profits. This is an obvious area for creative accounting.

Where profits have been seriously hit it is difficult to say that there is no impairment of goodwill. In 2008, the Royal Bank of Scotland charged a massive write-down of goodwill, which relieves subsequent years of impairment charges. In most circumstances impairment calculations are based on estimates of future cash flows that an acquired business will generate. Such calculations are not factual but are based on future estimates and on many assumptions that are very sensitive to slight changes. The scope for creatively selecting assumptions that are most appropriate for the desired result is obvious.

Reducing choices

In a number of areas, standard-setters are attempting to reduce the choices available to management by establishing criteria for deciding between alternatives. In the past there was often a free choice, but the criteria for making those choices have steadily become clearer, leaving less scope for creative accounting – or perhaps making the activities of the creative accountant more complex.

Development expenditure

There has long been a problem with expenditure on research and development and whether it should be written off as an expense when it is incurred, or whether it could be carried forward as an asset on the statement of financial position. The old SSAP 13 laid down that research expenditure should be written off when it is incurred, and that is still the case. But development expenditure *could* be carried forward as an asset on the statement of financial position *provided* it met certain criteria: companies could choose. Now, IAS 38 lays down that development expenditure *should* be recognized as an internally generated intangible asset (and carried forward on the statement of financial position, not immediately written off through the income statement), if, and only if, certain things can be demonstrated (such as that the project is technically feasible; that when completed it can be used or sold; how it will generate economic benefits; the availability of sufficient resources to complete it; and the ability to measure reliably the resources required to complete it). If these criteria are all met, then it should be recognized as an asset; there appears to be no choice. However, a company can choose whether (a) to put in sufficient effort and resources to demonstrate what is required; or (b) simply to write it off as an expense (as many pharmaceutical companies do).

Capitalization of interest

There are also areas where, currently, choices still remain. When a company constructs its own non-current assets (perhaps building a hotel) most of the costs are capitalized and become part of the cost of the non-current assets. A company is likely to borrow money while building, and to incur interest costs. Most traditional accountants might say that interest costs should be written off in the period in which they are incurred. But some would choose to capitalize them and treat interest as being part of the cost of the asset. IAS 23 specifies that writing off interest as an expense is the benchmark (or normal) treatment; but it is an allowed alternative treatment to include attributable interest payable as part of the cost of a non-current asset on the statement of financial position.

Revenue recognition

It is not always clear exactly when a sale takes place, and when the revenues from sales should be recognized. For bookkeeping convenience, a sale may be recognized in an accounting system when the invoice is sent to the customer. But sometimes, companies who are not doing very well are tempted to bring forward the date on which sales are recognized; this will have the effect of increasing the sales in the current period.[6] They might, for example, choose to recognize the revenue when an order for goods or services is first received, and this is allowed. The problem of 'revenue recognition' is explored more fully in Section 12.2 of Chapter 12. Currently, the issue is still 'work in progress' for the standard-setters. Meanwhile, some companies are choosing to recognize revenues as soon as a contract is signed, even though it might be years before a service is delivered and the cash flows appear.

Share options

If a company wants to minimize the amount of salaries that count as an expense, employees can be paid in share options instead of money. This became fairly common practice at the height of the dot-com boom (see Example 8.1).

Share options appear to cost the company nothing, and were not usually recorded as an expense. But existing shareholders do lose out: when someone exercises their options to buy, existing shareholders suddenly own a smaller portion of the company, and in a sense, the person who exercises the options has made a gain at their expense. Generally, such share option schemes are approved by shareholders at a general meeting and they will approve of such schemes if they believe the share option scheme will motivate directors and senior staff to focus upon increasing the company's share price. Such share options cannot be exercised within three years of the date they are granted and so senior management will benefit only if the share prices rise in that period. IFRS 2 now requires full reporting of share-based payments and detailed disclosure.

Suspicious treatments

Sometimes accountants are creative in producing profit figures that are not supported by the company's underlying performance. Perhaps people who work for the company know that it is going downhill; perhaps there are terrible delays in paying creditors. But still healthy-looking profit figures are produced.

One way of detecting questionable accounting is to compare the amount of tax a company is paying with its reported profit figures. If a company is paying virtually no corporation tax it must be

---

[6] If sales are brought forward to be included in this year, the sales figure for the following year is reduced.

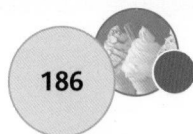

Example 8.1

Dorothy accepted a job with the e.vilwich company, selling potions on the internet. The job carried no salary or commission but she was given the option of buying 100,000 shares in the company for £1 each. When she joined the company the market price of the shares was only 50 pence. But before she left the company the market price had gone up to £11.

Dorothy bought her 100,000 shares for £100,000, and then immediately sold them for £1,100,000. She had received no salary; she had cost the company nothing; and she had become a millionairess.

telling HM Revenue and Customs that it is making virtually no profits. But if at the same time it is declaring substantial profits in its annual reports, it is worth further investigation. It may be that the company has invested heavily in non-current assets, and so has generous capital allowances for corporation tax purposes. Or it may be more suspicious. Companies might be engaging in questionable tax-saving schemes which might, in due course, be overturned by the courts.

A cash flow statement can also give indications of what is 'really' going on if profit figures seem questionable. It is easier to generate fictitious profit figures than to produce fictitious cash. Sooner or later a company is going to need more cash to keep going. A genuinely profitable company generates cash; and a healthy company can usually raise cash without much difficulty, typically by borrowing. But if a company keeps needing to borrow more, it may raise questions, and its statement of financial position will start to look very weak if burdened by too much debt. The company may try to borrow in ways that do not appear on the statement of financial position.

When a company wants more non-current assets it may:

1 borrow the money and buy the non-current assets;
2 lease the non-current assets.

In the first instance, there is clearly an asset and a liability; both appear on the statement of financial position. In the second instance, the financial effects are very similar: the company has the use of the asset just as if it owns it; and it has to make repayments, just as if it had borrowed the money. Leasing was seen as a way of, in effect, borrowing money, but keeping the borrowings off the statements of financial position. Creditors would not know the extent of the company's commitments to make payments under leasing agreements, and might be misled into lending more money.

But accounting standards (currently IAS 17) put a stop to this. Some leases are defined as 'finance leases' and treated just as if the company owned the non-current asset that it had leased: both the asset, and the liability to pay for it, had to be shown on the statement of financial position. One way of raising money 'off statement of financial position' had been ended. But companies sought other methods. The temptation to raise additional financing through dubious off statement of financial position arrangements was a key feature of the major accounting scandal with Enron in 2002, and its subsequent collapse.

Increasingly sophisticated, even devious, forms of off statement of financial position finance were developed, and the need to report the 'economic substance' of an arrangement rather than its legal form became accepted. Now, the requirements of IAS 32 and IAS 39 are detailed and complex. Whatever the legal technicalities might be, if a company has incurred a financial commitment it must be shown as such. In the USA the rules appear to be stricter, but the more strict and clear the rules are, the easier it is to create financial arrangements that just fall within the letter of the rules, but are a breach of the spirit of them. The UK approach errs on the side of principle rather than strict rules, and the idea of 'economic reality' takes priority over 'legal form'. It may be, however, that the international standards will be increasingly 'rules-based' in line with US standards.

Fuzzy rules

The accounting standard-setters have tried to move away from allowing companies a free choice between alternative treatments. They have done this by specifying the circumstances in which each should apply. Unfortunately, such specifications and rules tend to become fuzzy at the edges as some companies interpret them creatively.

The fuzzy rules, and the choice between the 'acquisition' (or 'purchase') and the 'merger' (or 'pooling of interests') methods of producing consolidated accounts, all but disappeared when strict criteria were specified for the use of the merger method. Now, with IFRS 3, there is no choice: the merger method is prohibited.

There are other areas where the standard-setters have tried to establish clear rules, including provisions; deferred tax; definition of associates; recognition of profits on uncompleted long-term contracts; the basis on which production overheads are included in inventory valuations; and defining exactly which leases should be shown on the statement of financial position. The rules appear to be clear; there appears to be no choice. But there is always some fuzziness in rules in marginal cases. And it is always possible that companies structure financial transactions in a particular way so as to be able to use the accounting treatment that shows their results in the best light.

Conclusion

Accounting standard-setters are steadily becoming more strict: they are reducing and eliminating choices; and more effective enforcement mechanisms are being implemented. But it seems unlikely that the problems of creative accounting will ever be completely solved. Perhaps it is unrealistic to expect (m)any problems to be completely solved. The present trend is for a steady increase in the length and complexity of accounting standards. But as the rules get fuller and more detailed, so some practitioners find increasingly complex ways around them. This in turn leads to the need for even more detailed standards to close loopholes that have been found. When these become pressing, financial reporting standards are frequently revised, and additional guidance is given. Finding ways around the additional guidance becomes more complex, and so it goes on. If present trends continue, by the time the average reader of this book reaches the present age of the writer, there will be more accounting and auditing standards, rules, principles and guidance than anyone could read in a lifetime. In July 2006 the IASB recognized the problem of too many standards being produced, 'constant tinkering' with them, and the need for preparers and users to catch up.

In spite of the efforts of the accountancy profession and the standard-setters, many would argue that creative accounting is still alive and well. A wide range of choices in the way that companies can measure and report their financial performance still remains.

8.4 How to Curtail Creative Accounting

Many different suggestions have been made for dealing with the problem of creative accounting, many of them building on what is already happening. The main ones are as follows.

Accounting standards

1 The production of clearer accounting standards that reduce or eliminate choices.
2 The 'benchmark' argument recognizes that there will never be 100 per cent agreement or standardization. There can be a single recommended treatment that is a 'benchmark'; where companies adopt a different treatment, the financial effects of doing this should be quantified and disclosed.
3 Stronger legal backing for accounting standards.

4 Enhancing the role of international accounting standards.

5 More effective monitoring and enforcement.

6 Principles rather than rules. The US approach seems to be more 'rules-based' – and it is always possible to find ways around the letter of the rule. The UK and international standards emphasize principles, and the importance of 'substance' (economic reality) rather than legal form.

7 Current cost accounting is favoured by some as a way of having clearer principles about asset valuation. But others see it as introducing more flexibility.

8 Cash flow accounting, if based simply on receipts and payments of cash, would reduce creativity. But there would be some subjectivity in classifying cash flows, and a serious loss of accruals-based information (like statement of financial positions).

The term 'cash flow accounting' is sometimes used to mean something quite different. Some people advocate the production of statements of financial position that use valuations based on the net present value of the future cash flows that an item is expected to generate. The amount of profit for a period would be based on the increase in the net asset value of the business between the two statement of financial position dates. This could lead to more creativity.

Auditing

There have been many criticisms of auditing arrangements, particularly relating to their perceived lack of independence from management. There is certainly a gap between what some people expect of auditors and what are more realistic expectations, as shown in Illustration 8.1.

Improvements might be made in a number of ways, such as the following:

1 Rotating senior audit partners more often so that they do not work too closely with management.

2 Audit fees being set by an independent body rather than being negotiated by management.

3 Auditors being appointed by an independent body.

4 Prohibiting auditors from non-audit work for audit clients.

5 Restricting companies in recruiting their accounting staff from the firms that audit them.

Punishing offenders

Where it is clear that illegal creative accounting has taken place there is a case for more transparent and effective punishment of offenders. Various voluntary codes exist in the UK for improved corporate governance, relying particularly on non-executive directors. These have achieved some success. In the USA the Sarbanes–Oxley Act (2002) is much stricter in making it clear who is responsible, and what sanctions are likely.

Radical proposals

Various more radical proposals have been made, both right wing and left wing.

Right wing

We could argue that the whole regulatory approach to accounting is a waste of time and money; it serves only to build up the bureaucratic empires of the regulators; it will always be unsatisfactory, and will always lead to demands for more resources for the regulators. Accounting and auditing is a matter for agreement between the shareholders and the directors.

A right-wing perspective could take a *laissez-faire* approach, or it could rely on freedom of access to information.

ILLUSTRATION 8.1

Expectation	More realistic
1 The financial statements are prepared by the auditors; the auditors agree with everything in them and are responsible for them	The directors are responsible for preparing the financial statements. Auditors agree only that they represent one of perhaps several possible 'true and fair' views
2 The financial statements are correct and accurate; a different auditor would produce the same financial statements from the same basic information	The auditors do not prepare the financial statements, and as there are many areas requiring judgement, different accountants would probably come to different conclusions (e.g. on rates of depreciation; or the appropriate provision for bad debts). The decisions belong to the directors
3 The financial statements show what a company is worth; assets have been properly valued	Most assets are shown at some variation of historic cost. Even if they were shown at some sort of current value, the value of the business as a whole would almost certainly be very different from the value of the separable assets less liabilities
4 The auditors have checked and ascertained that no significant fraud or irregularities have taken place	The auditors are on the look-out for fraud, but they are not responsible for finding it all. And even if they find some, provided it is not too enormous, they will still say that the financial statements show a true and fair view
5 The business is a going concern and is not likely to collapse or fail in the foreseeable future	The auditors check to see if there are any doubts about the business being a going concern, and report accordingly. But there can be no guarantee that it will not collapse in the near future
6 The management of the company is reputable, competent, efficient and effective	Auditors are usually happy to take fees from even the most hopeless managers and are not likely to disclose any incompetence!
7 The audit report draws attention to any doubts about the company's finances	If there are doubts about the company's immediate financial survival, the auditors should comment
8 Auditors are independent and cannot be got rid of by directors	In theory auditors have great security and independence. But directors can easily put an audit out to tender, and replace existing auditors
9 Auditors are controlled and disciplined by a professional body that clearly specifies what is required of them	This is a reasonable expectation
10 Auditors are more concerned with their duty to the public and their reputation than with maximizing their own remuneration	This is more a matter of opinion!
11 Auditors are experts and are competent to determine if the financial statements show a 'true and fair view'	In some industries, such as banking, some transactions, some assets and some liabilities are so highly specialized and their complexity so constantly evolving, that it is unlikely that most people in the industry, let alone the auditors, unreally fully understand them

1 *Laissez-faire* – The market-based argument is that there is no need for legislation or public involvement in the ways in which companies do their accounting, or in the existence, role or operations of auditing firms. Companies have a vested interest in supplying credible information to capital markets, and auditing firms have a financial interest in maintaining their reputations. Companies that supply duff information will be punished in the capital markets; share prices will collapse; the companies will be taken over at bargain basement prices; and the directors will lose their jobs when their more credible competitors take over. Similarly, auditing firms that give their names to incredible accounting treatments will soon lose credibility, and be of no use to their clients.

Eventually they will end up like Arthur Andersen – the major international accounting firm that collapsed with the Enron scandal. The market takes care of everything. There is no need for public involvement.

This argument is out of favour at present. As long as there are financial scandals, governments want to be seen to play a role in dealing with the problems. The UK approach tends to be gentle and consultative and the accountancy profession can usually talk governments around to their way of thinking. Following Enron, WorldCom and other scandals, the USA adopted very strong measures with the Sarbanes–Oxley Act.

2 *Freedom of access to information* – Financial statements provide summaries of transactions and of what can be a huge amount of financial data. In the early days of companies, when there were fewer shareholders and fewer financial transactions, it was practicable to open up the books of account to individuals[7] who could see all transactions for themselves. If someone chose to present 'creative' accounts of what had happened, it would be difficult to pull the wool over the eyes of shareholders who could inspect everything for themselves. Such an approach became impractical as the number of shareholders, and the number of financial transactions, increased enormously. Shareholders became dependent on the version of events that was created for them by account-ants, directors and auditors. But computerization may have changed all of that. When we read that schoolboys with computers in their bedrooms can penetrate the secrets of Pentagon defence sys-tems, and fraudsters or pranksters can penetrate the security of banking systems – perhaps just for fun – we can no longer pretend that company accounting systems are inviolate. The public need no longer be dependent on accountants as intermediaries to present company financial stories in ways that suit company directors.

Such open access to information is potentially revolutionary, and could be associated with a dramatic shift of power in society. There could be no secrets in relation to creative accounting. But, unfortunately, very few people seem to be interested in the details of company transactions.

Accounting and auditing arrangements are no longer a matter just for directors and shareholders. When companies are listed on stock markets, the listing agreement requires appropriate arrangements to be in place. A stock exchange does not want its reputation undermined by companies that have chosen to opt out of accounting regulations. The most substantial shareholders are institutional investors, such as pension funds. They are unlikely to invest in companies that lack normal accountability mechanisms.

Left wing

Many assume that there is a legitimate public interest in the numbers that purport to represent the profits, assets and liabilities of companies. This is because they are relevant in the allocation of resources in the economy, the amount of taxation paid by companies, or because of the importance attached to 'the system' and avoiding financial scandals. The left-wing view would be that it is bet-ter to rely on a public sector body to act in the public interest, rather than relying on the accounting profession, a variety of power groups and vested interests. When, as happens from time to time, there are accounting scandals, and financial reporting seems to be collapsing, there are increasing demands for more direct government/public control.

1 *HM Revenue and Customs Rules OK* – Many Europeans are surprised to find that, in this country, profits for financial reporting purposes do not simply follow the rules laid down by the govern-ment for taxation (and other) purposes, and that this is deemed to be quite legitimate. The idea that companies can choose to depreciate ships, or aircraft over 10 or 20 or 30 years – or almost any period they like – seems quite fantastic. Perhaps it is central to the Anglo-American notion of 'freedom', which includes freedom to be creative with accounting.

If we want to argue for clearer, more effective and enforceable accounting rules to curb crea-tive accounting, we can argue that this should come from the government, and it can build on

---

[7] Something similar happens with local authorities today.

what HM Revenue and Customs already does. To someone from Eastern Europe this would seem only natural. But the argument is rarely advanced in Anglo-American accounting cultures. It is argued that governments lack the necessary expertise in accounting, and that they would be too slow to respond to changing business and accounting circumstances and practices. Moreover, the tax regulations are not always designed with the intention of the accounts showing a 'true and fair view'. Accelerated capital allowances are arranged to encourage companies to acquire the latest technology, thereby improving productivity.

And if governments lack accounting expertise, they can easily buy it, as companies do. And if governments are slow to respond to changing circumstances they may be no worse than the accounting profession. The Chancellor of the Exchequer is usually criticized for producing too many changes in the taxation system too quickly, not for slowness to respond.

2 *A State Auditing Board* – It may be too extreme to suggest nationalizing the whole of the auditing profession. However, if auditing is seen as not operating in the public interest, but is, instead, operating for the benefit of vested interest groups, this must remain the ultimate solution. A State Auditing Board could do much to shift the balance of power without full nationalization. If there is a public interest in auditors being independent from directors (which is supposed to be the case), it is hard to defend a system where, in effect, the directors:

■ decide which firm of auditors should be appointed, and how long they should serve;

■ decide what level of remuneration to pay to auditors;

■ allocate substantial contracts to auditors for non-audit work.

A public or state auditing board could be responsible for appointing auditors to particular companies, determining the level of fees and the period of appointment, and deciding to whom non-audit work should be allocated.

Such a board would also have a vested interest in establishing and implementing clear-cut accounting rules that could be expected to minimize creative accounting.

Accountancy and power

Anyone who believes that there is such a thing as 'correct' accountancy is likely to favour existing accountancy arrangements whereby accounting standard-setters struggle with the problem of how particular items should be measured and reported. They then produce general reporting standards, and accountants and auditors have to ensure that these are properly applied.

But many accounting numbers and accounting standards are the result of negotiation, rather than being based on any underlying truth, principle or economic reality. Accounting standard-setters have changed their conclusions and recommendations on issues such as the amortization of goodwill, providing for deferred taxation, and capitalization of development expenditure. A negotiated settlement is reached, but it may be changed a few years later. No new 'truth' is discovered. In negotiations the strongest usually get their way, and the way in which accountancy is applied is as a result of bargaining among powerful interest groups. Any serious attempt to change the way in which accountancy is applied in practice would involve a change in the balance of power between the different vested interest groups in society that influence accounting.

8.5 Social and Environmental Reporting

Definition and overview

There has been increasing recognition of the idea that companies, and other organizations, should be more widely accountable:

■ To interest groups other than just shareholders and creditors

■ For social and environmental issues, not just financial

The Corporate Report, which was published by the Accounting Standards Steering Committee (ASSC) in 1975, adopted a very wide view of accountability. It took the view that every significant entity had an implicit responsibility to report publicly, and to a wide range of users. It defined the various user groups as:

1 equity investors;

2 loan creditors;

3 employees;

4 analysts and advisers, including financial analysts, economists, statisticians, researchers, trade unions, stockbrokers and credit rating agencies;

5 business contacts, including customers, trade creditors and suppliers, competitors, and those interested in mergers and takeovers;

6 the government, including tax authorities, central government departments and local authorities;

7 the public, including taxpayers, ratepayers, consumers, and community and environmental and other special interest groups.

This is a very wide view of who organizations should be accountable to, which seems to include just about everyone. In addition to existing members of the first three groups, they specifically included *potential* shareholders, loan creditors and employees. It is more difficult to specify what organizations should be accountable for.

The Corporate Report assumed that organizations would publish a single, multi-purpose report. As this was intended to meet the needs of such a diverse range of users, it was difficult to define their information needs, but six additional statements were advocated:

1 a statement of value added;

2 an employment report;

3 a statement of money exchanges with the government;

4 a statement of transactions in foreign currency;

5 a statement of future prospects;

6 a statement of corporate objectives.

The first two of these were fashionable for a few years; the second two did not catch on. The final two 'softer'[8] ones have been largely incorporated into directors' reports and operating and financial reviews. The *Corporate Report* had almost nothing to say about environmental issues: it was nearly 20 years before these concerns became fashionable.

In the decades following the publication of the *Corporate Report* there have been many attempts to define what is meant by 'social ' and to operationalize it.

Gray et al. (1987) define corporate social reporting as:

> *the process of communicating the social and environmental effects of organisations' economic actions to particular interest groups within society and to society at large. As such, it involves extending the accountability of organisations (particularly companies), beyond the traditional role of providing a financial account to the owners of capital, in particular shareholders. Such an extension is predicated upon the assumption that companies do have wider responsibilities than simply to make money for their shareholders.*

They use the abbreviation CSR to mean corporate social *reporting*; unfortunately, the same abbreviation is widely used to mean corporate social *responsibility* (see section below). Their definition is in no way limiting. Gray et al. (1996) say that CSR 'can take a potentially infinite range of forms . . . to fulfil

---

[8] 'Soft' in the sense that they do not include much 'hard' data like conventional accounting statements.

any one or more of a wide range of objectives. It can cover a myriad of different subjects ... It is not a systematic, regulated, or well-established activity.' It seems that CSR can be almost anything! It is necessary to distinguish between:

1 what some companies actually do. There are many companies that include some sort of social and/or environmental report with or in their normal annual reports. It may be a few paragraphs, or a supplementary booklet of a dozen or more pages;
2 what is advocated by a wide range of groups and individuals.

The term 'corporate social reporting' is reasonably clear. It means reporting by companies and other organizations on matters of concern to society and groups in society; it involves disclosing information in addition to conventional financial accounting statements; and at present it usually means mainly voluntary disclosure, although there are some matters of social concern that Companies Acts require to be disclosed. Those who argue in favour of corporate social reporting either:

1 advocate that legislation should require additional disclosures;
2 favour continued experimentation with voluntary disclosures.

Some advocate both, with experimentation continuing until a consensus on clear disclosure requirements emerges. Most advocate continuing research and experimentation. Many use corporate social reporting to include environmental (or 'green') reporting.

Social accounting is not helpful because its meaning is not clear. Sometimes it is used in relation to national income accounting. Sometimes it means public interest accounting. Gray (Centre for Social and Environmental Accounting Records (CSEAR)) identifies three aspects of social accounting:

1 Investigating the social effects of current accounting practice.
2 Investigating how to ameliorate some of the adverse effects.
3 Studying other possible ways of providing accounts of organizations.

This is a research agenda based on the idea that companies and other organizations should increasingly recognize their social responsibilities, and be accountable for them.

Corporate social responsibility

The idea that companies should increasingly recognize their social responsibilities is widely accepted. The government even has a corporate social responsibility website[9] that publishes its views. In a recent update, Stephen Timms, who was Minister for Corporate Social Responsibility (CSR), stated that the government wanted to see UK businesses taking account of their economic, social and environmental impacts, which it saw as supporting its strategy on sustainable development. The government took 'compliance with legal requirements' as the base for corporate social responsibility, but encouraged companies to go beyond that. There are no radical proposals for compulsory additional social and environmental disclosures, but it favours building on the statutory Operating and Financial Review.

Although politicians can produce fine-sounding statements on the subject, there is little commitment to specific proposals for corporate social *reporting*. The 2004 government update recognized that corporate social responsibility continued to be highly topical and much debated; that it has increasingly provided the focus for exploration of broad philosophical questions about the roles and responsibilities of companies, and about a range of (almost random!) questions about employee volunteering, health concerns about mobile phones, poverty eradication and even AIDS. The paper asks, perhaps rhetorically, 'Does this mean that CSR risks being about everything and nothing?'

It is recognized by the government paper that we are a long way from consensus on what CSR means, and its value, and it lists some of the different ways in which it is seen:

---

[9] www.csr.gov.uk

1 as glossy reports and public relations;

2 as a source of business opportunity and improved competitiveness;

3 as sound business practice;

4 as a distraction or a threat.

The government accepts the idea that many are concerned with the social and environmental impacts of companies, and refers to the idea of socially responsible investment (or ethical investment[10]). But it is cynical about the relationship between 'practice and communication'. In other words, there may be companies that are good at public relations, have a high public profile, and appear to take their social responsibilities seriously; but they may not be socially responsible businesses. Similarly, there may be other companies that concentrate on 'doing' CSR rather than reporting on it. Increased disclosure means increased transparency and accountability; but it does not necessarily make companies more socially responsible.

Employees

There are two distinct approaches to social reporting in relation to employees:

1 Giving information to employees. This may involve special employee reports that might be simplified versions of the usual annual report and accounts. It can also involve providing more detailed information about employment, performance and prospects at particular locations. It does not necessarily involve published reports: detailed information may be provided where it is requested by employees and their representatives.

2 Giving information about employees, perhaps mainly to investors. This was the approach adopted by the *Corporate Report,* which advocated the publication of an Employment Report showing:

   a numbers employed;

   b broad reasons for changes in numbers during the year;

   c age distribution and gender of employees;

   d functions of employees;

   e geographical locations of major employment centres;

   f major plant and site closures, disposals and acquisitions during the year;

   g hours worked and scheduled with detail for different groups;

   h costs and benefits of pension schemes and ability of schemes to meet commitments;

   i names of trade unions recognized for collective bargaining, and membership figures (or a statement that the trade union did not make the information available);

   j health and safety information including frequency and severity of accidents and incidence of occupational diseases;

   k selected ratios related to employment.

The 1970s saw many experiments in employment reports, and employee reporting. Today most companies disclose little more than the legal minimum in their annual reports. But there is usually a paragraph headed 'Employees' in which it is typically the chairman who pays tribute to all their good work.

The environment

Since the 1990s the popular concern has been with the environment, and 'green' issues. Companies do a lot to damage the environment, perhaps permanently or irretrievably, and they should stop it

---

[10] Some investors want to buy shares only in companies that behave ethically, and want companies to publish information to show how ethical they are. For example, does the company produce weapons or warfare, or use child labour?

at once! It is difficult to see how accountants could achieve this. Perhaps they can try to get others to measure the amounts of pollution, and put a cost on it, and then ensure that 'the polluter pays' by imposing appropriate taxation. Or reporting requirements could be imposed in the expectation that public shaming might inhibit their polluting behaviour. An alternative view would be that unacceptable pollution would be illegal, and it is for governments, rather than accountants, to establish and enforce such laws.

There are also concerns about over-exploitation of the world's natural resources, such as oil and other minerals, and companies should be committed to sustainable development. Perhaps accounting-type monitoring and reporting mechanisms could be applied to encourage companies to use sustainable raw materials. Those who believe in markets argue that, if oil is in short supply, its price will increase, and companies will continue to find ways of using less oil as its price increases. It may be that increases in oil prices have done more to encourage the development of the electric car than governments or accountants have done.

Most generation of electricity, however, also pollutes the environment. The amount of power that can be generated by wind, sun, water and tides, seems to be inadequate, and environmentalists complain about the appearance of wind farms, and fear for wildlife if an ambitious scheme like the River Severn Barrier is constructed. Nuclear power seems clean and almost infinite to many; but others consider it extremely dangerous to the environment because of the possibility of accidents, radiation leaks, terrorism, and the problem of what to do with radioactive waste, particularly at the end of the plant's life.

The potential problem of global warming was of major concern in the 1990s, and mathematical models[11] were constructed showing that, within a couple of generations, most of the planet would be uninhabitable. By the early years of the twenty-first century the cry of global warming was superseded by the cry of 'climate change'.[12] The conventional wisdom[13] today is that climate change is man-made, and that by reducing carbon emissions we can slow down the rate of global warming.[14] The pressure is on to reduce carbon emissions by using less electricity and oil, increasing the use of recycled materials, reducing air travel, and buying food locally rather than shipping it for thousands of miles. Accountants may have a role in calculating whether the carbon footprint is more increased by shipping food from the other side of the world than by growing it in the UK; and in assessing whether the benefits of recycling materials exceed the costs of so doing.

Environmentalists are concerned with a broad range of issues, many under the heading of sustainable procurement, production and development, and in developing measures of green accounting and environmental reporting. Issues include pollution, survival of different species, or biodiversity, and dealing with climate change. Accountants have most to offer in areas where objective measurement is required, especially if it is financial, and in reporting to the public.

Environmental accounting

Regardless of what is publicly reported, many companies have internal accounting systems that keep track of environmental impacts. Environmental accounting is defined as:

---

[11] In 1900 less sophisticated mathematical models showed that, if traffic continued to increase at the rate then prevailing, by 2000 London would be waist deep in horse manure. But the car replaced the horse! In the 1970s mathematical models showed that, if the accountancy profession continued to expand at the rate then prevailing, by the middle of the twenty-first century every man, woman and child in the UK would be an accountant. The main thing we learn from history is that we learn nothing from history!

[12] We cannot be certain about long-term forecasts of climate change, any more than we can be certain of short-term forecasts of weather.

[13] An alternative view is that, over the centuries, the world sometimes gets warmer, and sometimes colder, and that we do not really understand the reasons for this.

[14] King Canute knew that he could not stop the tide from coming in, and probably that he could not change the weather. Today, humankind is less humble, and seems to believe that it can change the climate.

The collection, analysis and assessment of environmental and financial performance data obtained from business management systems, environmental management and financial accounting systems. The taking of corrective management action to reduce environmental impacts and costs plus, where appropriate, the external reporting of the environmental and financial benefits in verified corporate environmental reports or published annual reports and accounts.

The government's Environment Agency produced this definition and stated the department's own commitment to develop an environmental accounting system to integrate environmental performance measures into core financial processes and to track internal environmentally significant expenditure. This is regarded as vital to assist in the management of environmental risks and operational costs. It is, of course, easier to collect and classify, and perhaps also to report, costs than it is to measure environmental impacts.

The definition is odd in that it assumes that separate corporate environmental reports would be 'verified' in some way, presumably in line with the way in which external financial reports are audited. Where environmental impacts and costs are included in the normal annual report and accounts, companies are free to report whatever information that they wish, in whatever way they wish, with no assumption that it should be included as part of the financial statements that are audited.

Who decides? Is it accountancy?

If companies are to produce corporate social reports someone has to decide what is to be included in them, and how it is to be defined, measured and reported. With financial disclosures, governments and the accounting standard-setters have determined what should be disclosed, and they are continually refining their standards. There are a few items, that are as much financial as social, that have to be disclosed by law, such as political and charitable donations, how long on average it takes a company to pay its trade creditors, and some information about employees. Otherwise, it is companies themselves that decide what kind of social and environmental disclosures they will make.

The danger of leaving it to companies to disclose what they wish is that many will use the idea of corporate social reporting mainly as a public relations opportunity. It is worth examining in detail the contents of companies' annual reports and analysing the extent to which they disclose information in a way that really holds them to account for their social responsibilities, and the extent to which these disclosures are designed mainly to enhance their image. Some companies have always used their annual reports as a public relations opportunity, and it may be of some benefit to society if they choose to boast about their social and environmental performance if that goes hand in hand with real improvements.

It may be that one day the accountancy profession will develop, promulgate and enforce accounting standards that require companies to report in specific ways on their social and environmental performance, and there are some moves in this direction. In general the accountancy profession has built on statutory requirements, with more detailed guidance on implementing Companies Acts for financial accounting purposes. There are already some legal requirements regarding social responsibilities that are, or could easily be, incorporated into annual reports. These relate to payment policies and timing in relation to trade payables; employment policies and number and gender of employees; numbers of industrial injuries; numbers of disabled employees; and political and charitable donations. Governments are perhaps more likely to increase companies' legal social responsibilities rather than reduce them. Where governments impose reporting requirements on companies, at least in relation to financial matters, it has long been the role of the accountancy profession to develop reporting recommendations and standards on how these should be implemented.

Additional *ad hoc* reporting requirements may well be introduced, but we are a long way from developing a comprehensive corporate reporting system, and many individuals and official, or semi-official, bodies have produced a variety of recommendations. Examples of such bodies are shown in Example 8.2.

Example 8.2

Social and environmental reporting: useful websites

- ACCA UK Awards for sustainability reporting:
  www.accaglobal.org.uk/sustainability
- AccountAbility:
  www.accountability.org.uk (e.g. AA 1000 standard)
- Accounting for Sustainability's Connected Reporting Framework:
  www.accountingforsustainability.org/home/
- Ethical trading initiative:
  www.ethicaltrade.org
- Ethical Investment Association:
  www.ethicalinvestment.org.uk
- FTSE4Good Index (evaluates social responsibility performance of companies):
  www.ftse.com/Indices/FTSE4Good_Index_Series/index.jsp
- Forum for the Future:
  www.forumforthefuture.org.uk
- Global Reporting Initiative's Sustainability Reporting Guidelines:
  www.globalreporting.org
- Good Corporation's Standard:
  www.goodcorporation.com/
- Green Globe Certification Standard:
  www.greenglobecertification.com
- ISO 14000 environmental standard:
  www.iso14000-iso14001-environmental-management.com/
- OECD Guidelines for Multinational Enterprises:
  www.oecd.org
- Social Accountability International SA 8000 Standard:
  www.sa-intl.org/
- UN Global Compact (e.g. International Standards of Accounting and Reporting (ISAR)): provides technical guidance on eco-efficiency indicators and corporate responsibility reporting:
  www.globalcompact.org
- Verite's Monitoring Guidelines:
  www.verite.org/

Corporate social reporting in practice

Most large companies include something on their social and/or environmental responsibilities and activities in their annual reports and accounts, but the quantity and quality of the information disclosed varies enormously. Some produce substantial additional reports while others include just a few paragraphs. Shell produced a 40-page, glossy 'Sustainability Report'.[15] If there is such a thing as a

---

[15] Shell, 2010.

'typical' report, it includes a paragraph or two under headings such as the following, some[16] of which are required by law:

1 safety;
2 environment;
3 communities;
4 building a sustainable energy system;
5 producing cleaner energy;
6 delivering energy responsibly;
7 raising living standards through enterprise;
8 making transport more sustainable.

Barratt Developments plc provides some details of its work on sustainability and social responsibility as shown in Illustration 8.2.

ILLUSTRATION 8.2

Extract from Barratt Developments plc annual report and accounts 2011:

Ethics Policy

1) INTRODUCTION AND OBJECTIVES

1. This Ethics Policy is supported by the Board of Barratt Developments PLC and shall be reviewed from time to time. The policy sets out standards of professionalism and integrity to be maintained by individuals in all the Group's operations.

2. Every employee in the Barratt Group (the "Group") has a right to expect the Group to maintain proper standards and in turn all employees have a duty to maintain these standards through their decisions, actions and communications. A heavier responsibility is borne by those who hold positions of authority. They must openly demonstrate leadership in applying the business practices outlined in this policy.

3. This policy provides guidance on the way all staff are expected to conduct themselves, operating with integrity, fairness and in compliance with the law and regulatory requirements as well as the Barratt Vision and Philosophies (the "Vision").

4. Whilst the policy applies primarily to directors and senior managers in Group functions, regions and divisions, it is also intended to apply to all employees of the business insofar as it is appropriate to their role.

5. All agents, joint venture and other partners, sub-contractors and suppliers are expected to adhere to the principles of this policy in their dealings with the Group. It must therefore be brought to their attention in your dealings with them. They must write to confirm receipt of the Policy and adherence to it and agree to confirm on an annual basis that this Policy has in fact been followed in their dealings with us and on our behalf by 1st September each year.

2) POLICY STATEMENT

6. The Group expects all of its staff to operate with integrity and to high standards of ethical conduct when carrying out their duties on behalf of the Group.

7. In particular they are expected to:
   ■ Behave honestly and fairly.
   ■ Comply with all legal and regulatory requirements.
   ■ Conduct themselves in a manner that will enhance the reputation of the Group.
   ■ Treat others with respect.
   ■ Safeguard the assets and property of the Group.
   ■ Follow the Barratt Vision & Philosophies.

Continued

---

[16] Items 1 and 8, and parts of 5 and 7 are required.

ILLUSTRATION 8.2 (Continued)

8. Staff must not:

- Use their authority or office for personal gain.
- Recruit or promote employees other than on their ability.
- Take unfair advantage of others through dishonest, unethical or illegal practices.
- Knowingly make any false or misleading statements.
- Mis-appropriate the assets or property of the Group.
- Seek to comply only with the letter of the law, rule or Group policy whilst ignoring the spirit, where such actions are not in accordance with this Ethics Policy and the Vision.
- Vary from this Ethics Policy or any Group policy simply on the basis of "commercial necessity".

9. If in doubt as to your responsibilities please ask (see section 13 below).

Source: www.barrattdevelopments.co.uk @ Barratt Developments plc (2011)

As outlined in the sections above the group has continued to make good progress on corporate responsibility throughout the year. In addition, it provides some information on health and safety including the number of reportable injuries to its employees, and of its standpoint on ethics as shown in Illustration 8.3.

Some companies have a preference for disclosing information that is easily quantified such as the number of complaints received per customer, perhaps comparing the number with the average for the industry. Some confine themselves to bland statements about being nice to one or more of employees, customers, suppliers, the environment and local communities. Often there are general statements about increasing the use of recyclable paper and other consumables, many of which are supported by quantitative statements and comparisons.

There have been attempts to quantify and compare, in financial terms, the total social and environmental good and harm that a company has done. But these are fraught with difficulties in deciding what should be disclosed, and with definitions and measurement. These may be compared with the difficulties in financial accounting, but corporate social and environmental reporting is at a much earlier stage in its development, and it remains to be seen how far it will go.

ILLUSTRATION 8.3

Extract from Barratt Developments plc annual report and accounts 2011:

HEALTH, SAFETY AND THE ENVIRONMENT

We continue to place a high priority on the safety of our employees, contractors, customers and the wider community within which we operate. During the financial year our Injury Incidence Rate ('IIR') was 539 (2010: 582) per 100,000 persons employed which is a 7.4% decrease on last year's figure. We remain committed to improving health and safety and have an Executive Health and Safety Committee, which reports to the Board, to drive further improvement.

We aim to secure a position as the lowest cost provider complying with the Code for Sustainable Homes (the 'Code'). During the year we built 3,071 homes to Code Level 3 or above and we are already starting to build developments at higher Code levels where required. We are establishing improved and lower cost methods which are allowing us to reduce the cost of compliance. We are well advanced with the development of ways of building a Code Level 4 house to satisfy the criteria without the need for renewable sources of energy.

We are progressing our development at Hanham Hall, the UK's first large-scale zero carbon housing development. We have cleared the site, built the first two zero carbon houses and commenced the renovation of the original listed Hanham Hall building.

As well as seeking technological solutions, we will continue to discuss with Government the most cost-effective way of meeting the environmental challenges facing the industry.

Source: www.barrattdevelopments.co.uk @ Barratt Developments plc (2011)

📖 Summary

Many accounting and financial scandals arise because of illegal (sometimes criminal) activity by company directors and others. It is often normal accounting and auditing routines and reports that uncover the problems.

Creative accounting also arises where the rules are not clear and so technically there is no wrong-doing. There will continue to be problems with creative accounting as long as directors have substantial control over the ways in which financial reports are presented. The problems of creative accounting can only be curbed, not cured; and the process may be slow, especially if reliance is placed on moderate, evolutionary changes. The UK is unlikely to implement radical right- or left-wing proposals, and will proceed by international consensus.

There may be potential for restricting creative accounting by requiring companies to use HM Revenue and Customs' taxation rules for measuring profit, as is (or was) the case in some European countries. But, somehow, the US–UK approach usually seems to win in any contest with European approaches. It may be unrealistic to expect a thorough, authoritative set of measurement rules to be developed and enforced that will close all the creative accounting loopholes. Substantial improvement can come from fuller and more clear-cut disclosure requirements. The most effective curbs would come from the most significant shifts of power over the presentation of accounting information.

The most likely outcome is that we will continue with gentle reforms, become increasingly international, and largely preserve the status quo. More effective changes come as statutory requirements for additional specific disclosures are increased; and from restricting the powers of directors over auditing and accounting. Those who have the power to do so create knowledge, accounting principles, and determine accounting practice. If creative accounting flourishes, it is because it is in the interest of those who have the power to allow it. Perhaps it can be effectively restricted only if there is a radical shift away from the existing power structures of the accountancy profession, standard-setters, directors and auditors.

Ever increasingly, however, either in response to regulation, recognition of pressure from interest groups or in recognition of the need for transparency and accountability, listed companies are increasing disclosure in the area of corporate social responsibility such as public safety, their impact upon the environment and their ethical stance on dealing with customers and the public.

➡ Review of key points

- The term 'creative accounting' is applied to a wide range of accounting practices.
- The exercise of judgement is inevitable in some areas of accounting, and it may be tempting to exercise it in a creative way, and to extend this to other areas.
- Some companies use questionable accounting practices to boost profits, to improve key ratios, to boost equity on the statement of financial position and to smooth out profits and losses from year to year.
- Problem areas have included exceptional and extraordinary items, provisions, goodwill and off statement of financial position finance.
- Accounting standard-setters have reduced the scope for creative accounting, but there are some 'fuzzy' rules, and some areas of choice remain.
- Moderate evolutionary changes are steadily reducing the scope for creative accounting.
- Creative accounting is still a problem and more radical solutions may be considered.
- Listed companies are disclosing information in a corporate social report on their impact on the environment and sustainability, about public safety issues and their ethical stance on such issues as the way staff are expected to conduct themselves through their decisions, actions and communications.

Self-testing questions

1 In what areas of accountancy has there always been a need for subjective judgement, and scope for creative accounting?

2 Give examples of techniques that have been used in 'creative accounting'.

3 Is creative accounting illegal?

4 In what ways can accounting standards be improved to restrict creative accounting?

5 In what ways have auditors been criticized for lack of independence?

6 The Platto Company produced the following draft income statements in early January year 9, shortly before being taken over by the Uppit Company in February year 9.

	Draft income statement for year ended 31 December year 8	Budgeted income statement for year ended 31 December year 9
	£000	£000
Sales revenue	800	790
Opening inventory	80	90
Purchases	650	636
	730	726
Closing inventory	(90)	(88)
Cost of sales	640	638
Gross profit	160	152
Depreciation	(40)	(38)
Operating expenses	(90)	(92)
Profit	30	22

In February year 9 the Uppit Company revised the draft accounts of the Platto Company for year 8 as follows:

a Closing inventories were written down to net realizable value, estimated at £50,000.

b Non-current assets in Chipping Sodbury were written down to an estimated fair value that led to an impairment charge of £55,000. The net book value of the assets was reduced from £120,000 to £65,000.

During year 9 the actual results of the Platto Company were much the same as had been budgeted, except that:

c Sales were reduced by £32,000 because inventories left from year 8, which were originally expected to be sold for £112,000, were, in fact, sold for £80,000.

d The non-current assets in Chipping Sodbury were sold for £90,000; as a result the total depreciation charge for year 9 was reduced from a budgeted level of £38,000 to an actual level of £26,000. The total of other operating expenses was unaffected.

Required:

i Show the summarized income statement for the Platto Company for year 8, as modified by the Uppit Company.

ii Show the summarized income statement for the Platto Company for year 9.

iii Explain and comment.

7 What information could annual reports include about the social performance of companies?

Assessment questions

1 In what ways are the problems of creative accounting being tackled at present?

2 What more radical solutions do you think should be considered?

3 In what areas is it particularly difficult to restrict creative accounting?

4 Examine the case for more government involvement in the setting and enforcing of accounting standards, and in the regulation of auditors.

5 What is likely to happen to a company that overstates its profits year after year?

6 Why should 'corporate social reporting' be considered as being part of the responsibility of accountants?

7 With regard to environmental issues, should accountants be more involved in:

   a Management accounting-type measurement of costs and impacts; or

   b External reporting?

Group activities and discussion questions

1 Obtain the annual reports of four companies, two being major, well-known companies, and two being much smaller. Compare the reports in terms of the public relations material and 'spin' that they put on the results. Can the reports be ranked on a scale indicating the extent of 'spin'? Do some reports contain little or nothing more than the minimum required? Why do some companies provide a lot more information, comment and explanation than is strictly required?

2 A company has a duty to maximize reported profits. If it uses creative accounting techniques to do so, it does not matter, as long as those profits have credibility. Discuss.

3 Examine a number of company accounts in detail. Express the taxation charge as a percentage of the profit before taxation, and compare the companies. Examine the cash flow statements of the companies. Do these comparisons reveal anything that causes you to question reported profit figures?

4 Produce a list of recent accounting standards, and select a few for detailed examination. Read the stated objectives in the standards, and try also to read between the lines. Can you suggest what 'creative accounting' techniques (if any) they are designed to address?

5 Should the rules for profit measurement be laid down by governments?

6 Select a few companies' annual reports and analyse their social and environmental reporting. Assess the value of the reported information.

7 To what extent, and in what ways, is a requirement to report particular information likely to affect the behaviour of companies?

8 Examine disclosures in the annual report of a listed company relating to the environment, sustainability and ethics and consider whether you believe businesses seeking to prosper in an economic slump and pay dividends to shareholders should be required to disclose such information.

Accounting in context

Discuss and comment on the following item taken from the press. What does it reveal about the increasing demands for non-traditional disclosures of information in the company annual report in addition to traditional financial measures of performance and the connection between them?

Puma monetises emissions

Can the sportswear company's environmental profit and loss statement show the true cost of its supply chain?

By Jessica Shankleman

Rising energy costs, new legislation and increasing stakeholder pressures are stirring a growing number of businesses to measure and report their carbon emissions. But while some companies are still getting to grips with the basics, Puma has taken the leap of creating its first environmental profit and loss (P&L) statement.

Working with PwC and Trucost, Puma has monetised its emissions, in the hope of identifying the "true cost" of the natural resources it uses. The first phase of Puma's environmental P&L statement focused on greenhouse gas emissions and water consumption. The next phase will include other impacts such as land use change and waste, while the third section is designed to reduce the company's growing so-called environmental debt, by factoring in economic and social benefits such as job creation and taxes.

Puma has estimated its greenhouse gas emissions and water consumption for 2010 at £94.4m (£83.7m), the vast majority of which occurred in the supply chain rather than the company's manufacturing. It paid about £66 per tonne of carbon in its environmental P&L statement, much higher than the £17 per tonne price in the European Union's emissions trading scheme.

Carbon reporting experts broadly applauded the company's efforts as an ambitious move that could prompt others to follow suit, despite a few questions about the validity of some aspects of the reporting. This year, Puma failed to release the environmental account with its other financial reports, but it claims that future information will form part of the financial accounts, subject to the same scrutiny from investors as its other year-end figures.

Frances Way, programme director of the Carbon Disclosure Project, a non-profit organisation which asks companies to report their emissions, told Financial Director that Puma's analysis would have been more significant if it were linked to financial results.

"If their intention is really to show environmental management in its operations, then Puma should combine the two reports to show how certain sensitivities would have an impact on its profits," she says.

Others have raised eyebrows over the fact that PwC is thought to be auditing the results, as the accounting company also helped collate and organise the information – although Puma told Financial Director that as the figures have yet to be audited, no decision on the firm has been made.

However, despite such discrepancies, Puma has been hailed as a trailblazer for its efforts. Alongside the environmental P&L statement, the company has published a breakdown of how it is measuring and monetising its impact to help others follow suit.

Alan McGill, the PwC partner who works on the Puma account, says stakeholders now have a more accurate picture of the company's business position, as it has identified where it uses resources and is able to act now to minimise future damage and reduce its carbon footprint.

"Even if you don't agree with the carbon impact on business and are faced with hard-nosed investors who are only interested in returns, this gives you the information now," he says.

Way admits that not every finance director would be ready or able to go to the expense that Puma has, but also maintains that they should still take a holistic view of the company's accounts.

"The FD who doesn't see this as part of his remit is going to run into trouble in the next 10 years," says Way.

Source: *Financial Director*, 7 July 2011

References and further reading

Accounting Standards Board (1999) *Statement of Principles*. ASB.

De la Torre, I. (2008) *Creative Accounting Exposed*. Basingstoke: Palgrave Macmillan.

Dearing Committee (1988) *The Making of Accounting Standards*. ICAEW.

Economica (monthly journal of the Institute of Chartered Accountants in England and Wales). Available online at www.icaew.com/economia.

Gilbert Welytok, J. (2006) *Sarbanes–Oxley for Dummies*. New York: Hungry Minds Inc.

Gray, R. (n.d.) *Discovering Social and Environmental Accounting*. Centre for Social and Environmental Accounting Research Website (St Andrews University).

Gray, R., D. Owen and C. Adams (1996) *Accounting and Accountability, Changes and Challenges in Corporate Social and Environmental Reporting*. Upper Saddle River, NJ: Prentice Hall.

Gray, R., D. Owen and K. Maunders (1987) *Corporate Social Reporting: Accounting and Accountability*. Upper Saddle River, NJ: Prentice Hall.

Griffiths, I. (1986) *Creative Accounting: How to Make Your Profits What You Want Them to Be*. London: Sidgwick and Jackson.

Griffiths, I. (1995) *New Creative Accounting*. Basingstoke: Macmillan.

Jameson, M. (1988) *A Practical Guide to Creative Accounting*. London: Kogan Page.

Jones, M. (2011) *Creative Accounting, Fraud and International Accounting Scandals*. New York: Wiley.

McBarnet, D. and C. Whelan (1999) *Creative Accounting and the Cross Eyed Javelin Thrower*. Chichester: Wiley.

Mulford, C.W. and E.E. Comiskey (2005) *The Financial Numbers Game: Detecting Creative Accounting Practices*. New York: Wiley.

Pijper, T. (1993) *Creative Accounting: The Effectiveness of Financial Reporting in the UK*. London: Macmillan.

Schilit, H. (2002) *Financial Shenanigans: How to Detect Accounting Gimmicks and Fraud in Financial Reports*. New York: McGraw-Hill.

Smith, T. and R. Hannah (1991) *Accounting for Growth*. London: UBS Phillips and Drew.

www.environment-agency.gov.uk/business/topics/performance

www.fasb.org

www.ifrs.org

Online LearningCentre

When you have read this chapter, log on to the Online Learning Centre website at *www.mcgraw-hill.co.uk/textbooks/leiwy* to explore chapter-by-chapter test questions, further reading and more online study tools.

Chapter

9

Bookkeeping to Trial Balance

Chapter contents

✓ Learning objectives

After studying Section 9.1 you will be able to:

☑ Record straightforward transactions using double-entry bookkeeping

☑ Prepare a trial balance summarizing those transactions

☑ Introduce closing inventory and convert the trial balance into a set of final accounts

After studying Section 9.2 you will be able to:

☑ Produce ledger accounts in a good format

☑ Record a wide range of transactions using double-entry bookkeeping, including discounts and returns

☑ Use a cash book and separate petty cash from bank transactions

After studying Section 9.3 you will be able to:

☑ Understand how accounting systems operate

☑ Appreciate the role of day books, ledgers and control accounts

☑ Prepare a simple bank reconciliation statement

9.1 Introduction

Consider the following example:

Keith opens a business, Keith Ltd, and opens a bank account in the name of the business. In the first week, the following transactions take place:

Day 1: Keith puts £1,000 of his own money into the bank account
Day 2: The business buys 100 shirts, each costing £10
Day 3: It sells 70 shirts for £30 each
Day 4: The business pays its shareholders a dividend of £100

In compiling accounts for the business, it is important to understand that every transaction affects two figures in the accounts.

In transaction 1, the bank balance goes up by £1,000. Why? Because the shareholders have purchased share capital from the business.

In transaction 2, the bank balance goes down by £1,000. Why? Because the asset inventory has risen by £1,000.

In transaction 3, the bank balance goes up by £2,100. Why? Because the business has sales totalling £2,100. Also, the inventory has reduced by £700 (70 shirts at £10). Why? Because 70 of the shirts are no longer assets; instead, they have been sold and the cost of the goods sold is £700.

And in transaction 4, the bank balance falls by £100. Why? Because the business has paid a dividend of £100 to the shareholders. In truth, this would not be possible in reality because we have ignored taxation and the legal restrictions on paying dividends.

We can see the accounts at the end of each day, and notice that, in relation to each transaction, two figures are affected (see Illustration 9.1).

You can see that:

1 Every transaction affects two figures.

2 The statement of financial position always balances.

ILLUSTRATION 9.1

Keith Ltd	£	£	£	£
	Day 1	Day 2	Day 3	Day 4
Statement of financial position at the end of day				
Assets:				
Inventory		1,000	300	300
Cash	1,000	–	2,100	20,000
Total assets	1,000	1,000	2,400	2,300
Share capital	1,000	1,000	1,000	1,000
Retained profits			1,400	1,300
Total equity	1,000	1,000	2,400	2,300
Income statement for the period ended	Day 1	Day 2	Day 3	Day 4
Sales			2,100	2,100
Cost of goods sold			700	700
Profit for the period			1,400	1,400
Dividends paid			–	100
Retained profits			1,400	1,300

3 The assets = equity + the liabilities (there are no liabilities in this example) but the equity is a liability of the company to its shareholders.

4 The profit increases the equity.

5 Opening equity + capital introduced + profit for the period – dividends = closing equity.

Or to rearrange that equation:

6 Profit for the period = closing equity – opening equity + dividends – capital introduced.

In this simple example, we have been able to prepare a statement of financial position, with a list of the various assets, equity and liabilities and an income statement after each transaction. However, in a real business, where there are hundreds or thousands of transactions of different types taking place, a system must be devised to record these transactions from which the two main accounting statements (the statement of financial position and the income statement) can be prepared from time to time.

Businesses use double-entry bookkeeping to record all transactions. For a very simple operation, it might be possible to keep only a cash account that records all the money that the business receives, and all the money that it pays out. But most businesses operate using credit (buying goods and paying for them at a later date; selling goods and receiving payment for them at a later date); they own non-current assets that have to be depreciated; and many are financed by borrowing. It is, therefore, necessary to keep account not only of what has been received and paid, but also of how much the business owes to various people, payables and other creditors, and of how much is owed to the business by customers (receivables), and other assets. Double-entry bookkeeping has developed to meet this need. It is also useful in producing a trial balance, which is a list of the various assets and liabilities and types of income, such as sales and the various expenses from which the two primary statements (the statement of financial position and income statement) will be prepared.

The rules for double-entry bookkeeping are straightforward: a few rules, consistently applied, are all that is needed. There are more detailed rules for anyone who wants to be a bookkeeper (introduced in Section 9.2). But the basic principles, outlined below, are not difficult.

Rule 1

A cash account shows all receipts of cash on the left-hand side (known as the debit side, *Dr*) and all payments of cash on the right-hand side (known as the credit side, *Cr*), as shown below.

Cash account

Receipts (Dr)			Payments (Cr)		
Date	Description	Amount	Date	Description	Amount
2013		£	2013		£
1 Jan	Capital – Catherine Fox	100,000	4 Jan	Rent	2,000
3 Jan	Loan from HSBC	50,000	5 Jan	Vehicle	20,000
8 Jan	Sales	3,300	6 Jan	Purchases of books	4,000

From the above cash account, it can easily be inferred what has happened.

Catherine Fox started a business (as a bookseller) on 1 January 2013 with £100,000 of her own capital, which she paid into a business bank account. The money was 'received' into the business cash or bank account. She then borrowed £50,000 from HSBC. The next day she paid rent of £2,000; then paid £20,000 to buy a vehicle; then she paid £4,000 to buy some books. Two days later she sold some books for £3,300.

Anyone with no training in accountancy would soon devise a system of record-keeping such as the above. Recording receipts and payments is essential to keep track of the business's money.

A professional bookkeeper would separate 'petty cash' (notes and coins) from money in the bank; but this need not trouble us here.[1] It is all money, and will be called cash. But the above cash account is too simple, and it is not double-entry bookkeeping.

Rule 2

Every transaction must be recorded twice: on the left-hand side of one account, and the right-hand side of another account. You can imagine these accounts as separate pages in a book, each of which is ruled in the shape of the letter 'T', hence they are known as 't-accounts'.

The next steps should follow naturally. Payments must be on the right-hand (Cr) side of the cash account; payments are usually to pay for assets, or expenses, or purchases of goods for resale. Separate t-accounts are needed for each of these, and the amounts will be recorded on the left-hand (Dr) side of the assets, expenses and purchases t-accounts.

Receipts must be on the left-hand (Dr) side of the cash account. They may be from the original capital provided, or from borrowings, but are mainly from sales. Separate accounts are needed for each of these, and the amounts will be recorded on the right-hand (Cr) side of the capital, loan and sales accounts.

These are illustrated below.

Capital account

Date	Description	Amount	Date	Description	Amount
Dr			Cr		
2013		£	2013		£
			1 Jan	Cash	100,000

HSBC loan account

Date	Description	Amount	Date	Description	Amount
Dr			Cr		
2013		£	2013		£
			3 Jan	Cash	50,000

Sales account

Date	Description	Amount	Date	Description	Amount
Dr			Cr		
2013		£	2013		£
			8 Jan	Cash	3,300

Rent account

Date	Description	Amount	Date	Description	Amount
Dr			Cr		
2013		£	2013		£
4 Jan	Cash	2,000			

[1] It is explained in Section 9.2.

Vehicle (Non-current asset) account

Date	Description	Amount	Date	Description	Amount
Dr			Cr		
2013		£	2013		£
5 Jan	Cash	20,000			

Purchases account

Date	Description	Amount	Date	Description	Amount
Dr			Cr		
2013		£	2013		£
6 Jan	Cash	4,000			

There should be no difficulty in deciding what description to use for a transaction: it is simply the name of the account where the other half of the double entry is to be found. Payments for purchases are shown on the right-hand (Cr) side of the cash account, and labelled as purchases; the transaction also appears on the left-hand (Dr) side of the purchases account, labelled as cash.

But many, or most, business transactions, are not conducted on a cash basis. Purchases are typically made on credit, and the payment is made a month or so later. Sales to other businesses are normally made on credit, and the money is received a month or so later. Purchases and sales that take place on a credit basis must not be shown on the cash account when the transaction first takes place. Entries in the cash account will be made when the cash is received or paid. But there is a need to record the sales and purchases as soon as they are made – not least because there is a need to keep track of how much is owed to suppliers, and how much is owed to the business by customers. Each t-account accumulates all the transactions of the same type so all transactions relating to the bank account are recorded in the cash t-account, while all transactions relating to purchases are recorded in the purchases t-account.

Rules 3 and 4 seem to follow naturally from what we have already seen.

Rule 3

The purchases account records all purchases that have been made, whether they are on a cash basis, or are on credit.

Rule 4

The sales account records all sales that have been made, whether they are on a cash basis, or on credit; in other words, all transactions of the same type or for the same reason are 'posted' to the t-account with that name or heading. It is much like in a postal sorting office where all letters and parcels going to Edinburgh will be put in the same place. Here, all the payments of rent will be recorded in a t-account called 'rent' and in that way, at the end of the year, we will know the total rent cost to the business.

Catherine Fox specializes in buying remaindered books on credit from UK publishers and selling them, on credit, to overseas colleges. Her purchases account and sales account for January are shown below.

Purchases Account

Date	Description	Amount	Date	Description	Amount
Dr			Cr		
2013		£	2013		£
6 Jan	Cash	4,000			
18 Jan	Pinwin Publishers	8,000			
22 Jan	Grohill Publishers	7,000			

Sales account

Date	Description	Amount	Date	Description	Amount
Dr			Cr		
2013		£	2013		£
			8 Jan	Cash	3,300
			10 Jan	College A	5,500
			27 Jan	College B	8,500

It is clear what has happened: she has bought books on credit from Pinwin Publishers and from Grohill Publishers, and she has sold books on credit to College A and to College B. No cash has changed hands in respect of these transactions (yet) and so the cash account is not affected. But she does need to keep track of her trade payables and trade receivables. She must also follow Rule 2, and complete the double entry, as shown below.

Purchases made on credit are shown on the left-hand (Dr) side of the purchases account, and on the right-hand (Cr) side of the payables account.

Pinwin Publishers (Payables) account

Date	Description	Amount	Date	Description	Amount
Dr			Cr		
2013		£	2013		£
			18 Jan	Purchases	8,000

Grohill Publishers (Payables) account

Date	Description	Amount	Date	Description	Amount
Dr			Cr		
2013		£	2013		£
			22 Jan	Purchases	7,000

Sales made on credit are shown on the right-hand (Cr) side of the sales account, and on the left-hand (Dr) side of the receivables account.

College A Receivables account

Date	Description	Amount	Date	Description	Amount
Dr			Cr		
2013		£	2013		£
10 Jan	Sales College A	5,500			

College B Receivables account

Date	Description	Amount	Date	Description	Amount
Dr			Cr		
2013		£	2013		£
27 Jan	Sales College B	8,500			

Catherine Fox will, in due course, pay some of what she owes to her suppliers, and these payments (like all payments) must be recorded on the cash account, as shown below.

Cash account

Date	Description	Amount	Date	Description	Amount
Dr			Cr		
2013		£	2013		£
1 Jan	Capital – Catherine Fox	100,000	4 Jan	Rent	2,000
3 Jan	Loan from HSBS	50,000	5 Jan	Vehicle	20,000
8 Jan	Sales	3,300	6 Jan	Purchases of books	4,000
			24 Feb	Pinwin Publishers	6,000
			25 Feb	Grohill Publishers	6,500

She also needs to complete the double-entry bookkeeping by recording the transactions on the left-hand (Dr) side of her suppliers' accounts, as shown below.

Pinwin Publishers (Payables) account

Date	Description	Amount	Date	Description	Amount
Dr			Cr		
2013		£	2013		£
25 Feb	Cash	6,000	18 Jan	Purchases	8,000

Grohill Publishers (Payables) account

Date	Description	Amount	Date	Description	Amount
Dr			Cr		
2013		£	2013		£
25 Feb	Cash	6,500	22 Jan	Purchases	7,000

The balance on Pinwin's account now shows that Catherine Fox owes it £2,000. The balance on Grohill's account now shows that Catherine Fox owes it £500.

The money owed to Catherine Fox by her credit customers should, in due course, be received. These receipts, like all receipts, must be recorded on the left-hand (Dr) side of the cash account, as shown below.

Cash account

Date	Description	Amount	Date	Description	Amount
Dr			Cr		
2013		£	2013		£
1 Jan	Capital – Catherine Fox	100,000	4 Jan	Rent	2,000
3 Jan	Loan from HSBC	50,000	5 Jan	Vehicle	20,000
8 Jan	Sales	3,300	6 Jan	Purchases of books	4,000
26 Feb	College A	3,000	24 Feb	Pinwin Publishers	6,000
28 Feb	College B	8,500	25 Feb	Grohill Publishers	6,500

Again, it is necessary to complete the double entry by recording the amount that has been received on the right-hand (Cr) side of the receivables (debtors) accounts, as shown below.

College A (Receivables) account

Date	Description	Amount	Date	Description	Amount
Dr			Cr		
2013		£	2013		£
10 Jan	Sales	5,500	26 Feb	Cash	3,000

College B (Receivables) account

Date	Description	Amount	Date	Description	Amount
Dr			Cr		
2013		£	2013		£
27 Jan	Sales	8,500	28 Feb	Cash	8,500

The balance on the College A account shows that it still owes £2,500. College B has paid in full and so there is no balance remaining on its account.

The above example shows most types of transaction. There may be dozens of different types of expense (rent, rates, insurance, postage, stationery, telephone, wages, salaries and so on), but in principle they are all the same. They are shown on the left-hand (Dr) side of an expense account, such as electricity, and on the right-hand (Cr) side of the cash account when they are paid.

It is not difficult to understand the words left and right. But the words 'debit' and 'credit' often seem to cause problems. But they are just more professional-sounding words for the same simple idea.

Rule 5

Recording a transaction on the left-hand side of an account is called debiting it. Recording a transaction on the right-hand side of an account is called crediting it. If an account has more debited to it than credited to it, it is said to have a debit balance. If an account has more credited to it than debited to it, it has a credit balance.

Enough transactions have been illustrated above to be able to make the following generalizations:

- A sales account has a credit balance.
- A purchases account has a debit balance.
- An expenses account, such as rent, has a debit balance.
- An asset account, such as receivables, has a debit balance.
- A creditors account, such as payables or a loan, has a credit balance (unless we have paid our suppliers too much by mistake!).
- A trade receivables account has a debit balance (unless our customers have paid us too much by mistake!).
- A cash or bank account has a debit balance, provided more has been received than paid out (an asset). If more has been paid out than received it will have a credit balance; that is, an overdraft (a liability).

If every transaction is recorded twice, on the debit side of one account, and on the credit side of another account, the totals of all the debits must equal the totals of all the credits. This can be checked and summarized in the form of a trial balance, which is simply a list of the balance on each t-account, as shown in Illustration 9.2.

ILLUSTRATION 9.2

Trial balance of Catherine Fox as at 28 February 2013

	Debit	Credit
	£	£
Capital		100,000
Loan		50,000
Vehicle	20,000	
Cash (£164,800 – £38,500)	126,300	
Pinwin (trade payable)		2,000
Grohill (trade payable)		500
College A (trade receivable)	2,500	
Rent	2,000	
Purchases	19,000	
Sales		17,300
	169,800	169,800

It is called a 'trial' balance because we are trying to see if it balances, or if there are errors and omissions. If it does not balance, there is definitely something wrong. If it does balance, there could still be some errors: items completely missing, or 'compensating errors', such as where a debit item and a credit item for the same amount have been omitted or where an entry has been 'posted' correctly but to the wrong account.

The trial balance is also useful in summarizing all transactions. Even if there have been hundreds of sales, we just have one figure for the total. A cash account may have hundreds of debits and credits, but on the trial balance we just show the one figure. In the above trial balance there are two trade payables; a normal business might have hundreds, but the trial balance would show just one figure for the total amount of the trade payables.

The trial balance provides the basis of the information that is needed to produce a statement of financial position and an income statement since it shows the sum total of the result of the transactions in the period. However, some additional information is usually needed and this leads to the adjustment of the figures appearing in the 'after all-transactions trial balance'. Each 'adjustment' to the trial balance must involve a debit and a credit, otherwise it would not balance. In any case, Rule 5 states every debit has a credit.

In the case of Catherine Fox, the figure for closing inventory (the amount of unsold books at the end of the period) must be added to the trial balance. It will appear on the statement of financial position as a current asset, and it will be deducted from purchases to arrive at the cost of goods sold on the income statement. If her closing inventory is £6,000, her income statement and statement of financial position can be prepared as shown in Illustration 9.3.

When looking at a statement of financial position and income statement like this for the first time, it is a good idea to check where each item has come from. It is important to note that the profit figure calculated at the end of the income statement account is added to the capital figure on the statement of financial position.[2]

Practice questions are provided in Self-testing questions (Carlos; Killip) at the end of this chapter (see p. 228), with answers at the end of the book (see p. 438). Additional practice questions (A Florist;

---

[2] In a company's income statement, any amount for dividends that shareholders receive is deducted to arrive at a 'retained' profit for the year. These items are shown on a separate 'statement of changes in equity' that links the income statement with the statement of financial position.

ILLUSTRATION 9.3

Income statement of Catherine Fox for the two months ended 28 February 2013

	£	£
Sales		17,300
Cost of goods sold		
Opening inventory	0	
Purchases	19,000	
	19,000	
Less Closing inventory	6,000	
		13,000
Gross profit		4,300
Expenses – rent		2,000
Net profit		2,300

Statement of financial position of Catherine Fox as at 28 February 2013

	£	£
Assets		
Non-current assets – van		20,000
Current assets		
Inventories	6,000	
Receivables	2,500	
Cash	126,300	134,800
Total assets		154,800
Liabilities and equity		
Current liabilities		
Payables		2,500
Non-current liabilities		
Loan from HSBC		50,000
Total liabilities		52,500
Equity		
Capital	100,000	
Profit for the period	2,300	
Total equity		102,300
Total liabilities and equity		154,800

Moorey) are also provided at the end of the chapter (see p. 229). These questions require production of double-entry accounts, a trial balance, and a statement of financial position and income statement. Questions in the Online Chapter 19 begin with the trial balance 'after all transactions' and do not require double-entry bookkeeping.

Remember the following:

1 Every debit has a credit.

2 Debits are increases to assets or expense or decreases to liabilities or revenues.

3 Credits are increases to liabilities or revenues or decreases to assets or expenses.

9.2 Bookkeeping in Practice

Section 9.1 provides enough information about bookkeeping to understand how a system works, to be able to record straightforward transactions and to understand how a trial balance is produced. In practice, bookkeeping systems are more sophisticated and this section explains how bookkeeping operates in practice.

Balancing accounts

In Section 9.1 there were very few transactions and it was easy to see what the balance on an account was. For example, in the account of a payable, Grohill Publishers, there was a debit item of £6,500 and a credit item of £7,000. As the credit item is greater than the debit item, we say that there is a credit balance on the account.

Where there are more transactions on the account (e.g. Catherine Fox's cash account), we have to add up all the debit items, which made a total of £164,800; then add up all the credit items, which made a total of (£38,500); then deduct the credit items from the debit items to arrive at the balance on the account, which is (£164,800 − £38,500 =) £126,300; this is a debit balance because the total of debits is greater than the total of credits.

Calculating the balance on an account is done at the end of a period, typically monthly, and the balance is recorded twice on the account (as a debit, and as a credit, keeping to the rules of double entry), and shown as a balance carried down (c/d), and then as a balance brought down (b/d), as shown in two of Catherine Fox's accounts below.

Grohill Publishers (Payables) account

Date	Description	Amount	Date	Description	Amount
Dr		£	Cr		£
25 Feb	Cash	6,500	18 Jan	Purchases	7,000
28 Feb	Balance c/d	500			———
		7,000			7,000
			1 Mar	Bal b/d	500

Cash account

Date	Description	Amount	Date	Description	Amount
Dr		£	Cr		£
1 Jan	Capital	100,000	4 Jan	Rent	2,000
3 Jan	Loan from HSBC	50,000	5 Jan	Vehicle	20,000
8 Jan	Sales	3,300	6 Jan	Purchases of books	4,000
26 Feb	College A	3,000	24 Feb	Pinwin Publishers	6,000
28 Feb	College B	8,500	25 Feb	Grohill Publishers	6,500
		———	28 Feb	Balance c/d	126,300
		164,800			164,800
1 Mar	Balance b/d	126,300			

Remaining balances on accounts, including receivables, payables, cash and other assets and liabilities, are summarized in the form of a statement of financial position that is, in effect, a statement of remaining balances. Accounts that deal with expenses and revenues are dealt with differently: the balances are transferred to the income statement, which is part of the double-entry bookkeeping system. The income statement is summarized and presented in the form of an income statement.

Cash and bank

Accountants often use the word 'cash' to include both petty cash (coins and notes) and money that is in the bank. But in practice it is necessary to record the two separately. Businesses are usually operated mainly through bank accounts recorded in the cash book, and it is necessary to keep a cash float to pay modest routine expenses (e.g. window cleaning, newspapers, coffee), such transactions being recorded in a petty cash book.

Discount allowed and discount received

Businesses often allow a cash discount of perhaps 2.5 per cent or 5 per cent for prompt settlement of accounts.

Discount allowed is an expense, and reduces the amount owed by debtors, and is accounted for as follows:

Debit: discount allowed account
Credit: the receivables (debtor's) personal account

The total on the discount allowed account is treated as an expense on the profit and loss account.

Discount received reduces the amount owed to creditors, and is treated as income to be added to gross profit, and is accounted for as follows:

Debit: the payables (creditor's) personal account
Credit: discount received

The amounts shown for sales and purchases are not affected by discounts allowed and received. The full amount (before deducting any cash discounts) is shown for sales and purchases. Discounts allowed and received are dealt with in the income statement, after calculating gross profit, and are included in the profit for the year shown on the income statement.

Discount allowed and received should not be confused with 'trade discounts'. Suppliers often charge higher prices to the general public than they do to wholesalers and other businesses. These trade discounts are not entered into the accounting system. The transactions are recorded at the price actually charged.

Returns inwards and returns outwards

Customers often return goods that they have received to the supplier for a variety of reasons and in such circumstances, a credit note (to all intents and purposes a 'minus' or 'negative' invoice) is issued. Generally speaking, such credit notes will be entered in the sales day book or the purchases day book as negative figures. Where the original sale was made on credit, the returns are accounted for as follows.

Returns inwards (or sales returns) are goods that a business has sold, but have then been returned by the customer.

Debit: sales account
Credit: the receivables personal account

And in that way, the returns inward is deducted from the total sales figure shown on the income statement.

Returns outwards (or purchases returns) are goods that a business has bought, but then returned to the supplier. They are recorded as follows:

Debit: payables (creditor's) personal account
Credit: purchases

In that way, the returns outward is deducted from the total purchases figure shown on the income statement.

The recording of discounts and returns is shown in Example 9.1.

Returns inwards are debited to sales, while returns outwards are credited to purchases and thereby affect the amount of gross profit. The figures to be included in the income statement from Example 9.1 are as follows:

	£
Sales	99,400
Purchases	25,500

Discounts received and allowed do not affect gross profit. Discount received is added to gross profit. Discount allowed is a normal expense shown after calculating gross profit.

Accruals and prepayments

The normal rules for double-entry bookkeeping apply to accruals and prepayments. For the purpose of preparing final accounts from a trial balance, particularly in an examination, the adjustments can

Example 9.1

Extracts from the ledger accounts of G. Maye

Sales account				Purchases account	
	1 Mar	Bal	51,000	1 Mar	Bal	17,000

S. Oldrick (Receivable)		Cass Hawin (Payable)	
1 Mar Bal 23,000			1 Mar Bal 11,000

During March the following transactions took place:

3 Mar	Sales on credit to S. Oldrick	£14,000
6 Mar	Purchases on credit from Cass Hawin	£7,000
12 Mar	Purchases on credit from Cass Hawin	£4,000
16 Mar	Returned goods to Cass Hawin	£2,500
19 Mar	Sales on credit to S. Oldrick	£21,000
21 Mar	S. Oldrick returned goods	£4,600
26 Mar	Sales on credit to S. Oldrick	£18,000
28 Mar	Paid the balance on Cass Hawin's account after taking 4% discount	
30 Mar	Received a cheque from S. Oldrick for £50,730 who had taken discount of £2,670	

Continued >>>

Example 9.1

Continued >>>

Solution

Purchases account

1 Mar	Bal	17,000				
6 Mar	C. Hawin	7,000				
12 Mar	C. Hawin	4,000	12 Mar	C. Hawin (return)	2,500	

Sales account

			1 Mar	Bal	51,000
			3 Mar	S. Oldrick	14,000
21 Mar	S. Oldrick (return)	4,600	19 Mar	S. Oldrick	21,000
			26 Mar	S. Oldrick	18,000

S. Oldrick (Receivables)

1 Mar	Bal	23,000	21 Mar	Returns inwards	4,600
3 Mar	Sales	14,000	30 Mar	Discount allowed	2,670
19 Mar	Sales	21,000	30 Mar	Cash	50,730
26 Mar	Sales	18,000	31 Mar	Bal c/d	18,000
		76,000			76,000
1 Apr	Bal b/d	18,000			

Cass Hawin (Payables)

16 Mar	Returns Outwards	2,500	1 Mar	Balance	11,000
28 Mar	Discount received[3]	780	6 Mar	Purchases	7,000
28 Mar	Cash	18,720	12 Mar	Purchases	4,000
		22,000			22,000

Discount allowed

30 Mar	S.Oldrick	2,670

Discount received

28 Mar	C. Hawin	780

be made directly onto the statement of financial position and/or income statement. But in practice full double entry is required, as shown below.

Accrual

A company pays its electricity bill quarterly, as follows:

3 April	£800
5 July	£600
4 October	£700

The company's year end is 31 December and the fourth electricity bill has not been received, recorded or paid by that date. It has to be accrued. An accrual is an expense incurred in one year but which is billed and paid for the following year. It may be estimated, or the actual bill, for example £750, may be used for the accrual. It is likely to be received early in January before the financial statements have been finalized. The three payments will have been recorded early in the year: debit electricity;[4] credit

---

[3] Four per cent of (£11,000 + £7,000 + £4,000 − £2,500) = £19,500 = £780.

[4] Alternatively, the account might be called 'lighting and heating'.

cash. Since the business has used this electricity, even though it has not paid for it or been invoiced for it by 31 December, nevertheless, the cost of this electricity must be accounted for. At the end of the year it is necessary to add £750 to the amount of the expense for electricity; it is also necessary to show £750 as a short-term creditor (an accrual) on the statement of financial position. The bookkeeping is done as follows:

Electricity account

Date Dr	Description	Amount £	Date Cr	Description	Amount £
3 Apr	Cash	800			
5 Jul	Cash	600			
4 Oct	Cash	700			
31 Dec	Accrual c/d	750	31 Dec	Income statement	2,850
		2,850			2,850
			1 Jan	Accrual b/d	750

This may seem a complicated way of proceeding, but it achieves three things:

1 The full amount of the electricity charge for the year (£2,850) is shown on the income statement (debit income statement; credit electricity account), although all of it has not yet been paid as at 31 December. This is because we are not accounting on a cash basis, but in accordance with the accruals concept.

2 The balance brought down at 1 January (a credit balance) is the balance that will be shown on the statement of financial position as an accrual, part of short-term creditors.

3 When the final bill for the year, £750, is actually paid, early in the following year, the bookkeeping will be: debit electricity; credit cash. The electricity account already shows a credit balance brought down of £750; this will offset the payment that is in respect of the previous year so that the new year, in effect, starts with a zero balance.

Prepayment

A company pays its rent bill quarterly, in advance, as follows:

3 January	£1,000	for January to March
25 March	£1,000	for April to June
24 June	£1,000	for July to September
29 September	£1,000	for October to December
24 December	£1,000	for January to March in the following year

The company's year end is 31 December and at the end of the year, the company has paid not only the rent for the year but also the rent for the following three months. This final payment is considered to be a prepayment, a payment in one year for which the benefits are going to arise in the following year. This sum of £1,000 is not considered to be an expense in this year but instead is regarded as a current asset, which will be 'consumed' in the following year. The accounting adjustment recording this prepayment is debit prepayments, credit rent. At the end of the year it is necessary to deduct £1,000 from the amount of the rent expense; it is also necessary to show £1,000 as a current asset (a prepayment) on the statement of financial position. The bookkeeping is done as follows:

Rent account

Date Dr	Description	Amount £	Date Cr	Description	Amount £
3 Jan	Cash	1,000			
25 Mar	Cash	1,000			
24 Jun	Cash	1,000			
29 Sep	Cash	1,000	31 Dec	Prepayment c/d	1,000
29 Sep	Cash	1,000	31 Dec	Income statement	4,000
		5,000			5,000
1 Jan	Prepayment b/d	1,000			

This may seem a complicated way of proceeding, but it achieves three things:

1 The full amount of the rent charge for the year (£4,000) is shown on the income statement[5] (debit: income statement; credit: rent account), although £5,000 has been paid in the year to 31 December.

2 The balance brought down at 1 January (a debit balance) is the balance that will be shown on the statement of financial position as a prepayment, part of current assets.

3 In the followings year's income statement, the rent for the months of January to March will be shown as part of the rent expense even though this was paid in the previous year. The rent account already shows a debit balance brought down of £1,000. As with electricity, we are not accounting on a cash basis but on the accruals basis (see p. 218).

Carriage inwards and carriage outwards

The cost of transporting goods, whether inwards or outwards, is an expense and is included on the trial balance as a debit. Often there is no cost for carriage inwards because the seller pays delivery costs. Where the buyer pays the delivery costs (or carriage inwards), the expense is added to the cost of purchases and so affects the gross profit figure.

The cost of carriage outwards does not affect the gross profit. It is a normal expense and is included in the income statement, often as part of 'distribution costs'.

Depreciation of non-current assets

Companies usually have a number of categories of non-current (or fixed) assets (e.g. land and buildings; plant and machinery; fixtures and fittings; vehicles). They should maintain two t-accounts for each category:

1 *Non-current assets at cost (or valuation)* – This shows all non-current assets that the company owns, usually at the original cost price; the account has a debit balance. Sometimes a non-current asset is revalued, then the amount on the non-current asset at cost is changed. If it is an increase in value, the non-current asset account is debited, and the increase is credited to revaluation reserve, which is shown as part of equity on the statement of financial position.

2 *Provision for depreciation* – This shows the cumulative (or aggregate) depreciation that has been built up over a number of years; the account has a credit balance. Each year the depreciation charge is debited to the income statement (to be included in expenses on the income statement), and credited to the provision for depreciation account. The credit balance on the provision for depreciation account increases each year until some non-current assets are sold.

---

[5] The term 'profit and loss account' is still sometimes used for recording transactions; the summary of it for final presentation is usually called an 'income statement'.

Example 9.2

The Salov Company bought a car for £20,000. The company's accounting policy is to depreciate cars over four years at 25 per cent per annum on a straight-line basis. The company estimates that the car will be sold for £2,000 at the end of its estimated economic life. The depreciation charge for each year will be (cost less estimated sale price, divided by four years, that is, £4,500 per annum. The company's non-current asset account and provision for depreciation account and depreciation expense account for the car are shown below.

The effect of these transactions and the depreciation adjustment are also shown below.

Car at cost account	
Cash £20,000	

Provision for depreciation on car account	
	Depreciation expense £4,500

Depreciation of car expense account	
Provision for depreciation (year 1) £4,500	Income statement £4,500

On the statement of financial position the amount shown for non-current assets is the net book value. The cumulative depreciation figure is deducted from the cost (or revalued amount) to give the net book value.

When a non-current asset is sold, it is necessary to remove its cost from the cost t-account and its accumulated depreciation from the provision for depreciation t-account. Both amounts are transferred to a 'disposal (or sale) of non-current asset account', as shown in Example 9.2.

Sale of non-current assets

When a non-current asset is sold, its cost and accumulated depreciation must be removed from the cost and the provision from t-accounts and transferred to a disposal of non-current asset t-account in order to compute the profit or loss on its disposal.

As can be seen in Example 9.3, the machine that is disposed of has to be removed from the machinery at cost account and transferred to the disposal of fixed asset account. This is done by crediting the machinery at cost account, and debiting the disposal of non-current asset account.

9.3 Bookkeeping Systems

Bookkeeping systems are designed, or have evolved over the years, so that they achieve a number of objectives:

1 All transactions and adjustments are recorded, using double entry.
2 They facilitate the production of trial balances and statement of financial position and income statements.
3 Transactions can be traced and verified by the organization's own staff, and by external auditors.
4 Errors can be identified, traced and corrected.

Example 9.3

The Salov Company bought a machine some years ago for £20,000; cumulative depreciation in respect of the machine amounts to £16,000. The machine was sold last week for £5,500. The company's non-current asset account and its provision for depreciation account had balances brought forward immediately before the disposal, as shown below.

Machinery at cost account		
Balance brought forward	£85,000	

Provision for depreciation on machinery account		
	Balance brought forward	£55,000

The accumulated depreciation in respect of the machine that is sold has to be removed from the provision for depreciation on machinery account, and transferred to the disposal of non-current asset account. This is done by debiting the provision for depreciation on machinery account, and crediting the disposal of non-current asset account.

The effect of these two transactions is shown below.

Machinery at cost account		
Balance brought forward	£85,000	Disposal of fixed asset	£20,000

Provision for depreciation on machinery account		
Disposal of non-current account	£16,000	Balance brought forward	£55,000

Disposal of non-current asset account		
Non-current asset at cost	£20,000	Provision for depreciation on machinery	£16,000

After these two transfers, the balance on the disposal of non-current fixed asset account is a debit of £4,000. This is the net book value of the machine. As the machine was sold for £5,500, a profit on sale of £1,500 was made. This profit is credited to the income statement, and debited to the disposal of non-current asset account. The cash received is debited to the cash account, and credited to the disposal of non-current asset account. The effect of these two transactions is shown below.

Disposal of non-current asset account		
Non-current asset at cost	£20,000	Provision for depreciation on machinery	£16,000
Income statement	£ 1,500	Cash	£ 5,500
	£21,500		£21,500

The effects of a sale of non-current assets is included in Self-testing question 6 (Ellie's Ltd) in Chapter 10 (p. 264).

5 Several different people can work on different parts of the system at the same time; there are separate books and ledgers for different parts of a system, whether it is handwritten or computerized.

6 One part of the system, or set of records, is used to check on another part of the system.

7 It is unlikely that one person, working alone, can commit fraud. It is more difficult to prevent or detect fraud where there is collusion between a number of different individuals.

Ledgers, day books and journals

All transactions end up being included in double-entry accounts in a 'ledger'. This is usually done on a computer using an accounting package. In a small business, with very few transactions, everything may be recorded in a single 'general ledger'. In a large organization there are likely to be several day books[6] and ledgers in which each individual transaction is recorded.

Where there are hundreds or thousands of items of sales, each item is usually recorded in a sales day book (or sales journal) and the total amount for a week's or a month's sales is shown in the ledger. Similarly, there is likely to be a purchases day book (or purchases journal). There might also be a purchases returns (or returns outwards) journal and a sales returns (or returns inwards) journal.

The main day books are:

1 Sales day book
2 Purchases day book
3 Cash book
4 Petty cash book
5 Journal

A journal may be used to record one-off or special transactions such as adjustments to the trial balance at the end of the period, or corrections of errors.

There may be several cash books and a petty cash book or a combined one. They may be analysed to show the amounts for different sorts of transaction (e.g. expenses, payments to trade payables, receipts from trade debtors). The cash book is regarded as being both a day book (showing each individual transaction) and a ledger account in its own right.

It is essential to keep a separate personal account for each individual trade receivable and each individual trade payable to be clear what transactions have taken place, and the net amount owed to or by each individual. Where a business has a large number of different suppliers and credit customers, their personal accounts are kept in two different ledgers:

1 The sales ledger (or sometimes called 'trade receivables' ledger)
2 The purchase ledger (or sometimes called the 'trade payables' or 'bought' ledger)

The remaining t-accounts will be recorded in a nominal ledger.

Control accounts

Where a business has many trade receivables, it is likely that some errors are made in individual personal accounts, and it is important that the bookkeeping system checks for such errors so that they can be corrected.

It is possible to arrive at the total figure for receivables at the end of a period without examining the individual receivables accounts. The figure can be arrived at by starting with the total amount of receivables at the beginning of the period, then adding all credit sales made during the period (minus any sales returns); from that is deducted any discount allowed to receivables, and any amounts of money received from them. The remaining balance should be equal to the total on the individual personal accounts.

It is useful to have this total on the receivables control account that can be used in the trial balance and to prepare the final accounts, even before errors on individual personal accounts have been corrected.

The position is similar with a trade payables control account (see Example 9.4), but the opposite way around. For example, the amount owed to payables is a credit balance (whereas the amount owed by receivables is a debit balance); payments are made to payables (whereas money is received from

---

[6] Or 'journals', or 'books of prime entry'.

Example 9.4

Trade receivables control account

Debit	£000	Credit	£000
Opening balances b/d	45	Cash received	197
Sales invoices total	210	Discounts allowed	2
Dishonoured cheques	2	Sales credit notes	6
		Bad debts	2
		Purchase ledger contra	3
		Closing balances c/d	47
	257		257
Opening balances b/d	47		

Trade payables control account

Debit	£000	Credit	£000
Cash paid	135	Opening balances b/d	26
Discounts received	2	Purchase invoices total	128
Purchase credit notes	4		
Sales ledger contra	3		
Closing balances c/d	10		
	154		154
		Opening balances b/d	10

receivables); discount may be received from payables (whereas discounts are allowed to receivables); and returns are made outwards to payables (whereas they are received inwards from receivables).

Bank reconciliations

The cash book, or the bank column of a cash book, shows the amount of money that the business has in its bank account. When a statement is received from the bank, the amount on that statement will, in theory, agree with the cash book. In reality, the balance in the cash book and the balance in the bank statement are very unlikely to agree for two main types of reason:[7]

1 First, the company might have made errors or omissions in recording its bank transactions. A business records all the transactions it is aware of but it might be unaware of some transactions until it reads the bank statement. For instance, it might not know what bank charges have been charged until the statement has been received. Or some customers might have paid money directly into the company's bank account through a direct banking system, which the company only learns about when reading the bank statement. Such 'missing' transactions must now be entered into the cash book.

---

[7] An additional factor is that, from the business's point of view, the money in the bank is an asset while from the bank's point of view, they owe the business money and, hence, the business is a liability. So, if the business pays £100 into a new bank account, this will be a debit balance in the books of the business while it will be a credit balance in the books of the bank. Transactions in the records of a business will be a mirror image of those same transactions in the records of the bank.

2   Second, cheques and other payments made by the company at the end of the month and moneys banked at the end of the month might not have cleared the BACS system (Banking Automated Clearing System) by the date of the last day of the month when the bank statement is produced. Such 'timing differences' must be entered in a 'bank reconciliation statement' in order to verify the corrected cash book balance with the bank statement balance.

The above adjustments are shown in Example 9.5.

Suspense accounts

Suspense accounts are t-accounts which arise for one or both of two different reasons. First, if extracting a trial balance after recording and posting transactions, the trial balance does not agree. Temporarily, and until the error is identified, a t-account is opened with the balance needed to make the trial balance agree. If the debit balances exceed the credit balances by, say, £500, then a suspense account with a credit balance of £500 is required, while if the credit balances exceed the debit balances by £500, then a debit balance will appear in the suspense account. The second cause of a suspense account is when one accounting entry is known but the other entry is not. For example, if a customer pays £1,000 directly into a company's bank account but the identity of that customer is unknown, then the t-account 'bank' will be debited. Since the company does not know which

Example 9.5

Grenaugh Ltd's cash book showed a debit balance of £13,000 on 31 December year 9.

   The bank sent it a statement, showing the same date, but that there was £16,400 in the bank.[8] Further investigation revealed the following:

1   Unpresented cheques, which had not cleared at 31 December, amounted to £5,000.
2   On 31 December Grenaugh Ltd had deposited £2,000 cash into the bank, but this was not shown on the bank statement until 5 January.
3   The bank statement showed dividends received of £500 that had not yet been recorded in the cash book.
4   The bank charges for December amounted to £100.

Cash book	
Balance according to cash book	£13,000
Add Dividends received not yet recorded (3)	500
Deduct Bank charges not yet recorded (4)	(100)
Updated cash book balance	£13,400
Bank reconciliation statement	
Balance according to bank statement at 31 Dec year 9	£16,400
Add Cash deposited on 31 Dec, not yet cleared (2)	2,000
Deduct Unpresented cheques, not yet cleared (1)	(5,000)
Updated bank statement balance	£13,400

---

[8] A credit balance of £16,400 in the bank's books.

customer's t-account in the receivables ledger should be credited, in order that the trial balance will agree and in order that 'every debit has a credit', the suspense account will be credited with £1,000. The suspense account is temporary and once the errors and unknowns' which gave rise to it have been remedied, as shown in Example 9.6, then the balance on the suspense account will be zero (or nil, whichever you prefer).

Example 9.6

The after all postings trial balance of Hue Limited at 31 December included a suspense account with a debit balance of £770. Further investigations reveal the following:

1 A payment by the company of £1,500 to supplier A Limited had been correctly entered in the cash book but had not been posted to A's account in the purchase ledger.
2 The purchases account in the ledger had been undercast[9] by £200.
3 When a receipt paid directly into the company's bank account of £930 was entered in the cash book, the company was unaware which customer had made the payment. It has now been established that Customer B Limited had made this payment to Hue Limited.

The steps required in order that the suspense account balance will be zero is to complete the debit or credit to correct the t-account which is wrong and the double entry will be posted to the suspense account.

Journal entries

		Debit	Credit
1.	Dr: Payables (A Ltd)	1,500	
	Cr: Suspense account		1,500
2.	Dr: Purchases	200	
	Cr: Suspense account		200
3.	Cr: Receivables (B Ltd)		930
	Dr: Suspense account	930	

Suspense accounts

		Debit			Credit
		£			£
	Opening balance	770			
1				Payables	1,500
2				Purchases	200
3	Receivables	930			
		1,700			1,700
	Closing balance	nil			

In each case, we have made the correction to the t-account with an existing error or an omission and the double entry, in each case, is to the suspense account.

---

[9] 'Casting' is the accounting term for 'adding up'. Undercasting is a total which is too low while overcasting is a total which is too high.

Summary

It is essential that all transactions are recorded accurately, and that bookkeeping systems are designed to ensure that every item can be traced and verified, and that most errors are shown up. Every transaction is recorded in a book of prime entry and then every transaction is recorded twice; once as a debit and once as a credit in the ledger t-accounts. The total of all credits must be equal to the total of all debits. Once the transactions have been recorded and summarized on a trial balance, adjustments to record accruals, prepayments, depreciation and the sale of non-current assets will be made. Bookkeeping systems are necessary to keep track of all assets and liabilities, and to ensure that there is an accurate record of all amounts owed to and by the business. They are also necessary to provide the basic information for producing statements of financial position and income statements. The first section of the chapter provided an outline of bookkeeping sufficient for most users of financial statements. More detail was provided in the second and third sections, including bank reconciliations, control accounts and suspense accounts.

⇨ Review of key points

- Every transaction is recorded twice, on the left-hand (debit) side of one account, and on the right-hand (credit) side of another, that is:

  Every debit has a credit.

- Debits are assets and expenses while credits are revenues and liabilities.
- All receipts of cash are recorded on the debit side of the cash account; all payments are recorded on the credit side.
- Not all transactions are shown in the cash account. In many businesses most sales and purchases take place on credit.
- The trial balance provides a summary of all transactions, and is the basis for producing a statement of financial position and income statement.
- Bookkeeping systems in practice include more detail than is shown in most textbook examples.
- The term 'cash' is often used loosely to include both bank transactions and petty cash transactions; the two must be recorded separately in practice.
- Bookkeeping systems include mechanisms such as bank reconciliation statements and control accounts as a check on accuracy and the removal of a suspense account which has arisen to reflect errors in the double entry or incomplete double entry.

! Self-testing questions

For the purpose of these questions there is no need to separate 'petty cash' from 'bank' transactions. They can be combined in a single 'cash account'.

1 Complete the double entry for each of the following transactions:
  a Sales made for cash are credited to the sales account and debited to the _____.
  b Sales made on credit to Smith are debited to the Smith account, and credited to the _____.

c Purchases made for cash are credited to the cash account, and debited to the _____.

d Purchases made on credit from Anirroc Company are debited to the purchases account, and credited to the _____.

e Smith, a trade receivable, pays us part of what he owes; the amount is credited to the Smith account and debited to the _____.

f The provision for bad debts is increased by £30. This amount is debited to the income statement (perhaps via an income statement) as an expense, and credited to the _____.

2 Which of the following accounts normally have a credit balance (as shown on a trial balance): sales, purchases, trade receivables, trade payables, non-current assets, share capital, share premium?

3 Which of the following accounts normally have a debit balance (as shown on a trial balance): expenses, non-current assets, receivables, cash at bank?

4 Which of the following statements is true?

a Accounts for assets and expenses have credit balances.

b Accounts for liabilities, share capital, retained earnings and overdrafts have credit balances.

5 Record the following transactions of Carlos using double-entry bookkeeping; summarize them in the form of a trial balance, and prepare an income statement for the three-month period, and a statement of financial position as at the end of the period.

1 Jul	Carlos started a business dealing in second-hand cars and opened a business bank account with £40,000
3 Jul	Carlos borrows £15,000 from the Spano Bank
5 Jul	Pays £5,000 to rent premises
8 Jul	Buys furniture and equipment for £11,000
13 Jul	Buys cars on credit from Motosales Ltd for £50,000
19 Jul	Pays general expenses of £2,500
27 Jul	Sells one car for £4,000 cash
3 Aug	Sells cars on credit to Minki Cabs for £18,000
10 Aug	Buys one car for £3,300 cash
16 Aug	Buys cars on credit from Motosales Ltd for £22,000
30 Aug	Pays £40,000 to Motosales Ltd
6 Sep	Pays general expenses of £3,300
14 Sep	Receives £15,000 from Minki Cabs
21 Sep	Sells cars for £24,000 cash

The inventory of unsold cars, the inventory, remaining at the end of September was £38,100 at cost. Ignore depreciation.

6 Record the following transactions of Killip using double-entry bookkeeping; summarize them in the form of a trial balance, and prepare an income statement for the one-month period and a statement of financial position at the end of that period.

1 Aug	Started business as a management consultant with £5,000 capital, which was paid into the bank
2 Aug	Paid £4,100 for a computer, printer, scanner and photocopier
4 Aug	Paid £500 rent for office for one month
6 Aug	Arranged advertising in the Journal of Man at a cost of £250, to be paid for a month later
7 Aug	Bought stationery on credit from Dubya Smith at a cost of £120
11 Aug	Received £650 for work done for two small clients
15 Aug	Paid travelling expenses of £135
20 Aug	Completed work for OneAlpha Ltd and invoiced them for £2,200
23 Aug	Paid £700 to a subcontractor
29 Aug	Paid £80 to Dubya Smith
31 Aug	Received £550 from OneAlpha Ltd

Depreciation should be ignored.

7 Cass Hawin's bookkeeper had not balanced the cash book on 31 March year 7. It received a bank statement, dated 31 March year 7, which showed an overdraft of £2,000. Further investigation revealed the following:

   a Unpresented cheques amounted to £1,500

   b On 31 March Cass Hawin had deposited £3,600 cash into the bank, but this was not shown on the bank statement

   c The bank statement showed interest received of £200, which had not yet been recorded in the cash book

   d The bank charges for December amounted to £150

   Required:

   i Show the necessary adjustments to the bank statement in a bank reconciliation statement; and

   ii Show what the cash book balance should be before making any necessary adjustments.

Assessment questions

1 Complete the double entry for each of the following transactions:

   a The owner of a business pays additional capital to the company; the cash account is debited and it is credited to the _____.

   b A business repays a loan; the cash account is credited and it is debited to the _____.

   c The provision for bad debts is reduced by £50; the provision for bad debts account is debited and it is credited to the _____.

   d Drawings paid are credited to the cash account and debited to the _____.

   e A loss arising on the sale of a non-current asset is debited to the income statement and credited to the _____.

   f Closing inventory is shown as a debit item on the statement of financial position and is credited to the _____.

   g A supplier allows a cash discount of £24; this is credited to the income statement and debited to the _____.

   h Costs of delivering goods to customers of £123 are incurred with Rodo Transport Ltd. This amount is credited to the Rodo Transport Ltd account and debited to the _____.

   i A customer returns goods as being unsatisfactory; the amount is debited to the sales account on the income statement. It is credited to the _____.

   j The cost of buying a new non-current asset (a car costing £20,000) has inadvertently been debited to the account for travelling expenses. To correct this error the travelling expenses account is credited and it is debited to the _____.

   k How would the answer to (j) differ if the car had been bought on credit from BWM Garages Ltd?

2 Record the following transactions of A Florist using double-entry bookkeeping; summarize them in the form of a trial balance, and prepare an income statement for the month of January, and a statement of financial position as at the end of the period.

1 Jan	Started business with £10,000 capital, paid into the bank
2 Jan	Bought second-hand van; paid £4,000 by cheque
3 Jan	Bought flowers on credit from Miss Daisy, £700
4 Jan	Sold flowers for cash, £120
5 Jan	Bought flowers, paying by cheque, £456
6 Jan	Paid one month's rent, £408
7 Jan	Sold flowers on credit to the University of Eastminster, £999
14 Jan	Sold flowers in Berwick Street Market for cash, £236
20 Jan	Paid Miss Daisy £400
28 Jan	Received a cheque from University of Eastminster for £899

At the end of January the closing inventory of flowers amounted to £210, at net realizable value. Depreciation should be ignored.

3 Record the following transactions of Moorey using double-entry bookkeeping; summarize them in the form of a trial balance, and prepare an income statement for the one-month period and a statement of financial position at the end of that period.

1 Apr	Started business selling electronic equipment with £800,000 capital that was paid into the bank
1 Apr	Paid £560,000 for a retail shop
2 Apr	Bought shop fittings on credit from Quirky Fitters for £101,000
3 Apr	Paid £460 for advertising
4 Apr	Purchased electronic goods from a car boot sale, paying cash, £800
5 Apr	Received £150 for first sales
7 Apr	Purchased goods on credit from Sinofacturers for £34,000
8 Apr	Sold goods on credit to Eccentainers amounting to £18,000
15 Apr	Cash sales, £230
24 Apr	Paid General Expenses, £333
28 Apr	Paid £51,000 to Quirky Fitters and £25,000 to Sinofacturers
31 Apr	Received £12,500 from Eccentainers

At the end of the month the inventory of goods remaining was £22,600. Depreciation should be ignored.

4 Banner Ltd's cash book showed a debit balance of £8,000 on 30 June Year 4. The bank sent it a statement, showing the same date, but that there was £11,800 in the bank.[10] Further investigation revealed the following:

a Unpresented cheques amounted to £6,000

b On 30 June Banner Ltd had deposited £3,000 cash into the bank, but this was not shown on the bank statement

c The bank statement showed dividends received of £1,000 that had not yet been recorded in the cash book

d The bank charges for December amounted to £200

Prepare a bank reconciliation statement showing the updated cash book and bank statement balances.

5 At 31 March 20X0, included in the trial balance of BC Limited were the following balances:

Purchase ledger control	170,367 (Cr)
Sales ledger control	236,703 (Dr)

---

[10] A credit balance of £11,800 in the bank's books.

The following additional information is given in relation to the y/e 31 March 20X1:

1. goods purchased in the year   633,570
2. goods returned in the year   16,665
3. sums paid to suppliers   599,997
4. discounts deducted from sums owing to creditors   3,270
5. goods sold to customers   996,633
6. good returned by customers   18,435
7. settled by receipt of   717,000
8. bad debts written off   10,032
9. discounts allowed to customers   7,200
10. at 31.3.X1, in relation to J. Smith, who is both a customer and a supplier, balances on the two ledgers are as follows:
    Sales ledger balance   5,340 Dr
    Purchase ledger balance   5,985 Cr

It has been decided to offset the sales ledger balance against the purchase ledger balance.

Required:

i Draw up sales and purchase ledger control accounts for the year ended 31 March 20X1.

ii Why might the balances on the purchase ledger control differ from the list of underlying balances?

6 In preparing the trial balance, you notice that the debit side exceeds the credit side by £970. Upon investigation, you identify the following mistakes:

1 Goods returned to suppliers amounting to £250 have been entered as a debit in the purchases account by mistake.

2 A cash payment for £560 has been entered in the cash book as £650.

3 A computer purchased for £2,000 as an office machine has been entered as a debit in the purchases account.

4 A credit note for £220 given to a customer has been credited twice in the customer's account.

5 A cheque for £780 received from a customer has been entered in the cash book and subsequently banked before the year end. However, no other entry has been made to the customer's account.

Required:

Explain how each of the above mistakes should be dealt with in a suspense account.

 ## Group activities and discussion questions

1 a Accountants cannot do their job effectively if they do not have a detailed understanding of the business' bookkeeping systems.

  b Bookkeeping is done by technicians and computers; it is not a matter for managers and accountants.

    Discuss these two statements. With which do you most agree, and why?

2 The power of accountants and accountancy lies mainly in their control of the official financial recording system. Discuss.

3 A French balloonist landed in a field somewhere in the south of England. He hailed a passer-by and said, 'Can you tell me where I am, please?' The passerby said, 'You are in a wicker basket in a field.' The Frenchman said, 'You are an accountant, aren't you?' The Englishman said, 'Yes. How do you know?' The Frenchman said, 'Because your information is totally accurate and totally useless.' Explain and comment.

4 What is the point of learning the principles of double entry and its application since generally, even in very small companies, the process of completing the accounting records and the preparation of annual accounts are both computerized?

Accounting in context

Discuss and comment on the following article from the press. Do you think that software can eliminate the need for accountants to be able to do bookkeeping?

On cloud nine

The adoption of online computing, or cloud computing, could not come at a better time with its money-saving and environmental capabilities. But why the slow uptake?

By Rachael Singh

According to Stefan Reid, a Forrester analyst, it is not a matter of if cloud computing will be adopted but how fast.

Technology companies, such as KashFlow and NetSuite, are even offering free trials, subscriptions and huge discounts but few firms have grabbed the bull by the horns to bring accountancy technology into the new millennium.

Ten years ago firms and businesses were falling over themselves to upgrade software in preparation for Y2K. At the time it was thought that any company that didn't would be crippled post-1999. But cloud computing has not been taken up with the same zeal.

The biggest block to cloud computing is the perceived security risk. Many feel data is not secure if they are not physically watching over it. Being given the financial information by clients is a huge responsibility that many feel they cannot relinquish to a third party data centre.

But the advantages to cloud computing are growing with every upgrade. Accountants have the ability to achieve real time information, constant dialogue with clients, 24-hour access to the finance function where mistakes can be corrected easily and quickly; reducing carbon footprints by cutting travel and even billing for work while sitting on a train – these are all possible with cloud computing.

Security concerns were raised when the government started to phase in online PAYE and self-assessment filing. There were doubts over the level of security measures for the introduction of chip and pin cards when many companies wanted to maintain signatures as payment authorisation.

But what happened to those companies that didn't adapt to the changes?

Source: Accountancy Age, 28 May 2009

References and further reading

Barrow, C. and J. Tracy (2011) *Understanding Business Accounting for Dummies* (3rd edn.). Chichester: Wiley

Black, G. (2009) *Introduction to Accounting and Finance* (2nd edn.). Upper Saddle River, NJ: FT Prentice Hall.

Monger, R. (2010) *Financial Accounting*. Chichester: Wiley.

Wood, F. and A. Sangster (2012) *Business Accounting* (vol. 1) (12th edn.). Upper Saddle River, NJ: FT Prentice Hall.

When you have read this chapter, log on to the Online Learning Centre website at *www.mcgraw-hill.co.uk/textbooks/leiwy* to explore chapter-by-chapter test questions, further reading and more online study tools.

Trial Balance to Final Accounts

Chapter contents

 Learning objectives

After studying this chapter you will be able to:

☑ Understand how a trial balance summarizes all transactions that have been recorded

☑ Classify items on a trial balance as being income, expenses, assets, liabilities or equity

☑ Produce statements of financial position and income statements from trial balances for sole traders, companies and partnerships

☑ Incorporate a wide range of adjustments into final accounts

☑ Deal with a variety of different profit-sharing arrangements in partnerships

10.1 Introduction

This chapter deals with the conversion of a trial balance to a set of final accounts, incorporating a range of different adjustments. A trial balance summarizes all the transactions that have been recorded by an organization and provides the main information for producing a set of 'final accounts'; that is, a statement of financial position and an income statement. Additional information and 'adjustments' are required to complete the process.

A statement of financial position shows assets, liabilities and equity. The way in which these are presented has been changed several times in recent history; most recently following the widespread adoption of International Accounting Standards (IASs). When dealing with trial balances it may be easiest to think of a statement of financial position as follows:

Debit	Credit
Assets	Liabilities
	Equity (liability of the business to the owners)

An income statement shows revenues (or income) and expenses, the difference being profit. The format for presenting these statements has varied over the years, but when dealing with trial balances it may be seen as follows:

Debit	Credit
Expenses	Income or revenues

If the above two simplified tables are combined, they begin to look a bit like a trial balance:

Debit	Credit
Assets	Liabilities
	Equity
Expenses	Revenue (or income)

The above table should help to avoid mistakes in dealing with items on a trial balance. Almost all debit items are either assets to be shown on the statement of financial position, or expenses to be shown on the income statement. Almost all credit items on a trial balance are either revenues (or income) to be shown on the income statement, or liabilities to be shown on the statement of financial position.

A long trial balance can be daunting but becomes more user-friendly if each item is labelled as being one of the above.

10.2 Sole Traders

The way in which a simplified trial balance can be converted into a statement of financial position and income statement is shown in Example 10.1.

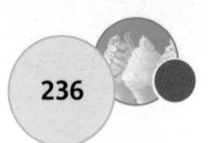

Example 10.1

A simplified trial balance might appear as follows:

Trial balance of Sim Pull as at 31 December year 8		
	Debit	Credit
	£	£
Land and buildings	200,000	
Payables (creditors)		10,000
Capital as at 1 January year 8		150,000
General expenses	80,000	
Sales revenue		120,000
	280,000	280,000

This would be easily converted into (not very well presented) final accounts, as follows:

Statement of financial position of Sim Pull as at 31 December year 8			
	£		£
Land and buildings	200,000	Payables	10,000
		Capital	150,000

Income statement of Sim Pull for year ended 31 December year 8			
	£		£
General expenses	80,000	Sales revenue	120,000

The above final accounts do not balance because a profit of £40,000 has been made, and this has to be shown on both the income statement and the statement of financial position, where it can be added to capital (if it is not a company), or shown as a separate item, as follows:

Statement of financial position of Sim Pull as at 31 December year 8			
	£		£
Land and buildings	200,000	Payables	10,000
		Capital	150,000
		Profit	40,000
	200,000		200,000

Income statement of Sim Pull for year ended 31 December year 8			
	£		£
General expenses	80,000	Sales revenue	120,000
Profit	40,000		
	120,000		120,000

Most trial balances look much more complex than Sim Pull's above because:

a there are more items; and
b there are adjustments to be made.

Additional items

The items that most frequently appear on trial balances are shown below, categorized under the main headings to indicate where they appear in final accounts.

Assets

Assets are usually classified as long term ('non-current assets') or short term ('current assets').

- Non-current assets
    - Premises, land, buildings
    - Furniture, fixtures, fittings
    - Plant, machinery
    - Vehicles, ships, aeroplanes
    - Goodwill

- Current assets
    - Inventories
    - Receivables
    - Prepayments or payments in advance
    - Cash and bank

Liabilities

- Short term
    - Payables
    - Accruals
    - Overdraft
    - Taxation
- Long term
    - Debentures, loans, mortgages

Equity

- Capital (called 'share capital' in a company)
- Retained profits
- Profit for the year
- Drawings (not in company accounts): these are a debit item, to be deducted from capital

Revenue (or income)

- Sales or turnover
- Dividends, interest, rent, commissions received or receivable
- Discount received

Expenses

There are probably hundreds of different expenses, sometimes grouped together under general headings such as distribution costs or administrative expenses. Examples of expenses include: wages, salaries, rent, rates, insurance, postage, telephone, stationery, travelling expenses, carriage inwards, carriage outwards and lighting and heating.

Provisions are either negative assets or estimated liabilities. A provision for depreciation is shown as a deduction from non-current assets on the statement of financial position. A provision for bad debts is shown as a deduction from receivables (or debtors) on the statement of financial position. A car manufacturer is likely to have a provision for warranty claims, an estimated liability.

How to tackle a trial balance question

There are many different ways of tackling a trial balance question, perhaps using an extended trial balance. The following stages often prove to be the fastest way of scoring marks in an examination:

1   Make sure that you have the format of a statement of financial position and income statement memorized. Set the format out, using a whole page for each statement and writing on alternate lines, leaving space for adjustments. You should then be clear where most items from the trial balance should appear, and there should be space for any additions or alterations. In a company, you will also need a note to the accounts called 'statement of movements in retained profits' showing the retained profits in the trial balance, plus the profit for the year (which will be the final total of the income statement) less the dividends paid in the year.

2   Copy each item from the trial balance onto the statement of financial position or income statement in the appropriate place (e.g. current assets or current liabilities).

   At this stage do not bother with adding up (the totals may have to be changed later, and there are not usually many marks in an examination for adding up), and do not try to do the adjustments until every item has been copied from the trial balance to the appropriate place. If you try to do adjustments before completing the copying-out of trial balance items, you may get confused or omit items, such as the second part of an adjustment.

3   Do each adjustment in turn, making sure that each item is dealt with twice; usually this is once on the income statement, and once on the statement of financial position.

4   Add up to produce subtotals under each heading, and profit figures, and to balance. There is no point in attempting to calculate profit until all the adjustments have been done.

Stages 2, 3 and 4 are demonstrated in Illustration 10.1 (Jimmy's Junk, p. 243).

   The 'extended trial balance' approach[1] is more time consuming, but it is also more systematic and thorough. Items are dealt with using several columns: debits and credits from the trial balance; adjustments; and columns to show the amounts for the statement of financial position and income statement.

Adjustments

The bookkeeping for dealing with these is shown on pages 242 and 246–249 but there is no need to do the detailed bookkeeping in order to produce correct final accounts from a trial balance in an examination.

1 Closing inventory

Most businesses are likely to have unsold inventory at the end of the period. A closing inventory is usually introduced in a question as an extra item after completing the trial balance. It has to appear twice in the final accounts as a:

■ debit on the statement of financial position, shown as a current asset;

■ credit on the income statement, deducted from the opening inventory and purchases in calculating cost of sales (or cost of goods sold); this can be shown directly on the income statement to avoid bothering with double-entry bookkeeping in an examination.

   Example 10.2 shows how to deal with the adjustment for closing inventory.

---

[1]   Illustrated on the website of this book.

Example 10.2

Trial balance of Rikki Bloderick as at 30 June year 2	Debit £	Credit £
Bank	56,000	
Capital		27,000
Lighting and heating	6,000	
Receivables	5,000	
Purchases	118,000	
Payables		13,000
Rent and rates	26,000	
Sales revenue		220,000
Inventories at 1 July year 1	12,000	
Wages and salaries	37,000	
	260,000	260,000

Adjustments:

1 Closing inventory as at 30 June year 2 amounted to £15,000

Prepare the income statement for the year ended 30 June year 2 and the statement of financial position as at that date.

Solution:

The first part of the income statement will compare the sales revenue figure for the year with the cost of goods sold to arrive at the gross profit.

The trial balance includes inventories available for sale at the beginning of the year (£12,000) and purchases made during the year (£118,000). The amount of goods available for sale was therefore (£118,000 + £12,000 =) £130,000, but not all those goods were sold during the year. We are told that the closing inventory of goods unsold at the end of the year amounted to £15,000. The cost of the goods that were sold during the year was therefore (£130,000 – £15,000 =) £115,000.

Income statement of Rikki Bloderick for the year ended 30 June Year 2	£	£
Sales revenue		220,000
Opening inventory	12,000	
Purchases	118,000	
	130,000	
Deduct Closing inventory	15,000	
Cost of goods sold		115,000
Gross profit		105,000
Lighting and heating	6,000	
Rent and rates	26,000	
Wages and salaries	37,000	69,000
Net profit		36,000

Continued >>>

Example 10.2

Continued >>>

Statement of financial position as at 30 June year 2	
	£
Current assets	
Inventory	15,000
Receivables	5,000
Bank	56,000
Total assets	76,000
Current liabilities	
Payables	13,000
Equity	
Capital as at 1 July Year 1	27,000
Add Profit for year	36,000
Total liabilities and equity	76,000

2 Depreciation

Most businesses have some non-current assets that should be depreciated each year. A trial balance usually includes a number of non-current assets that are shown at cost (debit items). It is best to leave this figure unchanged and to deal with 'provision for depreciation' as a separate item. A statement of financial position usually shows the original cost of the asset, and the provision for depreciation, and then the net book value, as follows:

Extract from statement of financial position as at 31 December year 6	
Plant and machinery at cost	£50,000
Deduct Provision for depreciation	£15,000
Net book value	£35,000

Trial balances include a provision for depreciation (a credit item), which is usually the figure left from the previous year. In the above example it could be that the £15,000 provision for depreciation figure on the trial balance was £10,000 (as at 31 December year 5); to that £5,000 is added (and charged as an expense, a debit, on the income statement) to give a new provision for depreciation as at 31 December year 6.

The bookkeeping for dealing with depreciation is shown in Chapter 9, Section 9.2; the idea of depreciation is explained in Chapter 2. Example 10.3 shows how to deal with the adjustment to the trial balance.

You should now be in a position to tackle Self-testing questions 1–4 (Noddy; Mona Ramsey; Sally Glen; Mary Rushen), which are to be found at the end of this chapter (see pp. 260–262). Answers are supplied at the end of the book.

Example 10.3

Extract from trial balance as at 31 December year 6		
	Debit	Credit
	£	£
Plant and machinery at cost	50,000	
Vehicles at cost	80,000	
Provision for depreciation on plant and machinery as at 31 December year 5		10,000
Provision for depreciation on vehicles as at 31 December year 5		35,000

Adjustments:

1 Provision for depreciation is to be made on plant and machinery at 10 per cent per annum on cost (straight-line basis).
2 Provision for depreciation is to be made on vehicles at 25 per cent per annum on a diminishing balance (or reducing balance) basis.

The calculations could be shown as a 'working' on the face of the statement of financial position, or a note, as follows:

Item	At cost	Provision for depreciation	£	Net book value
Plant and machinery		As at 31 Dec year 5	10,000	
		Charge for year	5,000	
	50,000	As at 31 Dec year 6	15,000	35,000
Vehicles		As at 31 Dec year 5	35,000	
		Charge for year	11,250	
	80,000	As at 31 Dec year 6	46,250	33,750

The net book value of the vehicles at the beginning of the year was (£80,000 – £35,000 =) £45,000. The depreciation charge for the year is 25 per cent of that balance (25% × £45,000) = £11,250.

3 Drawings

Most sole traders withdraw money from their businesses from time to time, especially if it is profitable. If drawings have already been recorded, the amount has been taken from the bank, and the amount withdrawn is shown as a debit item on the trial balance; that amount is then shown as a deduction from capital plus profit on the statement of financial position.

If drawings are shown as an adjustment, because they have not yet been recorded, the amount should be taken from the bank, and shown as a deduction from capital plus profit on the statement of financial position.

4 Accruals

There are usually some expenses (e.g. electricity) that have not yet been recorded or paid at the end of the year. The amount of the required adjustment is:

- shown as a debit on the income statement, increasing the amount of the expense that has already been recorded;
- shown as a credit on the statement of financial position, as a current liability.

Where an accrual already exists in the trial balance, this will be the accrual from the beginning of the year and it is usually necessary to change the amount at the end of the year.

When there is an *increase* in the accrual, the *amount of the increase* is included as an expense (a debit), to, say, electricity expense, on the income statement. The increase is added to (credited to) the existing accrual in the statement of financial position.

When there is a *reduction* in the accrual, the *amount of the reduction* is credited to the expense, electricity, in the income statement. The reduction is deducted from the accrual that is shown on the statement of financial position.

5 Prepayments

There are usually some expenses (e.g. rent) that have been paid in advance at the end of the year, so part of the expense that has already been recorded (and included on the trial balance) is in respect of the following year. The amount of the prepayment is:

- shown as a debit on the statement of financial position, as a current asset 'prepayments', underneath receivables;
- shown as a credit on the income statement, reducing the amount of the expense that has already been recorded.

Where a prepayment already exists in the trial balance, this will be the prepayment from the beginning of the year and it is usually necessary to change the amount at the end of the year.

When there is an *increase* in the prepayment, the *amount of the increase* is deducted (credited to) from expense, say rent, on the income statement. The increase is added to (debited to) the existing prepayment in the statement of financial position.

When there is a *reduction* in the prepayment, the *amount of the reduction* is debited to the expense, rent, in the income statement The reduction is deducted (credited) from the prepayment that is shown on the statement of financial position.

6 Bad debts written off

Bad debts written off are specific, where it is known that a specific trade receivable will not be paying, perhaps because of liquidation or bankruptcy. It is easier to keep the writing-off of specific bad debts separate from any provision for bad debts. The amount to be written off is:

- shown as a debit (an expense) on the income statement;
- treated as a credit on the statement of financial position by reducing the amount shown for receivables.

7 Provision for bad debts

Where a provision for bad debts already exists, it is usually necessary to change the amount at the end of the year.

When there is an *increase* in a provision for bad debts, the *amount of the increase* is included as an expense (a debit) on the income statement. The increase is added to (credited to) the existing provision for bad debts. This credit balance is shown as a deduction from receivables in the current assets on the statement of financial position.

ILLUSTRATION 10.1

Trial balance of Jimmy's Junk business as at 31 December year 9

	Debit	Credit
	£	£
Bank	18,010	
Capital as at 31 December year 8		90,950
Fixtures and fittings at cost	1,200	
General expenses	14,000	
Insurance	5,000	
Interest paid	7,000	
Inventory at 31 Dec year 8 (opening inventory)	3,000	
Lighting and heating	12,000	
Loan from Bank of Ruristan		100,000
Payables		32,000
Provision for bad debts		1,880
Provision for depreciation on delivery van as at 31 December year 8		9,760
Provision for depreciation on fixtures and fittings as at 31 December year 8		720
Provision for depreciation on premises as at 31 December year 8		24,000
Purchases	47,000	
Trade receivables	41,100	
Sales revenue		225,000
Shop premises at cost	300,000	
Delivery van at cost	20,000	
Wages	16,000	
	484,310	484,310

Adjustments

1 Closing inventory as at 31 December Year 9 amounted to £4,000.

2 Depreciation is to be provided on shop premises on a straight-line basis at 2 per cent per annum.

3 Depreciation is to be provided on fixtures and fittings on a straight-line basis at 10 per cent per annum.

4 Depreciation is to be provided on the delivery van at 20 per cent per annum on a diminishing balance basis.

5 The electricity bill for the three months ending on 28 February Year 10 amounts to £2,700, and has not yet been recorded in the accounts.

6 The amount shown for insurance includes £1,200 for the three-month period 1 November Year 9 to 31 January Year 10.

7 A specific debt of £1,100 is to be written off as irrecoverable.

8 The provision for bad debts is to be adjusted to be 5 per cent of receivables.

9 On 31 December Jimmy took drawings from the business of £18,000, which have not yet been recorded.

Prepare the income statement for the year ended 31 December Year 9 and the statement of financial position as at that date.

Solution in three stages

The following solution is designed to show three stages of producing final accounts from a trial balance. In stage 1 the figures that are taken from the trial balance are shown in normal type. Stage 2 adjustments are shown in **bold**. The results of the final stage, adding up, are shown in *italics*.

Continued

ILLUSTRATION 10.1 (Continued)

Income statement of Jimmy's Junk for the year ended 31 December year 9

	£	£	£
Sales revenue			225,000
Opening inventory		3,000	
Purchases		47,000	
		50,000	
Deduct Closing stock		4,000	
Cost of goods sold			46,000
Gross profit			179,000
General expenses		14,000	
Wages		16,000	
Interest		7,000	
Insurance	5,000		
	−400	4,600	
Light and heat	12,000		
	+900	12,900	
Bad debt written off		1,100	
Increase in provision for bad debts		120	
Depreciation: premises		6,000	
Depreciation: fixtures and fittings		120	
Depreciation: vehicle		2,048[2]	
			63,888
Net profit			115,112

Statement of financial position of Jimmy's Junk as at 31 December year 9

Non-current assets	Cost	Provision for depreciation	Net book value
Shop premises	300,000	24,000	
		+6,000	
		30,000	270,000
Fixtures and fittings	1,200	720	
		+120	
		840	360
Delivery van	20,000	9,760	
		+2,048	
		11,808	8,192
			278,552
Current assets			
Inventory		4,000	
Receivables	41,100		
Bad debt written off	−1,100		
	40,000		

Continued

---

[2] Van at cost £20,000, minus provision for depreciation as at 31 December year 8, £9,760, gives a net book value of £10,240 at the beginning of the year. The depreciation charge is 20 per cent of £10,240 = £2,048.

ILLUSTRATION 10.1 (Continued)				
Provision for bad debts	1,880			
Increase	+120	2,000	38,000	
Prepayment			400	
Bank	18,010			
Drawings	−18,000		10	
				42,410
Total assets				320,962
Liabilities and equity				
Current liabilities				
Accrual			900	
Payables			32,000	32,900
Non-current liabilities				
Loan from Bank of Ruristan				
				100,000
Total liabilities				132,900
Equity				
Capital as at 31 December year 8		90,950		
Add profit for year		115,112		
		206,062		
Deduct drawings		18,000		188,062
				320,962

When there is a *reduction* in a provision for bad debts, the *amount of the reduction* is credited to the income statement (as if it is additional income, or perhaps as a negative expense). The reduction is deducted from the provision for bad debts that is shown as a deduction from receivables in the current assets on the statement of financial position.

A provision for bad debts is general, estimated at perhaps 5 per cent of trade receivables. It is the trade receivables figure *after* writing off any bad debts referred to in adjustment 6, above.

These adjustments are illustrated in Illustration 10.1 (Jimmy's Junk).

Additional adjustments

There may be other adjustments when trial balances are produced in practice; for example, to correct errors. When a trial balance is first produced it is only a 'trial': the accountant is trying to see if it will balance. If not, a 'suspense account' is sometimes put in to make up the difference; errors are then traced, and each correction is debited to the correct account, and credited to the suspense account (or credited to the correct account, and debited to the suspense account) until the trial balance balances and the suspense account balance is zero.

Normal bookkeeping principles apply to all adjustments to the trial balance, and these are shown in Chapter 9.

10.3 Companies

In most ways the final accounts of companies are much the same as for sole traders. The main differences are as follows:

1 There are prescribed formats for company final accounts, as explained in Chapters 1 and 2. There is more freedom for sole traders to present financial statements in their own way.

2 The owners of companies receive payments *as dividends*; the equivalent payments to sole traders are called *drawings*.

3 In companies *share capital* is shown in an account that is kept separate from retained earnings and dividends. In sole traders profits are usually added to the figure for capital, and drawings are deducted from capital.

4 In companies there is a heading for *shareholders' funds,* which can include a number of items such as: *ordinary share capital, preference share capital, share premium, revaluation reserve and retained profits.* In sole traders a single capital account usually includes all that the owners have invested in the business, capital and profits.

5 Companies are liable to pay *corporation tax*, and a profit before tax figure is shown, and also a profit after tax figure. At the end of the year it is usually necessary to estimate the amount of corporation tax payable, and this is included as a debit in the income statement, usually as the final deduction before showing profit for the year. It is included as a credit, as a current liability on the statement of financial position (in the way that an accrual is treated). Sole traders are liable to pay income tax as individual people; there is no taxation on the profits of the business itself.

6 A trial balance often shows that a *dividend* has been paid (a debit item). Companies, particularly listed companies, pay an interim dividend in the second half of the financial year and after the year end, decide to pay a second dividend for the year, the final, or proposed dividend. This is usually approved by the shareholders at the annual general meeting. These days, dividends are accounted for on a cash basis; that is, only when actually paid. Dividends are shown in the 'statement of changes in equity' note to the accounts. The dividend paid is likely to comprise last year's proposed dividend, paid in the first half of this year and this year's interim dividend, paid in the second half of this year.

7 Legislation requires that many expenses are disclosed in company accounts; these are often shown as notes to the accounts. The specified formats for income statement accounts require relatively little disclosure. Examples of expenses that must be disclosed, although they are included within more general headings on the income statement, are directors' fees, auditors' fees and expenses. The income statements of sole traders usually disclose expenses in some detail, according to the preferences of the individual concerned.

8 Most companies have to pay some *interest* (finance expense), whether on long-term loans, such as *debentures,* or on overdrafts. It can be useful to show profit before charging interest ('operating profit') and profit after charging interest ('profit before taxation').

A simplified company trial balance question for Scarlett Ltd is shown in Illustration 10.2.

Additional adjustments

There may be other adjustments with company financial statements; for example, the issue or redemption of shares and debentures. There may be additional accruals for interest payable. Sometimes there might be revaluations of land, or impairment of goodwill. Closing inventories, for example, should be shown at the lower of cost and net realizable value. Any reduction in the amount shown for assets is

ILLUSTRATION 10.2

The trial balance of Scarlett Ltd as at 31 December year 4

	Debit	Credit
	£	£
Administrative expenses	24,000	
Cash	48,500	
Distribution costs	57,000	
Dividend paid	4,500	
Inventories at 31 December year 3	14,000	
Payables		53,000
Property and plant at cost	660,500	
Provision for depreciation on property and plant as at 31 December year 3		135,000
Purchases	730,500	
Retained earnings as at 31 December year 3		69,000
Receivables	68,000	
Sales		900,000
Share capital, ordinary £1 shares	——————	450,000
	1,607,000	1,607,000

Adjustments

1 Inventories as at 31 December year 4 cost £18,000.

2 The depreciation charge on plant and equipment for the year ended 31 December year 4 is to be £48,000.

3 Corporation tax of £15,000 is to be provided.

Income statement of Scarlett Ltd for the year ended 31 December year 4

	£	£
Revenue (from sales)		900,000
Cost of sales		
Opening inventory	14,000	
Purchases	730,500	
	744,500	
Deduct Closing inventory	18,000	726,500
Gross profit		173,500
Distribution costs	57,000	
Administrative expenses	24,000	
Depreciation	48,000	129,000
Profit before tax		44,500
Corporation tax		15,000
Profit for the year		29,500

Statement of changes in equity for the year ended 31 December year 4

Balance as at 31 December year 3 (450,000 + 69,000)	519,000
Profit for the period	29,500
Less: dividends paid	(4,500)
Balance as at 31 December year 4	544,000

Continued

ILLUSTRATION 10.2 (Continued)

Statement of financial position as at 31 December year 4

	£	£
Assets		
Non-current assets		
Property and plant at cost	660,500	
Deduct Provision for depreciation		
(135,000 + 48,000)		183,000
Net book value		477,500
Current assets		
Inventories	18,000	
Trade receivables	68,000	
Cash	48,500	
		134,500
Total assets		612,000
Liabilities and equity		
Current liabilities		
Payables (creditors)		53,000
Corporation tax		15,000
		68,000
Equity		
Ordinary share capital	450,000	
Retained earnings		
(69,000 + 29,500 – 4,500)	94,000	
		544,000
Total liabilities and equity		612,000

shown as a credit to the statement of financial position item (reducing the amount of the asset), and as a debit on the income statement (reducing profit). As always, normal bookkeeping principles apply to all adjustments. You should now be able to tackle Self-testing question 6 (Ellie's Ltd) at the end of this chapter (see p. 264). A solution is provided at the end of the book.

Summary of adjustments

1 **Inventory**

Dr: Cost of sales

Cr: Inventory with the opening inventory

Dr: Inventory

Cr: Cost of sales with the closing inventory

2 **Depreciation charge for the year**

Dr: Depreciation expense

Cr: Accumulated depreciation with depreciation charge for the year

3 **Bad debt written off**

Dr: Bad debt expense

Cr: Trade receivables

4 **Provision for bad debts**

Dr: Bad debt expense

Cr: Provision for bad debts

with increase in provision required based on given percentage of closing net trade receivables (or the opposite, if the provision is to be reduced).

5 **Accrued charges**

Dr: Electricity expense

Cr: Accrued charges

with an increase in the accrual, over and above any accrual in the trial balance from the beginning of the year. A decrease in the accrual is the opposite entry.

6 **Prepayments**

Dr: Prepayments

Cr: Rent

with an increase in the prepayment, over and above any prepayment left in the trial balance from the beginning of the year. A decrease in the prepayment is the opposite entry.

7 **Disposal of a non-current asset**

Dr: Disposal of non-current asset account

Cr: Cost of non-current assets

Dr: Accumulated depreciation of non-current asset

Cr: Disposal of non-current asset account

with the cost and accumulated depreciation of the asset sold, respectively.

8 **Revaluation of land**

Dr: Valuation of land in non-current assets

Cr: Revaluation reserve (in equity)

with an increase in carrying value of land

9 **Corporation tax**

Dr: Tax charge in income statement

Cr: Corporation tax creditor with corporation tax charge for the year

Extended trial balance

Another method of tackling the problem of producing accounts from a trial balance and adjustments is by extended trial balance (see Illustration 10.3).

You are given the following information:

1 Inventory at 31 December year 9 cost £450,000. Included in this is womenswear costing £120,000, which has become out of fashion. In order to sell these garments quickly, it has been decided to sell them at 70 per cent of their cost.

2 The land was purchased in year 2. It was revalued by ZTD, Commercial Property Agents, two years ago at £2,250,000. The directors decided to reflect the revalued amount in the statement of financial position. In December year 9, ZTD valued the land at £2,500,000 and the directors wish to include it at that amount in the statement of financial position.

3 Rent for the shops is payable quarterly in advance. The last quarterly payment of £120,000 was made on 1 December year 9. There were no other types of prepayment, other than rent, at 31 December year 8 or 31 December year 9.

ILLUSTRATION 10.3

Gadol Ltd is a distributor of imported clothes and accessories. The following is a list of balances extracted from its accounting records at 31 December year 9:

	Debit	Credit
	£000	£000
Land, at valuation	2,250	
Buildings: cost	3,200	
Buildings: accumulated depreciation at 1 January year 9		320
Inventory at 1 January Year 9	700	
Motor vans: cost	1,625	
Motor van: accumulated depreciation at 1 January year 9		975
Trade receivables	980	
Provision for doubtful debts at 1 January year 9		80
Prepayment rent at 1 January year 9	75	
Accrued heat and lighting		20
Cash	1,075	
Trade payables		630
8% debentures: year 14		800
Share capital: ordinary 50p shares		2,000
Share premium		1,000
Revaluation reserve		850
Retained earnings		1,270
Sales		9,050
Purchases	4,415	
Wages and salaries	1,150	
Heat and lighting	525	
Distribution costs	350	
Rent	480	
Insurance	56	
Interest paid	64	
Disposal account		130
Dividend paid	180	
	17,125	17,125

---

4   During the year, motor vans that were purchased on 30 June year 7 for £300,000 were sold for £130,000. The sales proceeds have been credited to the disposal account but no other entries have yet been made in the company's records with regard to this transaction. Details of the depreciation policy, on the motor vans, appears in note 5 below.

5   Land is not depreciated. Buildings are depreciated over 50 years to zero residual value. Motor vans are depreciated at a rate of 30 per cent on the reducing value basis. The company provides full depreciation in the year of acquisition and none in the year of disposal.

6   Accruals at 31 December year 8 relate to heat and lighting. The final heat and lighting payment in year 9 was paid up to 31 October 2009. The next heat and lighting invoice for the three months to 31 January year 10 was £150,000.

7 Included in trade receivables at 31 December year 9 is one of the company's customers that has recently gone into liquidation owing £60,000. Additionally, the provision for bad debts of 5 per cent of trade receivables is required.

8 Corporation tax of £230,000 on the current year's profits is to be provided.

9 The company issued 300,000 additional shares at 50p each on 30 December year 9. The proceeds of £310,000 were paid into a separate bank account and no entries have been made in the company's accounting records in respect of this transaction.

How to tackle an extended trial balance question

The following stages show how to produce the figures for an income statement and statement of financial position. The extended trial balance has four pairs of columns, each pair with a debit and a credit column. The first pair are the balance arising from the balances on each t-account arising from the transactions recorded in the ledgers at the year end. The second pair, headed *adjustments*, will record the accruals, prepayments, depreciation, and any other adjustments required at the year end arising from notes 1–9. Pairs 3 and 4 are headed *income statement* and *statement of financial position*.

1 List the balances from the question. You will notice that some of the balances are the sum total of transactions in the year: for example, sales, purchases and rent. Others are year end balances: for example, cash, receivables and payables. Other balances are balances at the beginning of the year, unchanged during the year: for example, inventory, prepayments, accruals and provision for bad debts. Remember that each row on the trial balance is the balances on t-accounts.

2 In the *adjustments* columns, complete the debits and credits arising from notes 1–9, bearing in mind our basic rules that 'every debit has a credit', and the nature of debits and credits. It might be that new rows will need to be added for assets, liabilities, revenues and expenses for which no balances appear in the 'after all transactions' columns. Check at the end of stage 2 that the total of debits column and the credit column agree. This will prove that you have done a debit for every credit.

3 Taking a ruler to each row on the trial balance, compute the arithmetic result of the row. If the result is a debit, if it is an asset, it will be 'extended' and be written as a debit in the statement of financial position columns, while if it is an expense, it will be 'extended' and be written as a debit in the income statement columns. If the result is a credit, if it is a liability, or equity, it will be 'extended' and be written as a credit in the statement of financial position columns, while if it is a revenue, it will be 'extended' and be written as a credit in the income statement columns.

4 When adding the two income statement columns, if the credits exceed the debits, the difference indicates the profit before tax. In this case, in the statement of financial position columns, the debits should exceed the credits by the same figure, and this difference also signifies the profit before tax. You will recall that the profit increases the retained profits, in the equity section of the statement of financial position.

5 And, finally, the figures in the income statement columns and the figures in the statement of financial position columns are simply copied onto the two statements in the standard formats.

	After all transactions		Adjustments Adjustments		Income statement		Balance sheet	
	Dr	Cr	Dr	Cr	Dr	Cr	Dr	Cr
Land: valuation	2250		250				2500	
Buildings: valuation	3200						3200	
Buildings: accrued Depreciation		320		64				384
Motor vans: cost	1625			300			1325	
Motor vans: accrued								

Depreciation		975	153	150.9				972.9
Inventory	700		414	700			414	
Trade receivables	980			60			920	
Provision for bad debts		80	34					46
Prepaid rent	75		5				80	
Cash	1075		310				1385	
Trade payables		630						630
Accrued heat and lighting		20		80				100
8% debentures		800						800
Share capital 50p shares		2000		150				2150
Share premium		1000		160				1160
Revaluation reserve		850		250				1100
Retained profits		1270						1270
Sales		9050				9050		
Purchases/cost of sales	4415		700	414	4701			
Wages	1150				1150			
Heat and lighting	525		80		605			
Distribution expenses	350				350			
Rent	480			5	475			
Insurance	56				56			
Interest expense	64				64			
Disposal account		130	300	153	17			
Dividend paid	180						180	
Depreciation expenses			64 + 150.9		214.9			
Bad debt expense			60		60			
Provision for bad debts:								
Decrease				34		34		
Totals	17125	17125	2520.9	2520.9	7692.9	9084	10004	8612.9
Difference (i.e. profit before tax)					1391.1			1391.1

1 The closing inventory is valued at the lower of cost and net realizable value. The net realizable value of the items costing £120,000 is £84,000; that is, a loss of £36,000. Hence the closing inventory is £414,000. So,

Dr: Cost of sales 700,000

Cr: Inventory 700,000

with the opening inventory

Dr: Inventory 414,000

Cr: Cost of sales 414,000

2 The land is to be revalued upwards by £250,000.

Dr: Land 250,000

Cr: Revaluation reserve 250,000

3 The rent paid in year 9 prepaid at the end of the year is two months out of the £120,000 paid in December. So the prepayment at the year end is £80,000. The prepayment already in the trial balance is £75,000, so the prepayment needs to be increased by £5,000.

| Dr: Prepayments | 5,000 |
| Cr: Rent | 5,000 |

4 The motor vans sold had cost £300,000. Depreciation in year 7 was 30 per cent of £300,000; that is, £90,000. The depreciation in year 8 was 30 per cent of £300,000–90,000); that is, £63,000. Hence, the accumulated depreciation on the vans sold is £153,000.

Dr: Disposal account	300,000
Cr: Motor vans: cost	300,000
Dr: Motor vans: accumulated depreciation	153,000
Cr: Disposal account	153,000

5 Depreciation on the buildings is £3.2m divided by 50; that is, £64,000. Depreciation on the remaining motor vans is 30 per cent of £1,325,000 less £822,000 (i.e. £975,000 – £153,000). The net book value is £503,000, so the depreciation is £150,900.

Dr: Depreciation expense	60,000
Cr: Buildings: accumulated depreciation	60,000
Dr: Depreciation expense	150,900
Cr: Motor vans: accumulated depreciation	150,900

6 Heat and lighting has been paid to October year 9. We need to accrue the two months of November and December. November to January cost £150,000 so the accrual will be two-thirds of £150,000; that is, £100,000. There is an accrual already in the trial balance of £20,000, so we need to increase the accrual by £80,000.

| Dr: Heat and lighting | 80,000 |
| Cr: Accrued charges | 80,000 |

7 A bad debt of £60,000 must be written off. The remaining receivables will be £920,000. The provision for bad debts is to be 5 per cent of £920,000, that is, £46,000. There is a provision in the trial balance of £80,000, so the provision must be *reduced* by £34,000.

Dr: Bad debt expense	60,000
Cr: Trade receivables	60,000
Dr: Bad debt provision	34,000
Cr: Reduction of provision expense	34,000

8 Corporation tax for the year is £230,000. Since the purpose of the extended trial balance is, among other things, to calculate the profit *before* tax, tax provisions are not adjusted on the trial balance but are put directly onto the income statement in the appropriate place in the standard format and shown in the statement of financial position as a current liability.

9 The cash increases by £310,000, the nominal value of the shares, 300,000 × 50p; that is, £150,000 increases the share capital while the excess sum raised over the par value increases share premium; that is, £160,000.

Dr: Cash	310,000
Cr: Share capital	150,000
Cr: Share premium	160,000

Income statement of Gadol Ltd for the year ended 31 December year 9

	£000	£000	£000
Sales revenue			9,050
Cost of goods sold			4,701
Gross profit			4,349
Wages		1,150	
Heat and lighting		605	
Distribution expenses		350	
Rent		475	
Insurance		56	
Interest		64	
Loss on disposal of van		17	
Depreciation		214.9	
Bad debts written off		60	
Decrease in bad debt provision		(34)	
			2,957.9
Profit before tax			1,391.1
Tax			230
Profit for the year			1,161.1

Statement of financial position of Gadol Ltd as at 31 December year 9

Non-current assets	£000 Cost	£000 Provision for depreciation	£000 Net book value
Land	2,500		2,500
Buildings	3,200	384	2,816
Motor vans	1,325	972.9	352.1
	7,025	1,356.9	5,668.1
Current assets			
Inventory		414	
Receivables	920		
Less: Bad debt provision	46	874	
Prepayment		80	
Bank		1,385	
			2,753
Total assests			8,421.1
Liabilites and equity			
Current liabilities			
Payables			630
Accrual			100
Corporation tax			230

		960
Non-current liabilities		800
Total liabilities		1,760
Equity		
Share capital	2,150	
Share premium	1,160	
Revaluation reserve	1,100	
Retained profits	2,251.1	
		6,661,1
Total equity and liabilities		8,421.1
Note: The retained profits is as follows:		
Balance at January year 9		1,270.0
Plus: profit for the year		1,161.1
Less: dividend paid		(180.0)
Balance at 31 December year 9		2,251.1

10.4 Partnerships

In most ways the final accounts of partnerships are much the same as for sole traders. The main differences arise because there is a need (a) to divide the profit between the partners and (b) to keep separate accounts for each of the partners, for capital, drawings and current transactions.

A partnership's income statement is prepared in the same way as for a sole trader until the net profit is arrived at. After that there is an 'appropriation account' on which the amount of profit due to each partner is calculated.

A partnership's statement of financial position is prepared in the same way as for a sole trader, except that (a) there is a separate capital account for each partner and (b) in addition to the capital accounts there is a 'current account' for each partner to keep track of the amounts of profits credited to each, and the amount of drawings taken.

In the simplified Illustration 10.4, it is assumed that there are no accruals or prepayments, and the only adjustments are for depreciation and closing inventory.

Other issues in partnership accounts

Partners can agree among themselves to share the work and benefits of the partnership business in any way they like, and this is best done with a formal written agreement. In the absence of any agreement to the contrary, the provisions of the 1890 Partnership Act apply, the key parts of which are that partners share profits and losses equally; they share equally in the management of the business; there are no partners' salaries, interest on capital or drawings; if a partner loans money to the business, interest will be allowed at 5 per cent per annum; and no new partner can be admitted unless all agree. The partnership is dissolved if one partner resigns, dies or becomes bankrupt or insane.

A general example of partnership accounts is provided in Illustration 10.5, with additional questions at the end of this chapter (see p. 258).

ILLUSTRATION 10.4

Trial balance of Orry, Mona and Michael as at 31 December year 7

	Debit £	Credit £
Cash	95,200	
Expenses	44,400	
Premises	280,000	
Provision for depreciation on premises at 31 December year 6		33,600
Purchases	240,000	
Sales		400,000
Inventory at 31 December year 6	25,000	
Capital accounts at 1 January year 7		
Orry		160,000
Mona		100,000
Michael		30,000
Current accounts at 1 January year 7		
Orry		30,000
Mona	40,000	
Michael	29,000	
	753,600	753,600

Adjustments

1 Inventory at 31 December year 7 amounted to £35,000.

2 The provision for depreciation on premises is to be increased by £5,600.

Income statement of Orry, Mona and Michael for the year ended 31 December year 7

	£	£
Sales revenue		400,000
Opening inventory	25,000	
Purchases	240,000	
	265,000	
Deduct Closing inventory	35,000	
Cost of sales		230,000
Gross profit		170,000
Expenses	44,400	
Depreciation	5,600	50,000
Net profit		120,000

Explanations

The profit is calculated in the same way as with a sole trader. In most cases there would be more assets and expenses, more adjustments, and additional items such as receivables (debtors) and payables (creditors).

In a sole trader the net profit is simply added to the capital account on the statement of financial position, which should then balance.

In a partnership it is necessary to know how the profit is to be divided between or amongst the partners. If there is £120,000 profit to be divided equally between three partners, it would be possible simply to credit £40,000 to each of the partner's capital accounts, and that would be the end of the matter. The statement of financial position (1) of Orry, Mona and Michael would balance if the £120,000 profit was added to the capital or current accounts.

Continued

ILLUSTRATION 10.4 (Continued)

More detail is usually required because:

1 The partners do not necessarily share the profits equally. In this example Orry has much more money invested in the business (£160,000 + £30,000 = £190,000) than Michael, who seems to draw almost as much money out of the business as he has invested in it. But perhaps it is Michael who does most of the work, and deserves a regular salary. Orry may be more or less retired ('a sleeping partner'), but as he has a substantial sum invested in the business (and perhaps he set it up in the first place), he deserves some extra return to reflect that. It might be agreed that Michael should have a 'salary' from the profits of £40,000 a year; that Orry should have half of the remaining profits; and that Mona and Michael should have one-quarter each. Statement of financial position (2), opposite, shows the effect of appropriating the profits in this way.

2 There are usually separate accounts for partners':

   a Capital, with the amounts remaining much the same from year to year, unless there is a major change

   b Current accounts, which change regularly each year as appropriations of profit are credited to them, and drawings debited to them

   c Drawings, which may be shown in a separate account, and debited to the current accounts at the end of the year

Statement of financial position (1) of Orry, Mona and Michael as at 31 December year 7 (before appropriation of profits)

				£	£
Non-current assets					
Premises					280,000
Deduct Provision for depreciation					39,200
(33,600 + 5,600)					
					240,800
Current assets					
Inventories				35,000	
Cash				95,200	
					130,200
Total assets					371,000
Capital accounts					

Orry	Mona	Michael			
£	£	£	£		
160,000	100,000	30,000	290,000		

Current accounts

Orry	Mona	Michael		
£	£	£		
30,000	(40,000)	(29,000)	(39,000)	
			251,000	

Statement of financial position (2) of Orry, Mona and Michael as at 31 December Year 7 (after appropriation of profits)

				£	£
Non-current assets					
Premises					280,000
Deduct Provision for depreciation					39,200
(33,600 + 5,600)					
					240,800
Current assets					
Inventories				35,000	
Cash				95,200	
					130,200
					371,000

Continued

ILLUSTRATION 10.4 (Continued)

Orry	Mona	Michael		
£	£	£		
160,000	100,000	30,000		290,000
Current accounts				

	Orry	Mona	Michael		
	£	£	£		
Opening balance	30,000	(40,000)	(29,000)		
Salary	–	–	40,000		
Profit	40,000	20,000	20,000		
	70,000	(20,000)	31,000	81,000	
					371,000

ILLUSTRATION 10.5

Before preparing the appropriation account, the profit and loss account of Knobby and Bee-Gears showed a net profit of £150,000, and their summarized statement of financial position as at 31 December year 2 was as follows:

	£	£
Net assets		700,000
Profit for year (before appropriation)		150,000
Capital accounts		
Knobby	500,000	
Bee-Gears	100,000	600,000
Current accounts		
Knobby	50,000	
Bee-Gears	(40,000)	10,000
Drawings accounts		
Knobby	(10,000)	
Bee-Gears	(50,000)	(60,000)
		700,000

The partnership agreement provides for charging interest on drawings at the rate of 10 per cent of the balances on the drawings accounts at the end of the year; interest on capital is to be 5 per cent per annum; Bee-Gears is to receive a salary of £30,000 a year; Knobby is to be credited with two-thirds of remaining profits and Bee-Gears with one-third.

ILLUSTRATION 10.6

Appropriation account of Knobby and Bee-Gears for the year ended 31 December year 2

	£	£
Net profit		150,000
Interest on drawings		
Knobby	1,000	
Bee-Gears	5,000	6,000
		156,000

Continued

ILLUSTRATION 10.6 (Continued)

Salary – Bee-Gears	30,000		
Interest on capital			
Knobby	25,000		
Bee-Gears	5,000	60,000	
		96,000	
Share of profit			
Knobby	64,000		
Bee-Gears	32,000	96,000	

Summarized statement of financial position of Knobby and Bee-Gears as at 31 December year 2

	Knobby	Bee-Gears	
Net assets			700,000
Capital accounts	Knobby	Bee-Gears	
	500,000 Cr	100,000 Cr	
			600,000 Cr
Current accounts	Knobby	Bee-Gears	
	50,000 Cr	(40,000) Dr	
Interest on drawings	(1,000) Dr	(5,000) Dr	
	49,000 Cr	(45,000) Dr	
Salary	–	30,000 Cr	
Interest on capital	25,000 Cr	5,000 Cr	
Share of profit	64,000 Cr	32,000 Cr	
	138,000 Cr	22,000 Cr	
Drawings	(10,000) (Dr)	(50,000) (Dr)	
	128,000 (Cr)	(28,000) (Dr)	100,000 Cr
			700,000

Explanations

The income statement and statement of financial position have already been prepared in the usual way, taking into account depreciation, accruals and other adjustments. The net profit to be allocated between the partners is £150,000, which is a credit balance remaining on the income statement. For each appropriation of profit (salary, interest on capital and share of profit), the bookkeeping is to debit the profit and loss appropriation account, and to credit the current account of each partner.

The idea of charging interest on drawings is rather different. The charge (the debit) is made to the partners' current accounts; the credit is to the profit and loss account, which has the effect of increasing the amount to be divided between the partners.

At the end of Year 2, the partners' drawings accounts can be netted off against their current accounts. The drawings accounts for Year 3 will then show only the drawings made in Year 3. Knobby may think that Bee-Gears ought to be charged more interest because he still has a debit balance on his current account in Year 3, even before making any drawings.

The partners' capital accounts usually remain unchanged from year to year, unless it is agreed that additional capital is introduced (or withdrawn).

📖 Summary

The basic recording of financial transactions, using double-entry bookkeeping, is the same with sole traders, companies and partnerships, and most of the adjustments to trial balances are much the same. Unincorporated businesses (sole traders and partnerships) are free to present their statements of financial position and income statements in traditional ways, often including expenses in some detail.

With sole traders it is acceptable for profits to be added to capital, and for drawings to be deducted from capital. In partnerships there are usually separate accounts for each partner's capital, current transactions and drawings.

> In company accounts share capital must be clearly separated from other reserves and retained earnings. Company financial statements are governed by Companies Acts and accounting standards; and the formats shown in IAS 1 for statements of financial position and income statements are generally being adopted.

⮕ Review of key points

- The trial balance is a summary of all transactions that have been recorded in the double-entry bookkeeping system, and is the basis for preparing statements of financial position and income statements.
- Adjustments and additional information are required to produce a statement of financial position and income statement. Each of these has to be dealt with twice: once as a debit, and once as a credit.
- Adjustments for closing inventory, depreciation, the disposal of non-current assets, revaluation of land, accruals, prepayments, bad debts written off and provisions for bad debts are the same in all types of organization.
- Drawings are deducted from capital in sole traders' accounts. In partnerships, drawings are shown separately from capital, and separately for each partner.
- A company's income statement concludes by showing profit for the period. Dividends are shown on a separate statement 'changes in equity for the period'.
- Statements of financial position and income statements for all types of organization are increasingly following the formats illustrated in IAS 1.

! Self-testing questions

1 The trial balance of Noddy's Business as at 31 December year 6 is as follows:

	Debit	Credit
	£	£
Shop premises	400,000	
Capital as at 1 December year 6		370,000
General expenses	120,000	
Payables (creditors)		20,000
Sales		130,000
	520,000	520,000

Prepare an income statement for the year ended 31 December year 6, and a statement of financial position as at that date.

2 The trial balance of Mona Ramsey as at 30 September year 3 was as follows.

	£	£
Bank	24,321	
Capital		27,000
General expenses	8,000	
Inventory at 1 October year 2	20,000	
Payables		13,000
Purchases	188,000	
Receivables	11,000	
Rent, rates and insurance	17,000	
Sales revenue		267,321
Wages	39,000	
	307,321	307,321

Adjustments

a Closing inventory as at 30 September year 3 amounted to £15,000.

Prepare an income statement for the year ended 30 September year 3, and a statement of financial position as at that date.

3 The trial balance of Sally Glen's business as at 31 December year 8 is as follows:

	£	£
Bank	23,000	
Capital as at 31 December year 7		370,000
General expenses	8,000	
Inventory at 31 December year 7	18,000	
Provision for depreciation on premises as at 31 December year 7		21,000
Provision for depreciation on delivery van as at 31 December year 7		14,000
Payables		20,000
Purchases	242,000	
Receivables	60,000	
Rent, rates and insurance	23,000	
Sales revenue		365,000
Shop premises at cost	350,000	
Delivery van at cost	32,000	
Wages	34,000	
	790,000	790,000

Adjustments

a Closing inventory as at 31 December year 8 amounted to £19,000.

b Depreciation is to be provided on shop premises on a straight-line basis at 2 per cent per annum.

c Depreciation is to be provided on the delivery van at 25 per cent per annum on a diminishing balance basis.

Prepare an income statement for the year ended 31 December year 8, and a statement of financial position as at that date.

4 The trial balance of Mary Rushen's business as at 30 June year 5 was as follows.

	£	£
Capital as at 30 June year 4		238,200
Cash and bank	7,400	
Fixtures and fittings at cost	44,000	
Freehold buildings at cost	400,000	
General expenses	13,000	
Inventory at 30 June year 4	12,000	
Payables		18,000
Provision for depreciation on freehold buildings as at 30 June year 4		80,000
Provision for depreciation on fixtures and fittings as at 30 June year 4		30,800
Purchases	155,000	
Receivables	8,000	
Repairs and maintenance	10,600	
Sales revenue		320,000
Wages	37,000	
	687,000	687,000

Adjustments

a Closing inventory as at 30 June year 5 amounted to £7,000.

b Depreciation is to be provided on freehold buildings on a straight-line basis at 2.5 per cent per annum.

c Depreciation is to be provided on the fixtures and fittings on a straight-line basis at 10 per cent per annum.

Prepare an income statement for the year ended 30 June year 5, and a statement of financial position as at that date.

5 The trial balance of Brad Head as at 31 December year 3 was as follows:

	£	£
Bank	6,400	
Capital as at 31 December year 2		35,000
Fixtures and fittings at cost	22,000	

General expenses	9,000	
Interest paid	3,500	
Inventory at 31 December year 2	28,000	
Heat and lighting	19,000	
Loan from SHC Bank		50,000
Payables		31,000
Plant and machinery at cost	220,000	
Provision for bad debts		1,800
Provision for depreciation on vehicles as at 31 December year 2		15,000
Provision for depreciation on fixtures and fittings at 31 December year 2		13,200
Provision for depreciation on plant and machinery as at 31 December year 2		24,000
Purchases	255,000	
Receivables	98,100	
Rent, rates, and insurance	65,000	
Sales revenue		660,000
Vehicles at cost	60,000	
Wages	44,000	
	830,000	830,000

Adjustments

a Closing inventory as at 31 December year 3 amounted to £13,000.

b Depreciation is to be provided on plant and machinery on a straight-line basis at 10 per cent per annum.

c Depreciation is to be provided on fixtures and fittings on a straight-line basis at 10 per cent per annum.

d Depreciation is to be provided on the delivery van at 20 per cent per annum on a diminishing balance basis.

e An electricity bill for the three months ending on 31 January year 4 amounts to £3,000 and has not yet been recorded in the accounts.

f Rent for the three months ending on 28 February year 4, amounting to £6,600, was paid at the beginning of December year 3.

g A specific debt of £2,100 is to be written off as irrecoverable.

h The provision for bad debts is to be adjusted to be 2.5 per cent of debtors.

i On 31 December year 3 Brad Head took drawings from the business of £6,000, which have not yet been recorded.

Prepare an income statement for the year ended 31 December year 3, and a statement of financial position as at that date.

6 The trial balance of Ellie's Ltd as at 31 December year 1 was as follows:

	Debit	Credit
	£	£
Inventory at 1 January year 1	19,500	
Trade receivables	61,000	
Trade payables		13,400
Share capital: 100 £1 shares		248,100
Share premium		11,600
Retained profits at 1 January year 1		17,100
Printing and stationery	2,400	
Provision for bad debts		600
Wages and salaries	12,300	
Purchases	167,000	
Sales revenue		248,300
Cash at bank	1,450	
Rent	1,500	
Electricity	1,100	
Fixtures and fittings at cost	12,000	
Fixtures and fittings: provision for depreciation at 31 December year 0		2,000
Van at cost	8,400	
Van: provision for depreciation at 31 December year 0		4,200
Van: disposal proceeds		4,750
Car at cost	20,000	
Car: provision for depreciation at 31 December year 0		5,000
General expenses	1,400	
	307,050	307,050

Additional information

a Inventories as at 31 December year 1 was £21,000.

b Rent prepaid as at 31 December year 1 was £400.

c Accrued electricity as at 31 December year 1 was £200.

d A receivable of £500 is to be written off.

e The provision for bad debts is to be increased to £650.

f Depreciation is to be provided for the year as follows: fixtures and fittings – 25 per cent per annum on a reducing balance basis; and vehicles – 25 per cent per annum on a straight-line basis.

g The company's accounting policy is to charge no depreciation in the year that a non-current asset is sold.

h Corporation tax of £15,000 is to be provided.

Prepare an income statement for the year ended 31 December year 1 and a statement of financial position as at that date.

7 The trial balance of Bulgham, Dhoon and Barony as at 31 December year 9 is as follows:

	£	£
Cash	47,000	
Furniture at cost	90,000	
General expenses	45,000	
Inventories as at 31 December year 8	37,000	
Provision for depreciation on furniture as at 31 December year 8		27,000
Purchases	320,000	
Rent	28,000	
Sales revenue		490,000
Capital accounts as at 1 January year 9		
Bulgham		40,000
Dhoon		30,000
Barony		20,000
Current accounts as at 1 January year 9		
Bulgham		10,000
Dhoon	22,000	
Barony	28,000	
	617,000	617,000

Adjustments

a Inventory as at 31 December year 9 amounted to £31,000.

b Furniture is to be depreciated on a straight-line basis at 10 per cent per annum.

c Rent of £6,000 was paid on 30 November year 9 for the three-month period ending on 28 February year 10.

d Profits are to be appropriated as follows:

  i 5 per cent interest on capital to each partner;

  ii salaries of £18,250 each to Dhoon and Barony;

  iii the remaining profits to be divided equally among the three partners.

There were no drawings during the year. Prepare an income statement for the year ended 31 December year 9, and a statement of financial position as at that date.

Assessment questions

1 The trial balance of E. Zee's Business as at 31 December year 7 was as follows.

	Debit	Credit
	£	£
Workshop	170,000	
Payables		15,000
Capital as at 1 January year 7		145,000
General expenses	50,000	
Sales revenue		60,000
	220,000	220,000

Prepare an income statement for the year ended 31 December year 7, and a statement of financial position as at that date.

2 The trial balance of Isabella Stanley as at 31 March year 9 was as follows:

	£	£
Administration expenses	43,000	
Bank	61,000	
Capital		30,000
Inventory as at 1 April year 8	18,000	
Payables		33,000
Purchases	234,000	
Receivables	17,000	
Sales revenue		370,000
Selling expenses	26,000	
Distribution costs	34,000	
	433,000	433,000

Adjustment

a Closing inventory as at 31 March year 9 amounted to £22,000.

Prepare an income statement for the year ended 31 March year 9, and a statement of financial position as at that date.

3 The trial balance of Michael Orry's business as at 31 March year 2 is as follows:

	£	£
Administrative expenses	43,000	
Capital as at 31 March year 1		250,000
Cash and bank	170,000	
Drawings	36,900	
Distribution costs	11,000	
Inventories as at 31 March year 1	18,000	
Payables		18,000
Plant and machinery at cost	180,000	
Provision for depreciation on plant and machinery as at 31 March year 1		108,000
Provision for depreciation on vehicles as at 31 March year 1		21,000

Purchases	120,000	
Receivables	16,000	
Repairs and maintenance	27,900	
Rent and rates	36,200	
Sales		390,000
Vehicles at cost	48,000	
Wages	80,000	
	787,000	787,000

Adjustments

a Closing inventory as at 31 March year 2 amounted to £21,000.

b Depreciation is to be provided on plant and machinery on a straight-line basis at 10 per cent per annum.

c Depreciation is to be provided on vehicles on a reducing balance basis at 25 per cent per annum.

Prepare an income statement for the year ended 31 March year 2, and a statement of financial position as at that date.

4 Andreas, Jude and Sandy are in business together, sharing profits in the proportion 3 : 2 : 1. Their partnership agreement provides for interest on their fixed capital balances of 8 per cent per annum, and that Sandy should receive a salary of £13,400 per annum. Their trial balance as at 30 June year 3 was as follows:

	£	£
Bank	42,800	
Business expenses	38,150	
Capital accounts as at 30 June year 2		
Andreas		120,000
Jude		150,000
Sandy		100,000
Payables		8,000
Current accounts as at 30 June year 2		
Andreas		15,000
Jude		13,000
Sandy	4,600	
Receivables	11,150	
Drawings accounts as at 30 June year 3		
Andreas	51,000	
Jude	72,000	
Sandy	38,400	
Plant and equipment at cost	290,000	
Goodwill	100,000	
Inventories as at 30 June year 2	12,000	
Provision for depreciation as at 30 June year 2		50,000
Purchases	78,900	
Sales		283,000
	739,000	739,000

Adjustments

a Non-current assets are to be depreciated at the rate of 20 per cent per annum on a reducing balance basis.

b Closing inventory amounted to £18,900.

c Business expenses of £2,735 have been incurred but not yet recorded.

d A provision for bad debts amounting to 10 per cent of receivables is to be created.

Prepare an income statement and an appropriation account for the year ending 30 June year 3, and a statement of financial position as at that date.

5 The trial balance of Faraway Retailers Ltd as at 31 December year 1 is shown below.

	Debit £000	Credit £000
Inventories as at 1 January year 1	545	
Trade receivables	705	
Trade payables		600
Share capital: £1 shares		1,500
Share premium		750
8% debentures		1,200
Retained profits at 1 January year 1		190
Printing and stationery	750	
Provision for bad debts		40
Wages and salaries	890	
Distribution costs	100	
Bad debt written off	20	
Purchases	3,350	
Sales		7,900
Cash at bank	51	
Rent and rates	320	
Electricity	55	
Debenture interest	48	
Land and buildings at cost	3,000	
Land and buildings provision for depreciation as at 31 December year 0		90
Fixtures and fittings at cost	1,500	
Fixtures and fittings provision for depreciation as at 31 December year 0		600
Plant and machinery at cost	2,800	
Plant and machinery provision for depreciation at 31 December year 0		1,264
	14,134	14,134

Additional information

a The stocktake on 31 December year 1 revealed the following:

	Cost	Net realizable value
	£000	£000
Home furnishing	500	1,000
Clothing	440	410

b Rent and rates includes a rent payment of £144,000 for the period 1 April year 1 to 31 March year 2.

c Electricity for the three months ended 31 January year 2 of £18,000 was paid in February year 2.

d A trade receivable of £5,000 is to be written off.

e The provision for bad debts is to be adjusted to be 5 per cent of trade receivables.

f Depreciation is to be provided for the year as follows: land and buildings – 2 per cent per annum, straight line; fixtures and fittings – 20 per cent per annum, straight line; plant and machinery – 25 per cent per annum, reducing balance.

g A full year's debenture interest is payable.

h Corporation tax of £615,000 is to be provided.

Prepare an income statement for the year ended 31 December year 1, and a statement of financial position as at that date.

Group activities and discussion questions

1 Would you rather be in business as a sole trader, in a partnership, or in a company? Why?

2 What are the various ways of sharing profits between partners, and why are they used?

3 Is there, or should there be, a standard format for the financial statements of unincorporated businesses? Why or why not?

4 Why is there a need for 'adjustments' to a trial balance at the year end?

5 Bookkeeping records transactions; trial balances, statement of financial positions and income statements summarize and present the results of those transactions. It is unrealistic to expect such summaries to be 'useful', except in a very narrow sense. Discuss. How useful would you like financial statements to be? How realistic is it to expect financial statements to meet the needs of various users of accounts, given the way in which they are derived?

Accounting in context

In relation to the following extract from the website of a well-known accounting software package developer and the article referring to this product, what advantages arise from using such a package instead of a manual system of accounting demonstrated Chapters 9 and 10? Do you think there are any differences in principle between accounting using a traditional approach and a computerized accounting system?

Background information on VT Software from the company website

VT Final Accounts, our final accounts software, runs in Microsoft Excel and produces professionally formatted company accounts (inc tax computation), sole trader accounts and partnership accounts from trial balance stage upwards. A trial balance can be entered directly into VT Final Accounts, or imported from the VT Transaction+ bookkeeping software package at the touch of a button. VT Final Accounts can also be used to generate an iXBRL account or tax computation file from any Excel workbook (the VT workbooks are pre-tagged).

• iXBRL • Extended trial balance • Automatic hiding of lines and notes with nil balances • Automatic note numbering • Automatic cash flow statement • Abbreviated accounts • Choice of audit or accountants report • Automatic export to tax software packages • Unlimited number of clients/companies

VT Transaction+ is an easy to use bookkeeping software package which runs directly in Windows. It can be used to process incomplete records or to record day to day transactions.

• Rapid data entry screen for posting a mixture of payments and receipts directly from bank statements • Transactions can be easily edited or deleted • Fully integrated cash book, sales, purchase and nominal ledgers • Profit and loss account and balance sheet in self assessment tax return format can be printed out or exported to tax software packages. Includes column for disallowable expenses • Unlimited number of clients/companies

VT Software is dedicated to producing easy to use and inexpensive bookkeeping and accounts production software.

Source: http://www.vtsoftware.co.uk

VT launches iXBRL final accounts program

By John Stokdyk

VT Software, developer of the popular Excel-based accounts production tool VT Final Accounts, released the iXBRL-equipped version on 31 January.

Like Sage and several other accounts production software developers, VT faced a big challenge to adapt its product for the new electronic filing format. The program is now ready, giving users two months to implement it and test their processes before online filing of Corporation Tax returns becomes mandatory.

VT managing director Philip Hodgson has been keeping members of AccountingWEB.co.uk updated on the program's progress and confirmed the planned 31 January launch date last month in the VT Software discussion group after rumours a rival developer had reportedly been circulating negative rumours about the product.

Costing £199 per user in the first year (and £150/year after that), VT Final Accounts includes a Generate iXBRL File command that can be used with any Excel

workbook, not just the pre-tagged VT templates. UK GAAP, UK IFRS and UK Corporation Tax taxonomies are supported and the software will also be able to "tag up" customisations to the standard templates, or other accounts spreadsheets.

This extra facility took a little time to get exactly right, Hodgson said: "We needed to build in the self tagging features so that users could customise the VT workbooks and it was only a little more work to make the self tagging features apply to any workbook."

"If you have already done your own thing in Excel, especially if you have a single template from which you derive all your accounts, then self tagging may well be the most efficient way forward."

The VT Final Accounts package will also include two tools that may help those determined to pursue the DIY tagging route:

• VT Fact Viewer – a tool that displays the tags in any iXBRL file.

• VT Taxonomy Viewer, which lists the tags available in any taxonomy.

Source: http://www.accountingweb.co.uk/topic/tax/vt-launches-ixbrl-final-accounts-program/476766

References and further reading

Barrow, C. and J. Tracy (2011) *Understanding Business Accounting for Dummies* (3rd edn.). Chichester: Wiley.

Black, G. (2009) *Introduction to Accounting and Finance* (2nd edn.). Upper Saddle River, NJ: FT Prentice Hall.

Monger, R. (2010) *Financial Accounting*. Chichester: Wiley.

Wood, F. and A. Sangster (2012) *Business Accounting* (vol. 1) (12th edn.). Upper Saddle River, FT Prentice Hall.

When you have read this chapter, log on to the Online Learning Centre website at *www.mcgraw-hill.co.uk/textbooks/leiwy* to explore chapter-by-chapter test questions, further reading and more online study tools.

Part 2

Financial Management

Financing a Business

Chapter contents

✓ Learning objectives

After studying this chapter you will be able to:

- ✓ Describe the main sources of finance used by companies

- ✓ Appreciate the differences between the various sources, and evaluate the appropriateness of each in different circumstances

- ✓ Understand the advantages and disadvantages of high gearing

- ✓ Evaluate different dividend policies

- ✓ Understand how published accounts indicate companies' financing needs and policies

- ✓ Take an overall view of the financing of businesses, combining a number of different approaches

11.1 Introduction

Businesses own a variety of different assets, and statements of financial position show how these have been financed. There are non-current assets (such as land and buildings, plant and machinery, furniture and fittings), and current assets (such as inventories, receivables and cash). These have been financed from three main sources:

1 *The money or capital that was put into the business by its owners* – In a company this is the share capital which is part of 'equity' or shareholders' funds.

2 *Borrowing* – A company may borrow money on a long-term basis (e.g. by issuing debentures), and on a short-term basis (e.g. as a bank overdraft).

3 *Retained profits* – A successful company makes profits, some of which are paid out to shareholders as dividends; what is left is retained in the business, financing an increase in net assets.

When starting a business the owners usually put in a large amount of their own money ('equity') and/or borrow substantial sums. If the business is to expand, they will need to make profits, retaining some within the business. There are, however, other ways of financing the setting-up of a business, and its subsequent growth. Although businesses tend to own the premises that they occupy and the vehicles and equipment that they use, they may choose to lease them instead. Although many businesses finance inventories of goods, many find that, by buying on credit, they do not need to provide the finance themselves. Similarly, many businesses finance 'receivables' themselves, whereas others manage to get their customers to pay cash (so that there are few, if any, debtors) or even to require them to pay in advance. It can be very expensive to finance a manufacturing facility (factory premises, plant and machinery; inventories of raw materials, components, work in progress and finished goods); an alternative is to subcontract (or 'outsource') the manufacturing, perhaps to a country where these things cost less, leaving the subcontractor to provide the finance.

The three main sources of finance to a business (share capital, borrowing and retained profits, as shown in Illustration 11.1) are examined in the first three parts of this chapter. But it is always worth considering other ways of financing. Careful control of working capital can substantially reduce financing requirements, and ways of doing this are examined in the fourth part of the chapter. Finally, 'other sources of finance' are considered, including other ways of doing business that reduce the need for external finance. In most situations a combination of different ways of financing the business is used.

In this instance the three long-term sources of finance are each £1,000, making a total of £3,000. There is also short-term funding (current liabilities, or payables) of £800. The £800 has financed most of the current assets; perhaps their inventory of goods has been financed by the company's trade payables. The £3,000 has financed all the long-term assets, leaving £200 for working capital.

11.2 Share Capital

Share capital is perhaps the most important source of finance for companies, and it is mostly 'ordinary' share capital. There are other types of shares, including a variety of preference shares.

Ordinary shares

When a company is established it issues a number of ordinary shares. With a small, new company, they may be issued only to a few family members. The shareholders are the owners of the company. They also bear most of the risk. If the company gets into financial difficulties, all the creditors have to be repaid before anything is returned to the shareholders. Shareholders can lose everything that they put into a company, but their liability is limited to that amount. There can be no call on the shareholders' personal assets to pay any amounts due to creditors; that is the nature of limited liability.

ILLUSTRATION 11.1

The three main sources of finance are shown in the following simplified company statement of financial position:

	£
Non-current assets	
Property, plant and equipment	2,600
Current assets	
Inventories, receivables and cash	1,200
Total assets	3,800
Liabilities and equity	
Current liabilities	
Payables	800
Non-current liabilities	
Debentures	1,000
Total liabilities	1,800
Equity	
Share capital	1,000
Retained earnings	1,000
	2,000
Total liabilities and equity	3,800

A company may start off as a small, private limited company, with a restricted number of shares. If it grows and wants more shareholders it becomes a public limited company. Very large plcs may become listed on a stock market (such as the London Stock Exchange) to raise additional finance from many more shareholders, with an Initial Public Offering (IPO) of shares.

The initial nominal (or par) value of the shares may be £1 each (or 50 pence, or 10 pence, or any amount). In a successful expanding company the market value of shares is likely to increase. New shareholders will not be invited to buy shares at an old, low price. New shares are normally issued at a premium, as shown in Example 11.1, where additional £1 shares are issued for £2.50; the premium is £1.50 per share.

There is no requirement for a company to pay dividends on ordinary shares. In a very small company, where there are only two or three shareholders, they may easily agree what dividends, if any, are to be paid. In large, listed companies the directors normally propose a dividend for approval by shareholders at the annual general meeting. There is usually an interim dividend paid part-way through the year, and a final dividend after the year end. Companies sometimes decide not to pay a dividend, perhaps because they have been making losses, or have some other financial problem. In 2011 British Airways (now part of ICAG) did not pay a dividend, and this has been the pattern in recent years. Similarly, Barratt Developments and many other companies do not pay dividends.

The fact that there is no requirement to pay a dividend may make ordinary shares seem to be an attractive, cost-free source of finance. But many shareholders, especially institutional shareholders (such as pension funds), expect and rely on a steady (and increasing) stream of income from dividends. The shareholders are the owners of the company, and directors who regularly disappoint shareholders are likely to find themselves out of a job. Many companies pay regular and increasing dividends.

Growing companies might not seek a full listing on the stock exchange to begin with. They may first invite a financial institution or venture capitalist to buy some shares. Companies such as venture capitalist 3i invest in growing companies that are not yet large enough for a stock market listing. The formalities, administrative burden and costs of a full stock market listing may be too much for

Example 11.1

Share premium

Big Company agrees to pay £2,500,000 to take over Little Company. Big Company's shares are highly regarded by investors and their market value is £2.50. The £2,500,000 is paid not in cash, but by the issue of one million £1 shares.

The effect of this transaction is that Big Company's statement of financial position will show £1,000,000 of additional share capital, and £1,500,000 of share premium. The total, £2,500,000, was issued in exchange for assets (the Little Company).

Shares may be issued in exchange for cash or any assets.

companies of modest size and they are likely to seek a listing on the Alternative Investment Market (AIM). AIM is regulated by the London Stock Exchange (LSE) but has less demanding rules, and a listing is less costly than being on the LSE's Official List.

Companies often increase their share capital a little each year, especially when there is some sort of incentive scheme for directors and other staff that provides them with shares. But any significant increase in funding through the issue of shares is a major event for a company, and does not happen very often. Similarly, a company may, from time to time, buy back some of its own shares and so reduce share capital. Companies do not keep a supply of shares for investors to buy and sell: investors buy and sell shares from each other, usually via a stock exchange. Investors cannot go to Marks & Spencer and buy a few shares along with their new underwear and microwave dinner! They have to go via some sort of stockbroker, and there are lots of easy and flexible ways of buying and selling shares via a range of banks and other financial institutions, and on the internet.

Rights issue

When a company wants to raise substantial additional funds by issuing shares it often makes a *rights issue* to existing shareholders. This usually means that it offers new shares at a price lower than the current market price (see Example 11.2).

A *rights issue* is the normal way in which established companies raise additional funds and it is intended to be attractive to existing shareholders. If the current market price of a company's shares is £2, the right to buy more shares at £1.50 each sounds attractive. After the rights issue the total value of the company will, in theory, be worth the amount it was worth before the rights issue, plus the amount of money raised from the rights issue. In practice, if investors believe that the additional funds will be invested sufficiently profitably, the total value of the company will increase by more than the amount of cash raised.

If shareholders take up all the rights to which they are entitled, they will continue to own the same proportion of the company. The right to buy shares cheaply may look attractive, but the record of rights issues is mixed. Sometimes it seems that companies make rights issues because they are in financial difficulties. Sometimes it is a sign of success and additional funds are needed for expansion.

Bonus issue

A bonus issue (or a scrip issue) is quite different: it raises no additional funds, and so should not really be included in a chapter on sources of finance!

Many shareholders like receiving a bonus issue, although they really receive nothing. Most people would probably rather have two pieces of cake than one. But if the second piece of cake is created just by cutting the original piece of cake in half, there is no gain. In effect that is what a bonus issue does. A one-for-one bonus issue means that everyone has twice as many shares, but nothing has changed;

Example 11.2

The Right Company has one million ordinary shares with a nominal value of 50 pence each, and a market value of £2 each. The company decides to make a rights issue, offering existing shareholders one share for every five that they already hold, at a price of £1.50 per share.

Shareholders might choose to exercise their rights (by buying the additional shares), or to sell them.

After the rights issue the theoretical value of the company will be:

Existing one million shares at £2 each	£2,000,000
Cash raised from rights issue 200,000 at £1.50	300,000
	£2,300,000
Number of shares after issue	1,200,000

Theoretical share price after rights issue:

$$\frac{£2,300,000}{1,200,000} = £1.92$$

each still owns the same proportion of the same total. In Example 11.3 there was a 'two-for-one' bonus issue. For example, anyone who held 200 shares would be given an additional 400 shares, giving them a total of 600 shares. The total number of shares the company had therefore increased from 2m to 6m; share capital was increased by £4m; retained earnings were reduced by £4m. But the assets (and liabilities) of the company are unchanged.

In practice a bonus issue is more likely to be one new share for every three, or four, or five shares already held. Shareholders may think that they will still receive the same amount of dividend per share, and so they will be better off. Bonus issues are often associated with good performance, and optimism, which could lead to an increase in demand for the shares, and so an increase in share price and in the total value of the company.

One of the justifications for bonus issues is that it is often said that share prices higher than about £8 or £10 become less 'marketable': shareholders would rather buy five shares at £2 each than one share for £10. But there are plenty of successful companies where the share price is £10 or £20 or more.

Preference shares

Preference shareholders take less risk, and can expect less reward than ordinary shareholders. Preference shares have a fixed rate of dividend, perhaps 7 per cent. This means that for each £1 preference share, investors receive a 7 pence dividend each year. Sometimes a company might decide not to pay the preference dividend (perhaps when profits are low). But if no preference dividend is paid, then no ordinary dividend can be paid either. The preference shareholders have preference over ordinary shareholders with payment of dividends.

Preference shares are usually *cumulative*, which means that if the preference dividend is not paid in some years, all arrears of preference dividends must be paid before any ordinary dividends can be paid. But preference shares are not very popular for a number of reasons. Ordinary shareholders always have the prospect that the company might do really well, and there could be a substantial increase in profits, dividends and share price: they might make loads of money! Preference shareholders are more secure, but their level of dividend is fixed, whether the company does well or badly.

Example 11.3

Scriptease plc	Before bonus issue	After bonus issue
	£000	£000
Non-current assets	5,300	5,300
Current assets		
Inventories and receivables	3,000	3,000
Cash	500	500
Total assets	8,800	8,800
Trade payables	300	300
Equity		
Share capital (£1 shares)	2,000	6,000
Retained earnings	6,500	2,500
	8,800	8,800

Preference shares can be made more attractive if they are *participating* and/or if they are *convertible*. Participating preference shares can participate in higher levels of dividend when the company does well, and ordinary dividends rise above some predetermined level. Convertible preference shares can be more attractive: they can be converted to ordinary shares, at a predetermined rate (see Example 11.4). Since preference shares are generally redeemable at some future date, they are viewed more like liabilities than like equity and, as a result, IAS 32 requires that preference shares are classified as liabilities and since there is an obligation to pay the preference share dividend, such dividends are classified much like interest payments.

The prospect of a substantial capital gain if the company is successful can make convertible preference shares seem very attractive to investors; they get a decent dividend in the short term, with reasonable security. But the dividend is likely to be very expensive to the company, mainly because dividends (unlike interest) are not allowable as an expense to be charged against taxation. If we assume a corporation tax rate of 30 per cent, then a company needs to earn £10 profit to pay a

Example 11.4

The Fastgro company issues £1 ordinary shares at a premium of 50 pence per share. On the same date it issues 6 per cent convertible £1 preference shares giving the shareholders the right to convert three preference shares into one ordinary share at any date they choose.

In the early years preference shareholders are unlikely to give up three preference shares, worth about £3, for one ordinary share, worth £1.50. But if the company is successful, the market price of the ordinary shares might increase steadily to, say, £10 per share. An investor with 900,000 preference shares, worth about £900,000, could then convert them to 300,000 ordinary shares worth £3m; this would give a profit of over £2m!

£7 dividend. It is cheaper for the company to borrow money: a company earning £10 profit could pay £7 in interest and still have £3 (pre-tax) profit left for shareholders.

Interpretation of statements of financial position

When interpreting statements of financial position, for most purposes the total figure for 'equity' is used. Equity (or ordinary shareholders' funds) includes all ordinary shareholders' funds (share capital, share premium and all reserves/retained profits) except preference share capital. This figure is used in calculating gearing, and in calculating the net assets per share. It is also used in calculating the profitability of ordinary shareholders' funds: net profit after tax (and after deducting any preference share dividends) is expressed as a percentage of equity. It is usually a mistake (often made by students) to use the share capital figure instead of including all shareholders' funds.

The nominal value of shares is of little or no importance except perhaps in calculating the number of shares that make up share capital. Calculations of earnings per share (EPS), dividend per share and net assets per share are based on the number of ordinary shares.

11.3 Borrowing

Some very prudent individuals and businesses may think that it is dangerous to borrow: the business may not be able to meet the interest and repayments, and there is always the risk of insolvency if the business gets into difficulties. Those who want to minimize risk probably want to minimize borrowing. But if they are so risk averse, they should probably not go into business, and will probably never make much money.

It is safest and easiest to put your money in a bank, and earn a steady, low rate of interest, with little or no risk. But people invest in businesses because they think that it is worth the risk in order to earn more money. If banks are paying, say, 5 per cent interest, investors hope to earn more than that by investing in companies. Perhaps they expect a return on capital employed (ROCE) of 10 per cent or more. A business could argue that, if the cost of borrowing is less than the ROCE that they can earn, then the more they borrow, the more profit they will make. If you can borrow money at 7 per cent per annum, and invest it to earn 10 per cent per annum, then the more money you borrow, the more profit you will make, as shown in Example 11.5.

Example 11.5

Two companies in the same industry each have a return on capital employed of 10 per cent, and they are each able to borrow money at an interest rate of 7 per cent.

Prudent plc borrows an extra £1m	
Cost of additional borrowings: £1m at 7%	£70,000 per annum
Additional earnings: £1m at 10%	£100,000 per annum
Net additional earnings	£30,000 per annum
Profitable plc borrows an extra £100m	
Cost of additional borrowings £100m at 7%	£7,000,000 per annum
Additional earnings: £100b at 10%	£10,000,000 per annum
Net additional earnings	£3,000,000 per annum

Example 11.6

Low-geared company	Capital structure		Equity	100m
			10% debentures	£10m
				£110m

	Year 1	Year 2		
	£m	£m		
EBIT	10	12	+20%	
Interest	1	1		
Pre-tax profit	9	11		
Tax (say) 30%	2.7	3.3		
Profit after-tax	6.3	7.7	+22.2%	

High-geared company	Capital structure		Equity	£50m
			10% debentures	£60m
				£110m
EBIT	10	12	+20%	
Interest	6	6		
Pre-tax profit	4	6		
Tax (say) 30%	1.2	1.8		
Profit after-tax	2.8	4.2	+50%	

Borrowing can increase the return to shareholders, as is demonstrated in Example 11.6. Borrowing can also be relatively cheap, and is a cheaper source of finance than issuing ordinary shares because the interest is allowable as an expense for tax purposes; and because shareholders expect a higher return as they are taking more risk than lenders. But what they expect and what they get can be very different.

In both cases EBIT (earnings before interest and taxation) increased by 20 per cent between years 1 and 2, but the effect of gearing was a larger increase in the profit after-tax earned for the ordinary shareholders. In the low-geared company the return earned for ordinary shareholders increased by 22.2 per cent. In the high-geared company it increased by 50 per cent.

There are other good reasons for borrowing rather than issuing more shares. In a family-controlled company the existing shareholders and directors might not want to risk issuing more shares if it would result in new and different people becoming shareholders and controlling the company. In spite of what some textbooks say, directors do not always make rational economic decisions: many like to keep their positions of power and influence, even if (by not issuing more shares) they restrict the growth and profitability of the company. The costs involved in issuing shares also tend to be higher than the costs in obtaining loans.

Another advantage of borrowing is that it comes in many forms, and can be very flexible. It may be short or long term. The most flexible way of borrowing is through an overdraft. Interest rates are negotiable, and are usually a number of percentage points above base rate. Individuals with unauthorized overdrafts may find that they are charged with ridiculously high interest rates, perhaps even 10 or 15 points above base rate. A company ought to be able to negotiate an overdraft interest rate just a little above base rate. Some businesses are seasonal and need to borrow at particular times of the year.

A business such as a seaside hotel is likely to be flush with cash in October, after the holiday season; but by March they need short-term borrowings until the money starts coming in for the next holiday season. Many businesses have plenty of money in the middle of the month, but need to borrow at the end of the month, when wages and salaries are paid. Overdrafts are most appropriate for such short-term financing because interest is payable only for the actual days that the overdraft facility is used. There is no point in having a fixed loan throughout the year, and paying interest throughout the year, if the money is needed only for a few days each month, or for a few months each year.

Although overdrafts are supposed to be a short-term source of finance, many individuals and companies seem to have significant (and increasing!) overdrafts that go on for years. Banks are interested in converting overdrafts into fixed loans for a few years, if they can earn more interest by so doing. Businesses need to work out carefully how much it is appropriate to borrow with fixed-term loans and fixed interest rates, and how much it is appropriate to use overdraft facilities for.

Debentures are a form of long-term borrowing (typically 5–10 years), usually with a fixed rate of interest, which can be listed on a stock market. Investors can therefore sell them when they wish, and the company can choose to buy them back on the market, if they have nothing better to do with their money. Debentures are usually 'secured' on some assets of the company; perhaps on land and buildings; perhaps a floating charge on most of the assets of the company, including inventory and receivables. The effect is a bit like taking out a mortgage: if the company does not meet its payments as they fall due, the debenture holders can eventually get their money back by selling off the company's assets.

Debentures are sometimes 'convertible' into ordinary shares, which can make them very attractive to investors if it is expected that the company's shares will do very well in the future. Investors in a new or expanding business may be attracted by the security of a debenture with a reasonable interest rate to begin with, together with the possibility of conversion to ordinary shares (and increases in the share price, and increasing dividends) once the venture has proved to be successful.

The main attraction of borrowing is the idea that the more you borrow, the more profit you can make. It may be an attractive idea, but there are a number of problems with ever-increasing borrowings:

1 Borrowing may be no problem as long as the company can be sure of always having earnings above the required level of interest payments. But businesses tend to have good years and bad years; the economy tends to run in cycles; some industries are particularly cyclical; some industries run into bad patches, with bad luck and/or bad management. If in some years the company does not earn enough to make the necessary interest payments, lenders may repossess vital assets and force the business to curtail its activities or close down.

2 The more you get into debt, the more difficult it is to borrow more money. There is probably always someone, or some bank, that will lend to you, but as you get more into debt, the higher the interest rates become to compensate the lender for additional risk.

3 Lenders usually look for some sort of security. It is easy to borrow money secured on land and buildings. Lenders may be happy to take some sort of 'floating charge' on whatever other assets the company has. But when all assets have already been used as security, it is increasingly difficult to borrow more money.

4 Those who have already lent money to the company often lay down conditions to restrict the ability of the company to borrow more. These 'restrictive covenants' may specify that a company's total borrowing must not exceed some (small, e.g. 1 or 1.5) multiple of the amount of equity.

5 Companies that are heavily in debt may get a reputation as being 'high risk', and other businesses may be reluctant to do business with them. Sometimes investors steer clear because the risk is too great.

A good, old-fashioned view might be that a company should keep increasing its borrowing, as long as it can get away with it. Theory suggests that eventually lenders will see that the company has borrowed too much (gearing is too high), and they will start to charge higher interest rates. As borrowing increases, interest rates increase until eventually the cost of borrowing is higher than the return that the company can generate from the borrowings. High levels of borrowing are also associated with high risk, and this can affect the share price, especially if it starts to look as if the company is so heavily in debt that it might be forced into liquidation. There is, thus, in this traditional view, an optimal level of borrowing (although it is difficult to establish what this level is).

A different perspective was offered by following Modigliani and Miller (1958) who suggested that the level of gearing has no effect on share price. Even if the amount of borrowing changes, it is still the same business, with the same earnings stream and the same business risk. Modigliani and Miller's presentation is sophisticated, but it depends on a number of unrealistic assumptions; and it is often misinterpreted. Their emphasis is on the value of the company, which depends on the investments that they have, and the cash flows that they will generate; how the company is financed is a secondary issue. More recent work, recognizing the impact of taxation (interest is an allowable expense for taxation, and so the cost of borrowing is likely to be lower than the cost of equity), together with lower interest rates, and the actual behaviour of companies, suggest that there may be some optimal level of gearing; but this is hard to find, and views about acceptable levels of gearing change from time to time.

In practice, many companies seem to borrow as much as they can get away with. Some companies constantly need additional funds because of expansion and development. But some companies (like some individuals!) do not seem to be able to live within their means, and borrow until they go bust.

In Illustration 11.1 (p. 266) the company had total long-term funds of £3,000, of which £1,000 was borrowed. In other words, one-third of its long-term funding was borrowed, or its gearing ratio was $33\frac{1}{3}$ per cent. There is, of course, no 'correct' or 'best' level of borrowing; nor is there a single correct way of measuring gearing.[1] Companies that are able to borrow extensively are likely to have a steady, secure income stream so that they can be confident about being able to pay the necessary interest every year. They are also likely to have lots of good quality assets (particularly land and buildings) to offer as security to lenders. Companies in very cyclical industries should avoid high gearing, but many do not, and they get into financial difficulties. The airline industry is noticeably susceptible to epidemics of war, terrorism and disease, sudden and rapid rises in the price of oil and the recent economic downturn; many airlines are highly geared; and many found themselves in serious financial difficulties in recent years.

When the telecommunications industry was expanding and share prices were booming at the end of the twentieth century, many companies got away with very high levels of borrowing for a while. Then the business climate turned against them, and many share prices collapsed. BT had a debt mountain of £30bn which did not look too bad in relation to the market value of their equity when share prices were high. But in comparison with the statement of financial position value of equity it looked terrible. And when telecommunications share prices took a nosedive, the amount of debt looked unsustainable in relation to the market value of equity. BT has taken decisive action, and has substantially reduced the debt.

As interest rates have remained low in recent years, higher levels of gearing have become acceptable. Sometimes one company buys another company and finances the purchase almost entirely by borrowing; this is called a 'leveraged buy-out'.[2]

11.4 Retained Profits

A successful company makes profits that materialize in the form of additional cash or other net assets. The company may choose to pay out all its profits as dividends, in which case profits will not be a source of funds. Most companies choose to pay out a proportion (perhaps around 40 per cent) of their

---

[1] If borrowing is represented as D, and equity is represented as E, gearing can be measured by taking D as a percentage of D + E; or as a percentage of E. D is sometimes taken to include overdrafts; sometimes it refers only to long-term borrowing.

[2] The purchase of another business can, instead, be financed by issuing additional ordinary shares.

profits as dividends; the rest are retained and used to finance the business. Obviously, the more profit a company makes, the greater is the potential for using retained profits as a source of finance. Raising finance through retained profits depends on how profitable the business is. It also depends on the company's dividend policy.

Dividend policy

In deciding how much dividend to pay, or what proportion of profits are to be paid out as dividends, companies need to consider some important matters. Dividend policy usually requires striking a balance between (a) paying out *all* profits as dividends, and (b) paying *no* dividends at all.

Pay out all profits as dividends

There is a case for paying out all profits as dividends: profits belong to the shareholders, not the directors. The directors might see retained profits as being too easy a source of finance, and not bother to ensure that they are reinvested in the company properly and profitably. As profits are earned, they may simply disappear into higher levels of inventories and receivables, or even cars and 'conference centres' for the comfort of directors.

Many companies find themselves with surplus funds that they invest in disastrous diversification (ad)ventures or waste on more or less (un)successful takeover bids and mergers. Northern Rock lost millions of pounds attempting to move from its secure base in retail banking into areas of wholesale banking where it had no experience. Marks & Spencer lost millions of pounds in spreading its operations overseas, and then withdrawing. Marconi wasted millions of pounds investing in overpriced telecommunications companies just before they collapsed. Some companies have a history of merging with others, and then demerging, or selling off the bits they no longer want (e.g. Kingfisher, Hays, Debenhams). The evidence so far suggests that a takeover is more likely to destroy shareholder value than to create it.

There are, of course, plenty of exceptions: well-managed companies that succeed in reinvesting retained profits year after year and which have a good record in increasing profits and dividends; some even succeed in increasing their return on capital employed, and, with a bit of luck, the company's share price. There are also many companies where the directors know that they are unable to do this. GEC sat on mountains of cash rather than risk wasting it on ill-advised investments. Other companies, knowing that there are limited opportunities for successful investment of surplus funds, simply return them to shareholders as special dividends; or they use the money to buy their own shares on the market and cancel them.[3]

Many companies, or their directors, cannot be trusted to invest retained profits successfully. But there are good reasons for not expecting companies to pay out all their profits as dividends:

1 Rising prices, or inflation, usually mean that companies need to retain some of their profits, not for expansion, but merely to maintain the existing level of operations. More funds are required to finance receivables (as selling prices increase); to finance inventories (as replacement costs increase) and to replace non-current assets as the cost of these increases. Inflation in the UK in recent years has been very low, and the cost of replacing many items (e.g. computers and electronic equipment) has actually fallen. But few businesses can afford to finance even their existing level of operations without retaining some profits.

2 Investors, particularly financial institutions, generally want to see dividends increasing steadily each year, preferably by rather more than the rate of inflation. Illustration 11.2 shows how company profits can fluctuate, but attempts are made to keep dividends steady.

3 Many companies boast that they have succeeded in increasing dividends every year since anyone can remember. Compared with dividend expectations, profits are less predictable, less controllable,

---

[3] This is a way of increasing EPS; even if total earnings do not increase, the number of shares decreases and so the EPS increases.

ILLUSTRATION 11.2

The EPS and the dividend per share of the Cycle Company for the last few years are shown below (in pence).

Year	1	2	3	4	5	6	7
EPS	100	134	60	116	180	10	191
Div	50	53	56	59	63	64	70
Cover	2	2.5	1.1	2.0	2.9	0.2	2.7

more cyclical, and more affected by one-off 'exceptional' items. Companies usually prefer to increase dividends only modestly in the very good years so that there is more scope for maintaining or increasing dividends in the lean years.

Pay out no dividends

There is a case for paying no dividends at all, even in successful companies. When a company is making serious losses, or when it has massive borrowings, scrapping the dividend for a year or two makes good sense. Companies at an early stage of their development need all the money that they can get hold of and so are not inclined to pay dividends. In the great dotcom and TMT[4] bubble of the late 1990s many companies did not pay dividends. A quick look at the *Financial Times* today will show which companies are not paying dividends; usually there are plenty of mining companies and pharmaceuticals and biotechnology companies that have not yet found their pot of gold or wonder drug, and are burning up cash in their efforts; there is unlikely to be a dividend until a worthwhile discovery has been developed.

If a company can invest the shareholders' money and earn a better rate of return than the shareholders can themselves, then there is a case for the company to keep the money, and not pay dividends. If the money stays within the company, the value of its shares should increase. If shareholders need some income, they can sell a few shares; and (they hope!) the value of their shares will increase because of all the retained profits being reinvested. If they sell a few shares they may have to pay capital gains tax; but for many shareholders the taxation of capital gains is lower than the taxation on income from dividends. Paying no dividends at all may suit some companies and some shareholders – sometimes.

Dividend policy in practice

When making a dividend decision, companies need to take into consideration a variety of often conflicting factors. First, from a legal perspective, a company can only distribute its retained profits. Second, it needs to have the cash in the bank in order to pay a dividend or an overdraft which will enable it to pay a dividend. Then, as will be seen in Chapter 14, if a company needs money to invest in attractive investment opportunities, that would tend to reduce its dividend payment since it needs that money for profitable investment. By the same token, if it has available cash but no significant investment opportunities, that would tend to argue in favour of paying a larger dividend. Furthermore, some companies tend to pay out a small dividend and that will attract shareholders who do not want a dividend but are attracted to companies which focus on growth, while other companies favour a high dividend policy which would tend to attract shareholders who are investing for high annual dividend income, perhaps the elderly.

Companies tend to follow a consistent dividend payout policy and so shareholders will be attracted to invest in companies with the dividend policy they prefer. Most companies do not opt for the extremes of no dividends, or 100 per cent distribution. Usually a proportion of profits is distributed. Listed companies typically pay out rather less than half of their profits as dividends. Recent figures for the FTSE 100 index and a number of companies are shown in Illustration 11.3.

---

[4] Technology, media and telecommunications.

ILLUSTRATION 11.3

	FTSE100	BAe Sys	Barclays Bank	United Utilities	ITV	BP	BT
Dividend cover	2.77	2.2	4.0	1.1	20.8	4.5	2.9
Proportion of profits distributed	34%	45%	25%	91%	5%	22%	34%

Source: Financial Times, 16 January 2012

Company profits tend to fluctuate from year to year, not least because of 'exceptional' items such as profits or losses arising from the sale of non-current assets, or closing down part of the business. As shown in Illustration 11.2, it makes more sense to try to maintain a record of steady and increasing dividends, rather than to pay out the same proportion of profits each year. Some companies pay an extra 'special' dividend in a particularly good year. But most try to keep an upward trend, even when profits fall. And many seem to increase their dividends more than the underlying profits justify; this results in the dividend cover declining over a number of years, and the dividend begins to look less safe.

In making dividend decisions, companies need to consider what 'signal' any change in dividends gives to investors. A sudden reduction in dividends suggests that directors are not confident about future years. Companies also need to consider what cash is available to pay dividends and their plans for expansion, investment and borrowing.

11.5 Other Sources of Finance

Companies are assumed to need funds to finance the purchase of fixed assets and inventories, and to pay expenses until the profits come rolling in, in the form of cash. In addition there is a need to finance working capital, but careful management of working capital can also be seen as a source of finance. If receivables or inventories are reduced, or if the time taken to pay trade payables is increased, funds are freed up to use for other purposes. The management of working capital is dealt with in Chapter 12.

There are various ways of avoiding, or minimizing, the need to raise finance:

1 Non-current assets can be leased instead of buying them. Obviously this applies to premises, but most machinery, equipment and vehicles can be leased if necessary. It is sometimes possible to arrange for an initial rent-free period to minimize initial funding requirements. But most lessors will not rent out equipment to any Tom, Dick or Harry: the lessee usually needs to produce evidence that they are creditworthy.

2 Sale and leaseback. A business can raise finance by selling assets that it owns and wants to continue using through a finance company (such as a bank or insurance company), and then leasing the asset back from that company. This is often done with premises, and many chains of retail shops no longer own the freehold of their premises: they made a sale and leaseback arrangement. This can make sense both for the finance company and for the retailer. The finance company gets a guaranteed return in rental income at the going rate (say 5–7 per cent per annum); the retailer continues to use the premises and raises additional funds at a reasonable cost. The transaction will look good if the premises are sold for more than their book value: the profit contributes to an increase in EPS. This may be further boosted if the funds raised are used to increase profits, or to reduce the number of shares.

A cautious proprietor may prefer to retain the freehold of business premises; it can be used to provide security for loans where additional finance is needed.

3 Businesses often find that they have more non-current assets than they need, especially when they find themselves in financial difficulties. Warehouses can be 'rationalized': the company may find that it can manage with two instead of six, and raise substantial sums by selling off uneconomic premises.

4 Outsourcing or subcontracting some activities (e.g. computing, accounting, catering, manufacture, cleaning, transport – indeed, almost anything) may free up surplus assets that can be sold to raise funds. It can also be used to minimize the finance required for expansion.

5 Careful management of working capital can effectively reduce the financing needs of a business; reductions in working capital can produce additional cash.

6 Factoring or invoice discounting the company's trade receivables. These involve borrowing funds from a 'factor', usually a department of a bank, equivalent to an agreed percentage of trade receivables. Usually, the factor will manage the collection of those debts from customers, while in invoice discounting, the company itself will manage credit control.

7 Increasing profits also generates additional funds. This can be done both by reducing costs (e.g. eliminating a layer of management, or transferring production to Morocco or Vietnam), or by increasing sales (the volume of sales, and/or selling prices).

8 Reducing dividends, or even not paying dividends for a year or two, is another way of making more funds available.

9 Careful cash budgeting can also make more funds available when needed by delaying major payments at times when there is a particular shortage of cash. Sometimes the easiest way to deal with a cash shortage is to delay capital expenditure programmes.

Businesses rely mostly on funds contributed by their owners (sole proprietors, partners or shareholders); on borrowing money; and on generating profits that are ploughed back into the business. But there are more creative ways of financing businesses.

📖 Summary

The published financial statements of companies show how they have been financed, and indicate the balance between safety and solvency, on the one hand, and risk and profitability, on the other. The safest way of financing a company is to issue more shares, but this can be an expensive business, and shareholders expect a high return. Borrowing is in many ways easier and cheaper, but excessive gearing can lead to excessive risk, which can adversely affect share prices, and increase the cost of borrowing. Retained profits are also an attractive source of funds, and companies need to have dividend policies that strike a balance between keeping shareholders happy, and retaining profits to finance expansion, where such reinvestment is justified. High gearing can enhance profitability, particularly during a period of low interest rates; but it also increases risk. Similar issues arise with the management of working capital. Minimizing levels of inventories and receivables can minimize the need for external finance, and enhance return on capital employed. But lowering levels of working capital make companies look less solvent. There are various more creative ways of financing a business, and there are no 'correct' solutions. Policies on gearing, dividends and working capital change as circumstances change, and a combination of several different approaches to financing a company is usually appropriate.

→ Review of key points

- The three main sources of funds for companies are share capital, borrowing and retained profits.
- There is no requirement to pay dividends to ordinary shareholders; they bear most of the risk of the business, and, if the business does well, will get substantial rewards.
- Borrowing can 'gear up' the return to the owners of the business, but excessive gearing is risky.
- Profits may be paid out to shareholders as dividends, or reinvested in the business as they are earned.
- Dividend policy strikes a balance between retaining funds within the business that are needed, and maintaining a payment record to satisfy shareholders.
- Much of business activity can be financed without using share capital, borrowing or retained profits.
- Published financials statements indicate the way in which a business has been financed, its dividend, gearing policies, and the effectiveness of its working capital management.

! Self-testing questions

1   What are the three main sources of finance for businesses?
2   What are the main differences between preference shares and ordinary shares?
3   Explain the advantages and disadvantages of a company increasing its gearing.
4   You are given the following information about two companies:

Summarized statements of financial position as at 31 December

| | TimeBall Company | | DownsPier Company | |
| | Year 6 | Year 7 | Year 6 | Year 7 |
	£000	£000	£000	£000
Total assets	350	402.2	400	354.1
Liabilities and equity				
Liabilities				
Current liabilities	50	60	100	70
9% debentures	100	140	100	50
	150	200	200	120
Equity				
Share capital	100	100	100	115
Share premium	–	–	–	15
Retained profits	100	102.2	100	104.1
Total equity	200	202.2	200	234.1
Total liabilities and equity	350	402.2	400	354.1

Summarized income statements for year ended 31 December

Sales	100	110	100	95
Gross profit	40	44	40	41
Operating profit	20	21.6	20	17.5
Interest	9	12.6	9	4.5
Pre-tax profit	11	9	11	13
Taxation	3.3	2.7	3.3	3.9
Profit after-tax	7.7	6.3	7.7	9.1
Dividends	4	4.1	4	5
Retained profit for the year	3.7	2.2	3.7	4.1

a You are required to calculate for each company for each year:
   i   capital gearing ratio;
   ii interest cover;
   iii dividend cover;
   iv proportion of profits paid out as dividends.
b Explain what each shows.
c Comment on the financial performance and position of the two companies making use of appropriate ratios.
5 Explain what factors affect a company's dividend distribution in a year.

Assessment questions

1 Why might a company issue convertible preference shares rather than debentures?
2 The capital structure of two companies is as follows:

	Loborough plc	Hiborough plc
	£m	£m
Equity	180	50
11% debentures	20	150
	200	200

The EBIT of both companies was as follows:

Year 1	£19m
Year 2	£22.8m
Year 3	£15.2m

The rate of corporation tax on profits is 25 per cent.

a Calculate the net profit after-tax earned for ordinary shareholders for each year and for each company.

b Comment on the effect that gearing has had on the results.

3 The directors of the Palazine Company are seeking funding of £50m to finance an expansion programme. The summarized financial statements for the most recent year are set out below:

Income statement for the year ended 31 December year 6		£000
Sales		120,000
Cost of sales		90,000
Gross profit		30,000
Distribution costs	8,000	
Administration expenses	12,000	(20,000)
Operating profit		10,000
Debenture interest		(5,000)
Net profit before taxation		5,000
Taxation		(3,000)
Net profit after taxation		2,000
Dividends		(1,000)
Retained profit for year		1,000

Statement of financial position as at 31 December year 6		£000
Non-current assets		
Land and buildings (market value £55m)		45,000
Plant and machinery		18,000
Investments at cost (market value £30m)		45,000
		108,000
Current assets		
Inventories	8,000	
Receivables	5,000	
Cash	1,000	14,000
Total assets		122,000
Current liabilities		
Payables		24,000
Non-current liabilities		
10% debentures (secured)		50,000
Equity		
Share capital	30,000	
Retained earnings	18,000	48,000
		122,000

The following suggestions have been made for raising the additional finance. You are required to explain the effects of each of the suggestions and to comment on their practicability.

The company could:

   i issue more debentures;

   ii make a sale and leaseback arrangement on its premises;

  iii sell its investments (although some directors object to this as it would involve a loss of £15m);

  iv reduce inventories by one half;

   v halve the period that receivables are allowed to pay (all sales are on credit);

  vi extend the period for paying payables by 50 per cent;

 vii use the reserves;

viii issue more ordinary shares;

  ix obtain a bank overdraft.

4 The earnings per share and the dividend per share of Uppen Down plc for the last few years are shown below (in pence):

	Year 1	Year 2	Year 3	Year 4	Year 5	Year 6	Year 7
EPS	20	25	18	30	10	13	24
Div	10	10.4	10.8	11.2	11.7	12.2	12.7
Share price	300	400	200	270	250	270	300

  a You are required to calculate the dividend cover for each year; the proportion of profits that was distributed as dividends; and the dividend yield based on the share price at the year end given above.

  b Comment on the company's dividend policy.

  c Since the end of year 7 the dividend yield, as shown in the *Financial Times*, has increased to 10 per cent. What is this likely to indicate?

5 An extract of Sky High plc's statement of financial position as at 1 October 20x6 is given below:

	£000
Ordinary share capital @ £1 each	1,000
Revaluation reserve	2,500
Retained profits	3,200
	6,700

On 1 January 20x7, the company issued 1 right share for every 5 in issue for £4 each when the market price was £5.

  a Show how the rights issue should be accounted for in the statement of financial position.

  b Calculate the theoretical share price of Sky High plc after the rights issue. Explain why in reality the share price may differ from the theoretical price.

 ## Group activities and discussion questions

1 What is the minimum amount of funding with which it is possible to start a business? Could a business be started with zero funds? What sort of business could each member of the group start, with little or no funding? Prepare a (very brief) business plan. Would it be necessary to raise substantial funding to develop the business so that it becomes large scale? How would you define 'large scale' (big enough to provide you with a suitable lifestyle; big enough for a stock market listing)?

2 Prepare a list of companies that are not currently paying dividends. (Look for shares with a zero yield in the *Financial Times*'s listing.) Why are these companies not paying dividends? Each member of the group could research a number of companies. Can the companies be classified into groups each with similar reasons for not paying dividends (e.g. developing new products/services; recent losses)?

3 Why are some companies high-geared, and others low-geared? Each member of the group should examine the statements of financial position of a number of companies, probably in different sectors. It may be easiest to do this using the companies' websites. The group should agree the way in which gearing should be measured (e.g. is short-term borrowing to be included with long-term borrowing?). Are utility companies more highly geared than retailers? Are breweries more highly geared than oil companies? Can you identify what factors seem to be associated with high gearing and low gearing?

4 Prepare a list of companies which have arranged bonus (scrip) issues in the last three months. (You can look at the *Financial Times* website for this information.) Note down the share price before and after the bonus issue and the market capitalization (shown in Monday's *Financial Times*) before and after the scrip issue. How much has the total value of the company (market capitalization) changed as a result of the bonus issue?

 ## Financial accounting in context

Discuss and comment on the following extract taken from the press with reference to the evolution in the sources of capital available to companies.

Companies challenged to quit bank addiction

Britain's businesses are being urged to unhook themselves from bank debt and make more use of alternative sources of finance.

By Richard Tyler

"It's been difficult for a CFO to go through the last three years that we have just had and not feel some element of stress. And yes, I am using English understatement," deadpans Philip Keller, chief financial officer of Intermediate Capital Group.

With £2bn to £2.5bn of borrowings outstanding at any one time, historically supplied by numerous syndicates of banks he didn't really know well, some stress is understandable. Yet Keller is among those treasurers taking their businesses through the corporate equivalent of The Priory. [...]

Dependency on banks when the banks themselves are far from healthy is one cause for the loss of corporate confidence, the Treasury argues. [...]

The Treasury is already planning to shoehorn £1bn of public money into co-investment funds that will lend directly to British companies. Bids from fund managers are due in February and the Treasury has allocated at least £150m to get the Business Finance Partnership scheme going.

It is likely to operate in a similar way to the M&G UK Companies Financing Fund, which raised £500m from Prudential – its parent – and over £900m from other insurance and pension funds, to lend directly to UK companies sums of between £30m and £100m, at rates of between 4pc and 6pc over Libor and maturities of typically around seven years.

A spokesman said the fund was gaining momentum after a slow start, backing nine companies such as Northgate, Stobart and Barratt Developments, since May 2010 with £780m in loans. The hope is that funds such as M&G's will be used by firms as a viable alternative source of finance. The attraction for mid-sized companies is that they don't have to secure a credit rating or subject themselves to the due diligence demanded of a bond issue on the public markets. The catch is that bank debt remains cheap for the right borrowers.

Martin O'Donovan, policy director at the Association of Corporate Treasurers, did some calculations on the relative cost of a bond issue over bank debt. He found that a company with a BBB rating could secure a £250m five-year bank loan at a rough margin of 1.1pc over Libor, which even he says is "surprisingly low". Arrangement fees of 0.75pc of the value of the loan and external advisory fees of roughly £50,000 all add up. As do new facility utilisation and commitment fees – the price now charged by banks for just having the facility without drawing on it fully. [. . .]

[M]id-sized companies should get used to the idea of paying a bit more to become less reliant on the banks. The savings from the longer refinancing cycle and the benefits of secure funds on long-term business planning should not be underestimated [...].

One company tackling its addiction head-on is Intermediate Capital Group, a senior debt and mezzanine finance provider to private equity deals. It borrows between £2bn and £2.5bn at any one time and so has to think about these things quite carefully. "Historically, that was bank finance but the world has changed dramatically," says Keller.

It means that whereas three years ago banks supplied two-thirds of ICG's finance, Keller expects that to settle at around 50pc in the future, with the bank debt all concentrated in around six banks rather than dozens in multiple syndicates.

The financial crisis is forcing ICG to innovate. It is used to tapping the US private-placement market, but has now begun exploring the UK – borrowing £75m in December from M&G and issuing a £35m retail bond to wealthy private investors via brokers such as Brewin Dolphin and Charles Stanley.

The M&G paper – with maturities ranging from five to seven years – helped Keller to manage the profile of ICG's debt. He doesn't want all its loans coming up for renewal at the same time. [. . .]

The likes of M&S and Tesco Bank can get retail bonds away relatively easily, but few had heard of ICG outside of the Square Mile. [. . .]

"The banks accept they are not able to lend to their favourite clients in the way they used to so they are starting to help."

In fact, if a bank can help a client to raise funds from private sources but retain its main facilities, then this could suit it down to the ground.

"It's a fact of life that the banks will want to lend less but eep all the goodies, the ancillary services," says Keller.

Source: The Sunday Telegraph, 29 January 2012

References and further reading

Boakes, K. (2010) *Reading and Understanding the Financial Times.* Upper Saddle River, NJ: FT Prentice Hall.

Financial Times (daily newspaper) www.ft.com

Hillier, D. and S. Ross et al. (2010) *Corporate Finance (*1st European edn.). Maidenhead: McGraw-Hill Education.

Investors Chronicle (weekly magazine).

McKenzie, W. (2010) *Financial Times Guide to Using and Interpreting Company Accounts* (4th edn.). Upper Saddle River, NJ: FT Prentice Hall.

Modigliani, F. and M. Miller (1958) The cost of capital, corporation finance and the theory of investment, *American Economic Review*, June, pp. 261–97.

Rees, B. (2011) *Financial Analysis* (3rd edn.). Upper Saddle River, NJ: FT Prentice Hall.

Vernimemen, P. et al. (2009) *Corporate Finance: Theory and Practice*. Chichester: Wiley.

www.londonstockexchange.com

When you have read this chapter, log on to the Online Learning Centre website at *www.mcgraw-hill.co.uk/textbooks/leiwy* to explore chapter-by-chapter test questions, further reading and more online study tools.

Chapter 12

Management of Working Capital

Chapter contents

✓ Learning objectives

After studying this chapter you will be able to:

- ✓ Define working capital and explain its importance in relation to solvency, overtrading and profitability
- ✓ Explain how to manage receivables and calculate the financial implications of different policies for managing receivables
- ✓ Discuss the control of inventories and apply the economic order quantity (EOQ) model
- ✓ Explain how to plan, control and manage cash, and how to manage and avoid cash crises
- ✓ Understand the role of control and management of payables

12.1 Introduction

The planning and management of working capital is an important part of the financing of a business. High levels of inventories and receivables tie up large amounts of finance; reductions in inventories and receivables, and increases in payables, provide extra finance for the business.

12.2 Definition and Importance of Working Capital

A large part of a company's capital is usually tied up in assets such as buildings and machinery for a period of years. But companies also need some capital to finance short-term assets such as inventories and receivables, and there is a need for some cash for day-to-day operations. The amount of long-term capital available after financing non-current assets is known as 'working capital', which may be defined as:

$$\text{Long-term funds} - \text{non-current assets} = \text{working capital}$$

From the statement of financial position in Illustration 12.1 we can see that working capital in year 1 was:

$$\text{Year 1} \quad 85,000 + 110,000 - 140,000 = \pounds55,000$$
$$\text{Year 2} \quad 88,000 + 135,000 - 138,000 = \pounds85,000$$

The more usual definition of working capital is:

$$\text{Current assets} - \text{current liabilities} = \text{working capital}$$

From the statement of financial position above we can see that working capital is:

$$\text{Year 1} \quad 175,000 - 120,000 = \pounds55,000$$
$$\text{Year 2} \quad 145,000 - 60,000 = \pounds85,000$$

The two definitions appear to be different, but provided all items on the statement of financial position are classified under the same five headings, the two approaches will produce the same figure.

Although most businesses finance their inventories and receivables partly from their long-term funds, current assets are also partly financed by payables and other current liabilities. In year 2 Solverham (Illustration 12.1) had inventories of £70,000; £60,000 of this was financed by current liabilities. In some companies, particularly retailers, inventories are wholly financed by short-term creditors.

How much working capital should a business have?

There is usually a relationship between a company's turnover, and the amount of working capital it has. In Chapter 4, ratios 14, 15 and 16 express inventories, receivables and payables in relation to the amount of (cost of) sales. As turnover increases we can expect working capital to increase in proportion. If turnover goes up by 25 per cent, it does not mean that the amount of cash coming into the business immediately goes up by 25 per cent: there is likely to be an increase in inventories and receivables (partly financed by an increase in creditors).

But companies should not simply watch working capital drift upwards: there is a need for proper planning and control. There is, however, no ideal level for working capital. It is a question of balancing (a) *solvency* against (b) *profitability*, that is, risk against reward.

A company that is very safe in terms of solvency will have lots more current assets than current liabilities. There will always be more than enough current assets, either in the form of cash or receivables (and even inventories) that will soon become cash, to meet short-term liabilities as they fall due. This short-term financial strength can be expressed in the form of *current ratios* and *liquidity ratios*. In Illustration 12.2, the first of the four companies (Alice Ltd) has most working capital, the strongest current ratio (3 : 1), and the strongest liquidity ratio (2 : 1). The fourth company (Dora Ltd) has the least working capital: a negative amount! Dora also has a very low current ratio (0.17 : 1) and a very low liquidity ratio (0.1 : 1).

ILLUSTRATION 12.1

Statements of financial position of Solverham Company Ltd as at 31 December

	Year 1	Year 2
	£000	£000
Non-current assets (at cost)	200	220
Provision for depreciation	(60)	(82)
Net book value	140	138
Current assets		
Inventories	95	70
Receivables	80	50
Cash	–	25
	175	145
Total assets	315	283
Current liabilities		
Payables	40	60
Overdraft	80	–
	120	60
Non-current liabilities		
12% debentures	110	135
Equity		
Share capital	50	50
Retained earnings	35	38
	85	88
Total liabilities plus equity	315	283

A company that is more concerned with profitability than with appearing to be solvent will concentrate on keeping down the amount of working capital. In order to maximize return on capital employed companies need not only to maximize profits or returns, but also to minimize capital employed (ROCE) in relation to profits. Other things being equal, companies that manage with the least working capital are likely to be the ones that are most profitable.

Each of the four companies in Illustration 12.2 has the same amount of non-current assets, and the same amount of profit. The only differences between the companies are the amounts of working capital. As working capital decreases, so the ROCE increases. The company with the lowest amount of working capital (Dora Ltd has £50,000 *negative* working capital) has the highest ROCE.

In terms of solvency or liquidity, however, Dora looks very weak. There are payables of £60,000, but current assets amount to only £10,000. Few businesses would have such a pattern of working capital (perhaps a florist's shop; inventories would be low because fresh flowers do not keep for long). Retailers tend to sell mostly on a cash basis, and so a low receivables figure is to be expected. Retailers buy mostly on credit and so a significant creditors' figure is normal.

Although there is no 'normal' level of working capital, we can see that higher levels of working capital are associated with higher levels of solvency; and lowering levels of working capital can increase profitability.

ILLUSTRATION 12.2

	Alice Ltd		Bertha Ltd		Colin Ltd		Dora Ltd	
	£000		£000		£000		£000	
Non-current assets		150		150		150		150
Current assets								
Inventories	100		50		100		4	
Receivables	150		80		150		2	
Bank/cash	50		10		–		4	
	300		140		250		10	
Current liabilities								
Payables	100		80		200		60	
Overdraft	–		–		50		–	
	100		80		250		60	
Working capital		200		60		–		(50)
Net assets = capital employed		350		210		150		100
Profit		35		35		35		35
Return on capital employed		10%		16.7%		23.3%		35%

Overtrading

Having too little working capital is associated with 'overtrading'. This occurs when a company is trying to do too much business with too little long-term capital. If a company is generating lots of cash, and manages its working capital carefully, it may survive and prosper even if it appears to be overtrading. But having insufficient liquid resources (or access to them) to meet liabilities as they fall due is fatal for businesses.

The problem can start with a major outflow of cash, perhaps to buy additional non-current assets or another business; to repay a loan; or paying too much out as dividends. It is sometimes the result of success: rapid expansion can lead to a rapid outflow of cash (inventories, receivables and non-current assets: all increase) before the cash comes in from customers. High levels of inflation make the problem worse: the amount of cash required to replace assets increases in line with inflation.

Overtrading can also be the result of failure. A company that makes substantial losses is likely to find that cash is haemorrhaging out of the business. A mild case of overtrading is easily treated with various tactics to bring in cash more quickly. Receivables can be pressed to pay more quickly; inventories can be reduced by control of new purchases and by extra efforts to clear inventory; and payments to creditors may be delayed.

A cash shortage, and the effects of reducing inventories and receivables, and increasing payables, soon show up in reducing a company's current ratio. A trend of falling current ratios is a matter for concern.

In a serious case of overtrading the symptoms get worse, and attempts to deal with it can lead to further deterioration. The overdraft limit can often be increased, but if an increased limit is breached, the bank soon loses patience with a business that seems unable to manage its cash. If a company reduces its inventories too much it will soon find that it is losing business because it is unable to supply what its customers want. Customers will go elsewhere, if they are pushed too hard to pay their bills too quickly. Trade payables will usually put up with a little delay, but most will not tolerate repeated or increased delays. If a company cannot pay its bills without excessive delay it soon finds that it is unable to obtain supplies on credit. If it is to continue in business it has to find cash to buy supplies, which makes the original problem worse.

Many of us have been in shops where the signs of overtrading are obvious. There is very little on the shelves because suppliers are no longer willing to sell to them on credit. Each day the shopkeeper hopes to bring in a few hundred pounds from customers so that they can go to their local cash and carry to replace what they have sold; they cannot buy very much because they have to use some of the cash to pay off some of the amounts due to whichever creditors are pressing hardest.

Often it is a wages bill that precipitates the crisis, especially at the stage when the bank is no longer willing to honour cheques because the business has (again!) exceeded its overdraft limit. At this stage desperate measures are needed. When difficulties first arise, surplus assets are sold off to raise cash. Towards the end it even has to sell essential assets, and sell off stocks at ridiculously low prices, just to bring in some cash to survive another day. At this stage the business has little chance of survival.

It is not difficult to spot the early symptoms of overtrading, and good financial planning and management can avoid a crisis. The usual problem is trying to do too much with too little money, especially where there is too little long-term finance. Solutions include raising more long-term capital, and careful management of working capital and profitability, with a particular emphasis on cash budgeting so that crises can be identified and averted before they become critical to survival (see Example 12.1).

A manufacturer buys goods on credit, uses those goods in production, sells those goods and then sells those goods. At each stage in this process, there is a time gap. It takes time between buying goods and production, between production and selling the goods, and the objective is to minimize the gap between each stage. Additionally, there is a time delay from each stage in its effect on cash. A business will try to minimize the time between paying for goods it has purchased to manufacture and sell and receipts of cash from its customers. In order to optimize its management of working capital and the effect of these time delays on its bank balance, it must control its stockholding and production process, its credit control by managing its receivables and the positive effect on its bank balance in paying its suppliers.

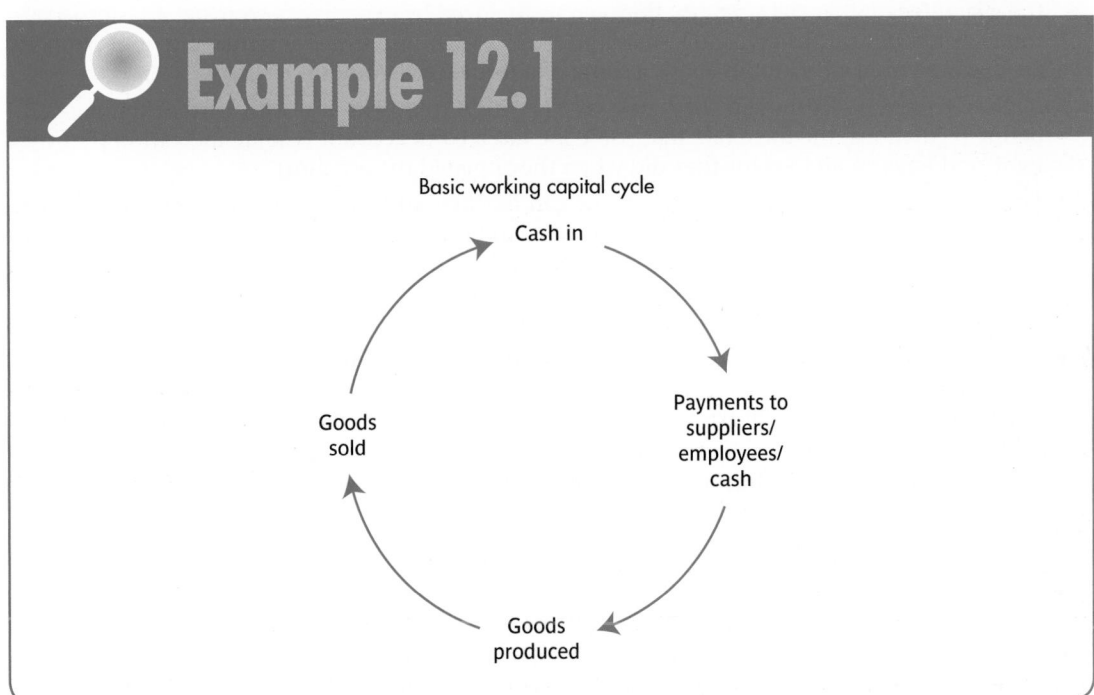

Example 12.1

Basic working capital cycle

Cash in

Goods sold

Payments to suppliers/ employees/ cash

Goods produced

Managing receivables

Financial managers may prefer to minimize the amounts tied up in receivables (debtors). This minimizes the requirements for external funding. If receivables are reduced, cash is brought into the business more quickly; the amount of capital employed is reduced; and profitability is increased.

Some businesses sell on a cash-only basis: there are no receivables. Some (such as mail order companies) require customers to pay in advance: their receivables can be negative. Others (particularly service providers such as airlines) require part of full payment in advance; this reduces the amount tied up in receivables.

Offering credit facilities to customers may be an important part of marketing strategy, and it is usually essential when supplying governments and other major organizations. But it has its costs: bad debts, administration of customers' accounts, credit control (chasing customers to pay on time), and the cost of capital (money tied up in receivables may be used more effectively elsewhere). If a company is partly financed by an overdraft that costs 10 per cent per annum, and the level of their receivables is £100,000, then the cost of financing those debtors is £10,000 per annum. It is worth calculating whether the costs of offering credit facilities are justified by the contribution earned by the additional business generated.

If a business decides that it will sell on credit, the following steps should be taken to encourage customers to pay on time, and to minimize losses through bad debts.

Accepting credit customers

It would be foolish to sell on credit to every Tom, Dick and Harry; there are always a few dodgy customers who will not pay up. There are various ways of deciding who is likely to be creditworthy:

1 *Personal judgement and the impression someone creates* – This is still important and no amount of investigation or calculation can eliminate the need for personal judgement. Even the most reputable companies and individuals (and even countries' governments) get into financial difficulties and are unable to pay their bills. But we should not rely on a smart suit and a flashy car being the guarantee of financial strength; they can be financed by excessive borrowing. A visit to a customer's premises can be revealing: many businesses with impressive internet sites and publicity are operated from a backroom above a shop, or a teenager's bedroom.

2 *Bankers' references* – Although they may say very little that is useful, with current money-laundering regulations, the mere fact that someone has a bank account is some indication that they exist, and have an address (or they did when they opened the account).

3 *Business annual reports and accounts* – These can be checked before accepting a credit customer, and show what liabilities a business already had, and indicate their financial strength and ability to pay liabilities as they fall due. It is also worth calculating their payables' ratio: how long they seem to take to pay existing creditors. It may be easier to rely on a credit rating agency to do the assessment.

4 *Ask other creditors how reliable a company is in paying its bills* – This can be done formally, by taking up trade references. It may be more revealing if done informally, through business contacts. Often it becomes widely known when a particular company becomes a slow payer.

5 *Credit-rating agencies* – Agencies such as Experian, Moodies and Standard and Poor provide information on the creditworthiness of individuals and firms; it can be done immediately by telephone or the internet.

How much credit to allow

The amount of credit allowed to customers should be limited in four ways:

1 *Time* – It is important to be clear about how long customers are allowed to pay, perhaps within 30 days. It is wise to have a contract with the agreed terms for payment, with penalties for delay.

2 *Amount of money* – There should be a credit limit for each customer, based on their size and creditworthiness. It could be millions of pounds for a government body, but perhaps only £100 for a student!

3 *Maximum for an individual receivable* – Many businesses rely too heavily on one or two major customers. If one such customer does not pay up, the business may go bankrupt. It is important for a business to know that there is not an individual receivable owing an amount large enough to bring the business down if they do not pay.

4 *Maximum total receivables figure* – It may be prudent to estimate the maximum total receivables figure that the business can afford to finance. Profitable expansion usually looks attractive, but if it involves additional working capital that the business cannot afford, it could be very risky.

Collecting in the money

The first step in collecting the money from trade receivables is to send out the paperwork promptly and correctly, and for it to be clear when payment is due. Small businesses are often lax about this: proprietors are often more keen on their product or service than they are on paperwork. Larger businesses usually have fairly tight – sometimes aggressive –credit control systems.

When payments come in, it is necessary to check carefully the amounts received; some customers are good at disputing invoices, delaying payments and taking discounts to which they are not entitled.

Offering cash discounts for prompt payment can be an effective way of encouraging customers to pay within, say, 14 days. But the cost of offering such discounts needs to be carefully calculated. A 10 per cent discount may encourage customers to pay up, say, one month early. But a 10 per cent discount for one month is very expensive – equivalent to 120 per cent per annum! Even a discount of 4 per cent may prove too expensive, as shown in Example 12.2. More modest discounts of, say, 1 per cent, may not be enough incentive for early payment. It might be more cost-effective to employ a competent credit controller to chase debtors to pay up promptly. Another approach is to charge interest on late payments.

It is important to have a credit control system that carefully monitors the payment record of customers, and what has been done about late payers. It is usual to produce an 'age analysis' of receivables, showing little detail where the sale took place only a month or two previously. But where

Example 12.2

Last year the Vinelia Building Company's turnover was £12m. All sales were made on credit. Their receivables figure was £3m at the statement of financial position date and that figure was typical of the figure throughout the year.

The company usually has a large overdraft and their cost of capital is 15 per cent per annum. The sales director recommends offering customers a 4 per cent discount for prompt payment and estimates that this would halve the receivables figure.

The costs and benefits of this proposal would be as follows:

Annual cost of discount: 4% × £12m	£480,000
Reduction in receivables: £1.5m	
Annual interest savings on reduction 15% × £1.5m	£225,000

The cost of offering the discount is more than the saving in interest.

Example 12.3

The Vinelia Building Company (as in Example 12.2) is considering employing a credit controller and instituting more effective procedures for collecting money from receivables. The annual cost of doing this is expected to be £40,000. If the average period taken by receivables to pay their bills is reduced from three months to two and a half months, would this expense be justified?

> Reduction in receivables: half of one month's sales = 500,000
> Annual saving in interest £500,000 × 15% = 75,000

Additional expenditure of £40,000 a year is justified if it has the effect of reducing the average level of receivables by £500,000, and reducing interest costs by £75,000 a year.

amounts have been outstanding for more than two or three months, the amounts and dates should be carefully detailed for each customer, together with what action had been taken, and what promises and payments have been received. The financial costs and benefits of a credit control system can be seen in Example 12.3.

When payments do not come in on time the next step is a prompt and polite reminder. Problems arise when customers have still not paid a few weeks after the due date. There are three main approaches to get customers to pay up:

1 *Phoning them, following up promises to pay and visiting them* – Sales staff are not usually keen on the sordid business of asking their customers for money. But continuing to supply customers who do not pay can be fatal to a business.

2 *Withdrawing supplies to customers* – Sometimes it may be best to negotiate a compromise: supplies will continue if the customer pays for them on delivery, and begins to pay off some of the amounts due for previous supplies.

3 *Threatening legal action* – The threat should be enough to frighten most customers into paying promptly. Legal action can be very expensive, but threats are cheap: a routine letter (that appears to come) from solicitors may be cost effective.

The costs and benefits of different approaches

The costs of having receivables include:

1 cost of capital;
2 administration;
3 bad debts;
4 discount allowed.

Companies need to evaluate the costs and benefits involved in different strategies. Sometimes they may want to increase sales by offering more attractive payment terms. If we know the contribution/sales ratio of a company[1] we can estimate the additional profits that will be brought in by an increase

---

[1] Contribution as a percentage of sales, as explained in Section 17.2.

Example 12.4

The Tightar Company specializes in surfacing driveways and minor roads. It has a strict credit control policy because it is short of funds, and depends on an overdraft that has an interest rate of 18 per cent per annum.

It does not undertake work for public institutions or building contractors because such customers are slow to pay, taking on average 10 weeks.

The company's annual turnover is £520,000, and its average receivables figure at any one time is £30,000.

The direct costs of surfacing a driveway amount to 40 per cent of the selling price.

Would it be worth extending its average credit period to 10 weeks if it could double turnover?

Direct costs as a proportion of turnover	40%	
Contribution as a proportion of turnover	60%	
Proposed additional sales	£520,000	
Additional contribution (60%)		<u>£312,000</u>
Existing receivables figure		£ 30,000
New receivables figure	$\dfrac{10\ \text{weeks}}{52\ \text{weeks}} \times £1,040,000 =$	<u>£200,000</u>
Increase in receivables		£ 170,000
Annual cost of increase in receivables	18% × £170,000 =	£ 30,600

It is worth while to pay interest on the necessary additional borrowings because the cost of the interest is substantially lower than the additional contribution generated.

in sales. We can also estimate the amount by which receivables will be increased by offering more attractive credit terms. If we also know the company's cost of capital, we can estimate the annual cost of an increase in debtors. We can then calculate if it appears to be worth while to offer more generous credit terms to customers, as shown in Example 12.4.

Factoring and invoice discounting

A business can outsource or subcontract almost any activity, including the management of receivables. With factoring, most of the money tied up in receivables (typically 75–80 per cent) can be turned into cash immediately. The factoring company provides the money, and charges interest for so doing; it also takes over the administration of the client's sales accounting, invoicing and credit control, for which they also charge a fee, typically of between 0.75 per cent and 2 per cent of turnover. These costs may be more than offset by savings in the business's own administration, and advantages in getting the money in more quickly so that it can be used for other, more profitable purposes. Factoring is likely to be particularly appropriate in small, rapidly growing businesses, where the business has relatively little expertise in credit control and the factor is likely to be more efficient and effective, with economies of scale in carrying out its specialist activity. Using a factor can mean that cash from debtors becomes readily available as the business expands; otherwise, the need to finance working capital can be a significant constraint on growth: increased sales usually require increases in inventory and receivables that are only partly financed by payables. Factoring can be a way of financing growth.

Factoring can be done confidentially so that customers do not know that a company's receivables are being collected by a third party. A business should be careful to calculate the costs and benefits of using a factor: it may seem to be more expensive, but if it is more effective in the long run, it may prove to be more economical. It usually has to be a long-term arrangement: once a business becomes reliant on getting the cash in quickly by using a factor, it is difficult to go back and establish a replacement source of finance, and to set up a credit control function again. Another disadvantage of factoring is that, sometimes, the factor may be unwilling to take on particular types of customer where it anticipates problems.

Invoice discounting is usually a short-term way of using receivables to make cash available quickly. In effect, the receivables are 'sold' to a financial institution that provides around 75 per cent of the amount immediately. The client (not the financial institution) continues with the administration of receivables and continues to bear any risks of bad debts. This usually applies only to selected receivables, and can be a useful source of short-term finance.

Managing inventories

Inventories of raw materials, work in progress and finished goods can be reduced by careful budgeting and planning, and the use of techniques such as the EOQ.

It is always handy to have lots of stuff in stock just in case it might be needed. But holding stock is a very expensive business. There are all the costs involved in providing storage space, including rent, rates, lighting, heating, insurance, security and administration. But the most substantial costs of holding stocks are:

1 *The cost of capital* – A company's cost of capital might typically be between 10–15 per cent per annum. This means that, just in terms of the cost of capital, it costs between £10,000 and £15,000 a year to have average inventory of £100,000.

2 *Obsolescence* – Clothes go out of fashion; publications go out of date; and technological items are soon superseded. Stocks of computers, software or mobile phones that are only a year or two old are worth very little. Inventories of goods for sale, and even raw materials and components, rapidly become out of date.

3 *Physical deterioration* – Inventories physically deteriorate – or even disappear – in various ways. Some things are eaten by rats and other creatures; some things evaporate, go mouldy, or become unusable in a variety of ways.

Holding inventories is expensive, typically costing perhaps 25 per cent per annum. A company that on average holds an inventory of £100,000 is likely to incur costs of about £25,000 a year. In order to maximize profitability, there is pressure to reduce inventory levels. Various approaches are used to achieve this.

Where inventory of finished goods appears to be excessive, there has presumably been a mismatch between the sales budget and the production budget – too much has been produced. This can be tackled by using appropriate control information more quickly, and considering special offers to clear existing inventories.

It is also worth concentrating only on the most valuable items in stock. Sometimes as much as 90 per cent of the value of inventory may be in only 10 per cent of the items. It may not be worth bothering too much about lots of small items of little value.

Economic order quantity (EOQ)

Various quantitative techniques are available for effective management of inventories. If the aim is to keep inventories at as low a level as practicable, there is a need to order small quantities at frequent intervals. But every time an order is placed, there are significant administrative costs: placing the order, checking what has been received, and checking and paying invoices. The administrative costs of ordering suggest that it would be better to order larger quantities less frequently. It is possible to balance these two factors, as shown in Example 12.5.

Example 12.5

The Chemvee company uses 10,000 special purpose disks each year, and pays 50 pence each for them. The administration cost associated with each order is £200, and annual stockholding costs are estimated at 25 per cent per annum. Calculate the EOQ.

$$EOQ = \sqrt{\frac{2 \times \text{annual demand} \times \text{ordering cost}}{\text{Price per unit} \times \text{stockholding cost}}}$$

$$= \sqrt{(2 \times 10{,}000 \times 200) \div (50p \times 0.25)}$$

$$= \sqrt{4{,}000{,}000 \div 0.125} = 5{,}657$$

The EOQ is 5,657 units.

If the company orders 5,657 units at a time it will have to order (10,000 ÷ 5,657 = 1.77) just less than twice a year: about once in 29 weeks. The average annual ordering cost will be 1.77 × £200 = £354 per annum.

When it receives each new order it will have 5,657 units in inventory that will be gradually whittled down to zero units. On average it will have half of 5,657 units in inventory (2,828½ each costing 50 pence) amounting to £1,414. Annual stockholding costs amount to 25 per cent of the amount of inventory (0.25 × £1,414 =) £354.

We can see that the EOQ is the quantity at which the annual inventory holding cost is equal to the annual ordering cost. If the company ordered more often, the annual cost of ordering would increase. If it ordered larger amounts, the annual inventory holding cost would increase.

A formula such as this is useful in drawing attention to two of the key variables in determining inventory levels, and providing rough guidelines. In practice it might be difficult to determine ordering costs and stockholding costs with the accuracy inherent in the use of the formula. Even annual demand may not be so predictable. A more serious weakness of the EOQ formula is that it ignores quantity discounts. It is often possible to negotiate price reductions in return for more substantial order quantities.

Just in time

The just-in-time approach to inventory planning and control is that goods are purchased or produced only when they are needed. A fine line is drawn so that inventories are neither too high, with the associated stockholding costs, or too low, so that customers cannot be supplied. A just-in-time policy is only suitable when there is reliable sales forecasting and when supply of materials and production are fast and reliable. Supermarkets have fresh bread delivered every day, just in time to meet customers' demand. Similarly, manufacturers can have components delivered just in time to meet production schedules; this minimizes the amounts of inventories held. It depends on managing good quality relationships with suppliers. Traditional managers may be tempted to keep large inventories 'just in case' they are needed. But the pressures of financial management lead to the use of a variety of approaches to minimizing inventory levels.

Managing cash

Planning and control of cash (and bank) is an essential part of financing a business. New and rapidly expanding businesses are often short of cash; unplanned overdrafts can incur very high rates of interest. In serious cases the bank may withdraw support and the business is then unable to meet its liabilities. In some businesses, excessive amounts of cash can be a problem and lead to underperformance. The business may earn interest on its deposits at modest rates (currently 4 or 5 per cent per annum),

but shareholders expect their funds to be used more profitably. Sometimes companies have large hoards of cash that they keep to be ready to buy another business; sometimes companies have surplus funds and they do not seem to know what to do with them; and sometimes these surplus funds are returned to shareholders as extra dividends, or the company buys up its own shares on the market and cancels them.

Careful planning and control of cash should ensure that sufficient long-term funds are available to finance all long-term assets; that additional funds are retained or raised to meet planned high levels of investment whether in non-current assets or acquiring other businesses; and that working capital is properly planned and financed, partly from current liabilities. Overdrafts are an appropriate source of finance to meet temporary or seasonal requirements. Cash budgeting is an essential tool of financial management, and businesses should plan their financing requirements over a three- to five-year period. Cash budgeting is dealt with in Chapter 7 and the main approaches to raising finance are outlined in this chapter. Liquidity problems become apparent in interpreting financial statements, as shown in Chapter 4, and cash flow statements can be used to review a company's performance, as shown in Chapter 7.

Where a company has liquidity problems, the ideal solution may be to raise more equity finance (by issuing shares); but a number of approaches suggested below may minimize the problem in the short term.

Liquidity problems can be minimized by good housekeeping. Prompt banking of all receipts will minimize cash shortages and interest charges. Centralized banking should ensure that any cash shortages in one part of the business are offset by surpluses elsewhere. Payments should not be made ahead of schedule and sending a cheque rather than using a bank transfer helps to retain funds within the business for a few more days. But customers should be encouraged to pay by the fastest means. Creditors should be paid at the time of the month when the business normally has most money in the bank, not at the same time as it pays wages and salaries. It is also important to maintain good relationships with bankers, letting them see budgets, and keeping within agreed limits; the role of bankers can be vital when times are tough. Careful planning and monitoring can avoid liquidity problems.

Where there are more serious liquidity problems, the business may need to take emergency measures that could include a desperate trip to the bank. Banks are always willing to help if they are sure that the customer will repay (and has assets as security), but can make high charges in situations that look risky, and may refuse to help if they have no confidence in the management of the business. Delaying payments to payables may be necessary. Receivables can be encouraged to pay more quickly. Selling off stocks at low prices will bring in cash, at the expense of profits. Capital expenditure can be postponed or cancelled. Surplus assets can be sold off: many businesses have some assets that are underutilized. Sometimes large companies, in times of crisis, suddenly appear to discover that they have expensive head office buildings in the centre of London, or country houses, or sports grounds (or even executive jets) that they do not really need. Smaller businesses can consider transferring their main administrative office to the spare bedroom at home! And businesses can free up cash by selling off company cars and using taxis or bicycles instead, especially when the only realistic alternative is bankruptcy. It may be possible or necessary to defer the payment of taxes; this can usually be negotiated with HM Revenue and Customs, although, of course, interest will be payable. The payment of dividends can also be delayed, or reduced, or cancelled, although it looks better if this is planned in advance.

Some short-term crisis measures can do more harm than good, especially if there is an underlying problem, such as overtrading. But tackling a problem promptly and harshly is better than undue optimism – a key cause of business failure.

Managing payables

To some extent inventories and receivables are financed by payables, and such trade credit is an attractive source of finance. It is cost-free, and the amount of payables tends to increase in line with increases in sales, inventories and receivables. When a company has short-term liquidity problems,

the easiest thing to do is to delay paying trade payables. This does not cause much of a problem if it is only for a week or two, especially if, after a short-term blip, the company goes back to paying its payables on time. But there is a danger that a company may be unable to resume normal payment periods, and that further delays will occur if it becomes too heavily dependent on creditors as a source of short-term funding.

Excessive delay in paying creditors is not cost-free. Payables soon lose patience with slow payers and are likely to cut off supplies, take legal action or add interest to the amount due. If supplies are cut off because of slow (or non-) payment, it may be difficult to get supplies on credit elsewhere, especially if a company gets a reputation as being a poor payer.

There is much to be said for cultivating good relationships with suppliers, keeping to the terms of the contract, and concentrating on the quality of the relationship including payment. A company that delays making payments is in a weak position when it comes to negotiating improvements in the quality of goods or service received from suppliers.

In some businesses, such as retailers, the amount of payables is greater than the total of current assets; in this case short-term creditors are, in effect, financing some of the company's long-term assets. But a 'normal' working capital cycle would show that inventories represent a number of days' sales; receivables represent a number of days' sales; and this is only partly offset by the number of days' sales represented by payables (see Example 12.6).

Example 12.6

Ground Limited is in business as a frozen food manufacturer. Figures from the annual accounts are as follows:

	20X2 £000	20X1 £000
Sales	3,427	2,981
Cost of goods sold	2,124	1,789
Inventory	500	374
Trade receivables	492	324
Trade payables	218	347

Chapter 4, ratios 14, 15 and 16 express inventories, receivables and payables in relation to the amount of (cost of) sales. These three ratios for the two years are as follows:

	20X2 days	20X1 days
Inventory period	86	76
Trade receivables period	52	40
Trade payables period	(37)	(71)
Working capital period	101	45

So, although the sales have increased, the working capital period has more than doubled and this is likely to put a strain on the ability of the business to survive with its existing level of capital.

📖 Summary

Working capital is the inventory, receivables, cash and payables tied up in the day-to-day operations of the business. It is vital for the optimal effectiveness of the business that there is neither too much money tied up in working capital nor too little. If there is too much in working capital that will be a drain on cash; it will affect the possibility of investing in new projects and buying new non-current assets or other businesses. On the other hand, if there is too little working capital, this is likely to affect relationships with suppliers; result in the inability to supply customers; and could result in overtrading and the collapse of the business. In this chapter, we have examined these issues, looked at the working capital cycle, how to optimize the quantity and reordering of inventory, the management of cash, credit control of receivables and issues relating to paying suppliers. These procedures and considerations will increase the company's efficiency.

➲ Review of key points

- Working capital is usually measured as current assets minus current liabilities.
- Insufficient working capital is likely to be associated with liquidity problems; excessive working capital restricts profitability.
- Receivables should be managed to minimize bad debts and to encourage debtors to pay up quickly.
- The cost-effectiveness of different ways of managing debtors should be assessed.
- Carrying excessive inventories is expensive for companies.
- Careful planning and control of cash is essential.
- Trade payables should be paid in accordance with agreed terms; some companies prefer the short-term financial advantage of delaying paying their creditors.
- Calculations and estimates can be made of the costs and benefits of different policies for managing each element of working capital.

❗ Self-testing questions

1. Why might a company want high levels of working capital?
2. Can a company operate with zero or negative levels of working capital?
3. How would you detect overtrading, and why does it matter?
4. What steps can be taken to speed up the collection of receivables? Why might a company deliberately allow an increase in the time taken for receivables to pay?
5. What factors are taken into consideration in the conventional model for calculating economic order quantities (EOQs)?
6. How can a company avoid having liquidity crises?
7. The Congle Company uses 40,000 wongles a year. Each wongle costs £1.25 to buy; stockholding costs are estimated to be 32 per cent per annum of the cost of the inventory held; each order costs £20 to place. What ordering quantity will minimize costs? How many orders will be placed each

year? How often will goods be delivered, and what is the average inventory level? What is the annual stockholding cost?

8 Fleshwick Traders has a large overdraft on which interest of 17 per cent per annum is being charged. The directors are considering offering cash discounts to customers to encourage prompt payment. Annual sales, all on credit, amount to £365,000, and the receivables figure at present is £90,000. The sales director considers that a discount of 2.5 per cent for settlement in 10 days would be taken up by about one-third of their customers. The finance director thinks that a larger discount would be required to achieve this result. Assuming that the sales level remained constant:

a Would it be worth offering the discount if the sales director is right?

b What is the largest discount the company could offer without a reduction in profits?

c Assume that each £1 of sales contributes 20 pence to non-current costs and profits. If the company decided to offer a 5 per cent cash discount for payment in 10 days, and it is taken up by one-third of its customers, how large an increase in sales would be required to maintain profits?

9 Stokeypokey Wholesalers Ltd is proposing to set up a branch in Northern Ireland. Experience elsewhere suggests that sales will start off at £100,000 a month in January, and then increase by £100,000 a month until reaching £400,000 in April. Then sales will increase by £80,000 a month until they reach £640,000 in July. In August sales are expected to reach £700,000 a month and remain at that level until the end of the year. Customers are expected to pay two months after the sales are made.

The cost of purchases is 80 per cent of the sales figure, and they are paid for in the month following the purchase. In January purchases will amount to £240,000; then, each month they purchase the amount of goods required for the following month.

Rent of £100,000 per quarter is payable at the beginning of January, and then in March, June, September and December. Other expenses, payable in the month that they are incurred, are expected to amount to £10,000 per month for the first four months; they will increase to £15,000 a month in May, and then to £16,000 a month in August–December.

The only capital expenditure is for purchase of fittings, with £50,000 payable in January and £50,000 in September. Depreciation is at 10 per cent per annum, with a full year's depreciation being charged in the first year.

The Northern Ireland branch starts business with an interest-free loan of £1 million from Stokeypokey Wholesalers, which is put into a separate bank account.

a Prepare a summarized income statement for the first year of business.

b Prepare a statement of financial position as at the end of the first year.

c Prepare a cash budget showing receipts and payments for each month for the year.

d Comment on the results, highlighting key learning points.

Assessment questions

1 How can a company operate with minimum levels of working capital?

2 Working capital should be managed to maximize profitability. Explain and comment.

3 What steps can be taken to minimize bad debts?

4 What are the main limitations of the EOQ model?

5 The Scottish Cake Company has annual sales of £1,200,000. Annual non-current costs are £150,000 and last year's profit was £50,000. At the year end the receivables figure was £100,000.

The company has been offered a contract for supplying cakes to the Swaysco Supermarket Group in England. Sales would be £300,000 in a year, and Swaysco would require three months' credit. The Scottish Cake Company's cost of capital is estimated at 15 per cent per annum. Is the proposed expansion worth while if all customers are given three months' credit? Is the proposed expansion worth while if only Swaysco is given three months' credit?

6 The summarized statement of financial position of the Warmel Trading Company as at 31 December last year was as follows:

	£	£
Non-current assets		3,000,000
Current assets		
Inventories	500,000	
Trade receivables	600,000	
Cash	10,000	1,110,000
Total assets		4,110,000
Current liabilities		
Trade payables		110,000
Equity		4,000,000
Total liabilities and equity		4,110,000

Last year sales amounted to £3,600,000 and net profit before tax was £600,000. The company's target ROCE is 15 per cent. It is estimated that variable costs amount to 50 per cent of sales, and that non-current costs amount to £1,200,000 per annum.

The purchasing manager is concerned about the very small amount of cash available and that the company may be unable to meet its current liabilities as they fall due.

The financial accountant says that the level of receivables is too high, and proposes to appoint a credit controller at an annual cost of £25,000. He reckons that by doing this the amount of receivables could be halved.

The sales manager believes that many customers are put off by the strict credit control policies, and would like to allow three months' credit to customers. If this policy was adopted he reckons that sales would increase by at least 10 per cent. The finance director estimates that such a policy would result in receivables taking, on average, four months to pay, that inventory and payables would each increase by 10 per cent, and that bad debts would increase by £18,000 per annum.

Required:

a Evaluate the comments made by:
   i the purchasing manager;
   ii the financial accountant;
   iii the sales manager and finance director.
b What would be your recommendation and why?

7 The following information has been extracted from the most recent annual report and accounts of Greyhound Leather Manufacturers Ltd:

Income statement	Year 1	Year 2
	£000	£000
Sales	20,000	22,000
Cost of sales	16,000	17,800
Gross profit	4,000	4,200
Operating profit	2,000	2,050
Net profit after tax	1,500	1,300
Statement of financial position		
Non-current assets	6,200	12,680
Inventories		
Raw materials	1,600	2,000
Work in progress	400	420
Finished goods	2,000	2,500
Receivables	5,000	3,200
Bank	2,000	–
Total assets	17,200	20,800
Current liabilities		
Payables	2,200	2,800
Overdraft	–	2,000
	2,200	4,800
Equity	15,000	16,000
Total liabilities and equity	17,200	20,800

a The finance director is pleased with the management of working capital, but the chairman is more concerned about profitability. Making use of appropriate calculations, you are required to analyse the financial management of the company and comment on the two points of view expressed.

b What is meant by the working capital cycle? Illustrate your answer with appropriate calculations for Greyhound Leather Manufacturers Ltd.

c What steps can a company take to improve inventory turnover?

d The company uses one million hides of leather a year, which it buys for £16 each. Stockholding costs are estimated to be 25 per cent per annum of the cost of the items in inventory. Administration costs for placing and receiving an order are estimated to be £50. How many hides should the company order at a time (i.e. calculate the EOQ)?

e Illustrate the financial effects of implementing the EOQ in practice and suggest its limitations.

8 The directors of Woebun Standard Components plc have been very successful in persuading their customers to pay, on average, in one month. However, they believe that this policy is restricting sales and that sales would increase by 15 per cent if the average collection period for receivables was allowed to increase from one month to two months.

The selling price of the component is £40 per unit and variable costs per unit are £30. Annual sales revenue is £6m. A sales increase of 15 per cent would lead to an increase in inventory of £400,000 and an increase in trade payables of £100,000.

Woebun expects a ROCE of 27 per cent per annum.

a On purely financial grounds, should the company allow its customers to enjoy the extended credit period of two months?

b Assess the practicability and financial viability of restricting the two months' credit to new customers only.

c What are the main causes and symptoms of *overtrading*? To what extent and in what ways can effective management of debtors avoid the problems of overtrading?

9 The Bonjarron Decorating Company uses 14,400 large-size cans of white gloss paint in a year. It uses different suppliers and on average pays £20 per can. It has limited storage space and reckons that the annual stockholding costs amount to 20 per cent of the cost of the stocks held. Administration costs amount to £50 per order placed.

a Calculate the EOQ.

b For what reasons might the company use (i) a much higher, or (ii) a much lower, ordering quantity?

Group activities and discussion questions

1 Many small businesses may be seen as 'overtrading'. Accountants are too conservative about such things. To be successful, a rapidly expanding small business needs to sail close to the wind. Discuss these views.

2 Large businesses should not have working capital problems. It is easy for them to borrow large sums on a long-term basis. The problem for large businesses is not working capital; it is excessive gearing. Discuss.

3 Discuss the effects on 'just in time' of increasing proportions of manufacturing (for the UK) taking place in Eastern Europe, Africa and Asia.

4 Can working capital, like manufacturing, be 'outsourced'? Could a company operate with zero or negative capital employed, make some profits, and therefore have a ROCE of infinity?

5 Large companies can bully small customers to pay up promptly, while they need not bother paying their own bills on time. Small companies have to pay up promptly if they are to continue to receive supplies, but they cannot force large customers to pay them promptly if they are to continue to make sales. Discuss these views.

6 How does cash budgeting for a business differ from the way in which you do your own, personal cash budgeting. Should it differ? (Other than the amounts of money being very different!)

7 Distinguish between factoring and invoice discounting. Explain the circumstances in which a company considering these two forms of finance would be likely to prefer factoring rather than invoice discounting.

Accounting in context

Discuss and comment on the following extract from the press with reference to alternative ways of controlling a company's working capital, such as using a company's assets to finance its operations.

Struggling to find credit? Invoice finance may be for you

Banks are pushing invoice finance as an alternative to overdrafts.

By Richard Tyler

"Giving a small business an overdraft is like handing a child a loaded gun," a leading business banker has told MPs in the Commons.

Without sensing that he might have said the wrong thing, the banker went on to advocate invoice finance as "a highly inexpensive form of finance if used properly".

Official surveys show demand from small businesses for overdrafts remains on the increase, with 35pc of firms applying in 2010 compared with only a quarter in 2007.

Banks, however, are less keen about overdrafts, as this banker speaking on condition of anonymity made clear. The part-nationalised banks – Royal Bank of Scotland and Lloyds Banking Group – may have pledged not to withdraw or alter the terms of agreed borrowing facilities before they mature, but that is not stopping them encouraging customers to shift onto other forms of finance.

While traditional bank lending to small businesses is still declining, lending against assets, like a company's invoices, is growing. They rose by 9pc to £12.4bn in the first quarter of 2011, according to the latest figures from the Asset Based Lending Association.

The shift comes as the cost to the banks of providing overdrafts increases as they have to hold more capital against the facilities even if they are not drawn down by customers.

The banks are also working harder to reduce bad debts on their loan books and prefer to monitor a customer's trading performance and reasons for needing credit, which invoice financing allows while an overdraft does not.

A significant change in the law in 2005 also meant that an overdraft is now classed as a fixed rather than a floating charge on a company's assets. If a company goes bust, its overdraft provider falls behind other preferential creditors in the queue to recover any remaining cash.

For small businesses keen to borrow to finance growth, asking for the right kind of finance has become more essential as banks remain highly selective about which ones they back.

A survey for the Business Department found that in 2010 more than a third of all small businesses needing finance were turned down by their bank, up from only 14pc before the financial crisis took hold.

Invoice finance works with a finance supplier auditing a company's customer base and setting credit limits on the amounts it is prepared to advance against business done with those customers.

Companies pay a fee when they draw down a percentage of the value of an invoice up until the date it is paid by the customer. The outstanding percentage of the invoice is then collected – either by the company's credit department (invoice discounting) or by the finance provider (factoring) directly – minus further fees and any insurance charges.

The latest ABFA statistics show that more than 41,000 companies used asset based finance in March, down 2pc year on year. [...]

Source: The Telegraph, 13 June 2011.

References and further reading

Atkinson, A., R. Kaplan, E. Matsumura and M. Young (2012) *Management Accounting* (6th edn.). Harlow: Pearson.

Dyson, J.R. (2010) *Accounting for Non-accounting Students* (8th edn.). Upper Saddle River, NJ: FT Prentice Hall.

Proctor, R. (2009) *Managerial Accounting for Business Decisions* (3rd edn.). Harlow: Pearson.

Seal, W., R.H. Garrison and E.W. Nooreen (2011) *Management Accounting* (4th edn.). Maidenhead: McGraw-Hill.

When you have read this chapter, log on to the Online Learning Centre website at *www.mcgraw-hill.co.uk/textbooks/leiwy* to explore chapter-by-chapter test questions, further reading and more online study tools.

Part **3**

Introduction to Management Accounting

Chapter 13

Introduction to Management Accounting

Chapter contents

✓ Learning objectives

After studying this chapter you will be able to:

- ✓ Distinguish between management accounting and financial accounting
- ✓ Outline the development of management accounting
- ✓ Appreciate the roles of budgets and budgetary control
- ✓ Understand manufacturing accounts and basic costing terminology
- ✓ Distinguish between absorption and marginal costing
- ✓ Outline the main areas of management accounting

13.1 Introduction

This chapter introduces the main areas of management accounting that are developed in subsequent chapters. Management accounting techniques have been developed to help managers make decisions affecting the performance of the company. These will include short-, medium- and long-term decisions. Short-term decisions are often those which must be made in a short period of time and, while they will affect the company's performance, they are unlikely to make or break the company. Such decisions include break-even analysis, which is dealt with in Chapter 17. Perhaps I am asked to run a graduation ball and need to decide how many tickets need to be sold in order to break even. Medium-term management accounting techniques include budgetary control and are examined in Chapter 15. Here, the company is creating a financial plan of its activities for each of the next few years. This will enable the company to determine its objectives, plan what resources it needs in terms of materials, labour and other 'inputs' such as indirect costs like rent, non-current assets and capital. And, as we will see, having established its budget, after the event, management will compare the 'actual' results with the 'budget' to establish what went right and what went wrong in order to improve the company's performance. Long-term management accounting techniques include capital investment appraisal when massive future projects are assessed. On an inner-city piece of land, should we build a shopping centre or an office block or sell the land to a property developer? Such decisions very often involve enormous sums of money and are likely to have a major impact on the company's future performance and survival. Capital investment appraisal is introduced in Chapter 14.

In this chapter, we examine the origins of management accounting, then distinguish management accounting from financial accounting and look briefly at budgetary control, manufacturing accounts, some important costing terminology, two different ways at looking at defining the cost of a unit of production – absorption costing and marginal costing – and then introduce standard costing and variance analysis. These techniques are introduced in this chapter but will be dealt with in subsequent chapters.

13.2 The Origins of Management Accounting

Management accounting[1] evolved during the twentieth century because managers needed systematic and reliable financial information to help them to *manage* their businesses. They needed financial information to make plans; to monitor the effectiveness of those plans;[2] and to help them to decide between alternative courses of action.

A small or new business can cope without management accounting, or perhaps without any accounting at all. As long as it keeps an eye on its bank statements, and make sure that the money it receives is more than it pays out, it will survive. But, sooner or later, it will need to calculate profit figures. HM Revenue and Customs will expect tax to be paid on any profits. Bankers or anyone lending to the business will expect to see conventional financial statements. If the business is large enough to have partners, or to become a company owned by a number of shareholders, the owners will want to know how much profit has been made, and how it is to be shared out between them.

Companies are required to produce annual reports, including income statements (showing profit for the year), statements of financial position and cash flow statements. But managers need to monitor and control the financial performance of their organizations more often than once a year. Even a very basic accounting system would include monthly financial statements. Managers would examine these monthly financial statements, and perhaps be pleased that they are better than expected. Or perhaps they would be disappointed if the results are poorer than expected. They presumably have *some* expectations – if only that they make a profit, or do better than the previous year.

---

[1] Or 'managerial accounting', if you think that sounds more impressive.

[2] Or to 'control' the business – by comparing actual results with planned results.

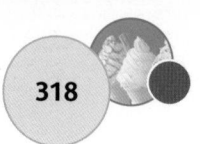

Financial plans, or budgets, detail the results that an organization is expected to achieve: its planned results. If the actual monthly results shown in the financial statements are then compared with the results that were intended, we have a rudimentary system of *budgetary control*. This basic ingredient of management accounting is examined in Chapter 15.

13.3 Management Accounting and Financial Accounting

Financial accounting has been developed within a framework of company law, mainly to provide information for shareholders and creditors rather than to provide information for the managers of a business. Managers can have whatever information they want as a basis for planning and controlling the business and making decisions. They do not need to rely on financial accounting, and systems of management accounting have been developed that differ from financial accounting in a number of ways, as shown in Illustration 13.1. Management accounting has developed from costing systems.

For many organizations, particularly those involved in manufacturing or producing a number of different products, financial accounting information does not provide sufficient information. In particular, they need to know the *costs* of the different products – or services – that they provide. Detailed costing systems were developed, particularly during the First World War, as a basis for determining how much companies should charge to the government for supplying armaments, clothing and other supplies necessary for war. Knowing how much it costs to produce each different product helps to determine the price to be paid for it. Early costing systems were based on 'cost plus' pricing: the government agreed to pay for the costs of direct materials and direct labour[3] plus a percentage to cover the manufacturer's overheads and to allow a profit. These costing systems were based on *absorption costing*, which is explained and illustrated in Chapter 16.

ILLUSTRATION 13.1

Comparison of financial accounting and management accounting

Financial accounting	Management accounting
Companies are required by law to produce financial accounting information	No formal requirements
The ways of producing and presenting the information are determined by company law and international financial reporting standards	No formal requirements. Statements are prepared in different formats for different purposes
Information is mainly a record of what has already happened	Information is a basis for decisions about the future and includes forecasts, plans and budgets
Emphasis on precise accuracy (statements of financial position must balance), although this leads to delays in producing information	Emphasis on relevance and immediacy; approximations are acceptable
Information is intended mainly for users outside the organization, especially shareholders and creditors	Information is intended for directors and managers within the organization
Information is public	Information may be private
Published information is for the company as a whole (with some additional information for main segments)	More emphasis on detailed analysis
Annual reporting is a requirement (but monthly reporting is normal)	Emphasis on frequent production of control information

---

[3] The terms 'direct materials' and 'direct labour' refer to the materials and labour in the production process and are explained further in Chapter 16.

Absorption costing is also necessary for financial accounting purposes. As explained in Chapter 15, gross profit is the difference between the sales figure for the year, and the cost of the goods that have been sold, as shown in Illustration 13.2 The *cost of sales* figure is calculated by adding opening inventory to purchases, then deducting closing inventory. The point is that costs have been incurred to buy some goods (in this instance, £50,000) that are not part of the cost of goods sold during year 10. They are to be carried forward as an expense for the following year: they will be opening inventory in year 11, and part of the cost of sales for that year.

In a retail business this is straightforward: it buys goods; it sells goods; and an adjustment for unsold inventories has to be made, as shown in Illustration 13.2.

In a manufacturing organization the principle is the same: we need to calculate the cost of the goods that have been sold. During a year all sorts of costs will be incurred, some of which are part of the cost of goods sold, and some of which have to be carried forward to the following period. In addition, there will be a range of other costs – overheads or operating expenses – which have to be written off as they are incurred. These are included in a manufacturing account, as shown in Illustration 13.3.

ILLUSTRATION 13.2

Income statement for 'a retailer' for year ended 31 December year 10

		£000
Sales revenue		300
Cost of sales		
Opening inventory	40	
Purchases	<u>260</u>	
	300	
Closing inventory	<u>(50)</u>	
		<u>250</u>
Gross profit		50
Operating expenses		<u>(35)</u>
Operating profit		15

ILLUSTRATION 13.3

Manufacturing account for 'a manufacturer' for year ended 31 December year 10

Direct materials	£000	£000
Inventory at 1 January year 10	12	
Purchases during year 10	<u>148</u>	
	160	
Inventory at 31 December year 10	<u>17</u>	
Cost of direct materials consumed		143
Direct wages		86
Direct expenses		<u>11</u>
Prime cost		240

Continued

ILLUSTRATION 13.3 (Continued)	
Production overheads	
Various	345
Total production costs incurred	585
Add work in progress 1 January year 10	35
	620
Deduct work in progress 31 December year 10	(50)
Production cost of goods completed	570
Transferred to income statement	

Income statement for 'a manufacturer' year ended 31st December year 10

		£000
Sales revenue		900
Cost of sales of finished goods		
Opening inventory	60	
Production cost	570	
	630	
Closing inventory	(80)	
		550
Gross profit		350
Operating expenses		(35)
Operating profit		315

13.4 Budgetary Control

Many businesses use financial accounting as a basis for planning future activities, making decisions between different courses of action, and for controlling their financial position and performance. They do not wait until the end of the year to see how things have turned out, after the statement of financial position and income statement have been produced. Instead, they plan ahead. They decide what they want next year's financial results to look like. They set themselves a target,[4] perhaps to increase the return on shareholders' funds to 16 per cent, or to increase earnings per share to 13 pence. These objectives may be set out in the form of a planned or budgeted set of final accounts for next year – perhaps with a budgeted income statement, statement of financial position and cash flow statement for each month. Then, as the year progresses, each month's actual results can be compared with what was planned. In this way some sort of financial control is established, and where the results that are actually achieved are not good enough, the need for some sort of corrective action becomes clear. This comparison and control takes place monthly, or more often.

Budgetary control is dealt with more fully in Chapter 15.

13.5 Manufacturing Accounts

Manufacturing accounts illustrate the link between financial accounting and management accounting. There is always a need to produce an income statement, but more detailed statements are required to arrive at the figure for cost of sales.

---

[4] They may have several targets, such as increasing market share, reducing short-term borrowings and increasing profitability.

At first sight a manufacturing account looks complicated. We need to see that there are three inventory adjustments for:

1 *Direct materials* – Calculate the cost of direct materials consumed during the period (as opposed to the direct materials *purchased* during the period).

2 *Work in progress* – Calculate the costs incurred in making finished goods (and to exclude the costs incurred in manufacturing items that are not completed during the period and so are not available for sale).

3 *Finished goods* – Calculate the cost of the goods that were actually sold (and to exclude closing inventories of finished goods that were available for sale, but not sold).

As with a retailer, there are unsold inventories at the end of a period, and these are not included in the cost of sales (they are shown as a deduction). A retailer's cost of sales is: opening inventories, *plus* purchases, *minus* closing inventories. The income statement of a manufacturer is the same, except that we are dealing with finished goods that they have made. It shows opening inventories of finished goods, *plus* the manufacturing cost of finished goods, *minus* closing inventories of finished goods.

Terminology

Prime cost includes all the direct production costs: direct materials, direct labour and direct expenses (if any).

All *prime costs* are part of *production cost* (which may also be called *manufacturing cost* or *factory cost*). Where a company makes a number of different products (e.g. tables, desks, chairs) prime costs are allocated directly to each different product so that it is possible to calculate the prime cost of manufacturing a table, or a chair, or a desk.

Production cost also includes *production[5] overheads*, which become part of the cost of finished goods. The costs are charged as an expense in the income statement (as part of cost of sales) when the items are sold. Costs incurred in making goods that are not sold are carried forward in closing inventory to be treated as an expense in the following period. It is not possible to allocate manufacturing overheads directly to individual items produced: they are usually apportioned in some way, perhaps in relation to direct labour costs.

Operating expenses include distribution costs and administrative expenses. These are not part of manufacturing costs and are not carried forward as part of closing inventories; they are *period costs*, which means that they must be charged as an expense during the period in which they are incurred. Finance expenses (or interest payable) are also a period cost and are not carried forward in closing inventories.

Fixed costs are costs which, within a stated range of output, do not vary. Fixed costs continue at much the same level, regardless of the volume of production. Such costs would include the rent, rates, lighting and heating of the factory, most of the costs of supervisory staff, and most machinery and maintenance costs. However, beyond that range, these fixed costs can increase. So it might be possible for a supervisor to manage the production of 10,000 cars but if production increases beyond that level, the company will need to employ another supervisor. Hence, supervisors' salaries will be '*stepped fixed costs*'.

Variable costs change directly in line with the volume of production. If the company stopped making desks, it would save all the costs of direct materials and direct labour. There would also be some reduction in production overheads – less power would be used, maintenance costs would probably be lower (if the machinery is used less), and there might be a reduction in 'indirect labour' costs (supervisors and others in the factory who are not direct labour). Variable costs are directly proportionate to activity or output within a stated range but can change beyond that range. In materials, there can be economies of scale whereby additional material can be purchased at a lower price per unit. On the other hand and with labour, there can be diseconomies of scale whereby workers work beyond their normal weekly hours and overtime is paid at a higher rate per hour.

Semi-variable costs are those with a fixed annual cost and a variable cost per unit consumed. Utility costs such as electricity, water and telephone are sometimes priced in this way.

---

[5] Which may be called manufacturing overheads or factory overheads.

Example 13.1

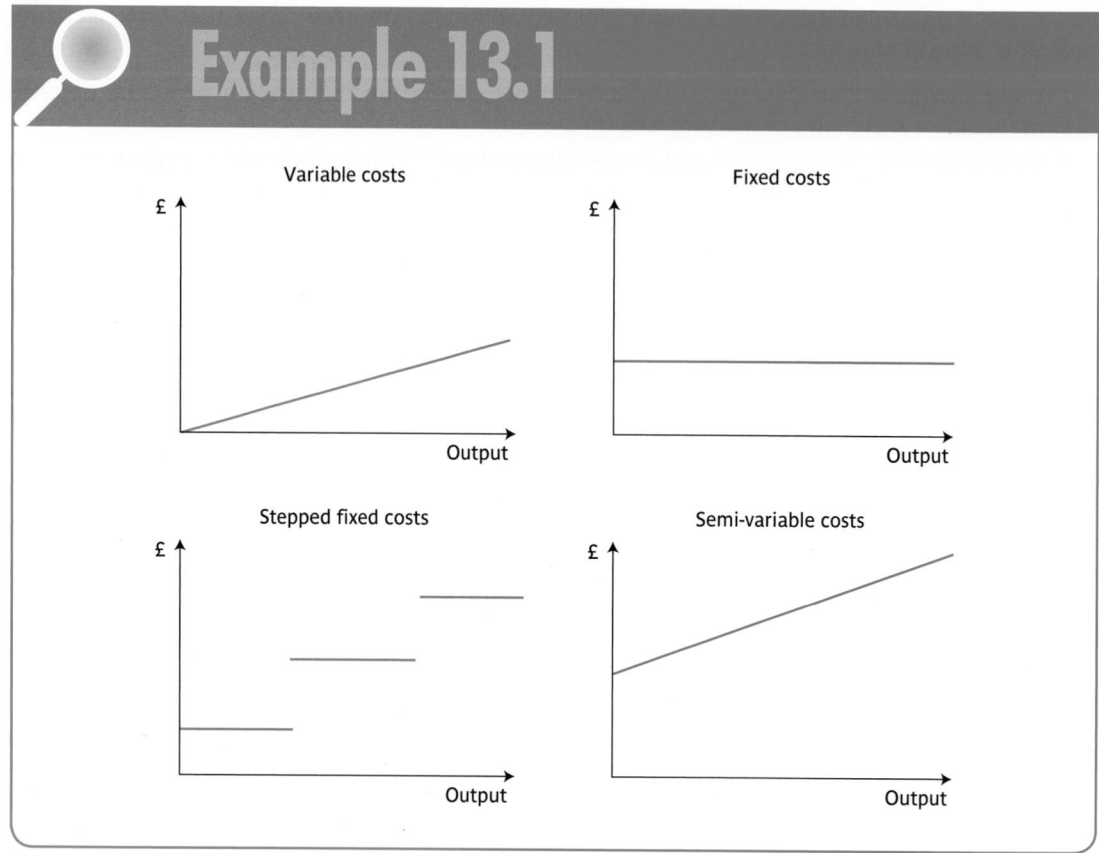

Direct costs are costs which can be identified with an individual cost unit. A cost unit could refer to a unit of production, such as a car or a cost unit could be a department of a business. In the case of a car, for example, direct costs would include materials and labour, while in the case of a department of a business, direct costs would also include the rent of the building.

Indirect costs, however, are costs which cannot be identified with the individual cost unit. The rent of the factory would be an indirect cost in determining the cost of a car.

Terminology, and issues arising are examined more thoroughly in Chapter 16.

13.6 Absorption and Marginal Costing

Traditional costing systems are based on *absorption costing*, where the costs shown for inventories of manufactured goods include their full share of manufacturing overheads.[6] This is necessary for financial accounting and the calculation of profit. Detailed costing systems enable companies to show the costs incurred in making particular products, providing different services, and engaging in a variety of different activities. Chapter 16 explains how this is done.

Marginal costing provides a different approach. It requires *fixed costs* to be separated from *variable costs*, and provides a more useful basis than absorption costing for making decisions. This is explained in Chapter 17.

---

[6] Manufacturing or production overheads include factory rent and electricity, and depreciation on the equipment used in production, and are explained further in Chapter 16.

ILLUSTRATION 13.4

Jeremy Paul set up in business selling hamburgers and hot dogs. He hired a van, and incurred total costs of £5,000 in April. He sold 1,000 hamburgers and hot dogs for £2,000.

Sales and costs in his first six months were as follows:

	Number sold	Total costs
		£
April	1,000	5,000
May	2,000	5,500
June	3,000	6,000
July	5,000	7,000
August	5,500	7,250
September	5,200	7,100

	Total costs incurred £	Number sold	Cost per item	Selling price per item	Profit/(loss) per item
April	5,000	1,000	£5	£2	(£3)
May	5,500	2,000	£2.75	£2	(£0.75)
June	6,000	3,000	£2.00	£2	0
July	7,000	5,000	£1.40	£2	£0.60
August	7,250	5,500	£1.32	£2	£0.68
September	7,100	5,200	£1.37	£2	£0.63

Although accountants try to produce costing figures that are accurate and reliable, costing systems do not necessarily produce a 'correct' cost for any particular purpose. A system can ensure that all costs are recorded, and that they are coded and allocated in particular ways to calculate what costs have been incurred by a particular activity, or in producing a particular product. But those costs are not necessarily relevant in making a particular decision.

In Illustration 13.4 if the total of *all* costs is divided by the number of items sold, the average cost per item sold was £5; but Jeremy Paul sold them for £2 each, and the business, at first Jeremy Paul sight, looks hopeless. But we should not assume that £5 will be the average cost per item sold in subsequent months; as shown in the illustration, the greater the volume of sales is, the lower the cost per unit is. This is normal in business.

The answer to the question 'How much does it cost to produce a hamburger?' depends on how many you produce.[7] It is easier to say how much it actually cost in (say) June, but the answer would be different for July. A costing system shows what something *did* cost, but projections of those costs into the future are fraught with danger.

In decision-making some costs are more relevant than others; it is usually better to separate fixed from variable costs (and use 'marginal costing') for making decisions. Costs should be calculated in whatever ways are most useful to management, and most 'relevant' to a particular decision.

13.7 Standard Costing and Variance Analysis

Some businesses use standard (or planned) costs rather than actual costs as a basis for making decisions, partly because actual costs can fluctuate a lot, and standard costs may provide a better guide. Where standard costs are used, together with budgets, it is important to compare actual costs with

---

[7] Perhaps the answer to most questions is, 'It depends on what assumptions you are making'.

what was planned. Variances can then be calculated to show where and why actual results were not what was expected, so that action can be taken to control the business.

13.8 Developments in Management Accounting

Management accounting is constantly changing and developing to meet the needs of particular businesses and circumstances. More accurate ways of identifying overhead costs with particular products and activities are required and more accurate activity-based costing has developed, which is outlined in Chapter 16.

As international businesses have become more competitive, and the life cycles of products have become shorter as new products are developed, a range of techniques has emerged. Some of these are outlined in Chapter 9.

📖 Summary

Management accounting is concerned with providing information that is useful to managers in planning and controlling their businesses. The following chapters develop the main areas of management accounting: Chapter 15 deals with budgetary control; Chapter 16 with absorption costing; Chapter 17 with marginal costing and decision-making; Chapter 18 with standard costing and variance analysis; and the Appendix introduces a range of other management accounting techniques.

⇒ Review of key points

- Financial accounting is concerned with meeting the needs of shareholders, creditors and others who are outside the business. Management accounting is concerned with meeting the needs of managers within the business.

- Financial accounting follows laws and accounting standards. Managers are free to develop management accounting and information systems that meet their particular needs.

- Management accounting is particularly concerned with providing information for planning, decision-making and control.

- Budgets are the usual tool for annual financial planning; budgetary control subsequently provides actual financial results for comparison with budget.

- Absorption costing ensures that all production overheads (variable and fixed) are 'absorbed' (charged to) products and included in closing inventories.

- Absorption costing is required to show the cost of closing inventories, but it is not usually the best basis for decision-making.

- Marginal costing separates fixed costs from variable costs and identifies 'contribution' as the difference between sales and variable costs.

- Marginal costing is a much better basis for decision-making, but is based on rather simplistic assumptions.

- Standard costing provides a systematic way of analysing 'variances', which are the difference between planned financial results and actual financial results.

- Many different management accounting techniques have been developed to meet the needs of particular circumstances.

Self-testing questions

1 Which of the following is true?

Management accounting, when compared with financial accounting, is:

a More subject to regulation

b More accurate and verifiable

c Focused more on the future

d Distributed more widely to shareholders

2 What is the difference between a direct and an indirect cost? Give an example of each.

3 In what circumstances is labour (a) a variable cost and (b) a fixed cost.

4 Which of the following is included in closing inventories of finished goods?

a Cost of direct materials consumed

b Finance costs

c Administrative expenses

d Selling and distribution costs

5 The trial balance of JackDannie, a manufacturer, as at 30 June year 7 was as follows:

	Debit	Credit
	£000	£000
Administrative expenses	420	
Bank	300	
Capital		370
Direct wages	270	
Direct materials: inventory as at 1 July year 6	64	
Distribution costs	320	
Factory electricity	11	
Factory rent	76	
Indirect manufacturing wages	90	
Finished goods: inventory as at 1 July year 6	70	
General factory expenses	12	
Machinery	140	
Payables		66
Provision for depreciation on machinery as at 1 July year 6		40
Purchases of direct materials	390	
Receivables	420	
Repairs to machinery	8	
Sales		2,200
Work in progress: inventory as at 1 July year 6	85	
	2,676	2,676

Additional information:

i Inventories at 30 June year 7 were:

	£000
Direct materials	67
Work in progress	78
Finished goods	92

ii Machinery is to be depreciated at 10 per cent per annum on a straight-line basis.

iii Ignore taxation.

You are required to prepare the manufacturing account and income statement for JackDannie for the year ended 30 June year 7, and a statement of financial position as at that date.

 ## Assessment questions

1 Which of the following is *not* true?
   Financial accounting, when compared with management accounting, is:
   a intended mainly for shareholders, creditors and others outside the business;
   b more accurate and verifible;
   c mainly concerned with providing information to managers;
   d a legal requirement.

2 Which of the following are included in *prime cost*?
   a manufacturing overheads;
   b direct materials;
   c direct labour;
   d distribution costs.

3 The trial balance of Stujerpa, a manufacturer, as at 31 March year 10 was as follows:

	Debit	Credit
	£000	£000
Administrative expenses	17,320	
Bank	15,068	
Capital		44,200
Direct wages	87,100	
Direct materials: inventory at 1 April year 9	2,500	
Distribution costs	9,100	

Factory power	850	
Factory rent, rates, insurance	8,400	
Factory supervisor's salary	35,600	
Finished goods: inventory as at 1 April year 9	380	
General factory expenses	1,340	
Machinery	29,000	
Maintenance of machinery	8,550	
Payables		26,760
Provision for depreciation on machinery as at 1 April year 9		5,800
Purchases of direct materials	92,510	
Receivables	44,231	
Sales		275,400
Work in progress: inventory as at 1 April year 9	211	
	352,160	352,160

Additional information:

1 Inventories as at 31 March Year 10 were:

	£000
Direct materials	2,200
Work in progress	189
Finished goods	444

2 Machinery is to be depreciated at 10 per cent per annum on a straight-line basis.

3 Ignore taxation.

You are required to prepare the manufacturing account and income statement for Stujerpa for the year ended 31 March year 10, and statement of financial position as at that date.

4 Explain the differences between financial accounting and management accounting.

5 Draw the following cost behaviour charts:

i A supervisor's salary.

ii Cost of raw materials at £15 per unit for the first 100 units, £10 per unit for the next 100 units and £5 per unit for the next 100 units.

iii Direct hourly labour with a 50 per cent surcharge for overtime.

iv The cost of water comprising an annual fixed charge and an amount for each cubic metre used.

Group activities and discussion questions

1 Would you rather be a management accountant or a financial accountant? Why?

2 Examine the idea that financial accountants act in the public interest but management accountants act only in the interest of managers.

3 Businesses have financial accounts, and bank statements. Why do they need additional information?

4 Discuss which of the costs of running a car are 'fixed' and which are 'variable' in relation to the number of miles run.

Accounting in context

Discuss and comment on the following article from the press with reference to impact on the profits and assets of a manufacturer according to whether inventory is valued on the absorption or marginal costing basis.

Gem may prove to be a real sparkler but hold for now

The eurozone crisis has hit diamond prices hard but history shows any recovery in the price is likely to be rapid.

By Garry White

Gem Diamonds, the owner of the Letseng mine in Lesotho, released a trading update yesterday that confirmed what we already know. Diamond prices slumped in the final quarter of 2012 because of fear generated by Europe's debt woes.

The average value of the Gem's production in the last three months of 2011 was $2,543 (£1,621) per carat, compared with $3,291 per carat in the equivalent period of 2010. Of course, some of this will be down to the mix – the size and clarity of diamonds sold – but the largest element is likely to be falling prices.

The company's Letseng mine is a very important asset. It produces some of the largest stones in the world – and this mine is the reason Laurence Graff, the art-collecting diamond billionaire, has built up a 15pc stake in the group.

Indeed, in October last year Gem sold a 550-carat stone called the Letseng Star for $16.5 m. Ten rough diamonds from the mine achieved a value in excess of $1 m each during the period. A total of 46 stones were sold for more than $20,000 a carat.

Letseng exported a total of 32,353 carats for sale during the fourth quarter, up 32pc on a year-on-year basis.

The company's Ellendale mine in Australia is renowned for fancy and vivid yellow diamonds. The colour is caused by the presence of nitrogen when the stones are being formed at high pressure. Gem has a supply agreement with Tiffany for these stones.

Ellendale achieved an average price of $4,269 a carat during the period, compared with $3,482 per carat in the final quarter of 2010.

So, all in all, production, sales and diamond prices in the period exceeded expectations, with Gem's 2012 guidance ahead of analysts' forecasts.

The company is guiding to 112,000 to 114,000 carats of diamonds recovered and 109,000 to 112,000 carats of diamonds sold.

In November Gem approved "Project Kholo" – Letseng's expansion plan. This involves building a third processing plant.

Phase 1 development of its Ghaghoo diamond mine in Botswana is progressing well and on budget and should start production in 2013.

▶

The group ended the period with a strong cash position of $141 m. The company does not pay a dividend and its shares are trading on a 2012 earnings multiple of 8.1 times.

The initial recommendation to buy into Gem was given too early and the shares are now down 26pc from the tip in January 2009.

Analysts are bullish, with the average target of the five City analysts monitored by Bloomberg being 275.4p. Of the eight analysts covering the shares, seven say buy and one says hold.

However, Questor still thinks Petra Diamonds, which has been named as a tip of 2012, is the preferred play in the diamonds sector. Petra has significant growth plans over the next few years, with production expected to increase from 1.1 m carats in the year to June 2011 to 4 m carats in the year to June 2014.

Therefore Questor continues to say hold.

Source: The Telegraph, 27 January 2012.

References and further reading

Atkinson, A., R. Kaplan, E. Matsumura and M. Young (2012) *Management Accounting* (6th edn.). Harlow: Pearson.

Bhimani, A.C.T., S.M. Datar, C.T. Horngren and G. Foster (2012) *Management and Cost Accounting* (5th edn.). Upper Saddle River, NJ: FT Prentice Hall.

Drury, C. (2008) *Management and Cost Accounting* (7th edn.). Andover: Cengage Learning.

Dyson, J.R. (2010) *Accounting for Non-accounting Students* (8th edn.). Upper Saddle River, NJ: FT Prentice Hall.

Proctor, R. (2009) *Managerial Accounting for Business Decisions* (3rd edn.). Harlow: Pearson.

Seal, W., R.H. Garrison and E.W. Nooreen (2011) *Management Accounting* (4th edn.). Maidenhead: McGraw-Hill.

Weetman, P. (2006) *Management Accounting: An Intro.* Upper Saddle River, NJ: FT Prentice Hall.

Online **LearningCentre**

When you have read this chapter, log on to the Online Learning Centre website at *www.mcgraw-hill.co.uk/textbooks/leiwy* to explore chapter-by-chapter test questions, further reading and more online study tools.

Chapter 14

Investment Appraisal

Chapter contents

✓ Learning objectives

After studying this chapter you will be able to:

✓ Understand the difference between using cash flow and profit in making investment appraisals

✓ Calculate and interpret the return on investment (ROI), or return on capital employed of a project and appreciate its uses and limitations

✓ Calculate and interpret the payback period of a project and appreciate its uses and limitations

✓ Understand the principles of discounting and calculate a project's net present value (NPV) and internal rate of return

✓ Evaluate the strengths and weaknesses of discounted cash flow (DCF) approaches to investment appraisal

✓ Understand which cash flows are relevant and should be included in a DCF calculation, and which are not

✓ Appreciate the importance of cost of capital in investment appraisal, and evaluate the relevance of cost of capital calculations

✓ Understand that there is always uncertainty and risk in investment appraisal and appreciate various ways of dealing with this

14.1 Introduction

Financial accounting is concerned with reporting to shareholders on the success of management in achieving what shareholders want. It may be assumed that the objective is to maximize shareholders' wealth. To achieve this they should use proper investment appraisal techniques to ensure that shareholders' funds are used only to finance activities that will produce an adequate return. They must strike a balance between high-risk projects that seem to promise a high return, and safer projects producing a lower return. They should also be aware of a company's cost of capital. A company with a cost of capital of 10 per cent per annum will find that projects yielding 12 per cent per annum are attractive and can increase the value of the company. Those with a higher cost of capital (e.g. 15 per cent) will find that fewer projects are attractive.

14.2 Investment

Individuals and companies invest money in the short term with the idea of getting back more, in the longer term, than the initial cost of the investment. This is a straightforward enough idea, but there are a number of issues that have to be addressed if we are to 'appraise' our investments properly.

1 How much do you need to get back to justify the amount invested?
2 How quickly does the money need to come back? If you can invest £100 today, and get back £300 after 50 years, the return might look brilliant, but the timing is terrible!
3 Risk. How sure are you that you will get back the amount suggested? There are various ways of allowing for risk and uncertainty in investment appraisal, but there is still a need for judgement, and to recognize that some uncertainty is inevitable in most businesses and projects.

Before considering the various approaches that are used in investment appraisal, it is necessary to be clear whether the returns that we expect an investment to make will be measured as:

a profit; or
b cash flow.

Profit and cash flow

Profits are measured in accordance with all the usual rules that apply to income statements. Profit, by definition, should always mean after depreciation has been charged as an expense. But as depreciation is not 'paid' (no cash goes out of the business), the annual *cash flows* from a project are usually much higher than the annual *profits*. This is clearly shown in Elizabeth's project in Example 14.1.

The first of our four methods of investment appraisal, ROI, uses profit. The other three methods use cash flow.

14.3 Methods of Investment Appraisal

a: ROI

The ROI, or accounting rate of return (ARR), is based on the ROCE.[1] It uses accounting profits that are calculated after charging depreciation.

---

[1] ROCE is usually applied to the business as a whole, but it can be applied to parts of the business or individual projects.

Example 14.1

Elizabeth was made redundant recently and was given a severance payment of £55,000 which she uses to buy a special purpose delivery vehicle. She employs a driver. Each year she receives money from customers for delivering goods; each year she pays all her expenses in cash (wages, petrol, repairs, insurance, etc.); and each year she pockets what is left: this amounts to £15,500 a year, which she reckons is a pretty good return on her initial capital of £55,000.

Unfortunately, Elizabeth forgot to allow for depreciation. After five years the vehicle is worn out, and she manages to sell it for £5,000. She should have allowed £10,000 a year for depreciation.

In terms of cash flow, Elizabeth made £15,500 a year. In terms of profit she made only £5,500 a year. In this simple business we can see that:

$$\text{Profit} + \text{Depreciation} = \text{Cash flow}$$
$$£5,500 + £10,000 = £15,500$$

It can be expressed as follows:

$$\frac{\text{Average annual profits}}{\text{Amount initially invested}} \times 100$$

The calculation of Elizabeth's return may be calculated as follows:

$$\frac{5,500}{55,000} \times 100 = 10\%$$

Using ROI is an appealing approach to investment appraisal in a number of ways. It is in many ways consistent with conventional financial accounting. If the performance of a company as a whole is judged on the basis of profitability, using return on capital employed, then it makes sense to judge the performance of each part of the business using ROCE. If a company wants to achieve a ROCE of, say, 15 per cent per annum, it can be sure of achieving this if every part of the business, and every project achieves this return.

But calculating the return on the *initial* amount invested is likely to understate the returns that a company subsequently achieves. If a project has no scrap value, that is, the capital employed at the end of its life is zero, then the average capital employed is exactly half of the initial capital employed. The return on average capital employed will be double the return on initial capital employed.

With Elizabeth's project, the initial amount invested is £55,000. After one year's depreciation the amount of the investment will be reduced to £45,000. After two years it will be £35,000. After three years it will be £25,000. After four years it will be £15,000. At the end of five years it will be down to £5,000. We can say that the *average* amount invested in the project is the amount halfway through its life; that is, after two and a half years. The average amount invested is £30,000, calculated as follows:

$$\text{Average capital employed} = \frac{\text{Initial capital employed} + \text{Value at end}}{2}$$

$$£30,000 = \frac{£55,000 + £5,000}{2}$$

$$\text{Return on average capital employed} = \frac{5,500}{30,000} \times 100 = 18.3\%$$

Example 14.2

The Trudo machine will cost £50,000, and will have a four-year life with zero scrap value at the end of five years. It will generate cash flows as follows:

Year 1	£10,000
Year 2	£16,000
Year 3	£20,000
Year 4	£20,000
Total	£66,000

To calculate average annual profit, it is necessary to calculate average annual depreciation charges.

There is no need to know what method or rate of depreciation will be used. The total amount to be written off, whatever method is used, is £50,000. The total cash flows are £66,000. The total profits must therefore be £16,000. Averaged over four years, the profits are £4,000 a year.

We could work out average annual profits as follows:

Average annual cash flows	£66,000 ÷ 4 = £16,500
Average annual depreciation	£50,000 ÷ 4 = £12,500
Average annual profit	£4,000

The return on initial amount of capital employed is:

$$\frac{£4,000}{£50,000} \times 100 = 8\%$$

The return on average capital employed is:

$$\frac{£4,000}{£25,000} \times 100 = 16\%$$

Elizabeth

Return on initial capital employed	10%
Return on average capital employed	18.3%

It may be better to use the *average* amount invested, rather than the *initial* amount invested. This is less prudent: using the *average* amount invested shows a higher return (see Example 14.2). Elizabeth should not reject what might be a perfectly good project on the basis that it achieves a return on initial investment of 'only' 10 per cent.

It is difficult to relate the ROI of a project to the company's cost of capital. It would be appealing to say that if a company's cost of capital is, say, 12 per cent, any project with a ROI of greater than 12 per cent should be accepted because it would increase the company's average return on capital employed, and so increase the value of the company. There are several important reasons why such a neat rule of thumb could lead to poor decisions:

1 There are different ways of calculating ROI and care is needed to ensure that like is compared with like.

2 ROI ignores the timing of future cash flows and profits. It simply averages profits over the life of the project. It assumes that making £10,000 profit next year is the same as making £10,000 profit after three years. But shareholders want to see results within a relatively short period of time. The problem is shown in Illustration 14.1 with two projects: one generates cash flows and profits more quickly; the other generates more profit and cash flow, but over a longer period.

In Illustration 14.1 the Jaggie project makes only £40 profit, but the Lardie project makes £45 profit. The ROI is therefore higher for the Lardie project than it is for the Jaggie project. But the Jaggie project makes the money much more quickly, and might be a better project.

3 Use of ROI is also criticized because it depends on all of the usual assumptions in financial accounting. The usefulness of ROI is limited by variations in accounting policies, the use of 'creative accounting', and any questionable assumptions in measuring profits or capital employed.

ROI, or ROCE, is the only method of investment appraisal that uses profit figures as opposed to cash flow figures. The 'return' means profit, and in calculating profit, depreciation has to be deducted.

Other methods of investment appraisal are based on cash flows, not profit. Depreciation is not deducted from cash flows when calculating payback period, or discounted cash flow.

b: Payback period

The easiest way to deal with the timing of future returns is to ask the simple question: how quickly do we get our money back? A project that gives you your money back in three years is likely to be better than one that takes five years.

ILLUSTRATION 14.1

	Jaggie project			Lardie project		
Year	Cash flow	Depreciation	Profit	Cash flow	Depreciation	Profit
0	(100)			(100)		
1	45	20	25	10	20	(10)
2	40	20	20	20	20	–
3	35	20	15	30	20	10
4	10	20	(10)	40	20	20
5	10	20	(10)	45	20	25
Total	140	100	40	145	100	45

	Jaggie	Lardie
Average annual profits	40 ÷ 5 = 8	45 ÷ 5 = 9
Average capital employed	50	50
Return on average investment	16%	18%

In deciding between Jaggie and Lardie, we need a method of investment appraisal that takes into account not just the amounts of cash flows or profits that a project generates, but also the timing of them. It is better to get our money back sooner rather than later.

In both of these projects there are years when no profit is being made. But as long as a project is generating positive net cash flows, it is usually worth continuing with.

A quick look at Jaggie and Lardie shows that both require an initial investment of £100, but Jaggie pays it back much more quickly. After only two years Jaggie has already produced cash flows of £95, and will have paid back the full £100 a couple of months into the third year. But Lardie is much slower: it has not repaid the full £100 until the end of the fourth year.

As a method of investment appraisal payback period has a number of clear advantages:

1 It is easy to calculate, easy to understand and easy to present.
2 It is based on cash flow, not profit, and so is seen as being more objective, with less dependence on questionable accounting assumptions.
3 It emphasizes the need for projects to repay quickly, which is important, especially if we take into account the cost of the funds invested in a project.
4 Projects with shorter payback periods are likely to be less risky than projects that take longer to pay back the initial investment. In forecasting the results of a project, we can be much more certain about costs and revenues in the first few years than we can be about what might happen 5 or 10 years into the future.

If we combine ROI with payback period we might make reasonable investment decisions. ROI takes into account all the profits that a project makes throughout its life; it ignores timing. Payback period considers only the length of time it takes for cash flows to amount to the amount of the original investment; it ignores cash flows after the payback period.

Using only the payback period as a method of investment appraisal could lead to really silly decisions, as Example 14.3 shows.

If the two investments were compared solely on the basis of payback period, Rudi's is clearly the better investment. But in this case it is worth waiting longer to get a lot more money back. Duri's project is the better one (unless the cost of capital is very high).

The disadvantages of using the payback period are:

1 It ignores cash flows after the initial amount has been paid back.
2 It does not consider the timing of cash flows in a systematic way.

Looking at the payback period may be a convenient way of screening out projects that take far too long to pay back, but it does not indicate whether or not a project is worth while. A project must produce enough total cash flows, as well as doing so within a reasonable period. It is important to consider the *timing* of cash flows more precisely; this is best done using discounted cash flow.

c: DCF: NPV

It is obviously better to receive £100 today than to receive £100 in one year's time, even if we ignore risk and inflation. £100 received today can be invested, and after a year it might be worth £104,

Example 14.3

Rudi pays £100,000 for a three-year lease on an office building that will generate cash inflows of £50,000 a year for three years, and then have no residual value.

Duri pays £100,000 for the freehold of some shop premises that will bring him cash inflows of £12,500 a year for many years into the future.

Rudi's payback period is two years.

Duri's payback period is eight years.

or more, depending on how successful the investment is. If we have to wait for the money we lose the opportunity of using it to generate a return, even if the return is only 4 per cent interest. But shareholders expect a higher return than they could get from putting their money in a bank, and might expect the company to 'make', say, 10 per cent per annum for them. Companies should have better investment opportunities than individuals.

If we have the choice of receiving £100 today, or £120 in a year's time, the decision is a little more difficult; but it is always worth waiting to receive money, *if* we are going to receive extra money to compensate for the delay. Indeed, that is the whole nature of investment: we pay out money in the short term in order to receive more back in the future. If a company's cost of capital[2] is 10 per cent, it is well worth waiting a year to receive £120 than having only £100 today. Where a company's cost of capital is 10 per cent per annum, then the cost of waiting to receive money is 10 per cent per annum, and DCF should be used to calculate if it is worth waiting for the expected returns.

If we know the cost of a project, and the future cash flows it will generate, then it is a matter of arithmetic to determine whether or not an investment is worth while. If the company's cost of capital is 10 per cent, we apply a 10 per cent discount rate to future cash flows. If we have to wait one year to receive £100, that is the equivalent of receiving £90.91 today. This is because, if we received £90.91 today, we could invest it at 10 per cent for a year, and then it would give us exactly £100 in a year's time.

If we have to wait two years for it, then the 'present value' is £82.64. If we have to wait three years for it, then the NPV is £75.13. If we have to wait four years for it, then the NPV is £68.30, and so on.

It is easy to check this. If we had £68.30 today, and it earned 10 per cent a year interest, at the end of four years it would amount to £68.30 × 1.1 × 1.1 × 1.1 × 1.1, which comes to £100.

If a company's cost of capital is 10 per cent per annum, we assume that it has investment opportunities that would enable £100 today to become £110 after one year. If this is the case, we can make the following statements:

1 Receiving £100 today is equivalent to receiving £110 after one year.

2 Waiting one year to receive £110 is equivalent to receiving £100 today.

3 Waiting one year to receive £100 is equivalent to receiving £90.91 today. This is because if we have £90.91 today, and we invest it at 10 per cent, we will make £9.09 interest in one year, which will give us (£90.91 + £9.09 =) £100 after one year.

4 Waiting two years to receive £100 is equivalent to receiving £82.64 today. This is because if we have £82.64 today, and we invest it at 10 per cent, we will make £8.26 interest in the first year, giving us (£82.64 + £8.26 =) about £90.90,[3] which, after another year at 10 per cent, will give us £100.

5 We can look at any future cash flows and discount them in this way.

This is all very important in investment appraisal. The nature of investment is that we pay out money now, and expect to get returns in the future. To start with we need to work out what those future returns are likely to be, and to assess the timing of them. Then we need to 'discount' the future cash flows to take into account the cost of having to wait for them. We will continue to assume that the cost is 10 per cent per annum, but equivalent calculations can be made for any 'discount rate'.

We have already established that receiving £100 after

1 year	is equivalent to receiving	£90.91 today
2 years	is equivalent to receiving	£82.64 today

---

[2] Cost of capital is the discount rate applied to the cash flows in calculating the net present value of a project.

[3] There are usually slight rounding differences with DCF.

We can continue as follows:

    3 years   £75.13

    4 years   £68.30, and so on

Another way to explain this is if the future value of £90.91 invested at 10% = $90.91 \times (1 + i)^n$

$$= 90.91 \times (1 + 0.1)^n$$
$$= 90.91 \times (1.1)^1$$
$$= £100$$

So to establish the 'present value' of £100 to be received at the end of year 1,

$$\text{the 'present value'} = 100 \times \frac{1}{(1 + i)^n}$$

$$= 100 \times \frac{1}{(1.1)^1}$$

$$= 100 \times 0.909$$

$$= £90.91$$

If the 'future value' of £82.64 invested at 10% = $82.64 \times (1 + i)^n$

$$= 82.64 \times (1 + 0.1)^2$$

$$= £100$$

So to establish the 'present value' of £100 to be received at the end of year 2,

$$\text{the 'present value'} = 100 \times \frac{1}{(1 + i)^n}$$

$$= 100 \times \frac{1}{(1.1)^2}$$

$$= 100 \times 0.826$$

$$= £82.64$$

The easiest way of finding these 'discount factors' is to look them up in a present value table, as shown in Illustration 14.2. Part 1 is the present values of £1, which equals $1/(1 + i)^n$, where i is the interest, or discount rate on the investment and n is the number of periods into the future where the £1 is to be received or paid. Part 2 is the present value of an annuity of £1 – an annuity is a regular sum of money to be received or paid at the end of period 1 and at the end of each succeeding year until year n. You will see from Part 1 that the present value of £1 received at the end of year 1 is £0.909, at the end of year 2 is £0.826 and at the end of year 3 is £0.751. The total present value of an annuity of £1 to be received at the end of years 1–3 is therefore £2.486. A quicker way to compute the present value of £1 to be received at the end of years 1–3 is to look at Part 2 where the PV of an annuity of £1 for all years up to year 3 is £2.487. The difference is a small rounding difference.

ILLUSTRATION 14.2

Part 1: Present value of £1

%	1	2	3	4	5	6	7	8	9	10
Period N										
1	0.990	0.980	0.971	0.962	0.952	0.943	0.935	0.926	0.917	0.909
2	0.980	0.961	0.943	0.925	0.907	0.890	0.873	0.857	0.842	0.826
3	0.971	0.942	0.915	0.889	0.864	0.840	0.816	0.794	0.772	0.751
4	0.961	0.924	0.888	0.855	0.823	0.792	0.763	0.735	0.708	0.683
5	0.951	0.906	0.863	0.822	0.784	0.747	0.713	0.681	0.650	0.621

%	11	12	13	14	15	16	17	18	19	20
Period										
1	0.901	0.893	0.885	0.877	0.870	0.862	0.855	0.847	0.840	0.833
2	0.812	0.797	0.783	0.769	0.756	0.743	0.731	0.718	0.706	0.694
3	0.731	0.712	0.693	0.675	0.658	0.641	0.624	0.609	0.593	0.579
4	0.659	0.636	0.613	0.592	0.572	0.552	0.534	0.516	0.499	0.482
5	0.593	0.567	0.543	0.519	0.497	0.476	0.456	0.437	0.419	0.402

Part 2: Present value of an annuity of £1

%	1	2	3	4	5	6	7	8	9	10
Period										
1	0.990	0.980	0.971	0.962	0.952	0.943	0.935	0.926	0.917	0.909
2	1.970	1.942	1.913	1.886	1.859	1.833	1.808	1.783	1.759	1.736
3	2.941	2.884	2.829	2.775	2.723	2.673	2.624	2.577	2.531	2.487
4	3.902	3.808	3.717	3.630	3.546	3.465	3.387	3.312	3.240	3.170
5	4.853	4.713	4.580	4.452	4.329	4.212	4.100	3.993	3.890	3.791

%	11	12	13	14	15	16	17	18	19	20
Period										
1	0.901	0.893	0.885	0.877	0.870	0.862	0.855	0.847	0.840	0.833
2	1.713	1.690	1.668	1.647	1.626	1.605	1.585	1.566	1.547	1.528
3	2.444	2.402	2.361	2.322	2.283	2.246	2.210	2.174	2.140	2.106
4	3.102	3.037	2.974	2.914	2.855	2.798	2.743	2.690	2.639	2.589
5	3.696	3.605	3.517	3.433	3.352	3.274	3.199	3.127	3.058	2.991

We can then apply these discount factors to the cash flows of a particular project to find the 'present value' of the future cash flows, assuming a cost of capital of 10 per cent. This is applied to Jaggie and Lardie as shown in Illustration 14.3. Clearly, the present value of £1 being paid out now (period 0) is £1. The present value of £1 received at the end of year 1 (period 1) is £0.909, at the end of year 2 (period 2) is £0.826, and so on.

Hence, adding the present value of all future cash inflows and deducting the present value of all outflows, using a 10 per cent discount factor, we can see that the total NPV for each of the projects is as follows:

Jaggie   (£113.31 – £100 =) £13.31
Lardie   (£103.42 – £100 =) £3.42

	Jaggie project			Lardie project		
Year	Cash flow	Discount factor	Net present value	Cash flow	Discount factor	Net present value
0	(100)	1	(100)	(100)	1	(100)
1	45	0.909	40.91	10	0.909	9.09
2	40	0.826	33.06	20	0.826	16.53
3	35	0.751	26.30	30	0.751	22.54
4	10	0.683	6.83	40	0.683	27.32
5	10	0.621	6.21	45	0.621	27.94
Total	140		+13.31	145		+3.42

ILLUSTRATION 14.3

Although Lardie brings in more money than Jaggie, it is not worth waiting for. Jaggie earns enough to cover the cost of capital, and an extra £13.31. Lardie also covers its cost of capital, and has a positive NPV. But Jaggie has a greater NPV, and so is the better investment.

Discount rates can be applied in this way to most projects. Once the discount rate or cost of capital has been decided, the best project is the one that produces the highest NPV.

If discount tables are not available, it is possible to work out the figures for Jaggie as shown in Example 14.4.

For those who are not particularly good at mathematics, it is easier to use discount tables. But if you want to do it without tables, here are the three easy steps:

1 Decide on the discount rate, and add it to 1, as follows:

5%	becomes	1.05
10%	becomes	1.1
15%	becomes	1.15

2 Multiply the figure given in (1) by itself once for year 1; twice for year 2; three times for year 3; four times for year 4, and so on.

3 Divide the cash flow for each year by the figure given in (2) above to 'discount' it to give the 'present value'.

When we have identified all the future cash flows, and then allowed for the delay in receiving them by 'discounting' them, we know the NPV of the future cash inflows. This can be compared with the amount of the initial outflow to see if the project has earned us the 10 per cent that we specified as the cost of capital. Investment decisions should be based on choosing those projects that give the maximum cash flows, after applying the appropriate discount rate. This is called the NPV.

The NPV decision rule is:

1 accept a project if the NPV is > 0;

2 reject a project if the NPV is < 0.

If choosing between mutually exclusive projects, accept the project with the highest NPV.

Part 2 of Illustration 14.2 shows the discount factors for the receipt of payment of the same sum of money for several years. For example, calculating the present value of £150 received at the end of year 1, year 2 and year 3, using the present value table, is:

$$(150 \times 0.909) + 150 \times 0.826) + 150 \times 0.753) = £373.20$$

Example 14.4

The cash flows in this illustration are from Illustration 14.3 in respect of Jaggie.

Year 1   Divide the cash flow by 1 + the discount rate. Divide the cash flow by 1.1 for a 10 per cent discount rate

$$\text{Cash flow } \frac{45}{1.1} = £40.91$$

Year 2   Divide the cash flow by 1.1 × 1.1 to allow for two years (i.e. 1.1 squared)

$$\text{Cash flow } \frac{40}{1.1 \quad 1.1} = £33.06$$

$$\text{or } \frac{40}{(1.1)^2}$$

Year 3   Divide the cash flow by 1.1 × 1.1 × 1.1 to allow for three years (i.e. 1.1 cubed, or 1.1^3)

$$\text{Cash flow } \frac{35}{(1.1) \times (1.1) \times (1.1)} = £26.30$$

Year 4   Divide the cash flow by 1.1 × 1.1 × 1.1 × 1.1 to allow for four years (i.e. 1.1^4)

$$\text{Cash flow } \frac{10}{(1.1) \times (1.1) \times (1.1) \times (1.1)} = £6.83$$

Year 5   Divide the cash flow by 1.1 multiplied by itself five times to allow for five years (i.e. 1.1^5)

$$\frac{10}{(1.1)^5} = £6.21$$

A quicker way of doing this calculation is using the present value of an annuity table.

Illustration 14.2, Part 2, shows that the present value of £1 received or paid in each of years 1, 2 and 3 is £2.487. The present value of £150 is:

$$£150 \times 2.487 = £373.05$$

The result is the same, of course, with a small rounding difference, but using the present value of an annuity table is a quicker route to the answer (see Illustration 14.4).

d: Discounted cash flow: internal rate of return (IRR)

With the NPV approach to investment appraisal, we need to select a discount rate; then the NPV of the project is calculated. With Jaggie, the NPV was £13.31. With Lardie, the NPV was £3.42. The answer will always be a sum of money (it could happen to be zero).[4]

---

[4] The sum of money could be positive, negative or zero.

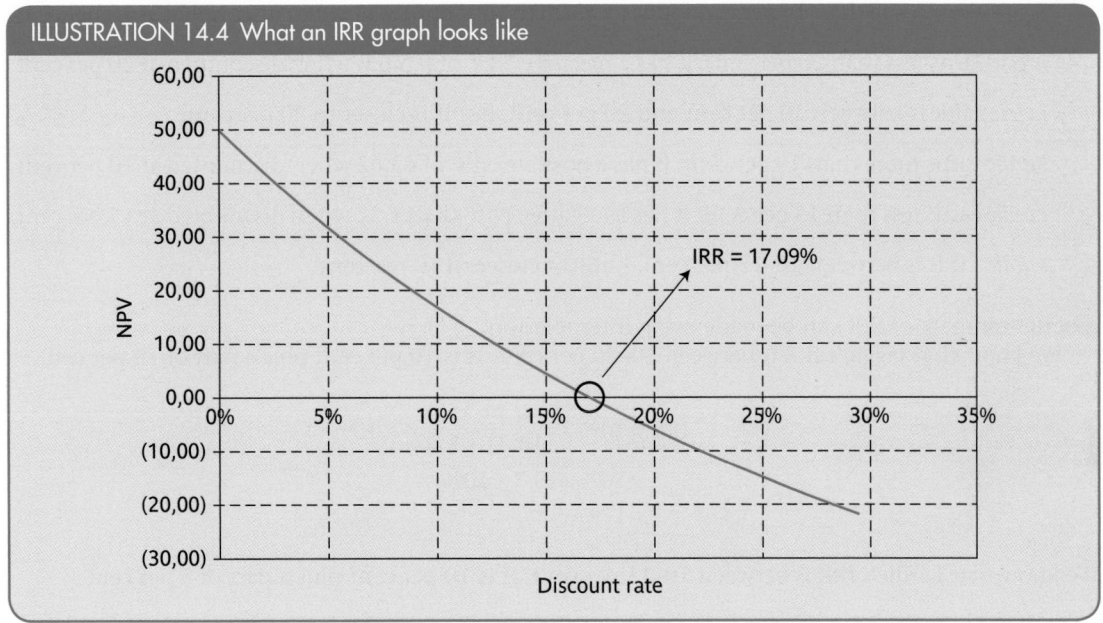

ILLUSTRATION 14.4 What an IRR graph looks like

IRR = 17.09%

NPV

Discount rate

If we do not know what discount rate to use, we could put the question the other way around: what discount rate would make future cash flows exactly equal to the amount of the initial investment? In other words, at what discount rate does the project break even, or give a zero NPV? The IRR is the 'yield' of the project. If the IRR equals or exceeds the company's required rate of return, that project is acceptable to the company.

With the IRR we do not assume a discount rate. Instead we try to find a discount rate at which the NPV of the project is zero. The answer will always be a percentage. A quick glance at Jaggie and Lardie suggests that the IRR of Jaggie is well above 10 per cent. As Lardie has a much smaller NPV, its IRR is likely to be not much above 10 per cent. In the calculations in Illustration 14.5, 20 per cent is chosen as a guess for Jaggie, and 15 per cent for Lardie.

When the cash flows of Jaggie and Lardie are discounted using higher discount rates, we can see that the totals amount to less than the £100 originally invested. Comparing these results with those shown using a 10 per cent discount rate, we can say that:

ILLUSTRATION 14.5

	Jaggie project			Lardie project		
Year	Cash flow	Discount factor 20%	Net present value	Cash flow	Discount factor 15%	Net present value
0	(100)	1	(100)	(100)	1	(100)
1	45	0.833	37.50	10	0.867	8.70
2	40	0.694	27.78	20	0.756	15.12
3	35	0.579	20.25	30	0.658	19.72
4	10	0.482	4.82	40	0.572	22.87
5	10	0.402	4.02	45	0.497	22.37
Total	+40		(5.63)	+45		(11.22)

Jaggie earns more than 10 per cent: it has a positive NPV of £13.31 when discounted at 10 per cent.

Jaggie earns less than 20 per cent: it has a negative NPV of (£5.63) when discounted at 20 per cent.

Jaggie's IRR is between 10 per cent and 20 per cent; but it is closer to 20 per cent.

Lardie earns more than 10 per cent: it has a positive NPV of £3.62 when discounted at 10 per cent.

Lardie earns less than 15 per cent: it has a negative NPV of £11.22 when discounted at 15 per cent.

Lardie's IRR is between 10–15 per cent; but it is closer to 10 per cent.

A better estimate of IRR can be made using interpolation.

We know that Jaggie's IRR is between 10–20 per cent. It is 10 per cent plus a part of 10 per cent.

$$\text{IRR} = 10\% + \frac{13.31}{(13.31 + 5.63)} \times 10\%$$
$$= 10\% + (0.7 \times 10\%)$$
$$= 17\%$$

We know that Lardie's IRR is between 10–15 per cent. It is 10 per cent plus a part of 5 per cent.

$$\text{IRR} = 10\% + \frac{3.62}{(3.62 + 11.12)} \times 5\%$$
$$= 10\% + (0.24 \times 5\%)$$
$$= 11.2\%$$

We can now compare the two investments, Jaggie and Lardie, using different approaches to investment appraisal.

	Jaggie	Lardie
Return on average investment	16%	18%
Payback period	2.14 years	4 years
Net present value at 10%	£13.31	£3.62
Internal rate of return	17%	11.2%

Jaggie is clearly the better project. Lardie showed a better return on investment because it produces slightly more profits. But because Jaggie produces cash flows more quickly, it shows a shorter payback period, and it is better using DCF.

Advantages of using internal rate of return are:

1 It deals properly with the timing of all cash flows; that is, the time value of money.
2 Seeing an answer as a percentage appears to be easy to understand and can be compared with a company's cost of capital.

The main disadvantages of using internal rate of return are:

1 It involves more calculations than other methods.
2 It is technically flawed and can lead to incorrect decisions. This is particularly true where there are irregular patterns of cash flows (perhaps with inflows coming before outflows) and high discount rates and, in those circumstances, there can be multiple IRRs.

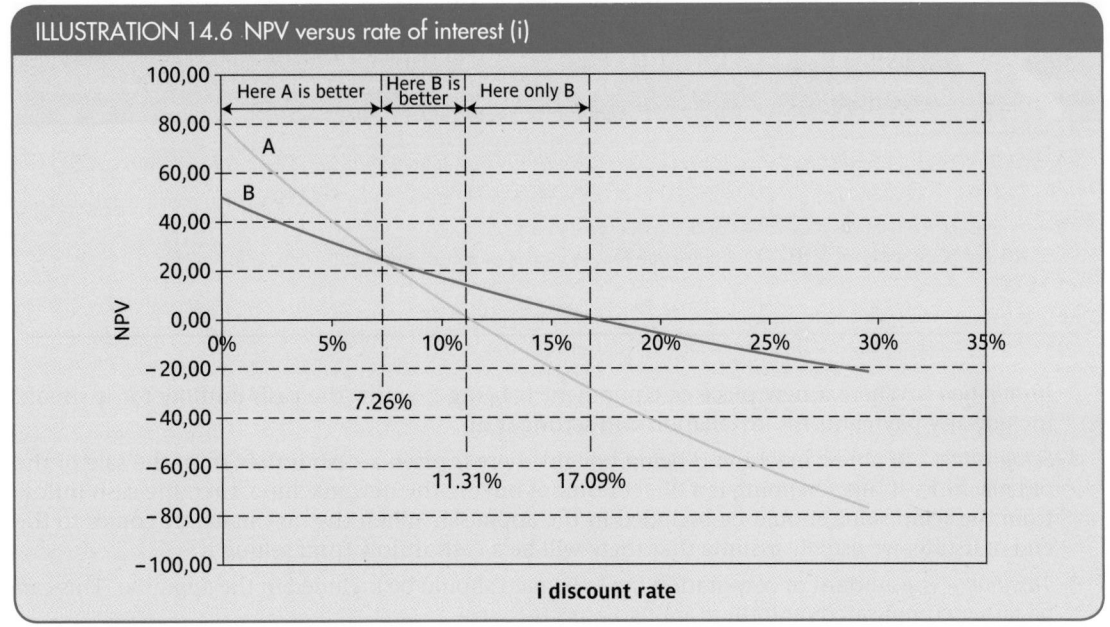

ILLUSTRATION 14.6 NPV versus rate of interest (i)

3 It cannot distinguish projects requiring large investment from those with small investment.

4 It cannot distinguish between projects involving investment from those requiring borrowing.

5 It cannot distinguish between mutually exclusive projects. We cannot assume that a project with a higher IRR is better than one with a lower IRR since the project with the higher IRR might have a lower NPV, as can be seen in Illustration 14.6.

A variety of different techniques for investment appraisal may be used. Sometimes the use of one technique rather than another can lead to a different, and perhaps a poor, investment decision. The best approach is to use DCF to calculate the NPV. In order to do this it is necessary to know what discount rate to use, or the 'cost of capital'.

Which cash flows to include: relevant costs

It is easy to get lost in the technicalities and complications of DCF and overlook the fact that the calculations can be no better than the basic data on which they are based. Estimates have to be made of the cost of the project, the timing and amount of future cash inflows and outflows that it will generate, and the cost of capital. There is always an element of risk and uncertainty.

The appraisal should take into account all cash flows that would result from the project being undertaken, and exclude all cash flows that would arise whether or not the project is undertaken. There are a number of problem areas, including those shown below. It is important not only to have the best estimates of the amounts of the cash flows, but also to be clear about the timing of them (see Example 14.5).

1 *Working capital* – Where a project involves expansion, there is usually a requirement for additional working capital (e.g. inventory and trade receivables) at the beginning, which is treated as a cash outflow. It is usually assumed that at the end of the project's life the additional working capital will no longer be required,[5] and so becomes a cash inflow.

---

[5] Inventories are sold; receivables pay up; there is an inflow of cash.

Example 14.5

A company owns a machine that it originally bought for £100,000 and on which depreciation of £80,000 has been charged. The company could sell it for scrap for £10,000; alternatively, it could hire it out to another manufacturer, and the net present value rentals receivable for doing this would be £15,000.

The net book value of £20,000 is irrelevant. The opportunity cost of using the machine for another purpose is £15,000.

2 *Installation* – Where a new piece of equipment is being bought, the cash outflow for it should include any payments for installation and setting it up.

3 *Scrap values* – If a new machine is being bought there is often a cash inflow from the sale of the old machine. If this scrapping is a direct result of buying the new machine, then the cash inflow from the scrap value should be included in the appraisal. When the new machine comes to the end of its life, we usually assume that there will be a cash inflow from selling it.

4 *Taxation* – The amount of corporation tax to be paid should be included in the appraisal. This can be rather complicated[6] and there are two aspects to it:

   a If the project makes additional profits (which is usually the intention), additional corporation tax is payable.

   b HM Revenue and Customs allows profits to be reduced for tax purposes by substantial 'capital allowances' for depreciation[7] (usually more generous than the amounts that the company charges in its financial accounts).

Example 14.6 shows two methods of dealing with these amounts. Method 1 shows a single tax payment each year, with capital allowances deducted from each year's profits. Method 2 deals with the writing-down allowances separately from the tax on additional annual profits by calculating the amount for each year, discounting them, then deducting them from the initial cost of the asset. Method 2 is useful in 'sensitivity analysis' where the effects of differing assumptions are calculated.

14.4 Cost of Capital

The preferred method of investment appraisal is DCF: NPV (see Section 14.3c), using a 'given' discount rate, perhaps 10 per cent. The best projects are those that show the highest NPV when discounted at 10 per cent. (In Illustration 14.6, Jaggie is better than Lardie.)

The choice of 10 per cent might almost be arbitrary and there is something to be said for having a clear policy: any project giving a positive NPV when discounted at 10 per cent is acceptable. This would work well if unlimited funds are available at a cost of no more than 10 per cent per annum. It is important to establish what the company's cost of capital is, to be used as a 'hurdle' rate, and there are various ways of approaching this.

---

[6] Sometimes profit is made in one year, and the tax is paid in the following year. The actual timing of payments has to be taken into account in DCF computations.

[7] And 'balancing allowances': any 'loss' when the asset is sold at the end of its life. If it is sold at a 'profit', tax is payable on the excess of the sale proceeds over the amount to which it is written down for tax purposes.

Example 14.6

DCF and taxation

Question:

A company is proposing to invest in a new machine that will cost £100,000. It will generate additional profits of £19,000 a year for five years. At the end of year 5 it is expected to have a scrap value of £10,000.

Corporation tax is 30% of taxable profits; capital allowance is a 'writing down allowance' of 25 per cent per annum.

Answer:

1   Calculate annual cash flows (before considering taxation)
    Annual profits will be £19,000
    Depreciation will be £90,000 ÷ 5 = £18,000 per annum
    Cash flows (before considering taxation) will be £18,000 + 19,000 = £37,000 a year for the first four years, with an additional £10,000 in year 5

2   Assuming that capital allowances is the writing down allowance of 25 per cent calculated on the diminishing balance basis, as follows:

Cost of asset	£100,000
Year 1 WDA 25%	25,000
	75,000
Year 2 WDA 25%	18,750
	56,250
Year 3 WDA 25%	14,062
	42,188
Year 4 WDA 25%	10,547
	31,641
Year 5 WDA 25%	7,910
	23,731
Proceeds of scrap	10,000
Balancing allowance	13,731

3   *Method 1* – Calculate amount of tax payable based on profits after deducting writing-down allowances. The DCF is then done on a single, all-embracing cash flow figure.

Year	0	1	2	3	4	5
Profit before deducting depreciation		37,000	37,000	37,000	37,000	37,000
WDA		25,000	18,750	14,062	10,547	7,910
Balancing allowance						13,731
Taxable profit		12,000	18,250	22,938	26,453	15,359
Cash flows						
Tax payable (30%)		(3,600)	(5,475)	(6,881)	(7,936)	(4,608)

Continued >>>

Example 14.6

Continued >>>

(Initial cost Annual CFs)	(100,000)	33,400	31,525	30,119	29,064	32,392
						10,000
						42,392
10% discount factor	1.0	0.909	0.826	0.751	0.683	0.621
DCF	(100,000)	30,361	26,040	22,619	19,851	26,325
NPV						125,196
						(100,000)
						25,196

4 *Method 2* – Two separate discounting calculations: (i) the cost of the asset together with the value of the taxation allowances, and the final scrap value; (ii) other cash flows, including profits, and the taxation on them.

Present value of writing-down allowances

Year	0	1	2	3	4	5	Total
WDA		25,000	18,750	14,062	10,547	7,910	
BA					13,731		
30% of WDA/BA		7,500	5,625	4,218	3,164	6,492	
10% discount factor	1.0	0.909	0.826	0.751	0.683	0.621	
NPV		6,817	4,646	3,168	2,161	4,032	20,824

Cost of machine	£100,000
NPV of WDAs and balancing allowance	(£20,824)
Net cost of machine (after deducting taxation allowances)	£ 79,176
Deduct NPV of final scrap value £10,000 × 0.621	£ 6,210
NPV of net cost of machine	£ 72,966
Annual pre-depreciation profits	£37,000
Deduct tax at 30%	£11,100
Annual cash flows after tax	£25,900
Annuity 10% for 5 years	× 3.791 = £ 98,187
NPV	£25,221

The two different methods produce the same positive net present value of £25,200. There are slight rounding differences. The second method facilitates 'sensitivity analysis': the results of lower sales or higher costs can be calculated without changing the cost of the machine.

5 *Incremental costs* – Some costs will be incurred, and the payments made, whether or not the project is undertaken. A project may be charged its share of fixed overheads (such as the costs of providing a factory and its administration), but as those costs will be incurred whether or not the project is undertaken, the cash flows for fixed overheads are usually excluded. Only incremental fixed costs, those which would arise as a result of this project, are relevant costs.

Continued >>>

Example 14.6

Continued >>>

6 *Sunk costs* – There are often significant payments for market research and feasibility studies that are undertaken before a decision is made on whether or not to go ahead. As those costs have already been incurred or paid (they are 'sunk'), or if the company is committed to paying these costs in the near future ('committed'), such costs are irrelevant in deciding whether or not to go ahead with the project and should be ignored in the project appraisal.

7 *Opportunity costs* – The cost of using an asset (or materials or labour) for a particular project is often the 'opportunity cost' of the best alternative use. If the asset or other input could be sold, if not used in the project under consideration, the selling price would be the relevant cost. Or if the resource is presently producing a contribution from its existing use, using it for the project under consideration, the contribution forgone would be the relevant cost.

8 *Costs of disposal* – If the cost of using a required material which is in stock but has no alternative use but would otherwise need to be safely disposed of, perhaps by health and safety regulations, a *cost saving* would arise in using it for the project equal to the cost of its safe disposal.

1 *Opportunity cost* – If there are plenty of projects available that show a positive NPV when discounted at 14 per cent, and only limited funds are available, then the hurdle rate should be 14 per cent, not 10 per cent. There is no point in tying up limited funds on projects that achieve only, say, 11 per cent, if there is the opportunity to invest in projects that achieve 14 per cent or more. In Illustration 14.6 the company should not invest in Lardie if they would then not have sufficient funds to invest in Jaggie.

It is important that a company has a sensible hurdle discount rate for investment appraisal. If it is set too low, perhaps at 7 per cent, then the company is likely to invest in projects that barely earn their keep; that disappoints the owners of the business; and that result in the value of the business falling. If it is set too high, perhaps at 22 per cent, then the company is likely to reject projects that more than earn their keep. If projects that earn a good return are rejected, then the business loses opportunities to increase its value.

2 *Weighted average cost of capital* – Companies are usually financed partly by borrowing, and partly by shareholders' funds. At first sight it is not difficult to establish the cost of borrowing: the interest rate on borrowings is usually specified. The cost of shareholders' funds is more difficult. As there is no requirement for companies to pay dividends on ordinary shares, we might be tempted to think that shareholders' funds have no real cost. They are 'free', and provided the company makes *some* profit, that is OK. But directors who do not meet shareholders' expectations in terms of profit will probably soon find themselves out of a job. Low profits lead to low share prices; low share prices invite takeover bids; and when another company acquires a company that is seen to be failing, it will soon get rid of the previous managers.

The cost of ordinary shareholders' funds depends on market expectations. The company should aim to invest in ways that increase the value of the company, not in ways that reduce it. Attempts to identify a company's cost of capital are attempts to identify the discount rate that projects must achieve in order to at least maintain the value of the company.

A company might be half-financed by borrowing, which costs 8 per cent per annum; and half-financed by shareholders' funds, which cost 14 per cent per annum. In this case the company's average cost of capital is 11 per cent.

Another company might be 25 per cent financed by borrowing, which costs 8 per cent per annum; and 75 per cent financed by shareholders' funds, which cost 14 per cent per annum. In this case the company's weighted average cost of capital is 12.5 per cent.

$$25\% \times 8\% = 2\%$$
$$75\% \times 14\% = \underline{10.5\%}$$
$$\underline{12.5\%}$$

In calculating the weighting of the different types of capital (e.g. shareholders' funds 75 per cent; loan capital 25 per cent), it may be better to use the *market* value of shareholders' funds, and the *market* value of borrowings rather than the amounts shown on the statement of financial position.

a *Cost of borrowing* – A company might have issued £1m of 10 per cent debentures, but that does not necessarily mean that the cost of those debentures is 10 per cent per annum. If the market value of debentures falls below the statement of financial position value, the amount of interest payable remains the same; but the *effective* rate (interest payable as a percentage of market value) will be higher. Similarly, if the market value of debentures increases, the effective interest rate declines. A number of other factors have to be taken into consideration:

  i Interest is an allowable expense for corporation tax purposes. If the company's effective rate of corporation tax is 25 per cent, then the effective cost of 10 per cent interest to the company is only 7.5 per cent.

  ii Most debentures are redeemable at some future date, perhaps 5 or 10 years into the future. They may be redeemable at par (which is book value, or face value); they may be redeemable at a discount (e.g. £100 debentures redeemable at £95); or they may be redeemable at a premium (e.g. £100 debentures redeemable at £110).

The calculation of the cost of debentures can look like doing a DCF calculation to arrive at the internal rate of return, as shown in Example 14.7.

b *Cost of equity (cost of ordinary shareholders' funds)* – Establishing the cost of equity is more difficult: there is no requirement to pay dividends, and it might be tempting to think that there is no cost attached to shareholders' funds. Shareholders have money invested in the business, and if they are lucky they will receive dividends, and the value of their shareholdings will increase. If they are unlucky there will be no dividends, and the value of their shareholdings will decline.

In a small company, perhaps where all the equity is owned by one or two directors, it can do what it likes. If it chooses to regard shareholders' funds as having zero cost, and to invest in duff projects, that is its own business.

If a listed company decided that shareholders' funds are cost-free, it might not produce enough profits or dividends; the market value of the shares would decline; and the directors will soon find their position threatened.

In order to determine the cost of a company's equity, we need to know what rate of return is needed to maintain, or increase, the value of the company. This really depends on shareholders' expectations. If they are expecting a return of 10 per cent, and the company generates 15 per cent, then the value of the company should increase. If they are expecting 15 per cent, and the company generates only 10 per cent, then we can expect the value of the company to decrease.

It is not clear how investors' expectations can be quantified. Even if we could find out what it is that determines future share prices, by the time we have found out, the picture would have changed; any model that predicts share prices, based on historic data, needs to be

Example 14.7

The market value today of Air UK's 6 per cent debentures is £80 for £100 par value. The debentures are redeemable at £105 four years from today. The company is profitable and its effective rate of taxation is 30 per cent.

The cost of interest each year is 70 per cent of £6, which is £4.20. At first sight the cost of the loan capital looks like 70 per cent of £6 per annum, that is, 4.2 per cent. But the effective cost is increased by the premium that is payable on redemption, and by the fact that the current market value of the debentures is well below the £100 par value.

The cash flows associated with it are shown in the second column below. As the cost of the debentures is likely to be more than 6 per cent, as a first guess we try discounting the cash flows at 10 per cent.

Year	Cash flow	Discount factor 10%	Net present value	Discount factor 15%	Net present value
0	(80)	1	(80)	1	(80)
1	4.2	0.909	3.81	0.870	3.65
2	4.2	0.826	3.47	0.756	3.18
3	4.2	0.751	3.15	0.658	2.76
4	109.2	0.683	74.59	0.572	62.44
			+ 5.02		(7.97)

When discounted at 10 per cent, the future cash flows associated with the debenture are more than the price of the debenture now. The cost of the debentures to the company (in relation to the current market value) is therefore more than 10 per cent per annum.

When discounted at 15 per cent, the future cash flows associated with the debenture are less than the price of the debenture now. The cost of the debentures to the company (in relation to the current market value) is therefore less than 15 per cent per annum.

$$\text{Interpolation suggests a cost of } 10\% + \frac{5.01}{(5.01 + 7.97)} \times 5$$
$$= 11.9\%$$

If the company has nothing better to do with its money, it should consider buying up the debentures on the stock market. But if the company's opportunity cost of capital is 12 per cent or more, it should be able to find a more profitable use of funds.

---

constantly updated to maintain credibility.[8] Sometimes companies seem to promise a lot, and their share price goes up and up. But if they then disappoint, the share price will collapse. It seems sensible to manage expectations: to plan and promise only what can be delivered with reasonable certainty.

In assessing shareholders' expectations, as in so many areas of accounting, we need to consider whether they should be expressed in terms of profit, or cash flow. ROCE and price/earnings (P/E) ratio are two indications of shareholders' expectations that are based on profits. The dividend growth model is based on dividends. The capital asset pricing model (CAPM) can also be used to assess a company's cost of capital. Companies should not undertake projects that are likely to lower the company's returns, and share price. When they cannot find

---

[8] There is more chance of maintaining credibility than of revealing truth!

sufficiently profitable opportunities for investing available funds, they should return those funds to shareholders as dividends, or use them to buy up the company's shares. There are plenty of examples of companies that have invested surplus funds unwisely, and so have reduced the value of the company.

3 *ROCE* – If a company has a ROCE of, say, 15 per cent, shareholders may expect this rate to continue in the future. If the company fails to achieve this, the share price is likely to fall. This does not, however, mean that the company's cost of capital for DCF purposes is 15 per cent. ROCE provides only a rough indication of shareholders' expectations, and there is no clear relationship between a company's ROCE and its cost of capital to be used for DCF.

4 *P/E* – A company's P/E ratio is also an indication of investors' expectations about the future profits of a company. Where substantial growth is expected, the share price is likely to be high in relation to the current level of profits; and so the P/E ratio is high. Where growth in earnings is expected to be low, then the company's share price is likely to be low in relation to the current level of profits; and so the P/E ratio is relatively low. There is, however, no easy way to convert the P/E ratio into a cost of capital figure.

5 *Dividend growth model* – A company's share price in relation to the last known level of dividends is also a good indicator of shareholders' expectations. If a company has a low dividend yield, this means that the share price is high in relation to the last known level of dividends; shareholders' expectations are high, and future dividends are expected to grow at a relatively high rate. The growth rate in dividends over recent years can be calculated, and incorporated into a 'model', or formula, that indicates the cost of a company's equity capital.

The cost of share capital is assumed to be the dividend yield on the shares (dividend expressed as a percentage of share price), adjusted for an assumed rate of growth (see Example 14.8).

6 *CAPM* – The CAPM assumes that the cost of capital is based on:

a a 'risk free' interest rate; to this is added

b an extra return to allow for the risk of investing in shares generally; this second element is adjusted to allow for

c the specific risk of a given company.

It is easy to find the 'risk-free' interest rate: it is the interest yield on government bonds, currently about 4 per cent.

Example 14.8

Last year's dividend per share: 20p
Current share price: £5
Assumed rate of dividend growth: 15 per cent per annum

1 Calculate next year's dividend: 20p + 15% = 23p
2 Express next year's dividend as a percentage of current share price: $\frac{23}{500} \times 100 = 4.6\%$
3 Add assumed rate of growth: 15% + 4.6% = 19.6%

Cost of capital is assumed to be 19.6 per cent.

The model obviously has limitations, and in this example a very high growth rate is assumed for dividends; this results in an unusually high cost of equity capital.

The second element is more difficult to estimate, but we might say that in recent decades investors in ordinary shares have had returns of about, say, 8 per cent over and above the rate on government bonds.

The specific risk of a given company is measured as a 'beta', which might be average (1.0), or above average (say, 1.2), or below average (say, 0.8).

The cost of capital of a company with high risk might be:

$$4\% + (8\% \times 1.2) = 4\% + 9.6\% = 13.6\%$$

The cost of capital of a company with low risk might be:

$$4\% + (8\% \times 0.8) = 4\% + 6.4\% = 10.4\%$$

Calculations are complex, but the answers produced seem to be reasonable: typically the cost of equity may be between 10–15 per cent per annum.

Evaluation of different approaches to cost of capital

It is difficult to establish the cost of ordinary shareholders' funds with any certainty, and without making some assumptions. Average returns on ordinary shares for the twentieth century can be calculated, and shareholders might expect this level of returns to continue. But in the first three years of the twenty-first century they were disappointed: returns on ordinary shares were negative, and share prices fell. In the following three years there was a return of growth. Although we do not know how long this will continue, it is reasonable to assume that there is little change in long-term expectations.

Estimates of the cost of borrowing are likely to be more accurate; and the cost of borrowing is likely to be lower than the cost of ordinary shareholders' funds because it is seen as being lower risk, and because interest is an allowable expense for corporation tax purposes.

Given that the cost of borrowing is likely to be lower than the cost of equity, it is worth calculating a weighted average cost of capital figure. This approach assumes that the more a company relies on borrowing, the lower its cost of capital is likely to be. But if a company relies too much on borrowing, the amount of risk increases; and this is likely to increase the cost of capital.

In practice many companies do not bother with the more sophisticated approaches to determining a 'correct' cost of capital figure. It is acceptable to choose a reasonable rate, and stick to it. For low-risk projects 10 per cent is acceptable. For higher-risk projects it could be increased up to about 15 per cent.

14.5 Uncertainty and Risk

All investment is based on assumptions about the future and there is usually some uncertainty about our forecasts, and a degree of risk. There are some 'risk-free' investments, such as lending money to the government by buying 'gilts'. But managers are more likely to be involved in evaluating projects where there is some uncertainty and risk in estimating:

1 The initial cost of the project: with major projects the initial capital expenditure often turns out to be much higher than was originally planned.
2 The cash inflows that the project will generate: forecasts may prove to be much too high, or much too low.
3 The cash outflows, including costs, that will be involved.

4 The timing: a project may take longer to be completed and to generate cash flows than was anticipated. And it is difficult to be sure how long a project will last. It is easy to 'assume' a five-year life, but difficult to know how long it will really continue.

There are various ways of dealing with risk and uncertainty, all of which involve some subjectivity, but which help to give credibility to forecasts and appraisals.

One approach is to use a higher discount rate for projects that are seen as involving more risk than others. This is appealing but it is difficult to know how much extra risk there is, and by how much the discount rate should be increased.

A second approach, where there are several possible outcomes, is to apply probability theory to arrive at an 'expected value'. For example, if there is a 20 per cent chance that a cash flow will be £10,000, a 45 per cent chance that it will be £20,000, and a 35 per cent chance that it will be £30,000, the 'expected' cash flow can be calculated as follows:

20% × £10,000	=	£2,000
45% × £20,000	=	£9,000
35% × £30,000	=	£10,500
Expected cash flow		£21,500

The actual cash flow for a particular project is unlikely to be the 'expected' figure calculated in this way. But if probabilities can be applied in this way to a number of different projects, on average the actual results are likely to be in line with what is expected. The problem is, of course, knowing what the probability is for any particular outcome.

A third approach is to recognize that a range of different outcomes is possible, and to produce one appraisal based on rather pessimistic assumptions; one based on rather optimistic assumptions; and one 'realistic' appraisal between these two extremes. This may be attractive in terms of saying (a) this is the worst that is likely to happen – this is the downside risk; (b) this is the best that is likely to happen; and (c) this is what is most likely to happen. If (a) looks pretty dreadful, then a pretty good (b) might be needed to make the risk look worth while. This may give a useful 'feel' for a project, and provide a basis for considering other likely outcomes. It may not be too difficult to get agreement on a range of likely outcomes, which can help to get decisions made. But it is very subjective. There is no way of determining how dreadful the pessimistic assumptions should be, or how brilliant the optimistic assumptions should be.

A fourth approach is to use 'sensitivity analysis' to consider a wider range of different possible outcomes. The appraisal can be done again and again, using different assumptions, to see how sensitive the decision is to particular changes in each variable. It may be uncertain whether a project will last for 5 years, or 10 years, or somewhere in-between. Sensitivity analysis might show that it is brilliant if it lasts for 10 years, but it is still viable if it lasts for only 5 years. It may be uncertain whether the initial project cost will be £1m, or £2m, or somewhere in-between. Sensitivity analysis might show that it is a brilliant project if it costs only £1m; a waste of money if it costs £2m; and that, provided it does not cost more than £1.6m, it is viable. Wherever there is uncertainty, the proposal can be recalculated to see how sensitive it is to a change in assumptions. This approach does not remove subjectivity, but it does enable the financial effects of particular uncertainties relating to each variable in the calculation to be quantified and provides a basis for judgement and decision-making.

📖 Summary

In theory managers use investment appraisal techniques to ensure that a company's funds are used in ways which maximize shareholders' wealth. In practice managers may have their own agendas, favouring particular projects, seeking to impress their superiors, enhancing their reputation, increasing their personal remuneration packages, and getting promotion by claiming credit for all that goes well, and blaming others for all that goes badly. It is easy to gain approval for a pet project by producing forecasts and appraisals that meet the company's criteria and show it as being viable. It is important that companies have 'post-investment appraisal' procedures in place that check if actual results are in line with the figures that were included in the appraisal that the company approved. Successful managers will have done some, or all, of the following:

1 Made sure that actual results are in line with the original appraisals.
2 Been promoted and transferred so that they are no longer around to take the blame.
3 Kept a careful record of all the forecasts that made up the appraisal, and made sure that someone else is responsible for each element that made up the total appraisal. If the project does not come up to expectations, it is Bill's fault because the sales forecasts were wrong; or Jane's fault because she underestimated the original cost; or Jo's fault because production costs were way out of line.

Successful investment projects are the key to the financial success of a company, and to maximizing shareholder value. Management cannot avoid the results of their investment activities being assessed by the outside world through their published financial statements. For individual managers, taking credit for successful investment projects is important to success. All managers need to understand investment appraisals if they are to be the ones who take the credit, and not the ones who end up taking the blame. Good managers ensure that decisions are taken on the basis of information that is as honest as possible, with risks and uncertainties specified and taken into account. Good decisions are taken by responsible groups of managers who understand the limitations of the data, and the techniques used for appraising the data.

➡ Review of key points

- The ROI of a project is calculated using profits, not cash flow, and is comparable with the return on capital employed for the company as a whole.
- The payback period is calculated using cash flows, not profits, and tells us how quickly a project is likely to pay for itself.
- DCF properly allows for the timing of cash flows.
- The NPV method of DCF is the preferred method of investment appraisal.
- It is necessary to know the company's cost of capital to use NPV.
- DCF calculations can be no better than the underlying data that are based on estimates, and there is always some risk and uncertainty.

Self-testing questions

1 How is ROI calculated?

2 The most recent annual report and accounts of the Row Sea Company shows that it made a profit after tax of £1m last year, and the statement of financial position shows total shareholders' funds of £10m. It is considering buying a ship that will cost £2m and that will generate operating profits (after charging depreciation) of £180,000 a year.

   Would the investment increase the company's return on capital employed?

3 The PBP company has £1m to invest, and is considering the following two projects:

   a Project A will generate annual net cash flows of £200,000 for eight years;

   b Project B will generate cash flows of £400,000 in year 1, £350,000 in year 2, £300,000 in year 3, £100,000 in year 4, £50,000 in year 5, and then about £5,000 a year for another few years.

   On the basis of this information, and without considering DCF, which of the two projects is better?

4 What are the main advantages and disadvantages of using the following methods of investment appraisal?

   a ROI

   b payback period

5 Is there a case for investing in the following project?

   A new machine costs £200,000 and will have a five-year life with no residual value at the end. It is expected to generate profits of £35,000 a year for five years.

   What is the highest cost of capital at which the project would be acceptable?

6 The Peel Company is considering two alternative investment opportunities: a Kippering Project and a Queenies Project. Each would involve an initial outlay of £50,000 and is expected to have a five-year life with no scrap value at the end. The additional cash flows (before deducting depreciation) that each project is expected to generate are as follows:

Year	Kippering £	Queenies £
1	25,000	5,000
2	20,000	15,000
3	15,000	25,000
4	10,000	25,000
5	5,000	20,000

You are required to calculate the following for each project, and suggest how a decision should be made between the two projects:

   a average annual profits;

   b return on initial capital employed;

   c return on average capital employed;

   d payback period;

   e NPV using 10 per cent discount factor;

   f NPV using 25 per cent discount factor;

   g an approximate internal rate of return.

7 The Maroc Production Company is considering manufacturing and selling an economy video camera for use by small retailers for security purposes. A firm of management consultants has carried out a feasibility study for them at a cost of £25,000, which has not yet been paid. There would be two requirements for machinery:

a Some existing machinery could be modified at a cost of £100,000 to undertake the first stage of production.

b For the second stage of production the company already has suitable machinery that is not in use; it has a book value of £80,000; it would be difficult to dismantle and dispose of, and its net realizable value at present is zero.

If the project goes ahead, maintenance costs of the machinery would be £10,000 per annum; there would be additional working capital requirements of £50,000 at the beginning of the project, which would be recovered at the end of four years; initial marketing costs, to be paid for as soon as soon as the project is approved would be £60,000; and annual marketing costs would be £20,000 per annum for the full four years.

The cost and selling price per unit is expected to be:

	£	£
Selling price		60
Materials	11	
Direct labour	6	
Variable overheads	13	
General fixed overheads	12	
Interest	2	
		44
Profit		16

The management consultants have suggested that the product would have a four-year life before being superseded by better cameras, and that the pattern of sales would be:

	Sales in units
Year 1	3,000
Year 2	7,000
Year 3	4,000
Year 4	1,000

The company's cost of capital is assumed to be 20 per cent per annum.

Making careful use of the above information, calculate the NPV of the project. Ignore taxation. Make and state appropriate assumptions where necessary.

8 Soderby plc has £10m of 10 per cent debentures that are due to be redeemed at par in five years' time. Their current market value is £98, and corporation tax is 30 per cent. What is the cost of the debt capital?

9 The market value of Chipperby's ordinary shares yesterday, immediately after paying a dividend of 40 pence, was £12. Dividends are expected to grow at the rate of 5 per cent per annum.

a   Calculate the cost of Chipperby's equity capital using the dividend growth model.

b   The return on ordinary shares in recent years has averaged 11 per cent; the risk-free interest rate at present is 3 per cent; and Chipperby's beta is 0.75. Calculate the cost of Chipperby's equity capital using the CAPM.

 ## Assessment questions

1   How is the payback period calculated? Why is it widely used although it can suggest wrong decisions?

2   The Leongwei Company decided that there would be no additional purchases of fixed assets unless they had been subject to investment appraisal and showed a positive NPV when discounted at 10 per cent. The policy was implemented five years ago, but the company's return on capital employed is still only 7 per cent per annum.

Explain the apparent inconsistency.

3   A project with an initial cost of £200,000 is expected to make profits of £44,000 per annum for five years, at the end of which it will have a scrap value of £20,000. Calculate:

a   average annual depreciation charge;

b   average annual cash flows;

c   payback period;

d   total profits made during the five years;

e   return on initial investment;

f   return on average investment;

g   NPV assuming a cost of capital of 20 per cent;

h   internal rate of return.

4   Respirer Ltd is a small company that specializes in the manufacture of electronic devices for surveillance purposes. Recently it has been involved in producing devices to detect drugs, and the presence of live animals or humans, in import and export consignments. It has designed and produced a prototype of a device that it is calling the 'Kensington' and that can be worn by lorry drivers.

A report from a large firm of management consultants suggests that in order to produce the device the company will need to set up a new production line at a cost of £600,000, and that an old assembly shop could be used. The assembly shop originally cost £500,000 and depreciation on it of £350,000 has been charged, but it has not been used for a number of years. The company was planning to sell it for £120,000, but the consultants' report recommends that it is used to produce the new device; modifications to the workshop for this purpose will cost £80,000.

The expected costs and selling price per unit of the Kensington are as follows:

	£	£
Selling price		110
Materials	18	
Labour	12	
Variable overheads	15	
General fixed overheads	8	
Interest	4	57
Profit		53

Anticipated sales in units are 5,000 in year 1; 10,000 in year 2; 16,000 in year 3; 12,000 in year 4; and 7,000 in year 5.

Additional working capital requirements will be £250,000, which will be recovered at the end of the project. An initial advertising campaign costing £400,000 will be required at the beginning of the project; continuing marketing costs will be £130,000 per annum.

It cost £80,000 to produce the prototype and those costs have been paid; the consultants' report cost £120,000, but those costs have not yet been paid.

The company's cost of capital is 15 per cent.

Making careful use of the above information, calculate the NPV of the project. Ignore taxation. Make and state appropriate assumptions where necessary.

5 The Bitchwood Company is considering two alternative investment proposals, details of which are as follows:

		Proposal 1 £	Proposal 2 £
Initial investment		100,000	120,000
Cash inflow	Year 1	35,000	30,000
	Year 2	30,000	30,000
	Year 3	30,000	35,000
	Year 4	25,000	50,000
	Year 5	15,000	40,000

Assume that the amount of the initial investment will be depreciated on a straight line basis over five years, and that there will be no residual value.

a Calculate for each proposal:
  i payback period;
  ii average annual profits;
  iii return on initial investment;
  iv NPV using discounted cash flow and assuming a cost of capital of 10 per cent;
  v internal rate of return.

b Which of the two projects would you recommend, and why?

6 Redderby plc has £12m of 11.43 per cent debentures that are due to be redeemed at a premium of 5 per cent in four years' time. Their current market value is £104, and corporation tax is 30 per cent. What is the cost of the debt capital?

7 The market value of Presterby's ordinary shares yesterday, immediately after paying a dividend of 15 pence, was £6. Dividends are expected to grow at the rate of 8 per cent per annum.

a Calculate the cost of Chipperby's equity capital using the dividend growth model.

b The return on ordinary shares in recent years has averaged 13 per cent; the risk-free interest rate at present is 3.5 per cent; and Chipperby's beta is 1.2. Calculate the cost of Chipperby's equity capital using the CAPM.

Group activities and discussion questions

1 'The acceptability of an investment proposal depends on the company's cost of capital; a project that is acceptable to one company may not be acceptable to another.'

   'Accurate assessments of cost of capital are not possible; choosing a figure of between 10 per cent and 15 per cent is a reasonable approximation.'

   Explain, contrast and attempt to reconcile these statements.

2 With many well-publicized projects it seems that proper investment appraisal techniques were not applied, were not possible or appropriate, or were ignored. Discuss this statement with reference to projects such as:

   a the Millennium Dome;

   b fees paid by telecommunications companies for third-generation licences;

   c the building for the Scottish Assembly in Edinburgh;

   d the building of Wembley Stadium or the 2012 Olympic sites.

3 To what extent is the proper use of investment appraisal techniques likely to stop the development of projects that are for the benefit of society?

4 Post-investment appraisal is essential to ensure that a company's investment appraisal techniques have been properly applied. But it is likely to reveal some uncomfortable facts. Discuss.

5 Sophisticated investment appraisal techniques are no substitute for sound judgement (or good luck). Discuss.

6 Effective managers usually succeed in getting approval for the projects that they want. A knowledge of the company's investment appraisal procedures enables them to produce figures that ensure that projects will be approved. The existence of sound investment appraisal procedures does not ensure that projected results are actually delivered. Discuss.

Accounting in context

Discuss what implications capital investment appraisal techniques will have had on the investment decisions taken by GlaxoSmithKline referred to in the following article appearing in the press.

GlaxoSmithKline to build £350m plant in Cumbria

Drug company GlaxoSmithKline today confirmed that it will invest £350m in building its first new British manufacturing site in almost four decades, revealing that the plant will be based in Cumbria.

By Rachel Cooper

Britain's biggest drug maker first announced the plan in 2009 after Labour's decision to introduce a "patent box" to promote research and development, offering a 10pc tax rate on income arising from UK patents.

When the Coalition reiterated its commitment to the policy in 2010, Glaxo said it would invest £500m in Britain, creating about 1,000 jobs.

After Wednesday's Budget confirmed that the patent box would be brought in from 2013, Glaxo announced that it will build a new plant in Ulverston. It will also invest in its two Scottish manufacturing plants and sites in Hertfordshire and County Durham.

Depending on "continued improvements in the environment for innovation in the UK", Glaxo

▶

added it could double its investment in Ulverston to about £700m.

Glaxo has always said that the investment is conditional on the patent box, indicating that if that tax cut was removed, it would reconsider its decision.

Coming just a day after the Budget, Government figures hailed the announcement as an endorsement of their plans to boost industry. Chancellor George Osborne told BBC's *Today* programme that Glaxo had opted to invest here "because the Budget has changed its view of Britain".

But Labour also claimed credit for the move, given they first introduced the idea of a patent box. Glaxo stressed that it had supported the proposal under both governments.

Source: *The Telegraph*, 22 March 2012.

References and further reading

Arnold, G. (2008) *Corporate Financial Management* (4th edn.). Upper Saddle River, NJ: FT Prentice Hall.

Brealey, R., S. Myers and F. Allen (2010) *Principles of Corporate Finance–Global Edition*. New York: McGraw-Hill.

Brealey, R.A., S.C. Myers and A.J. Marcus (2011) *Fundamentals of Corporate Finance* (7th edn.). New York: McGraw-Hill.

Das, S. (2012) *Extreme Money: The Masters of the Universe and the Cult of Risk*. Harlow: Pearson.

Drury, C. (2008) *Management and Cost Accounting* (7th edn.). Andover: Cengage Learning.

Vernimmen, P. et al. (2009) *Corporate Finance: Theory and Practice* (2nd edn.). Chichester: Wiley.

Watson, D. and A. Head (2009) *Corporate Finance Principles and Practice*. Harlow: Pearson.

Online **LearningCentre**

When you have read this chapter, log on to the Online Learning Centre website at *www.mcgraw-hill.co.uk/textbooks/leiwy* to explore chapter-by-chapter test questions, further reading and more online study tools.

Chapter 15

Budgetary Planning and Control

Chapter contents

✓ Learning objectives

After studying this chapter you will be able to:

- ✓ Define budgets and budgetary control and explain how they operate
- ✓ Explain and illustrate the use of budgets and control information
- ✓ Understand and demonstrate the use of flexible budgets
- ✓ Explain the role of cash budgets and produce and interpret practical examples
- ✓ Describe the main advantages of operating budgetary control
- ✓ Critically assess the operation of budgetary control in practice
- ✓ Understand the role and limitations of ZBB and of PPBS

15.1 Introduction

We all start off with some sort of plans in mind, however vague, and hope that they will come to fruition and that we fulfil our dreams (or some of them). Then, on a regular basis, we will compare what is actually happening in our lives with what we hoped for. Perhaps we find that all is as we had hoped; or we change our plans; or we decide what we need to do in order to fulfil our dreams, or attain our objectives. Some small businesses may operate in this way. But a well-managed business defines and quantifies its objectives, prepares detailed plans, and systematically compares the results that are actually achieved with those that were planned. Budgetary control does this in a systematic way and this chapter outlines how this is done in practice. Some of the difficulties in practice are discussed and two alternative approaches (ZBB and PPBS) are introduced.

15.2 Budgets and Budgetary Control

A starting point for preparing plans or budgets for next year is to look at the actual financial statements for this year, and estimate what is going to happen next year, probably adding a bit for inflation, and a bit for growth.

In Example 15.1 the directors of Daniel Dhoon are forecasting a 12 per cent increase in sales, and an increase in profits. This is to be achieved by instituting a delivery service. Unfortunately, this will lead to a substantial increase in distribution costs; it will also require the purchase of additional non-current assets (such as vans); and current assets (inventories and receivables) are likely to increase. Although a modest increase in net profit is expected, the increase in assets and equity is much greater. The end result is that return on equity will fall from 3 per cent to 2.5 per cent. This may be a reasonable estimate of what could happen, but it is not a satisfactory plan or budget.

Example 15.1 does not really show a budget. It looks as if someone has been asked to prepare financial statements on the basis that sales will increase by 12 per cent as a result of buying a vehicle for around £50,000, and spending £40,000 or so on employing a driver, petrol and other delivery costs. As a plan it is not satisfactory because it does not attain a particular objective: return on equity will fall instead of increase. It may be seen as a *draft* budget, providing a basis for revision. It can be changed again and again until it is more like a plan that can be implemented and which will succeed in increasing the return on equity.

Key words in the definition of a budget are that it is prepared and *approved* before the period to which it relates and that it is a plan intended to achieve *a given objective*.[1] There could even be several objectives, such as achieving a particular amount of earnings per share, reduction in borrowings or increase in sales. The point is that management must have approved of and be committed to the plan to ensure that it is implemented.

In revising the draft, consideration could[2] be given to the following:

1 Could the vehicle be hired instead of buying it? That would reduce the amount of capital employed, and, in turn, the return achieved.
2 Could the delivery function be outsourced?
3 Is an appropriate charge being made for delivery?

---

[1] If a budget is to be prepared and approved prior to (e.g.) year 8 (probably in November or December year 7), there is a problem in that the actual results for the whole of year 7 will not be available until after the end of the year. This is usually overcome by using actual results for January to October, and estimated results for November and December of year 7.

[2] It might be useful to start by applying and interpreting most of the set of ratios given in Chapter 4.

Example 15.1

Preparing budgeted income statement and statement of financial position

The directors of the Daniel Dhoon Company were not satisfied with results in recent years: growth had been sluggish, and return on equity was unsatisfactory. They planned to expand sales by starting a delivery service in year 8 in order to increase the return on equity. The draft budget for year 8, together with the actual results for year 7, are shown below.

Income statement for the year	Actual results Year 7 £	Forecast results Year 8 £	
1 Sales	400,000	448,000	12% increase
2 Cost of sales	300,000	318,000	
3 Gross profit	100,000	130,000	25% gross profit ratio, increasing to 29%
4 Distribution costs	(30,000)	(58,300)	
5 Administrative expenses	(53,000)	(54,000)	
6 Operating profit	17,000	17,700	
7 Finance expense	(8,000)	(8,000)	
8 Profit before taxation	9,000	9,700	
9 Taxation	(3,000)	(3,100)	
10 Profit for year	6,000	6,600	
Statement of financial position as at year end			
11 Non-current assets, net book value	270,000	315,000	
12 Current assets	60,000	85,000	
Total assets	330,000	400,000	
13 Current liabilities	30,000	36,000	
14 8% debentures	100,000	100,000	
15 Equity	200,000	264,000	
Total liabilities and equity	330,000	400,000	
Return on equity		2.5%	Line 10 as a % of line 15

4 Could the increase in current assets be held down[3] by restricting the amount customers are allowed to owe, or by reducing inventory levels?

5 Are there other ways of increasing sales that would require less (capital and revenue) expenditure?

A budget may be defined as:

> *A plan, quantified in monetary terms, prepared and approved prior to a defined period of time, usually showing planned income to be generated and/or expenditure to be incurred during that period, and the capital to be employed to attain a given objective.*

There is also a need to check if the draft budget is realistic, particularly in relation to sales and cash. It is likely that starting a delivery service will increase sales, but it is not clear why the gross profit

---

[3] Management of working capital is dealt with in Chapter 12.

ratio is expected to increase and this would need to be explained. Perhaps they expect lower buying prices because of bulk buying, but their estimates suggest a very optimistic increase in the gross profit ratio for a modest 5 per cent increase in sales. Perhaps they expect to be able to charge higher prices (but they need to be careful in view of their sluggish growth). Or perhaps their delivery service will concentrate on products with a higher margin. A detailed sales budget – showing planned sales for all the different product lines – would help to produce more realistic plans.

It is also necessary to know when and how the cash would become available, particularly for the purchase of the van. A detailed cash budget is required showing the receipts and payments expected for each month, and the balances available, or the overdraft (or other additional funding) that would be required.

After doing all the detailed work, it is possible that management would adopt the 'forecast' shown in Example 15.1 on the basis that it is worth accepting a short-term reduction in return on equity as a step towards improving sales and profitability in future years once the delivery service has been fully established. It is more likely, however, that management would require some modifications to the estimates before accepting it as the plan designed to achieve their objectives for the following year.

A full budgetary control system requires a whole set of different budgets, as shown in Section 15.3.

After the budget has been adopted as the plan that the organization intends to implement, it is necessary to monitor the actual results achieved each month.[4] This is the idea of 'control'. Usually the actual results achieved will be different from what was planned – that's life! Perhaps some sales and costs will be higher than planned, others will be lower, and overall the changes do not matter very much. But some results may be seriously out of line. In Example 15.1 the new delivery service may be a huge success – more than one van can cope with – and they will have to reconsider their options.[5] Or the service may be a failure with nowhere near enough additional sales to justify the costs. They may consider additional marketing initiatives that will help them to achieve their plans; or they could abandon their delivery service, or find other ways of doing it.[6] Control information provides information about *actual* results; these are compared with the plan; and where there are significant differences, action must be taken: either the budgets are changed, or additional effort has to be put in to achieve them.

Budgetary control may be defined as:

> *The establishment of budgets relating the responsibilities of executives to the requirements of a policy, and the continuous comparison of actual with budgeted results, either to secure by individual action the objective of that policy, or to provide a basis for its revision.*

A key part of the definition is that specified managers should be responsible for implementing particular parts of the budget. There is not much point in establishing plans and just hoping they will come to fruition. Someone must be responsible. In Example 15.1, someone would be responsible for implementing the delivery service – and would be 'given a budget' – an allocation of what they were authorized to spend. There would also be someone responsible for monitoring the sales and costs of the delivery service.[7]

It is important that the results that are actually achieved are compared with the original plan or budget to see if the business is on course. Where actual results are different from what was planned, some corrective action is required.

In addition to a budgeted income statement and statement of financial position, it is usually important to produce a cash budget; often this is required by the business's bankers who want to see when and how their loans and overdrafts can be repaid. Cash budgets are dealt with in Section 15.4.

---

[4] Or more frequently.

[5] Perhaps a second van; or making a delivery charge to reduce demand.

[6] Such as outsourcing.

[7] The delivery service could be cost centre, profit centre or investment centre in its own right.

A full and formal system of budgetary control involves the production of a set of detailed budgets to include all the business's activities and which all culminate in a budgeted income statement and a budgeted statement of financial position, and a cash budget. Managers in each area of the business are involved in setting the budgets. The system is supposed to express the intentions of top management, detailed as a financial plan, with a commitment from all managers to achieve the results expected.

15.3 Implementing Budgetary Control

Where budgets are used for planning and controlling a large and complex organization, different budgets have to be produced for each part of the organization, and for each major activity. Many people are involved in the process of setting budgets, and subsequently in dealing with the control information. Often it is necessary to produce a *budget manual*, specifying and standardizing how the budgets are to be produced. This will specify the various budgets that are used in compiling the *master budget*.

The starting point in producing the master budget is the sales budget. It is necessary to know the likely level of sales in order to know what direct materials need to be purchased, how much labour to employ, the amount of machinery, overheads, and so on. A typical set of budgets is shown below. In a large organization there may need to be budgets for each of a number of different product groups, and/or for a number of different geographic areas. Different managers will be responsible for producing (and later for monitoring the implementation of) each budget; managers are generally dependent on information from other budgets to plan their activities.

1 Sales budget: showing budgeted sales for each month.

2 Finished goods inventories and production budget: once the level of sales has been planned it is necessary to plan how much should be produced, making allowance for any inventories or finished goods.

3 Direct materials usage budget: once the level of production has been planned, it is necessary to plan what materials should be purchased (again making allowance for any inventories of direct materials).

4 Direct labour budget: obviously this is dependent on the planned level of production.

5 Production overhead budget: this is partly dependent on the planned level of production, but is also influenced by other factors, such as the purchase of better production facilities (capital expenditure budget).

6 Distribution cost budget.

7 Administration expense budget.

8 Budgeted income statement: all the above listed budgets are needed before a budgeted income statement can be produced.

9 Budgeted statement of financial position: even when all the above have been produced there is still not enough information to produce a budgeted statement of financial position. It is necessary, first, to produce the budgets listed below.

10 Capital expenditure budget: additional capital expenditure may be planned if there is to be an increase in production, or to reduce costs or improve quality. The capital expenditure budget will also include capital expenditure in relation to costs that are not directly linked to production, such as distribution costs and administrative expenses.

11 Cash budget: showing receipts and payments of cash, and the resulting balances, for each month (or more often).

This may seem a lot, but in a manufacturing organization they are necessary. There may be additional budgets, such as a budgeted cash flow statement, and a research and development budget. Many of the above budgets will be made up of a number of departmental budgets such as those for advertising or the human resources departments. The definition of budgetary control (given above) notes that budgets are 'relating the responsibilities of executives to the requirements of a policy'. In many organizations there is a separate departmental budget for each departmental manager. Ideally, this should detail what each manager is expected to achieve; in practice it often does little more than show how much money they are authorized to spend.

A *master budget*, or *summary budget*, is prepared from, and summarizes, all the other budgets. This is usually taken to mean the budgeted income statement and budgeted statement of financial position. It might be tempting to include the cash budget as part of the master budget; but the single figure for cash/bank on the statement of financial position cannot be properly produced without first producing a cash budget.

Budgeted figures are typically shown for each month. Sometimes the whole set of budgets is produced once a year, perhaps in November for the year beginning two months later in January. With *annual* budgeting, new budgets are not then produced until the following November. But many organizations produce *rolling budgets*. This means that the budget is produced for the following 12 months; then, each month, another month is added (and the old month taken out). Typically, in November year 7 the budget is produced for the year January to December year 8. In December year 7 the budget is produced for the 12 months February year 8 to January year 9. In January year 8 the budget is produced for the 12 months March year 8 to February year 9. In this way there are always budgets for the following 12 months.

A *fixed budget* assumes a given level of production and sales. The level may be different for each period during the year (many businesses are seasonal; and there may be plans for growth). There could be revisions to a fixed budget if circumstances change. But a fixed budget is quite different from a flexible budget.

One of the problems with fixed budgets is that actual cost figures are likely to be very different from budget, especially if output increases significantly. In Illustration 15.1 actual sales are 20 per cent up on budget, and, as we would expect, costs have increased. But not all costs should increase by 20 per cent: there may be some increases or decreases in efficiency; but some overheads (such as managers' salaries, or rents payable for premises) are 'fixed' – they do not increase as production increases. It is useful to separate 'fixed' costs from 'variable' costs, such as direct materials and direct wages, which are expected to increase in line with the volume of production. In this way we can produce a *flexed budget*, as shown in Illustration 15.2, using the principles of *flexible budgeting*.

A *flexible budget* may be most practicable where the levels of production and sales fluctuate a lot, and are hard to predict. The fixed budget shown in Illustration 15.1 shows that profit has increased to £15,000 compared with £8,000 shown in the budget. But this is not due to efficiency. Sales have increased by 20 per cent, and direct material and labour costs can be expected to increase by about 20 per cent. But overhead costs should increase by a smaller proportion because part of overheads are 'fixed': they do not increase as production increases.

In this instance it has been assumed that half of the overhead costs are fixed, and half are variable. In other words, when sales and production increase by 20 per cent, it is expected that overheads

ILLUSTRATION 15.1 A fixed budget		
January Year 9	Budget	Actual
	£000	£000
Sales	100	120
Direct materials	30	35
Direct labour	20	25
Production overheads	30	32
Administration and distribution overheads	12	13
Total costs	92	105
Profit	8	15

January Year 9	Budget £000	Flexed budget £000	Actual £000
Sales	100	120	120
Direct materials	30	36	35
Direct labour	20	24	25
Production overheads	30	33	32
Administration and distribution overheads	12	13.2	13
Total costs	92	106.2	105
Profit	8	13.8	15

ILLUSTRATION 15.2 A flexible budget

will increase by 10 per cent, and the 'flexed budget' column in Illustration 15.2 has been prepared on that basis. When sales increase by 20 per cent, total costs are expected to increase from £92,000 to £106,200. In this instance efficiency has increased: most costs have increased by less than the flexible budget would suggest (although direct labour costs have gone up by more than 20 per cent, indicating some decrease in efficiency).

A simple examination of the fixed budget in Illustration 15.2 shows that all costs have increased; but sales have increased, and so has profit. It appears that everything is alright. But such control information is not very useful. There is no indication of any increases or decreases in efficiency, which are revealed by using a flexible budget.

Another disadvantage of using a fixed budget is that overheads are charged out to different jobs and products on the basis of the original fixed budget. In this instance direct labour was originally budgeted at £20,000, and production overheads at £30,000. If absorption costing is used, production overheads could be charged to products at the rate of 150 per cent of direct labour. This means that the amount *charged* for overheads increases in line with the increase in output;[8] but the amount of overheads *incurred* would increase by a smaller proportion. In Illustration 15.1 the amount of production overhead incurred was £32,000, but the amount charged to particular jobs would be (150 per cent of £25,000[9] =) £37,500. Production overheads of £5,500 would be 'over-recovered'. Most of this problem is eliminated if marginal costing is used.

15.4 Cash Budgets

Most of us have some sort of cash budget in mind for our own personal receipts and payments. We like to know that each month there is enough coming in to meet the payments that we plan to make. Or we may plan it the other way around: we will spend no more than the cash that will be available to us. Failure to plan properly can lead to unexpected overdrafts and credit card borrowing with high charges.

It is a similar story for companies. They need to plan their monthly[10] receipts and payments for at least the next year. It may be that a company is very profitable, and expanding rapidly, but it may not be producing enough cash to meet its monthly commitments. Some companies make substantial profits, but at the year end have less cash than they had at the beginning of the year. Other companies may not be particularly profitable, but they generate lots of cash. Comparing a company's budgeted income statement with its cash budget for the coming year shows how its monthly cash flows differ

---

[8] Or, more accurately in this instance, in line with the increase in direct labour costs.

[9] The direct labour cost incurred.

[10] Or weekly or even daily.

from its monthly profits or losses, and why. The budgeted income statement gives a good indication of the viability of the business. The cash budget shows whether it is likely to have cash surpluses (which it may wish to invest); or whether there is going to be insufficient cash to get by. If a cash shortage problem is identified in advance, ways around the problem can be planned before it becomes a crisis. This can be seen by examining Example 15.2, the Holly Day Company.

 **Example 15.2**

Cash budget

Question:

The Holly Day Company manufactures seasonal goods for holiday-makers and supplies them to retailers in many seaside resorts. There has been little change in its seasonal sales patterns in recent years. Sales start off at £15,000 a month in January, and increase by £15,000 a month until they peak at £120,000 a month in August; they fall to £90,000 a month in September; £30,000 a month in October, and then to £15,000 a month in November and December. Customers pay for the goods, on average, two months after the sales are made.

The materials are bought and used in the month before sales take place; they are treated as an expense in the month that the finished goods to which they relate are sold; and they are paid for one month after purchase (i.e. in the month that the sale takes place). The cost of materials for making the goods amounts to one-third of the selling price.

There is a basic labour force costing £4,000 a month in October–January each year. This increases to £6,000 a month in February, and £8,000 a month in March. The labour costs in the busy time of the year are £16,000 a month, from April to September inclusive.

The only other expense is depreciation that amounts to £3,000 a month. One of the machines is getting towards the end of its life and will be replaced by a new one, costing £60,000, which will be paid for in June. Depreciation on the new machine will be charged at 20 per cent per annum on a straight-line basis. The old machine will be sold for £15,000 (which is its net book value) at the end of the year (in December).

Taxation of £50,000 is payable in March, and dividends of £55,000 will be paid in May.

Required:

a Prepare the income statement for the coming year, showing sales, expenses and profit for each month, and in total.

b Prepare the cash budget for the coming year, showing receipts and payments for each month; the net cash surplus or deficit for the month; and the bank balance at the end of each month. Assume that the business starts the year with £50,000 in the bank.

Answer:

a Budgeted income statement

Sales	15	30	45	60	75	90	105	120	90	30	15	15	690
Expenses													
Materials	5	10	15	20	25	30	35	40	30	10	5	5	230
Wages	4	6	8	16	16	16	16	16	16	4	4	4	126
Depreciation	3	3	3	3	3	4	4	4	4	4	4	4	43
	12	19	26	39	44	50	55	60	50	18	13	13	399
Profit	3	11	19	21	31	40	50	60	40	12	2	2	291

Continued >>>

Example 15.2

Continued >>>

b Cash budget of the Holly Day Company

	£000 Jan	£000 Feb	£000 Mar	£000 Apr	£000 May	£000 Jun	£000 Jul	£000 Aug	£000 Sep	£000 Oct	£000 Nov	£000 Dec	£000 Total
Receipts													
From debtors	15	15	15	30	45	60	75	90	105	120	90	30	690
Sale of machine	—	—	—	—	—	—	—	—	—	—	—	15	15
	15	15	15	30	45	60	75	90	105	120	90	45	705
Payments													
Materials	5	5	10	15	20	25	30	35	40	30	10	5	230
Wages	4	6	8	16	16	16	16	16	16	4	4	4	126
New machine						60							60
Taxation			50										50
Dividends	—	—		—	55	—		—		—	—	—	55
	9	11	68	31	91	101	46	51	56	34	14	9	521
Net receipts or (Deficit)	6	4	(53)	(1)	(46)	(41)	29	39	49	86	76	36	184
Opening balance	50	56	60	7	6	(40)	(81)	(52)	(13)	36	122	198	
Closing balance	56	60	7	6	(40)	(81)	(52)	(13)	36	122	198	234	234

A cash budget shows all the (planned or expected future) receipts and payments of an organization, typically on a monthly basis for the next year.

The receipts figure includes all cash that comes in directly from cash sales. It also includes receipts from customers (trade receivables); they usually come in a month or two after the sales are made, so the figure is different from that shown on an income statement. In Example 15.2 it was assumed that all sales were on credit. There may be other receipts such as money that comes in from dividends, interest, rent, commission and royalties. The cash budget will show the money as a receipt in the month when the money is expected. An income statement shows it in the month in which it is earned (or it 'accrues'), regardless of when the cash is received.

Some receipts do not appear on an income statement. These include receipts from issuing shares or debentures; borrowing money; and sales of non-current assets.[11]

---

[11] The profit arising on the sale of a non-current asset is included in the income statement. That is the differences between the net book value of the asset, and its sale proceeds.

The payments figure includes all the money that it is expected will be paid out. Payments for purchases are usually made a month or so after the purchases are made (and recorded for income statement purposes). The cash budget also shows payments for expenses that will also appear on the income statement. With most expenses the payment is made after the expense is incurred. Some expenses (such as rent, and perhaps advertising) are paid in advance. Again, in the cash budget, it is the period in which the payment is actually made that matters. In the income statement it is when the expense is incurred that matters.

The cash budget also shows when tax and dividends are to be paid. These items also appear on the income statement, but, again, the timing might be different. A company typically shows its tax charge on the income statement of one year, but the cash is actually paid in the following year. Similarly, a company typically decides on their final[12] dividend in one year and the cash is paid out in the following year.

Some payments do not appear at all on an income statement. Cash has to be paid out to acquire non-current assets (fixed assets), and there may be payments to buy investments such as shares in other businesses, and to repay loans.

A cash budget shows the change in the cash balance each month. There is an opening balance at the beginning of the month. Total receipts and total payments are calculated to give a figure for net receipts (or payments) for the month. Net receipts are added to the balance at the beginning of the month to show the closing balance for the month. That then becomes the opening balance for the next month.

Figures can, of course, be the other way around. If the budget shows an overdraft at the beginning of the month, net receipts for the month will reduce the overdraft.

The budget should also show the total increase, or decrease, in cash expected during the year. This will be different from the budgeted profit figure, and it is useful to compare the two to see how, and why, the profit figure for the year differs from the cash flow figure. This is illustrated in this chapter with the Holly Day Company (Example 15.2) and with Rachel's business (Self-testing question 6), and with Judas (Assessment question 5).

15.5 Advantages of Operating Budgetary Control Systems

Budgetary control (like many management techniques) is sometimes presented as if it is a panacea, a solution to all the problems of management. If it is operated well it has a number of functions and can certainly improve the management of an organization in a number of ways:

1 *Objectives* – It ensures that the objectives of an organization are defined, quantified and set down in plans in such a way that managers (and perhaps all staff) know what they are supposed to be achieving and the contribution that they are expected to make towards the attainment of the company's objectives.

2 *Limiting factors* – The budgeting process should ensure that any limiting factors are identified. Often it is the amount that the company is able to sell that is the limiting factor, and production volumes and expenses have to be planned on the basis of likely sales. But there could be different limiting factors, such as production capacity; where this is identified ways may be planned to overcome it, such as increasing capacity through shift working, or additional capital expenditure; or outsourcing. Alternatively, it may be possible to increase selling prices to reduce demand, and redirect the advertising budget to emphasize the quality of the higher-priced product. Availability of funding may also be a limiting factor: when the cash budget and the master budget have been prepared it may be that the company cannot afford to do what all the other budgets have suggested, and additional funding may be planned. The point is that, if limiting factors are identified a month or two before the year begins, there is a good chance of overcoming them in advance, which is better than waiting for a crisis to hit.

---

[12] Companies typically pay an interim dividend part way through the year, and a final divided after the end of the year.

3   *Authorizing* – Departmental managers are typically given budgets *authorizing* the amounts they can spend. This enables them to plan their expenditure in a systematic way, and avoids the need to seek permission for each item.

4   *Responsibility* – Budgetary control systems can help to define what each manager, or budget holder, is responsible for. Advertising managers are not just allowed to spend a given sum of money; they are expected to achieve a given level of sales. Human resources managers are not just allowed to spend money on recruitment: they are expected to ensure that the staff specified in the budget are actually recruited and in the jobs that were planned.

5   *Delegation* – Budgetary control facilitates the delegation of a great deal of responsibility to managers at different levels. The board of directors is usually seen as being responsible for the company achieving its objectives; but the overall objectives need to be broken down into individual chunks of responsibility, tasks and objectives that individual managers are expected to achieve. The board should know that managers are doing what their budgets specify, and leave them to get on with it.

6   *Management by exception* – Senior management should concentrate on the exceptions. They do not need to scrutinize piles of detailed reports for every part of the business and try to judge whether or not things are going well. Control information should highlight where actual results are significantly different from plan – the 'exceptions' – and where management need to take action. Where everything is going more or less according to plan, senior management can leave well alone. They can concentrate on managing the exceptions.

7   *Control* – It is possible to 'control' an organization only if there are plans or expectations of results to be achieved. Budgetary control systematically provides 'control' information comparing actual results with planned results.

8   *Motivation* – In some organizations employees do not have much motivation, especially where they do not know what is expected of them. Budgetary control should establish clearly what the objectives and plans are for each part of the organization. This can help to motivate managers and others to do their best to ensure that plans are implemented successfully. Budgetary control establishes targets and, provided these are realistic, they can improve motivation. Evidence shows that budgets should be 'tight but attainable'. If a car salesman who sold 100 cars last year is given a budget of 170 this year, he is likely to be utterly demotivated. But if he has a budget to sell 110 cars this year, he might consider this difficult but achievable and is likely to 'give it a go'.

9   *Performance evaluation* – There are often incentive schemes and bonuses designed to motivate employees to improve their performance. Budgets provide a useful basis for measuring performance so that good performance can be rewarded.

10   *Communication and co-ordination* – These should be improved. It is necessary for all parts of the organization to know what the plans are. It would cause problems if the sales team was busy securing orders that the company could not fulfil; or if the volume of production was being increased while the labour force was being reduced, and purchases of direct materials cut back. It is necessary for managers in every part of the organization to know what the plans are for the organization as a whole.

Much of the above could be summarized in a single word: planning. Preparing budgets, and operating a system providing regular feedback that compares actual results with budgeted results is essential for managing and controlling an organization. It can also help to achieve the benefits listed above.

15.6 Problems of Budgetary Control in Practice

In practice budgetary control may not be as successful as intended and there are many problems in implementing and operating successful budgetary control systems.

1 *Level of performance* – Realistic financial plans are needed to ensure that sufficient cash and other resources are available to meet the expected level of sales; and the budgeted level of sales should not be exaggerated, otherwise the organization would be in danger of arranging for too much labour and materials to be available, and resources will be wasted if the capacity that has been planned is not used. But if the budget is also intended to motivate staff, it may be necessary to set targets based on ambitious levels of performance, even if they are not likely to be achieved. Budgets that work in motivating staff are probably not a suitable basis for planning resources.

2 *Participation* – It is usually claimed that a budgetary control system works better if staff who are responsible for implementing particular parts of the plan are involved in establishing the plan. Where managers think that plans are realistic, and have been involved in establishing them, they are more likely to identify with them. But it may be difficult to get some managers to participate, especially those with little understanding of finance.

When a set of budgets has been produced, with effective participation, they are then put together as a master budget, which, it is hoped, will achieve the objectives that are established by the board of directors. Unfortunately, a set of budgets that results from extensive participation often does not show the results required; the board may decide that the profits shown are inadequate, and decide that all the budgets need to be revised. In particular, it might seek to reduce expenditure. All those managers who had conscientiously participated in determining what levels of expenditure are necessary may suddenly find that their proposed budgets are arbitrarily cut by a fixed percentage. This undermines the effectiveness of their participation, and may alienate some managers from the budgeting process.

3 *Reward schemes* – Where budgets are used as a basis for determining staff bonuses, promotion or other rewards, there are particular problems with participation and setting an appropriate level of performance. When sales managers are invited to participate in setting their budgets, if they think they can achieve sales of £5 m a year, they may keep that opinion quiet, and advocate a budget of only £4.5 m a year, because they know that they can easily achieve that level, and be rewarded accordingly. Similarly, advertising managers, who reckon they need an annual budget of £100,000 to achieve the budgeted sales level, are likely to press for budgets of perhaps £120,000 to make their life easier. In this way, where participation is encouraged, managers are inclined to build in *budgetary slack* so that it is fairly easy for them to achieve what the budgets require.

4 *Competition for resources* – Although the budgeting process is intended to improve co-operation and co-ordination within an organization, managers often find themselves competing for resources. It is only to be expected that heads of departments, such as advertising, human resources and research and development, want to maximize the resources available to them. Sometimes it could happen that all managers sit down and discuss idealistically how much the organization really needs to spend on each activity, and the resulting budget will be what is 'best' for the organization. More often there is likely to be some overall limit on what can be spent on these different activities, and managers will find themselves competing with each other to maximize their share, with a generous budget that authorizes how much they can spend in the coming year. Those managers who are most confident in dealing with finance may be the winners – perhaps at the expense of the organization as a whole.

5 *Incremental budgeting* – The easiest way to produce a budget is simply to base it on the previous year's actual results, and add a bit for inflation, and a bit more for growth. But this is *estimating* what is likely to happen; it is not *planning* to achieve desired results. It is likely to produce budgets that are easily achievable but this 'easy' approach is not best designed to help the organization to achieve its objectives. Sometimes managers are mainly motivated by empire building and ensuring that the budget allocated to them increases each year.

6 *A paperwork exercise* – Unless senior management enthusiastically endorse the budgets, and are determined to check that actual results are in line with plans, budgetary control can sometimes be little more than a paperwork exercise; something that the accounts department produces once a year, and of which no one takes much notice. This is particularly true where managers have little

understanding of or training in finance. Each month, vast quantities of control information are produced that most managers do not understand or use or care about. It is too much information, and may be too late to be of much use. Often managers produce their own 'control' information, and argue that the 'official' information is neither accurate nor relevant. A management account-ant has to be very able and determined to operate a budgetary control system effectively.

7 *Tendency to spend up to budget* – Where managers have a budget for some sort of expenditure, they sometimes treat it as if it were a bag of money that they have been given to spend within the year. Often, if they underspend their budget, that money is 'lost' to them, and they are likely to be given a smaller budget for the following year. Where managers are more interested in empire building than in doing what is best for the organization, they will tend to spend all that they can, and to seek a bigger budget allocation for the following year. In organizations where the year end is 31 March there is often a rush to spend money during February to ensure that the budget is used up by the end of the year, and that the budget will not be cut for the following year. Many suppliers expect such a rush from public sector organizations before their year end. Some find important conferences to go to in sunny climates, order large amounts of stationery or spend money on repairs (like repainting the inside of cupboards) just before the end of the financial year. The problem can be reduced if managers are allowed to 'carry forward' unspent balances to the following year. It is, however, more difficult to eliminate an empire-building attitude.

8 *An end in itself* – There is a danger that managers are expected 'only' to achieve what the budget shows, and that opportunities for more profitable activities are ignored because they are not in the budget. An unexpected, but potentially profitable, sales enquiry from China may be ignored because there is no money in the budget for the necessary travelling expenses. Similarly, an opportunity to take over a competitor at a knock-down price may be missed because it was not in the budget. Budgetary control can play a valuable role in helping an organization to achieve its objectives, but once budgets are approved they should not be set in stone: there must always be some flexibility when opportunities arise.

9 *Defining objectives* – For simplicity in setting budgets, a single objective may be assumed, such as achieving a given level of earnings, or return on capital employed. But often organizations have multiple and even conflicting objectives, such as to achieve sales growth (which might imply low selling prices), and to improve the quality of their products (which might imply higher selling prices). Sometimes different managers within an organization may seem to be pursuing differ-ent objectives. The problem of defining objectives, and measuring the extent to which they are achieved, is more difficult in a public sector or not-for-profit organization. In theory the budget-ing process ensures that objectives are defined and quantified, but in practice it may be difficult to secure agreement on objectives.

Most management techniques are more difficult in practice than their proponents would suggest. There are all the usual difficulties of the costs of implementation, and the need to train staff to operate the systems effectively. But budgetary control is well established in most medium and large organiza-tions and is operated with varying degrees of success.

Budgetary control is sometimes seen as a game in which the players (managers) are involved in setting their own budgets. Then the accountants put all the individual budgets together in a master budget: the budgeted income statement, statement of financial position and the cash budget. It may be that all the budgets fit neatly together revealing no cash shortages, and achieving all the intended targets. Similarly, pigs might fly. It is more likely that once the first draft of the master budget is prepared, the finance director or senior management will insist on revisions: expenditure to be cut back, sales to be increased, capital expenditure to be reduced and deferred. All the careful planning put in by individual managers is overturned. But experienced managers know that this will happen, and so they put some 'slack' into the first version of the budget because experience tells them that the final version will be tougher. And the finance director knows that they know, and that they have included slack, so tougher cut-backs are demanded. But very experienced managers know this, and

have included even more slack than the finance director would expect. But very experienced finance directors know this ... and so all is set for another round of the game of budgetary control.

One approach to making budgetary control more effective – and to avoid the tendency for expenditure to drift upwards every year ('incremental drift') – is to use *zero-based budgeting* (ZBB). This means that, instead of taking the previous year's figures as a basis for planning future expenditure, the basis is taken as zero. The starting point is that each activity will spend nothing in the coming year, unless it can be justified. This may be valuable in some areas: perhaps there is no need for company cars if it is cheaper to use taxis; perhaps there is no need for a mail room if most communication is done by email. But it is usually too much hassle, expense and bureaucracy to review every activity every year, and incremental budgeting still predominates.

If budgets are seen as the official expressions of the plans and intentions of top management, they are likely to be taken seriously, and provide an effective means of controlling the business. They are likely to be less effective if they are seen as being a paperwork exercise produced by the finance department; a pointless extra burden for management; a sterile figure-producing exercise that provides information that managers do not understand, is irrelevant to their needs, and arrives in too much detail, and too late for them to act on. If they are to be successful, management accountants must produce financial information that is relevant and effective in planning, decision-making and control in the business.

15.7 Zero-based Budgeting (ZBB)

ZBB is one way of tackling the inefficiencies and budgetary slack of traditional incremental budgeting. Instead of basing each budget on the equivalent budget for the previous year, with adjustments for known changes, each year and each budget begin with an assumption of zero expenditure. Instead of arguing for an increase of 5 per cent or 10 per cent, departmental managers have to argue for any budget at all. If the head of advertising cannot defend expenditure on advertising as being cost-effective, there will be no advertising budget. If the head of distribution cannot demonstrate that it is worth while for the company to operate its own fleet of vehicles, Royal Mail and others will be invited to put in tenders for taking over the distribution function. The finance director may be astute at self-defence (or may be fed up with running the finance department!) and be able to fight off proposals to outsource the finance function to a large firm of chartered accountants. But it is quite likely the payroll function will be outsourced. Even production departments may be given a zero budget (and be closed down) if it would be cheaper to cease manufacturing and buy in components, sub-assemblies or even finished goods – probably from some part of the world where production costs are lower.

The idea is to prepare a budget for each cost centre from a zero base, and every item has to be justified in its entirety if it is to be included in next year's budget. A questioning attitude is required to examine every item of expenditure, and to clear out any 'dead wood'. The company's activities should be divided into separate 'decision packages'. These are evaluated according to the costs incurred and benefits generated by each activity, and ranked in order of priority. Some activities will simply be closed down if they are hardly needed, generate little benefit, are outdated, or can be done more cost effectively in another way, perhaps by outsourcing. Candidates for axing might include: subsidized staff social clubs and canteens; typing pools; final salary pension schemes; printing and photocopying departments; car pools; and some retail outlets.

A number of advantages are claimed for ZBB. It helps to identify and remove obsolete, wasteful and inefficient operations and expenditure. It is a systematic way of responding to a changing business environment and can increase staff motivation towards greater efficiency. The systematic process and documentation challenges the status quo, appraises all operations, and ensures that alternatives such as outsourcing are considered. It should lead to a more efficient allocation of resources. And it is particularly useful in public sector and not-for-profit organizations where profitability is not an appropriate measure of efficiency and effectiveness.

ZBB is, however, expensive to apply. It involves a substantial volume of work and paper, and it seems excessive to do this every year. It can lead to rational economic decisions, but these decisions should perhaps be made on a long-term basis, within an overall framework, rather than on a short-term basis as part of an annual budgeting cycle. Systematic ZBB requires special training for staff, probably involving the use of consultants, and there is likely to be resistance if it seems likely to lead to redundancies. Existing information systems are likely to be inadequate, and it is difficult to evaluate the costs and benefits of all decision packages and functions.

Some of the questioning attitudes of ZBB can undoubtedly lead to the reduction and elimination of some activities and functions, improved resource allocation and greater profitability. But most organizations would not operate all their budgets from a zero base every year.

15.8 Planning and Programming Budgeting Systems (PPBS)

PPBS was developed particularly for public sector organizations such as defence. Some would argue that there is obviously a need for more defence, perhaps listing particular problem areas, and so it is necessary to spend more on defence. But it is difficult to assess the efficiency and effectiveness of that expenditure unless it is clearly targeted to particular 'programmes' where expenditure can be measured and success assessed.

If applied to a police force a number of programmes might be identified, such as (i) reducing drug crime in the Orriton area; (ii) reducing speeding and road accidents in the Searam area; (iii) reducing muggings in the Trandton area; (iv) reducing shop-lifting in the Brandwich area; and (v) reducing burglaries in the Julby area.

An important part of the planning process would be to define a number of programmes such as these, rather than simply to describe everything as 'policing'. Then budgets allocate resources to each programme, and expenditure is classified so that it is identified with particular programmes (rather than seeming to disappear down a black hole). We can budget to spend £200,000 a year on reducing muggings in the Trandton area. Subsequent control information might show that only £170,000 was actually spent. But, more important, the effectiveness of the programme in Trandton can be measured. By how much were muggings reduced? What percentage reduction can be aimed for next year, or in a comparable programme?

The overall management of the public sector organization can control how much was spent on each programme, and see how effective that expenditure was. This can provide a basis for reallocations in subsequent years in the light of actual experience of how effective different expenditure on different programmes has been in practice.

The phrase 'PPBS' is not particularly widely used, but, within the public sector, there is increasing emphasis on identifying 'programmes', and assessing the effectiveness of expenditure on different programme areas.

📖 Summary

Budgetary control is a well-established management accounting technique that is widely used in all but the smallest organizations. It defines objectives, establishes plans for achieving those objectives, and makes each area in the organization responsible for its part of the plan. Control information compares the results actually achieved with those that were planned on a regular basis. There are many 'behavioural' problems in practice with budgetary control that militate against the advantages that can be gained from an effective system.

➡ Review of key points

- Budgets are financial plans showing how the objectives of an organization can be achieved.
- Budgetary control provides regular feedback information.
- A budget manual details how budgetary control is to be applied in a particular organization, and shows all the different budgets to be produced.
- A master budget, the budgeted statement of financial position and income statement, shows the results of all the detailed budgets.
- A cash budget shows planned receipts and payments of cash, typically on a monthly basis for the next year.
- The budgeted net receipts of cash are likely to be very different from the budgeted profit figure.
- The availability of cash to meet liabilities as they fall due is essential to business survival.

❗ Self-testing questions

1 Define the term 'budget' and draw attention to the most important parts of the definition.
2 Distinguish between fixed budgets and flexible budgets.
3 The owner of a car servicing and repair business, with five employees, produces an annual statement of financial position and income statement, and monitors his bank statement on a monthly basis. Examine the case for and against introducing a system of budgetary control.
4 Produce a flexible budget for the Dhoon Glen Manufacturing Company and comment on the company's results for August. Assume that:
  a fixed production overheads are £100,000 per month;
  b fixed distribution costs are £20,000 per month;
  c fixed administration overheads are £50,000 per month.

	Budget August Year 6 £000	Flexed budget August Year 6 £000	Actual results August Year 6 £000
Sales	600		690
Direct materials	120		140
Direct labour	100		117
Production overheads	200		223
Distribution costs	80		95
Administrative overheads	60		70
Total costs	560		645
Profit	40		45

5 In what circumstances is a very profitable business likely to find that it has serious cash shortages?
6 Rachel owns a specialist boring-digging machine that she hires out, together with an operator/driver, to builders and farmers. A few years ago her accountant worked out that she should charge £500 a day and that should give her a comfortable living. In the last year demand has fallen, particularly in the winter months when the weather restricts the use of the machine, and in the

summer months when many people are on holiday. In the coming year (year 3) she estimates that she will have 10 days' work a month in January and February; 20 days' work a month in March, April, May and June. Then it will fall to 12 days a month in July and August. In September, October and November she expects 20 days' work a month, and only 5 days in December.

At the end of year 2 her debtors figure was £5,000, of which she expects to receive half in January and half in February.

On average customers pay two months after the work is done.

Operating expenses, including fuel and labour, amount to £100 per day.

Expenses are paid in the month that they are incurred.

Her fixed overheads, including depreciation, are £3,000 per month. The machine originally cost £140,000 and is expected to have a five-year life, with a residual value of £20,000. She uses straight-line depreciation.

At the end of last year she had only £1,000 in her business bank account.

Rachel would like to take £45,000 a year out of the business to cover her personal living expenses. But she does not want to have an overdraft; and she does not want to be living off capital.

Required:

a Prepare the income statement for the coming year, showing sales, expenses and profit for each month, and in total.

b Prepare the cash budget for the coming year, showing receipts and payments for each month; the net cash surplus or deficit for the month; and the bank balance at the end of each month. Assume that the business starts the year with £50,000 in the bank.

c Explain why the company has generated more cash than profit during the year.

d How much do you think that she can afford to take out of the business as drawings (or dividends if it is a company) during the year? Give your reasons.

Assessment questions

1 Define the term 'budgetary control' and draw attention to the most important parts of the definition.

2 Distinguish between annual budgets and rolling (or continuous) budgets.

3 What behavioural problems are likely to arise in operating a system of budgetary control?

4 Produce a flexible budget for the Gorrie Production Company and comment on the company's results for May. Assume that:

a fixed production overheads are £100,000 per month;

b fixed distribution costs are £20,000 per month;

c fixed administration overheads are £50,000 per month.

	Budget May Year 3 £000	Flexed budget August Year 3 £000	Actual results May Year 3 £000
Sales	900		810
Direct materials	200		178
Direct labour	250		227

Production overheads	240	210
Distribution costs	100	103
Administrative overheads	109	90
Total costs	899	808
Profit	1	2

5 Judas has developed a plan for a rapidly expanding business selling and installing software for individuals using computers at home. He will operate on a 100 per cent mark-up (50 per cent gross profit ratio) on the software that he sells, and will employ a team of highly paid technician/sales staff. He has piloted his business model on a number of customers and he knows that they are particularly afraid of computer viruses; he will provide a guarantee of 12 months free of viruses. But, somehow, after a year or so he knows that there will always be a return of viruses and most of his customers will request his services again. During the next 12 months he aims to build up his customer base, and make a small profit.

He has discussed his business plan with his accountant, and the following seems to be soundly based:

a Sales in January will be £220,000 and will then increase by £20,000 per month. Customers pay two months after the sale is made.

b Suppliers are paid one month after purchases are made. Stocks amounting to £100,000 will be bought in the first month and maintained at that level. Purchases will be made each month that are sufficient to supply sales for that month.

c Wages and expenses will be £100,000 a month for the first four months of the year; then they will increase to £150,000 a month for the following three months; then they will be £200,000 a month for the next five months. They are paid during the month that they are incurred.

d At the beginning of the year he will spend £840,000 on non-current assets. All non-current assets are depreciated over 10 years. Depreciation is charged on a monthly basis. In June additional fixed assets of £360,000 will be bought.

His accountant advises him that, although the business should make a modest profit, there will be substantial cash outflows to begin with. She prepared a monthly budgeted income statement, and a monthly cash budget. But Judas had £1 m available to finance the business and reckoned that there would be no problem. He refused to pay her fees and so she did not show him the monthly budgets.

Required:

i Prepare a monthly income statement for the first year of the business, showing the profit or loss each month, and for the year in total.

ii Prepare a cash budget for the year, showing the receipts and payments for each month, and the cash surplus or deficit each month.

iii Explain and comment on the results.

Group activities and discussion questions

1 What plans do you have for this year? Would it be helpful to define and quantify them? What do you do when what actually happens is very different from what you had planned?

2 If you have work experience, did you see evidence that your employer operated a system of budgetary control? What were the attitudes of your colleagues towards budgets and budgetary control?

3 Do you prepare a cash budget for yourself for the coming year? What is the case for and against bothering to do this? Is it *essential* for a company to prepare a cash budget? Is it *essential* for you?

4 Should large companies publish their budgets for the coming year? Do companies publish any forecasts?

5 Is budgetary control too idealistic? Is it inevitable that powerful employees will feather their own nests and empire-build rather than working to achieve the objectives of the company?

Accounting in context

Discuss and comment on the following extract from the press with reference to the importance of budgetary control even in not-for-profit organizations.

I work on ...

saving money for RAF Air Command

As deputy command secretary, resources, at RAF Air Command, I led the team tasked with a two-year programme to reduce costs in the central finance and planning functions by a third. The task to cut the budget by £3.8 m was actually achieved within half the allotted time.

The decision to move so quickly on the project was partly to show leadership to the rest of RAF Air Command HQ, which, in turn, had been set identical budget cuts of a third, so it was right that we should also embark on that course.

We still had to deliver our outputs and products, and continued to steer the Command to come in on budget against its wider £3bn operating budget, which included delivering multi-million pound savings across the RAF.

We were also able to deliver more analytical services across the Command as we became slicker with process.

My appointment to the task is an endorsement of CIMA professional skills. Exposure to organisation design and relationship management in the CIMA qualification has certainly helped me.

Simply put, the qualification instils credibility, confidence and competence. On top of that, CIMA-qualified individuals helped deliver positive change and a "human face".

I also co-led the overall redesign of the Command's HQ with an air commodore colleague. Central to the redesign was to increase effectiveness in the finance and planning functions – consolidating budgeting and enhancing forecasting capabilities.

I have now been appointed as the head of the defence financial management reform programme tasked with delivering financial improvement across departments.

Key deliverables will be giving responsibility to the service chiefs for the budget and planning of their equipment programmes, designing and delivering a smaller, more strategic head office finance function and improving the generation and analysis of financial information.

I can't think of a more challenging and motivating job to be taking on at this time. [...]

Source: Financial Management, March 2012

References and further reading

Atkinson, A., R. Kaplan, E. Matsumura and M. Young (2012) *Management Accounting* (6th edn.). Harlow: Pearson.

Bhimani, A.C.T., S.M. Datar, C.T. Horngren and G. Foster (2012) *Management and Cost Accounting* (5th edn.). Upper Saddle River, NJ: FT Prentice Hall.

Drury, C. (2008) *Management and Cost Accounting* (7th edn.). Andover: Cengage Learning.

Dyson, J.R. (2010) *Accounting for Non-accounting Students* (8th edn.). Upper Saddle River, NJ: FT Prentice Hall.

Proctor, R. (2009) *Managerial Accounting for Business Decisions* (3rd edn.). Harlow: Pearson.

Seal, W., R.H. Garrison and E.W. Nooreen (2011) *Management Accounting* (4th edn.). Maidenhead: McGraw-Hill.

When you have read this chapter, log on to the Online Learning Centre website at *www.mcgraw-hill.co.uk/textbooks/leiwy* to explore chapter-by-chapter test questions, further reading and more online study tools.

Chapter 16

Absorption Costing

Chapter contents

✓ Learning objectives

After studying this chapter you will be able to:

- ✓ Explain how absorption costing developed
- ✓ Understand how product costs are accumulated using absorption costing
- ✓ Apply the main classifications of costs
- ✓ Understand and apply the main pricing systems for materials issued
- ✓ Calculate production overheads using different methods
- ✓ Evaluate absorption costing
- ✓ Understand and apply ABC

16.1 Introduction

Costing systems are used to determine the cost of producing something, usually a 'cost unit'. It might be a car, a piece of furniture, a thousand bricks, a house, or the product of a service organization such as a haircut, a successful student, or a task undertaken by a firm of solicitors. The two main systems of costing are *absorption costing*, sometimes known as *full costing*, which is examined in this chapter; and *marginal costing*, which is dealt with in Chapter 17.

16.2 Role and Origins of Costing Systems

Most costing systems have developed gradually during the last 100 years in response to the needs of management who need to establish a cost for closing inventories; to price goods for sale; to make a variety of different decisions about which products to make; and to plan and control costs.

In financial accounting it is necessary to establish the cost[1] of closing inventories. This is needed for calculating profit. Gross profit is the difference between the revenue earned from sales, and the cost of the goods that have been sold. The cost of goods that have not been sold ('closing inventory') is carried forward to be shown as an expense in the following period; it is not charged as an expense until the goods sold. Costs that have been incurred therefore have to be allocated between (a) cost of sales, which is treated as an expense on the income statement; and (b) closing inventory, which is carried forward on the statement of financial position as a current asset. For this purpose costs include all production (or manufacturing costs), which include not only direct materials and direct labour, but all production overheads. All these costs have to be attributed to what has been produced, in a fair and reasonable manner, so that the cost of sales and the cost of closing inventory include the total of all manufacturing costs.[2]

It is important to establish the costs of producing different products,[3] if only to give some indication of what price should be charged for each product. During the First World War 'cost plus' pricing systems were developed for businesses that supplied goods for the war effort (such as weapons, uniforms, vehicles), direct material and direct labour costs were carefully recorded, and a percentage was agreed (the 'plus') to cover overheads and profit. Companies wanted to ensure that all their costs, and a margin for profit, were covered in the price agreed.

In some ways this 'cost plus' approach lives on. Costing systems typically record and classify direct material and direct labour costs in detail, then a percentage is added to cover production overheads, and then perhaps another percentage to cover other overheads and profit. This approach is now usually too crude. As manufacturing processes have become more automated, direct labour has become a smaller proportion of production costs, and production overheads have become a much larger proportion. Moreover, competition means that it is not usually possible simply to calculate the costs and then add some percentages, and then determine a price that covers everything; somehow costs have to be planned and managed with a price in mind that the market will bear.

It is, of course, important to know what it costs to produce something so that relevant decisions can be made: whether to produce more or less of a particular product, or to abandon some, or increase prices. But absorption costing is not a good basis for making such decisions; marginal costing is usually more appropriate. Care should be taken in deciding to eliminate a 'loss-making' product (such as desks in Illustration 16.1). This is explained more fully in Chapter 17. Absorption costing is a necessary basis for some decisions, such as quoting a price for major construction

---

[1] Closing inventory should be shown at the lower of cost and net realizable value. It is therefore necessary to know both the cost, and the net realizable value, in order to establish which is the lower.

[2] But manufacturing costs exclude administration costs, selling and distribution overheads, and finance costs.

[3] Products or services or orders or contracts.

ILLUSTRATION 16.1 Absorption costing

	Total	Tables	Desks	Chairs
	£000	£000	£000	£000
Sales	757	254	276	227
Direct materials	300	100	120	80
Direct labour	160	50	60	50
Prime cost	460	150	180	130
Production overheads	160	50	60	50
Production cost	620	200	240	180
Distribution and administrative overheads	124	40	48	36
Total costs	744	240	288	216
Profit	13	14	(12)	11

---

projects (such as the Channel Tunnel, or Crossrail, or the facilities for the Olympic Games in London). Sometimes it might make good business sense to agree selling prices that do not cover full production costs; but scope for this is limited. Somehow a business must have selling prices that cover not only all production costs, but also all administration, distribution and finance costs, and also make a profit. Where selling prices do not cover all such costs, businesses soon fail – as so many did in 2008/9.

Absorption costing is also important in planning and controlling costs. A budgetary control system includes budgets for all costs, and involves regular comparisons of actual costs with those that were planned. Ideally, control systems are designed so that managers who are responsible for particular costs can actually control those costs. It is too easy to say that an individual production manager cannot control some production overheads because they are predetermined and relatively fixed. But someone has to be responsible for all costs, and all costs should be planned and controlled. Absorption costing can help to ensure that someone is responsible for all costs.

16.3 Classification of Costs

Accounting systems are designed to classify and record costs in various ways that are useful. Typically, as costs are incurred, they are given code numbers; these code numbers may indicate a number of things, such as:

1 the nature of the cost (e.g. rent, insurance, wages, materials, utilities, maintenance);

2 whether it is a production cost (which may be included in closing inventories), or a period cost, which must be charged as an expense during the period in which it is incurred;

3 who is responsible for authorizing the cost. This can be related to cost centres, budget centres and the whole business of budgetary control.

In a manufacturing organization, production costs are classified as direct costs (direct material, direct labour and direct expenses) and as production overheads, as shown in the manufacturing account in Chapter 17.

Costs can be defined and classified in many different ways. It is useful to identify sunk costs and relevant costs when making decisions (see Glossary).

16.4 Direct Materials and Pricing

Direct materials are materials and components that become part of the finished product, and which are charged to individual jobs. In a garage repair business, a new fan belt for Mrs Shah's car is a direct material cost of the repairs for Mrs Shah. In a building business, for any particular job, the direct materials would include bricks, timber and partly-made items such as staircases and window frames. In a manufacturing business, the direct materials could include the metal, timber, glass and chemicals that are incorporated into a particular product.

It is necessary to record which materials are used for which particular job or product so that the total cost of that job or product can be calculated. Where 'just-in-time' purchasing is used, purchases can be charged directly to a particular job as soon as they are ordered. Where purchases go into stores before being issued to production, some sort of 'requisition' note must be used each time materials are issued from stores; this will specify which job the materials are required for to ensure that they are charged to that job.

There may also be 'indirect materials' where it is not worth the time and trouble of charging them to individual jobs. These include lubricants, cleaning materials and items of low value (perhaps adhesives or nails) that are included in general production overheads.

In a modern manufacturing environment, direct materials and components are, ideally, delivered to the factory 'just in time' to be used for a particular job, batch, product or contract. From the moment that the materials are ordered, it is known for which product they are intended, and there is no need for complicated costing procedures: all materials are allocated directly to jobs.

In some traditional manufacturing environments, large inventories of many different materials and components are kept 'just in case' they are needed. This is particularly true in many 'jobbing' industries where there is a regular demand for materials such as particular lengths of wood, metal, various screws, rivets, and so on. A problem can arise when identical materials are bought at different dates and different prices. In Illustration 16.2 below different quantities of an item are bought during March, with the price paid varying between £11 per unit and £14 per unit.

A problem with all these methods is that the cost shown for a particular item varies from one date to another. It could happen that a job completed on one date is shown as being profitable, but an identical job completed on a different date is shown as being unprofitable, and the difference between the two is due only to the issue prices changing; and that in turn is due only to the pricing system used.

If some of the materials are then issued from the stores, on 28 March, there are different ways of pricing those issues, as follows:

1   It could be assumed that the earliest prices (£12) are charged first until all 1,000 items have been issued; then subsequent issues are charged at £11 until 2,000 have been used up. This method is called first in first out, or FIFO. It is probably a sensible method of physically handling the goods (use up the oldest first), but where items are identical this may not be possible. In any case, the way in which issues are priced can be different from the way in which they are physically handled.

ILLUSTRATION 16.2				
Date	Units purchased	Cost price per unit	Amount	Total
1 March	1,000	£12	£12,000	£12,000
13 March	2,000	£11	£22,000	£34,000
26 March	500	£14	£7,000	£41,000

2 It could be assumed that the most recent prices (£14) are charged first until all 500 items have been issued; then subsequent issues are charged at £11 until 2,000 have been used up. This method is last in first out, or LIFO.

3 An averaging system could be used. There are 3,500 items in stock that have cost £41,000; that is an average price of (about) £11.71. That average price could be used for all issues. The average could be recalculated on a regular basis (e.g. monthly or quarterly), or each time a new delivery is received.

4 Standard cost: a 'fairer' system of charging direct materials to jobs might be to use a standard price for all components, with that price being revised annually. This is normal when a standard costing system is used. In Illustration 16.2, it could be decided that the standard cost is £12 per item (or perhaps £12.50 to allow for a bit of inflation), regardless of the cost of different purchases during the year.

5 Replacement cost is sometimes used, based on the current cost of purchasing more items at the date the item is to be used. This is likely to give more realistic decisions, especially where major long-term production is being considered, rather than relying on the chance of what happens to have been bought in the past.

During a period of rising prices, FIFO has the advantage that closing inventories tend to be at recent prices, which are likely to be relatively high, and fairly realistic. But the items that are issued to production are likely to be at the oldest, and so probably the lowest, prices; costs of production are likely to be understated, and any further orders for the same product could not be produced at the same cost.

With LIFO it is the other way around. During a period of rising prices, LIFO has the advantage that it is the most recent prices that are charged to production, and these are likely to be fairly realistic.[4] But what is left as inventory will be shown at old, low and unrealistic prices – a prudent version of 'cost' when applied to valuing inventory.

An averaging system is likely to be 'fairer', but costs are still subject to the chance of what happens to have been purchased in the past. Standard cost is not only 'fair'; it is also as realistic as the standard price selected; but standards can rapidly become out of date. Replacement cost is likely to provide the best basis for decision-making, but it would often be too much trouble to establish and record replacement costs for every little item issued from stores. In general, accountancy is based on costs actually incurred and recorded; there is continuing debate about the extent to which it is worth moving to more 'relevant' figures.

16.5 Direct Labour

Direct labour costs are wages and employment costs that are charged directly to particular jobs. It may be that some employees work exclusively on one product (perhaps making standard tables), and so their wages are charged to that product. Other direct labour employees may have their time allocated to different products using some sort of time sheet. Such a system is used in many professional offices where lawyers or accountants have to complete time sheets showing how many hours were spent on each job so that their time can be charged accordingly.

'Indirect labour' costs are those costs of employing people that cannot be charged to particular individual jobs or products. Some indirect labour costs are part of production overheads; others are part of administrative expenses or distribution costs.

---

[4] But if ever the whole inventory of an item is used up, the oldest, lowest costs would be charged to production; this could result in costs being seriously understated.

16.6 Direct Expenses

Most 'expenses' such as hire and maintenance of machinery, or use of patents and trademarks, may be included in production overheads rather than being charged to individual products or customers. A builder is likely to have a lot of machinery and equipment that is used on all jobs. But when it is necessary to hire a crane to build a high office block, the cost of hiring the crane would be a 'direct expense' that is charged directly to a particular job rather than being included in production overheads.

With materials, labour and expenses, the test is the same: they are 'direct' if they can properly be charged to individual jobs rather than being included in production overheads.

16.7 Production Overheads

Production overheads include all the costs of operating a factory or other production facility that cannot be charged to individual products or customers. They are the costs of the facilities that most or all products use to some extent. It is necessary to charge them indirectly to different products. They include the costs of providing and operating the factory, such as rent, rates, insurance, maintenance, lighting and heating; the costs of providing and operating the machinery and equipment, including depreciation, maintenance, lubrication and power; and the costs of employing all those who work in the factory who cannot be charged as direct labour, including supervisors, maintenance staff, storekeepers, cleaners and operators of fork-lift trucks and other lifting equipment.

The total cost of production overheads is easy to establish, but it is difficult to decide how much should be charged to each different product or job, and what basis would be 'fair'. In Illustration 16.1 total production overheads for the period amount to £160,000, and it so happens that the total direct labour costs for the period are also £160,000. An easy way to charge production overheads to the three different products is to say that for each £1 of labour cost that they incur, they will be charged £1 for production overheads. Production overheads are charged on the basis of direct labour cost; in this instance it is 100 per cent of direct labour cost.

Percentage on direct labour cost

The percentage to be charged has to be recalculated each year, based on budgets for the forthcoming year. If the budget shows production overheads for the forthcoming year as £250,000, and labour costs as being £100,000, the percentage on direct labour will be 250 per cent, as shown in Example 16.1.

Example 16.1

	Budget for next year		
	Total	Machining workers	Assembly workers
Hours to be worked	10,000	2,000	8,000
Total direct labour cost	£100,000	£36,000	£64,000
Total production overheads	£250,000		
Production overheads as a % of direct labour	250%		
Direct labour hour rate	£25		

The rate calculated before the year begins will be charged on all jobs throughout the year. When the end of the year comes there are two main possibilities:

a Overheads will have been under-recovered. Perhaps actual labour costs were only £90,000; production overheads charged would be 250 per cent of that, which is £225,000. But actual overheads incurred might have been £265,000. Under-recovered overheads would be £40,000 – an extra charge when profits are calculated.

b Overheads will have been over-recovered. Perhaps actual labour costs were £112,000; production overhead charges would be 250 per cent of that, which is £280,000. Even if actual overheads incurred had increased to £260,000, there would still be over-recovered overheads of £20,000 – an extra credit when profits are calculated.

Direct labour hour rate

Charging production overheads on the basis of a direct labour hour rate seems much the same as charging them as a percentage of direct labour cost. In Example 16.1, if only the total column is used (and so assuming that direct labour is paid at £10 per hour) the two methods will give the same answer (see Example 16.2).

If a percentage on direct labour cost is used, and different workers are paid at different hourly rates, the amount of overheads charged will be different. In Example 16.2, machining workers are paid at £18 per hour, and assembly workers are paid at £8 per hour. The production overhead cost of Job 123A would have to be calculated based on the labour cost.

Labour cost	Machining	5 hours @ £18 =	£ 90
		15 hours @ £9 =	£135
			£225
Production overheads 250% of £225			£562.50

The *average* labour cost in the factory was £10 per hour; this particular product required 20 hours of labour, which cost £225. If overheads are charged in accordance with the specific labour cost, then a higher overhead charge results.

Example 16.2

Question:
Job 123A requires 20 hours of direct labour (5 hours machining, 15 hours assembly). Calculate the amount of production overheads to be charged to that job using the following methods:

1 Percentage on direct labour cost
2 Direct labour hour rate

Answer:

1 20 hours of labour at £10 = £200. 250% of £200 = £500
2 20 hours @ £25 per hour = £500

If a direct labour hour rate is calculated for production overheads that rate (£25 in this instance) is charged for all hours worked.

In order to have more accurate charging of production overheads factories are often divided into different cost centres, with different overhead rates for each. In Example 16.2 it would probably be sensible to divide the factory into a Machining Department and an Assembly Department. Each would have different rates of overhead recovery, and perhaps even different methods.

Machine hour rate

Where there is machinery that is particularly expensive to operate, there may be a separate cost centre for a particular machine or group of machines.

A factory has an electronic testing machine in a separate cost centre. The production overheads for that cost centre are £80,000 a year. The machine is expected to operate for 2,000 hours per annum.

The machine hour rate is £80,000 ÷ 2,000 = £40 per hour.

Each product is charged (in this instance) £40 for production overheads for each hour that the machine is used.

Other methods

Various other methods of charging production overheads to different products are possible. Overheads could be charged per unit produced, but usually only where all units produced are identical. They could be charged as a percentage of direct material costs, or of prime costs. For vehicles, they could be charged per mile.

The management (or accountants on their behalf) should determine which methods are most appropriate in their particular circumstances, and the first three methods described above are the most usual. Obviously, the use of different methods is going to produce different product costs. One method might show a particular product as being profitable while a different method shows it as being unprofitable. It is perhaps inevitable that, whatever method is used, some products will sometimes be treated unfairly. Accountants are constantly seeking more accurate methods (such as ABC, as described later in this chapter); but every method is based on assumptions that may sometimes be of questionable validity. There is no such thing as a single 'correct' overhead cost. Those who use costing information should always be aware of the assumptions on which it is based, and be prepared to question them.

16.8 Allocation, Apportionment and Absorption

Where a factory operates a number of separate cost centres (perhaps different workshops), the production overheads for each cost centre can be separately calculated.

Some costs can be directly *allocated* to different cost centres very accurately. Some members of staff ('indirect labour') may work exclusively in one cost centre, or their time can be specifically allocated between cost centres. Each cost centre can be separately metered to give accurate figures for lighting, heating and power. Machinery may be located exclusively in specific cost centres and so the cost of depreciation and maintenance of that machinery can be specifically allocated to that cost centre.

Other costs are more difficult to identify with particular cost centres and need to be *apportioned* to them in some equitable way. The cost of rent, rates, depreciation and repairs for the factory building may be apportioned to different cost centres on the basis of the square metres occupied. (This may also be done for lighting and heating where separate metering is not possible.) Some costs may be apportioned to cost centres on the basis of the number of employees in that cost centre; this might include some costs of supervision and indirect labour, and the costs of operating a canteen. Other costs may be apportioned on the basis of usage; perhaps the number of times a facility is used, or the number of hours that a facility is used.

The costs of individual products are accumulated by adding together direct materials, direct labour (and perhaps some direct expense), and then the amount of production overheads (based on calculations such as those shown in Section 16.7) is *absorbed* by the product to give its total production costs.

It is sometimes useful to estimate the amount of administration, selling and distribution overheads that are incurred by a particular product; but these are period costs,[5] and do not become part of product costs.[6]

16.9 Evaluation of Absorption Costing

Absorption costing is the required method for valuing closing inventory. It is also useful in ensuring that all costs are 'recovered': that means charging every cost to a job or customer. If a business allocates only some of its costs to jobs, it could end up showing that all its jobs make some sort of contribution to overheads, but overall it makes a loss.

The process of charging out all costs inevitably involves approximations and arbitrary elements. The basis for charging is usually established at the beginning of the year, based on budgeted figures. As the year goes by, actual figures are likely to be different from budgeted figures, and the amount of overheads charged to jobs during the year is likely to be different from the amount of overheads actually incurred. At the end of the year there are usually 'under-recovered' or 'over-recovered' overheads.

In the long run a business must ensure that its sales revenue covers all of its production costs. Absorption costing is a method of attributing all production costs to individual products in the expectation that they will be covered by sales revenue. It is a method of recording and classifying costs that does not necessarily provide a suitable basis for short-term decisions.

16.10 Activity-based Costing

Partly because of the inadequacies and inaccuracies of absorption costing, developments such as ABC are intended to make overhead charges more accurate. In Example 16.3 central overhead costs are allocated to three different cost centres on a single, simple basis (as a percentage of sales revenue), which ignores the factors that really 'drive' costs. ABC attempts to identify the 'drivers' for each cost, so that, for example, delivery costs are allocated to the different depots on the basis of miles covered (rather than being lumped in with other costs and allocated on the basis of sales revenue).

So, the overheads are allocated to the three locations according to what 'drives' or causes those costs. In that way, the overheads are more accurately allocated than in the 'traditional' methods of overhead absorption. However, whatever methods of allocating overheads are used, and however complex they are, there is inevitably an arbitrary element, and, in making any particular decision, it is best to ensure that only the most appropriate or relevant specific costing information is used for that particular purpose. It is not possible to develop a costing system that produces costs that are accurate for all purposes. And, of course, ABC is more costly to complex and costly to implement so, when comparing ABC to the traditional methods of overhead absorption, the costs and benefits need to be considered.

---

[5] To be written off during the period in which they are incurred, whether or not the product is sold.

[6] Which are carried forward in the cost of closing inventory if the product is not sold in the current period.

Example 16.3

The Brigstow Autoparts Company operates from a main warehouse in Brigstow and imports spare parts for specialist sports cars and sells them via three distribution depots: one in England, one in Wales and one in Scotland. The company's budget for the coming year is summarized as follows:

	England £000	Wales £000	Scotland £000
Sales	10,000	8,000	6,000
Cost of sales	5,600	4,600	3,800
Gross profit	4,400	3,400	2,200
Local operating costs	2,720	2,660	1,620
Operating profit	1,680	740	580
Brigstow: Central costs			
Warehouse			
Depreciation	200		
Storage	160		
Operating and despatch	240		
Delivery	600		
Head office			
Salaries	400		
Advertising	160		
Establishment	240		
	2,000		

Central costs are allocated to the three distribution depots as a percentage of the sales revenue of each depot, as follows:

	£000
Total sales	24,000
Total central costs	2,000
Central costs as a percentage of sales	8.33% (one-twelfth)

	England £	Wales £	Scotland £
Central costs	833	667	500
Operating profit	1,680	740	580
Net profit (loss)	847	73	80
Total £1,000,000			

Continued >>>

Example 16.3

Continued >>>

Following the popularity of activity-based costing, management have decided their usual approach to allocating central overheads to the different distribution depots is too crude and simplistic, and that each category of central costs should be allocated in accordance with cost drivers (what it is that really incurs the costs at each depot). These have been defined as follows:

Depreciation: in proportion to the amount of space occupied
Storage: in proportion to the amount of space occupied
Operations and despatch: in proportion to the number of despatches
Delivery: in proportion to the number of delivery miles
Salaries: 10 per cent of their time is spent on warehouse issues; the remainder is divided equally between the three depots
Advertising: to be allocated in proportion to sales
Establishment: to be allocated on the same basis as salaries

The necessary information for the three depots is as follows

	England	Wales	Scotland
Number of despatches	550	450	520
Total delivery distances (000 miles)	70	50	90
Storage space occupied (%)	40	30	30

Required:

Prepare a schedule showing the costs and profit of each depot using activity-based costing as specified above.

Answer:

Brigstow Autoparts Company

	England £000	Wales £000	Scotland £000
Sales	10,000	8,000	6,000
Cost of sales	5,600	4,600	3,800
Gross profit	4,400	3,400	2,200
Local operating costs	2,720	2,660	1,620
Operating profit	1,680	740	580
Central costs			
Depreciation (40:30:30)	80	60	60
Storage (40:30:30)	64	48	48

Continued >>>

Example 16.3

Continued >>>

Operating and despatch (550:450:520)		86.8	71.1	82.1
Delivery (70:50:90)		200	142.9	257.1
Salaries	Warehouse			
(10:30:30:30)	40	120	120	120
Advertising (5,000:4,000:3,000)		66.7	53.3	40
Establishment (10:30:30:30)	24	72	72	72
Reallocation (550:450:520)	64	23.2	18.9	21.9
		712.7	586.2	701.1
Net profit		967.3	153.8	(121.1)
Total £1,000,000				

📖 Summary

Absorption costing developed as a method of applying all production costs to individual products or jobs. This is needed partly to separate the costs of sales from closing inventories, and so for profit calculation. Absorption costing is not usually appropriate for short-term decision-making. In the long term it can help to ensure that all costs are 'absorbed' by products, and to avoid selling at a loss. ABC is a more accurate but by no means perfect system for allocating overheads on the basis of cost drivers.

⮕ Review of key points

- Absorption costing is needed for valuing closing inventories rather than for short-term decision-making.
- Direct materials and direct labour can be allocated directly to the costs of individual products or jobs.
- Production overheads have to be absorbed by individual products or jobs on the basis of an hourly rate or a percentage addition that is 'fair'.
- The production cost shown for a particular product will be different if a different method of recovering overheads or pricing materials is used.
- Production overheads are allocated directly to cost centres where this is possible, otherwise they are apportioned to cost centres on an equitable basis.

- The production overheads for a cost centre are absorbed by products using different overhead recovery rates (and perhaps methods) for each cost centre.
- ABC is an absorption costing method in which fixed costs are allocated to products on the basis of what drives those costs.

Self-testing questions

1 Give examples of direct materials and indirect materials, and explain why and how they are treated differently.

2 The budget for the Mooarport Manufacturing Company for the coming year shows total production overheads as £23m. They plan to work 1.4 million hours.

  a Calculate the production overhead rate per hour.

    Total labour costs for the year are budgeted at £23m.

  b Calculate the average wage rate per hour.

  c Calculate the production overhead recovery rate as a percentage of direct labour cost.

    The factory is divided into three departments; the budgets for each show:

	Department A	Department B	Department C
Production overheads	£1m	£2m	£20m
Hours worked	500,000	500,000	400,000
Direct wages	£5m	£8m	£10m

  d Calculate the production overhead rate per hour for each department.

  e Calculate the average wage rate per hour for each department.

  f Calculate the overhead recovery rate as a percentage of direct labour cost for each department.

    The company makes a product called PQ that requires 13 hours of direct labour.

  g Calculate the production overheads for product PQ using the production overhead rate per hour for the factory as a whole, as in (a) above.

3 The Baldrine Company made the following purchases of Component WX:

Date	Units purchased	Cost price per unit	Amount	Total
1 March	1,000	£12	£12,000	£12,000
13 March	2,000	£11	£22,000	£34,000
26 March	500	£14	£7,000	£41,000

The company then undertook two contracts; one on 28 March, and the second on 31 March. Each used 1,500 units of component WX. Show the price that would be charged to each job using each of the following methods:

  a FIFO;

  b LIFO;

  c weighted average.

4 Distinguish between allocation, apportionment and absorption of production overheads.

5 In what ways are administrative overheads and selling and distribution costs absorbed by different products?

6 The Canters Riding Centre is based in Cheshire. It offers three types of course. These are Pony Trekking, General Lessons and Advanced Riding Skills. The following budgeted figures relate to the year 2014.

	No. of courses per year	Staff hours per course	Brochures per course	Admin events per course	Insurance clauses per course
Pony trekking	40	25	30	10	14.15
General lessons	3000	2	1	4	1.5
Advanced riding skills	100	2	5	6	5

The centre currently uses the total number of participant days per year to absorb fixed overheads. Budgeted fixed overheads for 2014 are expected to be as follows (£):

Staff salaries	108,000
Administration	33,800
Brochures	7,050
Insurance	139,150

Required:
a Calculate the overhead absorption rate used by the centre.
b Calculate the cost of each course using traditional absorption costing.
c Reallocate the overheads using the most appropriate cost driver available, and calculate the cost of each course using ABC.
d Briefly discuss the advantages and disadvantages of ABC over traditional absorption costing.

7 The Breakaway Holiday Company has overheads totalling £800,000. Until recently it had applied its overheads on a traditional volume basis, based on the number of holidays sold. It sells two major products, package tours and adventure holidays.

Type of holidays	Number of holidays sold	Number of enquiries	Total number of brochures printed per holiday	Number of couriers on a holiday
Package tour	2,000	7	34	2
Adventure	1,200	5	10	1

Overheads have been split into the following activities:

	£
Enquiries	180,000
Publicity brochures	320,000
Courier trips	300,000
Total	800,000

Required:

a Calculate to the nearest £, the overhead cost of a holiday based on the traditional volume-based method.

b Recalculate the overhead costs of *both types of holiday*, using an activity-based costing approach, showing how the costs differ from (a) above.

c Indicate what advantages and possible disadvantages an activity-based costing approach can bring to an organization.

Assessment questions

1 Give examples of direct labour and indirect labour, and explain why and how they are treated differently.

2 The Rumsea Production Company has annual production overheads of £1,000,000 and 50,000 direct labour hours per annum are worked, made up as follows:

Machining operatives	10,000 hours at £20 per hour
Assembly operatives	25,000 hours at £10 per hour
Finishing operatives	15,000 hours at £15 per hour

a Calculate, for the factory as a whole, the overhead recovery rates as a percentage of direct labour.

b The production overheads for each department are as follows:

Machining	£500,000
Assembly	£200,000
Finishing	£300,000

Calculate the overhead recovery rate as a percentage of direct labour for each department.

c A new product, the Rumbo, will require 10 hours of machining, 4 hours of assembly and 4 hours of finishing. How much production overhead should be charged? Explain and justify your calculations.

3 The Ballorna Company made the following purchases of component LMS:

Date	Units purchased	Cost price per unit	Amount	Total
11 Feb	500	£20	£10,000	£10,000
17 Feb	200	£22	£4,400	£14,400
21 Feb	300	£24	£7,200	£21,600
25 Feb	400	£23	£9,200	£30,800

The company completed two contracts, one on 28 February, and the second on 11 March. Each used 600 units of component LMS. Show the price that would be charged to each job using each of the following methods:

a FIFO;

b LIFO;

c weighted average.

4 What are 'cost centres' and why are they used?

5 GamesRus PLC manufactures three types of electronic game. These are 'Dungeons and Druids', 'Alien Invader Force' and 'Sorcerers' Revenge'. The factory is set up to produce the games in batches of 1,000, and it plans to manufacture 1 million of each type of game during the year 2009 (i.e. 1,000 batches of 1,000 games each). In each case, the cost unit is a batch of 1,000 games.

The budgeted direct costs of manufacture are as follows:

Product	Direct labour hours per batch	Raw material costs per batch
Dungeons and Druids	3	£250
Alien Invader Force	5	£360
Sorcerers' Revenge	4	£270

Direct labour is paid at £8 per hour.

Total production overheads for 2009 are budgeted as follows:

	£
Machine set-up costs	405,000
Maintenance costs	155,000
Quality control costs	200,000
Packaging costs	140,000
	900,000

At present the company uses direct labour hours as a base to absorb these production overheads.

The company has started to investigate the possibility of using ABC and has identified some data that could be used to calculate cost driver rates. The following cost driver information is expected for *each batch of 1,000 games*:

	Number of set-ups per batch	Number of quality inspections per batch	Number of packaging steps per batch	No. of maintenance events per year
Dungeons and Druids	2	2	1	10
Alien Invader Force	3	1	2	10
Sorcerers' Revenge	4	2	4	20

Required:

a For each product, calculate *the total production cost* for each batch of 1,000 games for each product using traditional absorption costing for the year 2009.

b Calculate *the total production cost* for each batch of 1,000 games for each product using ABC for the year 2009.

c Briefly discuss the advantages and disadvantages of ABC over traditional absorption costing. Your discussion should include a reference to the ways in which managers could use the cost information produced by ABC more meaningfully.

Activities and discussion questions

1 Costs based on absorption costing are not wholly accurate, and do not provide an appropriate basis for decision making. Discuss.

2 Why is absorption costing widely used?

3 Cost accounting is a system of recording, classifying and accumulating costs; there is no reason why this should be useful in management accounting. Discuss.

4 Absorption costing is often used in the pricing of long-term government contracts, as in the case of the building of submarines for the Royal Navy. Discuss and identify the reasons for this.

Accounting in context

Discuss and comment on the following extract from the press with reference to reducing costs, including overheads, in improving a company's performance.

Spirax-Sarco should steam ahead even in a downturn

By Josephine Moulds

Thomas Savery clocked the fact that steam was an efficient way of transferring energy back in 1698, when he invented the first crude steam engine. More than 300 years later and steam is still used in almost every industrial process.

FTSE 250 company Sprirax-Sarco Engineering has built its business on this discovery, and now boasts that it is the world leader in steam management.

It is a solid business that, unusually for an engineering group, proves relatively resilient in a downturn. That is because about 50pc of its revenues come from providing companies with replacement products, which often they cannot do without.

It is not, therefore, dependent on businesses splashing out on new equipment from tightly monitored capital expenditure budgets. Instead it depends on the day-to-day approvals for maintenance projects, paid out of companies' operating budgets, which tend to have rather looser purse strings.

Spirax has a hugely diverse customer base, spanning breweries to oil refineries, paper mills and dairies. Its largest sector is food, which represents just 10pc of sales. Customers are also spread across the world, with a sizeable 38pc of revenues coming from emerging markets.

Demand is driven by high energy prices and increasingly stringent environmental legislation.

Spirax products are energy-efficient and the company advises customers on improving their systems, cutting energy use and curbing their emissions. As a result, it does well when energy prices rise and companies look around for ways to rein in their costs. As Mark Vernon, chief executive, said: "We like high energy prices, as long as they don't dampen consumer spending overall."

Spirax also benefits from the trend for outsourcing, as it can take on maintenance contracts to look after its own products, bolstering the services business.

The results on Tuesday spoke for themselves. Pre-tax profits were hit by non-cash elements, such as the revaluation of a joint venture it bought out, which boosted profits in 2010 by £8 m. Stripping that out, pre-tax profits for the six months to June 2011 rose 15pc to £63m.

The operating margin inched up to almost 20pc. Revenues were 11pc higher, and organic sales growth 10pc. What's more, Spirax still has cost savings to come through from moving its plants in Cheltenham on to one site.

Mr Vernon did sound a warning note. Spirax may be resilient compared with other engineering groups but everything is relative. While its peers saw sales drop by between 15pc and 30pc in 2009, Spirax sales were off by 8pc.

▶

Mr Vernon said the company has a short order book, so it has limited insight into sales in the future. "We'll just have to see how the next six months play out," he said cautiously.

If history is anything to go by, he should not be too worried. Spirax has grown sales by an average 9pc a year over the past 25 years – even the tougher past five years it has managed an average 8pc a year. It is a hugely cash generative business, and has held or increased its dividend for the past 44 years.

With that track record, the shares look cheap on 12.5 times next year's earnings, particularly for a company that beats its peers in a downturn. A strong buy.

Source: The Telegraph, 24 August 2011.

References and further reading

Atkinson, A., R. Kaplan, E. Matsumura and M. Young (2012) *Management Accounting* (6th edn.). Harlow: Pearson.

Bhimani, A.C.T., S.M. Datar, C.T. Horngren and G. Foster (2012) *Management and Cost Accounting* (5th edn.). Upper Saddle River: FT Prentice Hall.

Drury, C. (2008) *Management and Cost Accounting* (7th edn.). Andover: Cengage Learning.

Dyson, J.R. (2010) *Accounting for Non-accounting Students* (8th edn.). Upper Saddle River, NJ: FT Prentice Hall.

Proctor, R. (2009) *Managerial Accounting for Business Decisions* (3rd edn.). Harlow: Pearson.

Seal, W., R.H. Garrison and E.W. Nooreen (2011) *Management Accounting* (4th edn.). Maidenhead: McGraw-Hill.

Online
LearningCentre

When you have read this chapter, log on to the Online Learning Centre website at *www.mcgraw-hill.co.uk/textbooks/leiwy* to explore chapter-by-chapter test questions, further reading and more online study tools.

Chapter 17

Marginal Costing and Decision-making

Chapter contents

✓ Learning objectives

After studying this chapter you will be able to:

- ✓ Distinguish between fixed and variable costs
- ✓ Calculate contribution and understand its meaning
- ✓ Understand the relevance, uses and assumptions of marginal costing
- ✓ Use marginal costing for a range of short-term decisions including break-even analysis, make and buy decisions and optimal use of scarce resource (limiting factor) decisions
- ✓ Be able to identify the advantages and limitations of marginal costing

17.1 Introduction

Absorption costing provides a means of ensuring that all products and services bear their fair share of costs; but it is not helpful in decision-making. The full cost of producing desks may be £240,000 a year, but that does not mean that £240,000 a year would be saved if the production of desks was stopped. Nor does it mean that the costs would go up or down by 10 per cent if the volume of production was increased or decreased by 10 per cent. In decision-making it is important the know the *behaviour* of costs so that questions such as the following can be answered.

What will happen to costs if

1 the volume of output is increased or decreased?
2 a production line is terminated?
3 a new product is introduced (and what volume of production and sales will be required to cover costs)?
4 new and better machinery is installed?

The key to establishing the behaviour of costs is to separate fixed costs from variable costs.

Fixed costs continue at much the same level, regardless of the volume of production. Such costs would include the rent, rates, lighting and heating of the factory, most of the costs of supervisory staff, and most machinery and maintenance costs.

Variable costs change directly in line with the volume of production. If the company stopped making desks, it would save all the costs of direct materials and direct labour. There would also be some reduction in production overheads – less power would be used, maintenance costs would probably be lower (if the machinery is used less), and there might be a reduction in 'indirect labour' costs (supervisors and others in the factory who are not direct labour).

17.2 Marginal Costing Presentation and Contribution

Marginal costing information can be presented for a business as a whole, or separately for each product, or combined, as shown in Illustration 17.1. Sales figures are shown first, then all variable costs are deducted to show the 'contribution' that each product makes towards fixed costs and profits.

When using costing information to make decisions, it is useful to be able to separate fixed costs from variable costs. Ways of doing this are outlined in the section on marginal costing below. The figures from Illustration 17.3 are presented in a marginal costing format in Illustration 17.4. Here, it is assumed that production overheads are half-fixed and half-variable; and that distribution and administrative overheads are mainly fixed (£78,000 fixed; £46,000 variable).

The following points emerge from the marginal costing presentation:

1 Each of the three products makes a 'contribution' towards fixed costs. Those costs will be incurred whether or not desks are made.
2 Desks make a contribution of £48,000. It might be 'fairer' if desks made a larger contribution. But if the company stops making desks it will be £48,000 worse off[1]; and its (modest) overall profit would become a loss.
3 Using marginal costing, variable costs are charged to each product; but fixed costs are dealt with only in total (not charged to individual products).
4 *Contribution* may be defined as sales minus variable costs, and it is worth calculating it for each product.

---

[1] Unless it replaces desks with a more profitable product, or increases the selling price of desks.

ILLUSTRATION 17.1 Marginal costing

	Total £000	Tables £000	Desks £000	Chairs £000
Sales	757	254	276	227
Variable costs				
Direct materials	300	100	120	80
Direct labour	160	50	60	50
Production overheads	80	25	30	25
Production costs	540	175	210	155
Distribution and administrative overheads[2]	46	15	18	13
Total variable costs	586	190	228	168
Contribution	171	64	48	59
Fixed costs				
Production overheads	80			
Distribution and administrative overheads	78			
Total fixed costs	158			
Profit	13			

5 *Contribution* is also equal to fixed costs plus profit; but fixed cost and profit are not shown for each product.

6 The above may be summarized as sales minus variable costs equals contribution, which equals fixed costs plus profit. This may be expressed as:

$$S - V = C = F + P$$

$$\text{or} \quad S - V = F + P = C$$

Absorption costing and marginal costing systems each provide information that is useful for different purposes.

17.3 Separating Fixed and Variable Costs

There are a number of ways of separating fixed from variable costs:

1 *Inspection, line by line* – Each item of expenditure can be examined and assessed as fixed or variable. Many items such as direct materials, direct labour, and some production overheads such as the power used to drive machinery are mainly variable. Other items such as rent, rates, insurance and most salaries are mainly fixed. The main problem with this approach is that some items are semi-fixed; for example, salaries where there is a bonus for higher levels of output or sales; and some items are semi-variable; for example, repairs to machinery and inspection of manufactured goods, which are likely to increase somewhat, but not by as much as the increase in production.

---

[2] Distribution and administrative overheads have been allocated to each product in proportion to total variable production costs. £46,000 is 8.52 per cent of £540,000; that percentage has been applied to the total variable production cost for each item: 8.52 per cent of 175,000 is £14,900, rounded to £15,000; 8.52 per cent of £210,000 is £17,900; 8.52 per cent of £155,000 is £13,200. Businesses are free to allocate overheads on whatever basis seems most appropriate to them.

2 *Comparing two periods* – Where the level of profit and sales is known for two periods, a lot of information can be deduced by comparing the two periods.

Illustration 17.2 does not seem to contain much information: sales have increased by 20 per cent; profits have increased by 50 per cent; the higher increase in profits is due to the incidence of fixed costs. In Illustration 17.3 a line for total costs (the difference between sales and profit) has been inserted, and the amount of change between March–April is shown. When sales increased by £20,000, variable costs increased by £15,000. We assume that fixed costs did not increase (because they are fixed), and so the whole of the increase in costs is an increase in variable costs. The relationship between variable costs and sales is therefore established: variable costs are 75 per cent of sales; this is shown in the fourth line of figures in Illustration 17.3. As total costs are made up of the two items (fixed costs; variable costs), the amount of fixed costs is simply the difference between line (iii) and line (iv); and it must be the same amount (in this case it is £15,000) for each month.

3 *Comparing several periods* – To see if the pattern suggested by just two periods is representative, it is more realistic to compare the level of costs with the level of output over a number of periods. This can be done in several ways:

a The measurements can be plotted on a graph, with a visual attempt at plotting a line that best fits the measurements. Cost levels at various levels of output can be read from the graph. Continuing that line down to a zero level of output suggests the amount of fixed costs (which is presumed to be the amount of costs the line shows at a zero level of output).

b Every measurement. Only two are considered – the highest level of output and the lowest. The calculation is then done using the highest and the lowest levels of production, using the method shown above for comparing two periods.

c Regression analysis, using the 'least squares' method, can be used to obtain a line of best fit, which takes all the available measurements into account. It assumes a straight-line relationship.

Greater mathematical precision in calculating the relationship in previous periods does not mean that the figures that are produced will provide better bases for decision-making. The usefulness of all costing information, when used for decision-making, depends on what assumptions are made (particularly about future cost levels). Realistic assumptions are more important than more refined and detailed mathematical accuracy in measuring previous relationships between costs.

ILLUSTRATION 17.2 Separating fixed and variable costs

	March £	April £
Sales	100,000	120,000
Profit	10,000	15,000

ILLUSTRATION 17.3 Separating fixed and variable costs

	March £	April £	Change £
i Sales	100,000	120,000	20,000
ii Profit	10,000	15,000	
iii Total costs	90,000	105,000	15,000
iv Variable costs	75,000	90,000	
v Fixed costs	15,000	15,000	

17.4 Break-even Analysis

Once we have separated fixed costs from variable costs, in a given situation we can calculate *contribution, break-even point* and *margin of safety*.

We know that profit is the difference between sales and costs; if we identify the two types of cost we can say that:

SALES minus VARIABLE COSTS minus FIXED COSTS equals PROFIT

This can be rearranged as:

SALES minus VARIABLE COSTS equals FIXED COSTS plus PROFIT

$$S - V = F + P = \text{Contribution}$$

That gives us two definitions of contribution:

Contribution is   Sales minus variable costs

or   Fixed costs plus profit

Each definition of 'contribution' should give the same answer. This can be illustrated using the figures for March from Illustration 17.3:

Sales minus variable costs

£100,000 – £75,000 = £25,000

Fixed costs plus profit

£15,000 + £10,000 = £25,000

The contribution/sales ratio can also be calculated. Expressed as a percentage it is contribution as a percentage of sales. It can also be expressed as contribution ÷ sales. Using the figures for March from Illustration 17.3, the contribution/sales ratio is:

$$\frac{£25,000}{£100,000} \text{ which is 25\%, of 0.25}$$

The *break-even point* is the level of sales at which neither profit nor loss is made. The sales revenue is equal to the costs incurred. Where a business makes many units that are identical, it can be expressed in terms of the number of units sold. Where a business makes a number of different products, it is expressed as the amount of sales in £'s rather than units. The calculation is as follows:

Break-even point in units

Fixed costs per annum ÷ contribution per unit

Break-even point in £'s sales

Fixed costs per annum ÷ contribution/sales ratio

The *margin of safety* is the amount by which sales can fall before reaching the break-even point. If sales fall by more than the margin of safety, losses will be incurred. In Example 17.2, the expected level of sales is 50,000 units a year and the margin of safety is 16,667 units because sales can fall to the break-even point, 33,333, before losses are made.

Example 17.1

The volume of production in units, and total production costs of the Soldrick Manufacturing Company in recent weeks were as follows:

Week	Number of units produced	Total production costs
1	80,000	176,000
2	76,000	170,000
3	82,000	177,000
4	84,000	180,000
5	77,000	170,750
6	82,000	176,500
7	79,000	106,200

The highest level of production was 84 in week 4 at a cost of £180,000
The lowest level of production was 76 in week 2 at a cost of £170,000

	Week 4	Week 2	Change
Production in units	84,000	76,000	8,000
Production costs	£180,000	£170,000	£10,000

It cost £10,000 to produce an extra 8,000 units. The variable cost per unit is therefore $\dfrac{£10,000}{8,000} = £1.25$ per unit

Production costs can now be split between fixed costs and variable costs, as follows:

	Week 4	Week 2
Variable costs	£105,000	£95,000
Fixed costs	£75,000	£75,000

Example 17.2

Break-even point

The Dulby company produces and sells 50,000 dulbies a year for £25 each. Variable costs amount to £16 per unit. Annual fixed costs are £300,000.

The contribution per unit is £25 − £16 = £9 per unit.
The break-even point in units is:

$$\frac{\text{Fixed costs}}{\text{Contribution per unit}} = \frac{£300,000}{£9} = 33,333 \text{ units}$$

Continued >>>

Example 17.2

Continued >>>

The contribution/sales ratio is £9 ÷ £25 = 36% or 0.36
    The break-even point in sales revenue is:

$$\frac{\text{Fixed costs}}{\text{Contribution / sales ratio}} = \frac{£300,000}{0.36} = £833,33$$

The sale of 33,333 units at £25 each would yield sales revenue of £833,333

The margin of safety can also be expressed in £'s of sales revenue. In Example 17.2 the level of sales is (50,000 × £25 =) £1,250,000; this can fall to £833,333, giving a margin of safety of £416,667 (which is 16,667 units).

17.5 Break-even Charts and Profit/Volume Graphs

ILLUSTRATION 17.4 Break-even chart of Dalby Company

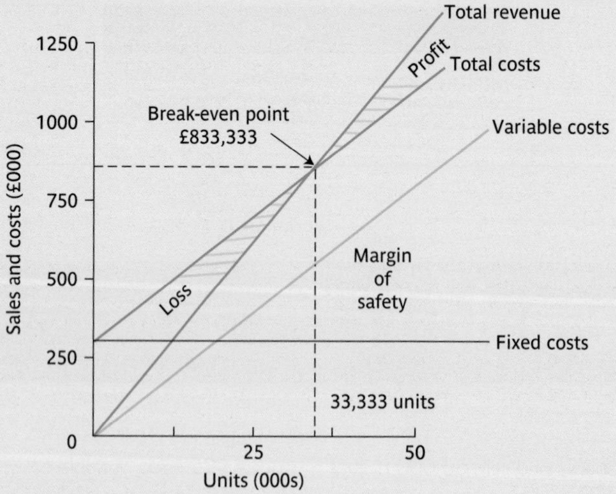

Note:

Break-even point is where total cost = total revenue

333,33 units and sales revenue of £833,325 : Margin of safety = expected output – break-even point

= 50000 – 33,333 units = 16,667 units

= £1,250,000 – 833,333 = £416,667 sales revenue

= 33%

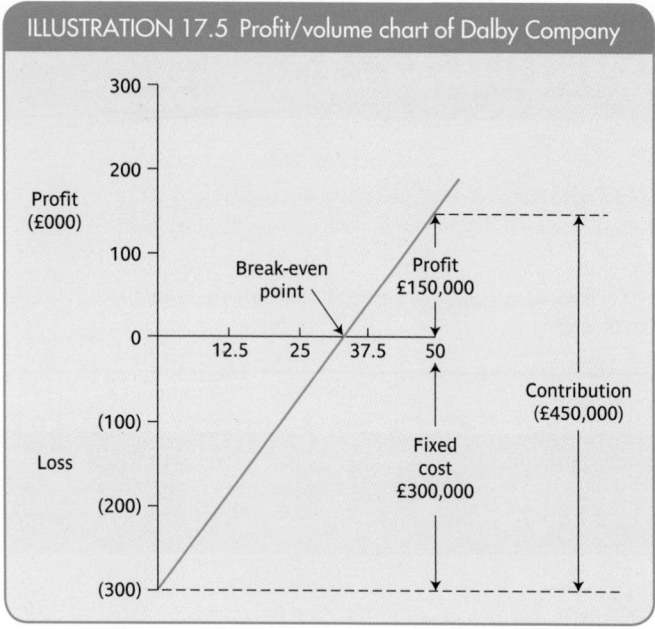

ILLUSTRATION 17.5 Profit/volume chart of Dalby Company

17.6 Marginal Costing and Decision-making

Once fixed costs have been separated from variable costs, it is possible to answer questions such as the following:

1 When launching a new product, what sales level is needed to ensure that all costs are covered?
2 When planning a price reduction, how many additional sales are required to make up for lost revenue?
3 By how much can the existing level of sales fall before the business starts to make losses?
4 What sales level is required to achieve a profit of, say, £50,000?
5 How can we maximize profitability when production is restricted by a limiting factor (such as limited machine capacity)?
6 Should we manufacture components in-house or buy them from outside ('make or buy' decisions)?

Examples of answers to the above six questions are shown in Examples 17.3–17.8. A break-even chart (Illustration 17.4) or a profit/volume chart (Illustration 17.5) can show answers to the first four questions.

17.7 Advantages of Marginal Costing

The main advantage of marginal costing is in decision-making: it focuses on how costs will behave as a result of changes in the volume of production. It takes no account of the effect of fixed costs which, within a specified range of output, are assumed not to change, and the existence of economies of scale (e.g. materials), where the unit purchase price might fall, as quantities increase or diseconomies of scale (e.g. labour), where the production increases, overtime rates might increase the unit cost. The

Example 17.3

Question:
The Burjy Company is planning to launch a new type of burjy that will sell for £100 each. Fixed costs are £80,000 per annum; variable costs are £60 per unit. How many do they need to sell to break even?

Answer:
Contribution is (£100 – £60) = £40 per unit; need enough contribution to cover fixed costs of £80,000. £80,000 ÷ £40 = 2,000 units to break even.

Example 17.4

Question:
The Mulby Company is planning to reduce the selling price of mulbies from £60 per unit to £50 per unit. Fixed costs are £900,000 per annum; variable costs are £30 per unit; 50,000 units per annum are made and sold. How many additional units must be sold to make up for the price reduction?

Answer:

Existing sales revenue	50,000 @ £60	£3,000,000
Existing costs 50,000 @ £30 = 1,500,000 + 900,000		£2,400,000
Existing profit		£600,000
Proposed contribution per unit (£50 – £30)		£20
Contribution required:		
Fixed costs	£900,000	
Profit	£600,000	
	£1,500,000	

Sales units required to make that contribution
£1,500,000 ÷ £20 = 75,000
An increase of 25,000 units is required

greater the volume of production, the more units there are, while the unit costs will not change, the total contribution will increase in direct proportion to the level of output. The focus is not on the 'profit' each product makes. It is on the 'contribution' that each product makes towards fixed costs that will be incurred regardless of the volume of production, and towards profit. A product may appear to be running at a loss (when absorption costing is used), but it is making a positive contribution to the fixed costs and profit of a business. In Illustration 16.1 absorption costing showed desks losing £12,000 a year. But if the business stopped making them, it would be £48,000 worse off because desks make a contribution of £48,000 a year (Illustration 17.1).

Example 17.5

Question:
The Gurby Company make and sells 1 million gurbies a year that sell for £20 each. Fixed costs are £600,000 a year and variable costs are £18 per unit. By how much can the existing level of sales fall before the company starts to make losses?

Answer using sales revenue:

Existing sales revenue 1 million @ £20 = £20,000,000

Contribution/sales ratio	£2 ÷ £20 = 10% or 0.1
Break-even point:	Fixed costs ÷ contribution sales ratio
	£600,000 ÷ 0.1 = £6,000,000

Sales can fall by £14m.

Answer using units:

Existing sales units	1,000,000
Contribution per unit	£2
Break-even point	= fixed costs ÷ £2

£600,000 ÷ £2 = 300,000 units

Sales can fall by 700,000 units.

Comparing two answers: 700,000 units @ £20 = £14m sales revenue

Example 17.6

Question:
The summarized results of the Pulby Company are as follows:

	£
Sales 10,000 units at £30 each	300,000
Variable costs at £25 each	250,000
Fixed costs	45,000
Profit	5,000

How many more units does it need to sell to make a profit of £50,000?

Answer:
It needs £45,000 additional contribution. Contribution is £5 per unit. It needs to sell an extra 9,000 units.

Example 17.7

Limiting factors

The Wink Company produces three types of wink: Fenwinks, Garwinks and Hoodwinks, details of which are as follows:

	Fenwinks	Garwinks	Hoodwinks
Demand in units per annum	100,000	140,000	200,000
	£	£	£
Selling price per unit	50	80	100
Variable costs per unit	20	40	55
Contribution per unit	30	40	45

If the company had unlimited production facilities, it would produce all it could sell. If demand were limited to 350,000 units per annum, it would produce all the Hoodwinks and Garwinks it could (340,000 units) because they each make the greatest contribution. It would produce only 10,000 Fenwinks.

Its problem is that, because of health and safety regulations, all products have to be treated by their safety-wink machine, which has a capacity of only 400,000 hours per annum. The time taken to treat each product is as follows:

Fenwinks	1 hour
Garwinks	1½ hours
Hoodwinks	2 hours

If it concentrated on producing only Hoodwinks (because they have the highest contribution per unit) its total production would be 200,000 units, using all the capacity of the safety-wink machine, which would give a contribution of 200,000 × £45 = £9,000,000.

Instead, it should concentrate on producing the items that give the greatest contribution per unit of limiting factor; that is, the greatest contribution per hour of the safety-wink machine.

	Fenwinks	Garwinks	Hoodwinks
Demand in units per annum	100,000	140,000	200,000
Contribution per unit	£30	£40	£45
Time on safety-wink machine	1 hour	1½ hours	2 hours
Contribution per hour of safety wink machine	£30	£26.67	£22.50

The production plan should be as follows:

	Number produced	Contribution generated	Safety-wink hours used	Safety-wink hours remaining
Fenwinks	100,000	£3,000,000	100,000	300,000
Garwinks	140,000	£5,600,000	210,000	90,000
Hoodwinks	45,000	£2,430,000	90,000	0
Total contribution		£11,030,000		

Continued >>>

Example 17.7

Continued >>>

By concentrating on making items that maximize the contribution per unit[3] of the limiting factor it has made a total contribution of just over £11m. If it had simply concentrated on producing items that maximized the contribution *per item of production*, the total contribution would have been only £9m.

However, this analysis assumed that there is no interrelated demand among these three products. If, for example, Nike were selling three products – trainers, t-shirts and caps – and the trainers had the lowest contribution per unit of scarce resource, it will still be necessary to make and sell this product because it is the trainers that create the demand for the other two products. Additionally, of course, it might be possible to remove or mitigate the constraint by acquiring another machine, finding another source for a scarce material or finding additional labour from abroad.

Ranking products in order of their contribution per unit of the limiting factor is the strategy when there is only *one* scarce resource; if there is more than one scarce resource, we then have to resort to *linear programming*, an operational research technique.

Sometimes a business wants to quote low prices, perhaps in order to penetrate a new export market, or as a 'loss leader' to encourage customers to buy other products. By identifying the marginal cost of a product, it is possible to see the minimum selling price that would not produce a loss. Where pricing decisions consider only full absorption costs, there is little flexibility, and it is difficult to see the effects of different pricing decisions.

Example 17.8

Question:
The Baldwynne Company manufactures almost all of the components it uses in-house. An important component, the wynngie, costs £50 to produce. An outside supplier can provide wynngies at a price of £43 each. The production cost of a wynngie is as follows:

	£
Direct materials	14
Direct labour	12
Production overheads	24
	50

Production overheads, one-third of which are variable, are charged at 200 per cent of direct labour costs.
Should the company continue to produce, or buy in wynngies?

Answer:
The variable costs of production are £14 + £12 + £8 = £34 per unit. It is cheaper to make them than buy them (unless production capacity is limited, and an alternative product can make a greater contribution).

---

[3] In this case the unit of limiting factor is hours. It could be, for example, litres or kilo, if only a limited amount of a raw material was available.

Break-even analysis clearly identifies the effects of changes in volume, the break-even point and the margin of safety.

Where marginal costing is used for valuing closing inventories, the resulting profit figures will be different from absorption costing and, arguably, more realistic. In Illustration 17.6 (a), closing inventories are shown at full absorption cost of £80 per unit, and gross profit is £18,000. In Illustration 17.6 (b), closing inventories are shown at marginal cost, which is £30, and gross profit is only £13,000. The difference arises because, in absorption costing, closing inventories include their share of fixed production overheads; these are carried forward to be treated as an expense in the following year. In marginal costing, closing inventories include only variable production costs; the whole of the fixed production overheads is written off as an expense in the current year. In Illustrations 17.6 (a) and 17.6 (b) closing inventory is 100 units, and fixed production overheads are £50 per unit: this amounts to £5,000, which is the difference in gross profit between the two methods.

Which method is 'better' is debatable. Normal financial accounting standards require the use of absorption costing, so that closing inventories include their fair share of fixed production overheads. But if the net realizable value of closing inventories is less than the cost figure shown (in this case £8,000), they should be written down to realizable value.

17.8 Limitations of Marginal Costing

1   Marginal costing is not acceptable for the valuation of closing inventories in financial accounting.
2   The use of marginal costing might encourage selling at prices that are too low to cover fixed costs and to make a profit. The view might be taken that all orders are worth while, provided the price

ILLUSTRATION 17.6 (a) Absorption costing

		£
Sales	900 @ £100 each	90,000
	Opening inventory	0
	Absorption cost of production 1,000 @ £80 each	80,000
	Closing inventory 100 @ £80 each	(8,000)
Production cost of goods sold		(72,000)
Gross profit		18,000

ILLUSTRATION 17.6 (b) Marginal costing

		£
Sales	900 @ £100 each	90,000
	Opening inventory	0
	Variable cost of production 1,000 @ £30 each	30,000
	Closing inventory 100 @ £30 each	(3,000)
Marginal cost of goods sold		(27,000)
Contribution		63,000
Fixed production overheads		(50,000)
Gross profit		13,000

covers variable costs, and makes a positive contribution. But if there are too many orders that make only a small contribution, fixed costs will not be covered, and the business will make a loss. There are often occasions when it is worth taking some orders that make only a small contribution; but there will be serious problems if a company does not make a sufficient contribution overall.

3   The main danger of marginal costing and break-even analysis is that it is based on simplifying assumptions and can lead to oversimplistic interpretation, and to bad decisions. The following assumptions may be reasonable where only modest changes are expected, but would not be true in respect of major changes in levels of production.

   a   Cost behaviour is linear; that is, total costs vary in line with the level of output, as shown on profit/volume graphs and break-even charts. In practice the line of total costs would often be curved, or go up in steps (e.g. when new production facilities come on stream).

   b   Variable costs per unit remain constant. In practice direct material costs per unit might decrease as output increases because of economies from bulk buying. Labour costs per unit might also decrease as employees become more efficient (the 'learning curve' effect). But in some circumstances increased production may lead to material and labour shortages, and increased costs. Break-even analysis usually assumes that there are no changes in efficiency or productivity.

   c   All costs can be classified as fixed or variable. Although the behaviour of costs can be plotted over a period of time, and relationships assumed, those relationships can easily change as circumstances change.

   d   Fixed costs remain constant. This is unlikely to be true in the long run. If production is to increase beyond the capacity of current capacity, there will have to be a step up to increase production facilities. If production declines sufficiently, factories will close, and 'fixed' costs will be reduced. In the long run most 'fixed' costs are variable.

   e   Variable costs vary in line with production. This may be true when there is time to adjust. But direct labour cannot usually be switched on and off instantly because of people's contracts of employment. In the short term direct labour costs may be more like fixed costs.

If these limitations are borne in mind marginal costing should provide a better basis for decision-making than absorption costing.

📖 Summary

Fixed costs do not change with the level of output within a given range, while marginal costs vary with the level of output. In marginal costing, fixed costs are not associated with a unit of output and absorbed into the cost of a unit but are treated as period costs. Contribution per unit is the selling price less the variable costs and the contribution per unit is a contribution towards covering the company's fixed costs and after having covered the fixed costs (i.e. having broken even), each additional unit sold makes a profit equivalent to the unit contribution. Marginal or variable costs and contribution can be used to establish the number of units required to make a given profit, to calculate the number of units required to break even, and to help in making such decisions as whether to make or buy goods and what to make in the event that there are insufficient resources, materials or labour, for instance, to satisfy the demand for the company's output.

Like all management accounting models, marginal costing makes various assumptions and has some limitations but it is a very useful way of making several types of short-term decision.

⇒ Review of key points

- Fixed costs are costs that do not vary with the level of production within a specified range of output and/or time.
- Variable costs are costs that vary with production.
- Contribution per unit = selling price – variable cost.
- PV ratio = contribution per unit/selling price per unit × 100.
- Break-even point = fixed costs/selling price per unit.
- Margin of safety = budgeted or expected output – break-even point.
- Break-even point and margin of safety can be determined graphically as well as in a computation.
- With limiting factors, products should be 'ranked' in order of their contribution per unit of scarce resource.
- Marginal costing assumes that costs can be classified according to whether they are fixed or variable.
- It is assumed that there are no economies or diseconomies of scale and that fixed costs, variable costs and revenues are all linear, varying in proportion to output.

! Self-testing questions

1 Define 'contribution', 'break-even point' and 'margin of safety'?

2 How can fixed costs be estimated or measured separately from variable costs?

3 The Dannidhoon Company is planning to launch a new type of dhoon that will sell for £60 each. Fixed costs are £700,000 per annum; variable costs are £35 per unit. How many does it need to sell to break even?

	September	October
	£000	£000
Sales	600	650
Profit	100	120

From the above information calculate total costs for each month, variable costs as a percentage of sales, fixed costs, contribution/sales ratio and break-even point.

4 The Paradise Island Building Company builds three types of residence, details of which are shown below. It has always concentrated on the luxury end of the market where prices and profits are highest. Recently the government has required work permits for all building workers, and the company is allowed to use only (a) 30,000 hours a year or (b) 51,000 hours. What other factors might be taken into consideration in the decision?

	Holiday chalets	Terraced houses	Luxury villas
Annual demand	20	30	10
Labour hours to build a home	300	600	3,000
	£000	£000	£000
Selling price per home	100	200	800
Variable costs per home	70	120	420

You are required to calculate:

a the contribution for each type of home;

b the amount of contribution per unit of limiting factor, assuming first there are 30,000 labour hours available and, second, there are 51,000 labour hours available;

c its optimum building plan, and the total contribution it would generate;

d any other factors you think should be taken into consideration in making this decision.

5 Eagle Sandwiches makes and sells sandwiches in a local light industrial zone. The average variable cost of a sandwich is £1, while the average selling price is £3. Weekly fixed costs are £4,000, while budgeted sales are 2,400 units. Calculate the profit at the forecast level of sales, the break-even point in terms of both units and sales revenue, the margin of safety in terms of both units and sales revenue and as a percentage of sales revenue, and draw a break-even chart reflecting this decision.

 ## Assessment questions

1 Define 'fixed costs' and 'variable costs'.

2 How does marginal costing differ from absorption costing?

3 The Cornay Company is planning to reduce the selling price of cornays from £110 per unit to £99 per unit. Fixed costs are £3,600,000 per annum; variable costs are £40 per unit; 80,000 units per annum are made and sold. How many additional units must be sold to make up for the price reduction?

4 The summarized results of the Poterin Company are as follows:

	£
Sales 6,000 units at £150 each	900,000
Variable costs at £130 each	780,000
Fixed costs	100,000
Profit	20,000

How many more units does it need to sell to make a profit of £90,000?

	February	March
	£	£
Sales	120,000	150,000
Profit	24,000	34,000

From the above information calculate total costs for each month, variable costs as a percentage of sales, fixed costs, contribution/sales ratio and break-even point.

5 Persie Limited is dedicated to the production and sale of highly fashionable sunglasses. The company's budgeted monthly production is 3,000 units. Variable manufacturing costs are £16 per unit, while variable selling costs are £4 per unit. Fixed selling costs are £24,000 per month, while monthly fixed manufacturing costs are £30,000. Each pair of sunglasses sells for £40. The company values stock on a first-in-first-out basis.

Other data relating to July and August were as follows:

Number of units	July	August
Opening inventory	400	100
Production	3,400	3,300
Sales	3,700	2,800
Closing inventory	100	600

Required:

a Prepare an income statement for Persie Limited for both July and August using:

  i   marginal costing;

  ii absorption costing.

b Present a calculation explaining the differences between the profits arising from the two methods.

Group activities and discussion questions

1 'Break-even analysis is pointless, given the unrealistic and simplistic assumptions of the model.' Identify these assumptions and discuss this statement.

2 Increasingly, companies are outsourcing activities that were previously handled in-house by employees. What activities do you believe are subject to such a policy? What are the advantages and disadvantages of such a policy?

3 In the circumstances that a manufacturer is operating with scarce resources, what are the dangers of determining production on the basis of the ranking of the products according to their contribution per unit of that scarce resource?

4 Absorption costing overstates the profit of a manufacturer when compared to margin costing. Discuss why this might be argued.

Accounting in context

Discuss and comment on the following article from the press with reference to effect on break-even point and margin of safety arising from expected changes in selling price and expected increases in production and sales units.

Avocet beats guidance

When it comes to production guidance, the best thing mining companies can do is under-promise and over-deliver. This is what Avocet Mining has done.

By Garry White

The gold mining company, which owns 90pc of the Inata gold mine in Burkina Faso, issued a production update on the final quarter of last year that smashed expectations. Avocet produced 46,102 ounces of ▶

gold in the three months ending December – 39pc more than the previous quarter. Guidance was for 40,000 ounces.

This brought total production for the year to 166,744 ounces, compared with guidance of 160,000 to 165,000 ounces. For 2012, the guidance is a conservative 160,000 ounces.

The company has had a busy couple of years – selling off its South East Asian gold mines for £200m to focus on West Africa. As well as Inata, the group has a pipeline of exploration projects in Burkina Faso, Guinea and Mali.

Avocet is ramping up Inata production and this is going to consume most of the cash that it throws off over the next couple of years. However, gold prices are likely to stay at elevated levels for some time.

Indeed, the prospect of more quantitative easing in the US, as hinted at by Ben Bernanke, Federal Reserve chairman, on Wednesday, sent the gold price once again above $1,700 an ounce. Guidance for the cash cost of producing each ounce at Inata is $800 to $850 an ounce this year.

Most gold miners have underperformed over the past year or so but the view is building that they could have a better 2012. This includes Avocet. Indeed, last week Nomura named Avocet as one of its top three picks in the sector.

The group should continue to throw off cash and, although one should never buy a share on bid hopes alone, some analysts regard it as a prime acquisition target.

Avocet does not currently pay a dividend and it is likely to use its cash flow to invest in new projects, so Questor does not expect any payments soon.

The shares are trading on a December 2012 multiple of 14.1, falling to 8.1 in 2013.

Last tipped at 190p on June 28 last year the shares are up 19pc compared with a FTSE 100 up less than 1pc since that date.

The shares are a buy.

Source: The Telegraph, 27 January 2012.

References and further reading

Atkinson, A., R. Kaplan, E. Matsumura and M. Young (2012) *Management Accounting* (6th edn.). Harlow: Pearson.

Bhimani, A.C.T., S.M. Datar, C.T. Horngren and G. Foster (2012) *Management and Cost Accounting* (5th edn.). Upper Saddle River, NJ: FT Prentice Hall.

Drury, C. (2008) *Management and Cost Accounting* (7th edn.). Andover: Cengage Learning.

Dyson, J.R. (2010) *Accounting for Non-accounting Students* (8th edn.). Upper Saddle River, NJ: FT Prentice Hall.

Harris, E. (1995) *Marginal Costing.* London: CIMA Publishing.

Proctor, R. (2009) *Managerial Accounting for Business Decisions* (3rd edn.). Harlow: Pearson.

Seal, W., R.H. Garrison and E.W. Nooreen (2011) *Management Accounting* (4th edn.). Maidenhead: McGraw-Hill.

Online LearningCentre

When you have read this chapter, log on to the Online Learning Centre website at *www.mcgraw-hill.co.uk/textbooks/leiwy* to explore chapter-by-chapter test questions, further reading and more online study tools.

Chapter 18

Standard Costing and Variance Analysis

Chapter contents

✓ Learning objectives

After studying this chapter you will be able to:

- ✓ Understand the role of standard costing and variance analysis
- ✓ Calculate, analyse and interpret direct material, direct labour and overhead variances
- ✓ Calculate, analyse and interpret sales margin variances
- ✓ Use variances to analyse and explain differences between budgeted profit and actual profit
- ✓ Evaluate the role, strengths and weaknesses of standard costing and variance analysis

18.1 Introduction

Chapter 15 showed how budgeting can be used to 'control' a business. Plans or budgets that show how the company's objectives can be achieved are set down and approved. They provide the basis for controlling the business. Actual results are then compared with planned results to see how they differ and what changes need to be made.

Where actual profits turn out to be very different from those that were planned, the problems are to do with costs, and with sales revenues. If costs and sales are not at the levels that they *should be*, the reasons must be identified, and, if possible, corrective action taken. Standard costing shows what costs *should be*. Where actual costs are different from standard costs there are one or more 'variances'. Variance analysis can also be identified for sales.

It is possible to calculate a set of cost variances and sales margin variances that explain the difference between budgeted profits and actual profits achieved. The variances are intended to point management in the direction of improved performance. In Examples 18.1 and 18.2 it is not surprising that profits are higher than budget because the volume of sales and the selling price are both higher than budget. But the increase in profit compared with budget is modest (only £1,000). Variance analysis can identify where their performance is unsatisfactory or inefficient, and where they have done well.

Example 18.1

Busy Airports plc plans to produce 100,000 meals per month and to sell them at £3.50 each. The standard cost of production per meal is:

	£	
Direct materials	1.00	1/2kg @ £2 per kg
Direct labour	0.50	3 minutes @ £10 per hour
Variable overheads	0.75	£15 per hour
Total variable costs	2.25	
Fixed overheads	0.80	£80,000 per month
	3.05	

Budgeted profit is 100,000 meals @ 45 pence = £45,000
Its actual costs and revenues last month were:

	£	£
Sales 110,000 meals @ £3.60		396,000
Direct materials 54 kg	118,000	
Direct labour 5,200 hours	53,000	
Variable overheads	87,000	
Fixed overheads	82,000	
Total costs		340,000
Profit		56,000

Example 18.2

	Per unit	Standard costs Total for 100,000 meals	Flexed budget Total for 110,000 meals		Actual results Total for 110,000 meals	Per unit
	£	£	£		£	£
Sales	3.50	350,000	385,000	54 kg	396,000	3.60
Direct materials	1.00	100,000	110,000	5,200 hrs	118,000	1.073
Direct labour	0.50	50,000	55,000		53,000	0.482
Variable overheads	0.75	75,000	82,500		87,000	0.791
Fixed overheads	0.80	80,000	80,000		82,000	0.745
Total costs	3.05	305,000	327,500		340,000	3.091
Profit	0.45	45,000	57,500		56,000	0.509

Direct material and direct labour variances are very similar. If actual costs are higher than standard costs it is due to one or both of the following:

1 More materials or labour have been used than standard (direct material usage variance; direct labour efficiency variance); and/or

2 The price of materials or labour is higher than standard (direct material price variance; direct labour rate variance).

Variable overhead variances are typically in proportion to direct labour variances (variable overheads are typically charged as a proportion of direct labour hours).

When calculating cost variances it is important to compare actual costs with standard costs; and to remember that the standard cost of production is what it should have cost to produce the amount that was *actually produced*; that is, using the flexed budget. Of course it costs more to produce more. The important question is: have costs gone up more, or less, than would be expected for *that volume* of production.

18.2 Direct Material Variances

As direct material costs should be £1 per meal, and 110,000 meals were produced, the cost should have been £110,000; but the actual cost was £118,000. This was not due to food being wasted; indeed, they used only 54 kg of food whereas the standard amount (for that volume of output) was 55 kg. The reduction in the amount of food saved was £2,000; that is the direct material usage variance. But the cost of buying food increased. It bought 54 kg of food, which should have cost £108,000 but actually cost £118,000. This extra £10,000 is the direct material price variance and is due to price increases (see Illustration 18.1).

Managers need to consider why the variances have arisen. Perhaps the favourable usage variance was because less food was wasted (and maybe the quality of the meals suffered). Perhaps the adverse price variance was due to the demand suddenly increasing, and having to buy extra food at short notice from more expensive suppliers. Or perhaps market prices had increased generally.

In other circumstances where there is an increase in production, it might be expected that the variances would be the other way around. Purchasing greater quantities can mean obtaining bulk

ILLUSTRATION 18.1 Direct material variances

Actual cost		Actual quantities @ planned price		Standard cost
		54 kg @ £2 per kg		110,000 meals @ £1 each
£118,000		£108,000		£110,000
	Direct material price variance £10,000 adverse		Direct material usage variance £2,000 favourable	
		Direct material cost variance £8,000 adverse		
In sum:				
Direct materials	Price	AQ × (AP − SP)		
Variances	Usage	SP × (AQ − SQ)		

discounts, and favourable direct material price variances. And a sudden need to work more quickly can lead to more materials being wasted, and an adverse direct material usage variance. Perhaps the price and usage variances are interrelated; if there is a favourable price variance and an adverse usage variance, perhaps lower quality materials were purchased and that led to greater wastage.

The important thing for management is to identify what has gone wrong, why and what can be done about it.

Direct material cost variances can be analysed in more detail, identifying price and usage variances for each category of direct material. Where different direct materials are mixed together, it is possible to subdivide the usage variance into a mix variance (due to a change in the proportions used in the mixing), and yield variance (due to a higher or lower amount of end products emerging from the process). It is also possible to subdivide the price variance to see which materials have increased most in price, and perhaps which have gone down.

18.3 Direct Labour Variances

As direct labour costs should be 50 pence per meal, and 110,000 meals were produced, the cost should have been £55,000; but the actual cost was only £53,000. Clearly the workers were not lazy or inefficient; indeed, they needed to work for only 5,200 hours to produce 110,000 meals. The standard amount of time specified for producing that number of meals is 5,500 hours.

In this example production can be measured in units: number of meals. In a business that produces many different products, 'units' may not be comparable. Another way of measuring output is the 'standard hour'. This is the amount of production that should be achieved in one hour. As each meal is expected to take three minutes to produce, in one hour 20 meals should be produced. Therefore 110,000 meals should take $110,000 \div 20 = 55,000$ hours. The actual amount produced was 5,500 standard hours (or 110,000 meals).

Illustration 18.2 shows the calculation of variances using units, which is probably easier. Illustration 18.3 shows the calculation of variances using standard hours as the measure of output, which is probably harder, but it is often the only method possible.

The rate variance (like a direct material price variance) is not too difficult. It is based on the actual number of hours worked (regardless of what was produced), and compares the planned rate of pay with what was actually paid. In this instance 5,200 hours were worked; that should have cost £10 per hour; the cost should have been £52,000. The actual cost was £53,000. There is an adverse direct

ILLUSTRATION 18.2 Direct labour variances

Actual cost	Actual hours @ planned rate	Standard cost
	5,200 hours @ £10 per hour	110,000 meals @ 50p each
£53,000	£52,000	£55,000

Direct labour rate variance £1,000 adverse

Direct labour efficiency variance £3,000 favourable

Direct labour cost variance £2,000 favourable

ILLUSTRATION 18.3 Direct labour variances

Actual cost	Actual hours @ planned rate	Standard cost
		Standard hours for actual production 5,500 hours @ £10 per hour
	5,200 hours @ £10 per hour	
£53,000	£52,000	£55,000

Direct labour rate variance £1,000 adverse

Direct labour efficiency variance £3,000 favourable

Direct labour cost variance £2,000 favourable

In sum:

Direct labour variances: rate: AH × (AR − SR)

efficiency: SR × (AH − SH)

---

labour rate variance of £1,000. There is no need to calculate the actual hourly rate of pay; the calculation can be done simply using the total amount paid.

The efficiency variance is based on the amount actually produced. It compares what that output should have cost with the hours actually taken to produce that. The amount actually produced can be calculated using *units*, as shown in Illustration 18.2, or *standard hours*, as shown in Illustration 18.3.

Using units, production was 110,000 meals, which, at £0.50 each, should have cost £55,000.

Using 'standard hours' as the measure, the production amounted to 5,500 hours, which should have cost £55,000.

The standard cost of production (£55,000 worth of production) is then compared with the actual number of hours it took to achieve that level of production (charged at the standard hourly rate): 5,200 hours were worked, which at £10 per hour, should have cost £52,000. The difference between the £53,000 and the £55,000 is the direct labour efficiency variance, which in this instance is favourable.

Any changes in the actual rate of pay are ignored in calculating the direct labour efficiency variance; they are separately calculated in the direct labour rate variance.

There is no need for the more complicated calculations used by those who like formulae.[1] The main variances can be calculated by using the three columns shown. On the left is the actual cost – easy

---

[1] For example, we could calculate that the actual rate of pay was £53,000 ÷ 52,000 hours = £10.192307 per hour. The standard rate of pay was £10 per hour. The variance in the rate per hour was £0.192307. As 52,000 hours were worked, the total adverse labour rate variance is 52,000 × £0.192307 = £999.99.

enough. On the right is the standard cost: the only difficulty is to remember that it is the *actual* volume of production shown at what it should have cost. The middle column is more difficult: it is the actual number of hours, multiplied by the standard rate per hour.

The left-hand column and the middle column both include the actual hours worked: the only difference is that the left has been calculated using the actual rate of pay per hour; the middle column shows the standard rate of pay. The difference between the two columns is the rate variance.

It is worth investigating the causes of the variances. It is possible that workers were more efficient because they were paid more. Or perhaps there are some greater efficiencies with an increased volume of production. The adverse rate variance may have been because of the need to work overtime with higher rates of pay. Perhaps the rate and efficiency variances are interrelated; if there is a favourable rate variance and an adverse efficiency variance, perhaps lower grade workers were used and that led to inefficiencies.

It is also possible that the original standards specified were unrealistic.

18.4 Variable Overhead Variances

Variable overheads are in proportion to labour costs. In this illustration, labour costs are £10 per hour; variable overheads are £15 per hour. Although they worked only 5,200 hours, the amount of production achieved was 5,500 standard hours. The standard cost of the amount actually produced was 5,500 at £15 (the variable overhead recovery rate), which is £82,500. They were efficient, as with labour, in producing more 'hours worth' (or standard hours) of production than the number of hours they worked: 300 hours at £15 per hour is £4,500; that is the variable overhead efficiency variance.

Although variable overheads should have been £78,000 for the number of hours worked, they were, in fact, £9,000 more. Possible explanations for this would include an increase in the price of items within variable overheads, and perhaps the need for more supervision, inspection, transport, administration, and so on as a result of the increased output. It is possible to analyse the variable overhead expenditure variance to see the extent to which it is due to price increases, and the extent to which it is due to a greater volume of expenditure (see Illustration 18.4).

ILLUSTRATION 18.4 Variable overhead variances

Actual cost	Actual hours @ planned rate	Standard cost
£87,000	5,200 hours @ £15 per hour £78,000	110,000 meals @ 75p each £82,500
	Variable overhead expenditure variance £9,000 adverse	Variable overhead efficiency variance £4,500 favourable
	Variable overhead cost variance £4,500 favourable	

In sum:

Variable overhead	Price	$AQ \times (AP - SP)$
Variances	Efficiency	$SP \times (AQ - SQ)$

18.5 Fixed Overhead Variances

Fixed overheads are not expected to vary with the amount of production. The company planned to spend £80,000 during the month, but actually spent £82,000. This adverse expenditure variance could be due to particularly large expenses having to be paid that month (rent, rates, maintenance); or to inflationary pressures (e.g. salary increases); or it could be that fixed overheads were not as fixed as had been thought, and some expenditure increased as production increased.

The standard cost of production (£88,000) is expected to be more than the amount budgeted because more was produced. Even if fixed overheads are totally fixed, using absorption costing, fixed overheads are still charged out at £16 per hour. If 10 per cent more is produced, the costing records will show that it cost 10 per cent more because of the way that costs are charged out. (The budget was £80,000; the standard cost was £88,000.)

In the following table the difference between the Budget column and the Standard column arises because the volume of production was greater than had been budgeted. This is the fixed overhead volume variance. The company budgeted to work for 5,000 hours; it produced 5,500 hours worth of production. The favourable volume variance is 500 hours at £16, which is £8,000.

The volume variance is partly due to working more hours than specified in the budget (5,200 hours instead of 5,500 hours); and partly because the staff worked more efficiently.

The efficiency variance arises because they worked only 5,200 hours to produce 5,500 standard hours worth of production. This mirrors the direct labour and variable overhead efficiency variances; each is at a different rate per hour. Fixed overheads are charged at £16 per hour, and so the fixed overhead efficiency variance is 300 hrs × £16 = £4,800 favourable. The capacity utilization variance arises because they used more of their capacity than they planned. They worked for 5,200 hours instead of the 5,000 hours budgeted. This meant that more overheads were charged out, which is 'favourable'.

One advantage of calculating the variances using the columns shown in Illustration 18.5 is that it is easy to see which variances are favourable, and which are adverse. If actual costs (on the left) are lower than standard costs (on the right), that is favourable. Indeed, if any item to the left is lower, that is favourable.

18.6 Sales Margin Variances

The amount of sales revenue earned during a period may be different from the amount budgeted because (a) the volume of sales is different from budget; and/or (b) the price of sales is different from budget. But in calculating the variances it is not the sales revenue that matters. What matters is the effect of changes in sales volume and sales price on profit; it is the margin between costs and selling price that is used in calculating sales variances. All cost variances should already have been identified; sales margin variances base the margin on standard costs; and on the margin between standard cost and actual selling price.

It is legitimate to refer to sales volume variance and sales price variance. But adding the word 'margin' to the names of the variances is a useful reminder that they are not based on sales revenues, but on the margins, or amounts of profit, that would be generated.

The sales margin price variance measures the effect of a change in price. The first and third columns in the following table both show the actual volume of sales. The difference between them is that the first is based on the actual selling price; and the third is based on the budgeted selling price.

The sales margin volume variance measures the effect of a change in volume. The third and fifth columns in the table both show the budgeted profit margin. The difference between them is that the third column shows the actual volume of sales, and the fifth column shows the budgeted volume of sales.

ILLUSTRATION 18.5 Fixed overhead variances

Actual cost	Budgeted hours @ planned rate	Capacity used (hours worked)	Standard cost
	5,000 hours @ £16 per hour	5,200 hours @ £16 per hour	110,000 meals[2] @ 80p each
£82,000	£80,000	83,200	£88,000

Fixed overhead expenditure variance £2,000 adverse

Fixed overhead capacity utilization variance £3,200 favourable

Fixed overhead efficiency variance £4,800 favourable

Fixed overhead volume variance £8,000 favourable

Fixed overhead cost variance £6,000 favourable

Fixed overhead variances can be further analysed by showing, for example, separate variances for fixed production, administration and selling and distribution overheads.

In simple terms:

Fixed overheads	Expenditure	Actual FO – budgeted FO
Variances	Volume	Budgeted FO – (AQ × SP per unit)

In Illustration 18.6 all the sales margin variances are based on the assumption that the cost of production was £3.05 per meal. The planned profit margin for each meal was 45 pence; but the actual selling price was 10 pence higher and so the actual profit margin was 10 pence higher.

Using the table if the figures to the left are higher, that is favourable. With costs it is obviously the other way around: if actual costs to the left are higher, that is adverse.

As with most variances it is possible to subdivide them. This illustration assumes that there is only one product. Where there are a number of different products, price variances can be calculated for

ILLUSTRATION 18.6 *Margin* approach

Actual sales @ actual margin	Actual sales @ planned margin	Budgeted sales @ budgeted margin
110,000	110,000 hours	100,000 meals
@ 55 p	@ 45 p	@ 45 p each
£60,500	£49,500	£45,000

Sales price variance £11,000 favourable

Sales margin volume variance £4,500 favourable

Total sales variance £15,500 favourable

[2] As with direct labour and variable overhead variances, the standard cost of production can be measured in standard hours. The standard hours of production is 5,500 hours, which, at the hourly rate of £16, is £88,000.

each. It is also likely that the actual mix of products sold will be different from what was budgeted; it is then possible to divide the volume variance into a mix variance and a quantity variance.

18.7 Summary of Variances

Where both cost and sales margin variances are calculated, the sum of all the variances should equal the difference between the budgeted profit for the period and the actual profit achieved and can be summarized in a 'performance report'. See Illustration 18.7.

Interpretation of these variances

The firm made £11,000 more profit than it had planned. This was overwhelmingly due to a favourable sales performance. It increased both the volume of sales, and the selling price, which would have increased profits by £15,500. There were, however, some adverse cost variances.

There were adverse expenditure variances on both fixed and variable overheads amounting to £11,000. This may have been due partly to cost increases with respect to various overhead items (e.g. increases in rents, rates, electricity); it may be that they spent a lot more on marketing to achieve the higher sales levels; and it could be that the distinction between fixed and variable overheads had not accurately been determined.

In other areas there were efficiency gains with savings on material usage, and due to the efficiency of labour.

ILLUSTRATION 18.7 Performance report: margin approach

	£	£	£
Budgeted profit for period			45,000
Sales price variance	11,000 favourable		
Sales margin volume variance	4,500 favourable		
Total sales margin variance		15,500 favourable	
Direct material price variance	10,000 adverse		
Direct material usage variance	2,000 favourable		
Direct material cost variance		8,000 adverse	
Direct labour rate variance	1,000 adverse		
Direct labour efficiency variance	3,000 favourable		
Direct labour cost variance		2,000 favourable	
Variable overhead expenditure variance	9,000 adverse		
Variable overhead efficiency variance	4,500 favourable		
Variable overhead cost variance		4,500 adverse	
Fixed overhead expenditure variance	2,000 adverse		
Fixed capacity utilization variance	3,200 favourable		
Fixed efficiency variance	4,800 favourable		
Fixed overhead volume variance	8,000 favourable		
Fixed overhead cost variance		6,000 favourable	
Total variances			11,000 favourable
Actual profit for the period			56,000

18.8 Another Approach

Sales contribution variance

An alternative approach to the sales margin variance is the sales contribution variance, where the focus is upon the contribution variance rather than the change in margin. With the sales volume contribution variance, we are trying to isolate the change in the contribution of the business arising from a change in sales units. With this approach, the fixed overhead variance is simply the variance on fixed overhead expenditure; there is no need to calculate the fixed overhead volume variances.

The sales price variance measures the effect of a change in price. The first and third columns in Illustration 18.8 both show the actual volume of sales. The difference between them is that the first is based on the actual selling price; and the third is based on the budgeted selling price.

The sales contribution volume variance measures the effect of a change in volume. The third and fifth columns in the table both show the budgeted contribution. The difference between them is that the third column shows the actual volume of sales, and the fifth column shows the budgeted volume of sales.

In Illustration 18.8 all the sales contribution variances are based on the assumption that the variable cost of production was £2.25 per meal. The planned contribution for each meal was £1.25; but the actual selling price was 10 pence higher and so the actual contribution was 10 pence higher.

Summary of variances

Where both cost and sales contribution variances are calculated, the sum of all the variances should equal the difference between the budgeted profit for the period and the actual profit achieved and can be summarized in a performance report (see Illustration 18.9).

Interpretation of these variances

The firm made £11,000 more profit than it had planned. This was overwhelmingly due to a favourable sales performance. The firm increased both the volume of sales, and the selling price, which would have increased profits by £23,500. There were, however, some adverse cost variances.

There were adverse expenditure variances on both fixed and variable overheads amounting to £6,500. This may have been due partly to cost increases with respect to various overhead items (e.g. increases in rents, rates, electricity); it may be that it spent a lot more on marketing to achieve the higher sales levels; and it could be that the distinction between fixed and variable overheads had not accurately been determined.

ILLUSTRATION 18.8 *Contribution* approach

Actual sales @ actual contribution	Actual sales @ planned contribution	Budgeted sales @ budgeted contribution
110,000 @ £1.35	110,000 meals @ £1.25	100,000 meals @ £1.25 each
£148,500	£137,500	£125,000
Sales price variance		Sales contribution volume variance
£11,000 favourable		£12,500 favourable
Total sales variance £23,500 favourable		

ILLUSTRATION 18.9 Performance report: contribution approach

	£	£	£
Budgeted profit for period			45,000
Sales price variance	11,000 favourable		
Sales contribution volume variance	12,500 favourable		
Total sales margin variance		23,500 favourable	
Direct material price variance	10,000 adverse		
Direct material usage variance	2,000 favourable		
Direct material cost variance		8,000 adverse	
Direct labour rate variance	1,000 adverse		
Direct labour efficiency variance	3,000 favourable		
Direct labour cost variance		2,000 favourable	
Variable overhead expenditure variance	9,000 adverse		
Variable overhead efficiency variance	4,500 favourable		
Variable overhead cost variance		4,500 adverse	
Fixed overhead expenditure variance		2,000 adverse	
Total variances			11,000 favourable
Actual profit for the period			56,000

In other areas there were efficiency gains with savings on material usage, and due to the efficiency of labour.

In sum there are two approaches to the sales variances:

Sales	Price	$AQ \times (AP - SP)$
	Contribution volume	$SC \times (AQ - SQ)$
	or margin volume	$SM \times (AQ - SQ)$

18.9 Evaluation

Role and functions

The main appeal of standard costing and variance analysis is that it is a control mechanism that provides a systematic analysis of differences between planned performance and actual performance. It is intended to do so in such a way that, for each variance, it is possible to establish:

1 which managers are responsible for performance not being according to plan;
2 which variances are unavoidable, and which are due to inefficiency;
3 where it is possible to take actions to improve performance;
4 which variances are significant or important, and which are small and of little consequence;
5 which variances are favourable, and whether they are at the expense of adverse performance elsewhere;
6 which variances are adverse, and whether they are offset by favourable variances elsewhere;
7 a systematic basis for further investigation into the causes of poor performance.

Standard costing establishes a range of expected costs that can be used for a variety of purposes, in planning and making decisions. When planning new products it is straightforward to obtain the costs of the various direct materials and components. It may be possible to use synthetic standards in planning labour costs. Traditionally standard costing developed from the era of 'scientific management', and time and motion study (work study) techniques were used to develop standards, and assess the speed at which people should work. In recent years the development of 'target costing' has required renewed emphasis on minimizing labour costs. Standards can provide target costs that help to motivate staff towards greater efficiency.

Standard costing, particularly with labour costs, can also be used as a basis for remuneration, with bonuses, piece-work, and a range of schemes for performance-related pay. In traditional work study, people were expected to perform at a rate equivalent to walking at four miles an hour. Those who could walk (or work) faster would be paid more.

Overall, it is intended that standard costing and variance analysis should enhance efficiency. It can help in developing budgets, facilitate 'management by exception', and perhaps even improve staff motivation because expected levels of performance are defined.

In some organizations, standard costs are used as the basis for valuing inventories of work in progress and finished goods for financial accounting purposes.

Problems and limitations

Unfortunately, it is not always possible to establish 'standards' in a scientific or objective way. How long it should take to do a particular piece of work is often disputed. Moreover, it is not clear on what basis standards should be established, and the following are sometimes suggested:

1 Ideal standards, which are a very high target to aim for. It assumes working under ideal conditions with no wastage or hold-ups. In theory this may be what is aimed for, but it can be very demotivating if standards are set that are more like targets that cannot realistically be attained.

2 Attainable standards, which are stretching, but make some allowance for inevitable inefficiencies.

3 Current standards are based on what is currently happening with no expectation of significant improvement. These provide a realistic basis for planning, decision-making and valuing inventories.

4 Basic standards remain the same for long periods of time and can be useful for comparing efficiency from year to year.

Standard costs are sometimes discredited, especially when they are used as a basis for remuneration, and some people find ways around them. It is necessary to keep standards current, alive and real otherwise they can become discredited and unrealistic. When there are significant changes in the costs of raw materials and components, it is always a problem to know how often to change standards. Standard costing has tended to concentrate on direct materials and direct labour, but in modern manufacturing production, overheads are often much greater than direct costs, and are more difficult to control. The need for just-in-time manufacturing has also tended to de-emphasize standard costing. There is a need for continuous improvement across the board, rather than aiming for standards that are sometimes out of date and not very soundly based.

Summary

Standard costing is still widely used in manufacturing organizations, although it is seen as being a traditional technique, and has been much criticized. It can also be used in a range of professional and service organizations. The idea of establishing a standard, what something *should* cost, is inherently appealing, and provides a basis for control information. Once standards and budgets are established, it is possible to calculate 'variances' showing how actual performance differs from what it should be. Variance analysis provides a systematic approach to explaining differences. It does not provide all the answers; it points to where further investigation is likely to prove fruitful.

Summary of variance formulae

Sales	Price	AQ × (AP − SP)
	Contribution volume	SC × (AQ − SQ)
	or margin volume	SM × (AQ − SQ)
Direct materials	Price	AQ × (AP − SP)
	Usage	SP × (AQ − SQ)
Direct labour	Rate	AH × (AR − SR)
	Efficiency	SR × (AH − SH)
Variable overhead	Price	AQ × (AP − SP)
	Efficiency	SP × (AQ − SQ)
Fixed overheads	Expenditure	Actual FO − budgeted FO
	Volume (when using the margin approach)	Budgeted FO − (AQ × SP per unit)

⮕ Review of key points

- Standard costing establishes standard costs for materials, labour and overheads and is the basis of a systematic control system.

- Variance analysis compares actual costs with standard costs to help establish where, how and why actual performance differs from standard performance.

- Analysis shows in many areas where differences are due to changes in efficiency or in price.

- Variances can also be calculated for sales.

- A comprehensive set of variances should explain the difference between planned performance and actual performance.

- Standard costing has a number of useful functions, but is only as good as the standards on which it is based.

! Self-testing questions

1 Corrina planned to spend £10 to buy 10 kg of dough to make 10 loaves of bread.[3] Actually she spent £10.50 and bought 10.4 kg of dough and made 11 loaves of bread.

a Calculate and explain the direct materials cost variance.

b Calculate and explain the direct materials price and usage variances.

2 Anomelg solicitors employed Maggie to do their conveyancing work; she is treated as 'direct labour'. They planned to pay her £30 per hour for 100 hours a month and expect her to complete 10 conveyances.

---

[3] The standard cost (of materials) was therefore £1 per loaf.

During April they paid her £2,400 for 84 hours work and she completed seven conveyances.

a Calculate and explain the direct labour cost variance.

b Calculate and explain the direct labour rate and efficiency variances.

3 The Wee Lee Cycle Company planned to produce 120,000 bicycles a year (10,000 a month) at a total cost of £80 each, and to sell them for £100 each.
  Last month it produced 11,000 bicycles at a total cost of £902,000, and sold them for £979,000.

a Calculate the budgeted profit for the month.

b Calculate the actual profit for the month.

c Calculate sales margin and cost variances in as much detail as the information permits.

d Evaluate the information disclosed.

4 The Wool Witch Company manufactures woollen dolls that sell for £28 each and the company plans to manufacture and sell 5,000 a month. The standard production costs per doll are:

Direct materials	1 kg at £3 per kg
Direct labour	1 hour at £10 per hour
Fixed overheads	£10,000 per month

Last month the company made and sold 4,000 dolls for £108,000. Its costs were:

Direct materials	3,900 kg costing £12,200
Direct labour	3,850 hours costing £39,500
Fixed overheads	£9,500

a Calculate the budgeted profit for the month.

b Calculate the actual profit for the month.

c Calculate cost and sales contribution variances in as much detail as the information permits.

d Evaluate the information disclosed.

5 Poleg Limited manufactures kitchen cupboards. The standard cost of each unit is £120, comprising:

		£
Direct materials	15 sq metres at £4.50 per sq metre	67.50
Direct labour	5 hours at £6 per hour	30.00
Variable overheads	5 hours at £3 per labour hour	15.00
Fixed overheads		7.50
		£120.00

The company had budgeted to make and sell 1,000 cupboards at a selling price of £150 in June. However, in June, the actual figures were as follows:

		£
Production and sales:	1,400 units	212,800
Direct materials	22,000 sq metres	121,000
Direct labour	6,800 hours	34,000
Variable overheads		15,000
Fixed overheads		6,000

Prepare a performance report reconciling the budgeted profit to the actual profit showing all the variances arising. Write a brief report advising management on your finding and possible reasons why each variance arose.

Assessment questions

1 Mary planned to pay Tom £50 for 5 hours to wash 20 cars.[4]

  Last week Tom and a number of customers were on holiday. She actually paid Fred £45 for four hours to wash 15 cars.

  a Calculate and explain the direct labour cost variance.

  b Calculate and explain the direct labour rate and usage variances.

2 The Aanroc Manufacturing Company budget for May shows the following:

Fixed overheads	£256,000
Number of labour hours to be worked	16,000
Number of aanrocs to be produced	10,000

  Actual results for May were as follows:

Fixed overhead costs	£266,000
Number of labour hours worked	17,000
Number of aanrocs actually produced	11,000

  Required:

  a Calculate and explain the fixed overhead cost variance.

  b Explain and illustrate how the standard cost of production can be measured (i) in units, and (ii) in standard hours.

  c Calculate and explain the fixed overhead expenditure, volume, capacity utilization and efficiency variances.

3 The standard cost of producing one kiredo is as follows:

Direct materials	5 kg at £12 per kg	£60
Direct labour	2 hours at £16 per hour	£32
Variable overheads	2 hours at £8 per hour	£16

  Fixed overheads are expected to be £180,000 per annum, and the plan is to produce 12,000 kiredos per annum.

  Last month 1,200 kiredos were produced and the costs incurred were:

Direct materials 5,900 kg costing	£70,000
Direct labour 2,000 hours costing	£44,000
Variable overheads	£18,600
Fixed overheads	£15,500

  Calculate the cost variances in as much detail as the information permits and comment on the results.

4 The Nire Company plans to sell 2,000 nires a month, the standard marginal cost of which is £60 each, at a selling price of £80 each. Last month it sold 2,100 nires for £161,700.

  Calculate the sales contribution price variance and the sales contribution volume variance.

---

[4] The standard labour cost of washing one car was therefore £50 ÷ 20 = £2.50.

5 The following is extracted from the standard unit cost card of RNM Ltd for the quarter ended 31 December 20X9:

Selling price per unit	£25
Direct materials (2 kg @ £1 per kg)	2
Skilled labour 1 hour @ £8 per hour	8
Variable overheads	3
Fixed overheads	2
Net profit per unit	10
Budgeted sales	10,000 units

Variable overheads are determined by using the skilled labour hours, while fixed overheads are absorbed on the budgeted sale units. For the quarter ended 31 December 2009, the following results were reviewed:

	£
Sales (9,000 units)	234,000
Direct materials (16,000 kg)	20,000
Skilled labour (9,500 hours)	71,250
Variable overheads	30,875
Fixed overheads	22,000

Required:

Calculate the actual and budgeted profit for the quarter ended 31 December 20X9. Reconcile these profit figures by providing the appropriate variances in a performance report.

What explanations would you give regarding the discrepancies between the actual and the budgeted results?

Group activities and discussion questions

1 How widely do you think standard costing could be applied? Discuss possible examples from non-manufacturing organizations.

2 Do you have any 'standard costs' in mind in your own life (e.g. the standard cost of buying lunch, or cooking dinner)? Is it useful to have such costs in mind?

3 If you were expected to produce something (e.g. a picnic, or a student newspaper) under a 'standard costing' system, would you find ways round the system? How?

4 What do you think of the idea that everyone should work at the same speed (or produce the same amount in a given time)?

 Accounting in context

Discuss and comment on the following extract from the press with reference to the need for a company to regularly review 'standard price' and budgeted profit in the light of changes in costs, selling price and demand caused by factors outside its control.

Kenmare mines profitable seam as titanium shines

After a period of slight under-performance, shares in Kenmare have started moving again in the past few weeks. It's all due to an interesting read-across from an Australian company called Iluka.

By Garry White

Kenmare is a Mozambique-based titanium miner. About 95pc of the global supply of titanium is used in white pigments and lightweight alloys. The main mineral sources of the metal are ilmenite and rutile, but Kenmare's mine also produces high-value zircon, which is used to make laboratory-grown diamonds.

Last week, Iluka revealed that it had agreed significant price increases with its customers for the provision of zircon and rutile in the second half of 2011.

After extensive talks, price increases of between 70pc and 75pc were agreed for rutile. Talks with zircon customers are ongoing, but Iluka said it expected price increases of 35pc to 40pc.

This demonstrates the strong pricing environment for producers as demand rises – and Kenmare is already developing a 50pc expansion project at its flagship Moma mine.

The company says it has negotiated "significant" price increases with customers for 2011. However, a number of legacy contracts exist but they continue to expire.

This means the company can push through price rises when the chance arises, but much of its production is already committed on volume and price. Next year, however, the new production from its expansion should be able to lock in these higher prices.

Kenmare is one of the few UK listed companies that is producing the mineral. Supplies of titanium oxides are expected to be lower than demand by 2013, unless there is another steep downturn in the global economy. However, we are unlikely to see prices fall to the nadir seen in 2008 and 2009.

The resource life at Moma is about 100 years, so once the current 50pc expansion plans are implemented, it is likely that there could be a further ramp-up in future years, too.

Margins should improve significantly as the selling price rises. The mine is a low-cost operation because the titanium oxides are recovered through dredging in settlement ponds. Kenmare even owns docks for loading ships, within sight of the mining operation.

In the year to December, revenues rose to $91.6m (£57m) from $26.7m and the pre-tax loss narrowed to $16.3m from $30.4m. The group is expected to swing into pre-tax profits in the current year. The group is not paying a dividend at the moment as it is investing in its growth and, at its recent AGM, the company said it would prefer to pay down debt before starting payments.

The company was also included in the FTSE 250 index in August last year. The shares are trading on a December 2011 earnings multiple of 41.1, falling to 9.5 in 2012 and just 6.1 in 2013.

They are up 153pc since being tipped on September 5 last year at 18¾p, compared with a FTSE 100 up 4pc. [. . .]

Source: The Telegraph, 17 June 2011.

References and further reading

Atkinson, A., R. Kaplan, E. Matsumura and M. Young (2012) *Management Accounting* (6th edn.). Harlow: Pearson.

Bhimani, A.C.T., S.M. Datar, C.T. Horngren and G. Foster (2012) *Management and Cost Accounting* (5th edn.). Upper Saddle River, NJ: FT Prentice Hall.

Drury, C. (2008) *Management and Cost Accounting* (7th edn.). Andover: Cengage Learning.

Dyson, J.R. (2010) *Accounting for Non-accounting Students* (8th edn.). Upper Saddle River, NJ: FT Prentice Hall.

Proctor, R. (2009) *Managerial Accounting for Business Decisions* (3rd edn.). Harlow: Pearson.

Seal, W., R.H. Garrison and E.W. Nooreen (2011) *Management Accounting* (4th edn.). Maidenhead: McGraw-Hill.

When you have read this chapter, log on to the Online Learning Centre website at *www.mcgraw-hill.co.uk/textbooks/leiwy* to explore chapter-by-chapter test questions, further reading and more online study tools.

Answers to Self-testing Questions

Chapter 1

1 A statement of financial position shows assets, liabilities and share capital. Expenses, sales and profit for the year are shown on the income statement.

2 Non-current assets (fixed assets) are intended to be retained and used by the business for more than a year.

Current assets are cash and things that are intended for conversion into cash within a year.

3 Land and buildings; plant and machinery; furniture, fixtures and fittings; vehicles, ships and aircraft.

Furniture owned by a furniture shop and intended for sale is a current asset. Vehicles owned by a garage and intended for sale are a current asset.

4 Assets minus liabilities equals equity.

5 Individual assets may be worth more or less than the statement of financial position value.

A successful business as a whole (including unrecorded goodwill) should be worth more than the statement of financial position shows because of the profits that it now produces, and expectations for the future.

6 a Current ratio = current assets : current liabilities

$$45,000 : 22,000 = 2.05 : 1$$

   b Liquidity ratio = current assets excluding inventories : current liabilities

$$21,000 : 22,000 = 0.95 : 1$$

   c

	Existing		Revised	
	£	£	£	£
Non-current assets		50,000		50,000
Current assets				
Inventories (at cost)	24,000		20,000	
Trade receivables	12,000		12,000	
Cash	9,000	45,000	17,000	49,000
Total assets		95,000		99,000
Current liabilities				
Trade payables		22,000		22,000
Equity				
Share capital	50,000		50,000	
Retained earnings	23,000	73,000	27,000	77,000
		95,000		99,000

   d Current ratio = 49,000 : 22,000 = 2.2 : 1

Liquidity ratio = 29,000 : 22,000 = 1.3 : 1

As the business now has £4,000 less inventory, and £8,000 more cash, both the current ratio and the liquidity ratio have improved, or become stronger.

7 a £83,000, being the increase in shareholders' funds

   b £83,000 + £10,000 − £20,000 − £30,000 = £43,000

8

	Domer Castle	Warmer Castle
Current ratio	34 : 17 = 2 : 1	34 : 17 = 2 : 1
Liquidity ratio	26 : 17 = 1.5 : 1	15 : 17 = 0.88 : 1
$\frac{\text{Debentures}}{\text{Debentures + Equity}}$	100 ÷ 331 = 30.2%	200 ÷ 331 = 60.4%
EBIT ÷ Interest payable	31,000 ÷ 10,000 = 3.1 times	32,000 ÷ 20,000 = 1.6 times

Warmer appears to be weaker. The two companies have the same current ratio, but a large part of Warmer's current assets is stocks and so it has a much lower liquidity ratio. Warmer also has much higher capital gearing and its interest cover is low.

9 a i Non-current assets – £ 80,000
       Cash + £ 100,000
       Retained earnings + £ 20,000
  ii Inventories – £ 30,000
       Receivables + £ 80,000
       Retained earnings + £ 50,000
  iii Cash – £ 40,000
       Payables – £ 40,000

b

	Existing		Revised	
	£	£	£	£
Non-current assets		158,000		78,000
Current assets				
Inventories (at cost)	110,000		80,000	
Trade receivables	120,000		200,000	
Cash	20,000	250,000	80,000	360,000
Total assets		408,000		438,000
Current liabilities				
Trade payables		120,000		80,000
Equity				
Share capital	250,000		250,000	
Retained earnings	38,000	288,000	108,000	358,000
		408,000		438,000

Chapter 2

1 The statement of financial position is as at a particular date. An income statement is for a particular *period*, such as for a year.

  a A statement of financial position shows assets, liabilities and equity (which includes all retained profits).

  b An income statement shows revenues, expenses and the current year's profit.

2 An expense is the cost incurred in earning the revenues of a particular period. Some assets become expenses. Assets such as unsold inventories and non-current (fixed) assets may be seen as stores of value that have not yet been used up in generating revenues. Fixed assets become recognized as expenses as they are depreciated. Inventories become expenses when they are sold. Receivables become expenses if they are written off as bad debts.

3 Closing inventories are shown at the lower of cost and net realizable value. The valuation of closing stock has a direct effect on profits. If closing stock is overstated by £1m, then profits are overstated by £1m.

If closing inventories were shown at selling price, the company would be taking credit for profits before sales are made; it is not a good idea to claim profits that have not yet been earned.

4 Depreciation is charged to write off the cost of the fixed asset over a number of years, depending on its economic life. If an asset is shown at a revalued amount rather than at cost, then the revalued amount is written off in the same way.

5 Capital expenditure adds to fixed assets that are then written off (depreciated; an expense) over a number of years. Examples would include a retail shop buying a new delivery vehicle, having an extension to the shop built and buying new tills. Revenue expenditure is written off during the period in which it is incurred. Examples include lighting, heating and cleaning. (Some revenue expenditure is included in closing inventories that are carried forward and written off in the period in which they are sold.)

6 Profit after tax for the year, £12,000. This is because:

a it is the amount that has been earned for them after charging all expenses and taxation; and

b it is the basis for dividend decisions; dividends are the amounts actually paid to shareholders.

7 Kingsdun Company1158150

	Delivery van £	Boring machine £
Cost	25,000	25,000
Year 1 depreciation	6,250	2,500
Net book value at end of year 1	18,750	22,500
Year 2 depreciation	4,688	2,500
Net book value at end of year 2	14,062	20,000
Year 3 depreciation	3,516	2,500
Net book value at end of year 3	10,546	17,500
Year 4 depreciation	2,636	2,500
Net book value at end of year 4	7,910	15,000

8 Dargate Retailing Company

Product	Cost price £	Mark-up %	Selling price £	Gross profit %
Fargs	100	25	125	20
Gargs	100	10	110	9.09
Hargs	50	100	100	50
Jargs	40	100	80	50
Kargs	80	50	120	33 1/3
Largs	50	20	60	16 2/3
Margs	30.77	30	40	23.1
Nargs	45	11.11	50	10
Pargs	75	33 1/3	100	25

9 Banterbury Company Ltd

	Year 3		Year 4	
	£000	%	£000	%
Turnover	100	100	120	100
Cost of sales	60	60	73	60.83
Gross profit	40	40	47	39.17
Distribution costs	(12)	12	(14)	11.67
Administration expenses	(9)	9	(12)	10
Operating profit	19	19	21	17.5
Interest payable	(3)	3	(3)	2.5
Profit before taxation	16	16	18	15
Tax on profit for year	(4)	4	(3)	2.5
Profit after tax for the year	12	12	15	12.5

Turnover has increased by 20 per cent, but most costs have increased by a larger percentage than sales. Expressing all items as a percentage of sales, we can see that cost of sales has increased slightly, and so gross profit has gone down. There has been an increase in operating costs as a percentage of sales, and so operating profit as a percentage of sales has gone down. There has been no change in interest costs, and the company is fortunate that the amount of tax payable has gone down: the effect of these two is that there has been an increase in profit after tax as a proportion of sales.

The small improvement in profit as a percentage of sales is mainly due to the lower tax charge. Cost of sales and operating costs have both increased by a bigger proportion than sales. These results suggest that management have not been very successful in getting more profits out of the increase in sales.

Shareholders' funds are £109,000, and the profit after tax earned for them is £15,000, a return on shareholders' capital employed of 13.8 per cent, which is satisfactory.

Chapter 3

1 The main users of financial accounting information are: shareholders, potential shareholders and investors generally; creditors, and suppliers; lenders (such as banks and debenture holders); employees, and potential employees; customers; government and public sector bodies; HM Revenue and Customs; the company's managers and directors; financial analysts and advisers; competitors; and the public.

Different users may have a wide variety of different information needs, but financial accounting tends to concentrate on what investors want to know about the security of their company and its future prospects, as well as receiving an account of the directors' stewardship. Creditors also want to know about the security or solvency, and its future prospects as an indicator of how likely it is to be able to repay the amounts it owes.

2 An asset is a resource controlled by the enterprise as a result of past events and from which future economic benefits are expected to flow to the enterprise.

A liability is a present obligation of the enterprise arising from past events, the settlement of which is expected to result in an outflow from the enterprise of resources embodying economic benefits.

3 Provisions are a problem because the Companies Act, and conventional practice, are more liberal than the definition and treatment established by accounting standards. The Companies Act 1985 defined provisions as 'amounts retained as reasonably necessary to cover any liability or loss which is either likely or certain to be incurred'. Provisions were often created for future reorganizations, redundancies, legal liabilities, decommissioning costs, and future costs and losses of various sorts. This would exclude current *proposals* to incur liabilities or losses in future periods. IAS 37 defined a provision as 'a liability of uncertain timing or amount' and indicates that it must be a liability, a present obligation. This means that many traditional provisions are not allowed. But there is some flexibility because the provision can include an obligation that is 'constructive', where there are no legal commitments, but where the company has by its actions and announcements committed itself to a course of action.

4 IFRS 3 defines goodwill as 'future economic benefits arising from assets that are not capable of being individually identified and separately recognized'. It arises where one business has paid more for that business than the fair value of its assets.

5 'Pure' historic cost accounting would show all assets on the statement of financial position at cost price. Non-current assets need to be depreciated. Inventories have to be shown at net realizable value where this is below cost price. A provision for bad debts may have to be deducted from receivables. Some assets such as property and investments may be revalued.

6 Revenues are the amounts credited to the income statement in respect of the main activities of the business (sales, fees earned). Income includes any other amounts generated, for example from rentals or investments. Gains can be of any type, including revenues and income; they also include gains arising on revaluation of assets, which may be realized or unrealized.

7 Profit is seen as being important because: (a) it provides a guide to dividend decisions; (b) it indicates how much cash a company has generated; (c) it indicates how successful, or otherwise, a company and its management are; (d) it provides a basis for levying corporation tax; (e) it provides a guide to investors in choosing what shares to buy and sell; (f) it gives an indication to creditors about the company's ability to pay its liabilities; it indicates economic efficiency; and (g) it is of interest to different groups, including employees, politicians, customers and others who may be concerned about companies making excessive profits.

Chapter 4

1 a Current assets: current liabilities (e.g. 1.8 : 1)

   b Current assets minus stocks : current liabilities (e.g. 0.9 : 1)

   c Capital requiring a fixed return (e.g. debentures) as a percentage of total long-term capital (equity plus debentures). This is often expressed as: $\dfrac{D}{D+E}$ e.g. 35%

   It may also be expressed as $\dfrac{D}{E}$

   It is usually calculated using statement of financial position values. It may be calculated using market values. Preference shares and all borrowings may be included with D.

   d Earnings before interest and taxation ÷ interest payable (e.g. five times)

2 It might take a long time to convert stocks into cash; they are not a very 'liquid' asset.

3 Net profit for the year, after taxation, as a percentage of equity (including all reserves and retained earnings) as shown on the statement of financial position.

4 The 'return' is earnings before interest and taxation. If debentures are included as part of capital employed, the interest payable on them should be included as part of the return on capital employed (ROCE). It is important that the numerator and the denominator are consistent: where borrowings are included in the denominator, the interest on those borrowings should be included in the numerator. Return on ordinary shareholders' capital employed is usually measured after charging taxation for the year. If borrowings are included in capital employed, an earnings before interest and taxes (EBIT) is used as the numerator, it is taken before charging taxation; this is a matter of convenience, not a matter of principle.

5 An increase in the gross profit ratio does not tell us anything for sure about sales. They may have increased; selling prices may have increased. But an increase in the gross profit ratio may be entirely attributable to a reduction in cost of sales as a percentage of sales, which could be due to more effective buying, or reductions in purchase prices.

6 The company's financial position looks reasonably strong with some improvement in year 2. The current ratio is lower, but the liquidity ratio has increased. The gearing looks rather high, but has reduced; the company has reduced its long-term borrowing slightly; shareholders' funds have increased slightly; and interest cover has increased.

The company's current assets look rather high, and this can have an effect on profitability. It has generated substantial amounts of cash, and the cash balance is now excessive and should be used profitably. It may be the company's intention to further reduce its long-term borrowing.

The company has managed to increase its profitability slightly: both measures of ROCE have improved. But it appears to be struggling with sales and costs. Sales have increased slightly (5 per cent), but the gross profit margin has gone down a little. Operating costs have been kept under control (a slight decrease); and because of reduced borrowings, there has been a significant reduction in interest payable. After taxation, there has been an improvement in net profit as a percentage of sales.

Overall utilization of capital employed has hardly changed, but there have been improvements in the management of stocks and debtors. Stock turnover looks very slow, but has been improved substantially. The length of time that debtors take to pay has also been reduced substantially.

More detailed analysis of each item of expense as a percentage of sales could be undertaken; more detailed analysis of each item of assets and liabilities in relation to sales could be made. But the analysis shown below brings out the main points outlined above. The overall impression might be of reasonably successful financial management struggling to improve financial performance in difficult market conditions.

Solvency	Year 1	Year 2
Current ratio	1,868 : 434	2,100 : 600
	4.3 : 1	3.5 : 1
Liquidity ratio	688 : 434	1,100 : 600
	1.6 : 1	1.8 : 1
Gearing ratio	1,000 ÷ 2,434	900 ÷ 2,400
	41%	37.5%
Interest cover	295 ÷ 100	305 ÷ 90
	2.95 times	3.39 times
Profitability		
Return on ordinary shareholders' capital employed	135 ÷ 1,434	150 ÷ 1,500
	9.4%	10%
EBIT as a percentage of long-term capital employed	295 ÷ 2,434	305 ÷ 2,400
	12.1%	12.7%
Gross profit ratio	375 ÷ 3,600	384 ÷ 3,780
	10.42%	10.16%
Operating profit/sales	295 ÷ 3,600	305 ÷ 3,780
	8.19%	8.07%
Net profit after-tax sales	135 ÷ 3,600	150 ÷ 3,780
	3.75%	3.97%
Sales net assets	3,600 ÷ 1,434	3,780 ÷ 1,500
	2.51 times	2.52 times
Inventory turnover (days)	$\frac{1,200}{3,225} \times 365$	$\frac{1,000}{3,396} \times 365$
	136 days	107 days
Receivables ratio (days)	$\frac{600}{3,600} \times 365$	$\frac{500}{3,780} \times 365$
	61 days	48 days

Chapter 5

1 The three ratios may be calculated on a 'per share' basis, or for the company as a whole. The results should be the same.

  a The price/earnings (P/E) ratio indicates whether the share price is expensive or cheap in relation to the most recent profits. It is calculated by dividing the share price by the earnings per share (EPS). A high P/E ratio (e.g. 30+) suggests that investors are optimistic about future increases in earnings. A low P/E ratio (e.g. 10 or less) suggests that investors are not very optimistic about future growth.

b The dividend yield indicates whether the share price is expensive or cheap in relation to the most recent dividends. It is calculated by dividing the most recent year's dividend per share by the share price. A high dividend yield (e.g. 5 per cent or more) suggests that shares are cheap in relation to the most recent dividend. A very high dividend yield (e.g. 8 per cent or more) suggests that there are serious concerns about the company: perhaps the share price has collapsed, and/or the level of dividends is not expected to be maintained at last year's level. A low dividend yield (e.g. 2 per cent or less) suggests that investors are optimistic about future growth.

c The dividend times cover relates the most recent year's dividends to the amount of profits earned in that period. It helps to indicate how 'safe' the dividends are. It is calculated by dividing the amount of earnings by the amount of dividends. A high cover (e.g. 2.5 or more) suggests that dividends are relatively safe. A low cover (e.g. 1.2, or even less than 1) suggests that the company would have difficulty maintaining the dividend, especially if there was a fall in earnings.

2 The market value of a successful company is likely to be higher than its statement of financial position value. This is partly because statement of financial position values may be understated. It is mainly because the market value of a business is largely influenced by its profitability, and expectations that it will be at least maintained, and will probably increase. The value of a successful business as a whole, as a going concern, with internally generated goodwill that is unrecorded, is normally higher than the value of a collection of dead assets.

Sometimes the market value of a company falls below the net asset value, especially when the company is doing badly. In these circumstances the company may unwittingly attract an asset-stripping takeover bid. Another company may be attracted to buy up the assets of the company at a low price, and then split up the various parts of the company and sell them at a profit.

In some companies (e.g. property companies) assets may be fully valued, and prospects for growth in earnings are limited; the market value may then be lower than the net asset value.

3 The dividend yield refers to the last known dividend. The next dividend may be lower, or it may be zero. High dividend yields are associated with low share prices, and question marks about how likely the dividend is to be maintained.

4 The figures are shown in full below.

	Alemouth plc	Beermouth plc
Share capital (20p shares)	£1,600,000	£2,000,000
Retained earnings	£3,200,000	£18,000,000
	£4,800,000	£20,000,000
Net profit after tax for year	£3,520,000	£1,200,000
Dividends for year	£3,200,000	£800,000
Number of shares	8,000,000	10,000,000
Market price of shares	£4.40	£1.80
Market capitalization	£35,200,000	£18,000,000
EPS	£0.44	£0.12
Dividend per share	£0.40	£0.08
P/E ratio	10	15
Dividend times cover	1.1 times	1.5 times
Dividend yield	9.09%	4.44%
Net assets per share	£0.60	£2.00

5 The dividend yield of Alemouth plc is very high, which is associated with a low share price (the P/E ratio is only 10), a low dividend cover (1.1 times) and pessimism about future prospects.

6 The market capitalization of Beermouth is only £18m, although its net asset value is £20m. In most companies the market value is higher than the net asset value. There could be something seriously wrong with Beermouth's statement of financial position: perhaps the assets are overvalued, or there is a significant unrecorded liability; perhaps the company is about to be used for something. It is more likely that the market value of the company

is very low because the company is expected to be making losses. The company's return on capital employed (ROCE) (£1,200,000/£20,000,000) was only 6 per cent last year. If the company makes losses of more than £2m in the current year, the net asset value would soon fall below the current market capitalization (which might then rise or fall, depending on investors' expectations).

Chapter 6

1 The accruals concept means that profit is not based on cash flows; it is not the difference between cash received during a period, and cash paid out during that period. The accruals basis of accounting means that profit is the difference between revenues earned during a period, and the costs incurred in earning those revenues. Revenues (sales and other income) are recognized when they are earned, not when the cash is received. Similarly, expenses are not recognized when payments are made; instead, they are 'matched' against the revenues earned during the period.

The accruals concept is important in financial accounting because profits are different from cash flows; a business can be profitable and expanding, but be short of cash. A business can generate cash (e.g. by selling off assets), but be running at a loss.

If business accounts were based entirely on 'receipts and payments', there would be no statement of financial position, and no measurement of profit. The accruals concept is essential for the preparation of statements of financial position and income statements.

2 A very successful business will have serious cash shortages if its profits are poured into additional assets. This may be a healthy expansion of inventories and receivables in line with sales; and investment in additional non-current assets, and buying shares in other companies. It may be unhealthy if poor control results in too many assets being bought, excessive inventory levels, and fixed assets that are not profitably utilized.

The situation could also arise if substantial loans are repaid, and if the company pays out more as dividends than it earns as profits.

3 If a company's depreciation charge is greater than its losses, it can still produce a positive cash flow. If a business is declining, additional cash could come in from reducing asset levels (inventories are sold off, receivables pay up and excess non-current assets are sold). But this could not continue indefinitely. Eventually non-current assets will be fully depreciated and/or sold off, leaving little more than a cash shell.

4 Free cash flow is the amount of cash flow that a company has generated during a period, which it is free to spend as it wishes. It is based on cash flow from operations after deducting non-discretionary payments such as interest and taxation (and including any dividends received). The company is free to spend as much of this free cash flow as it wishes on additional investments in fixed assets, paying dividends and repaying loans. The figure should be reduced to allow for the fact that there is usually some *essential* replacement of non-current assets.

a £7,000 minus essential asset replacement = approximately zero

b £4,100 minus, say, £3,100 = £1,000; £5,500 minus, say, £2,200 = £3,300

5 It is true that Deek Lining plc produced positive cash flows in year 4, but this was mainly as a result of reducing assets. Reducing stocks and debtors produced £500,000, and sales of fixed assets produced £1,100,000. The increase in the amount owed to creditors produced another £100,000.

It is also true that additional non-current assets were bought, but this amounted to only £150,000, while the proceeds of selling non-current assets were £1,100,000.

Borrowings were substantially reduced, as the chairman stated, and, as a result, there was a reduction in the amount of interest paid.

The most serious feature of year 4 was the substantial loss (£1.2m), compared with a profit of £3.4m in year 3. This demonstrates clearly the difference between cash flow and profit: although it made a loss in year 4, it produced a positive cash flow.

Year 3 generally looked more healthy, with a substantial profit, although it ended the year with less cash than it had at the beginning. It may be that it overexpanded in year 3 (with too much cash going into additional assets) and that some rationalization and careful housekeeping (including control of working capital) was required in year 4.

The increase in dividend is not justified by earnings: the company made a loss in year 4.

Although the chairman's statements are correct, it is difficult to justify the overall view that the company had a successful year in year 4. It made a substantial loss, and seemed to be selling off assets in order to raise additional cash.

6

Daubyhaven Ltd. Cash flow statement for year ended 31 December year 2		
Cash generated from operating activities	£	£
1 Operating profit	35,000	
2 Depreciation*	20,000	
3 Other items: profit on sale of machine	(1,500)	
		53,500
Increase in working capital		
4 Increase in inventories	(20,000)	
5 Increase in receivables	(5,000)	
6 Decrease in payables	(2,000)	
		(27,000)
7 Interest paid	(2,000)	
8 Taxation paid	(8,000)	
		(10,000)
		16,500
Cash used in investing activities		
9 Purchase of non-current assets**	(15,000)	
10 Disposal of non-current assets	4,500	
		(10,500)
Cash used in financing activities		
11 Repayment of loan	(10,000)	
12 Dividends paid	(18,000)	
		(28,000)
		(22,000)
Decrease in cash during year		
Opening balance		10,000
Closing balance		(12,000)

*At the beginning of the year the provision for depreciation was £60,000 During the year it was reduced by £12,000 in respect of a machine that was sold, to £48,000. It ended the year as £68,000, which means that it must have increased by £20,000, being the depreciation charge.

**At the beginning of the year machinery at cost was £130,000. During the year it was reduced by £15,000 in respect of a machine that was sold, to £115,000. It ended the year as £130,000, which means that it must have increased by £15,000, being the additional purchases of machinery.

7

Fistard Neash plc	£	£
Cash generated from operating activities		
1 Operating profit	20	
2 Depreciation*	24	
3 Impairment of goodwill	10	
Profit on sale of Scottish factory	(7)	
		47

Increase in working capital

4 Increase in inventories	(25)		
5 Decrease in receivables	5		
6 Decrease in payables	(5)	(25)	
7 Interest paid	(2)		
8 Taxation paid	(4)	(6)	
		16	

Cash used in investing activities

9 Purchase of fixed assets**	(44)	
10 Disposal of fixed assets	23	

Cash used in financing activities

		(21)	
11 Redemption of debentures	(49)		
Issue of shares***	60		
12 Dividends paid	(8)	3	
		(2)	

Decrease in cash during year

Opening balance	10
Closing balance	8

*At the beginning of the year the provision for depreciation was £50m. During the year it was reduced by £8m in respect of the Scottish factory that was sold, to £42m. It ended the year as £66m, which means that it must have increased by £24m, being the year's depreciation charge.

**At the beginning of the year plant, property and equipment at cost was £120m. During the year it was reduced by £24m, in respect of the Scottish factory that was sold, to £96m. It ended the year as £140,000, which means that it must have increased by £44m, being the additional purchases of property, plant and equipment.

***Share capital increased by £20m, and share premium increased by £40m. This indicates that shares with a nominal value of £20m were issued for £60m.

Chapter 7

1 Marks & Spencer

Ratio	2011	2011	2010	2010
1 Current ratio	$\dfrac{1,647.7}{2,210.2}$	0.7	$\dfrac{1,520.2}{1,890.5}$	0.8
2 Liquidity (quick) ratio	$\dfrac{956.4}{2,210.2}$	0.4	$\dfrac{907.0}{1,890.5}$	0.5
3 Capital gearing ratio	$\dfrac{2,456.5}{2,673.5}$	92%	$\dfrac{3,076.8}{2,168.6}$	142%
	$\dfrac{2,456.5}{2,456.5+2,673.5}$	48%	$\dfrac{3,076.8}{3,076.8+2,168.6}$	59%
4 Interest times cover	$\dfrac{836.9+42.3}{98.6}$	8.9 times	$\dfrac{852.9+12.9}{162.2}$	5.3 times
5 Return on shareholders' funds	$\dfrac{598.6}{2,673.5}$	22%	$\dfrac{523.0}{2,168.6}$	24%

6 Return on total long-term capital	$\dfrac{836.9 + 42.3}{2,456.5 + 2,673.5}$	17%	$\dfrac{852.9 + 12.9}{3,076.8 + 2,168.6}$	16%
7 Operating profit as a % of sales	$\dfrac{836.9}{9,740.3}$	9%	$\dfrac{852.9}{9,536.6}$	9%
8 Asset turnover	$\dfrac{9,740.3}{7,344.1 - 2,210.2}$	1.9 times	$\dfrac{9,536.6}{7,153.2 - 1,890.5}$	1.8 times
9 Gross profit ratio	$\dfrac{3,724.7}{9,740.3}$	38%	$\dfrac{3,618.5}{9,536.6}$	38%
10 Selling and administrative expenses as % of sales	$\dfrac{2,959.7}{9,740.3}$	30%	$\dfrac{2,831.5}{9,536.6}$	30%
11 Other operating expenses as a % of sales	not shown		not shown	
12 Sales/non-current assets	$\dfrac{9,740.3}{5,702.4}$	1.7 times	$\dfrac{9,536.6}{5,633.0}$	1.7 times
13 Sales/current assets	$\dfrac{9,740.3}{1,641.7}$	5.9 times	$\dfrac{9,536.6}{1,520.2}$	6.3 times
14 Inventory turnover ratio	$\dfrac{685.3 \times 365}{6,015.6}$	42 days	$\dfrac{613.2 \times 365}{5,918.1}$	38 days
15 Receivables ratio	$\dfrac{98.3 \times 365}{9,740.3}$	3 days	$\dfrac{88.5 \times 365}{9,536.6}$	3 days
16 Payables ratio	$\dfrac{919.2 \times 365}{6,015.6}$	56 days	$\dfrac{792.2 \times 365}{5,918.1}$	49 days
17 Price/earnings ratio	$\dfrac{337}{38.8}$	8.7	$\dfrac{370}{33.5}$	11.0
18 Dividend yield	$\dfrac{15.7}{337}$	4.7%	$\dfrac{15.0}{370}$	4.1%
19 Dividend cover	$\dfrac{523.0}{247.5}$	2.2 times	$\dfrac{523.0}{236.0}$	2.2 times
20 Net assets per share	$\dfrac{2,673.5}{1,584.9}$	£1.69	$\dfrac{2,168.6}{1,582.3}$	£1.37

When asked to 'write a report on the financial position and performance' of a company, it is not sufficient just to comment on each ratio. An attempt should be made to analyse and comment of key themes – perhaps more fully than that provided below.

Report on the financial position and performance of Marks and Spencer plc for the years 2010/2011, which should be read in conjunction with the analysis of the 2010 figures appearing after Illustration 7.2.

- *Introduction* – This report is based on 20 ratios calculated from the published annual report of Marks & Spencer for 2011.

- *Financial position* – The current and quick ratios of the company have fallen but are still higher than Tesco's liquidity ratios. While the control of inventory has deteriorated, the company is taking longer than in 2010 to pay its suppliers. There has been a small increase in share capital, the details of which appear in Note 26 to the Annual Report but further details show that this increase arises ony from directors and other staff exercising share options. It is becoming increasingly common for large companies to delay in paying their suppliers and, while there is a cash flow benefit, ethical questions arise. There has been a substantial reduction in borrowing and the gearing ratio has fallen accordingly. Although gearing was on the high side, Marks & Spencer does however have the strength and reputation to maintain such a level of gearing; clearly a decision has been taken to reduce gearing. Associated with this reduction in gearing, the interest cover has risen. Overall, this indicates that shareholders' risk has fallen.

■ *Overall profitability* – There was 2.1 per cent increase in sales revenue and a 1.8 per cent fall in operating profit. Although the return on capital employed has fallen from the previous year, the profitability of the company, including the gross margin at 38 per cent has otherwise remained steady. The asset turnover has also improved.

■ *Stock market* – The share price fell by 9 per cent while the FTSE 100 rose by 4 per cent in this year. The P/E ratio fell substantially, indicating the market's fall in confidence about the future prospects of the shares. The dividend yield has risen largely as a result of the fall in the share price. The dividend cover indicates that the company has maintained its policy of maintaining the proportion of profits distributed to shareholders. Even though the net assets per share have risen by 23 per cent, the market seems to have lost Confidence in Marks & Spencer shares as an investment during this year.

2 Current ratio; liquidity ratio; capital gearing; interest cover. Profits, quality of assets and cash flows are also important. Z–scores take into account various combinations of similar information including working capital, total gross assets, retained earnings, earnings before interest and tax, market value of equity and book value of debt.

3 Group statement of financial position of Grand plc and its subsidiary at 31 December year 6

	£m	Workings
Non-current assets	255	180 + 75
Goodwill	10	90 – 60% (45 + 55) = 30
		30 – 20 impairment
Current assets	100	80 + 20
Total assets	365	
Current liabilities	45	30 + 15
Minority interest	32	40% (45 + 35)
Ordinary share capital	150	Grand only
Retained earnings		Grand 170. Deduct share of post-acquisitions loss 60% (55 – 35) = 12 Impairment 20
	138	170 – 12 – 20
Liabilities and equity	365	

4 Turnover, operating profit and net assets for each class of business and for each geographic sector.

5

	2011 UK	2011 UK	2011 International	2011 International	2011 Total	2011 Total	2010 UK	2010 UK	2010 International	2010 International	2010 Total	2010 Total
Operating profit as a % of sales	$\frac{679}{8,733}$	88%	$\frac{158}{1,007}$	16%	$\frac{837}{9,740}$	9%	$\frac{701}{8,568}$	8%	$\frac{151}{969}$	16%	$\frac{852}{9,537}$	9%
Sales/ Assets	$\frac{8,733}{6,288}$	1.39 times	$\frac{1,007}{1,057}$	0.96 times	$\frac{9,740}{7,344}$	1.33 times	$\frac{8,568}{6,243}$	1.37 times	$\frac{969}{910}$	1.06 times	$\frac{9,537}{7,153}$	1.33 times
Operating profit/ Assets	$\frac{679}{6,288}$	11%	$\frac{158}{1,057}$	15%	$\frac{837}{7,344}$	11%	$\frac{701}{6,243}$	11%	$\frac{151}{910}$	17%	$\frac{852}{7,153}$	12%

In 2011, the profitability in total and of the UK activity and the international activities have remained the same. The profitability of the International activity remains much higher than that of the UK but, of course, the UK activity dwarfs the International activity. The utilization of assets is unaltered in the business, as a whole, but the UK assets utilization has improved while the International asset utilization has deteriorated. The return of assets has deteriorated during 2011 mostly because of a fall in the International segment. Even if, to a small extent, the profitability and use of assets in the International segment have fallen slightly, they exceed those of the UK segment. The changes between 2010 and 2011 are very small but it is evident that the international segment performs better than the UK segment in terms of profitability and use of assets and this might explain why Marks & Spencer is pursuing a policy of international expansion.

6 The key ratios for Gobbiediggan International plc are calculated as follows:

Segment	UK		Africa		South America	
	Year 1	Year 2	Year 1	Year 2	Year 1	Year 2
Operating profit	80 900	78 760	40 200	44 175	20 40	21 60
Operating assets	8.9%	10.26%	20%	25.1%	50%	35%
Operating profit	80 800	78 860	40 300	44 270	20 100	21 180
Sales	10%	9.1%	13.3%	16.3%	20%	11.7%
Sales	800 900	860 760	300 200	270 175	100 40	180 60
Operating assets	0.89	1.13	1.5	1.54	2.5	3.0

It is true that profits in the UK are declining, in spite of a modest increase in sales. However, the UK produces the bulk of the company's profits; the amount of capital employed has declined, and the profitability of the UK (in terms of return on capital employed, ROCE) has increased. The UK may be a mature market, with limited long-term prospects, but for the foreseeable future it is still very important and profitable to the company.

It is true that sales are declining in the Africa market; but profits are increasing; profitability (in terms of ROCE) is higher than the UK and is increasing. The decline in sales may be a one-off blip, and the company should investigate its causes, and try to increase sales before abandoning the market.

It is true that the South America market has had additional investment of £20,000; but this sum is small compared with the substantial increase in sales, and the high level of profitability. The ROCE declined, but this may be because it will take a little while for the additional investment to generate substantial additional profits.

The ratios may suggest that the company has a reasonable balance of different markets. It may also suggest priorities for developing each of the markets.

7

	£m	Weighting		
Current assets	1,520			
Current liabilities	(1,891)			
Working capital (WC)	(371)			
Non-current assets	5,633			
Current assets	1,520			
Total assets (TGA)	7,153			
Retained profits (RP)	5,282			
Profit before interest and tax (PBIT)	852			
Market capitalization (MV)				
1,582 million @ £3.70	5,853			
Current liabilities	1,891			
Non-current liabilities	3,079			
Total liabilities (BV)	4,970			
Sales	9,537			
1 WC/TGA	$\frac{(371)}{7,153}$ = (0.052)	1.2	(0.062)	

2 RP/TGA	$\dfrac{5,282}{7,153} = 0.738$	1.4	1.034
3 PBIT/TGA	$\dfrac{852}{7,153} = 0.119$	3.3	0.393
4 MV of equity/BV of debt	$\dfrac{5,853}{4,970} = 1.178$	0.6	0.707
5 Sales/TGV	$\dfrac{9,537}{7,153} = 1.333$	1.0	1.333
Z-score			3.405

As with 2011 when the Z-score was 3.416, this is well above the 'safe level' of 2.99.

Chapter 8

1 Depreciation, valuation of inventories, the distinction between capital expenditure and revenue expenditure, provisions for bad debts, other provisions, impairment of goodwill.

2 Low depreciation figures; profits/losses on sales of non-current assets; other exceptional items; provisions; asset (re)valuations; capitalizing items in the grey area between capital and revenue expenditure; showing alternative earnings per share figures.

3 There is no agreed definition of creative accounting. At the moderate end of the spectrum of creative accounting practices, some exercise of judgement is perfectly legal. At the other extreme, deception is illegal.

4 Accounting standards could reduce or eliminate choices of accounting policy, and require additional disclosures. More effective systems for monitoring and enforcement could also be developed.

5 There may be a conflict of interest between the auditors' wish to earn additional fees from consultancy and their need to remain independent from directors. In practice it is the directors who determine the appointment and remuneration of auditors, although this is subject to approval by the shareholders. Many of the problems are criticisms of the arrangements for auditing rather than of the auditors themselves.

6 The Platto Company

	Draft income statement for year ended 31 December Year 8	Budgeted income statement for year ended 31 December Year 9	Answer (i) Revised income statement for year ended 31 December Year 8	Answer (ii) Actual income statement for year ended 31 December Year 9
	£000	£000	£000	£000
Sales revenue	800	790	800	758
Opening inventory	80	90	80	50
Purchases	650	636	650	636
	730	726	730	686
Closing inventory	(90)	(88)	(50)	(88)
Cost of sales	640	638	680	598
Gross profit	160	152	120	160
Profit on sale of asset				25
				185
Impairment			(55)	
Depreciation	(40)	(38)	(40)	(26)
Operating expenses	(90)	(92)	(90)	(92)
Profit	30	22	(65)	67

iii When the Uppit Company took over the Platto company it looked as if Platto's profits were steadily declining (from £30,000 in year 8 to £22,000 in year 9). Uppit produced a rapid improvement: it showed that Platto was not making a profit at all – it made a loss of £65,000 in year 8. By year 9, Uppit had turned this around: a profit of £67,000 was produced. But this was all done by 'creative accounting': there was no real improvement in the company's performance. Two extra charges were made against profits in year 8 (writing-down inventories, impairment of non-current assets); this led to extra profits in year 9 (a lower opening inventory figure; a profit on sale of non-current assets). Both of the additional charges in year 8 proved to be too high: the inventories sold for more than their supposed net realizable value; and the assets in Chipping Sodbury sold for more than their supposed fair value. There was no real improvement in performance (and it no longer has Chipping Sodbury!).

7 Information to appear in published accounts should help the various users to make informed decisions and since a company has a relationship with society in general, these days, that will include so-called 'corporate social reporting'. Thus, it is a relatively recent concern for accountants. An alternate view is that a business' primary responsibility is to maximize profit and while it will have to follow the law, there is no reason or requirement to go any further in terms of social responsibility and disclosure.

- The company might produce additional data since it might foresee imminent government regulations.
- The company might wish to build a reputation with the public (e.g. The Body Shop).
- The company might wish to demonstrate it is considering the needs of various user groups.
- The company might feel under pressure from various pressure groups (e.g. Shell).

Among the information that might be disclosed:

- About employees: numbers, salaries, benefits, conditions in developing countries, industrial accidents, policies on employing disabled workers, involvement with and secondment of staff to local charities.

Chapter 9

1 a Sales made for cash are credited to the sales account and debited to the *cash account.*

b Sales made on credit to Smith are debited to the Smith account, and credited to the *sales account.*

c Purchases made for cash are credited to the cash account, and debited to the *purchases account.*

d Purchases made on credit from Anirroc Company are debited to the purchases account and credited to the *Anirroc Company* (Anirroc is a creditor).

e Smith, a debtor, pays us part of what he owes; the amount is credited to the Smith account and debited to the *cash account.*

f The provision for bad debts is increased by £30. This amount is debited to the income statement as an expense, and credited to the *provision for bad debts account.*

2 Sales, creditors, share capital, share premium.

3 All of them.

4 Statement (b) is true.

5

Carlos cash account					
Date	Description	Amount	Date	Description	Amount
		£			£
1 Jul	Capital	40,000	5 Jul	Expenses (rent)	5,000
3 Jul	Spano Bank	15,000	8 Jul	Furniture and equipment	11,000
27 Jul	Sales	4,000	19 Jul	Expenses	2,500
14 Sep	Minki Cabs	15,000	10 Aug	Purchases	3,300
21 Sep	Sales	24,000	30 Aug	Motosales	40,000
			6 Sep	General expenses	3,300

Carlos capital account

Date	Description	Amount £	Date	Description	Amount £
			1 Jul	Cash	40,000

General expenses account

Date	Description	Amount £	Date	Description	Amount £
5 Jul	Cash (rent)	5,000			
19 Jul	Cash	2,500			
6 Sep	Cash	3,300			

Furniture and equipment account

Date	Description	Amount £	Date	Description	Amount £
2004					
8 Jul	Cash	11,000			

Purchases account

Date	Description	Amount £	Date	Description	Amount £
13 Jul	Motosales Ltd	50,000			
10 Aug	Cash	3,300			
16 Aug	Motosales	22,000			

Motosales Ltd (payables) account

Date	Description	Amount £	Date	Description	Amount £
30 Aug	Cash	40,000	13 Jul	Purchases	50,000
			16 Aug	Purchases	22,000

Sales account

Date	Description	Amount £	Date	Description	Amount £
			27 Jul	Cash	4,000
			3 Aug	Minki Cabs	18,000
			21 Sep	Cash	24,000

Minki Cabs (receivables) account

Date	Description	Amount £	Date	Description	Amount £
3 Aug	Sales	18,000	14 Sep	Cash	15,000

Trial balance as at 30 September

	Debit	Credit
	£	£
Capital		40,000
Spano Bank loan		15,000
Cash	32,900	
General expenses	10,800	
Furniture and equipment	11,000	
Purchases	75,300	
Payable (Motosales)	32,000	
Sales		46,000
Receivables (Minki Cabs)	3,000	
	133,000	133,000

Income statement of Carlos for the three months ending 30 September

	£	£
Sales		46,000
Cost of sales		
Opening inventory	0	
Purchases	75,300	
Deduct Closing inventory	38,100	
Cost of goods sold		37,200
Gross profit		8,800
General expenses		10,800
Loss		2,000

Statement of financial position of Carlos as at 30 September

Fixed assets

	£	£
Furniture and equipment		11,000
Current assets		
Inventory	38,100	
Receivables	3,000	
Cash	32,900	
		74,000
Total assests		85,000
Capital	40,000	
Loss	(2,000)	
		38,000
Loan		15,000
Payables (creditors)		32,000
		85,000

6   Killip's ledger accounts

Cash account

Date	Description	Amount £	Date	Description	Amount £
1 Aug	Capital	5,000	2 Aug	Office equipment	4,100
11 Aug	Sales	650	4 Aug	Office expenses (rent)	500
31 Aug	OneAlpha Ltd	550	15 Aug	Travelling expenses	135
			23 Aug	Salaries and subcontracting	700
			29 Aug	Dubya Smith	80

Capital account

Date	Description	Amount £	Date	Description	Amount £
			1 Aug	Cash	5,000

Office equipment account

Date	Description	Amount £	Date	Description	Amount £
2 Aug	Cash	4,100			

Office expenses account

Date	Description	Amount £	Date	Description	Amount £
4 Aug	Cash (rent)	500			
7 Aug	Dubya Smith (stationery)	120			

Advertising account

Date	Description	Amount £	Date	Description	Amount £
6 Aug	Journal of Man	250			

Journal of Man (payable) account

Date	Description	Amount £	Date	Description	Amount £
			6 Aug	Advertising	250

Dubya Smith (receivable) account

Date	Description	Amount £	Date	Description	Amount £
29 Aug	Cash	80	7 Aug	Office expenses	120

Sales account

Date	Description	Amount £	Date	Description	Amount £
			11 Aug	Cash	650
			20 Aug	OneAlphaLtd	2,200

Travelling expenses account

Date	Description	Amount £	Date	Description	Amount £
15 Aug	Cash	135			

OneAlpha Ltd (receivable) account

Date	Description	Amount £	Date	Description	Amount £
20 Aug	Sales	2,200	31 Aug	Cash	550

Salaries and subcontracting account

Date	Description	Amount £	Date	Description	Amount £
23 Aug	Cash	700			

Trial balance as at 31 August

	Debit	Credit	Calculation of balances
Cash	685		6,200 – 5,515
Capital		5,000	
Office equipment	4,100		
Office expenses	620		500 + 120
Advertising	250		
Journal of Man		250	
Dubya Smith		40	120 – 80
Sales		2,850	650 + 2,200
Travelling expenses	135		
OneAlpha Ltd	1,650		2,200 – 550
Salaries and subcontracting	700		
	8,140	8,140	

Income statement for month ending 31 August		Statement of financial position as at 31 August	
Sales	2,850	Non-current assets	
Office expenses	620	Office equipment	4,100

			Current assets		
Advertising	250		Debtors	1,650	
Travelling expenses	135		Cash	685	2,335
Sales and subcontracting	700	1,705	Total assets		6,435
Profit		1,145	Current liabilities		
			Journal of Man	250	
			Dubya Smith	40	290
			Equity		6,145
			Capital	5,000	
			Profit	1,145	
					6,145
					6,435

7 Cass Hawin

Cass Hawin: bank reconciliation	
Balance according to cash book	£ **
Add Interest received	200
Deduct Bank charges	(150)
Updated cash book balance	£100
Balance according to bank statement	£(2,000)
Unpresented cheques	(1,500) increasing the overdraft
Add Cash deposited on 31 March	3,600 reducing the overdraft
Updated bank statement balance	£100

**The balance in the cash book would be £50 (debit) before recording the interest received (debit) and the bank charges (credit).

Chapter 10

1 Noddy

Income statement of Noddy's business for the year ended 31 December year 6		Statement of financial position as at 31 December year 6		
	£			£
Sales	130,000	Shop premises		400,000
General expenses	(120,000)	Total assets		400,000
Profit	10,000	Payables		20,000
		Capital	370,000	
		Profit	10,000	
		Equity		380,000
		Total liabilities and equity		400,000

2 Mona Ramsey

Income statement of Mona Ramsey for the year ended 30 September year 3			Statement of financial position as at 30 September year 3		
		£			£
Sales revenue		267,321	Current assets		
Opening inventory	20,000		Inventory	15,000	
Purchases	188,000		Receivables	11,000	
	208,000		Bank	24,321	50,321
			Total assets		50,321
Deduct Closing inventory	15,000		Current liabilities		
Cost of goods sold		193,000	Payables		13,000
Gross profit		74,321	Equity		
General expenses	8,000		Capital at 1 October year 2	27,000	
Rent, rates, insurance	17,000		Profit for year	10,321	37,321
Wages	39,000	64,000			50,321
Net profit		10,321			

3 Sally Glen

Income statement of Sally Glen for the year ended 31 December year 8		
	£	£
Sales revenue		365,000
Opening inventory	18,000	
Purchases	242,000	
	260,000	
Deduct Closing inventory	19,000	
Cost of goods sold		241,000
Gross profit		124,000
General expenses	8,000	
Rent, rates, insurance	23,000	
Wages	34,000	
Depreciation: premises	7,000	
Depreciation: vehicle	4,500[1]	
		76,500
Net profit		47,500

Statement of financial position of Sally Glen as at 31 December year 8			
Non-current assets	Cost	Provision for depreciation	Net book value
	£	£	£
Shop premises	350,000	21,000	
		+7,000	
		28,000	322,000

[1] Van at cost £32,000 minus provision for depreciation at 31 December year 7, £14,000, gives a net book value of £18,000 at the beginning of the year. The depreciation charge is 25 per cent of 18,000 = £4,500.

Delivery van	32,000	14,000		
		+4,500		
		18,500	13,500	
			335,500	
Current assets				
Inventory	19,000			
Receivables	60,000			
Bank	23,000		102,000	
Total assets			437,500	
Current liabilities				
Payables			20,000	
Equity				
Capital as at 31 Dec year 7		370,000		
Add Profit for year		47,500		
			417,500	
Total liabilities and equity			437,500	

4 Mary Rushen

Income statement of Mary Rushen for the year ended 30 June year 5		
	£	£
Sales		320,000
Opening inventory	12,000	
Purchases	155,000	
	167,000	
Deduct Closing inventory	7,000	
Cost of goods sold		160,000
Gross profit		160,000
General expenses	13,000	
Repairs and maintenance	10,600	
Wages	37,000	
Depreciation: freehold buildings	10,000	
Depreciation: fixtures and fittings	4,400	
		75,000
Net profit		85,000

Statement of financial postion of Mary Rushen as at 30 June year 5			
Fixed assets	Cost	Provision for depreciation	Net book value
	£	£	£
Freehold buildings	400,000	80,000	
		+ 10,000	310,000
Fixtures and fittings	44,000	90,000	

		30,800	
		+4,400	8,800
		35,200	318,800
Current assets			
Inventory	7,000		
Receivables	8,000		
Cash and bank	7,400		22,400
Total assets			341,200
Current liabilities			
Payables			18,000
Equity			
Capital as at 30 June year 4	238,200		
Add Profit for year	85,000		323,200
			341,200

5 Brad Head

Income statement of Brad Head for year ended 31 December year 3		
	£	£
Sales revenue		660,000
Opening inventory	28,000	
Purchases	255,000	
	283,000	
Closing inventory	13,000	
Cost of sales		270,000
Gross profit		390,000
General expenses		9,000
Light and heating 19,000 + 2,000		21,000
Rent, rates, insurance 65,000 – 4,400		60,600
Wages		44,000
Depreciation:		
fixtures and fittings		2,200
Depreciation: MV		9,000
Depreciation:		
plant and machinery		22,000
Increase in provision for bad debts		600
Bad debt written off		2,100
Total expenses		170,500
Operating profit		219,500
Interest paid		3,500
Profit for the year		216,000

Statement of financial position as at 31 December year 3

Non-current assets	Cost £	Depn £	NBV £
Fixtures and fittings	22,000	13,200	
		2,200	6,600
Plant and machinery	220,000	24,000	
		22,000	174,000
Vehicles	60,000	15,000	
		9,000	36,000
			216,600
Current assets			
Inventories			13,000
Receivables (98,100 – 2,100)	96,000		
Provision for bad debts (1,800 + 600)	(2,400)		93,600
Prepayment			4,400
Cash (6,400 – 6,000)			400
Total assets			328,000
Equity			
Capital as at 31 December year 2	35,000		
Profit for year	216,000		
Drawings	(6,000)		245,000
Current liabilities			
Payables	31,000		
Accruals	2,000		33,000
Non-current liabilities			
Bank loan			50,000
			328,000

6 **Ellie's Ltd**

Income statement of Ellie's Ltd as at 31 December year 1	£	£
Sales		248,300
Cost of goods sold		
Opening inventory	19,500	
Purchases	167,000	
	186,500	
Less Closing inventory	21,000	165,500
Gross profit		82,800
Printing and stationery	2,400	
Wages	12,300	
Bad debt written off	500	

Increase in provision for bad debts (650 – 600)		50	
Rent (1,500 – 400)		1,100	
Electricity (1,100 + 200)		1,300	
Depreciation on furniture and fittings (25% × 10,000)		2,500	
Depreciation on cars (25% × 20,000)		5,000	
Profit on disposal of van (8,400 – 4,200 – 4,750)		(550)	
General expenses		1,400	26,000
Operating profit			56,800
Corporation tax			15,000
Profit after tax			41,800

Statement of financial position of Ellie's as at 31 December year 1

Fixed assets	Cost	Accumulated depreciation	Net book value
	£	£	£
Fixtures and fittings	12,000	4,500	7,500
Vehicles	20,000	10,000	10,000
			17,500
Current assets			
Inventories		21,000	
Receivables (61,000 – 500)	60,500		
Less Provision for bad debts	(650)	59,850	
Prepaid rent		400	
Cash		450	
Total assets		81,700	
Current liabilities		99,200	
Payables	13,400	13,400	
Accruals	200	200	
Taxation	15,000	15,000	
		28,600	
Equity			
Share capital		100	
Share premium		11,600	
Retained profits as at 31 December year 0	17,100		
For year to 31 December year 1	41,800		58,900
			70,600
			99,200

Note

Dividends payable are now not normally recognized until after they have been approved by shareholders. It may be assumed that the above financial statements were finalized after the annual general meeting.

7 Bulgham, Dhoon and Barony

Income statement of Bulgham, Dhoon and Barony for the year ended 31 December year 9		
	£	£
Sales revenue		490,000
Opening inventory	37,000	
Purchases	320,000	
	357,000	
Deduct Closing stock	31,000	
Cost of sales		326,000
Gross profit		164,000
General expenses	45,000	
Rent (28,000 – 4,000)	24,000	
Depreciation	9,000	78,000
Net profit		86,000
Profit and loss appropriation account		
Interest on capital		
Bulgham	2,000	
Dhoon	1,500	
Barony	1,000	4,500
Salaries		
Dhoon	18,250	
Barony	18,250	36,500
Profit share		
Bulgham	15,000	
Dhoon	15,000	
Barony	15,000	45,000
		86,000

Statement of financial position as at 31 December year 9

Non-current assets		
Furniture at cost		90,000
Deduct Provision for depreciation (27,000 + 9,000)		36,000
		54,000
Current assets		
Inventories	31,000	
Prepayment	4,000	
Cash	47,000	
		82,000
Total assets		136,000

Capital accounts:	Bulgham	Dhoon	Barony

		40,000	30,000	20,000	90,000
Current accounts:		Bulgham	Dhoon	Barony	
		10,000	22,000 Dr	28,000 Dr	
Interest		2,000	1,500	1,000	
Salaries		–	18,250	18,250	
Share of profit		15,000	15,000	15,000	
		27,000	12,750	6,250	46,000
					136,000

Chapter 11

1 ■ Owners' capital, which is share capital in the case of a company

■ Borrowing, which may be short term (e.g. overdraft) or long term (e.g. debentures)

■ Retained profits

In addition, expansion can be funded in a variety of ways such as factoring debtors, sale and leaseback of premises.

2 Preference shareholders receive a fixed rate of dividend. No dividend can be paid to ordinary shareholders unless the preference dividend has been paid. There is no fixed rate of dividend for ordinary shareholders: they may receive very substantial dividends, or none at all.

Preference shares are usually *cumulative*, which means that if their dividend is not paid for one or more years, all arrears of preference dividends must be paid before any ordinary dividends are paid.

3 The main advantages of gearing (or borrowing) are that, if the company is successful, it can 'gear up' the return to ordinary shareholders. If a company can borrow money at, say, 7 per cent, and invest it to earn, say, 10 per cent, the whole of the extra profits belongs to the ordinary shareholders. The more the company borrows, the more profit it will make. Such borrowing also has the advantage that it enables companies to finance expansion relatively quickly, and at a relatively modest cost. Interest is an allowable expense for corporation tax purposes. If the alternative to borrowing is to issue ordinary shares, the issue costs of shares are likely to be higher, and shareholders are likely to expect a higher return in due course.

The main disadvantage of gearing is the risk of borrowing too much, and the company getting into difficulty. If a company has excessive borrowing, suppliers and lenders may be reluctant to do business with it. As long as a company has to pay only, say, 7 per cent for its borrowing, and is able to earn, say, 10 per cent, it should be alright. But if interest rates rise very much, or (more likely) if earnings are significantly reduced – or the company has no earnings – in particular years, it is likely to get into serious financial difficulties. Substantial borrowing is usually secured on some of the company's assets, and if the company is unable to meet the repayments, the lenders may require the assets to be sold, and the company could be forced into liquidation.

High gearing exaggerates the effects of changes in earnings before interest and taxes (EBIT) on earnings for ordinary shareholders. When EBIT is good, it is very, very good for the ordinary shareholders. But when EBIT is bad, it can be horrid for the ordinary shareholders – there may be no dividends and the share price may collapse. High gearing is associated with high risk.

4 a

	TimeBall Co		DownsPier Co	
	Year 6	Year 7	Year 6	Year 7
Debentures	100	140	100	50
Debentures + equity	300	342.2	300	284.1
i Capital gearing ratio	33⅓%	40.9%	33⅓%	17.6%

Operating profit	20	21.6	20	17.5
÷ interest	9	12.6	9	4.5
ii Interest cover	2.2 times	1.7 times	2.2 times	3.9 times
Profit after tax	7.7	6.3	7.7	9.1
Dividend	4	4.1	4	5
iii Dividend cover	1.9 times	1.5 times	1.9 times	1.8 times
iv Proportion of profit paid as dividend	36%	46%	36%	38%

b i The capital gearing ratio shows the proportion of net assets financed by borrowing. The TimeBall Company increased its fixed assets plus current assets less current liabilities; a small part of this was financed by retained profits; it was mainly financed by additional borrowing. It became a higher risk company.

The DownsPier Company reduced its fixed assets plus current assets less current liabilities; this was needed, plus an issue of additional shares, and a small amount of profit retained during the year, to provide enough to pay off half of the borrowing. The company's risk was reduced.

ii The interest times cover shows how much the company is earning in relation to the amount of interest payable. In year 6 the interest cover of both companies was very low (2.2 times), which means that nearly half of their EBIT was committed to interest payments. A serious dip in EBIT could make it very difficult for the company to pay the necessary interest.

In year 7 the TimeBall Company's interest cover was lower, meaning that the situation became more risky. The DownsPier Company's interest cover increased significantly (though it is still on the low side), and risk was reduced.

iii The dividend cover shows how much profit after tax was available to pay the dividend that the company chose to pay. The TimeBall Company's profit after tax was lower in year 7 than in year 6, and there was a very small increase in dividend, both of which reduced the cover.

The DownsPier Company's profit after tax increased significantly (by 18 per cent), but the increase in dividend was more substantial (25 per cent) and so the dividend cover was reduced.

iv The proportion of profits paid out as the dividend is the same information as in (iii) above, but expressed the other way around (the reciprocal expressed as a percentage).

c

	TimeBall Co		DownsPier Co	
	Year 6	Year 7	Year 6	Year 7
Return on shareholders' capital employed				
Profit after tax	7.7	6.3	7.7	9.1
Shareholders'				
capital employed	200	202.2	200	234.1
ROSCE	3.85%	3.1%	3.85%	3.9%
Return on total long-term capital employed				
Operating profit	20	21.6	20	17.5
Debentures + equity	300	342.2	300	284.1
Return	6.7%	6.3%	6.7%	6.2%

In year 7 the TimeBall Company increased its operating profit, but because of extra debenture interest, its profitability was reduced.

In year 7 the DownsPier Company managed a small increase in the return on ordinary shareholders' capital employed; although its operating profit was lower than in the previous year, its debenture interest was halved. The ordinary shareholders had put more money into the company, and they earned just enough to make it worth while.

Gross profit/sales (%)	40	40	40	43
Operating profit/sales (%)	20	19.6	20	18.4

The TimeBall Company maintained the same gross profit ratio from year 6 to year 7, but its operating profit as a percentage of sales declined; this must have been due to operating expenses increasing more than sales.

The DownsPier Company's gross profit ratio increased from year 6 to year 7; perhaps it concentrated on its most profitable lines, and the total amount of sales declined. Its operating profit as a percentage of sales declined, although the gross profit had increased. This was because operating expenses had increased, both as a percentage of sales, and in total.

The TimeBall Company expanded sales and borrowing in year 6, and its financial position was weaker, as shown by the gearing ratio and interest times cover. But the expansion was not (yet?) worth while, and profitability declined. It managed a small increase in dividends, but this was not justified by profits.

The DownsPier Company seems a little safer. Sales declined, and borrowing was reduced, and the gross profit ratio increased, and the amount of net profit increased. The return on ordinary shareholders' capital increased very slightly and there was a substantial increase in dividend – more than was justified by the increase in profits.

5

- Legal position: balance of retained profits is the maximum sum payable.
- Cash flow position: there must be money available to pay a dividend.
- Investment opportunities: if cash is required for profitable investment, that would tend to reduce sums available to pay a dividend. And vice versa.
- Consistency of dividend policy: companies tend to follow a consistent payout policy and investors who approve of that policy would be attracted to become shareholders.
- Signal to the stock market: a company with poor performance this year might maintain its dividend in order to convey its confidence in its future performance.

Chapter 12

1 High levels of working capital make life easier for managers. Sales can be made to anyone without worrying about collecting the money in. Having large amounts of stock is convenient to satisfy all demands. Having substantial sums of money in the bank is also very convenient – there is no need to plan it properly, and there is always money available. High levels of working capital also lead to high current ratios, which make the company look financially stronger in terms of its ability to pay its creditors as they fall due.

2 Receivables can be reduced to little or nothing (or even negative) if customers are required to pay in advance. Some businesses have no inventories, or ensure that deliveries are 'just in time'. If there is a significant trade payables figure, then working capital can be negative. This is not unusual with retailers.

3 At first it arises with attempts to expand with insufficient long-term capital. There might be significant increases in non-current assets, inventory and receivables; but then the business finds that it is unable to finance these. Payables increase; current and liquidity ratios fall; and the company runs out of money. It may then have to operate on a cash only basis, and start to sell off assets.

4 Prompt paperwork, with invoices and reminders; follow-up letters and telephone calls; personal visits. Threatening to cut off supplies and/or legal action. Implementing threats. Offering cash discounts for early payment. Charging interest on late payment.

A company might deliberately increase the length of time that customers are allowed to pay if this is likely to lead to increases in sales, and to generate additional profits greater than the cost of financing the additional debtors.

5 Inventory holding costs; and the costs of ordering (which may include placing the order, monitoring receipt and payment of invoice). It also considers the volume of usage during the year, and the price per unit.

6 By careful planning and monitoring of cash receipts and payments; ensuring that there are sufficient funds to meet all planned requirements; and not authorizing unplanned payments.

7 Congle.

Applying the EOQ formula the ordering quantity will be the square root of the placed orders:

$$\sqrt{\frac{2 \times 40,000 \times £20}{1.25 \times 0.32}} = \sqrt{\frac{1,600,000}{0.4}} = \sqrt{4,000,000} = 2,000$$

The number of orders each year will be $40,000 \div 2,000 = 20$.

The annual ordering cost = $£20 \times 20$ times per annum = £400.

Goods will be delivered ($365 \div 20 =$) every 18 days.

The average inventory level will be half of the amount delivered, i.e.

$$\frac{1}{2} \times 2,000 \times £1.25 = £1,250$$

The annual inventory holding cost is $£1,250 \times 32\% = £400$.

8 Fleshwick Traders

Annual cost of receivables now: $£90,000 \times 17\% = £15,300$.

Annual sales are £365,000, i.e. £1,000 per day.

Existing receivables figure is £90,000, i.e. 90 days.

Expected reduction in receivables applies to one-third of receivables, i.e. £30,000.

Reduction is from 90 days to 10 days, i.e. a reduction of (eight-ninths).

Eight ninths of £30,000 is £26,667.

Annual interest saved is 17 per cent of £26,667 = £4,533.

Annual cost of discount on one-third of annual sales is $£121,667 \times 2.5\% = £3,042$.

a It is worth offering the discount because the amount of interest saved is greater than the cost of the discount offered.

b The annual interest saved is £4,533; discount costing up to £4,533 could be offered without reducing profits. £4,533 as a percentage of eight-ninths (one-third of annual sales) of £121,667 is 3.726%.

c Five per cent discount to one-third of existing customers would cost £6,085.

   The annual interest saved would be £4,533.

   The additional cost would be £6,085.

   The additional contribution required would be £1,552.

   Additional annual sales to achieve this contribution (contribution is one-fifth of sales) is $5 \times £1,552 = £7,760$.

This is near enough for most purposes, but for the mathematically inclined it is rather simplistic.

A more accurate calculation would be as follows:

Let I = the increase in sales required to finance the discount.

The cost of the discount is one-third $(365,000 + I) \times 0.05$, less the interest saving, which is 17 per cent of eight-ninths of one-third of $(365,000 + I)$. This will be equal to the amount of the additional contribution required, which is 20 per cent of the additional sales. We can say, therefore, that

$$\left[\frac{1}{3}(365,000 + I) \times 0.05\right] - \left[0.17 \times \frac{8}{9} \times \frac{1}{3} \times \frac{90}{365}(365,000 + I)\right] = 0.2 \times I$$

The amount of the additional contribution required (solving the above equation) is £7,913.

9 Stokeypokey

a **Income statement**

	£000
Sales		6,180
Cost of sales		4,944
Gross profit		1,236
Rent	400	
Other expenses	165	
Depreciation	10	575
Net profit		661

b **Statement of financial position as at end of year**

Non-current assets at cost		100
Less provision for depreciation		10
		90
Current assets		
Inventories	560	
Receivables	1,400	
Prepayment	100	
Cash	71	2,131
Total assets		2,221
Liabilities and equity		
Payables		560
Loan		1,000
Branch profit		661
		2,221

c

	Jan £000	Feb £000	Mar £000	Apr £000	May £000	Jun £000	Jul £000	Aug £000	Sep £000	Oct £000	Nov £000	Dec £000
Receipts												
from receivables	–	–	100	200	300	400	480	560	640	700	700	700
Payments for												
purchases		240	240	320	384	448	512	560	560	560	560	560
Rent	100		100			100			100			100
Fittings	50								50			
Expenses	10	10	10	10	15	15	15	16	16	16	16	16
Opening												
balance	1,000	840	590	340	210	111	(52)	(99)	(115)	(201)	(77)	47
Net receipts	(160)	(250)	(250)	(130)	(99)	(163)	(47)	(16)	(86)	124	124	24
	840	590	340	210	111	(52)	(99)	(115)	(201)	(77)	47	71

Workings												
	Jan	Feb	Mar	Apr	May	Jun	Jul	Aug	Sep	Oct	Nov	Dec
Sales	100	200	300	400	480	560	640	700	700	700	700	700
Purchases	240	240	320	384	448	512	560	560	560	560	560	560

d The business looks highly profitable. Stokeypokey plans to put £1m into the Northern Ireland branch and expects to earn £661,000 profit: a return on capital of just over 66 per cent per annum.

The gross profit ratio is expected to be 20 per cent. The net profit/sales ratio is expected to be 10.7 per cent. The main reason for the high ROCE that capital employed is fairly low, partly because the premises are rented.

Although profits look very good, it will take a little longer to generate cash flows to match. Rapid expansion in sales means that cash receipts from receivables tend to lag behind payments. A rapidly expanding and profitable business is often 'cash hungry' in the early stages. In this venture the branch pays out more cash than it receives in each of the first nine months, and the initial £1m will not be sufficient to avoid an overdraft by September.

By careful planning it might be possible to avoid an overdraft. Perhaps it could arrange to delay some payments in September, such as for the additional fittings, or make an extra effort to get debtors to pay more quickly in August.

Depreciation is an expense in calculating profit, but it is not a cash payment.

Chapter 13

1 Only (c) is true.

2 Direct costs are directly attributable to a particular job, product or service. Indirect costs are costs that cannot be identified with the individual cost unit.

3 Hourly paid staff are a variable cost, while employees on a monthly salary are fixed costs.

4 Only (a) is true.

5 Manufacturing account for JackDannie for year ended 30 June year 7

	£000	£000
Direct materials		
Inventory as at 1 July year 6	64	
Purchases during years 6 and 7	390	
	454	
Inventory as at 30 June year 7	(67)	
Cost of direct materials consumed		387
Direct wages		270
Prime cost		657
Manufacturing overheads		
Factory electricity	11	
Factory rent	76	
Indirect manufacturing wages	90	
General factory expenses	12	
Depreciation on machinery	14	
Repairs to machinery	8	211
		868

Total manufacturing costs incurred

Add Work in progress 1 July year 6	85
	953
Deduct Work in progress 30 June year 7	(78)
Manufacturing cost of goods completed	875
Transferred to income statement	

Income statement for JackDannie year ended 30 June year 7

		£000
Sales revenue		2,200
Cost of sales of finished goods		
Opening inventory	70	
Manufacturing cost	875	
	945	
Closing inventory	(92)	
		853
Gross profit		1,347
Administrative expenses		(420)
Distribution costs		(320)
Profit		607

Statement of financial position of JackDannie as at 30 June year 7

Non-current assets			
Machinery at cost			140
Provision for depreciation	40		
	14		(54)
			86
Current assets			
Inventories direct materials		67	
Work-in-progress		78	
Finished goods		92	
		237	
Receivables		420	
Bank		300	957
Total assets			1,043
Current liabilities			
Payables			66
Capital as at 1 July year 6	370		
Profit for year	607		977
			1,043

Chapter 14

1 The return on investment (ROI) takes the average annual profits during the life of a project and expresses them as a percentage of the capital employed in the project. It is sometimes based on the initial capital employed, and sometimes on the average capital employed over the life of the project.

2 The company's return on capital employed (ROCE) is 10 per cent (£1m as a percentage of £10m).

The ROI of the proposed project is 9 per cent (£180,000 as a percentage of £2m). But these figures are not strictly comparable: the £1m is after tax; and the £180,000 is operating profit (before tax).

If the company had surplus funds, the new ship would increase the company's ROCE because there would be no increase in capital employed, and profits would increase. If the £2m needed was in the bank, the increase in profits would depend on the amount of interest receivable that was lost as a result of buying the ship.

If the company had to raise additional equity, the total return on equity would be lowered because (a) the 9 per cent return is lower than the existing 10 per cent return; and (b) the additional £180,000 is operating profit: it would be less after tax.

If the ship was financed by borrowing, the company's return on equity would increase, assuming that the cost of borrowing was less than 9 per cent per annum.

3 Cash flows

Year	Project A £000	Project B £000
0	(1,000)	(1,000)
1	200	400
2	200	350
3	200	300
4	200	100
5	200	50
6	200	5
7	200	5
8	200	5
Total	1,600	1,215

The payback period of Project A is five years. The payback period of Project B is just less than three years.

Project A produces substantially more cash flows than Project B. If the time value of money is not considered, Project A is much better.

If the discounted cash flow (DCF) was used, whether or not it is worth waiting for the extra money would depend on the discount rate used.

4 a ROI is based on profits and so is compatible with financial accounts. The answer is expressed as a percentage which appears to be easy to understand. It is relatively easily calculated and understood.

However, the approach ignores the timing of the cash flows. A project may have a good ROI but not be worth while if the delay in receiving it is too long.

b Payback period is easy to understand and easy to calculate. It uses cash flows rather than profits, and the emphasis is on getting back the money quickly.

But payback period ignores cash flows received after the end of the payback period. Use of payback period could lead to a project being accepted that makes very little money, but pays back quickly; and a very profitable project could be rejected because it takes a little longer to pay back.

5 The project will generate £35,000 profits a year for five years, giving total profits of £175,000. This looks poor.

But, profits are measured after charging depreciation, which amounts to £40,000 a year. Annual cash flows are therefore £75,000 a year.

Using a discount rate of 10 per cent, the project gives a net present value (NPV) of about £84,300, as follows:

Year 1   0.909 × 75,000 = 68,175
Year 2   0.826 × 75,000 = 61,950
Year 3   0.751 × 75,000 = 56,325
Year 4   0.683 × 75,000 = 51,225
Year 5   0.621 × 75,000 = 46,575
         3.790 × 75,000 = 284,300

After deducting the initial cost of the investment (£284,300 – £200,000) the NPV of the project is £84,300, which makes it acceptable if the company's cost of capital is 10 per cent.

The project would still be just about acceptable with a cost of capital of 25 per cent (£75,000 × 2.689 = £201,675) because the net present values of the future cash flows would still be slightly above the initial cost.

6

					Kippering	Queenies
a	Average annual profits				£	£
	Total cash flows				75,000	90,000
	Total depreciation				50,000	50,000
	Total profits				25,000	40,000
	Average annual profits				5,000	8,000
b	Return on initial capital employed				10%	16%
c	Return on average capital employed				20%	32%
d	Payback period				2 ⅓ years	3.2 years
				£000		£000
e	NPV using 10%	1	0.909	25	22,727	5	4,545
		2	0.826	20	16,528	15	12,396
		3	0.751	15	11,269	25	18,782
		4	0.683	10	6,830	25	17,075
		5	0.621	5	3,105	20	12,418
					60,459		65,216
					(50,000)		(50,000)
	NPV				10,459		15,216
f	NPV using 25%	1	0.800	25	20,000	5	4,000
		2	0.640	20	12,800	15	9,600
		3	0.512	15	7,680	25	12,800
		4	0.410	10	4,100	25	10,250
		5	0.328	5	1,640	20	6,560
					46,220		43,210
					(50,000)		(50,000)
	NPV				(3,780)		(6,790)

g Approximate internal rate of return

10% plus a proportion of 15%	10,459	15,216
	(10,459 + 3,780)	(15,216 + 6,790)
	0.735 × 15	0.691 × 15
	11.02	10.36
+ 10	21.02%	20.36%

7 If it is decided to go ahead with the proposal the additional cash outflows at the beginning of the project would be:

Modifications to existing machinery	£100,000
Additional working capital	£50,000
Initial marketing costs	£60,000
	£210,000

The book value of the other machine is irrelevant; it has no alternative use or disposal value and so there is no 'opportunity cost'.

The cost of the consultants' report has already been incurred whether the project goes ahead or not, and so is irrelevant.

The cash flows generated by each unit of sales are:

Selling price		£60
Variable costs		
Materials	11	
Labour	6	
Variable overheads	13	£30
		£30

The costs of general fixed overheads and of interest will be incurred whether or not the project goes ahead and so they are not relevant.

	Year 0	Year 1	Year 2	Year 3	Year 4
Sales (units)	–	3,000	7,000	4,000	1,000
'Contribution' at £30 per unit		90,000	210,000	120,000	30,000
Machinery	(100,000)				
Working capital	(50,000)				50,000
Marketing	(60,000)	(20,000)	(20,000)	(20,000)	(20,000)
Maintenance		(10,000)	(10,000)	(10,000)	(10,000)
Net cash flow	(210,000)	60,000	180,000	90,000	50,000
20% discount factor	1.0	0.833	0.694	0.579	0.482
Present value	(210,000)	50,000	124,920	52,110	24,100

The NPV of the project discounted at 20 per cent is (£251,130 – £210,000 =) £41,130

8 Soderby plc cost of debt capital

Year	Cash flow	Discount factor 10%	NPV	Discount factor 5%	NPV
0	(98)	1	(98)	1	(98)
1	7	0.909	6.36	0.952	6.664

2	7	0.826		5.78	0.907	6.349
3	7	0.751		5.26	0.864	6.048
4	7	0.683		4.78	0.823	5.761
5	107	0.621		66.45	0.784	83.888
				(9.4)		10.71

$$\text{Interpolation suggests the IRR is} \quad 5\% + \frac{10.7}{(9.4 + 10.7)} \times 5$$

$$7.66\%$$

9 a i Next year's dividend: 40 pence × 1.05 = 42 pence

ii Next year's dividend as a % of current share price: $\dfrac{£0.42}{12} = 3.5\%$

iii Add assumed rate of growth: 5% + 3.5% = 8.5%

b i Risk free 3%

ii Return on shares generally 11%; deduct risk free rate of 3% = market risk premium: 8%

iii Adjust for Beta 8% × 0.75 = 6%; add risk free rate: 6% + 3% = 9%

Chapter 15

1 A budget may be defined as:

> 'A plan, quantified in monetary terms, prepared and approved prior to a defined period of time, usually showing planned income to be generated and/or expenditure to be incurred during that period, and the capital to be employed to attaining a given objective.'

Important parts of the definition are that a budget is a *plan* designed to attain a given *objective* and that it should be *approved* prior to a defined period of time.

2 A fixed budget is based on a planned level of output. A flexible budget (distinguishing between fixed and variable costs) has different versions that vary according to different levels of output.

3 Many advantages are claimed for operating a system of budgetary control, as shown in Section 13.4. In such a small business the amount of work to operate a detailed budgetary control system would probably not be worth while. As the organization is too small to have a management structure (there would be just one boss) issues of authorizing expenditure, delegation of responsibility, communication and co-ordination would scarcely arise: it would all be in one person's head. However, even in such a small organization, it would be worth defining objectives (perhaps a given sales and profit level for the year, or even for each month), and keeping an eye on actual results on a regular basis (control). It might not be necessary to produce monthly income statements. Monitoring receipts from sales, and payments of expenses (using bank statements) might provide sufficient control information.

4

	Budget	Flexed budget	Actual results	Workings for flexed budget
	August Year 6	August Year 6	August Year 6	
	£000	£000	£000	
Sales	600	690	690	
Direct materials	120	138	140	120 + 15%
Direct labour	100	115	117	100 + 15%
Production overheads	200	215	223	100 + (100 + 15%)
Distribution costs	80	89	95	20 + (60 + 15%)

Administrative overheads	60	51.5	70	50+(10+15%)
Total costs	560	608.5	645	
Profit	40	81.5	45	

The fixed budget showed that sales increased from £600,000 to £690,000 and profits increased from £40,000 to £45,000. Some people might be satisfied with an increase in profits of more than 10 per cent when sales increase by 15 per cent. However, as many costs tend to be 'fixed', profits should have increased by significantly more than 15 per cent. The flexed budget shows that profits should have more than doubled.

As there was a 15 per cent increase in sales, a 15 per cent increase in variable costs is expected in the flexed budget. But direct material and direct labour costs increased by £4,000 more than expected. Moreover, all overhead costs increased by more than the flexed budget specified. Overall, costs increased by £85,000 when they should have increased by only £48,500. It seems that, in the effort to increase output by 15 per cent, insufficient attention was paid to the control of costs.

5 A very successful business will have serious cash shortages if its profits are poured into additional assets. This may be a healthy expansion of inventories and receivables in line with sales; and investment in additional non-current assets, and buying shares in other companies. It may be unhealthy if poor control results in too many assets being bought, excessive inventory levels and fixed assets that are not profitably utilized.

The situation could also arise if substantial loans are repaid, and if the company pays out more as dividends than it earns as profits.

6 Rachel

a **Budgeted income statement**

£m	Jan	Feb	Mar	Apr	May	Jun	Jul	Aug	Sep	Oct	Nov	Dec	Total
Sales	5,000	5,000	10,000	10,000	10,000	10,000	6,000	6,000	10,000	10,000	10,000	2,500	94,500
Expenses													
Operating expenses	1,000	1,000	2,000	2,000	2,000	2,000	1,200	1,200	2,000	2,000	2,000	500	18,900
Fixed overheads	3,000	3,000	3,000	3,000	3,000	3,000	3,000	3,000	3,000	3,000	3,000	3,000	36,000
	4,000	4,000	5,000	5,000	5,000	5,000	4,200	4,200	5,000	5,000	5,000	3,500	54,900
Profit	1,000	1,000	5,000	5,000	5,000	5,000	1,800	1,800	5,000	5,000	5,000	(1,000)	39,600

b **Cash budget**

£	Jan	Feb	Mar	Apr	May	Jun	Jul	Aug	Sep	Oct	Nov	Dec	Total
Receipts													
From receivables	2,500	2,500	5,000	5,000	10,000	10,000	10,000	10,000	6,000	6,000	10,000	10,000	87,000
Payments													
Operating expenses	1,000	1,000	2,000	2,000	2,000	2,000	1,200	1,200	2,000	2,000	2,000	500	18,900
Fixed overheads	1,000	1,000	1,000	1,000	1,000	1,000	1,000	1,000	1,000	1,000	1,000	1,000	12,000
	2,000	2,000	3,000	3,000	3,000	3,000	2,200	2,200	3,000	3,000	3,000	1,500	30,900
Net receipts or deficits	500	500	2,000	2,000	7,000	7,000	7,800	7,800	3,000	3,000	7,000	8,500	56,100
Opening balance	1,000	1,500	2,000	4,000	6,000	13,000	20,000	27,800	35,600	38,600	41,600	48,600	1,000
Closing balance	1,500	2,000	4,000	6,000	13,000	20,000	27,800	35,600	38,600	41,600	48,600	57,100	57,100

c

	£
Profit	39,600
Depreciation	24,000
	63,600
Increase in receivables	
(£12,500 – £5,000)	7,500
Increase in cash	56,100

d Drawings should not exceed profit of £39,600

Chapter 16

1 Most wood, metal and components and sub-assemblies would be treated as direct materials. Cleaning materials, lubricants, and many widely used items of low value such as glue, screws and nails would be treated as indirect materials. Anything that becomes part of the finished item is really a direct material, but with items of low value it is often not worth the trouble of charging them to different jobs. Materials used in the factory which do not become part of the finished item are part of production overheads.

2 a £23m ÷ 1.4m = £16.42867, or £16.43 per hour

   b £23m ÷ 1.4m = £16.42867, or £16.43 per hour

   The budgeted production overheads for the year are the same as the budgeted wages for the year, so the answers to (a) and (b) are the same.

   c 100%

   i Dept A £1m ÷ 500,000 hrs = £2 per hour

   Dept B £2m ÷ 500,000 hrs = £4 per hour

   Dept C £20m ÷ 400,000 hrs = £50 per hour

   ii Dept A £5m ÷ 500,000 hrs = £10 per hour

   Dept B £8m ÷ 500,000 hrs = £16 per hour

   Dept C £10m ÷ 400,000 hrs = £25 per hour

   iii Dept A £2 ÷ £10 = 20%

   Dept B £4 ÷ £16 = 25%

   Dept C £50 ÷ £25 = 200%

   d 13 hrs × £16.43 = £213.59

   e Labour cost 13 hrs × £16.43 = £213.59 × 100% = £213.59

   f Dept A 3 hrs @ £2 = £6

   Dept B 6 hrs @ £4 = £24

   Dept C 4 hrs @ £50 = £200 __£230__

   g Labour cost

   Dept A 3 hrs @ £10 = £ 30 × 20% = £ 6

   Dept B 6 hrs @ £16 = £ 96 × 25% = £ 24

   Dept C 4 hrs @ £25 = £100 × 200% = __£200__ £230

In this example it is assumed that the same wage rate is paid to all operatives within a department is; using percentage on direct labour cost therefore gives the same answer as using a direct labour hour rate. If different operatives within a department were paid different hourly rates, the two methods would give different answers.

3

Contract 1	Contract 2
a FIFO 1,000 @ £12 = £12,000	1,500 @ £11 = £16,500
500 @ £11 = £ 5,500	
£17,500	
b LIFO 500 @ £14 = £ 7,000	1,000 @ £11 = £11,000
1,000 @ £11 = £11,000	500 @ £12 = £ 6,000
£18,000	£17,000

   c Average weighted average = £41,000 ÷ 3,500 = £11.714285

   1,500 @ £11.71 = £17,565[2]   1,500 @ £11.71 = £17,565

4 Production overheads are directly allocated to particular cost centres where this is possible; for example, where a machine or a member of staff exclusively belongs to one cost centre. Production overheads are apportioned to cost centres where this is not possible, perhaps on the basis of the number of square metres occupied, or the

---

[2] The answer is inaccurate due to rounding. The correct answer would be £17,571.43.

number of employees. After total production overheads have been calculated they are charged to particular jobs or products, which are said to absorb them.

5 Administrative expenses and selling and distribution costs are not absorbed by products. They are not part of product costs; they are not included in closing inventory; they are charged against profits in the period in which they are incurred.

6 a Overhead absorption rate = total overheads £288,000/total number of staff hours 7200* = £40 per hour*

*(25 × 40) + (3,000 × 2) + (100 × 2) = 7,200 staff hours.

Cost per course:

Pony trekking 25 × 40 = £1,000

General lesson 2 × 40 = £ 80
Advanced riding skills 2 × 40 = £ 80

(Check: 40 pony trekking courses cost £40,000, 3,000 general lessons cost £240,000, 100 advanced riding skills cost 8,000, total £288,000.)

b Staff costs driven by total number of staff hours (40 × 25) + (3,000 × 2) + (100 × 2) = 7,200 hours. £108,000/7,200 = £15 per hour

Number of brochures (40 × 30) + (3,000 × 1) + (100 × 5) = 4,700. £7,050/4,700 = £1.50 per brochure.

Admin costs driven by number of events (40 × 10) + (3,000 × 4) + (100 × 6) = 13,000 events. £33,800/13,000 = £2.60 per event.

Insurance driven by number of clauses (40 × 14.15) + (3,000 × 1.5) + (100 × 5) = 5,566.

£139,150/5,566 = £25 per clause.

c Reallocation of overheads using ABC:

Pony trekking: (25 staff hours × £15) + (30 brochures × £1.50) + (10 admin events × £2.60) + (14.15 insurance clauses × £25) = £375 + £45 + £26 + £353.75 = £799.75

General lessons: (2 staff hours × £15) + (1 brochure × £1.50) + (4 admin events × £2.60 + (1.5 insurance clauses × £25) = £30 + £1.50 + £10.40 + £37.50 = £79.40

Advanced riding skills: (2 staff hours × £15) + (5 brochures × £1.50) + (6 admin events × £2.60 + (5 insurance clauses × £25) = £30 + £7.50 + £15.6 + £125 = £178.10

Check (£799.75 × 40 courses) + (£79.40 × 3,000 courses) + (£172.90 × 100 courses) = £31,990 + £238,200 + £17,810 = £288,000

d **General advantages**

■ More accurate and meaningful product cost information can be determined.

■ There is an improvement in management's understanding of costs and their causes.

■ Improved management information in terms of performance measurement prevails in budgeting, new products/processes and general cost reduction.

Specific advantages

■ Provides quality service at low cost.

■ Horizontal view, quality chains.

■ Activity-based budgeting can result from this.

■ Develop into activity-based management.

Disadvantages

■ Behavioural issues, for example, resistance to change.

■ Selling benefits to managers.

■ Willingness to participate.

■ Effect of new performance measures.

7

a *Traditional volume-based absorption costing*

using no. of holidays

Overhead absorption rate:

total overheads | 800,000
basis (i.e. no. of holidays) | 3,200
Overhead absorption rate: | £250 per holiday

b *ABC approach*

Enquiries	180,000	
Adventure: 1,200 × 5 = 6,000		
Package tour: 2,000 × 7 = 14,000	20,000	£9 per enquiry
Brochure	320,000	
Adventure: 1,200 × 10 = 12,000		
Package tour: 2,000 × 34 = 68,000	80,000	£4 per brochure
Courier trips	300,000	
Adventure: 1,200 × 1 = 1,200		
Package tour: 2,000 × 2 = 4,000	5,200	£57.69 per courier

so, total overheads per holiday

	Adventure holiday	Package holiday
Enquiries @ £9 × 5	45.00	
@ £9 × 7		63.00
Brochures @ £4 × 10	40.00	
@ £4 × 34		136.00
Couriers @ £57.69 × 1	57.69	
@ £57.69 × 2		115.38
	142.69	314.38

c ABC:

Benefits	Pitfalls
More meaningful product costs	It's just another method of cost absorption
Improves understanding of overhead costs	
Helps development of non-financial performance	Selection of cost drivers may be problematical
Targets cost reduction	
Assists in the design of new products and services	The time and cost of implementation may be prohibitive

Chapter 17

1 Contribution is: sales less variable costs.

Contribution per unit is: selling price less variable costs per unit.

Break-even point is: fixed costs/contribution per unit.

Margin of safety is: expected (or budgeted) sales less break-even point.

2 Fixed costs can be separated from variable costs according to:

a whether they vary with output;

b a given range of output or time.

For example, to manufacture up to 100,000 machines a company might need one supervisor, but beyond 100,000 they might need two supervisors. Hence, the fixed costs will rise in steps as output exceeds expected boundaries.

3 Dannidoon's contribution is (£60 – £35) = £25 per unit; need enough contribution to cover fixed costs of £700,000.

$$£700,000 ÷ £25 = 28,000 \text{ units to break even}$$

4

	September	October	Change
	£000	£000	£000
Sales	600	650	50
Profit	100	120	
Total costs	500	530	30
Variable costs 60% of sales	360	390	
Fixed cost	140	140	
Contribution	240	260	

Contribution/sales ratio September 240 ÷ 600 = 40% or 0.4

October 260 ÷ 650 = 40% or 0.4

Break-even point 140 ÷ 0.4 = £350,000

a with 30,000 hours

		Holiday chalets	Terraced houses	Luxury villas
		£000	£000	£000
Selling price		100	200	800
Variables costs		70	120	420
Contribution per unit		30	80	380
Hours to build a unit		300	600	3,000
Contribution per labour hour		100.00	133.33	126.67
Ranking	3rd	1st	2nd	
Maximum sales	20	30	10	
Optimal production	0	30	4	
Labour hour required	–	18,000	12,000	30,000
Contribution	0	2,400	1,520	Total 3920
				i.e. £3,920,000

If it built 10 luxury villas it would use 30,000 labour hours, which is all that are available. The contribution would be £3,920,000.

b with 51,000 hours

	Holiday chalets £000	Terraced houses £000	Luxury villas £000		
Selling price	100	200	800		
Variables costs	70	120	420		
Contribution per unit	30	80	380		
Hours to build a unit	300	600	3,000		
Contribution per labour hour	100.00	133.33	126.67		
Ranking	3rd	1st	2nd		
Maximum sales	20	30	10		
Optimal production	10	30	10		
Labour hour required	3,000	18,000	30,000		51,000
Contribution	300	2,400	3,800	Total	6500
				i.e. £6,500,000	

With 51,000 hours it would build 30 terraced houses, 10 luxury villas and 10 holiday chalets. The contribution would be £6.5m.

This analysis assumes that there is no interrelated demand and also that, with only 30,000 labour hours, the company believes that it is prepared to cut production of what hitherto it has considered its key product, luxury villas.

c If it built 10 luxury villas it would use 30,000 labour hours, which is all that are available. The contribution would be £3,920,000.

d It would build 30 terraced houses producing a contribution of £2,400,000, and 4 luxury villas producing a contribution of £1,520,000. The total contribution would be £3,920,000.

5

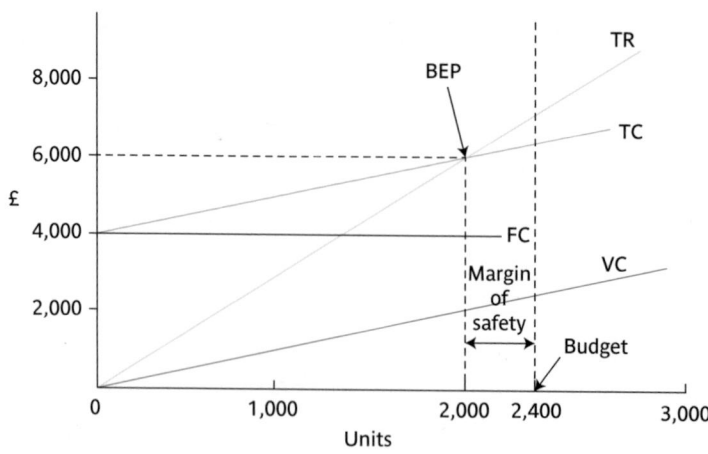

$$BEP = \frac{Fixed\ costs}{Contribution\ per\ unit}$$

$$Fixed\ costs = £4,000$$

$$Contribution\ per\ unit = £2$$

$$BEP = 2,000\ units$$

$$= £6,000$$

$$\begin{aligned}
\text{Margin of safety} &= \text{Budget} - \text{BEP} \\
&= 2{,}400 - 2{,}000 \\
&= 400 \text{ units} \\
&= \pounds 1{,}200 \\
&= 16.7\%
\end{aligned}$$

Chapter 18

1 Corrina made 11 loaves instead of 10, and so it is not surprising that the cost of her materials was more than the £10 she had planned. But her material cost variance was *favourable*. This is because she spent only £10.50 to make 11 loaves whereas the standard cost of making 11 loaves would be £11.

a Direct materials cost variance

Actual cost	Standard cost
	11 loaves @ £1
£10.50	£11

Direct material cost variance

b Direct materials price and usage variances

Actual cost	Actual quantities at standard (or cost budgeted) cost per kg	Standard cost
	10.4 kg @ £1 per kg	11 loaves @ £1
£10.50	£10.40	£11
	Direct material price variance	Direct material usage variance
	10p adverse	60p favourable
	Direct material cost variance 50p favourable	

The price of dough was higher than expected, but this was more than offset by efficient usage. Perhaps she made smaller loaves.

2 Anomelg

Actual cost	Actual hours at standard (or budgeted) rate per hour	Standard cost
	84 hours @	7 @ £300
	£30	£2.50
£2,400	£2,520	£2,100
	Direct labour rate variance	Direct labour efficiency variance
	£120 favourable	£420 adverse
	Total direct labour cost variance £300 adverse	

a There was an adverse labour cost variance of £300 because it cost more to do seven conveyances than it should have done.

b The adverse cost variance was due to inefficiency. She took 84 hours to do seven conveyances that should have taken only 70 hours. This was partly offset by a reduction in her rate of pay per hour.

3 Wee Lee Cycle Company

a Budget

	£
Sales 10,000 bicycles at £100 each	1,000,000
Costs 10,000 bicycles at £80 each	800,000
Profit	£ 200,000

b Actual

Sales 11,000 bicycles	979,000
Costs 11,000 bicycles	902,000
Profit	£ 77,000

c Budgeted profit margin £100 – £80 = £20

Actual profit margin £979,000 ÷ 11,000 = 89. £89 – £80 = £9. Assumes standard cost of production. Cost variances are separately identified.

Actual volume of sales at actual margin per unit		Actual volume of sales at budgeted margin per unit		Budgeted volume of sales at budgeted margin per unit
11,000 units		11,000 units		10,000 units
@ £9 per unit		@ £20 per unit		@ £20 per unit
£99,000		£220,000		£200,000
	Sales margin price variance		Sales margin volume variance	
	£121,000 adverse		£20,000 favourable	
	Total sales margin variance £101,000 adverse			

Actual cost of producing the actual number that were produced		Standard cost of producing the actual number that were produced
£902,000		11,000 × £80 = 880,000
	Total cost variance	
	£22,000 adverse	

d Difference between budgeted and actual profit £200,000 – £77,000 = £123,000

Total of variances	Sales margin variances	£101,000 Adverse
	Cost variances	£ 22,000 Adverse
		£123,000

The most striking features of the results are:

i a lot more bicycles were sold than planned (11,000 instead of 10,000); and

ii profit was a lot lower than planned (£77,000 instead of £200,000).

The problem with sales was not the *volume* of sales, but the *price* of the units sold. The sales revenue was £979,000 for 11,000 bicycles: that is £89 per bicycle instead of £100 per bicycle. The *volume variance* was favourable, but the price variance was unfavourable.

It was planned that each bicycle would generate a profit (or 'margin') of £20. If nothing had changed other than the volume of sales, the additional profit generated would have been 1,000 extra bicycles at £20 each, which is £20,000: there was a favourable sales margin volume variance of £20,000.

Unfortunately, there was also an unfavourable variance because of the average price being reduced from £100 to £89. Instead of making a profit of £20 per bicycle, they made only (£89 – £80 =) £9 per bicycle, or £11 less than planned. The result of the price reduction was that each bicycle sold (11,000) made £11 less than expected. In other words, there was an adverse sales margin price variance of (11,000 × £11=) £121,000.

There was also a problem with costs. Each bicycle was expected to cost £80 to produce. As 11,000 units were produced, total costs should have been (11,000 × 80 =) £880,000. But the actual costs for the month amounted to £902,000.[3] There was an adverse total cost variance of £22,000.[4]

4 Wool Witch Company

			£		£
a	Budgeted profit	5,000 @ £13			65,000
b	Actual profit	Sales		108,000	
	DM	12,200			
	DL	39,500			
	O	9,500		61,200	46,800
	Total variance				18,200

c Direct materials

Actual cost		Actual quantities @ planned price		Standard cost
		3,900 kg @ £3 per kg		4,000 @ £3
£12,200		£11,700		£12,000
	Direct material price variance £500 adverse		Direct material usage variance £300 favourable	
		Direct material cost variance £200 favourable		

Direct labour

Actual cost		Actual hours @ planned rate		Standard cost
		3,850 hrs @ £10 per hr		4,000 @ £10
£39,500		38,500		£40,000
	Direct labour rate variance £1,000 adverse		Direct labour efficiency variance £1,500 favourable	
		Direct labour cost variance £500 favourable		

Overheads Actual cost		Budgeted hours @ planned rate		Actual hours @ planned rate		Standard cost
		5,000 @ £2 per hr		3,850 @ £2 per hr		4,000 @ £2
£9,500		£10,000		£7,700		£8,000
	Overhead		Overhead		Overhead	

---

[3] Normally, we expect costs per unit to decrease as the volume of production increases (because fixed costs are spread among more units – what economists call 'economies of scale'). In this example costs per unit have increased although the volume of production has increased.

[4] It cost £902,000 to produce 11,000 units, that is, £82 per unit, on £2 per unit more than planned. As 11,000 units were produced; the total adverse cost variance was 11,000 × £2 = £22,000.

expenditure variance	capacity utilization variance	efficiency variance
£500 favourable	£2,300 adverse	£300 favourable

Overhead volume variance £2,000 adverse
Overhead cost variance £1,500 adverse

Sales margin variances

Selling price	£28
Standard cost DM + DL + O: £3 + £10 + £2 = £15	
Planned margin	£13

Actual selling price £108,000 ÷ 4,000 = £27
Margin (assuming standard cost)
£27 − £15 = £12

Actual sales	Actual sales @ planned margin	Budgeted sales @ budgeted margin
4,000 @ £12	4,000 @ £13	5,000 @ £13
£48,000	£52,000	£65,000

Sales margin variance £4,000 adverse

Sales margin volume variance £13,000 adverse

Direct material cost variance £17,000

d **Summary of variances**

	£	£
Direct material price variance	500 adverse	
Direct material usage variance	300 favourable	
Direct material cost variance		200 adverse
Direct labour rate variance	1,000 adverse	
Direct labour efficiency variance	1,500 favourable	
Direct labour cost variance		500 favoured
Overhead expenditure variance	500 favourable	
Overhead capacity utilization variance	2,300 adverse	
Overhead efficiency variance	300 favourable	
Overhead cost variance		1,500 adverse
Sales margin price variance	4,000 adverse	
Sales margin volume variance	13,000 adverse	17,000 adverse
Total variances		18,200 adverse

Efficiency and usage variances were all favourable, which suggests good cost control. There were adverse price variances for materials and labour, which may have been outside the company's control. The main problems were with not producing and selling enough. There was a substantial adverse capacity utilization variance, and also an adverse selling price variance. But the largest adverse variance was in sales volume. Even price reductions failed to produce sales at the planned level.

5 Poleg Limited

	Unit	Original budget	Flexed budget	Actual	Fav	Adv
Units		1,000	1,400	1,400		
Sales	150	150,000	210,000	212,800		
Materials	67.5	67,500	94,500	121,000		
Labour	30	30,000	42,000	34,000		
VO	15	15,000	21,000	15,000		
Total VCs	112.5	112,500	157,500	170,000		
Contribution	37.5	37,500	52,500	42,800		
FO	7.5	7,500	7,500	6,000		
Profit (*i.e.* margin)	30	30,000	45,000	36,800		

					Fav	Adv
Budgeted profit						30,000
Sales price variance	AQ(AP – SP)	1,400(152 – 150)	1,400 × 2		2,800	
Sales volume contribution variance	SCntn(AQ – SQ)	37.50 (1,400 – 1,000)	37.50 × 400		15,000	
Standard contribution for actual sales						47,800
Materials						
price	AQ(AP – SP)	121,000 – (22,000 × 4.50)	121,000 – 99,000			22,000
efficiency	SP(AQ – SQ)	4.50 (22,000 – 1,400 × 15)	4.50 × (22,000 – 21000)		4,500	
Labour						
rate	AH(AR – SR)	34,000 – (6,800 × 6)	34,000 – 40,800		6,800	
efficiency	SP(AH – SH)	6[(6,800 – 1,400 × 5)]	6(6,800 – 7,000)		1,200	
		245 – (250 × 1.25)				
Variable overheads						
rate	AH(AR – SR)	15,000 – (6,800 × 3)	15,000 – 20,400		5,400	
efficiency	SR(AH – SH)	3[(6,800 – (1,400*5)]	3 × (6,800 – 7,000)		600	
Fixed overheads						
expenditure	Actual – Budget	7,500 – 6,000			1,500	
					15,500	26,500
						(11,000)
Actual profit						36,800

Answers to Chapter 4 Activities

4.1 Druisdale plc

Ratio	Year 5		Year 6		Comment
1 Current ratio	120 : 60	2 : 1	120 : 80	1.5 : 1	Looks weaker because of increased current liabilities
2 Liquidity ratio	60 : 60	1 : 1	60 : 80	0.75 : 1	Looks weaker because of increased current liabilities
3 Gearing ratio	60/240	25%	40/240	16.7%	Lower, less risky, because of reduced borrowings
4 Interest cover	60/5	12 times	69/4	17¼ times	Higher, less risky, because of reduced borrowings, reduced interest and increased operating profit

4.2 Druisdale plc

Ratio	Year 5		Year 6		Comment
5 Return on share-holders' capital employed	40/180	22.2%	50/200	25%	Profitability for shareholders has increased because profits have increased more than the increase in shareholders' capital employed
6 Return on total long-term capital employed	60/240	25%	69/240	28.75%	Overall profitability in the use of assets has increased
7 Operating profit as a percentage of sales	60/300	20%	69/350	19.7%	Profit as a percentage has declined, indicating an increase in costs as a percentage of sales
8 Asset turnover	300/240	1.25 times	350/240	1.46 times	Overall increase in profitability is due to improved utilization of assets (sales have increased; assets have not)

Relationship between ratios 6, 7 and 8
Year 5 25 ÷ 20 = 1.25
Year 6 28.75 ÷ 19.7 = 1.46

4.3 Druisdale plc

Ratio	Year 5		Year 6		Comment
9 Gross profit ratio	100/300	33⅓%	120/350	34.3%	The margin between buying prices has improved by increasing selling prices and/or reducing the cost of purchase
10 Distribution costs as a % of sales	15/300	5%	20/350	5.7%	Distribution costs have increased by a bigger proportion than sales
11 Administrative expenses as a % of sales	25/300	8⅓%	31/350	8.9%	Administrative expenses have increased by a bigger proportion than sales

4.4 Druisdale plc

Ratio	Year 5		Year 6		Comment
12 Sales/non-current assets	300/180	1.67 times	350/200	1.75 times	Sales have increased by a bigger proportion than fixed assets, thus improving the utilization of fixed assets
13 Sales/current assets	300/120	2.5 times	350/120	2.92 times	Sales have increased, current assets have not, thus improving the utilization of current assets
14 Inventory turnover ratio	$60 \div 200 \times 365$	109.5 days	$60 \div 230 \times 365$	95.2 days	Stock levels have remained constant while turnover has increased
15 Receivables ratio	$40 \div 300 \times 365$	48.7 days	$50 \div 350 \times 365$	52 days	Debtors have increased by a bigger proportion than sales, indicating that it is taking a few days longer to get money in from debtors
16 Payables ratio	$60 \div 200 \times 365$	109.5 days	$80 \div 230 \times 365$	127 days	Creditors have increased by a bigger proportion than cost of sales, and it is taking even longer than an already long period to pay them

Comments on profitability

Overall profitability (measured as return on capital employed, ratios 5 and 6) increased from year 5 to year 6. This was not due to an improvement in the profitability of sales, which declined (ratio 7). It was due to improved utilization of assets (asset turnover, ratio 8, increased).

The problems with the profitability of sales were due to an increase in distribution costs and administrative expenses; the gross profit ratio increased, suggesting that there was not a problem with the cost of sales or selling prices.

The improved utilization of assets applied to both non-current assets and current assets. Inventory turnover increased, although this was offset by a slowing-down in the collection of receivables. The period taken to pay creditors is excessive, and increased; but this increasing reliance on funding by receivables contributed to the increase in profitability.

4.5 Druisdale plc

Ratio	Year 5		Year 6		Comment
17 Price/earnings (P/E) ratio	£5.60 ÷ 40p	14	£7.50 ÷ 50p	15	Share price has increased by an even bigger proportion than earnings per share (EPS)
18 Dividend yield	25p ÷ £5.60 × 100	4.5%	30p ÷ £7.50 × 100	4%	Dividend has increased by a significant proportion, but the share price has increased by an even bigger proportion so that dividend is a smaller proportion of the share price

| 19 | Dividend cover | 40/25 | 1.60 times | 50/30 | 1.67 times | Dividends have increased almost in line with profits, but there is a slight increase in cover |
| 20 | Net assets per share | £180/100 | £1.80 | £200/100 | £2.00 | Net assets per share have increased as profits have been retained; but the market price is much higher than the underlying asset value |

4.6 Garwick Ltd

Ratio	Year 7	Year 8
1 Current ratio	2.47 : 1	1.5 : 1
2 Liquidity ratio	1.88 : 1	0.85 : 1
3 Capital gearing ratio	53.3%	42.9%
4 Interest times cover	4.75 times	7.67 times
5 Return on shareholders' funds	31.4%	37.5%
6 Return on total long-term capital employed	25.3%	32.9%
7 Operating profit as a % of sales	18.8%	21%
8 Asset turnover	1.35 times	1.57 times
9 Gross profit ratio	30.7%	32.7%
10 Distribution costs as a % of sales	6.9%	6.4%
11 Administrative expenses as a % of sales	5%	5.5%
12 Sales/non-current assets	2.02 times	1.83 times
13 Sales/current assets	2.4 times	3.67 times
14 Inventory turnover ratio	52.1 days	64.1 days
15 Receivables ratio	50.6 days	53.1 days
16 Payables ratio	88.6 days	98.6 days
17 (P/E) ratio	17	19
18 Dividend yield	4.3%	3.5%
19 Dividend cover	1.4 times	1.5 times
20 Net assets per share	£0.35	£0.40

Comments

In year 7 the current and liquidity ratios were strong, but they had declined to worrying levels in year 8.

In year 7 the gearing ratio was high, and the interest times cover was low, indicating heavy reliance on long-term borrowing. The level of gearing was lower (safer), and the interest cover was stronger in year 8.

The company had reduced its reliance on long-term borrowing mainly by reducing the amount of cash held.

The level of overall profitability was high, and increased in year 8 (ratios 5 and 6). The increase was due both to an increase in the profitability of sales (ratio 7) and in the utilization of assets (ratio 8).

The increase in the profitability of sales was due both to an increase in the gross profit ratio, and to a decrease in distribution costs as a percentage of sales; this was offset by an increase in administrative expenses as a percentage of sales.

The improvement in the utilization of assets was due entirely to an increase in the turnover of current assets; the utilization of non-current assets declined (because the amount of non-current assets increased by a bigger proportion (20 per cent[1]) than the increase in sales (just less than 10 per cent[2]),

The improvement in the utilization of current assets was due partly to the reduction in the amount of cash, and partly to the increase in stock turnover; these were offset by the deterioration in the debtors ratio. The amount of net assets was also reduced (and so capital employed was reduced[3]) by the increase in creditors.

Overall, there was a good improvement in profitability, but some concern about solvency and excessive liabilities remains.

The share price increased substantially, and the increase in the P/E ratio indicates investors' optimism about the company. The amount of dividend paid by the company increased substantially (by 25 per cent), but the share price increased by a greater proportion, and so the dividend yield declined; a reduction in dividend yield may be seen as an indicator of the market's confidence in the company. There may be questions about the sustainability of dividends (cover was only 1.4 times in year 7), but this improved a little in year 8.

The market value of the company is much higher than the statement of financial position value of it (the share price is much higher than the net assets per share).

---

[1] From £50,000 to £60,000.
[2] From £101,000 to £110,000.
[3] And so return on capital employed was increased.

Glossary

The word 'company' is used in this glossary although most of the definitions apply to other businesses and entities.

A

Absorption costing A traditional costing method in which individual products bear their share of both fixed and variable production costs.

Accounting policies The specific bases, conventions, rules and practices applied by an entity in preparing and presenting financial statements.

Accounting rate of return (ARR) The average accounting profit divided by the initial (or average) investment, expressed as a percentage (also called return on investment (ROI)).

Accounting standards Quasi-legal regulations defining terms and explaining how figures are to be calculated or disclosed in external financial accounts. These have been issued as **SSAPs**, **FRSs** (UK and Ireland) **IASs** and **IFRSs** (international).

Accrual An accrual is an expense that has been incurred but not yet recorded at the year end; the trial balance has to be adjusted to include accruals as an adjustment to the expense and as a current liability. Accruals are only a small part of the accruals concept.

Accruals concept On an income statement revenue is recorded in the period when it is earned and not when the cash is received; expenses are recorded in the period in which they are incurred and not when they are paid; expenses are matched against revenues. This is distinct from the cash (or receipts and payments) basis of accounting. Additionally, costs are matched with revenues.

Acid test *See liquidity ratio.*

Activity-based costing (ABC) A method of costing in which the fixed costs are allocated to products or other cost objects on the basis of the activities that drive them.

Articles of association The internal constitution of a company including the rights of shareholders.

Assets A resource controlled by the enterprise as a result of past transactions or events and from which future economic benefits are expected to flow to the enterprise.

Associate An associate company is not a subsidiary company but it is one over which an investing company has significant influence, usually by owning between 20–50 per cent of its shares.

Audit report A report appearing in a company's annual report, written and signed by the independent auditor and addressed to the shareholders expressing their opinion on whether the accounts show a 'true and fair view' and comply with the Companies Act and other specified regulations such as IFRSs.

Auditing An external annual process whereby all but small companies are subject to independent and expert assessment of their financial records and statements and systems of internal control, to express an opinion on whether the accounts have been prepared in accordance with the Companies Act and relevant accounting standards and regulations, and show a true and fair view.

B

Balance sheet A statement of *assets*, *liabilities* and *equity* as at a given date, typically at the end of a year, or a month. Often now called the statement of financial position.

Bank reconciliation A statement in which bank receipts and payments which have not yet cleared the banking system are added and subtracted from the balance per the bank statement in order to confirm the cash book balance is correct.

Bonus (or scrip) issue An issue of shares to existing shareholders in proportion to their existing shareholding. No money changes hands. Reserves or retained earnings are redesignated as share capital and the market value per share reduces in proportion to the proportionate increase in the number of shares.

Break-even point Number of units sold, or sales revenue whereby total revenue equals total cost and where profit is zero.

Budget A quantitative plan showing forecast sales and costs such as direct materials, direct labour and overheads, purchases, inventory and cash for a future period which is used for planning, co-ordination, control and motivation.

Business entity concept Financial accounts report the activities, assets and liability of the business and not those of the owner.

C

Capital expenditure Expenditure incurred in buying, creating or adding to non-current assets.

Cash A current asset; it includes petty cash and bank. It can be negative, usually shown as an overdraft, a *current liability*.

Cash book A book of prime entry in which the bank receipts and bank payments are listed by date and analysed with details of the name of payer or payee and the bank balance is shown. This will be reconciled to the bank statement from time to time on a *bank reconciliation*.

Cash flow The term has no precise meaning but is sometimes used as if it means profit plus depreciation. Cash flow statements show separately cash flows from operating activities, investing activities and financing activities.

Cash flow statement One of the principal statements in a published set of accounts, it shows cash inflows and outflows in operating activities, investing activities and financing activities, the net result of these three categories being the increase or decrease in the cash balances.

Company A separate legal entity, owned by shareholders and managed by directors. The shareholders usually have limited liability and the company is required to produce annual accounts which must be sent to the shareholders and are filed at Companies House where they are available for public scrutiny.

Concepts The ideas and conventions which underpin the financial accounting process. The idea of four fundamental accounting concepts (prudence, consistency, accruals and going concern) has been superseded by emphasis on qualitative characteristics, relevance and reliability, comparability and understandability.

Consistency Consistent accounting policies or treatment is applied to similar items within a given year and from year to year.

Consolidated financial statements Financial statements of a group of companies that includes 100 per cent of the assets, liabilities, revenues and expenditure of all subsidiary companies, even if they are only, say, 60 per cent owned. The amounts in respect of *minority interests* are separately shown on the financial statements. The consolidated statement of financial position shows all the assets and liabilities controlled by the parent company.

Consolidated (or Group) accounts This is a report of a parent company and its subsidiaries, as if it was one reporting entity, showing all the assets and liabilities and profits controlled by the parent company.

Consolidated profits The parent's own profits together with the group share of the post-acquisition profits of the subsidiary less impairment of goodwill on consolidation.

Contingent liability A possible obligation from past events or transactions which will be confirmed by the occurrence or non-occurrence of a future uncertain event that are not within the control of the company (e.g. a pending court case).

Contribution Sales revenue less variables costs.

Control accounts A statement including the day book totals for invoices and payments in which the total arising agrees with the total of the individual balances in the sales ledger and purchase ledger, thereby proving the accuracy and completeness of the two ledgers.

Corporate governance The system by which companies are directed and controlled, involving law and other regulation and convention, and the roles and relationships between a company's directors, management and shareholders and other stakeholders, and the company's objectives.

Cost centre A unit to which only costs are charged and apportioned and are considered the responsibility of the manager (e.g. a department, a process, a service).

Cost driver A factor which causes a change in the cost of a cost object.

Cost object Anything we wish to know the cost of (e.g. a product, an activity, a process, a department).

Cost of capital The rate used to discount the project cash flows in a net present value computation.

Cost of sales In a retailing organization, this is opening inventory plus purchases minus closing inventory. In a manufacturing organization, it is opening inventories plus costs of production, minus closing inventories. Also known as cost of goods sold. It is deducted from sales revenue to arrive at *gross profit*.

Costs Costs may be classified as *fixed costs* and *variable costs*; or as *production costs* (which include *production overheads*) and other *overheads*, which include distribution costs (selling and distribution overheads), and administration overheads. Production costs may be classified as *direct materials*, *direct labour* and *production overheads*. *Prime cost of production* comprises direct materials and direct labour (and *direct expenses*, if any). *See also opportunity cost*.

Creditors *See payables*. Future financial obligations arising from past transactions or events.

Creditors: amounts falling due after more than one year These are now called *non-current liabilities*.

Creditors: amounts falling due within one year These are now called *current liabilities*.

Creditors' ratio The relationship between trade payables (creditors) and purchases (or cost of sales) usually expressed as a number of days.

Current assets *Assets* such as *inventories*, *receivables* and *cash*, which are held short term (less than one year) and expected to be converted into cash within a year.

Current cost accounting (CCA) A system of accounting that adjusts for changing values following SSAP 16.

Current liabilities Amounts expected to be paid within a year.

Current purchasing power accounting (CPP) A system of accounting that adjusts for inflation following (P)SSAP 7.

Current ratio The ratio of *current assets* to *current liabilities* that indicates a company's ability to meet its current liabilities as they fall due.

D

Day books Books in which the financial transactions are first recorded in the accounting records. Day books include the sales day book, the purchase day book, the cash book and the petty cash book.

Debenture Long-term loan, usually with a fixed rate of interest and often secured on fixed property or the floating assets such as inventory and trade receivables.

Debtors (receivables) period The relationship between trade receivables (debtors) and sales, usually expressed as a number of days.

Depreciation The systematic allocation or writing-down of the carrying amount (cost or revaluation) of a non-current asset, as an expense, over its expected economic life as the economic benefits arise.

The depreciation expense for the year is shown in the income statement, while the accumulated depreciation is deducted from the carrying amount to show the asset's net book value in the statement of financial position.

Direct expenses (Much less frequently encountered than direct labour and direct materials.) Costs of the type that would normally be treated as part of *production overheads*, but instead are treated as part of *prime cost of production* because they are directly attributable to a particular job, product or service. For example, a car repair business would normally treat machinery costs as being part of production overheads; but if a special-purpose machine has to be hired to repair a specialist car, the cost of hiring that machine would be treated as part of the cost of repairing that car, and not included in general production overheads.

Direct labour The costs of remunerating employees who work directly on a product or service to be sold; these labour costs are separately identified and charged to particular products or services (as opposed to being treated as part of *production overheads*). Part of *prime cost of production* which, when *production overheads* are added, make up total *production cost*.

Direct materials The cost of direct materials and components that are separately identifiable and enter into and become constituent elements of a product or service to be sold. Part of *prime cost of production* which, when *production overheads* are added, make up total *production cost*.

Director A person appointed by the shareholders to manage a company.

Director's remuneration Compensation of a director comprising of a salary, fees, bonus or use of a company's property.

Discounted cash flow (DCF) A method of capital investment appraisal in which the relevant expected cash inflows and outflows of a project are discounted to their present value using the time value of money. DCF techniques include net present value (NPV) and internal rate of return (IRR).

Dividend cover Net profit after tax (or profit available to pay dividends) divided by dividends payable for the year.

Dividends Amounts distributed (or paid out as a scrip dividend) to shareholders from distributable profits, usually twice a year (interim dividend, final dividend). Sometimes companies pay more dividends than they have earned as profits in the year in which case retained profits from previous years are being distributed.

Dividend yield The most recent annual dividend per share as a percentage of share price.

Double entry The system whereby accounting transactions and adjustments are recorded in the ledger, both as a debit and as a credit entry. Debits are increases to assets and expenses while credits are increases to liabilities and revenues.

E

Economic order quantity (EOQ) A technique in which the optimal reorder quantity is computed using ordering and holding costs of inventory.

Equity The total of shareholders' funds including ordinary share capital, share *premium*, and other reserves and retained earnings.

Exceptional items The term now has no precise definition but there is usually separate disclosure of unusual or non-recurring items, such as write-downs of inventories, impairment of property, plant and equipment, restructuring, profits or losses on disposal of investments or tangible non-current assets. They must be separately disclosed because of their abnormal incidence or size. All these affect earnings per share.

Expectations gap The difference between what many seem to expect of auditors and what they actually do.

Extraordinary items These have in effect been abolished as a category of cost in external annual reports.

F

Fair value of a non-current asset This is the amount for which it could be exchanged in an arm's length transaction.

Finance cost Interest payable.

Finance income Interest receivable.

Financial Reporting Standards (FRSs) These were issued by the Accounting Standards Board, but have now been superseded by *IASs*.

Fixed assets Now normally known as *non-current assets*.

Fixed costs Costs (such as rent for the premises, or most salaries) that tend to remain at the same level when there are changes in the volume of production or sales. In *marginal costing* fixed costs are separated from *variable costs*. (Some costs are semi-variable.)

G

Gearing The extent to which a company's long-term finance relies upon debt (such as debentures) as compared to equity. The first of these is often represented as D; and the second as E. It may be calculated showing D as a percentage of D plus E; or, more simply, showing D as a percentage of E. Also

known as capital gearing or *leverage*.

Going concern The assumption that the business will continue in operational existence for the foreseeable future and, as a result, it is assumed, in the financial accounts, that the non-current assets will be used and the inventory sold in a relaxed manner and not sold in a liquidation.

Goodwill The amount paid to acquire a business over and above the fair value of its net separable assets. It is an intangible asset and subject to annual impairment reviews.

Goodwill on consolidation This is the consideration given by parent company for the controlling interest in the shares of the subsidiary, in excess of the fair value of the separable net assets underlying those shares. It must be revalued each year and any impairment of its value will be written off against group reserves.

Gross profit Sales revenue minus *cost of sales*.

Gross profit ratio Gross profit as a percentage of sales.

Group accounts *See consolidated financial statements*.

I

Impairment Goodwill is not now systematically amortized; it is subject to an annual impairment review.

Income statement A statement of sales revenue, costs and net profit for a period (e.g. one year). Used to be known as a profit and loss account.

Incomplete records Some small businesses do not keep proper double-entry accounting records and accountants need to construct statements of financial position and income statements from incomplete records that usually comprise bank statements and a variety of documents such as invoices, and unpaid receivables and

payables and inventory at the statement of financial position date.

Indirect costs These are costs which cannot be identified with the individual cost unit.

Intangible asset An asset with no physical substance.

Interest cover Operating profit (or profit available to pay interest) divided by interest payable.

Interest times cover Profit available for paying interest (usually operating profit) divided by the amount of interest payable (finance costs).

Internal rate of return (IRR) The discount rate at which the net present value of expected outflows and inflows from a project are zero.

International Accounting Standards (IASs) These have been superseded by *IFRSs*.

International Financial Reporting Standards (IFRSs) These are issued by the International Accounting Standards Board.

Inventories Raw materials, components, work in progress, finished goods and goods held for resale. Formerly known as *stocks*.

Investment centre Much like a cost centre or profit centre but here, the manager is responsible for and answerable for costs, revenues and investments.

J

Joint venture A business jointly owned by several other business, none of whom has a controlling interest.

L

Leverage *See gearing*.

Liabilities A present financial obligation arising from past events, the settlement of which is expected to result in an outflow from the enterprise embodying economic benefits.

Limited liability The liability of the company's shareholders is limited to any sum they have not paid into the company for the purchase of shares. In the event of a liquidation, if the shareholders have fully paid for their shares, they have no further liability for any debts of the company.

Limiting factor An input factor which is temporarily unavailable.

Liquidity The ease and speed with which assets can be turned into cash to pay imminent liabilities.

Liquidity (or quick, or acid-test) ratio The ratio of current assets excluding inventories to *current liabilities* that indicates a company's immediate ability to meet its current liabilities as they fall due. Liquid assets include cash and receivables, but exclude inventories.

M

Margin of safety Expected sales less break-even point.

Marginal costing A costing system in which individual products are charged with variable but not fixed production overheads; useful in decision-making and break-even analysis.

Mark-up Percentage added to cost price to arrive at selling price. This is not the same as gross profit (or margin) ratio.

Memorandum of association A document setting out a company's name, its objects and its registered share capital.

Minority interest The share of the net assets (or capital and reserves) of a subsidiary at the statement of financial position date, attributable to the non-group shareholders.

N

Nominal value *See par value.*

Non-current assets Formerly known as *fixed assets*. Assets that are held for long-term use (more than one year) including tangible assets such as property, plant and equipment; intangible assets, such as *goodwill*, patents and trademarks: and financial assets that are investments such as shares and debentures. The non-current assets were not purchased in order to sell them.

Non-current liabilities Formerly known as *creditors: amounts falling due after more than one year*. These are liabilities which are due for repayment in the long term (more than one year after the statement of financial position date, and include long-term bank loans and debentures.

O

Operating costs These are the main difference between gross profit and profit before tax. These operating costs are usually designated and disclosed as distribution costs and administrative expenses.

Opportunity cost The value of a benefit sacrificed in favour of an alternative course of action. If a business owns premises that are currently unoccupied, the cost of using them for a particular purpose should not be regarded as zero; the 'opportunity cost' of using them for that purpose is the amount that they could have earned from the best alternative use (e.g. renting them out).

Overheads All costs other than *direct materials, direct labour* (and *direct expenses*, if any). There are *production overheads*, distribution costs (which comprise selling and distribution overheads) and administration overheads.

Overtrading A rapid expansion in business activity with insufficient long-term capital to finance it, which often leads to difficulty in paying liabilities as they fall due.

P

Par value Each share has a theoretical, or par, or nominal value that is of little importance other than it appears on the statement of financial position.

Partnership A business owned and controlled by a number of people in partnership with a view to profit. It is not incorporated and so not subject to Companies Act requirements in terms of formation, limited liability or public accounting disclosure.

Payables Amounts that a business owes and is required to pay, for example trade payables (creditors).

Payback period Capital investment appraisal technique which measures how long it will take to recover the initial investment; that is, when the cash inflows will equal the cash outflows.

Preference shares Shares with a predetermined rate of dividend which must be fully paid before any dividend is paid to ordinary shareholders and the par value of which will be paid to its shareholders before any ordinary shareholder receives any distribution in the event of a liquidation. Now usually classified as non-current liabilities.

Premium Shares are often issued at a premium above their nominal or par value. For example, a 20 pence share might be issued for 30 pence, which means the premium is 10 pence. On a balance sheet, share premium is very much like share capital.

Prepayment A current asset representing the amount to which an expense has been paid in advance at the statement of financial position date.

Price/earnings ratio (P/E ratio) This is share price divided by earnings per share.

Prime cost of production The total of *direct materials, direct labour* (and *direct expenses*, if any). It excludes production and other overheads.

Production cost This includes *prime cost of production* and *production overheads*.

Production overheads The costs of providing a production or manufacturing facility that are not directly attributable to individual products or services. It includes rent and rates for the factory premises, depreciation and repairs for machinery, and wages and salaries for people in the factory who are not part of *direct labour*. These costs are allocated and apportioned to individual products in an *absorption costing* system.

Profit and loss account Now usually known as an income statement. The term 'profit and loss account' may still be used in conversation, as part of the double-entry bookkeeping system, and in the process of producing the final statement that is called an *income statement*.

Profit centre Much the same as a cost centre except here, both costs and revenues are charged and allocated and are considered the responsibility of the manager.

Provision A liability of uncertain timing or amount.

Prudence Prudence was regarded as a fundamental accounting concept. Profits should not be recognized until realized, while expenses must be recognized as soon as they can be anticipated with a reasonable degree of probability. It no longer has the same degree of force.

Q

Quick assets ratio See *liquidity ratio*.

R

Receivables Money expected to be received from customers who may be referred to as trade debtors. Part of current assets.

Relevant costs Expected future incremental cash costs arising from a project.

Return on shareholders' funds (ROSF) or return on equity (ROE) Net profit after tax as a percentage of equity.

Return on total long-term capital employed Operating profit as a percentage of long-term funding (equity plus long-term borrowings).

Revenue expenditure Costs incurred in earning revenues during the period; it excludes *capital expenditure*.

Rights issue An issue of shares to existing shareholders at a price below the current market price. These rights can be sold by the existing shareholder to a third party.

S

Segmental reporting Diversified companies report separate figures for sales, operating profit and net assets for each of their business and geographic segments.

Sensitivity analysis An assessment of those variables in a project which will have the most profound impact on its suitability. Those variables to which the project is most sensitive will then be given most focus in further analysis (e.g. 'What if labour rates increase by 10 per cent?).

Share capital The part of the company's equity that has been sold to shareholders for cash or an equivalent item of capital value. The share capital appears in the statement of financial position at its par/nominal/authorized value. The shares can be sold by the existing shareholder to another person.

Share premium See *premium*.

Sole trader A business owned and controlled by one person. It is unincorporated and so not subject to Companies Act requirements in terms of formation, limited liability and public accounting disclosure.

Statement of changes in equity Statement showing the changes during the year in each of the elements in equity shown on the statement of

financial position. This includes increases and decreases in share capital and share premium, movements in revaluations reserves and movements in the retained profits such as profits and dividends paid as well as unrealized gains.

Statement of financial position A statement of assets, liabilities and equity as at a given date, typically at the end of a year, or a month. Formerly and still sometimes called the balance sheet.

Statements of Standard Accounting Practice (SSAPs) These were issued by the Accounting Standards Committee, but have now been superseded by *FRSs*.

Stewardship Directors are assumed to be stewards of shareholders' funds and so directors are accountable to shareholders.

Stocks See *inventories*.

Stock turnover ratio The relationship between inventories (stocks) and cost of sales (or purchases) usually expressed as a number of days.

Subsidiary company A company controlled by another company (a parent company), which usually owns (or controls in another way) more than 50 per cent of its shares.

Sunk costs Past costs which are irrelevant in a net present value calculation since they will not be affected whether or not the project proceeds.

Suspense account A t-account used to correct errors such as trial balance differences and when it is not known to which t-account a transaction should be posted. In due course, these errors and 'unknowns' must be corrected by journal entries which post the entries to the correct t-account and remove all the postings into the suspense account. The suspense account balance will then be zero.

T

Time value of money The value of money, not in absolute terms, but taking into consideration when it flows and the interest rate expected to prevail in the meantime. A sum received now is worth more than the same sum received at some future time.

Trial balance A list of balances extracted from each ledger account, some of which will be debits (the assets and expenses) and some credits (liabilities and revenues) in which the total of the debit balances and the credit balances will agree. The trial balance can be *extended* to include adjustments, such as depreciation and bad debt provisions, to produce the figures which will appear in the final statement of financial position and income statement.

V

Variable costs These costs (e.g. *direct material* costs) tend to vary in proportion to the level of production or sales. In *marginal costing*, variable costs are separated from *fixed costs*. Some costs may be regarded as semi-variable, or semi-fixed.

Variance The difference between the budgeted figures and the actual figures.

W

Working capital The excess of *current assets* over *current liabilities*. It can be negative.

Working capital ratio *See* *current ratio*.

Z

Z-score A combination of ratios that can predict financial distress.

Index

Critical successful Factors

Price   Volume   Cannibalization   Raw material cost

Produ